DISTINGUISHED
CLASSICS
OF REFERENCE
PUBLISHING

DISTINGUISHED
CLASSICS
OF REFERENCE
PUBLISHING

Edited By
JAMES RETTIG

ORYX PRESS
1992

The rare Arabian Oryx is believed to have insprired the myth of the unicorn. This desert antelope became virtually extinct in the early 1960s. At that time several groups of international conservationists arranged to have 9 animals sent to the Phoenix Zoo to be the nucleus of a captive breeding herd. Today the Oryx population is over 400, and nearly 800 have been returned to reserves in the Middle East.

Copyright © 1992 by James Rettig
Published by The Oryx Press
4041 North Central at Indian School Road
Phoenix, Arizona 85012-3397

Published simultaneously in Canada

Printed and Bound in the United States of America

∞ The paper used in this publication meets the minimum requirements of American National Standard for Information Science—Permanence of Paper for Printed Library Materials, ANSI Z39.48, 1984.

Library of Congress Cataloging-in-Publication Data
Distinguished classics of reference publishing / edited by James
   Rettig; foreword by Charles Scribner, Jr.
      p.   cm.
   Includes bibliographical references and index.
   ISBN 0-89774-640-6
   1. Bibliography—Best books—Reference books. 2. Reference books-
   -Publishing—History. 3. Reference books—Bibliography.
   I. Rettig, James.
   Z1035.1.D57 1992   91-33629
   011′.02—dc20   CIP

With love and gratitude,
the editor dedicates this book to Monica Mary Rettig
"I'm so lucky to be loving you."

Contents

Foreword: Publishing the *Dictionary of Scientific Biography*

Charles Scribner, Jr.

Distinguished Classics of Reference Publishing relates the stories of 31 major reference works, many of them very ambitious undertakings that from concept to completion spanned years or even decades. One must have great admiration for the dedicated, hard working editors who created them. The *Dictionary of Scientific Biography* was the most ambitious publishing project that I ever dreamt up. As a schoolboy I was greatly impressed by the history of Chartres Cathedral and used to marvel at the dedication of the ancient French townspeople who were willing to commence a building that none of them would live to see finished. Frankly, I am a little less amazed now by that part of the story. It is obvious that they expected to see it finished. My own experience as a publisher of the *DSB* has given me a good deal of insight into the planning of long-term projects. The truth of the matter is that at the start no one can imagine how long they are going to take. Perhaps it is just as well that our chronological depth perception fails us so often when we look into the future. We might never begin many worthwhile projects if we knew ahead of time their actual completion dates. Dan Boorstin, the Librarian of Congress, commented on this remark saying that it constituted a proof of the existence of God.

Although the *DSB* was conceived, planned, written, and edited almost entirely by historians of science, it was our original hope that it would also serve a wide readership outside that special field. We hoped that it would be useful and interesting to historians in other fields as well as to teachers and students, journalists, and general readers.

It was natural that the idea for a biographical dictionary of science should have been taken up enthusiastically by Scribners. In the earliest years of our company's history we were active in publishing multi-volume reference works in such fields as literature, religion, and history. At one time—over a hundred years ago, as noted elsewhere in this book—we published the ninth edition of the *Encyclopaedia Britannica* in the United States. In the 1920s we entered into an agreement with the American Council of Learned Societies to publish the *Dictionary of American Biography* and in the 1950s we had begun to be active in publishing books on science for the general reader. My own interest in history of science had been greatly stimulated by a little book by James B. Conant entitled *Science and Common Sense* (New Haven: Yale University Press, 1951). He proposed that the study of history of science would be valuable in science teaching and especially so for beginners who would find it easier to grasp the purposes and methods of science by reading case histories taken from the earlier and simpler periods in the development of various sciences.

With all those ideas somewhat confusedly in mind, I wrote to Dr. Charles Gillispie at Princeton University asking to see him. I had not met him but was familiar with his splendid book in history of science entitled *The Edge of Objectivity* (Princeton: Princeton University

Press, 1960). I told him that I wanted to discuss some publishing ideas in his field and had been "nursing the hope" that he would assist us as an advisory editor. Dr. Gillispie responded courteously, and I visited him at Princeton a few days later. In the story of the *DSB* I consider that visit as eventful as Dr. Watson's first meeting with Sherlock Holmes. (Incidentally, Dr. Gillispie said, "Which one of us is Sherlock Holmes?" I said, "You, of course.") We talked about the possibility of Scribners publishing a series of books in history of science. Dr. Gillispie was obviously doubtful and pointed out that most of his colleagues were already over-committed as far as writing was concerned. In the following days I brooded over the difficulty of launching any major effort in history of science. In hindsight, now, given our success in commissioning articles from leading historians for the *Dictionary of American Biography,* it seems almost inevitable that the idea for a *DAB* of scientists would dawn on us. But the inevitable is not always perceived promptly. In any case, that idea did finally occur to me. Considering the subject, I have later thought it very auspicious that this inspiration took place one morning in the bathtub. I did not rush out shouting "Eureka!" I telephoned Dr. Gillispie almost immediately to see what he thought of a dictionary approach. His response was unhesitating and splendidly positive. He liked the idea and was willing to help. His favorable reaction was the decisive event in the creation of the *DSB*. Without his enthusiasm the idea would almost certainly have aborted; with his support it had every chance of success.

During the next few months a number of steps were taken—all of them important to our moving ahead on the project. A luncheon meeting of prominent historians of science resulted in a request that the American Council of Learned Societies take the *DSB* under its wing in the same way it had taken the *DAB*. A detailed grant proposal was prepared by Dr. Gillispie, which was then submitted by the ACLS to the National Science Foundation. All this sounds very complicated if not Byzantine,

but it was absolutely necessary given the scale of the work and the strong sponsorships it would need to enlist the cooperation of scholars all over the world. In such a situation the publisher must emulate the cuckoo and lay its egg in another bird's nest for hatching.

Once the National Science Foundation responded affirmatively with what was the largest publication grant it had made until then, the *DSB* was a going concern. An editorial board was appointed under the chairmanship of Charles Gillispie and steps were taken to make a working list of subjects—that is, names of scientists—for inclusion in the *Dictionary.* The original estimate had been around 2,600 articles. The final list contained twice as many, a tolerable margin of error for reference books and cathedrals. I might add that in the very tentative first list of names that was typed up at Scribners, a shocking clerical mistake was made between the "M's" and the "N's" with the result that Sir Isaac Newton was left out. That was inauspicious—to say the least—and I never felt we enjoyed the full confidence of physics editor Thomas Kuhn after that. I hasten to add that Newton *is* in the *DSB*.

Each of the major reference works included in *Distinguished Classics of Reference Publishing* has generated its share of interesting stories. So has the *DSB*. To describe in any detail the events and trials of the decade and a half in which the successive volumes of the *DSB* were published, from Abelard to Zwelfer, would take a book in itself. But I shall share a couple of anecdotes given me by managing editor Marshall DeBruhl.

It was the policy for the *DSB* to include no living subject, but it was not always easy to ascertain whether a particular scientist was still alive or not. For example, Dame Kathleen Lonsdale was asked to write the article on Ralph Wyckoff, which she did. A fact checker discovered no grounds for thinking the man had died, which would disqualify him. Meanwhile, Dame Kathleen died. We thereupon wrote to Wyckoff—at his last known address—and asked him to write the article on her. He agreed but had to give up the assignment because of ill health. It was the first case of the "author is dead, but the subject is alive." Also, if he could have completed the article on Dame Kathleen, and then died, we would have had a real first in biographical publishing. Incidentally, Wyckoff did not die in time for the W volume. We held the article on him for a future supplement.

The article on Max Planck was translated from the German language and in one passage the author seemed to be going on and on about Planck's knowing everything. The copy editor asked if he would let us reduce the paragraph to stating that Planck had a reputation for omniscience. The author replied "Omniscience is not sufficient."

Planning and producing the index for the *DSB* turned out to be a much more difficult task than we had anticipated. It would have been comparatively easy had we limited ourselves to proper names, but given the organization of the *Dictionary*, which is biographical, we considered it all the more necessary that the index be thoroughly topical as well. For a while we hoped that it would be possible to produce the index entirely by computer. In fact, we conferred with some of the experts at IBM to explore that possibility. But we soon learned that computers were not up to such a job—however well they may play chess. There seemed to be no way to develop a foolproof program that could cope with such statements as "Darwin was a man of great personal *gravity*" or "Pasteur had boundless *energy* as a researcher." Computers are strong in *l'esprit de geometrie* but weak in *l'esprit de finesse*.

In the end, the longest way around turned out to be the shortest way home and we engaged a top-notch indexer, Julia McVaugh, to take on the job in the old-fashioned way. Working at Chapel Hill with a small staff of assistants, she produced the index in ten years. The completed job required 65,000 cards for 75,000 entries. When these were shipped up to New York in three batches by train we did not dare let them out of our sight, but provided an escort for each shipment. This part of the *DSB* was almost as

time-consuming and costly as our original estimates for the entire work. So much for our ability to foretell the completion of our cathedral!

Although the principal purpose of the *DSB* is to describe the achievements of individual scientists from the earliest times to the present day, I believe that it is as much a humanistic as a scientific work—that is, if one accepts the idea that humanism is essentially a point of view that can be taken towards all departments of knowledge, including science. From the humanistic point of view, the creation of increasingly comprehensive and beautiful conceptual schemes in science, the production of more and more precise scientific data, and the continual application of scientific knowledge to practical human needs, are all to be seen as coordinated achievements in the life of the mind and additions to the contents of human experience.

I would say further that no matter how complex or unfamiliar the subject matter of a particular science may become or how far its concepts and assumptions may be at variance with our ordinary intuition, the thought processes of scientists are not fundamentally different from those of other researchers in other departments of knowledge who must apply imagination, reason, and factual investigation to whatever difficulties of understanding may arise in their work. In this connection one thinks of the simple definition of scientific method proposed by Percy Bridgman. He called it "Doing your damnedest with your mind—no holds barred." One of the advantages of the biographical approach to the history of science is that it consistently reminds the reader that science has no life of its own apart from the minds of the men and women who study or create it. That point is made implicitly by more than 5,000 articles in the *DSB*, and we have been fortunate to find a large enough pool of experts who have kept it going through its supplements.

Similarly, the biographical information about the creators of the 31 landmark reference works whose stories are told in *Distinguished Classics of Reference Publishing* demonstrate that these books, so often taken for granted, owe their existence to the hard work—no holds barred—of their editors. Anyone who has worked on a project like the *DSB* can empathize with the difficulties the editors of these other great reference works encountered and tri-umphed over. Users of these indispensable works, while they might not be able to empathize, will surely sympathize. All will welcome the opportunity *Distinguished Classics of Reference Publishing* offers to deepen acquaintance with these books and to learn more about the stories behind them.

Introduction

> "If there is such a thing as a work of reference that I cannot read through, I have yet to find it. Catalogues, timetables, chronicles of alumnus and alumna, Companions and Concordances of every kind—all are a joy to me."*

This is a book for everyone who derives such unbounded joy from reference works. *Distinguished Classics of Reference Publishing* tells the story of 31 reference books or families of reference books that have stood the test of time and become so indispensable that if any one of them did not exist, we would need to create it. Many of them have established the standards of excellence for their respective reference genres and all have proved themselves invaluable. And they have, even if not read through from cover to cover (or through many volumes), provided their users more than a bit of joy over the years. Through an amusing example, a striking photograph, a carefully drawn map, and in innumerable other ways, all these books have been ever fresh springs of knowledge and of the joy reference works uniquely give. *Distinguished Classics of Reference Publishing* shares with its readers that joy and explains how a select number of notable reference books have evolved and refined themselves to provide joy, knowledge, and information in abundance.

Any collection of this sort is bound to engender differences of opinion about what items ought to have been included or excluded. The 31 books and families of books were chosen because they have proved themselves again and again. Although other reference books have similarly proved their enduring value, those included here were selected because they illustrate the value of reference works in a variety of broad subject areas and specific reference types. Indeed, they were selected from a much longer list that the editor and Oryx Press editorial staff considered initially. The selection is meant to be representative, not exhaustive. Especially significant reference types (e.g., dictionaries and encyclopedias) are represented by more than one example. For other genre, more difficult choices had to be made to select a single representative title to keep the scope of the project and size of the finished book manageable. For example, the category of national and trade bibliographies, represented here by the *National Union Catalog,* could well have been represented by the *Union List of Serials* or *Books in Print.* Choices had to be made. The editor and publisher hope there will be opportunity in another volume to treat those significant reference works not selected for this book.

With one exception, all of the books treated are English-language books. The single exception is the Baedeker family of travel guides. These were included because of their shaping influence on the *vade mecum* travel guide genre and because they have long been available in English editions. The absence of electronic reference works should not be interpreted as a slight; these worthy tools are simply outside the scope of this book.

In most cases a single visionary person with determination, fortitude, and unflagging

---

*John Russell, "Larousse's Dictionary Is Smart and Concise," *New York Times* (18 April 1982), p. D29. This passage is the opening of a review of the *Larousse Dictionary of Painters.*

dedication merits credit for the creation and maturation of each of the reference works. In others, for example, the *National Union Catalog*, teams of individuals made them possible from the start. With few exceptions, such as Post's *Etiquette* and Bartlett's *Familiar Quotations*, all have become institutionalized and are today the products of many minds and hands. But all are alike in one telling characteristic; all meet day-to-day needs for thousands of ordinary people. Furthermore, all have been refined and rendered with such care and quality that they are unquestionably, beyond any similar works (for none is the only book of its kind), a joy to their users, year after year, edition after edition.

Distinguished Classics of Reference Publishing offers glimpses behind the scenes. The essays tell about the people who often overcame seemingly insurmountable obstacles to bring these works into being, and the people who have carried them on and made them better over decades or generations. They explain how and why the characteristics of each new title came over time to define its genre, and how these reference works, many products of pen-and-paper processes in the nineteenth century, have thrived and positioned themselves in the electronic age to move productively into the twenty-first century.

The 31 chapters are organized alphabetically by the titles of the books treated. Each chapter has a four-part structure. The first and most important section is an analytical historical essay. This essay traces the origin of the book, places it in its historical context, and describes its present state and likely future directions. The second section is a bibliographic history of publication, recording various editions, title changes, etc. These publication histories vary in form and content so as to accommodate the complexities of and variations among the histories of the 31 books. None of these publication histories should be construed as an exhaustive bibliographic description or final bibliographic history of any of these titles; telling the stories of the books

and their value through narrative, not enumerating the niceties of their bibliographic histories, is the primary purpose of this book. The third section is a selective bibliography, rarely numbering more than 25 entries, of secondary works about the title discussed. A headnote introduces each bibliography, points out highlights, and explains the particular value of the most significant items in the list. The fourth section is the chapter notes; these are grouped at the end of each chapter. As the chapter notes show, the contributors consulted current editors for information about present operations and future plans of their particular publications. This information was gathered through correspondence and telephone calls and, in the case of the editors of the *New York Times Index*, through an on-site interview. On behalf of the contributors, this book's editor thanks these busy editors for their cooperation and hopes that each one will be pleased with the chapter describing their respective reference classic.

The essays vary in length. This variation results sometimes from the the relative significance of the work in question, sometimes from the extent of the secondary literature extant, but usually from both. For example, little information other than reviews has been recorded about either *Granger's Index* or the *Guide to Reference Books*. On the other hand, works such as the Webster dictionaries or the short title catalogs have been the subject of numerous reports, articles, essays, and reviews, only the most significant of which could be cited in their essays or listed in their bibliographies.

As one who in the past ten years has reviewed more than 2,000 reference books and has read even more reference book introductions, I am well acquainted with statements by editors of collective works in which they humbly assign credit for their books' virtues to their contributors and accept responsibility for any defects. After reading hundreds of these statements, many of them virtually interchangeable, one could easily be tempted to dismiss them as *pro forma*. However, after having assembled a group of busy contributors and cajoled them to meet deadlines, and to revise several times work they considered finished, this editor has gained a profound appreciation of the sincerity and veracity of those statements. Truly, the book's virtues lie in the individual essays, and its editor humbly accepts responsibility for any shortcomings it may have.

Many persons deserve thanks for their contributions. First and foremost I wish to thank the 31 other contributors; without them there would be no *Distinguished Classics of Reference Publishing*. On their behalf I thank the many individuals, too numerous to name individually, who assisted the contributors in their work by critiquing early drafts, offering advice, etc. Art Stickney, director of editorial development of The Oryx Press, merits special thanks for conceiving the idea for this book. I am grateful to him that he asked me to carry out his fine idea and that he and his colleagues at The Oryx Press were patient enough to let me complete several other projects before taking on this one. Both Anne Thompson and John Wagner, the editors at The Oryx Press who guided me through the project, have provided wise counsel and encouragement; and their sense of humor has provided some laughs along the way. Special thanks are also due to Charles Scribner, Jr., truly a living legend in reference publishing, for graciously providing the Foreword. I am grateful to the College of William and Mary for awarding me a research grant to cover expenses related to the project. My fine colleagues at Swem Library at William and Mary have been supportive and have taken an interest in the book's progress. At various times Andrew Magpantay, James Wilson, Patrick Page, and Bob Richardson converted files that contributors produced on IBM microcomputers so I could read and edit them on a Macin-

tosh computer; they also provided other technical assistance. Glenda Page, as fine a secretary as one could wish for, helped prepare mailings, send fax messages, field telephone calls from contributors, and tend to other inglorious-yet-essential chores along the way.

By providing invaluable legal advice, Philip G. Rettig proved one more time that his favorite *pro bono* client is his grateful son. Profound gratitude goes to the late Ann J. Rettig, who, through her tireless reading to a young boy, instilled in him a love of books so strong that today he is decidedly one to whom "Catalogs, timetables . . . Companions and Concordance of every kind" are a never ending source of joy. She knew of this book in its early stages; I wish she were here to see it finished. My children, Chris, Tony, and Katie—children who witness the infinite variety of reference books as newly published review copies ebb and flow in and out of the house almost daily—have taken an interest in the progress of the book even though they have expressed deep doubts that any book about books (especially when some of those books are in turn about yet other books!) could be interesting to anyone. For their good humor I am grateful; I hope their doubts are ill-founded and that some day each of them may open this volume at least in curiosity, if not with burning desire to read it cover to cover. Along with editors' statements of responsibility for their books' shortcomings, editors' expressions of gratitude to patient, long suffering spouses appear to be *de rigueur* in reference book introductions. But it is with a sense of obligation genuinely incurred rather than obeisance to convention that I express my deepest gratitude to my wife, Monica Rettig, for her encouragement and support throughout this project. Without that support, it would not have been completed as soon nor as well.

—*James Rettig*

DISTINGUISHED
CLASSICS
OF REFERENCE
PUBLISHING

Documenting the Travel Experience: Baedeker Guidebooks

Harold M. Otness

DEVELOPMENT AND HISTORY

Above average" was the phrase recently used by a *Booklist* reviewer to evaluate the latest Baedeker guidebook. A few years ago such words would have been unthinkable for this venerable series because Baedeker was the unquestioned leader in the guidebook field. "Kings and governments may err," went the jingle of A.P. Herbert, "but never Mr. Baedeker."[1] One of the many bits of lore concerning this series is the story of Kaiser Wilhelm interrupting a high-level conference at the palace in Potsdam to appear at a window because, as he explained, "You see, it says in Baedeker that at this hour I always do."[2] So dominant was the series that the very name "Baedeker" became the generic term for all guidebooks, much like Kleenex and Xerox have become identified with their types of products.

It is not that Baedekers have fallen so low, but rather that in recent years a fair number of guidebook series have risen to the level of thoroughness and objectivity that Baedeker established over a century ago. Baedekers still are among the best of the genre, and they remain the gauge against which other guidebooks continue to be measured. The older Baedekers have considerable historical reference value to attractions that no longer exist, while the current volumes provide a vast array of information on what is available for the traveler today both in terms of what to see and do, and the practical information of how to get there, where to stay, and where to eat and be entertained.

Baedeker Beginnings

Baedeker is an author (actually four generations of the family), a publishing company, and the title of a guidebook series, as well as a generic name for all guidebooks. The father of the series was the first Karl Baedeker who was born in 1801 in Essen. He studied at Heidelberg University and did some local traveling before settling into the book selling business in Coblenz in 1827. Five years later he bought out a bankrupt publishing house whose titles included a somewhat scholarly survey of the history and art of the Rhine by Professor Johann August Klein entitled *Rheinreise von Mainz bis Koln* (Coblenz: F. Roehling, 1828). In 1835 Baedeker revised this work, extending the geographical range and adding to it the practical information on transportation, lodging, food, and health needed by travelers. In 1839 Baedeker for the first time put his name on the title page of another revision of this work. Any of these three dates could be argued as the beginning of the Baedeker guidebook dynasty.

None of these dates, however, mark the beginning of the guidebook format. The credit for this is often given to Pausanias, a scholar who compiled a landmark description of the Greek world in the second century A.D., of which only fragments have survived. In medieval times guidebooks were published for pilgrims visiting holy shrines. Guidebooks were a response to the increased number of travelers; as the world become more settled and safe, more people began traveling for pleasure and education. In broad terms such travel was one impetus of the Renaissance and its consequent rapid spread of knowledge throughout and beyond Europe. The grandees of Renaissance tourism, traveling with retinues of servants from court to court became the "Grand Tour" aristocracy of later centuries. By the early nineteenth century, the emerging middle class began to venture abroad without servants, tutors, and interpreters, and a need thus arose for guidebooks.

By the beginning of the nineteenth century, a fair number of local guidebooks were available, but most of these concentrated on describing the sights and their histories, rather than providing the practical information to get the traveler there. Another early guidebook format was the "itinerary" book, which simply listed the distances between places with a record of the post stops where teams of coach horses were changed. With the advent of railways, travelers could go faster and to more places and guidebooks were organized for the train traveler along railroad routes. Baekeker appeared at the beginning of this era of travel.

Murray's Contribution

While Baedeker is often credited with creating the modern guidebook, a combination of practical travel information and a description of things to experience, the original Karl Baedeker credited his English rival John Murray (also both a personal name and the name of a famous family publishing business) with perfecting the format. The second John Murray (his father was Lord Byron's publisher) took a trip as a young man around northern Europe, and while doing so he compiled notes organized by routes which in 1836 his father published as *A Hand Book for Travellers in Holland, Belgium, and along the Rhine, and throughout Northern Germany*

(London: John Murray). It was a success, quickly followed by similar works on southern Germany, Austria, Hungary, and Switzerland. Baedeker was so impressed by the utility of these books that he copied the format, including eventual use of the term "handbook" and the flexible red covers for his own German-language guidebooks. For years afterwards he sent updated information from his travels to the grateful John Murray, since at this time Murray's guidebooks were published only in English, and Baedeker's only in German.[3]

Baedeker followed his Rhine guidebook with *Holland* (1839), *Belgium* (1839), and *Germany* (1842) and each quickly became the standard for German-speaking travelers. The series soon spread over all of Europe. By 1846 the firm was translating its titles into French, and by 1861 into English. By 1862, when Baedeker brought out his first London guidebook (in German), the warmth between the Baedeker and Murray firms had cooled, and the former had achieved a dominance which was to last until the beginning of World War II.

A Family Enterprise

The compiling of guidebooks, which Karl Baedeker had done almost single-handedly on the spot, passed on to his capable sons and grandsons, as well as to such outsiders as Francis Muirhead, who authored the volumes on the United States and Canada and served as the English-language editor for many years. (Translated editions were not just literal translations but actually reworked texts to satisfy the needs and interests of other language groups.) The last family member with the name Baedeker to be active in the venture, Eva Baedeker, passed away in 1984. This multigenerational continuity has been the key to the long-time standardization and high quality of the series.

From the beginning, the strength of the Baedekers resulted from at least five factors:

1. The thoroughness of coverage, with even small, out-of-the-way places at least mentioned.
2. The up-to-dateness of coverage, with substantial revision taking place between editions, which appeared every two or three years for most titles.
3. The wealth of detailed maps, and especially city plans, included in all titles. Baedekers became virtual small-format atlases with their foldout maps, panoramas, and detachable index plans.
4. The authoritative and often scholarly introductory essays to the history and arts of the places covered. Some of these were signed essays, mostly by German academics, and they added to the accuracy and prestige of the series.
5. The unbending objectivity in the description and rating of sights (an asterisk system was used to denote relative merit) and in the listing of facilities. The early Baedekers traveled anonymously and, unlike many guidebook writers today, would never accept "freebies," or other favors, nor would they accept advertising of any kind. The standard warning in the turn-of-the-century guidebooks stated: "To hotel-proprietors, tradesmen, and others the Editor begs to intimate that a character for fair dealing and courtesy towards travellers forms the sole passport to his commendation . . . . Hotel-keepers are also warned against persons representing themselves as agents for Baedeker's Handbooks."

The Baedekers always placed the well-being and fair treatment of the traveler first, and there was almost a paternal tone in the handing out of advise on health, safety, and where to get best value for the money. They have never been tools of the travel industry, puffing travel destinations and facilities; but display an integrity not matched in many of today's guidebooks. Generations of travelers came to rely upon the Baedekers, and people walking around with the little red volumes in hand became common to the tourist landscape.

Tributes to Baedeker Quality

Because of their excellence, Baedekers were heavily mined, often without acknowledgement, by compilers of competing guidebooks, and by authors of popular travel books of the day. Baedekers figured prominently in Graham Greene's *Stamboul Train: An Entertainment* and E.M. Forster's *Room with a View*. T.E. Lawrence is said to have used them in the Middle East.[4]

They were complimented by Evelyn Waugh ("With his unfailing discernment Baedeker points firmly and inobstrusively to the essential."[5]) and Theodore Dreiser ("Let me here and now, once and for all, sing my praises of Baedeker and his books."[6]). Bertrand Russell was influenced by their clear and direct prose style.[7] (However Aldous Huxley took a swipe when he wrote "How often I have cursed Baron Baedeker for sending me through the dust to see some nauseating Sodoma or drearily respectable Andrea del Sarto! How angry I have been with him for starring what is old merely because it is old."[8]) Mark Twain had great fun with them: "I was aware that the movement of glaciers is an established fact, for I had read it in Baedeker; so I resolved to take the passage for Zermatt on the Gorner Glacier."[9] Indeed Baedekers were an integral part of both the travel experience and its resulting literature.

Baedekers and Two World Wars

In 1872 Baedeker moved from Coblenz to the German book center of Leipzig where it evolved into a large publishing organization with extensive book-making and geographical information resources. By the beginning of World War I Baedeker coverage had extended to North Africa, the Middle East, across Russia and through Siberia as far as Peking, the Indian subcontinent, and North America, and worldwide coverage seemed near. But the war halted growth of the series, and anti-German sentiment in the 1920s encouraged the development of other guidebook series including the excellent *Blue Guides* (edited by a former Baedeker editor), which were near clones. The Italian Touring Club lured away Baedeker's skilled map lithographers to work on their own extensive series of guidebooks to Italy and its then expanding territories. The French published several competent series of guidebooks, including the *Michelins* which today dominate the crowded European guidebook market. The "golden era" of Baedekers had passed, but during that era an estimated two million copies, in three languages, had been sold.

Between the wars the firm updated some titles, but concentrated on regional guidebooks to Germany for the local market. It also began to restructure the guidebooks for the emerging automobile traveler.

World War II was an even greater disaster for the firm. In ways it could not envision, the firm played a role in the war's destruction. The Baedeker on Scandinavia was said to be instrumental in General Von Falkenhorst's planning for the 1940 invasion of Norway. In 1942, following the Royal Air Force's bombing of Lubeck, Goering supposedly ordered the Luftwaffe to destroy every historical building in Great Britain marked in Baedeker with asterisks. The resulting bombings of cathedrals and other monuments became known as "Baedeker raids." Then, on December 3, 1943, a massive R.A.F. raid reduced Leipzig, including the Baedeker plant, to rubble. Irreplaceable printing plates, inventory, and extensive files were destroyed.

Baedekers after World War II

The firm rose from the ashes under the direction of Karl Baedeker, grandson of the founder. In 1948 he issued a guidebook to Leipzig, which was in the Russian zone of divided Germany. But because—with characteristic family thoroughness—he showed the location of some sensitive facilities on the city plan, the occupying Soviets quickly censored the book. This repressive environment caused the firm to shift to West Germany where, with the infusion of a fourth generation of Baedeker family members, the firm finally found solid footing in Freiburg in 1956.

The post-World War II Baedekers have been aimed at the automobile travelers and group tourists who prevail today. This manner of travel requires a different approach because of the faster pace and special needs of the motorist. Some of today's titles convey less history and less detailed description of artistic works, but more on the mechanics of getting about. Some exceptions to their policy of not carrying advertising have been made, but commercial influence is not nearly as intrusive as it is in most guidebook series. If Baedekers are not what they were, they are in many ways more suitable for today's travelers.

Their Enduring Value

Old Baedekers have gained in utility as research sources—both for what is no longer there, and as social history. There is no better source for study of the evolution of tourism than a century and a half of Baedekers. They document how people traveled, what they saw, and what they thought about what they saw. From reading them we can determine national attitudes, measure our expanding knowledge of other countries and cultures, and mark the impact of technology on the development of globalization.

What can be found in these old volumes? A plan of Budapest at the turn of the century before it was drastically altered by industrialization, wars, the automobile, and Sovietization. A description of the major cultural monuments of Berlin later destroyed in the wars. A plan of a Paris cemetery showing the graves of famous people. A floor plan of a museum in

Amsterdam including a listing of the artworks then displayed by location. A survey of the rigors of travel in Albania, including the kind of food one was likely to encounter and the general state of sanitation and public health. A scholarly outline of the history of Egypt. A geological description of the Alps actually written by a geologist. The price of a meal, a glass of the local wine, a night's lodging in a modest country inn, the schedule of the "Orient Express," and the fair price of a taxi ride in Rome. Recommendations on health precautions and cures. Descriptions of the local economy. Comments on the differences of cultures, as then perceived. And more.

Most major reference books are impressively large, but the old Baedekers measured a mere 6¼" x 4¼," and never exceeded 1 1/3" in thickness; yet what they contained is astounding. Through the use of thin "bible paper," small but varied typefaces, and a compact style of writing that included many abbreviations, some of these volumes contained over 500 pages of dense description and up to 30 pages of double-column index entries.

The number of maps is also impressive. *Great Britain* (1910 ed.) had 28 maps, 65 plans, and a panorama; *Rhine* (1906 ed.) had 52 maps and 29 plans; and *Switzerland* (1911 ed.) had 75 maps, 20 plans, and 12 panoramas. These were veritable atlases. The larger maps, some as much as 16 inches high and wide, were folded and were either tipped in or inserted in back pockets. The city plans were particularly rich in detail and even showed such things as streetcar routes and individual trees along boulevards. By the turn of the century, most maps and plans were colored, highly readable and attractive, and rigorously updated with each new edition. There were also numerous black-and-white floor plans of cathedrals and museums. The Baedeker maps and plans are indexed in *Index to Nineteenth Century City Plans Appearing in Guidebooks,* and *Index to Early Twentieth Century City Plans Appearing in Guidebooks*, both published by the Western Association of Map Libraries.

Most major public and academic libraries keep a reference set of the old Baedekers, often set aside in special collections because of their increasing market value. Thieves value their maps, which can, unfortunately, easily be cut out and sold separately. Baedekers are collected avidly. The titles which never enjoyed great sales, such as *Russia* (the first and only English edition appeared in the unhappy year of 1914); *Indien* (also published in 1914 and never in English); and *Maderia* (issued in 1934 in German and 1939 in English) now bring several hundred dollars apiece when they come on the market. Others, such as the 1929 edition of *Egypt* with its excellent plans of monuments now underwater and often claimed to be the best guidebook ever written; *Greece* with its strong historical description; and the *United States* are also highly valued. The most common titles are those concerning Italy, France, Germany, and Great Britain. Several Baedekers have been reprinted and efforts are being made to translate some of the early German editions into English. Greenwood Press issued a collection of 266 English-language volumes up to World War II on 1,898 microfiche, with printed index. This set is now available in microfiche from University Publications of America for $3,545.[10]

Today's Baedekers have a decidedly more modern look with a larger format, two sizes (country guides being larger than city guides), glossy paper, and abundant color photographs. The flexible red covers remain (but of a different design and material) and they still fit in the pocket or camera bag. The practical information appears at the back on bright yellow pages. The city guides are arranged alphabetically by attraction and no longer have comprehensive indexes. Each volume has a large fold-out map in back. The recent publication history of the Baedekers is complex, and is best told by Alex Hinrichsen in "An Account of the History of the Firm of Baedeker."[11] Cooperative ventures were first struck with the large German map publisher Mairs of Stuttgart in 1951, and the Autoguides were done by this firm for many years. For a while there were actually two separate firms issuing Baedekers, one centered in Freiburg (Karl Baedeker Verlag, a part of the Langenscheidt publishing group), and one in Kemnat, near Stuttgart (Baedeker's Autoguides, a part of the Mairs publishing group). In 1987 the two ventures were merged under the name of Karl Baedeker GmbH, with headquarters at Kemnat. The ownership is split 50-50 between Langenscheidt and Mairs. The series continues to evolve. Both Asia and the western hemisphere are receiving more coverage, but western Europe and the Mediterranean continue to be the strength of the series.

The revisions are more difficult to identify today. The edition numbering has unfortunately been dropped and one must search the verso of the title page for a copyright date, but one is not always present. However the Baedeker tradition of rigorous revision appears to be maintained.

Today the Baedekers are unique reference tools in that both the current editions and the older editions can be justified in a library's reference collection, a claim none of its many imitators can yet make.

PUBLICATION HISTORY

Over 200 distinct titles in German, French, and English have been issued with the Baedeker imprint over the last century and a half. There have been several German, British, French, and American publishers' imprints over the years, and some editions have been joint publications with the (British) Automobile Association, Lufthansa, Shell, and others. The definitive list of titles, along with a useful numbering system for them, is Hinrichsen's *Baedeker-Katalog*.

Pre-World War I English-Language Guidebooks

Austria-Hungary
Belgium and Holland

The Eastern Alps
Egypt
France:
Paris and its Environs
Northern France
Southern France

Germany:
Berlin and its Environs
Northern Germany
The Rhine
Southern Germany

Great Britain:
England, Wales, and Scotland
London and its Environs

Greece
Italy:
Central Italy and Rome
Italy from the Alps to Naples
Nothern Italy
Southern Italy

The Mediterranean
Norway, Sweden, and Denmark
Palestine and Syria
Russia
Spain and Portugal
Switzerland
The United States, with excursions to Mexico,
    Cuba, Puerto Rico, and Alaska

Modern Guidebooks

Today's list of Baedeker offerings is comparable. There has been some restructuring of the guidebook series and geographical areas are redefined from time to time. Some titles are not currently distributed in the United States. The following are recent titles offered through the American distributor Prentice-Hall:

Country Guidebooks:

Denmark	Great Britain
Egypt	Greece
France	Ireland
Germany	Israel

Italy	Switzerland
Japan	Yugoslavia
Mexico	

Multi-Nation and Regional Guidebooks

Caribbean	Rhine
Costa Brava	Scandinavia
Greek Islands	Turkish Coast
Islands of the	Tuscany
Mediterranean	
Loire	
Netherlands, Belgium,	
Luxembourg	

City Guidebooks

Amsterdam	Madrid
Athens	Moscow
Bangkok	Munich
Berlin	New York
Brussels	Paris
Copenhagen	Rome
Florence	San Francisco
Frankfurt	Singapore
Hamburg	Tokyo
Hong Kong	Venice
Jerusalem	Vienna
London	

Baedeker also offers a *Rail Guide to Europe!* and a series of maps under the Baedeker name is distributed in the United States by Gousha.

BIBLIOGRAPHY

The Germans are particularly keen enthusiasts of Baekeders, and they have conducted seminars featuring papers by academics and collectors from several countries (a recent one included a cruise on the Rhine while reading aloud appropriate passages from an early guidebook). The Hinrichsens, in addition to their excellent history and bibliography, publish "Reiseleben" (in German only, write for subscription information). In England Michael Wild, a dealer in old Baedekers, publishes an informative newsletter "Baedekeriana" (write for current subscription information—21 Nursery Grove, Lincoln, LN2 1RS). Another Englishman, L. Lawrence Boyle, a professor of physics at the University of Kent, has written extensively on Baedekers and is working on a book that promises to be a major contribution.

In the United States, Herbert Warren Wind's article in the *New Yorker* is the best written and most carefully researched of the numerous magazine articles that have appeared over the years.

This bibliography is not comprehensive, due to the vastness, and in some cases, super-ficial nature of the literature. Many slick travel pieces have been based on the series, or otherwise make use of it, but these are often derivative. Yet there are substantial writings, and there will be more as appreciation of the series continues to grow. Listed here are some of the best writings, and in some cases the representative and more unusual writings, that have been published in English (with the exception of the Hinrichsen work).

Ayrton, Michael. "The Traveler Incognito." *Harpers Bazaar* (June, 1959): 92 +.

"Baedeker and the Modern World." *The Bookman* XVII (July, 1903): 495–97.

Constable, W. G. "Three Stars for Baedeker." *Harpers* 206 (April, 1953): 76–83.

Dunbar, Gary S. "The Way It Was Done in Leipzig: A Comment on Baedeker's First Century." *Landscape* 19 (May, 1975): 11–13.

"Enlisting Baedeker in the Army." *Literary Digest* 58 (June, 1918): 31.

Gebhard, Bruno. "The Doctor Travels with Karl Baedeker." *Bulletin of the New York Academy of Medicine* 46 (June, 1970): 469–78.

Hinrichsen, Alex W. *An Account of the History of the Firm of Baedeker*. Translated into English by Michael Wild (photocopied typescript, 1988).

———. *Baedeker-Katalog; verzeichnis aller Baedeker-Reisefuhrer von 1832–1987.*

Holzminden, West Germany: Ursula Hinrichsen Verlag, 1988.

Holroyd, James Edward. "Baedeker and Baker Street." *Cornhill Magazine* 173 (Winter, 1962–63): 139–45.

Knoles, George Harmon. "Baedeker's United States." *Pacific Historical Review* XIII (March, 1944): 1–9.

Mendelson, Edward. "Baedeker's Universe." *Yale Review* 74 (Spring, 1985): 386–403.

Muirhead, James F. *America, the Land of Contrasts; a Briton's View of His American Kin.* New York: John Lane, 1911. Chapter XII, 219-72, is titled "Baedekeriana."

———. "Baedeker in the Making." *Atlantic Monthly* 97 (May, 1906): 648–60.

———. "The House of Baedeker." *Outlook* 83 (May, 1906): 224–30.

Otness, Harold M. "Baedeker's One-Star American Libraries." *Journal of Library History, Phi-losophy and Comparative Librarianship* XXI (Summer, 1977): 222–34.

———. *Index to Nineteenth Century City Plans Appearing in Guidebooks.* Santa Cruz, CA: Western Association of Map Libraries, 1980.

———. *Index to Twentieth Century City Plans Appearing in Guidebooks.* Santa Cruz, CA: Western Association of Map Libraries, 1978.

Smiles, Samuel. *Memoirs and Correspondence of the Late John Murray, With an Account of the Origin and Progress of the House, 1768–1843.* London: John Murray, 1891. Chapter V, 459-83, is titled "Murray's Handbooks."

Wallace, Irving. *The Saturday Gentleman.* New York: Simon & Schuster, 1965. Chapter 8, 183-200, is titled "Tourist Bible."

Wind, Herbert Warren. "The House of Baedeker." *New Yorker* 51 (September 22, 1975): 42+.

NOTES

[1] These kinds of anecdotes appear in many sources. The most reliable source for this one, and several others which follow, is Herbert Warren Wind, "The House of Baedeker," *New Yorker* 51 (22 September 1975): 42+.

[2] Ibid., 49.

[3] Samuel Smiles, *Memoirs and Correspondence of the Late John Murray, with an Account of the Origin and Progress of the House, 1768-1843* (London: John Murray, 1891).

[4] Wind, 49.

[5] Evelyn Waugh, *Labels, a Mediterranean Journal* (London: Duckworth, 1930), 56.

[6] Theodore Dreiser, *A Traveler at Forty* (New York: Century, 1914), 307.

[7] Wind, 49.

[8] Aldous Huxley, *Jesting Pilate; Notes and Essays of a Tourist* (New York: Duran, 1926), 37.

[9] Mark Twain, *A Tramp Abroad* (New York: Gabriel Wells, 1923), 127.

[10] *Baedeker's Handbook(s) for Travelers: The Complete Collection of 266 Editions Published in English Prior to World War II:* (Bethesda, MD: University Publications of America, 1975.)

[11] Alex W. Hinrichsen, *An Account of the History of the Firm of Baedeker.* Translated into English by Michael Wild (processed, 1988).

"The Most Famous Book of Its Kind": Bartlett's *Familiar Quotations*

Kerry L. Cochrane

DEVELOPMENT AND HISTORY

John Bartlett, editor, publisher, and lexicographer, was born in Plymouth, Massachusetts, on June 14, 1820. He gave early evidence of a love for reading: he was able to read a Bible verse to his mother at the age of three; by nine he had read the entire Bible aloud. He left the Plymouth public school at 16 to become a clerk in the University Book Store in Cambridge. This bookstore, where the early works of Longfellow and Lowell had been published, faced the campus of Harvard College. Although employment signaled the end of his formal education, the acquaintance with books and Harvard professors which the bookstore made possible was the equivalent of a university education for Bartlett. His self-acquired erudition earned him the respect of the literary community, and Bartlett made the University Book Store a cultural meeting place for faculty and students who loved books. By 1849, at the age of 29, Bartlett had become the proprietor of the University Book Store, which he managed for ten more years. In 1851 he married Hannah Staniford Willard, daughter of the Harvard professor of Hebrew and granddaughter of Harvard's thirteenth president.

Bartlett became a publisher of scholarly works, including Harvard textbooks of classical languages and authors such as Thoreau and Emerson. His regular customers were allowed access to the back room, where they could discuss their reading, and Bartlett indulgently permitted college students to take books away and pay when they could. His voracious reading and near-total recall so impressed his literary friends that it was soon standard practice to "ask John Bartlett" when the provenance of a quotation was in doubt. Such requests became so frequent that Bartlett began noting in a commonplace book memorable passages and literary quotations from his wide reading. The references in this notebook, arranged chronologically and listing the sources, would become the basis for the first *Collection of Familiar Quotations*.

The Early Editions

With the help of Harvard student Henry W. Haynes, Bartlett compiled and published the *Collection of Familiar Quotations* in 1855 as a service to his friends. Bartlett published the first three editions of his work himself from the University Book Store, and then in 1863 he joined the Boston publishing firm of Little, Brown & Co., which published the fourth edition of *Familiar Quotations* that same year. He edited his book through six more editions, all of which bear the imprint of Little, Brown & Co., and eventually became senior partner of the firm. In recognition of his work, Harvard in 1871 awarded Bartlett an honorary Master of Arts degree. He was made a fellow of the Academy of Arts and Sciences, and held honorary membership in Phi Beta Kappa. Bartlett retired from Little, Brown in 1889 to write his *Complete Concordance to Shakespeare's Dramatic Works and Plays*, which appeared in

1894. He died 11 years later at the age of 85. According to Nathan Haskell Dole, editor of the tenth edition (1914), the first nine editions of *Familiar Quotations* had sold 300,000 copies before Bartlett's death.

In the preface to the first edition, Bartlett modestly mentioned that although the work was not originally intended for publication, if it were to be favorably received "endeavors will be made to make it more worthy of the approbation of the public in a future edition."[1] The public's approbation was immediate. The 1,000 copies of the first edition sold out within three months. *Harvard Magazine* described Bartlett's work this way:

> The book, like a good rule, works both ways; it not only gives every facility for the detection of careless copyists, but it also enables one to sprinkle his conversation, his writing, and his public speaking, with the choicest selections from the best authors,—the very nutmeg of the English language. . . . It is a boon, an absolute boon, to lawyers, newspaper editors, politicians, literary people, drawing-room belles, young gentlemen of limited conversational powers, and, above all, for students.[2]

The second edition, appearing in 1856, and 63 pages longer, was just as popular. *Familiar Quotations* increased in size with each subsequent edition: the third edition (1858) was 446 pages long, almost twice the size of the first; the fourth edition (1863) was 480 pages long, the fifth (1868) and sixth (1874) each had 778 pages. The ninth edition (1891), the final one compiled by Bartlett, contained 1,158 pages.

The work has continued to attract praise over the years and is considered a basic reference source. Eugene Sheehy calls *Familiar Quotations* "one of the best books of quotations with a long history"; it has also been called "the most famous American book of its kind, and in many respects the best."[3] *American Reference Books Annual* said of *Familiar Quotations*: "A fairly common definition of a 'reference book' is a book that is 'consulted, but not read.' But one always has to hasten to add that many kinds of reference books *are*

read, at least by certain kinds of people. Dictionaries of quotations are perhaps the best example, and Bartlett continues to be the best of such dictionaries."[4] In a review of the eleventh edition the *Christian Science Monitor* called *Familiar Quotations* an institution, saying, "What the Cambridge History of Literature is to English and American letters, Webster to the American language, the Britannica to encyclopedias in English, Bartlett is to English quotations. . . . This is, of course, primarily a reference book, but it is also a fascinating anthology of memorabilia. It is an ideal book for the bedside table, the waiting room, for random moments when you haven't time to settle down to a real read. It's an admirable book in which to browse."[5]

Significant Features

Two features contribute to the "readability" of *Familiar Quotations*: its chronological arrangement, and its thorough cross-referencing. The chronological arrangement provides a sense of historical context and of the progression of an author's thought over time which is not present in works arranged thematically or alphabetically. Authors are arranged in birth date order; quotations within each author are chronological by date of publication. The author index at the beginning provides birth and death dates as well as the page number of each author's first citation. The extensive footnotes allow the reader to follow the evolution of an idea through the writings of several authors, or trace how different ages and cultures have employed similar sayings. Footnotes can also give information about a quote such as identifying its translator and the version in the original language, if appropriate, and any cross-references. The exhaustive keyword index lists short forms of each phrase being indexed, with page references.

The purpose of *Familiar Quotations* was, according to Bartlett's preface, "to show, to some extent, the obligations our language owes to various authors for numerous phrases and familiar quotations which have become 'household words.'"[6] More than just a reference source, *Familiar Quotations* is a living document which records the development of American literary taste over more than 125 years. In the first edition, more than one third of the quotations were drawn from the Bible and Shakespeare, with the balance of the book comprised mainly of citations to English poets such as Byron, Milton, and Wordsworth. In 1855 these were the primary cultural references of the educated American. This stock of common culture—what Americans considered "familiar"—has widened with every edition of *Familiar Quotations*. Through the first ten editions the guiding principle for selection remained the same: the book included only those words which the general reader could recognize as familiar. With the eleventh edition, under the editorship of Christopher Morley, *Familiar Quotations* departed from this principle. Morley was the first editor to make a conscious effort to include what he thought was worthy of *becoming* familiar: references to contemporary literature and, in the twelfth edition, to contemporary politics. This is the model that has been followed to the present day.

Bartlett edited the first nine editions of *Familiar Quotations* essentially by adding to his original work new quotations he considered worthy of inclusion. One reviewer remarked, "The well-known taste which has from the first presided over the formation of this incomparable collection, and the genuinely familiar character of the quotations that have found admission to its pages, make this book the surest of guides, if not to the popularity, at least to the comparative quotability, of the great authors of our language."[7] References to the *Bible*, the *Book of Common Prayer*, and Shakespeare accounted for only one-fifth of the ninth edition, because so many new sources had been added. Authors quoted for the first time included Matthew Arnold, Epictetus, Marcus Aurelius, and both the El-

der and the Younger Pliny. Not yet represented, however, were Rossetti, Swinburne, Mark Twain, Hawthorne, Melville, Emily Dickinson, Thoreau, and Walt Whitman. One of the most significant enhancements introduced in the ninth edition was the systematic inclusion of translated quotations both from ancient authors and from early modern writers such as Rabelais, Montaigne, and Cervantes. The translations had comprised only 8 pages of the eighth edition, but made up 120 of the ninth. Bartlett also greatly increased the amount of parallel references given in footnotes and in the appendix.

Newer Editions, New Editors

Bartlett seems to have intended the ninth edition to be the last, since he began the preface by saying, "The small thin volume, the first to bear the title of this collection, after passing through eight editions, each enlarged, now culminates in its ninth,—and with it, closes its tentative life."[8] But 1914 saw the publication of a tenth edition, edited by the poet and translator Nathan Haskell Dole, which was six times the size of the original. In all its years of publication, *Familiar Quotations* had been enlarged but never revised. Dole left the bulk of Bartlett's original work intact, stating as his purpose "to incorporate in the work quotations from those writers whose place in literature has been achieved since the issue of the ninth edition in 1891."[9] He attempted to apply Bartlett's requirement that a quotation be "distinctly worthy of perpetuation," claiming that "ephemeral quotations will not be found included in its pages."[10] Noteworthy among newly elected authors were Nietzsche, Shaw, George Eliot, Lewis Carroll, Hardy, Swinburne, and Kipling. Blake, Hawthorne, Melville, James, and Emily Dickinson were still not recognized.

The eleventh edition, published in 1937, was edited by the writer and poet Christopher Morley in collaboration with associate editor Louella D. Everett, a quotation-finder for the

"Queries and Answers" department of the *New York Times Book Review*. Under Morley's editorship *Familiar Quotations* entered a new era. In revising the tenth edition, Dole had simply brought the book up to date, while attempting to judge new quotations as its original compiler might have done. The new editors, however, not only added quotations from authors who had become famous since 1914, but examined the rest of the book as well, inserting quotations in every historical period. Morley also was the first to delete entries which had proven less memorable than originally thought; this became standard practice in subsequent editions.

In the most important departure from precedent, the editors no longer adhered to Bartlett's requirement that quotations "have the seal of popular approval." According to Morley, "We have tried to make literary power the criterion, rather than the width and vulgarity of fame."[11] This interpretation of his mission as editor allowed Morley to add the broadest range of contemporary writers ever seen in Bartlett's. He included references to Auden, Pound, Langston Hughes, Bertrand Russell, Sinclair Lewis, T.S. Eliot, and Willa Cather, and finally cited Blake, Hawthorne, Melville, and Emily Dickinson. As the *Christian Science Monitor* review of this edition stated, "They're all here: poets, novelists, essayists, college presidents, columnists and critics, kings and dictators, and all the editors of the *Saturday Review*."[12] Morley was the first editor of *Familiar Quotations* to impose his own vision on the work. Under Morley's editorship Bartlett's began to anticipate an author's fame rather than merely reaffirm it. As Morley said in the preface, one of the pleasures of this cooperative effort was that "one collaborator, by long experience with inquiries for the affable familiar ghosts of print, knows acutely what readers want; and the other believes himself to know what they ought to want."[13] The size of the book reflected this new spirit of inclusiveness. Even after its pruning, the eleventh edition contains some 20,000 quotations, nearly double the number in the previous edition.

Since the tenth and the eleventh editions had each appeared 23 years after their respective predecessors, Morley predicted that his 1937 revision should last until 1960. But the upheavals of the war years made him reconsider this remark as early as 1940. "Man in his Penultimate War was saying words that had to be recorded,"[14] Morley wrote. He and Everett had been noting possible inclusions throughout the Second World War, and in 1948 they produced a twelfth edition which reflected the advent of the atomic age. Sir Winston Churchill, unrepresented in the 1937 edition, was given 60 entries. By comparison, Bartlett had not felt a similar inclination to add Lincoln to the fifth edition, published three years after his assassination. Again, Morley included much of this new material because he considered it important, not because it was necessarily familiar. This edition included words made famous by recent events, such as Einstein's statement that the use of the atom bomb "brought into the world the most revolutionary force since man's discovery of fire." It also contained passages which had become significant by hindsight, such as a prescient reference to atomic weapons from H. G. Wells's *The World Set Free*, written over 30 years before Hiroshima: "The catastrophe of the atomic bombs which shook men out of cities and businesses and economic relations, shook them also out of their old-established habits of thought, and out of the lightly held beliefs and prejudices that came down to them from the past."

The editors and publishers all agreed that this revision should have as its aim not the complete reworking of the book but simply the addition of new material. The twelfth edition is therefore identical with the eleventh through the entries on Kipling (page 787), after which it is entirely new.

Little, Brown & Co. decided to reexamine the entire text of *Familiar Quotations* for a centennial edition, published in 1955. While the previous two editions had borne the stamp of Morley's personality and literary taste, this one was virtually edited by committee. Emily Morison Beck, who would become the editor of the fourteenth and fifteenth editions, was hired to organize the deletions and additions to the centennial edition, and a former assistant in the Harvard English department, Jack Rackliffe, became copy editor. According to Beck, Rackliffe was able to rectify omissions from English literature from Shakespeare through Yeats. As she puts it, "the editing of the centennial edition was turned upside down, with the fellow on the bottom emerging as the true savant and arbiter, with me, the tyro who was cutting her teeth on quotations, in the middle, and with the casual, uncritical editors at the top."[15]

The thirteenth edition contained a variety of songs, ballads, nursery rhymes, and proverbs, reflecting the taste for the folkloric prevalent at the time. In addition, there were a number of stylistic changes. Pages were divided into two columns and running heads were added to the index pages. Ancient and non-English authors who had formerly been in a separate section in the back of the book were incorporated into the main body of the text, arranged chronologically and dated whenever possible. The *New York Times* review of this edition noted an indication of significant change in American taste: "One thing is certain: in the last hundred years our general fund of quotation has both changed direction (away from the stuffy toward the trivial, gay and light-hearted) and increased in size."[16] This edition increased the amount of space given to Shakespeare, and the section of Biblical references increased by 19 pages over the previous edition, although such references now comprised only one-ninth of the book.

At the request of Little, Brown & Co., Emily Morison Beck agreed to edit the fourteenth edition of *Familiar Quotations*, which was published in 1968. She accepted on condition that she be allowed to hire a staff of scholars and experts in various fields to help her select quotes. Beck saw the fourteenth edition as one informed by the social upheavals of the late 1950s and early 1960s, which had given us new terms like the beat generation, brinkmanship, the multiversity, and cybernetics. For this edition she also reexamined the classical quotations whose translations dated from the nineteenth century and were considered outdated. Homer appears in direct translation for the first time, rather than in Pope's verse. Zeph Stewart, professor of Greek and Latin at Harvard, produced new translations of classical authors for the fourteenth edition, and in passing corrected the omission of "Man is the measure of all things" from Protagoras. A broadening of interest in Eastern cultures was reflected in the insertion of quotes from Confucius, Gandhi, and Lao-tzu.

This edition was also the first to be indexed by computer. Computerized cross-indexing greatly improved access to the 20,421 quotes, and also cut production time dramatically. Indexes to early editions of *Familiar Quotations* had been alphabetized by hand, which took 20 people about six months; the computerized alphabetizing of the fourteenth edition took about three hours.

Little, Brown & Co. published the fifteenth and current edition, also edited by Beck, in 1980. Essentially an updating of the previous edition, it includes over 400 new authors (both contemporary and historical), expands coverage of the Koran as well as ancient Buddhist texts, and carries fresh translations of non-English works. Beck again compiled the work with the help of a staff of subject specialists in various areas, and the experts acknowledged in the preface represent such timely fields as ecology, the environment, and Latin American literature. Beck included more quotations produced by women and minorities or inspired by social movements, and she also introduced more popular culture into *Familiar Quotations* than it had ever seen. The fifteenth is the first edition to contain the words of rock musicians, and the only one to carry a quote from a cartoonist, the popular "Keep on truckin'" by Robert Crumb, creator of Mr. Natural and Fritz the Cat. There are lines from songs by Bob Dylan ("For the times they are a-changin'"), Simon and Garfunkel ("Here's to you, Mrs. Robinson"), Mick Jagger ("Well, we all need someone we can lean on") , and Janis Joplin ("Lord, won't you buy me a Mercedes-Benz"). The play *Hair* is quoted, as are *My Fair Lady*, *Camelot,* and *West Side Story*. Paddy Chayevsky is represented by one line from the screenplay to *Network*, ("I'm mad as hell and I'm not going to take it anymore"). In the preface Beck says, "Time will judge the validity of the fifteenth edition's choices from contemporary life and literature."[17] Some critics have objected to this seeming bid for "relevance" at the expense of actual literary or cultural merit, questioning the enduring value of such quotes as Helen Reddy's "I am strong, I am invincible, I am woman." As one reviewer put it, "Reading the recent entries in this edition is like reading the 10th anniversary issue of *Rolling Stone*.[18] Beck maintained that the best way to gather quotations is to list important people who are unrepresented or underrepresented in the work, and then to cull their works for good lines. Others have criticized Beck's editions of *Familiar Quotations* for avoiding topics which seem harsh, cynical, or unpleasant. According to one critic, the book

> emerges as a one-sided chronicle, conspicuously void of We Dare Not Speak Its Names. The expanded coverage of the environment, for example, includes no mention of nuclear power, and the references to nuclear warfare have a certain A-bomb archaism. Cancer doesn't appear even as a metaphor in a volume that purports to represent modern science. . . . *Bartlett's* creates the impression, by quoting exclusively from *The Colossus of Maroussi*, that Henry Miller is a travel writer.[19]

The Future

Justin Kaplan, who is currently preparing the sixteenth edition of *Familiar Quotations* for publication in 1992, plans to rectify this impression. Kaplan's view of what *Familiar Quotations* should include is the most accessible yet: "Generally, it should be useful, timely and entertaining. Useful as a reference book, timely as a guide to a lot of current usage—even if ephemeral, but so is everything else—and it ought to be fun to read."[20] A Pulitzer Prize-winning biographer of Whitman, Twain, and Lincoln Steffens, Kaplan intends to remove what he considers its New England stuffiness. He sees evidence for this in the book's neglect of Shakespeare's comedies in favor of the tragedies, and its focus on the more uplifting pronouncements of politicians. His revision will contain more references to the comedies, and remarks like Tammany Hall politician George Washington Plunkitt's, "I seen my opportunities and I took 'em." In order to add some 3,000 new quotes while keeping the book approximately at its current size, Kaplan is deleting what he calls "Harvard-derived allusions, outworn sentiments, and excerpts from commencement speeches." He is trimming the amount of space given to contemporary poetry in response to the criticism that it is overrepresented in the fifteenth edition. His edition will reflect a broader cultural base by including more quotes from world literature and international figures. Kaplan also wants to include more phrases which have become part of our everyday speech, from Henny Youngman's "Take my wife . . . please" to the fast-food advertising slogan "Where's the beef?" The new edition will contain more song lyrics and lines from movies, but Kaplan found that neither television nor contemporary politics has produced much in the way of memorable quotes. For example, Ronald Reagan's entries in the new *Familiar Quotations* will not be due to his oratory but to his own quotations of movie lines such as "Win one for the Gipper" and "Make my day."

On the university lecture circuit, Kaplan says, audiences typically do not recognize the occasional Biblical or Shakespearean quotation. The technology of mass communication provides a constant flow of ephemeral "familiar" references, while the numbers of Americans for whom Shakespeare's words are truly familiar seems to be decreasing. One of the difficulties he faced was balancing quotes from the masterpieces of the English language with the popular references of the day. "For *Bartlett's* to be useful," Kaplan says, "it has to reflect the fact that a great deal of current discourse is popular language—from movies, television, sports. Yet one of the essential elements of *Bartlett's* is to act as a sort of home concordance and to retain the major sources of our language, such as the Romantic poets."[21] According to Kaplan, quotations can reinforce a sense of community or; they can exclude; they enrich discourse; and they are powerful means of communicating.

Now, *Familiar Quotations* continues to be a printed information source. However, future editions of this classic might be produced in CD-ROM or hypermedia format, allowing for still more complete indexing and faster access to quotations. A hypertext *Familiar Quotations* could include all editions of the work with their various prefaces, digitized graphics for images of persons who have been the sources of quotations, and even audible examples of the music that has provided quotable references. From its private first printing to its present status as the standard American quotation source, *Familiar Quotations* has recorded the shared culture of our world throughout the upheavals of 135 years. We can only hope this "most famous book of its kind" will continue to be with us as long as a common heritage is valued.

PUBLICATION HISTORY

Bartlett, John. *A Collection of Familiar Quotations, with Complete Indices of Authors and Subjects.* Cambridge, MA: John Bartlett, 1855. 295p.

Bartlett, John. *A Collection of Familiar Quotations, with Complete Indices of Authors and Subjects.* New ed. Cambridge, MA: John Bartlett, 1856. 358p.

Bartlett, John. *A Collection of Familiar Quotations with Complete Indices of Authors and Subjects.* 3rd ed. with supplement. Cambridge, MA: John Bartlett, 1858. 446p.

Bartlett, John. *Familiar Quotations; Being an Attempt to Trace to their Source, Passages and Phrases in Common Use.* 4th ed. Boston: Little, Brown & Co., 1863. 480p.

Bartlett, John. *Familiar Quotations; Being an Attempt to Trace to their Source Passages and Phrases in Common Use.* 5th ed. Boston: Little, Brown and Company, 1868. 778p.

Bartlett, John. *Familiar Quotations; Being an Attempt to Trace to their Source, Passages and Phrases in Common Use.* 6th ed. Boston: Little, Brown, 1872. 778p.

Bartlett, John. *Familiar Quotations: Being an Attempt to Trace to their Source, Passages and Phrases in Common Use.* 7th ed. Boston: Little, Brown & Co., 1875. 864p.

Bartlett, John. *Familiar Quotations; Being an Attempt to Trace to their Sources Passages and Phrases in Common Use.* 8th ed. Boston: Little, Brown and Company, 1882. 904p.

Bartlett, John. *Familiar Quotations: A Collection of Passages, Phrases, and Proverbs Traced to their Sources in Ancient and Modern Literature.* 9th ed. Boston: Little, Brown and Company, 1891. 1,158p.

Bartlett, John. *Familiar Quotations: A Collection of Passages, Phrases, and Proverbs Traced to their Sources in Ancient and Modern Literature.* 10th ed. revised and enlarged by Nathan Haskell Dole. Boston: Little, Brown and Company, 1914. 1,454p.

Bartlett, John. *Familiar Quotations: A Collection of Passages, Phrases, and Proverbs Traced to their Sources in Ancient and Modern Literature.* 11th ed., revised and enlarged, edited by Christopher Morley, and Louella D. Everett, associate editor. Boston: Little, Brown and Company, 1937. 1,578p.

Bartlett, John. *Familiar Quotations: A Collection of Passages, Phrases, and Proverbs Traced to their Sources in Ancient and Modern Literature.* 12th ed., revised and enlarged, edited by Christopher Morley, and Louella D. Everett, associate editor. Boston: Little, Brown, 1948. 1,831p.

Bartlett, John. *Familiar Quotations: A Collection of Passages, Phrases, and Proverbs Traced to their Sources in Ancient and Modern Literature.* 13th and centennial ed., completely rev. Boston: Little, Brown, 1955. 1,614p.

Bartlett, John. *Familiar Quotations: A Collection of Passages, Phrases, and Proverbs Traced to their Sources in Ancient and Modern Literature.* 14th ed., edited by Emily Morison Beck. Boston: Little, Brown & Co., 1968. 1,750p.

Bartlett, John. *Familiar Quotations: A Collection of Passages, Phrases, and Proverbs Traced to their Sources in Ancient and Modern Litera-* *ture.* 15th and 125th anniversary ed., edited by Emily Morison Beck. Boston: Little, Brown & Co., 1980. 1,540p.

BIBLIOGRAPHY

Although Bartlett's work has received many reviews over the years, most of them are brief and limited to comparison between new editions and their predecessors. The items listed below, have been chosen because they offer the reader more than the typical book review. Some of these are especially useful for historical or editorial background. Both Marshall and Reynolds provide biographical information on John Bartlett and discuss the history of his book. These two articles are invaluable sources of information on the development of *Familiar Quotations*. For contrasting behind-the-scenes views of the work, compare McWhorter's irreverent analysis of *Familiar Quotations* editorial practices to the article by Beck, its former editor.

Anderson, Melville B. "The New 'Bartlett's Quotations.'" *Dial* 12 (December, 1991): 268–78.

Atlas, James. "A New Bartlett's Quotations, Familiar and Otherwise." *New York Times Book Review* (March 29, 1981): 9.

Beck, Emily Morison. "The Long, Happy Life of 'Bartlett's Familiar Quotations.'" *American Heritage* 35 (August-September, 1984): 102–07.

"The Booklist Interview: Justin Kaplan on *Bartlett's Familiar Quotations*," *Booklist* 87 (February 1, 1991): 1152–53.

Goldberg, Isaac. "Who Said It?" *Saturday Review* 17 (December 4, 1937): 9–10.

"Ideas." *Newsweek* (March 12, 1990): 75-76.

Marshall, John David. "John Bartlett and His Quotation Book, 1855-1955." *Wilson Library Bulletin* 30 (November, 1955): 250-52.

McWhorter, Diane. "Bartlett's Hall of Fame." *Harper's* (May, 1981): 75-78.

Mitgang, Herbert. "A Bartlett's of Henny Youngman as Well as Shakespeare and Frost." *New York Times Book Review* (November 21, 1988): 15.

Review of *Collection of Familiar Quotations*, by John Bartlett. *Harvard Magazine* 6 (1855): 293-94.

Review of *Familiar Quotations*, 5th ed., by John Bartlett. *North American Review* 109 (July, 1869): 293-98.

Review of *Familiar Quotations*, 9th ed., by John Bartlett. *Writer* 7 (1894): 90–92.

Review of *Familiar Quotations*, 11th ed., edited by Christopher Morley. *Christian Science Monitor* (January 5, 1938): 11.

Review of *Familiar Quotations*, 15th ed., edited by Emily Morison Beck. *Choice* 18 (January, 1981): 631.

Reynolds, Horace. "A Name as Familiar as One's Own." *New York Times Book Review* (November 13, 1955): 1.

NOTES

[1] Facsimile of preface to first edition, *Familiar Quotations*, 12th ed., rev. by Christopher Morley and Louella D. Everett (Boston: Little, Brown & Co., 1948), ix.

[2] Review of *Collection of Familiar Quotations*, by John Bartlett, 1855, *Harvard Magazine* 6 (1855): 294.

[3] Eugene P. Sheehy, *Guide to Reference Books*, 10th ed. (Chicago and London: American Library Association 1986), 417-18; *Literary World* 15 (29 November 1884): 418.

[4] D. Bernard Theall, review of *Familiar Quotations*, 15th ed., ed. by Emily Morison Beck, *American Reference Books Annual* 13 (1982): 69.

[5] Review of *Familiar Quotations*, 11th ed., ed. by Christopher Morley and Louella D. Everett, 1937, *Christian Science Monitor* (5 January 1938): 11.

[6] Facsimile of preface to first edition, *Familiar Quotations*, 12th ed., ix.

[7] Melville B. Anderson, "The New 'Bartlett's Familiar Quotations,'" *Dial* 12 (December 1991): 269-70.

[8] "Preface to the Ninth Edition," in *Familiar Quotations*, 9th ed., by John Bartlett (Boston: Little, Brown & Co., 1891).

[9] "Preface to the Tenth Edition," in *Familiar Quotations*, 10th ed., ed. by Nathan Haskell Dole (Boston: Little, Brown & Co., 1914).

[10] Ibid.

[11] "Preface to the Eleventh Edition," in *Familiar Quotations*, 11th ed., ed. by Christopher Morley and Louella D. Everett (Boston: Little, Brown & Co., 1937).

[12] Review of *Familiar Quotations*, 11th ed., *Christian Science Monitor* (5 January 1938): 11.

[13] "Preface to the Eleventh Edition."

[14] "Preface to the Twelfth Edition," in *Familiar Quotations*, 12th ed., ed. by Christopher Morley and Louella D. Everett (Boston: Little, Brown & Co., 1948).

[15] Emily Morison Beck, "The Long, Happy Life of 'Bartlett's Familiar Quotations,'" *American Heritage* 35 (August-September 1984): 102.

[16] Horace Reynolds, "A Name as Familiar as One's Own," *New York Times Book Review* (13 November 1955): 1.

[17] "Preface to the Fifteenth Edition," in *Familiar Quotations*, 15th ed., ed. by Emily Morison Beck (Boston: Little, Brown & Co., 1980).

[18] James Atlas, "A New Bartlett's Quotations, Familiar and Otherwise," *New York Times Book Review* (29 March 1981): 9.

[19] Diane McWhorter, "Bartlett's Hall of Fame," *Harper's* 262 (May 1981): 76, 78.

[20] Herbert Mitgang, "A Bartlett's of Henny Youngman as Well as Shakespeare and Frost," *New York Times Book Review* (21 November 1988): 20.

[21] Ibid.

Black's Law Dictionary: Ninety-Nine Years, 1891–1990

DEVELOPMENT AND HISTORY

A brief history of the English and American predecessors to *Black's Law Dictionary* provides insight to some of the characteristics of early law dictionaries and the tradition from which *Black's* evolved. English law dictionaries date back to sixteenth-century England when John Rastell, brother-in-law of Sir Thomas More, authored the *Expositiones terminorum legum Anglorum* (1527). This compilation included only 208 entries chosen and designed to explain obscure terms to students of law. The entries were mostly in Latin and the text was almost exclusively French.[1] An expanded version of Rastell's work, known as *Terms de la ley*, was later published in parallel French and English columns.

Early English-Language Antecedents

In 1607 John Cowell published the first edition of *The Interpreter*. Like Rastell's work, the title was designed for those learning about the law, but there the similarities ended. Rastell was a practicing lawyer, whereas Cowell was a former professor of civil law at Cambridge. Cowell wrote his dictionary in English and included not only "obscure" words but almost "all" law words that needed explanation.[2] *The Interpreter* was a larger volume than Rastell's and a more scholarly one, and it included lay terms such as "fish," "spices," and "furres."[3] According to Cowell, entries not related to the art of the law were included so that lawyers would not be ignorant of such things as beasts or fowls.

In 1670 Thomas Blount, the author of a general English dictionary, issued the one-volume *Nomo-Lexikon*. As an antiquarian, Blount enjoyed oddities of the English legal past and included them in the *Nomo-Lexikon*. An example of this was his inclusion of an entry on "doitkin," defined as a coin of small value prohibited since 1416, and the source of the phrase, "not worth a doitkin."[4]

Giles Jacob's *New Law Dictionary*, published in 1729, was an important representative of its time. This huge tome was intended to serve as a substitute for a legal education. It included legal forms and reflected the decline of sophisticated schools for barristers, the expense of law books, and the increasing number of attorneys without formal education. Jacob's work, paralleling a phenomenon in general language dictionaries, copied from its predecessors by adding ordinary words to make a larger and more impressive volume for the consumers.

English law dictionaries were used in the United States until 1839, when John Bouvier published a two-volume American law dictionary entitled *A Law Dictionary Adapted to the Constitution and Laws of the United States of America and of Several States of the American Union* (Philadelphia: T. and J. W. Johnson). Bouvier was critical of the English law dictionaries because they were outdated and contained entries copied from earlier titles without much alteration. In his preface Bouvier noted that most of the matter in English law dictionaries was written while the feudal law was in full vigor and was not appropriate for the nineteenth century. Based on these criticisms, Bouvier omitted much from his dictionary that English law dictionaries had included.

Like Jacob, Bouvier wrote a work that also offered a legal education. There was need for such a work in the early United States; most lawyers learned about law through an apprenticeship rather than through formal education at a university. Some attorneys just studied the law on their own. Bouvier's *Law Dictionary* was in use when Black wrote the first edition of his famous work.

Henry Campbell Black

Henry Campbell Black, a legal scholar, was born on October 17, 1860, in Ossining, New York. Black's parents were the Reverend John Henry Black and Caroline Campbell Black. After studying the Greek and Latin classics, Black entered Trinity College, graduating in 1880 with an A.B. A member of Phi Beta Kappa, Black received his A.M. in 1887 from Trinity College and an honorary degree of Doctor of Laws in 1916.

In 1883 Black was admitted to the Bar of Lycoming County, Pennsylvania. He practiced law in Williamsport, Pennsylvania, and subsequently moved to St. Paul, Minnesota, where he continued his law practice. But Black's true interest was in legal theory, and that led him to publish his first important book, *An Essay on the Constitutional Prohibitions Against Legislation Impairing the Obligation of Contracts, and Against Retroactive and Ex Post Facto Laws* (Boston: Little, Brown, 1887). It was accepted by the legal profession as an authoritative source on the subject.

In 1888 Black moved to Washington, D.C., where he came in contact with some of the most prominent members of his profession, as well as with many others with intellec-

tual interests. In this stimulating environment Black devoted his time to authorship. He was most interested in studying the Constitution of the United States, and he wrote books about constitutional law as well as other legal topics. Black also authored articles for law journals and encyclopedias, and he served as the editor of *The Constitutional Law Review* from 1917 until his death in 1927.

In January 1891 Dr. Black published his first book with West Publishing Company, a major legal publisher in St. Paul, Minnesota. *Black on Judgments* was an immediate success, requiring reprints in April 1891, and again later in the year.

Black's Dictionary

Today, Henry Campbell Black is best known for his law dictionary, which was first published by West in 1891 under the title *A Dictionary of Law*. Black's one-volume dictionary still is a very important West publication. The dictionary includes ancient and modern terms, phrases, and maxims used in American and English law. In the first edition's preface Black stated that for, "the terms appertaining to old and middle English law and the feudal polity, recourse has been had freely to the older English law dictionaries, (such as those of Cowell, Spelman, Blount, Jacob, Cunningham, Whishaw, Skene, Tomlins, and the 'Terms de la Ley,') as also to the writings of Bracton, Littleton, Coke and other sages of the early law."[5]

Black relied upon other dictionaries and writings of legal scholars for terms from Roman and modern civil law as well as for the terms and phrases from French, Spanish, and Scotch law. Modern American and English law terms were derived from codes, statutes, reports, legal textbooks, works by legal scholars, and recent English and American dictionaries. Quoted material was indented in an entry and set in smaller type along with the source of the reference. Black did not provide an exhaustive list of sources consulted in compiling the *Dictionary*; however, he made acknowledgements in entries when aid was "directly levied from those sources."[6] Black also wrote many new definitions, for his stated aim was "to present a definition at once concise, comprehensive, accurate, and lucid."[7]

The first edition, which was intended for the student and the professional, had two supplementary sections. One was a list of older principal law dictionaries and the second was a list of British regnal years. The *Dictionary* contained no place or personal name entries, illustrations, or pronunciation aids, and usually gave no indication of the parts of speech for an entry. Abbreviations generally appeared at the beginning of each alphabetical section. Synonyms and antonyms were included under the word entries and important variations in meanings were noted. For example, the entry on "death" distinguished between the meaning of a "natural" death and a "civil" death.[8] The entry on "debt" included a five-paragraph section on synonyms.[9]

An unsigned review of the first edition praised it as a "useful book" and criticized it for including too many words merely because they had been involved in a decision of a case.[10] Examples included "dead-head," "father," and "female."[11] The critic believed it superfluous to include words that laity and lawyers used in exactly the same manner. But the reviewer praised Black for confining himself to definitions and not trying to offer a legal education by including essays, as Bouvier had.

In the second edition, published in 1910, Black wrote about the changes to his work. In response to demands, Black added a number of references to cases in which terms or phrases of the law were judicially defined. Black rewrote many definitions because he had received "helpful criticism" or because he otherwise saw a need for change.[12] The second edition also included terms new to the law which had come into use since the first edition was published. Black included medical terminology when appropriate and acknowledged

the assistance of Dr. Fielding H. Garrison. A new supplementary section, a table of abbreviations, appeared in the second edition. The 70 page table primarily contained abbreviations or reference sources cited in the *Dictionary*'s entries.

Another change in the second edition was a new system of arrangement which grouped all compound and descriptive terms under the respective headings from which they were derived. The placement of the entry on "straw bail" was an example of this new arrangement. In the first edition, the entry on "bail" did not include a description of "straw bail,"[13] which appeared instead in a separate entry in the "S" alphabetical section.[14] In the second edition, however, the term "straw bail" was defined within the entry on "bail," and a *see* reference under "straw bail" pointed to "bail."[15] This new arrangement was praised by a reviewer who also liked the book's physical appearance and stated that the title was "well worthy of being pronounced the best American single volume dictionary of the law."[16]

The third edition of the *Dictionary* came out in 1933, six years after Black's death. In the preface the publisher briefly explained the changes in the work. New words were added and modernized definitions were included, along with references to updated authorities supporting new uses of a term. The third edition was the first to be titled *Black's Law Dictionary*.

Criticism of the Dictionary

The reviews of the third edition were generally very positive; however, Alexander Hamilton Frey wrote that a random look at *Black's* disclosed many lay terms that did not have any unique legal definition.[17] He listed "alehouse," "aristocracy," "chain," "double," "gentlewoman," and "monogram" as examples." Frey even suggested that the "padding" of the *Dictionary* may have been for a commercial reason.[18]

Typographical changes were made in the fourth edition in 1951 to accommodate the enlarged contents. The type was completely reset and arranged in wider columns, making the text more attractive and readable. The publishers added a five-page guide to the pronunciation of primarily Latin words and phrases. As in earlier editions, the *Dictionary* included definitions found in the works of early legal scholars along with new and updated definitions.

In 1968 West published a revised fourth edition, which included some changed and updated entries. Several new supplementary sections were added: the Code of Professional Responsibility, the Code of Judicial Conduct, and a table of the minimum requirements for admission to legal practice in the United States.

The fifth edition, published by West in 1979, was produced on an IBM computer composition system.[19] This edition's preface clearly summarized its improvements and changes, crediting two individuals and the West editorial staff for the major improvements. Joseph R. Nolan, Associate Justice of the Massachusetts Supreme Court, was primarily responsible for the 10,000 new or revised entries, and M. J. Connolly, Associate Professor of Linguistics and Eastern Languages at Boston College, developed the pronunciation guides for all entries which posed pronunciation difficulties. The Code of Professional Conduct, the Code of Judicial Conduct, the five-page guide to pronunciation, and the table listing the requirements for admission to legal practice were removed. The Constitution of the United States, the United States government organization chart, and a listing of the U.S. Supreme Court justices and their terms were included in the appendices.

An abridged fifth edition of *Black's* containing over 16,000 definitions was published in 1983. The publisher created this abridged edition in response to the need for a compact law dictionary that could be conveniently carried and used away from a library or office. Also in 1983, the fifth edition of *Black's* was first offered online through WESTLAW, a system of databases produced and made available by West Publishing.[20] The *WESTLAW*

Reference Manual explains the general database search techniques and provides searching tips for use with *Black's*.

The reviews of the fifth edition in the printed format were generally positive. Richard Sloane, Law Librarian and Professor of Law at the University of Pennsylvania Law School, pointed out the work's notable virtues and main short-comings, compared 16 specific entries in *Black's* to another current law dictionary, and provided several proposals for improvement.[21] These proposals included deleting a large proportion of *Black's* ancient terms and its general or specialized nonlegal terms. Sloane felt the references to cases were helpful; however, the date the case was decided needed to be included. He stated that references made to some cases and treatises were outdated, and more timely references could be made. Finally, Sloane suggested emphasizing new terms and concepts emerging in expanding branches of the law.

Sloane recognized that a publisher would hesitate to tamper with success; however, he felt that a future edition of Black's would benefit from his ideas. Sloane's comparative review identified the *Dictionary's* strengths and weaknesses and, importantly, reaffirmed its preeminence among American law dictionaries.

The Current Edition

In mid-1990 the sixth edition of *Black's* was published. In this new edition the publisher addressed points raised in Professor Sloane's review of the fifth edition. Many nonlegal terms were deleted and new terms were added. The work contains more than 5,000 new, revised, or updated words and terms. The publisher has expanded examples of word usages, added cross-references to related terms, and added updated citations.[22] The preface explains that new tax, finance, and accounting terms have been added due to the expanding importance of financial terminology. A certified public accountant served as a contributing author and reviewed the tax and accounting terms.

The appendices include an expanded table of abbreviations, the Constitution of the United States, a time chart of the United States Supreme Court, a United States government organization chart, and a table of British regnal years. The pronunciation guides were updated by the linguistics professor who also contributed to the fifth edition.

The importance of *Black's* among law dictionaries is evident when reviewing current bibliographies of legal reference works. Although there are many specialized and foreign-language legal dictionaries, *Black's* is the one most often cited as the most desirable general law dictionary. Legal scholars, practitioners, and students will benefit from the updated edition of this well known and respected title.

PUBLICATION HISTORY

A Dictionary of Law, Containing Definitions of the Terms and Phrases of American and English Jurisprudence, Ancient and Modern; Including the Principal Terms of International, Constitutional, and Commercial Law; With a Collection of Legal Maxims and Numerous Select Titles from the Civil Law and Other Foreign Systems, by Henry Campbell Black. St. Paul, MN: West Publishing Co., 1891. 1,253p.

A Law Dictionary Containing Definitions of the Terms and Phrases of American and English Jurisprudence, Ancient and Modern; And Including the Principal Terms of International, Constitutional, Ecclesiastical, and Commercial Law, and Medical Jurisprudence, with a Collection of Legal Maxims, Numerous Select Titles from the Roman, Modern Civil, Scotch, French, Spanish, and Mexican Law, and other Foreign Systems, and a Table of Abbreviations, by Henry Campbell Black. 2nd ed. St. Paul, MN: West Publishing Co., 1910. 1,314p. Spine title: *Black's Law Dictionary.*

Black's Law Dictionary Containing Definitions of the Terms and Phrases of American and English Jurisprudence, Ancient and Modern, and Including the Principal Terms of International, Constitutional, Ecclesiastical and Commercial Law, and Medical Jurisprudence, with a Collection of Legal Maxims, Numerous Select Titles from the Roman, Modern Civil, Scotch, French, Spanish, and Mexican Law, and Other Foreign Systems, and a Table of Abbreviations, by the publisher's editorial staff. 3rd ed. St. Paul, MN: West Publishing Co., 1933. 1,944p.

Black's Law Dictionary; Definitions of the Terms and Phrases of American and English Jurisprudence, Ancient and Modern, with Guide to Pronunciation, by the publisher's editorial staff. 4th ed. St. Paul, MN: West Publishing Co., 1951. 1,882p.

Black's Law Dictionary; Definitions of the Terms and Phrases of American and English Jurisprudence, Ancient and Modern, by the publisher's editorial staff. Rev. 4th ed. St. Paul, MN: West Publishing Co., 1968. 1,882p.

Black's Law Dictionary; Definitions of the Terms and Phrases of American and English Jurisprudence, Ancient and Modern, by the publisher's editorial staff, contributing authors Joseph R. Nolan and M. J. Connolly. 5th ed. St. Paul, MN: West Publishing Co., 1979. 1,511p.

Black's Law Dictionary; Definitions of the Terms and Phrases of American and English Jurisprudence, Ancient and Modern, by the publisher's editorial staff, contributing authors Joseph R. Nolan and M.J. Connolly. Abridged 5th ed. St. Paul, MN: West Publishing Co., 1983. 855p.

Black's Law Dictionary; Definitions of the Terms and Phrases of American and English Jurisprudence, Ancient and Modern, by the publisher's editorial staff, coauthors Joseph R. Nolan and Jacqueline M. Nolan-Haley, contributing authors M. J. Connolly, Stephen C. Hicks, and Martina N. Alibrandi. 6th ed. St. Paul, MN: West Publishing Co., 1990. 1,657.

BIBLIOGRAPHY

Reviews of *Black's Law Dictionary* have generally been short and most biographical data on Henry Campbell Black are brief. Two notable exceptions are Richard Sloane's review of the fifth edition in the *University of Toledo Law Review* and David Hill's summary of Dr. Black's life in *The Constitutional Review*.

Adams, Oscar Fay. *A Dictionary of American Authors.* 5th ed., rev. and enl. Boston: Houghton, Mifflin and Co., 1904.

Alexander, Arthur A. Review of *Black's Law Dictionary*, 3rd ed., by the publisher's editorial staff.

Georgetown Law Journal 22 (March, 1934): 657-58.

Anderson, William C. "Law Dictionaries." *American Law Review* 28 (July-August 1894): 531-46.

Dick, Terry S. *WESTLAW Reference Manual*. 3rd ed. St. Paul, MN: West Publishing Co., 1989.

Frey, Alexander Hamilton. Review of *Black's Law Dictionary*, 3rd ed., by the publisher's editorial staff. *University of Pennsylvania Law Review* 82 (June 1934): 886-87.

Hill, David Jayne. "In Memoriam Doctor Henry Campbell Black." *The Constitutional Review* 11 (April, 1927): 67-76.

Mellinkoff, David. "The Myth of Precision and the Law Dictionary." *UCLA Law Review* 31 (December, 1983): 423-42.

Review of *A Dictionary of Law, Containing Definitions of the Terms and Phrases of American and English Jurisprudence, Ancient and Modern; Including the Principal Terms of International, Constitutional, and Commercial Law; With a Collection of Legal Maxims and Numerous Select Titles from the Civil Law and Other Foreign Systems*, by Henry Campbell Black. *The Nation* 53 (December 17, 1891): 469-70.

Review of *A Law Dictionary Containing Definitions of the Terms and Phrases of American and English Jurisprudence, Ancient and Modern; And Including the Principal Terms of International, Constitutional, Ecclesiastical, and Commercial Law, and Medical Jurisprudence, With a Collection of Legal Maxims, Numerous Select Titles from the Roman, Modern Civil, Scotch, French, Spanish, and Mexican Law, and Other Foreign Systems, and a Table of Abbreviations*, 2nd ed., by Henry Campbell Black. *The American Political Science Review* 5 (May, 1911): 284.

Sloane, Richard. Review of *Black's Law Dictionary*, 5th ed., by the publisher's editorial staff. *University of Toledo Law Review* 11 (Winter, 1980): 322-30.

"A Symposium of Law Publishers." *American Law Review* 23 (May-June, 1889): 396-44.

Who Was Who in America. Vol. 1, 1897-1942. Chicago: Marquis Who's Who, 1943.

NOTES

[1] David Mellinkoff, "The Myth of Precision and the Law Dictionary," *UCLA Law Review* 31 (December 1983): 426.

[2] Ibid., 427.

[3] Ibid., 428.

[4] Ibid.

[5] Henry Campbell Black, "Preface," in *A Dictionary of Law Containing Definitions of the Terms and Phrases of American and English Jurisprudence, Ancient and Modern* (St. Paul, MN: West Publishing Co., 1891), iv.

[6] Ibid.

[7] Ibid.

[8] Black, *Dictionary of Law*, 335.

[9] Ibid., 337.

[10] Review of *A Dictionary of Law Containing Definitions of the Terms and Phrases of American and English Jurisprudence, Ancient and Modern*, by Henry Campbell Black, The Nation 53 (17 December 1891): 470.

[11] Ibid.

[12] Henry Campbell Black, "Preface," in *A Law Dictionary Containing Definitions of the Terms and Phrases of American and English Jurisprudence, Ancient and Modern; And Including the Principal Terms of International, Constitutional, Ecclesiastical, and Commercial Law, and Medical Jurisprudence, with a Collection of Legal Maxims, Numerous Select Titles from the Roman, Modern Civil, Scotch, French, Spanish, and Mexican Law, and Other Foreign Systems, and a Table of Abbreviations*, 2nd ed. (St. Paul, MN: West Publishing Co., 1910), iii.

[13] Black, *Dictionary of Law*, 113.

[14] Ibid., 1127.

[15] Black, *A Law Dictionary*, 113, 1113.

[16] Review of *A Law Dictionary*, 2nd ed., by Henry Campbell Black, *The American Political Science Review* 5 (May 1911): 284.

[17] Arthur A. Alexander, review of *Black's Law Dictionary*, 3rd ed., by the publisher's editorial staff, *Georgetown Law Journal* 22 (March 1934): 657-58; Alexander Hamilton Frey, review of *Black's Law Dictionary*, 3rd ed., by the publisher's editorial staff, *University of Pennsylvania Law Review* 82 (June 1934): 886-87; Review of *Black's Law Dictionary*, 3rd ed., by the publisher's editorial staff, *Harvard Law Review* 47 (November 1933): 170.

[18] Frey, review of *Black's*, 886.

[19] Kenneth G. Heimbach, Managing Editor, West Publishing Co., letter to the author, March 30, 1990.

[20] Ibid.

[21] Richard Sloane, review of *Black's Law Dictionary*, 5th ed., by the publisher's editorial staff, *University of Toledo Law Review* 11 (Winter 1980): 322-30; Dan Henke, review of *Black's Law Dictionary*, 5th ed., by the publisher's editorial staff, *American Bar Association Journal* 65 (September 1979): 1378-80; Leonard Schulte, "About Dictionaries," *Florida Bar Journal* 56 (February 1982): 153.

[22] Kenneth G. Heimbach, Managing Editor, West Publishing Co., letter to the author, 22 May 1990.

An "Alms-Basket" of "Bric-A-Brac": *Brewer's Dictionary of Phrase and Fable*

Charles Bunge

DEVELOPMENT AND HISTORY

The first edition of *Brewer's Dictionary of Phrase and Fable* was published in the year that Charles Dickens died. It was as firmly rooted in and reflective of the literary, intellectual, and social concerns of Victorian England as were the novels of Dickens, and, like them, Brewer's *Dictionary* has entertained and informed successive generations to the present day. Both Dickens and Brewer addressed social problems—in Brewer's case the need to make the fruits of nineteenth-century scholarship accessible to an ever widening range of readers—but they were also willing to respond to the Victorian hunger for diversion and entertainment, a formula that has stood them both in good stead for over a century.

Ebenezer Cobham Brewer was born in 1810 into the family of a Norwich schoolmaster. He worked his way through college at Trinity Hall, Cambridge, graduating with first-class honors in 1836. In 1848 he was awarded the LL.D. He entered the priesthood in 1838, probably hoping this would be an entrée into a university or scholarly career. However, after graduating from college, he assisted his father at the family's boarding school, becoming its headmaster when his father retired. He traveled extensively on the Continent and lived for a while in Paris. He read very widely and had excellent facility with languages.[1]

Around 1840, Brewer's *Guide to Science* (London: Jerrold) launched a successful career of writing informational and instructional materials for a popular audience. The *Guide* sold several hundred thousand copies and was translated into numerous languages. In the early 1860s Brewer started what would be a long and fruitful association with the publishing house of John Cassell. By then, Cassell, social reformer and former temperance lecturer, had firmly established his publishing company and its policy of publishing good educational and recreational reading for the working man.[2]

Undoubtedly, Brewer's experience as a schoolmaster and his proven ability as an educational writer were particularly attractive to the publisher. Brewer had an office at Cassell's La Bell Sauvage quarters, where he wrote and edited many of the firm's popular works for adults and children.[3] He was the compiler of such reference books as the *Reader's Handbook of Famous Names in Fiction* (London: Chatto & Windus) and the *Historic Notebook* (London: Smith, Elder), which were considered standard sources for many years.

The Dictionary's Antecedents

Brewer's grandson, P.M.C. Hayman, writes that Brewer himself attributed the genesis of the *Dictionary of Phrase and Fable* to "his boyhood habit of notetaking, which he continued all his life."[4] This habit of making and saving notes from one's reading, along with correspondence between authors and their readers, seems to have been common in Brewer's day. Brewer wrote that the popularity of his *Guide to Science* "brought me a large number of questions on all imaginary matters." He accumulated the answers to these questions, along with other notes and references, in A-Z pigeonholes, and they became the nucleus of the *Dictionary*.[5]

The *Dictionary of Phrase and Fable* also had roots in antiquarianism and the miscellanies of folk custom, beliefs, and curiosities it produced, including Hone's *Every-Day Book* (London: Hunt & Clarke, 1825-26), John Timbs' *Things Not Generally Known* (London: David Borgue, 1856) and other works, and Robert Chambers' *Book of Days* (Edinburgh: W. & R. Chambers, 1862-64). Brewer called his miscellany "bric-a-brac" and said that his entries drew in the "curious . . ., historical trifles . . ., and references to Scandinavian and other mythology."[6] If the *Dictionary* had a tap root, it surely fed on the nineteenth-century philology that produced many etymological dictionaries in Brewer's day, culminating in the *Oxford English Dictionary*. He wrote that etymology "forms a staple of the book," especially etymologies and explanations of familiar phrases, allusions that would puzzle the common reader, and "words that have a tale to tell."[7] And there was the Victorian impulse toward self-improvement and Brewer's concern for making knowledge and literature accessible to the increasingly literate working class. He called his work an "alms-basket," alms being gifts for the less fortunate, and said that he selected from his mass of notes those items that he thought were "best suited for popular purposes."[8] The second ("New") edition was published in 13 installments (hence, the frequent references to it as the 1894-95 edition), a common nineteenth-century strategy for making books affordable to working-class people.

John Buchanan-Brown, former manager of Cassell's Reference Department, points out that a more immediate inspiration for Brewer was William Adolphus Wheeler's *Noted Names in Fiction* (Boston: Ticknor and Fields).[9] Buchanan-Brown believes that Wheeler was not only the source for some of Brewer's entries, but that he challenged Brewer to provide information on such things as "celebrated customs and phrases" that represented what Wheeler called "too vast a field of enquiry" for him to have undertaken. Indeed, Brewer's first edition does contain entries for phrases that Wheeler used as examples of his exclusions, such as "flap-dragon" and "to carry coals to Newcastle."[10]

Brewer's, in turn, has influenced other reference works, especially literary handbooks. For example, Henrietta Gerwig, in the preface to *Crowell's Handbook for Readers and Writers*, acknowledged her debt to the *Dictionary*, and a number of her entries were taken directly from it.[11] William Rose Benét, in his preface to the *Handbook's* successor, *The Reader's Encyclopedia*, expressed his pleasure with this association, noting that *Brewer's* was among the reference books in his father's library.[12]

Critical Reception

Reference book reviewers have treated *Brewer's* well over the years. Early printings contained a page of "Selections from Notices of the Press" that quoted complimentary notes from newspapers and periodicals of the day. These notes pointed out features that would be mentioned again and again for the next 120 years. The writer in *The Daily Telegraph* noted that the *Dictionary* offered "the rare attraction in a book of reference of being thoroughly readable," and others noted that it would provide much pleasure and amusement. The *West Sussex Gazette* and *The Manchester Examiner* recommended the work to students, speakers, writers, and general readers who needed explanations of allusions or "who are in want of pertinent illustrations," while another reviewer characterized the knowledge in the volume as "one of the very best means of effecting a pleasant diversion from the dull level of commonplace small-talk in ordinary company." From the first printing onward, reviewers agreed that *Brewer's* should "find a place in every library, whether public or private."[13]

Reviewers greeted each successive major revision with notes of from one to several paragraphs. The *London Quarterly* review of the 1894-95 edition is typical among these. It notes *Brewer's* "enormous popularity," its improvement through updating and correction of old entries and the addition of new ones, its delights for lovers of the curious, and its general usefulness to other readers.[14] The *Reference Books Bulletin* note on the 1989 edition strikes a similar tone.[15] In between these, reviewers took special note of the 1970 centenary edition. For example, B. Hunter Smeaton, writing in *Library Journal*, reflected on *Brewer's* particular usefulness for items that are likely to be absent from other reference books,[16] and the reviewer in *The Times Literary Supplement* wished that the new edition had concentrated on such items, leaving "all the other terms to works which cover them more fully and knowledgeably...."[17]

Such reviews both reflected and confirmed *Brewer's* early-won status as a standard reference book. The same is true of its treatment in lists of recommended reference works. As early as 1877, Justin Winsor included it on a list of reference books for small libraries, albeit with note of its borrowings from Wheeler mentioned above.[18] Alice B. Kroeger included it in her 1902 *Guide to the Study and Use of Reference Books*, (Boston: American Library Association) as has every edition of "Mudge" (or "Winchell" or "Sheehy," depending on one's generation). Likewise, Bessie Graham included it in the first edition of her *Bookman's Manual* (New York: Bowker, 1921), and it is still listed in the latest edition of *The Reader's Adviser* (New

York: Bowker, 1986-88). British guides have been equally consistent in listing it.

Not surprisingly, *Brewer's* is included among the tools that are taught in courses on reference materials in library schools, and is among the tools considered "vital" for all types and sizes of libraries in a study conducted by Wallace Bonk to see what sources all library school students should be taught.[19] And John C. Larsen found that most library schools included *Brewer's* among the "tried-and-true" titles in their humanities literature or bibliography courses.[20] Various reference course textbooks, from Shores to Katz, have also included *Brewer's*.

Evolution and Editions

No sooner was the first printing of the *Dictionary* off the press than Brewer was noting needed corrections and addenda. While the pagination and most of the entries remained constant through the 1870 version's numerous printings (called "editions" through at least 26), some corrections and additions were made on the pages, and many printings had one or more pages of "addenda et corrigenda." Many of these had been suggested in letters from readers of the volume, whom Brewer acknowledged in additions to the preface. After several printings, the publisher added a "Bibliographic Appendix," which was a listing of English authors and their works, based on W. Davenport Adams' *Dictionary of English Literature* (2nd ed., London: Cassell, Petter, & Galpin, 1878). This appendix was discontinued with the 1923 edition.

By 1894, the needed correction and additions were beyond what could be done "with such clipping and verbal changes as can be made in stereotyped plates," and a completely reset "New Edition" was published.[21] By this time, the publishers claimed that 100,000 copies of the volume had been produced, and the title page of printings of the new edition indicated increases in this number (e.g., "110th

Thousand" in 1899, "129th Thousand" in 1905).

Brewer expanded the size of his dictionary by a third in the second edition. He also corrected many entries and substituted new items for less useful ones. His preface to the new edition credits two sources for these corrections and expansions. First, there were "many hundreds of correspondents," some of whom seem to have gone through the first edition painstakingly, suggesting corrections, quotations, and other changes. The other source was the wealth of material coming out of what Brewer dubbed "The Era of English Philology." He wrote that he took advantage of "this great literary movement from every available source," very probably including the early installments of the *New English Dictionary*.[22]

The 1894–95 edition was reprinted numerous times up through World War I. Another "New Edition" was published in 1923. Buchanan-Brown says that Lawrence H. Dawson edited this version, though he is not mentioned on the title page or elsewhere in the volume.[23] Revisions consisted mainly of dropping numerous terms and allusions that had fallen out of use since the 1890s, and the addition of new terms and phrases.

By the end of World War II, *Brewer's* was much in need of revision again, and it was the first of the Cassell reference books to receive attention after the turmoil of the war period subsided.[24] Cassell's chairman, Desmond Flower, took personal interest in the revision, and a "Revised & Enlarged" edition came out in 1952.[25] The unnamed editor wrote in the volume's "Editor's Note" that the new edition had been "brought up to date by the inclusion of many forms of expression that have arisen during the past years," including phrases that came into use during the war, such as "blood, toil, tears, and sweat" and the V-for-victory symbol.

With the 1952 edition, the publishers again adopted the practice of referring to printings as editions. The "fifth edition" of 1959 contained minor revisions within the same page set-up, and in 1963 a "Revised Edition" (also referred to as the eighth edition) was published "in order to keep pace with the coinage of new phrases."[26]

In 1963 Desmond Flower appointed Ivor H. Evans editor of what was to be the 1970 "Centenary Edition." Evans was recommended by S. H. Steinberg, Cassell's editor in charge of dictionaries, with whom Evans had worked on the *Dictionary of British History* (New York: St Martin's).[27] Evans, like Brewer, was a school teacher. He was educated at King's College, London, and the University of London Institute of Education.

Evans completely revised the *Dictionary*. He discarded many entries that seemed inappropriate to Brewer's original conception, especially technical expressions and other terms for which one would be likely to consult a general dictionary or encyclopedia.[28] Many remaining entries were rewritten for accuracy, clarity, and conciseness. Some 2,000 new entries for recent and current phrases were added, and an improved system of cross-referencing was used.

Ivor Evans has remained editor through two subsequent editions, the 1981 "Revised Edition" and the 1989 "Fourteenth Edition." His methods of collecting materials for the *Dictionary* are strikingly similar to those used by Brewer himself. "I have always read extensively and have been blessed with a good memory and always register anything that might be worth space in *Brewer's*, either as an entry or a worthwhile quotation. I work on the principle of Captain Cuttle in Dickens's *Dombey and Son*, 'When found make a note of . . .'" He also picks up expressions from conversation, newspapers, periodicals, and correspondence. Each potential new entry is carefully checked in several sources and weighed as to its appropriateness for Brewer's. Entries that pass the test are placed in Evans' equivalent of Brewer's pigeonholes to await the next revision.[29]

American publishers have published editions and printings of *Brewer's* parallel to those of Cassell. Except for the title pages, these versions have been exactly the same as

Cassell's. The firm of Claxton, Remsen and Heffelfinger was the American publisher into the 1880s, and Lippincott published the volume through the 1923 edition. In 1952 George W. Jones added the *Dictionary* to Harper & Row's list of "staples," where it has more than met the criteria of being practical and informative and having long-term sales potential.[30] Various publishers have also found *Brewer's* an attractive title to reprint. The 1894-95 edition appeared as one of Henry Altemus' cheap reprint editions in 1898, and Avenel Books published a reprint of the same edition in 1978 (both with a curious extraneous quotation mark in their printed transcriptions of Brewer's handwritten preface that was in early printings of the 1894-95 edition as a facsimile).

The Current Edition

The 1989 edition of *Brewer's* is quite similar to that of 1870. Several small sections of the alphabet (100 entries) in the 1989 edition were examined by this author, as were the same sections of the 1870 edition (97 entries). Fifty-six entries are in both editions, 37 of them largely the same in content and wording. Reflections of successive generations of scholarship and changes in usage can be found by tracing such entries as "Stonehenge," "Barbecue," and those under "Oil" through various editions. The first edition contains 41 entries that have not survived into the "fourteenth" edition, e.g., "Hegemony," "New-fangled," "Papa," and "Swiss Family Robinson." The latest edition contains 44 entries not found in the first edition, e.g., "Blurb," "Heidelberg Man," "In the Swim," and "Switched on." The 1989 edition adds a 20-page index that will supplement the volume's cross-references.

Its Enduring Value

Why has a work that was so much a product of its age survived to serve eras that have been so different in characteristics and needs? The answer lies in its combination of two features that were pointed out by reviewers of the first edition. First, Brewer emphasized practical reference usefulness. Through the years, the volume has helped a broad range of readers and writers, from the student or the self-educated reader who wished to understand literary allusions and to share the culture they represent, to the scholar or the well-educated writer who needed to verify a half-remembered phrase or its source. The *Dictionary* has been especially useful for phrases and adages that often get left out of general dictionaries and for lists of such phenomena as patron saints, national anthems, or dogs of note. Certainly, a key to the volume's continued usefulness has been Cassell's willingness to support revisions, so that users could find recently coined phrases, along with now obscure allusions found in literature from the past.

The second feature that has accounted for *Brewer's* remarkable success over the years is its delights for the browser. It is a disciplined user, indeed, who can look up one phrase in the *Dictionary* and put the book down immediately. Curiosity is a timeless human trait, whether in the Victorian antiquarian or in the trivia buff of the 1990s, and Brewer's has always spoken to it. Librarians who have bought the book for reference collections, readers who have perused it in libraries, and those who have it on their shelves at home will admit, with only a little hesitation, that the book may have been bought for its reference value but that it is loved for its hours (or moments, however fleeting) of browsing enjoyment.

To keep "Brewer's" from the fate of "Webster's" and "Roget's," Cassell's has registered the name as a British trademark. On the other hand, the publisher would like to take advantage of the widespread familiarity with "Brewer's" as a name, perhaps using it to enhance the acceptance of a similar reference tool for young people and another with a political emphasis.[31] Since the latest edition of the *Dictionary* has come out very recently, it is too early for the publisher to have formulated definite plans for yet another revision. However, allusions to fables of the past and the coinage of phrases will surely continue apace. Just as surely, *Brewer's Dictionary of Phrase and Fable* will continue to offer alms to readers (and listeners and viewers) of the twenty-first century who need help in sorting out the bric-a-brac of their past and present.

PUBLICATION HISTORY

Dictionary of Phrase and Fable, Giving the Derivation, Source, or Origin of Common Phrases, Allusions, and Words that have a Tale to Tell, by E. Cobham Brewer. London: Cassell, Petter, & Galpin, 1870. 976p.

Dictionary of Phrase and Fable, Giving the Derivation, Source, or Origin of Common Phrases, Allusions, and Words that have a Tale to Tell, by E. Cobham Brewer. New Edition, Revised, Corrected, and Enlarged, to which is added A Concise Bibliography of English Literature. London: Cassell, 1895. 1,440p.

A Dictionary of Phrase and Fable, by E. Cobham Brewer. New Edition. London: Cassell, 1923. 1,157p.

Brewer's Dictionary of Phrase & Fable. Revised & Enlarged. London: Cassell, 1952. 977p.

Brewer's Dictionary of Phrase & Fable. Revised Edition. London: Cassell, 1963. 970p.

Brewer's Dictionary of Phrase and Fable. Centenary Edition, revised by Ivor H. Evans. London: Cassell, 1970. 1,175p.

Brewer's Dictionary of Phrase and Fable. Revised Edition, by Ivor H. Evans. London: Cassell, 1981. 1,213p.

Brewer's Dictionary of Phrase and Fable. Fourteenth edition, by Ivor H. Evans. London: Cassell, 1989. 1,220p.

BIBLIOGRAPHY

Neither primary nor secondary sources regarding E. Cobham Brewer and his *Dictionary* are plentiful. Most of the relevant Cassell archives were destroyed in the air raid that destroyed La Belle Sauvage in 1941. The only easily accessible biography is the "brief memoir" by his grandson, P. M. C. Hayman, that is part of the introductory material in the 1970 Centenary Edition of the *Dictionary*. John Buchanan-Brown, former manager of Cassell's Reference Department, has provided a useful introduction to the 1981 and 1989 editions that places the work in its cultural context. Ivor H. Evans' editor's preface to the 1970, 1981, and 1989 editions provides brief information on the history of *Brewer's* and on his revisions. An understanding of John Cassell's background and activities in publishing informational and educational materials for working-class people is important to understanding the cultural context of *Brewer's*, and Nowell-Smith's book on Cassell's publishing house will provide useful and interesting insights in this regard. Likewise, good treatments of education and reading in the Victorian era, such as those by Richard Altick, will provide context very helpful to understanding Brewer and his works.

Altick, Richard D. *The English Common Reader: A Social History of the Mass Reading Public 1800–1900.* Chicago: University of Chicago Press, 1957.

Buchanan-Brown, John. "Introduction." In *Brewer's Dictionary of Phrase and Fable,* edited by Ivor H. Evans, ix-xvi. 14th ed. London: Cassell, 1989.

Collison, Robert. *Encyclopedias: Their History Throughout the Ages.* New York: Hafner, 1966.

Hayman, P. M. C. "E. Cobham Brewer LL.D.: A Brief Memoir by His Grandson." In *Brewer's Dictionary of Phrase and Fable,* edited by Ivor H. Evans, vii-xii. Centenary ed. London: Cassell, 1970.

McArthur, Tom. *Worlds of Reference: Lexicography, Learning and Language from the Clay Tablet to the Computer.* Cambridge: Cambridge University Press, 1986.

Nowell-Smith, Simon. *The House of Cassell, 1848–1958.* London: Cassell, 1958.

NOTES

1. P.M.C. Hayman, "E. Cobham Brewer LL.D.: A Brief Memoir by His Grandson," in *Brewer's Dictionary of Phrase and Fable*, Centenary ed., ed. by Ivor H. Evans (London: Cassell, 1970), vii-xii.

2. Simon Nowell-Smith, *The House of Cassell, 1848–1958* (London: Cassell, 1958), 36–49.

3. John Buchanan-Brown, "Introduction," in *Brewer's Dictionary of Phrase and Fable*, 14th ed., ed. by Ivor H. Evans (London: Cassell, 1989), xii.

4. Hayman, ix-x.

5. Ibid.

6. E. Cobham Brewer, "Preface," in *Dictionary of Phrase and Fable* (London: Cassell, Petter, & Galpin, 1870), v-viii.

7. Ibid.

8. Ibid.

9. Buchanan-Brown, xi-xii.

10. William A. Wheeler, *An Explanatory and Pronouncing Dictionary of the Noted Names of Fiction* (Boston: Ticknor and Fields, 1866), v-vi.

11. Henrietta Gerwig, *Crowell's Handbook for Readers and Writers* (New York: Crowell, 1925), v. See, for example, entries for "Abigail," and "Abracadabra."

12. William Rose Benét, "Preface to the First Edition," in *The Reader's Encyclopedia*, 2nd ed. (New York: Crowell, 1965), unpaged.

13. "Selections from Notices of the Press," in *Dictionary of Phrase and Fable*, 3rd ed, by E. Cobham Brewer (London: Cassell, Petter, & Galpin, 1872), unpaged.

14. Review of *Dictionary of Phrase and Fable*, *London Quarterly and Holborn Review* 86 (July 1896): 389-90.

15. Review of *Brewer's Dictionary of Phrase and Fable*, *Booklist* 86 (1 March 1990): 1380–81.

16. B. Hunter Smeaton, Review of *Brewer's Dictionary of Phrase and Fable*, *Library Journal* 97 (15 March 1972): 1002.

17. "As They Brew . . . ," The *Times Literary Supplement* no. 3581 (16 October 1970): 7.

18. Justin Winsor, "Reference Books in English," *Library Journal* 1 (31 March 1877): 247–49.

19. Wallace J. Bonk, *Use of Basic Reference Sources in Libraries* (Ann Arbor: University of Michigan, 1963), 116–28.

20. John C. Larsen, "Titles Currently Studied in Humanities Courses," *Journal of Education for Librarianship* 10 (Fall 1969): 120–28.

21. E. Cobham Brewer, "Preface," in *Dictionary of Phrase and Fable*, New ed. (London: Cassell, 1895), unpaged.

22. Ibid.

23. Buchanan-Brown, xv.

24. Nowell-Smith, 243.

25. Buchanan-Brown, xv.

26. "Preface," in Rev. ed. (London: Cassell, 1963), v.

27. Ivor H. Evans, letter to the author, 17 February, 1990.

28. Ivor H. Evans, "Editor's Preface," in *Brewer's Dictionary of Phrase and Fable*, Centenary ed. (London: Cassell, 1970), v-vi.

29. Evans, letter to author, 17 February 1990.

30. Eugene Exman, *The House of Harper* (New York: Harper & Row, 1967), 240, 283.

31. Steven Cook, Assistant Editor, Reference, Cassell Publishers, Ltd., telephone conversation with author, 2 February, 1990.

"The Indispensable Guide": *The Chicago Manual of Style*

Richard D. DeBacher

HISTORY AND DEVELOPMENT

"It is often thought of as "The Bible" in terms of editorial style; I don't know an experienced editor who does not know it."
—Nancy N. Clemente, Managing Editor, Harvard University Press

"We like it. It is well organized, well thought out. What else can I say after I've said, 'I love you'?" —Sophie Sorkin, Vice President and Director of Copy Editing, Simon & Schuster[1]

Editors and writers commonly make affectionate reference to *The Chicago Manual of Style* and often regard it with gospel-like reverence. In fact one review of the most recent edition bore the title, "Look-it-up heaven for the writer."[2] While the principal authors of that edition, Bruce Young and Catharine Seybold, find such remarks hyperbolic and somewhat embarrassing, few of their professional colleagues would argue with Naomi Pascal, editor-in-chief of the University of Washington Press, who called it, "the indispensable guide for us scholarly publishers,"[3] or with Laurence Urdang, whose review in *Verbatim* concluded, "it must be conceded to be the most useful editorial tool available."[4]

The *Chicago Manual* quickly rose to its definitive status in North America shortly after publication of the first edition in 1906. Like the thirteenth edition, the first appeared as a revolution in printing technology was unfolding. Then as now, changes in the ways books were produced created a demand for new standards in the preparation of manuscripts, the editing of text, and the setting of type. The *Chicago Manual* met this need and subsequent editions changed over the years as printing technology evolved further. Thus, as Mark Carroll observed in his review of the thirteenth edition, "This grand tool is, as it always has been since its first edition in 1906, reflective of change and adaptation of the publication and printing process."[5]

These same trends shaped the market for the *Manual*, and, over the years, the primary focus has shifted from the needs of typesetters and their proofreaders to those of authors and their editors. Whereas the first line under the title of the original edition read, "Being a Compilation of the Typographical Rules . . .," the line had evolved by the eleventh edition (1949) to read, "containing typographical and other rules for authors, printers, and publishers." The twelfth (1969) and the thirteenth (1982) editions claim to serve, "Authors, Editors, and Copywriters," and all reference to typesetting has vanished from the title page.

In John Howell's words, the various editions of the *Chicago Manual* reflect "the process by which the printer's manual evolved into the editor's and author's manual."[6] The *Chicago Manual* was not written to cover matters of style that are the province of other well known works such as *The Elements of Style*, 3rd ed., by William Strunk, Jr., and E. B. White (New York: Macmillan, 1979) or the various prescriptive guides to grammatical usage. Rather, *The Chicago Manual of Style* covers "typographical style. . . . it tells you not how to say or write something, but how it should appear on the page."[7] According to Catharine Seybold, the *Manual* aims to serve editors and authors who need a reference tool that will

> help them decide what to capitalize, italicize, put in quotation marks; how to abbreviate all kinds of terms, to quote from other sources, to punctuate, to form plurals of numbers, names, etc., to compile and edit tables and indexes, to deal with footnotes and bibliographies and reference lists. . . . The accepted, and acceptable, ways of coping with these matters in good writing and good bookmaking, together with the University of Chicago Press preference where there was an alternative, had really always been chiefly what was meant by the word *style* in the title of the *Manual*.[8]

Today, most manuscripts are prepared with word processing software, and the author's "output" on magnetic floppy disks is frequently used in the copy editing process and to drive typesetting equipment. With desktop publishing software, the same machine used to write a document can be used edit it and set it in type. Technology has blurred the line that once clearly separated the writing, editing, and typesetting functions. The next edition of *The Chicago Manual of Style* is sure to reflect the changes brought about by this continuing technological evolution.

Early History of the Chicago Manual

The history of *The Chicago Manual of Style* is intimately tied to the history of the University of Chicago Press, which, in turn, traces its origins to those of the University itself in 1892.[9] The founding President of the University of Chicago, William Rainey Harper, believed that the basic mission of his new university should include not only teaching and a strong emphasis on research, but the dissemination of the fruits of scholarship as well. Thus, "From the time the University of

Chicago opened its doors in 1892, its press has been a department of the university. . . . to carry the wisdom of the university beyond its own student body."[10]

The new university press was assigned a variety of tasks, including the publication of scholarly books and journals containing the research results of the university's faculty as well as that of other researchers. To accomplish the challenging printing assignments, Newman Miller, who served as the director of the Press from 1900 to 1919, aimed to employ the new technology that was effecting a revolution in typesetting at the end of the nineteenth century. Miller persuaded the University Board of Trustees of the economic advantage of the Mergenthaler Linotype and the Lanston Monotype composing machines.

Faced not only with mastering these new machines but with using them to publish scholarly works in Greek, Hebrew, Syriac, Arabic, and Ethiopic, as well as technical and scientific research, the printing department of the Press established a copy editing and proofreading section under the direction of Louis Warming. As Seybold recounts it:

> Professors brought their handwritten manuscripts directly to the compositors, who did their best to decipher them and set them in an acceptable form. Rough proofs from this operation were turned over to a growing band of proofreaders, referred to as the 'brainery' by the typesetters because they endeavored to correct not only typographical errors but stylistic inconsistencies and even the grammatical lapses of the distinguished authors. To these hard-working souls, it inevitably became apparent that some guidelines were needed in their business. So, true to the pioneer spirit of the new university growing around them, they drew up their own 'style sheet' with a little help from interested members of the English department and others. This was printed in a small pamphlet and distributed to the professorial journal editors and others in the university community."[11]

This small pamphlet, first produced in 1901, became the seed from which the first edition of *The Chicago Manual of Style* would grow. Newman Miller perceived both the editorial and economic potential of the style sheet and urged the governing board of the Press to approve its issuance as a regular Press publication:

> It is recommended by the Publication Committee that this pamphlet be issued as a regular publication of the Press. . . . It is believed . . . that the work will be valuable to many persons not connected with the University, and in order to take it out of the class of documents which are usually given away it has been thought wise to put a price upon it and endeavor to sell it through general trade channels, without special promotional efforts being put upon it."[12]

The First Edition of the Manual

Accordingly, in 1906, the Press issued a 200-page book with a two-color title page which read, "MANUAL OF STYLE. Being a compilation of the typographical rules in force at the University of Chicago Press, to which are appended SPECIMENS OF TYPES IN USE." Some 80 pages of this first *Manual* cover type specimens and elaborate ornaments. Seventy-five pages are devoted to Rules of Composition; 12 pages to technical terms; and 10 pages to an appendix offering what are called "Hints." The latter begin assertively, "Manuscripts should be either typewritten or in a perfectly clear handwriting. The former is preferable." To proofreaders it advises, "The *Manual of Style* is primarily meant for you. Learn its rules by heart." To copyholders (those who read aloud to proofreaders the material being checked) it counsels, "cultivate a low, soft, clear, reading voice."

The following passage from the first *Manual,* which Seybold ascribes to Louis Warming, is quoted in full in the preface to the thirteenth edition:

> "Rules and regulations such as these . . . cannot be endowed with the fixity of rock-ribbed law. They . . . must be applied with a certain degree of elasticity. . . . Throughout this book it is assumed that no regulation contained therein is absolutely inviolable. Wherever the peculiar nature of the subject-matter, the desirability of throwing into relief a certain part of the argument, the reasonable preference of a writer or a typographical contingency suggests a deviation, such deviation may legitimately be made. Each case of this character must largely be decided upon its own merits. Generally it may be stated that, where no question of good taste or good logic is involved, deference should be shown to the expressed wishes of the author."[13]

Later Editions

The *Manual's* early success was noted by the preface to the second edition (1910): "The merit of the Manual is best evidenced by its very general adoption and use in editorial offices and proofrooms throughout the United States and Canada."[14] A third edition was published a year later, and its preface by Newman Miller attributed the need for still further revision of the manual in part to "the recent development of the profession of librarian, with the attendant uniformity of practice recommended by the national association of librarians, and the added experience resulting from a daily application of these rules to a very varied list of publications."[15]

The second, third, and fourth (1914) editions of the *Manual* were produced under the guidance of John A. Powell, successor to Warming as chief proofreader. The stature of this position is suggested by Powell's background. A world traveler, he held a degree from the University of London and a Ph.D. from the University of Berlin.

The fifth (1917), sixth (1919), and seventh (1920) editions of the *Manual* were produced under the editorial guidance of Powell's successors including Lilian E. Bridgen. Seybold notes "this frequency of new editions in the early days of the Press was due largely to additions of new typefaces by the printing department."[16] The seventh edition, says Seybold, "shows no vast difference from the third. Somewhere, however the article "A" was added before the title: 'A MANUAL OF STYLE.'"[17]

Commercial Viability

Press memoranda and correspondence now stored in the Special Collections of Regenstein Library at the University of Chicago shed light on the commercial viability of the early editions of the *Manual*. For instance, before the fourth edition was issued in 1914, Newman Miller exchanged a series of memos with Gordon Laing, for many years general editor of the Press, about whether to publish the *Manual* in cloth, paperback, or both.

On November 6, 1913, Miller wrote to Laing, "I believe that we ought to work toward a single edition of the *Manual of Style* to be put out in cloth. . . . I am disposed to think it will sell just as well in cloth although the paper edition has sold rather better in the past." Laing responded in pencil on Miller's typed memo, "The figures show that the demand is for the paper edition. On the face of it, it seems to me that it would be wise to abandon the cloth edition." Miller prevailed, and in a directive to Laing dated November 19, 1913, he ordered the new revision to be issued in a single clothbound edition. Miller then directed Laing to revise the text "carefully . . . so that we can now look upon it as final for the next few years, at least."[18]

Miller's concerns about the cost of updating the *Manual* are explained in other Press documents that detail the several purposes for which the book was being used. Figure 1 reproduces the data presented on a document dated April 26, 1917, relating to the proposed fifth edition.

Despite its widespread acceptance, sales revenue for the *Manual* (called "returns" in Figure 1) failed to cover production costs for any edition but the fourth. Still, the *Manual* served an important commercial and public relations purpose for the Press, a function Miller felt compelled to explain to T.E. Donnelly, chair of the subcommittee of the University of Chicago's Board of Trustees that oversaw Press operations, as he sought that body's approval for a new edition:

> This title has been an evolution, at first a convenience to the office and later developing into a publicity asset of considerable importance. It has finally come to have a steady sale through our trade channels, and it is only justice to those who have contributed to the compilation of the book to say that in many quarters it is looked upon as an authority in matters of style. . . .

Donnelly urged Miller to increase the price to $2. Miller resisted, thinking $1.50 to be the price ceiling. Donnelly gave in and approved the publication of 1,000 copies of the fifth edition with a list price of $1.50. Miller hoped the book could be made self-sustaining and that "future corrections will not be heavy," but these hopes seemed lost when he wrote to the Board on September 8, 1920:

> It has always been considered as more or less of a promotion scheme, and many copies have been and still are given away to authors and editors of our books and journals. The nature of the book of course requires a constant revision, and the manufacturing cost of each impression is therefore considerably above that of an average book. For both of these reasons it has never been a paying book.

The Eighth and Ninth Editions

The birth of the eighth edition of 1925, the most complete revision of the *Manual* to date was not to be an easy one. Laing's memo to the file summarizes a conference held in January 1924 at which it was decided that David H. Stevens of the English department would be "asked to revise the Manual of Style from the academic point of view, and that Mr. Kittredge of the Donnelley Company should be requested to make suggestions on the typographic part of the book." From the new edition, an abridgment was to be produced, "to consist of a small pamphlet of from 32–64 pages which we can send to authors whose books we are publishing."

Stevens finished his work on August 26, 1924, and asked for $400 for his services. Laing and Donald P. Bean, manager of the Publication Department, had expected to pay

April 26, 1917

Manual of Style

	First Edition	Second Edition	Third Edition	Fourth Edition
Published	Nov. 1906	Mar. 1910	Dec. 1911	Feb. 1914
No. Produced				
Paper	1002	999	1026	--
Cloth	--	--	460	1024
Sales	579	742	1144	955
Free	423	257	223	32
On hand	--	--	119	37
Cost	$583.50	$848.50	$1159.20	$563.01
Est. Returns	415.30	519.40	800.00	694.40

Total cost--$3,154.21
" Est. Ret.--$2,429.10

Proposed Fifth Edition

Number of Copies--1000
Estimated cost--Corrections-- $350.00
Printing-- 360.00
$710.00
Estimated returns-- 600.00

Figure 1.
Replication of 1917 Internal Document Regarding Sales Figures And Projections for the *Manual*

from $50 to $100, and Bean's memo to Laing of August 29, 1924, calls the invoice "preposterous." Worse, Stevens' work was not acceptable and had to be rewritten, largely by Jessie D. Whittern, head of the proofroom. Ultimately, Laing offered Stevens $100 and a $.20 per copy royalty on the first 2,000 copies sold. Stevens accepted.

According to Seybold, the design of the eighth edition was the joint effort of designer Robert O. Ballou and A.C. McFarland, manager of the Printing Department. It is not clear whether the renowned Mr. Kittredge of the Donnelley Company contributed to the effort. Seybold states that the design was "noticed with approval by *Publishers' Weekly*, which . . . mistakenly credited R.R. Donnelley's typographer for the improvement."[19]

The preface to the eighth edition specified the intended users as "authors, editors, advertising men, printers, proofreaders, and publishers."[20] The new *Manual* contained a section on selecting typography and relating the parts (preliminaries, text, back matter, running heads, page numbers, etc.) which together create "the personality of a book." The rules for composition offered instructions on dealing with legends and captions, mathematical formulas, and complex indexes. The "Hints" moved from the appendix to the text, comprising 18 pages.

Seybold detects and laments "a new, self-assured air about the instructions addressed to authors and other ignorant readers." For instance, the author is admonished that in submitting copy, "he may ordinarily rely on the judgment of his publisher with regard to typographical style. Vexation and delay are the usual results of interference with one who is a specialist in book-making."[21] Manuscripts submitted "in a perfectly clear hand" are still acceptable, although typewritten manuscripts are "preferable for many reasons." Handwritten manuscripts were not forbidden altogether until the eleventh edition.

The ninth edition (1927) was unchanged save for the addition of ten pages of type specimens. Discussion of a tenth edition appeared in Press documents as early as 1935. A Professor David Gustafson of the Carnegie Institute of Technology Department of Printing hoped to adopt an updated *Manual* for his classes. By April of that year, however, Laing wrote regretfully, that "financial conditions prevent our revising the book at present." The next year, Professor Gregory Paine of the English department of the University of North Carolina wrote to the Press on the letterhead of the Modern Language Association, offering a number of suggestions for the next edition. His letter was addressed to Mary D. Alexander, since 1925 head of the proofroom and the principal force behind both the tenth and the eleventh editions.

Paine recommended (1) an expanded chapter on footnotes; (2) a separate chapter on bibliographies; (3) a revised list of foreign words recognizing the "change from italics to roman and the omission of accents"; and (4) a less "confusing" general index, eliminating "the double references to page and paragraph numbers." Finally, he added, "I wish that you could publish a book that could sell for about two dollars so that I could use in [it] freely as a textbook. Why not omit *Specimens of Type*, pages 221-361? These pages are of use only to printers. . . . The *Manual* will not be purchased by students or writers at three-fifty a copy."

The Tenth and Eleventh Editions

Alexander, whose forceful style and strong personality contributed significantly to the corporate culture of the Press for 50 years, chose not to incorporate all of Paine's suggestions. The tenth edition (1937) included greatly expanded "Rules for Preparation of Copy," a new chapter on bibliography, and a list of proper forms for addressing prominent persons. By the eleventh edition (1949), a largely revised "Hints" section reflected Alexander's

touch and, according to Seybold, "the no-nonsense tone has become a bit sharper." Authors were told:

> No amount of careful preparation of a dull manuscript will disguise its basic shortcomings. But even a brilliant piece of writing will have difficulty finding a publisher if the author has neglected to dress his manuscript decently. On the assumption that the author has produced something worth printing, the suggestions offered here might well be entitled "How to Win a Publisher."[22]

Authors are also admonished to keep their footnotes to a minimum because "footnotes add nothing to the appearance of the printed page." Furthermore, they were told to avoid changes in their proofs "as such changes are expensive. Remember, to make a change in manuscript requires only a few strokes of the pen; to make a change in proofs, a skilled operator must be employed."[23]

In her summary remarks on the eighth through the eleventh editions, Seybold observes and regrets a growing tendency to regard the rules for composition promulgated by the University of Chicago Press as irrevocable, as the only sensible way, and, contrary to the disclaimer still in the preface, as now indeed "endowed with the fixity of unchanging law." To be sure, this attitude was undoubtedly encouraged by users of the *Manual* who followed its every dictate and over the years turned to the Press for answers to questions not covered in its pages. Its sometimes schoolmarmish tone aside, however, this eleventh *Manual* was a most useful reference tool, and it served the Press and its wider audience for a longer period than had any of its predecessors."[24]

The Modern Manual

The next major revision of the *Manual* was undertaken after important changes in the organization and structure of the Press had been made in the 1950s, a period of rapid expansion under then director Roger Shugg. At the outset of this period, the Printing Department of the University, which was no longer a part of the Press, was still copy editing, designing, and producing most of the books and journals published by the Press. Shugg created a new manuscript editing department within the Press in 1956 and added a design and production department two years later.

The new organizational scheme was not implemented without resistance or difficulty. Seybold witnessed the transition, having been hired in 1956 as the first "chief manuscript editor" within the Press:

> The new manuscript editors, in Shugg's plan, were to go beyond the traditional "mechanical" kind of editing—such as regularizing spelling, punctuation, capitalization, and the like—to perform "substantive editing where desirable and to work with authors to improve the quality and clarity of the Press books." They also were not to be rigidly bound by the strictures of the printing department's widely used *Manual of Style* . . . To the proofreaders on the fourth floor such a lax approach would be nothing short of blasphemous."[25]

Understandably, "a new edition of the Manual more suitable to the current state of affairs was a subject frequently discussed by the staff"[26] during this period. Finally, in 1968, the new director of the Press, Morris Philipson, suggested that Seybold, then senior manuscript editor, and Bruce Young, the managing editor, take time off to produce a new edition of the *Manual*, three months being thought sufficient for the task. "Some eight grueling months later," notes Seybold, "we produced a manuscript."[27]

John Grossman, another Press manuscript editor, revised the chapter on punctuation; another staff editor wrote a new chapter on citing public documents. Young and Seybold divided the rest of the work between them, aiming to make the twelfth edition "more relevant to the needs of authors and editors than to those of typographers and printers."[28] The new edition was designed by Cameron Poulter, head of the design and production department.

The heart of the old *Manual*, what had been called Rules for Composition in the first ten editions and Rules for Preparation of Copy in the eleventh, was now simply called "Style," by which was meant "the accepted and acceptable ways of coping with these [editorial] matters in good writing and good bookmaking, together with the University of Chicago Press preference where there was an alternative."[29]

Other parts were completely revised or omitted altogether, including, at last, the type specimens, which had occupied nearly half the pages of the preceding edition. With some regret Young and Seybold abolished the "Hints" section and incorporated these tips into an expanded section called "Bookmaking." It explained what went into the various parts of a book and how to assemble them, the preparation of copy for the printer, and authors' and publishers' responsibilities regarding copyright.

Now truly a success both critically and commercially, the first printing of 20,000 copies of the twelfth edition sold out before publication. From its appearance in January 1969 through August 1982, this edition sold 153,501 copies, a sum nearly equal to the combined sales of the first eleven editions.[30]

Work on the thirteenth edition began in 1975 when Young and Seybold sent a questionnaire to some 75 professional colleagues, inviting their suggestions for the new work. To their surprise, 129 questionnaires were returned, a number of recipients having copied the document to permit eager colleagues to contribute to the effort.

Challenges for the Editors

A variety of important developments, legal, cultural, and technological, came to bear on this edition. First, changes in the federal copyright regulations had been adopted in 1978 and needed to be interpreted in language understandable to authors and editors.

Second, the women's movement had called attention to the deleterious effects of sexist language. Young and Seybold were inclined to be cautious in responding to the emerging trend, and, more than a year before the new edition appeared, they stated in a published article that they would be "only giving a nod to the continuing controversy over sexist language: A footnote will explain that the pronoun 'he' will be used in the generic sense throughout the guide."[31] Once word of their decision spread, the outcry convinced Seybold to make a more radical change: "The traditional single generic pronoun in the English language could no longer safely be used to refer to an author or an editor of either sex. And the twelfth edition of the Manual suddenly was perceived to be filled with this pronoun. I persuaded my male colleague that we must 'desex' our new text altogether or risk the dire consequences of offending more than half our readers. How? Well, we used a lot of plurals."[32]

Finally, typesetting and printing methods were once again changing rapidly, and the new *Manual* had to take these developments into account. The old "hot lead" typesetters were being replaced by phototypesetting and computer-driven alternatives. Authors were beginning to use stand-alone word processors or campus computers to produce machine-readable manuscripts on magnetic tape or floppy disks. While the personal computer did not yet play an important role in the revolution, its impact soon was to explode upon the scene. These still emerging trends held profound implications for writers, editors, and publishers.

It was, perhaps, impossible in the late 1970s and early 1980s to anticipate the needs of the microcomputer age. Still, at least one otherwise admiring reviewer of the thirteenth edition, Laurence Urdang, criticized the new editior for its lean coverage of the new technology:

> There is a great deal more to be said about automatic typesetting than is even suggested in the *Chicago Manual* . . . . It is not my

intention to write that segment of the Style Manual here, only to point out that the coverage given is niggardly, especially when one considers that many of those functions formerly the provine of the compositor are now becoming the responsibility of the editor and often of the author."[33]

The thirteenth edition, greatly expanded and completely revised in nearly every area, now included a new chapter by Bruce Young on the history and current methods of composition, printing, and binding. Seybold's efforts focused on revising and amplifying the material on documentation of scholarly works. The new edition was published in August 1982 in a volume of 748 pages, 102 more than its predecessor. It has broken all previous sales records, having sold 203,000 copies to date, and it continues to sell more copies each year.

Not long thereafter, work began on an altogether new guide to set standards for authors who employed microcomputers and other electronic systems in preparing manuscripts for publication. *The Chicago Guide to Preparing Electronic Manuscripts* was prepared under the direction of Jennie Lightner, senior manuscript editor, and Pamely Pokorney, then senior production controller. The *Guide* was published in 1987, addressing the need Urdang had cited in his review of the thirteenth edition of the *Manual*. In their preface, Lightner and Pokorney proclaim: "Our focus is on manuscript preparation—how it should be done when computers are used—and on the procedures that should be followed by author and publisher so that the author's electronic medium can be used for typesetting."[34] Like the *Manual,* the new *Guide* evolved from "guidelines for authors of electronic manuscripts that were distributed to Press authors," which were subsequently expanded for publication.[35]

Present and Future

Later, the *Manual* was selected to be one of the reference books published on CD-ROM as an element in Microsoft's revolutionary *Bookshelf* product. Used in conjunction with a word processing program, *Bookshelf* permits its users to conduct onscreen look-ups in the text of the *Manual* as they write. It does not automatically proofread, edit, or stylize a manuscript, but hints of such capabilities are on the horizon, and some programs now on the market exhibit extraordinary powers.

For instance, Oberson Resources' "Notebook II *Plus*" textual data and bibliographic reference system can, among other things, "generate bibliographies and reference lists, automatically, in any of over 650 publishing styles." The Modern Language Association now offers *Editor* which it calls a program for "checking usage, mechanics, vocabulary, and structure." As such powerful writing tools emerge to serve scholarly writers, the author-editor relationship is sure to continue evolving.

Still, suitable organizations need to review, revise, and devise appropriate standards for the preparation of manuscripts, electronic or otherwise, if research results and other scholarly work are to be communicated clearly and effectively. *The Chicago Manual of Style* will likely retain its place as "indispensable guide" to such standards for the forseeable future.

As this essay is written, work has begun on a fourteenth edition of the *Manual*. It will be prepared by John Grossman, now managing editor of the Press. He has compressed the three chapters on documentation to two. The chapter on rights and permissions will be updated to cover new rulings of the past decade. The chapter on indexing will make more reference to computer tools. More detailed coverage of electronic manuscripts will be offered in the next edition of the *Chicago Guide to Preparing Electronic Manuscripts*. A publication date for the fourteenth edition of *The Chicago Manual of Style* has not yet been announced, but its appearance is sure to be greeted with gratitude by thousands of loyal users.

PUBLICATION HISTORY

Manual of Style. Chicago: University of Chicago Press, 1906. 201p.

Manual of Style. 2nd ed. Chicago: University of Chicago Press, 1910. 115p.

Manual of Style. 3rd ed. Chicago: University of Chicago Press, 1911. 118p.

Manual of Style. 4th ed. Chicago: University of Chicago Press, 1914. 141p.

Manual of Style. 5th ed. Chicago: University of Chicago Press, 1917. 300p.

Manual of Style. 6th ed. Chicago: University of Chicago Press, 1919. 292p.

Manual of Style. 7th ed. Chicago: University of Chicago Press, 1920. 300p.

Manual of Style. 8th ed. Chicago: University of Chicago Press, 1925. 391p.

Manual of Style. 9th ed. Chicago: University of Chicago Press, 1927. 400p.

A Manual of Style. 10th ed. Chicago: The University of Chicago Press, 1937. 394p.

A Manual of Style. 11th ed. Chicago: The University of Chicago Press, 1949. 498p.

A Manual of Style. 12th ed., rev. Chicago: The University of Chicago Press, 1969. 546p.

The Chicago Manual of Style. 13th ed., rev. and expanded. Chicago: The University of Chicago Press, 1982. 738p.

BIBLIOGRAPHY

Aside from reviews, the secondary literature on the *Manual* is not extensive. Catharine Seybold, coauthor of the twelfth and thirteenth editions, has published one invaluable article, cited below. She subsequently updated and revised that work for an unpublished speech, a copy of which she provided to this chapter's author. Additional valuable information on the history of the *Manual* can be found in her unpublished history of the University of Chicago Press to 1956, a copy of which is available in the Special Collections Department of Regenstein Library. Stacy Michelle's "The Book of Style," published in a Chicago weekly newspaper, the *Reader*, is well worth reading, however back issues of that paper are not readily available outside Chicago.

Pascal, Naomi B. "Chicago's Thirteenth." *Scholarly Publishing* 13 (October, 1982): 87-95.

Seybold, Catharine. "A Brief History of *The Chicago Manual of Style*." *Scholarly Publishing* 14 (February, 1983): 163-77.

———. "History of the *Manual of Style* through its 13th Edition." Unpublished speech (1984). Courtesy of the author.

———. "The University of Chicago Press: A Brief History, 1891-1965." Unpublished manuscript available in Special Collections, Regenstein Library, University of Chicago, 1983.

Stacy, Michelle. "The Book of Style." *Reader* 12 (November 12, 1982): 1-10.

Trett, Garald. "Two Stylebooks: An Editor's View; or, The Outlook in the Trenches." *Review* 6 (1984): 202-34.

NOTES

[1] Larry Green, " 'Bible' of Editorial Style—Now 77 Years Old—Is Last Word on Words," *Los Angeles Times*, 18 February 1983.

[2] Henry Kisor, "Look-It-Up Heaven for the Writer," *Chicago Sun Times Book Week*, 3 April 1988.

[3] Naomi B. Pascal, "Chicago's Thirteenth," *Scholarly Publishing* 14 (October 1982): 87.

[4] Laurence Urdang, review of *The Chicago Manual of Style*, 13th ed., *Verbatim* 9 (Autumn 1982).

[5] Mark Carroll, *Letter of the Society for Scholarly Publishing* 5 (1983).

[6] John Bruce Howell, *Style Manuals of the English-Speaking World: A Guide* (Phoenix: Oryx Press, 1983), xi.

[7] Catharine Seybold, "A Brief History of *The Chicago Manual of Style*," *Scholarly Publishing* 14 (February 1983): 172.

[8] Catharine Seybold, "History of the *Manual of Style* through its 13th Edition," unpublished speech, 1984, courtesy of the author, 11.

[9] Catharine Seybold, "The University of Chicago Press: A Brief History, 1891-1965," unpublished paper, Special Collections, Regenstein Library, University of Chicago.

[10] Seybold, "History of the *Manual of Style* through its 13th Edition," 1.

[11] Ibid., 3.

[12] Ibid., 4-5.

[13] *The Chicago Manual of Style*, 13th ed. rev. and expanded (Chicago: University of Chicago Press, 1982), viii.

[14] *Manual of Style*, 2nd ed. (Chicago: University of Chicago Press, 1910).

[15] *Manual of Style*, 3rd ed. (Chicago: University of Chicago Press, 1911).

[16] Seybold, "The University of Chicago Press: A Brief History, 1891-1965," 57.

[17] Seybold, "A Brief History of *The Chicago Manual of Style*," 166.

[18] Memoranda and correspondence cited from this period of the Press are available in the Special Collections of Regenstein Library at the University of Chicago.

[19] Seybold, "The University of Chicago Press: A Brief History, 1891-1965," 80.

[20] Seybold, "History of the *Manual of Style* through its 13th Edition," 7.

[21] Ibid., 7.

[22] Ibid., 8.

[23] *A Manual of Style*, 10th ed. (Chicago: University of Chicago Press, 1937).

[24] Seybold, "History of the *Manual of Style* through its 13th Edition," 9.

[25] Seybold, "The University of Chicago Press: A Brief History, 1891-1965," 146-47.

[26] Seybold, "History of the *Manual of Style* through its 13th Edition," 10.

[27] Ibid.

[28] Ibid., 10-11.

[29] Ibid., 11

[30] Ibid., 13.

[31] Rosalynne Harty, "Setting the Style for Publishers," *Chicago Tribune Book World*, 4 May 1980.

[32] Seybold, "History of the *Manual of Style* through the 13th Edition," 14.

[33] Urdang.

[34] *Chicago Guide to Preparing Electronic Manuscripts* (Chicago: University of Chicago Press, 1987), x.

[35] Ibid., x.

The "Instinctive Grammatical Moralizer": H. W. Fowler and His *Dictionary of Modern English Usage*

William A. McHugh

DEVELOPMENT AND HISTORY

H.W. Fowler's *Dictionary of Modern English Usage* has long been regarded as the final authority for writers seeking guidance on the questions they inevitably face in their work, from the proper use of a particular word to the way out of an awkward construction. Often cited as *MEU*, or simply as Fowler, the book has had its legion of admirers. Harold Ross, founder and long-time editor of the *New Yorker*, held it in high regard.[1] Evelyn Waugh admonished young writers to keep the book at their elbow.[2] Winston Churchill, irritated at the misuse of a particular word by his director of military operations, asked him "Why must you write 'intensive' here? 'Intense' is the right word. You should read Fowler's *Modern English Usage* on the use of the two words."[3] And T.S. Eliot, reviewing the book in 1927, mirrored the sentiments of many later devotees when he wrote: "As for Mr. Fowler's *Dictionary of Modern English Usage*, every person who wishes to write ought to read *in* it (for it is inexhaustible) for a quarter of an hour every night before going to bed."[4]

Few reference books so much reflect the character of their creator as does the *Dictionary of Modern English Usage*. Fowler has been described as "one of those eccentrics who seem to be a special product of England—not the wild surrealist eccentrics, but the logical eccentrics, who decide exactly what to do in a large number of situations, [and] do it with relentless consistency."[5] Fowler had a strong sense of duty, and much of the authority of the book derives from his sense of morality and propriety, which quickly becomes evident to the reader. Critic Marie Borroff has noted that

> to read Fowler is to be made vividly, indeed uncomfortably, aware of the morality of usage. . . . For Fowler, the writing of clear, expressive English is a battle, and the inner strength and courage of the good soldier are signified by the ungrudging acceptance of discipline in matters of external appearance. Fowler zeros in on the 'slipshod,' the 'slovenly,' the 'untidy' in language; he takes us to task for being lazy, childishly vain, or weak.[6]

Fowler's Early Life

On the surface, though, there is little in Fowler's early life to suggest that he would become, as he has been called, the "arbiter of the entire English language."[7] Henry W. Fowler[8] was born in 1858, the son of a schoolmaster and the eldest of eight children. He was educated at Rugby and at Balliol College, Oxford, though his record at Balliol showed no great distinction. The first part of his adult life was spent as a schoolmaster in British public schools, for 17 years at Sedbergh in Yorkshire. At Sedbergh Fowler was known as

"Joey Stinker" because he always smelled of tobacco. Fowler was a reserved man, a quality that does not always make for a popular teacher. One of his students wrote of him:

> I don't think I or any one else in the form ever got through his shell to know him as a human being. I for one respected him immensely, but in those days I should have said he lacked humanity. . . . On the whole, I think his defects as a schoolmaster all arose from shyness, coupled with his great fastidiousness (moral and intellectual) and something in the Sedbergh atmosphere that kept a barrier between boys and masters. I used to think that Fowler lacked humanity, and it was only . . . in later years that I learned that this was not so.[9]

Fowler's moral fastidiousness led him to leave Sedbergh in 1899. He had been in line for a position as house master, but the position included preparing boys for confirmation in the Church of England. Fowler was an agnostic and did not feel he could fulfill this duty in good conscience; the headmaster, H.G. Hart, did not feel he could remove this duty from the position. Though the two remained friends, neither would modify his position. Fowler left behind "a name for Spartan discipline and omniscience."[10]

Fowler then moved to London to begin a literary career, relying on the modest income of 120 pounds a year from an inheritance. "I'm not going to do anything *useful* again," he wrote to a friend.[11] He published a few articles, as well as three books of essays at his own expense, but these won him little success. After a few years he moved to the island of Guernsey, to a small cottage near that of his brother Frank G. Fowler, who raised tomatoes there. The two then began their productive literary partnership with a translation of the Greek poet Lucian. This translation in turn began the authors' long association with the Oxford University Press, publisher of the volume.

The King's English

The brothers next began work on a manual for writers which would emphasize the common blunders and infelicities found in writing, particularly journalistic writing; the book was to be copiously illustrated with examples of bad writing. *The King's English* (Oxford: Clarendon Press, 1906) is often seen merely as a precursor to the *Dictionary of Modern English Usage*, but it is an important book in its own right, and has continued in print to this day. Its arrangement as a handbook, with chapters on various aspects of writing, often makes it the easier book in which to find an extended discussion of a topic. The book's appeal was very much beyond the "sixth form boys and journalists" its authors supposed it would appeal to; "mature writers found parts of it difficult, and parts perverse, but for anybody who had ever tried to put pen to paper it was either an indispensable guide or a threat to mental health. . . . The only reassuring aspect of the book was the abundant evidence it provided that everybody made mistakes."[12] And as the *Times* noted in its obituary of H.W. Fowler, it "took the world by storm."[13]

Lexicographic Projects

The brothers' next project was the *Concise Oxford Dictionary of Current English* (Oxford: Clarendon Press, 1911), a one volume dictionary drawn insofar as possible from the *Oxford English Dictionary*, since only the A-S volumes were then published. The last part of the *COD* was based on other sources, for the brothers were working in seclusion in Guernsey, and had no contact with the *OED* staff in Oxford. This was the first of their lexicographical projects, and the writing of dictionaries was a very congenial and successful enterprise for the brothers. The writing of brief and precise definitions is not a common skill, and is one that the *COD* reveals in abundance. This dictionary was published in 1911; the brothers then began working on an even briefer dictionary, which was to become the *Pocket Oxford Dictionary*.[14]

In 1908, at the age of 50, Henry married a nurse a few years his junior. The marriage was an unusually happy one, though his wife was as outgoing and unscholarly as he was scholarly and reclusive. Fowler characteristically chose to abandon this increasingly successful and contented life when he felt duty obliged him to do so. Henry had been something of a pacifist, and the outbreak of World War I took him by surprise. Nonetheless, shocked by the invasion of Belgium, he began first to preach recruitment, and then to feel that it was not fair for him to urge others to a sacrifice he was not willing to make himself. He was 57 at the time, but physically the equal of a much younger man. Since his days at Sedbergh he had begun his day with a run of several miles, followed by a swim in any kind of weather, breaking the ice if necessary. Once, in London on Christmas Day, a friend encountered him with his chest bleeding from this effort. Giving his age as 44, he enlisted as a private, then persuaded his brother to follow him. Neither was allowed on the front lines once their true ages were discovered, and they spent the war washing dishes and hauling coal. Henry was eventually discharged due to gout. Frank contracted tuberculosis during his service and died shortly after the war.

Advent of the Dictionary

Henry continued work on the *Pocket Oxford Dictionary of Current English* (Oxford: Clarendon Press, 1924); it was the last book to list both brothers as authors. He also continued work on a project the brothers had planned earlier, originally described as a "Dictionary of Idioms." Henry had proposed the book to R.W. Chapman of the Oxford University Press in 1909. The book would treat the more difficult or problematic words from the *Concise Oxford Dictionary*, and "give in detail the information about constructions, synonyms, &c., that in *The King's English* can only be hinted at with a scanty selection of examples. We should assume a cheerful attitude of infallibility." Chapman had written back that "a Utopian Dictionary would sell very well—in

Utopia," a reply that discouraged the brothers. However, Chapman had not intended the remark to be taken so seriously, for two years later he asked what had become of the project, much to the brothers' surprise.[15]

By the mid-1920s the work was nearing completion, and a new title needed to be found, because the scope of the work had expanded beyond idioms to cover a variety of points of composition and grammar. Fowler, stung by a newspaper reference to "the pedantic brothers Fowler," at one point suggested *Oxford Pedantics*, but the title *Dictionary of English Usage* was finally chosen. Fowler added the word "modern" at the last moment, lest the book seem to promise coverage of historical usage.[16] Though the book bore only the name of H. W. Fowler as author, its preface contained a dedication to the younger brother that noted "The present book accordingly contains none of his actual writing; but, having been designed in consultation with him, it is the last fruit of a partnership that began in 1903 with our translation of Lucian."[17]

Critical Reception

The book was an immediate success, though critics often were puzzled by its idiosyncrasies. "It is difficult to describe this book" began one reviewer,[18] a sentiment many have surely shared. Its originality was not so much in doing an entirely new thing, but in doing it with much greater thoroughness and exactitude than had earlier usage dictionaries and style manuals. "Most treatises written to correct the evil [of poor writing] have been either dusty little compilations of errors, or rather florid school-boy discourses based on Latin grammar," noted another reviewer. "Mr. Fowler's book, thank heaven, is neither of these."[19] The expertise gained in writing dictionaries certainly helped the author; Joseph Epstein has noted that this is "clearly the book that all Fowler's previous experience led him to write."[20] Fowler also had the entire *OED*, then newly completed, to draw upon for etymologies and for evidence in the use of particular words. The impression of thoroughness is enhanced by Fowler's copious use of examples of the proper or (more often) improper use of a word, or of certain problematic constructions; as many as 10 or 20 examples may be used in a single article.

More puzzling was the arrangement of material. George Krapp was perhaps the first to note that "though it is called a dictionary, it is so mainly in the respect that the materials in it are arranged in alphabetical dictionary order."[21] Many entries do simply treat a single word or a group of related words. These entries range from several pages for such troublesome words as "only" (one page, double column) or "that" (nine pages), to a line or two to note the pronunciation or spelling of a particular word, or distinguish among various words liable to confusion. We can, for example, go to Fowler to find out that a toy-shop is a store where toys are sold, while a toy shop is a "child's mock shop"; or to find "unsubstantial" recommended over "insubstantial."[22]

Intermingled with these are a series of topical entries. At the front of the book is a list of 455 "General Articles," which includes both the topical entries and the longer entries for troublesome words. The list is presumably to aid the reader in finding a particular discussion, and there are indeed some entries a reader would readily recognize, such as "Parallel-Sentence Dangers," "Hyphens," or "Sequence of Tenses." Many entries are much less clear, however, with names like "Swapping Horses," "Out of the Frying-Pan," "Pairs & Snares," and "Cannibalism." "Swapping Horses" covers such problems as changing the sense in which a word is used in mid-sentence, and "Cannibalism" discusses instances where a common word such as "that" is needed twice in a sentence, but used only once. "Out of the Frying-Pan" treats instances where a writer, attempting to avoid some questionable construction, winds up with something worse; this is one of Fowler's favorite themes. A long article called "French Words" gives the pronunciation for many French words and phrases that have found their way into English, and an article called "Technical Terms" gives definitions for many rhetorical and literary terms. Liberal cross references are given to these general articles, though this does not always make it easy to find the discussion of a particular problem or construction.

The Author's Imprint

The true originality of the book comes not from its arrangement, however, but from the author's personality, which forcefully impresses itself upon the reader in article after article. The dictionary article form finally gave Fowler his voice,[23] and what an unmistakable voice it is, as the passages below demonstrate:

> *From the article "Salad Days"*: Whether the point [of this phrase] is that youth, like salad, is raw, or that salad is highly flavoured & youth loves high flavours, or that innocent herbs are youth's food as milk is babes' & meat is men's, few of those who use the phrase could perhaps tell us; if so, it is fitter for parrots' than for human speech.[24]

> *From "Love of the Long Word"*: "A few lines of the long-word style we know so well are added: *Vigorous condemnation is passed on the foreign policy of the Prime Minister, 'whose temperamental inaptitude for diplomacy & preoccupation with domestic issues have rendered his participation in external negotiations gravely detrimental to the public welfare'.* Vigorous indeed; a charging hippopotamus hardly more so.[25]

> *From "Italics"*: The practiced writer is aware that his business is to secure prominence for what he regards as the essence of his communication by so marshalling his sentences that they shall lead up to a climax, or group themselves round a centre, or be worded with different degrees of impressiveness as the need of emphasis varies; he knows too that it is an insult to the reader's intelligence to admonish him periodically by a change of type, like a bad teacher imploring his boys to attend for a moment, that he cannot safely go

to sleep just now. . . . To italicize whole sentences or large parts of them as a guarantee that some portion of what one has written is really worth attending to is a miserable confession that the rest is negligible.[26]

Small wonder many reacted as did Henry Fuller, the reviewer for the *New York Times*: "After a few hours' browsing through these many hundreds of pages, one reaches the state where he hardly dares attempt to write English."[27] Fowler's liberal use of negative examples certainly reinforced the impression of him as an astringent critic. Eric Partridge, who would later write his own book on English usage, was a junior lecturer at the University of Manchester when Fowler's book appeared, and has noted the "stir made by this austere work. Students and other irreverent persons delighted in Fowler's pillorying, both of the *Times* and other important periodicals and of celebrated writers."[28] Partridge added, however, that Fowler was motivated not "to puncture this reputation or that, nor yet to show how clever he was, . . . but simply in order to perform a public service."[29] Fowler in reality remained the schoolmaster, carefully and thoroughly explaining to the reader how a particular word is to be used, or why a particular construction should be preferred to another.[30] He could be sensitive to criticism at times, but tried to view it with equanimity, as he demonstrated when he republished one of his early volumes of essays after he had become a famous man. Fowler introduced the book with excerpts from both the positive and negative reviews of the earlier edition, including such notices as "This group of self-conscious, verbose essays."[31]

A Prescriptivist Grammarian?

Fowler has been criticized as a narrow prescriptivist grammarian, attempting to legislate language usage, and also praised as a great liberal, freeing English usage from the petty and arbitrary rules of Victorian schoolmasters and grammarians. The truth is somewhere in between. One perhaps looks in vain for absolutely consistent principles in Fowler's work; as one critic noted "he often took away with one hand the principle he had offered with the other."[32] He certainly enjoyed demolishing the many traditional rules that did more harm than good. The fear of ending a sentence with a preposition is a "superstition . . . . The fact is that the remarkable freedom enjoyed by English in putting its prepositions late & omitting its relatives is an important element in the flexibility of the language."[33] Split infinitives also are permissible; those who split infinitives unawares "are a happy folk . . . 'to really understand' comes readier to their lips & pens than 'really to understand', they see no reason why they should not say it (small blame to them, seeing that reasons are not their critics' strong point.)" What Fowler really wanted, however, was for his reader to be able to discriminate when to split them: "We will split infinitives sooner than be ambiguous or artificial; more than that, we will freely admit that sufficient recasting will get rid of any s. i. without involving either of those faults, & yet reserve to ourselves the right of deciding in each case whether recasting is worth while."[34] Fowler even defended the placement of the word "only" in such sentences as "He only died yesterday," rather than the more strictly logical "He died only yesterday," because there is no danger of confusion and it is more natural English.[35] Certainly in these and in many other opinions he defied the strict conventions of most Victorian style manuals, and for that matter of many editors and English teachers to this day. Sir Ernest Gowers recalled that when the book appeared it was hailed "as a gust of common sense that swept away the cobwebs of grammarians' fetishes."[36]

A Deference to Latin

Yet Fowler certainly was a prescriptivist who felt that there were correct and incorrect ways of using English, and there were times when he defended causes it would perhaps have been wiser to abandon. He particularly could be led astray when English usage began to offend against Latin grammatical principles and etymologies.[37] An oft-cited example is Fowler's treatment of the word "meticulous." Fowler objected to the use of the word "meticulous" unless accompanied by the meaning of "timid" or "fearful." He objected partly because the word was otherwise simply an unnecessary replacement for "scrupulous" and "punctilious," but also because the word derived from the Latin root "metus," meaning fearful.[38] On the first ground Fowler was at least generally consistent: he often objected to words he considered superfluous, particularly when longer or more pretentious words had taken the places of simpler ones, as "faience" for "porcelain," or "habitude" for "habit."[39] He also tended to argue for preserving fine distinctions between words; he carefully explained the distinctions between "accessary" and "accessory," or advised when "individual" may properly be used as a noun, and even attempted to differentiate "slush" and "slosh," or "slaver" and "slobber."[40] But on the second ground he was less consistent. He often condemned as pedantic the too strict construction of a word's meaning when it flies in the face of common usage; for example, of the use of "America" to mean the United States, we read, "It will continue to be protested against by purists & patriots, & will doubtless survive the protests."[41]

Fowler's deference to Latin is perhaps even more striking in his treatment of grammar, which many have found the weakest aspect of his work. One of the first to take Fowler to task in this regard was the noted Danish grammarian and scholar of English Otto Jespersen, who attacked Fowler's treatment of the fused participle. *The King's English* gave this name to such constructions as "without the man telling us" (rather than "without the man's telling us," which the Fowlers regarded as correct).[42] H.W. Fowler published these views in an expanded form as a tract of the Society for Pure English in 1925, and this discussion reappeared in the *Dictionary of Modern English Usage*.[43] Fowler had two basic objections to the construction: that it tended to produce ambiguous and cumbersome sentences, and that it was ungrammatical—by which he essentially meant that it could not be analyzed by the rules of traditional Latin grammar. Jespersen argued that the construction had been long (and idiomatically) used in English, and could be explained grammatically, if not by traditional Latin-based grammar.[44] The significance of this somewhat esoteric debate is that Jespersen, whose case is certainly the more convincing, identified one of Fowler's most significant weaknesses: "If [certain constructions in English] cannot be analyzed according to Latin grammar, the reply is obviously that there are many things in English as well as in other languages that cannot be understood from the Latin grammar we were taught in our youth."[45] Jespersen called Fowler an "instinctive grammatical moralizer,"[46] and this title has stayed with Fowler. Fowler seems to have been entirely unaware of and unsympathetic toward the work of scholars such as Jespersen, who were attempting to replace traditional Latin-based English grammar with a more purely descriptive grammar. In his reply to Jespersen, he defended the application of Latin grammar to English; "our [English] grammatical conscience has by this time a Latin element inextricably compounded in it."[47] Jespersen was not the only writer of the time to fault Fowler on this point. The Dutch scholar Kruisinga authored a devastating review on this part of Fowler's work, using the occasion to attack the neglect of linguistic studies in English academic circles. "To expect Mr. Fowler to consult a book of a real grammarian . . . is misunderstanding his state of mind completely."[48] Another review from the Continent, in a more balanced appraisal, complained that the "grammar part is altogether unsatisfactory, because Mr. Fowler has not the slightest notion of what English and continental scholars have written on the subjects treated by him."[49] More recently, linguist Randolph

Quirk has noted that in his "fused particle" argument, Fowler defended views that had been discredited as many as 50 years earlier.[50]

Other Issues

Fowler certainly can be criticized for other excesses. His article "Genteelisms" sensibly condemned the use of "domestic" for "servant," or "save" for "except," but also endorsed "belly" for "stomach," and "corn-cutter" for "chiropodist."[51] And Fowler sometimes seems too much a man of his time. Kenneth Stiles was perhaps the first to note that "from these pages emerges an admirable portrait of an English gentleman. Conservative; respectful of tradition, yet an individualist . . . polite to inferiors, while perfectly conscious of their inferiority; distrustful of display; insular."[52] This may help explain Fowler's frequent distrust of new usages until they were established, as well as his condemnation of the "pedantry" of sticking too much to outworn rules. He distrusted displays of learning, as with the scholar who prefers the form "Mohammed" to the good English "Mahomet," but he also seemed to distrust those ignorant of the Latin derivation of such words as "meticulous." More modern sensibilities may not be comfortable with his frequent condemnation of a given word or usage as "illiterate," or his characterization of the use of the word "aggravate" to mean "annoy" as "a feminine or childish colloquialism."[53] Fowler himself was not entirely unaware of his insularity; the discussion of "shall" and "will" in *The King's English* begins "It is unfortunate that the idiomatic use, while it comes by nature to southern Englishman (who will find most of this section superfluous), is so complicated that those who are not to the manner born can hardly acquire it; and for them the section is in danger of being useless."[54]

One can also criticize Fowler's own style. W. Somerset Maugham greatly admired the book, but complained that "Fowler had no ear.

He did not see that simplicity may sometimes make concessions to euphony."[55] And Fowler was not always the master of simplicity; sometimes his desire to drive home a point, and to express a complex notion with precision, makes for very difficult prose. C.T. Onions, who read the proofs of the book for the Oxford University Press, complained that "Fowler's ingenuity has surpassed itself, with the not infrequent result of mere obscurity."[56] And one can complain that the book, even when it came out, was slightly out of date, or that it reflected written rather than oral speech.

Yet Fowler cannot be so easily dismissed. Kemp Malone's review is often quoted by the linguistic critics of Fowler: "At bottom his book is unsound. It gives us the conclusions of a learned and charming dilettante rather than those of a man of science. It is a collection of linguistic prejudices persuasively presented by a clever advocate; it is not an objective, scientific presentation of the facts of English usage." But Malone's review concluded: "Mr. Fowler's volume belongs rather with books like Mr. Mencken's *American Language* than with works of exact scholarship. But when I say this, I am not condemning the book. One the contrary, I am praising it. Grammarian and layman alike ought to have it on their shelves, and if they fail to find it highly enjoyable and highly stimulating, there is something wrong with them."[57]

Fowler's Contribution and Influence

So where does Fowler's contribution lie? Much of it certainly lies in his consistent unmasking of pretentious, empty, and thoughtless writing for what it is. He is at his best in articles such as "Love of the Long Word" or "Polysyllabic Humor," or in revealing pretensions and humbugs of all kinds. The use of antiquated words such as "anent" or "wellnigh" is treated in the article "Wardour Street," named after a street in London occupied principally by antique dealers. Literary critics are castigated for the use of words such as "actuality" and "inevitable," shorn of their meaning by thoughtless over-use; "vogue-words," such as "feasible," "mentality" or "acid test," are condemned for the same reason.[58] Fowler drives home his point with ruthless analysis and numerous examples; three columns of type are used to condemn the vogue-word "unthinkable," a word loved by "all who like to combine the most forcible sound with the haziest meaning."[59] To these contributions must also be added his remarkably sure sense of English idiom, and his relentless analysis of the many pitfalls the writer faces. Who else could advise us so well (and so thoroughly) on the proper use of the problematic word "as," or distinguish whether to use "bloom" or "blossom?" Even Jespersen found that there was more in the book to admire than to condemn,[60] and W. Somerset Maugham wrote "I do not think anyone writes so well that he cannot learn much from [Fowler]."[61]

And, of course, there is the force of the author's personality. Fowler takes the task of writing seriously, and invites the reader to do so too. Jespersen was certainly correct in calling him a "moralizer," but he is more than simply that. Marshall McLuhan has noted that "Fowler approached language in the spirit of gamesmanship (and even of one-upmanship) and his instruments varied from the precision rifle to the butterfly net and the X-ray. . . Fowler never fails in his most censorious moments to direct a very perceptible wink at his readers."[62] It is not a book that yields its wealth to the hurried reader who needs to find a quick answer to some question of language or style, but rather to the reader willing to learn what the author has to offer, and to share his passion for the English language.

What influence has Fowler had? The claim, originating in the *Times Literary Supplement*, that "probably Henry Fowler has more powerfully affected the development of English prose style since 1926 than Bridges, Kipling, Shaw or any of his contemporary masters"[63] is of course impossible to prove or disprove. His advocacy of a plain, direct, and unadorned style had obvious appeal to many writers of the twentieth century. Randolph Quirk has distinguished between Fowler's influence over details, which has perhaps been slight—words such as "meticulous" flourish, and no one today says "corn-cutter" for "chiropodist"—and his influence in principle, which "is perhaps quite extensive. We are probably more self-critical in the use of hackneyed phrases, hyphens, gallicisms, and even Unequal Yokefellows and Cannibalisms than the first readers of *The King's English* and *Modern English Usage*. The Fowler brothers . . . heightened the sense of style and personal responsibility for expression among writers in the English-speaking world."[64]

Revision

"To tamper with Fowler has taken both humility and courage—or perhaps foolhardiness."[65] These words were written by Fowler's first reviser, Margaret Nicholson, and point up the difficulty of revising a work so much the product of one man's personality. Nicholson was an editor for the American branch of the Oxford University Press, and her book, published in 1957, is actually an adaptation for the American reader, called *A Dictionary of American-English Usage*. The work was also intended as a simplification of Fowler; indeed, the publisher promoted it as a "Faster Fowler." It was shorter by about a third. Nicholson did try to "retain as much of the original as space allowed," but cut many of Fowler's numerous examples and lengthy explanations.

A basic problem with this revision was that it tried to make the book into something it was never intended to be. Fowler certainly was fundamentally British; as one critic noted, "you cannot hope to retain 'as much of the original as space allowed' and expect to produce a meaningful description of something else."[66] Mixed in with Nicholson's advice on American usage are portions retained from Fowler's original, with their British examples and tone. Nor is it easy to make a book like

Fowler's into a model of quick reference; "it is Fowler for people whom H.W. Fowler did not choose to take into account—the hasty, the arbitrary and the half-educated who want rules rather than reason."[67] And many reviewers found that Nicholson did not command a sufficiently good sense of American idiom, and had not identified many of the places where usage had changed since Fowler's day. She retained, for example, his strictures that "a Chinaman" is common and preferred usage, and that "on the carpet" means "under discussion."[68] Some found her more arbitrary and prescriptive than Fowler had ever been.[69]

Gowers' Revision

The very mixed success of Nicholson's work did not dampen the desire of the Oxford University Press to publish an entirely new edition of the work. This revision, the second edition of *Modern English Usage*, fell to Sir Ernest Gowers and was published in 1965. Gowers was a career civil servant who produced a guide to good English for use by British civil servants. This guide was published as *Plain Words* (London: H.M. Stationery Officer, 1948), and attained a far wider audience than its original purpose suggested. Gowers seemed the perfect candidate to revise Fowler. Like Fowler, he approached *Modern English Usage* late in life, revising it during his retirement at his Hampshire estate. He added much new material, making space by eliminating many short entries that merely established spelling or pronunciation of a word, since this information could be found in ordinary dictionaries. The long articles on "Technical Terms" and "French Words" were omitted, though some of the material was retained in short entries under the various terms. Many of Fowler's judgments were, of course, modified; Gowers gave up the battle against using "aggravate" to mean "annoy," and noted that it is useless to force "meticulous" into "an etymological strait-jacket."[70] We are no longer enjoined to avoid "stomach" and "chiropodist" as genteelisms, nor are lo-

cutions condemned as "illiterate" or "feminine." Gowers rewrote a few of Fowler's more convoluted explanations, and eliminated some of the excessive examples, though not to the drastic degree Nicholson had. A classified guide to the general articles was provided to aid the user in finding the discussion of a particular point. However, the book is still not always easy to use for reference, a fact made evident by the publication four years later of a thorough index called *Find It in Fowler* (Princeton, NJ: Wolfhart Book Co., 1969).

Gowers, however, took care to insure that the revision would retain the stamp of the original. As much of Fowler's text as possible was kept; "rewrite him and he ceases to be Fowler," Gowers noted.[71] Gowers's revision is remarkable for catching the tone of the original while bringing it up to date. It is difficult at times to tell where the original leaves off and the revision begins, and many of the new articles have an almost Fowleresque tone, if not quite with the bite or the playfulness of Fowler's style.

This revision was quite well received, though some reviewers worried about the wisdom of trying to patch Fowler in this way, skillfully as it had been done. The *Times* noted that Fowler's old-fashioned language was "not a language in which it seems aesthetically fitting to discuss the modern English usage of 1965."[72] Another critic complained that "Fowler's attitude is not a possible one for a good mind in the 1960's, and the attempt at modernization leads Gowers into irreconcilable conflicts."[73] Gowers reprinted in full Fowler's article on the fused participle, for example, but added comments of his own to modify Fowler's strictures and to summarize the famous dispute with Jespersen. Some critics still found the work lacking in its awareness of current work in grammar and linguistics.[74]

Fowler's Relevance Today

What relevance does Fowler's book have today? R.W. Burchfield, who is now at work on a third edition, observed a few years ago that—despite criticism of the work by grammarians—scholars and writers of all kinds continue to rely on Fowler for guidance.[75] Demand for the book justified a paperback edition in 1983. The need for a thorough revision, however, certainly becomes apparent as the language changes. Marie Borroff recently observed that "Fowler remains a classic, indispensable, yet of little practical help in the day-to-day scuffle."[76] Burchfield, though appreciative of Gowers's revision,[77] realizes that a new edition cannot be approached in the same way. The "verdicts and evidence of [Fowler] now needed to be replaced, not just modified here and there." He promises that the book, to be published in 1992, will be "mildly prescriptive, dogmatic in my own manner, and thoroughly up to date." As with Gowers's revision, American usage will be given some prominence, but, as with the earlier editions (omitting of course Nicholson's adaptation), British usage will remain the chief focus.[78] There will be some who question whether such a thoroughly rewritten Fowler should bear the name of this idiosyncratic author, perhaps making his name an eponym on the order of Webster's or Roget's. But certainly there is a need to replicate in the late twentieth century Fowler's achievement three-quarters of a century earlier. Burchfield, as editor of the four-volume supplement to the *Oxford English Dictionary*, revives the connection between pure lexicography and the *MEU* that Fowler himself began, and one can only wish him the same success.

PUBLICATION HISTORY

Fowler, H.W. *A Dictionary of Modern English Usage*. Oxford: Clarendon Press; London: H. Milford, 1926. 742p.

Nicholson, Margaret. *A Dictionary of American-English Usage, Based on Fowler's Modern English Usage*. New York: Oxford University Press, 1957. 671p.

Fowler, H.W. *A Dictionary of Modern English Usage*. 2nd ed., rev. by Sir Ernest Gowers. New York: Oxford University Press, 1965. 725p.

BIBLIOGRAPHY

The standard treatment of Fowler's life was written by his close friend, G.G. Coulton. Accounts of the publication of the *Dictionary of Modern English Usage* can be found in Peter Sutcliffe's history of the Oxford University Press and in the article "Fowler and His 'Modern English Usage'" from the *Times Literary Supplement*. The articles by Otto Jespersen and E. Kruisinga represent the two most famous contemporary attacks on Fowler's weaknesses. A great many laudatory articles appeared in decades following the publication of the first edition; notable are those by Eric Partridge, Gilbert Highet, and Jacques Barzun, and the article "Auspice Aucupe" from the *TLS*. The article by Barzun, however, is primarily an attack upon Nicholson's revision. Randolph Quirk offers an appreciative but critical evaluation from the point of view of a modern linguist and grammarian.

The two primary revisers of Fowler's work—Gowers and Burchfield—each served as president of the English Association and devoted their presidential addresses to evaluations of Fowler's work. An interview with Gowers concerning his revision can be found under the title "Our Man in Trotton" in the *New Yorker*. The publication of Gowers's revision prompted reviews by a number of prominent writers; those of Marshall McLuhan, David Daiches, and Anthony Burgess are of particular interest. The review from the *TLS*, "How Modern is Your English Usage," presents an interesting and rather negative view of the revision. More recent articles by Marie Borroff and Joseph Epstein assess the continuing value of various dictionaries of English usage, with particular attention to Fowler's.

"Auspice Aucupe." *Times Literary Supplement* no. 2892 (August 2, 1957): 471.

Barzun, Jacques. "Fowler's Generation." *American Scholar* 26 (Summer, 1957): 315–23.

Borroff, Marie. "'Fowler and the Rest.'" *Yale Review* 74 (Spring, 1985): 353–67.

Burchfield, Robert W. *The Fowlers: Their Achievements in Lexicography and Grammar*. English Association Presidential Address. London: English Association, 1979.

Burgess, Anthony. "Switched-On Fowler." *Observer* no. 9071 (May 9, 1965): 27.

Coulton, G.G. *H. W. Fowler*. S. P. E. Tract no.43. Oxford: Clarendon Press, 1934.

Daiches, David. "Speaking of Books: H.W. Fowler." *New York Times Book Review* 70 (August 15, 1965): 2.

Dangerfield, George. "The Brothers Fowler." *Bookman* 75 (June/July, 1932): 209–17.

Epstein, Joseph. "What's the Usage?" *New Criterion* 6 (June, 1988): 9–20.

"Fowler and His 'Modern English Usage.'" *Times Literary Supplement* no. 2935 (May 30, 1958): 302.

Gowers, Sir Ernest. *H. W. Fowler: The Man and His Teaching*. English Association Presidential Address. London: English Association, 1957.

Greenwood, J. Arthur. *Find It in Fowler: An Alphabetical Index to the Second Edition (1965) of H. W. Fowler's Modern English Usage*. Princeton, NJ: Wolfhart Book Co., 1969.

Highet, Gilbert. "Henry Fowler: Modern English Usage." In *People Places and Books*, 3-12. New York: Oxford University Press, 1953.

"How Modern is Your English Usage." *Times Literary Supplement* no. 3299 (May 20, 1965): 395.

Jespersen, Otto. "On Some Disputed Points in English Grammar." S. P. E. Tract no. 25. Oxford: Clarendon Press, 1926.

John, V.V. "Fowler: Forty Years After." *Literary Criterion* 7 (1966): 11–20.

Kronenberger, Louis. "How Not to Write, What Not to Say." *Atlantic Monthly* 216 (September, 1965): 97–100.

Kruisinga, E. "English Grammar as She is Taught at Oxford." *English Studies* 8 (December, 1926): 181–85.

McLuhan, Marshall. "Wordfowling in Blunderland." *Saturday Night* 80 (August, 1965): 23–27.

Nicholson, Harold. "Two Acute Linguists." *Listener* 59 (April 10, 1958): 619, 622.

"Our Man in Trotton." *New Yorker* 41 (August 14, 1965): 20–23.

Partridge, Eric. "Henry Watson Fowler." In *A Charm of Words: Essays and Papers on Language*, 63–67. London: Hamish Hamilton, 1960. Originally published in slightly shorter form as "To the English-Using World He Counseled Perfection," *New York Times Book Review* 63 (March 9, 1958): 5.

Pyles, Thomas. "The New Fowler." *Sewanee Review* 74 (Spring, 1966): 540–44.

Quirk, Randolph. "The Toils of Fowler and Moral Gowers." Chapter 9 in *The English Language and Images of Matter*. London: Oxford University Press, 1972. Portions originally published as "Fowler's Toils," Listener 59 (March 13, 1958): 449–51, and as "Fowler's Net," *New Statesman* 69 (May 21, 1965): 812–13.

Stiles, Kenneth. "H. W. Fowler's Englishman." *Spectator* 159 (July2, 1937):12–13.

Sutcliffe, Peter. *The Oxford University Press: An Informal History*. Oxford: Clarendon Press, 1978.

NOTES

1 Gilbert Highet, "Henry Fowler: Modern English Usage," in *People Places and Books* (New York: Oxford University Press, 1953), 4.

2 Quoted in "Fowler's English," *Commonweal* 67 (21 March 1958): 630.

3 George Frazier, "Fowler's Love Affair with the Language," *Life* 59 (20 August 1965): 8.

4 T. S. Eliot, "Books of the Quarter," *New Criterion* 5 (January 1927): 124. Italics in original.

5 Highet, 4.

6 Marie Borroff, "'Fowler and the Rest,'" *Yale Review* 74 (Spring 1985): 361.

7 Joseph Epstein, "What's the Usage?" *New Criterion* 6 (June 1988): 12.

8 Except where otherwise indicated, details about Fowler's life are taken from G. G. Coulton, *H. W. Fowler*, S. P. E. Tract no. 43 (Oxford: Clarendon Press, 1934).

9 Sir Alexander Lawrence, quoted in Coulton, 104–05.

10 "Henry Watson Fowler," *Sedberghian* (March 1934): 4.

11 Coulton, 117. Italics in original.

12 Peter Sutcliffe, *The Oxford University Press: An Informal History* (Oxford: Clarendon Press, 1978), 152.

13 "Mr. H. W. Fowler: A Lexicographical Genius," *Times*, 28 December 1933, 12.

14 Robert W. Burchfield, *The Fowlers: Their Achievements in Lexicography and Grammar*, English Association Presidential Address (London: English Association: 1979), 11–14.

15 "Fowler and his 'Modern English Usage,'" *Times Literary Supplement* no. 2935 (30 May 1958): 302.

16 Ibid.

17 H.W. Fowler, *A Dictionary of Modern English Usage* (Oxford: Clarendon Press; London: Humphrey Milford, 1926), iii.

[18] F. Sidgwick, review of *Dictionary of Modern English Usage*, by H. W. Fowler, *Review of English Studies* 2 (October 1926): 490.

[19] George N. Shuster, review of *Dictionary of Modern English Usage*, by H. W. Fowler, *Commonweal* 5 (23 February 1927): 443.

[20] Epstein, 14.

[21] George Philip Krapp, "P's and Q's," *Saturday Review of Literature* 2 (17 July 1926): 933.

[22] H.W. Fowler, *A Dictionary of Modern English Usage*, see "Toy" and "Insubstantial."

[23] Epstein, 14.

[24] Fowler, *Modern English Usage*, see "Salad Days."

[25] Ibid., see "Love of the Long Word." Italics in original.

[26] Ibid., see "Italics."

[27] "Henry B. Fuller, "Even Syntax Provides Comic Relief," *New York Times Book Review* 76 (2 January 1927): 2.

[28] Eric Partridge, "Henry Watson Fowler," in *A Charm of Words: Essays and Papers on Language* (London: Hamish Hamilton, 1960), 65–66.

[29] Ibid., 66.

[30] David Daiches, "Speaking of Books: H. W. Fowler," *New York Times Book Review* 70 (15 August 1965): 2; Sutcliffe, 153.

[31] Review of *"Si Mihi—!"* by H. W. Fowler, *Yorkshire Observer*, quoted in H. W. Fowler, *If Wishes Were Horses* (London: George Allen & Unwin, 1929), 4.

[32] F.G. Cassidy, review of *Dictionary of American-English Usage*, by Margaret Nicholson, *Archivum Linguisticum* 10 (1958): 144.

[33] H.W. Fowler, *Modern English Usage*, see "Preposition at End."

[34] Ibid., see "Split Infinitive."

[35] Ibid., see "Only."

[36] Sir Ernest Gowers, *H. W. Fowler: The Man and His Teaching*, English Association, Presidential Address (London: English Association, 1957), 10.

[37] Kenneth Stiles, "H. W. Fowler's Englishman," *Spectator* 159 (2 July 1937): 12; Randolph Quirk, "The Toils of Fowler and Moral Gowers," in *The English Language and Images of Matter* (London: Oxford University Press, 1972), 91.

[38] Fowler, *Modern English Usage*, see "Meticulous."

[39] Ibid., see "Superfluous Words."

[40] Ibid., see "Accessary, Accessory," "Individual," "Slush, Sludge, Slosh," and "Slaver, Slobber, Slubber."

[41] Ibid., see "America(n)."

[42] H.W. Fowler and F.G. Fowler, *The King's English*, 2nd ed. (Oxford: Clarendon Press, 1919), 116–25.

[43] H. W. Fowler, "Fused Participle," *S. P. E. Tract* no. 22 (1925): 43-47; Fowler, *Modern English Usage*, see "Fused Participle."

[44] Otto Jespersen, *On Some Disputed Points in English Grammar*, *S. P. E. Tract* no. 25 (Oxford: Clarendon Press, 1926).

[45] Ibid., 170.

[46] Ibid., 148.

[47] H.W. Fowler, "On -ing: Professor Jespersen and 'The Instinctive Grammatical Moralizer,'" *S. P. E. Tract* no. 26 (1927): 195.

[48] E. Kruisinga, "English Grammar as She is Taught at Oxford," *English Studies* 8 (December 1926): 181–85.

[49] P. Fijn van Draat, review of *Dictionary of Modern English Usage*, by H. W. Fowler, *Englische Studien* 63 (September 1928): 85. Also of interest is G. van Langenhove, review of *Dictionary of Modern English Usage*, by H. W. Fowler, *Revue belge de philologie et d'histoire* 6 (1927), 841-44.

[50] Quirk, 93.

[51] Fowler, *Modern English Usage*, see "Genteelism."

[52] Stiles, 12.

[53] Fowler, *Modern English Usage*, see "Aggravate."

[54] Fowler and Fowler, *King's English*, 133.

[55] W. Somerset Maugham, *The Summing Up* (London: William Heinemann, 1938), 42.

[56] "Fowler and his 'Modern English Usage,'" 302.

[57] Kemp Malone, review of *Dictionary of Modern English Usage*, by H. W. Fowler, *Modern Language Notes* 42 (March 1927): 201–02.

[58] Fowler, *Modern English Usage*, see "Literary Critics' words" and "Vogue-words."

[59] Ibid., see "Unthinkable."

[60] Jespersen, 142.

[61] Maugham, 41.

[62] Marshall McLuhan, "Wordfowling in Blunderland," *Saturday Night* 80 (August 1965): 23.

[63] "Auspice Aucupe," *Times Literary Supplement* no. 2892 (2 August 1957): 471.

[64] Quirk, 94-95.

[65] Margaret Nicholson, *A Dictionary of American-English Usage, Based on Fowler's "Modern English Usage"* (New York: Oxford University Press, 1957), v.

[66] C. K. Thomas, review of *Dictionary of American-English Usage*, by Margaret Nicholson, *Quarterly Journal of Speech* 44 (April 1958): 200.

[67] Robertson Davies, "The Stream and the Creek," *Saturday Night* 72 (26 October 1957): 26.

[68] Nicholson, see "Chinaman" and "Carpet." For criticisms of this aspect of Nicholson's work, see Jacques Barzun, "Fowler's Generation," *American Scholar* 26 (Summer 1957): 315–23; Dwight MacDonald, "Sweet Are the Uses of Usage," *New Yorker* 34 (17 May 1958): 136–54; Cassidy, review, 143–47.

[69] Cassidy, 145. Also critical of prescriptive tendencies in Nicholson is R.W. Zandvoort, review of *Dictionary of American-English Usage*, by Margaret Nicholson, *English Studies* 41 (June 1960): 213–15. For a more positive view of Nicholson's work, see Harold Whitehall, "The Elusive Word," *Kenyon Review* 19 (Autumn 1957): 641–43.

[70] H.W. Fowler, *A Dictionary of Modern English Usage*, 2nd ed., rev. by Sir Ernest Gowers (Oxford: Clarendon Press, 1965), see "Meticulous."

[71] Sir Ernest Gowers, "Preface" to H. W. Fowler, *Modern English Usage*, 2nd ed., ix.

[72] "How Modern is Your English Usage?" *Times Literary Supplement* no. 3299 (20 May 1965): 395.

[73] Barbara M. H. Strang, review of *Dictionary of Modern English Usage*, by H.W. Fowler, *Modern Language Review* 61 (April 1966): 264.

[74] Ewald Standop, "Sprachwissenschaft und Sprachpflege: zur Neubearbeitung von Fowlers *Modern English Usage*," *Anglia* 83 (1965): 390–410; L. F. Brosnahan, review of *Dictionary of Modern En-

glish Usage, by H.W. Fowler, *AUMLA* no. 26 (November 1966): 343–45; Yvan Lebrun, "Fowler revu par Gowers," *Revue des langues vivantes* 32 (1966): 324–27.

[75] Burchfield, *The Fowlers*, 19–20.

[76] Borroff, 367.

[77] R. W. Burchfield, review of *Dictionary of Modern English Usage*, by H. W. Fowler, *Listener* 73 (6 May 1965): 675.

[78] R.W. Burchfield, letter to the author, 24 April 1990.

"The Most Amusing Book in the Language": The *Dictionary of National Biography*

Johannah Sherrer

DEVELOPMENT AND HISTORY

In 1893 Leslie Stephen called the *Dictionary of National Biography* "the most amusing book in the language."[1] One might argue that as its first editor Stephen was too close to the *DNB* to make an objective judgment. The passage of time, however, has tested his words and proven them true. No other national biography possesses the color, quality, charm, clever turns of phrases, eccentricity, or outright pizazz that characterize the *Dictionary of National Biography*. Begun in 1885 and current to date, the *DNB* is remarkable on many levels, not the least of which are its conception, origin, aims, and intent.

Precursors

The genre of biography and specifically that of collective biography can be traced back many hundreds of years. British attempts at producing biographical dictionaries included the *Biographia Britannica* published in seven folios between 1747 and 1766. The first important English work came out in eleven volumes in 1761 and was titled *The New and General Biographical Dictionary*.[2] Several editions followed, but the edition published between 1812–1817 with Alexander Chalmers as editor, marked that title's pin-nacle of achievement.[3] Between 1839 and 1847 Rose's *New General Biographical Dictionary* appeared in twelve volumes. More than half of the twelve volumes were consumed by the letters A, B, and C and the articles were mainly abridgements from other dictionaries.[4] None of the above efforts were considered an appropriate reflection of British scholarship nor were they deemed effective universal biographies.[5] While these universal or general biographies were being published, smaller thematic collections were also appearing.

Biographical dictionaries, both thematic and universal, were published in some abundance both in England and throughout the Continent. The first successful national biography appeared in Sweden between 1835 and 1857 and accumulated to 23 volumes. The Dutch introduced a 24-volume set between 1852 and 1878, Austria completed 35 volumes between 1856 and 1891, and Germany 45 volumes between 1875 and 1900.[6] In France, the *Biographie universelle* comprised 40 volumes completed between 1843 and 1863. A British national biographical dictionary was not even contemplated until the early 1850s. John Murray's prestigious publishing firm considered such a publication, but investigation into the feasibility of the project soon indicated that such a venture could not recover costs let alone provide a profit. The successful attempts on the Continent were either heavily or completely funded through government subsidy, and Murray's firm abandoned the project. In an 1884 article, the *Quarterly Review* bemoaned Great Britain's failure to produce a successful, reliable, collective biography and questioned the ultimate feasibility of such an attempt.[7] It was into this scenario that circumstances placed three singularly talented individuals.

George Smith

George Smith, Leslie Stephen, and Sidney Lee are the men responsible for what has been called "the most important reference work for English biography."[8] The series of circumstances that made such a venture possible, as well as the ability of all three individuals to share a common vision and work toward it in harmony are indeed remarkable. All three men would have secured places in the literary annals of Victorian Britain without the *DNB*, but the monumental *DNB* might not have come into being without the unique collaboration of this triumvirate.

George M. Smith (1824–1901) had been head of Smith, Elder and Company since 1845, when, in his early twenties, he succeeded his father as head of the firm. The company was a diversified one that dealt primarily in the India trade; publishing was only a small facet of the company. Hard work and solid business acumen escalated Smith's establishment into the ranks of prosperous firms. Under his leadership, Smith, Elder published the works of William Thackeray, Harriett Martineau, Matthew Arnold, John Ruskin, Charlotte Brontë, and Brontë's biographer, Mrs. Gaskell. The firm is credited with discovering Charlotte Brontë who, up to that point, had been rejected by several other houses.[9]

In 1857, with his company on secure financial footing, Smith to focused his personal efforts on the publishing division. He founded the *Cornhill Magazine* in 1860 and appointed William Thackeray editor. In 1865 he founded the *Pall Mall Gazette*,[10] through which he first met Leslie Stephen.

Leslie Stephen

Leslie Stephen (1834–1904), one of the eminent Victorians and a man of letters, was regarded by his contemporaries as both brilliant and versatile. He was well known to the Victorian intelligentsia for his scholarly pursuits in eighteenth-century literature and philosophy. Outside of literary circles, his feats as a mountain climber and as an ardent (some might say fanatical) walker made him a well known figure in his day both in England and on the Continent. Twentieth-century students of the Victorian era know him as the father of Virginia Woolf and Vanessa Bell.

Leslie Stephen had been a tutor and fellow at Cambridge. His gradual disinclination to accept Christianity made his Cambridge appointment tenuous and in 1862 he was asked to resign.[11] He decided to pursue a living as a journalist and arrived in London in 1865. Stephen soon became a regular contributor to the *Pall Mall Gazette*, and it was in this capacity that he and Smith met and soon formed a relationship that would continue for the rest of their lives. In March 1871 Stephen was offered the editorship of *Fraser's Magazine*. He sought the advice of George Smith, who countered with an offer to edit *Cornhill Magazine*.

Smith, while keeping his hand in other business ventures, relished his position and friendships in the literary world. His concern and respect for men and women of letters became a source of personal reward and satisfaction, and accounted for his desire to see good literature published even at minimal monetary returns for the firm. His success in other ventures allowed him the freedom, for instance, to operate the *Cornhill Magazine* at a loss under Stephen's editorship. The readership of the *Cornhill Magazine* had been declining for some time. Stephen believed that the quality of the magazine was still constant but that public taste was changing. Since he was not inclined to compromise his standards or alter his current editorial practices to accommodate a changing public, both he and Smith agreed that a new editor was needed. It was at this time that Smith proposed his idea concerning a universal biography and the role he wanted Stephen to take in the project.[12]

From the very beginning Smith intended the dictionary to be his legacy to the British people.[13] He understood the monetary commitment and was well aware of previous attempts and failures.

> Why did I undertake a scheme discredited by so many failures? For one thing these very failures tempted me. They challenged my pride. Then, too, I liked the idea of a private individual undertaking a work which was really national, and which outside England is only possible by virtue of the resources of the State. There are national biographies in continental literature, but they are never the result of private enterprise. The State undertakes them and pays for them. Or they are made possible by the aid of ancient and richly endowed libraries. It was something that a private Englishman should undertake a work which, elsewhere, needed the authority and resources of the nation for its accomplishment.[14]

George Smith's fortune was the result of his keen overall business sense, which he displayed in 1872 when he secured for his firm the British concession from a bottled water firm in Germany. The water, sold under the name of Appollinaris, became very popular and eventually earned a return in excess of one million pounds.[15] This financial security permitted Smith to consider the dictionary idea and to commit to its completion. Although his original idea was to produce a compendium of universal biography, he was persuaded by Stephen to limit the scope to a national biography.

Smith's choice of Stephen as editor was not based as much on friendship as on Smith's unwavering belief that Stephen could define the parameters and produce an unequalled literary achievement. He believed that Stephen was "a master of clear and exact English" and

he knew from the *Cornhill* experience that his standards would never waiver.[16] Stephen accepted responsibility for the project in the fall of 1882. In March 1883 Sidney Lee was selected assistant editor. The choice of Lee proved to be pivotal to the project's success.

Sidney Lee

Sidney Lee (1859–1926), was born Solomon Lazarus Lee, the son of a London merchant. He studied at the City of London School under Dr. Edwin Abbot who nurtured his interest in Elizabethan literature. He entered Oxford in 1878 and graduated from Balliol College in 1882. While an undergraduate, he published two articles on Shakespearean topics, both well received in scholarly circles. His Shakespearean scholarship brought him to the attention of Frederick James Furnivall who commissioned him to work on an assignment for the Early English Text Society. Lee was considering a lectureship in a German university when the *DNB* position became available, and gave him the opportunity to remain in England. Brought to Stephen's attention by Dr. Furnivall, Lee's selection as assistant editor was certainly one of Stephen's most astute and valuable contributions to the effort.

The importance of the collaboration of these three men cannot be overstated. The *Dictionary* owes not only its existence but its very essence to these individuals. George Smith's willingness to fund the project at an estimated loss of 50,000–60,000 pounds was critical to the project's success.[17] Leslie Stephen's ability to define the parameters of the endeavor and to rigorously enforce high editorial standards set the tone for the entire run, while Lee, responsible for the day-to-day operations, the proofreading, and the management of the editorial staff, ultimately carried the project through to its successful completion.

Both Lee and Stephen had extraordinary scholarly expectations for the final entries. They stressed attention to detail, accuracy, good writing, and strict adherence to schedules. Each man, while shouldering his editorial responsibilities, also contributed entries to the work. Stephen valued Lee, a Shakespearean scholar, for his expertise in the sixteenth and seventeenth centuries while his own recognition and acclaim rested in the eighteenth and nineteenth centuries. Stephen contributed a total of 378 articles,[18] placing at least one in all but 3 of the 63 volumes.[19] Most noted among his entries are those on George Eliot, Joseph Addison, Charles Dickens, Thomas Babbington McCaulay, Thomas Carlyle, Alexander Pope, and William Wordsworth. Lee's knowledge of Elizabethan sources and bibliography were unequalled. He contributed 820 articles, including his entries on William Shakespeare, Edward VII, and Queen Victoria.

Stephen and Lee took two years to organize and to set into motion the process that would accommodate the innumerable details needed to produce a successful effort. All three men were well aware of previous British and Continental efforts and all were driven by the desire to complete the *Dictionary* in a timely yet scholarly manner. The first volume appeared in January 1885. It had been delayed several months by Smith's concern over a myriad of misprints resulting from poor proofreading and the late detection of a plagiarized article.[20] The article in question was Alexander Balloch Grosart's biography of Richard Alleine, for which Grosart used material he had previously submitted to *Encyclopaedia Britannica* for an article on Alleine. The undetected error sent chills through George Smith. His Victorian ethical standards dictated delaying the project until an honorable solution could be worked out with the publishing firm of the *Encyclopaedia* and until he was confident that editorial procedures were in place to detect similar problems much earlier in the publishing process. Thereafter, the staff of the *DNB* punctually delivered a new volume for quarterly publication for the next 16 years! It became a hallmark of unparalleled dedica-tion, pride, and shared responsibility between publisher, editors, and contributors.

The Dictionary's Purpose

The aim of the *Dictionary* was to commemorate the nation's past through biography. Both Lee and Stephen wrote and lectured widely on the significance of biography and on its relationship to history.[21] Neither wanted to continue in the tradition of the antiquaries or the "Dryasdusts" who had previously attempted to record British lives. The *Dictionary* was to serve as a compendium of lives that would reflect the nation's growth, development, and character. Stephen and Lee deliberately set out to redefine biography in terms of methodology and to present a collective national biography in a manner both uniform and consistent with known facts. Stephen was concerned that the growth and documentation of raw historical sources were accumulating at a rate that was exceeding the scholars' ability to make them accessible. He viewed the *Dictionary* as a tool that would alleviate the problem for biographical research.

The process for selecting entrants for the compendium was initiated by Stephen in an article published in the *Anthenaeum* in December 1882.[22] The process continued to evolve as time went on, but the initial limits were set at this time. From the beginning Stephen excluded the names of living persons. He also excluded names that were only names, meaning those individuals whose main claim to fame was simply having appeared in a list or bibliography. It was also his intention to limit the entrants to real people rather than mythical personalities. The definition was designed, however, to leave the door open to individuals of lesser fame. Both Lee and Stephen believed that it was the chronicling of lesser individuals that would give their work the lasting depth and importance they intended it to achieve. According to Stephen: "It is the second-rate people; the people whose lives have to be reconstructed from obituary notices, or from references in memoirs and collections of let-ters; or sought in prefaces to posthumous works; or sometimes painfully dug out of collections of manuscripts, and who really become generally accessible through the dic-tionary alone; that provide really useful read-ing."[23] The process of identifying these names progressed alphabetically. The first list of proposed candidates came from John Murray's publishing firm. Although he had declined to proceed with the venture for financial reasons, he graciously turned over the notes that had been started on the project, including a list of about 200 names. It was with this list that Stephen began his project.

The *Dictionary* was to include English, Scotch, and Irish names from the earliest times. It was intended that Americans and natives of India who were British subjects would also be included, but eventually the editors decided that eighteenth-century Ameri-can colonists would have to wait for their own national biography.

The *Anthenaeum* agreed to publish a list of proposed names twice a year and the public was invited to add to this list. Each list con-tained about 1,000 names that had been culled from some 200 reference works, all of the volumes of the *Gentlemen's Quarterly,* and, of course, the *The Times* obituary list. After each list appeared in the *Anthenaeum* it was published as a pamphlet by the Smith, Elder Company. This pamphlet was sent to con-tributors who then submitted forms for the contributions they wished to write. They were also invited to identify additional names that may have been omitted from the original screening.[24]

Writing assignments were handed out two years before actual publication. The contribu-tors, however, had up to six months to com-plete their work. The editorial work that fol-lowed the submitted articles was often exten-sive. The articles were checked for accuracy, especially for dates, and often factual material was supplied only at the editorial level. It was believed that as much time was spent editing the articles as was spent in writing them.[25]

Editorial Standards

Both Lee and Stephen had developed the writing of biography into an art. They strove to attain both accuracy and abundance in the delivery of facts; stressed the importance of primary sources, including personal knowl-edge of the subject; and sought to discover the character of an individual without elaborate or critical analysis while valuing succinctness and readability. Stephen believed that "The epitaph should give in the smallest possible number of words the very essence of a man's character and of his claims upon the memory of posterity."[26]

The writers were instructed to be in sym-pathy with their subject but to keep eulogy within bounds. In the 1882 *Anthenaeum* ar-ticle Stephen concluded his remarks with the words: "The editor of such a work must, by the necessity of the case, be autocratic. He will do his best to be a considerate autocrat."[27]

Both Lee and Stephen kept in close con-tact with their contributors. The general un-derstanding at that time was that an editor could omit segments from a signed article without an author's consent but he could not add to the work. The editorial policy at the *DNB* was quite different. The editors felt free to add details, especially factual information, and to supplement biographical detail and physical descriptions of the entrants. Over the years the editorial staff became noted for their proficiency in tracking genealogical informa-tion and for their files of personal contacts for county and church record information.[28]

Adherence to schedules and timetables was taken quite seriously. If a contributor failed to meet a deadline or to correct per-ceived inadequacies in writing and research, the article was produced inhouse and submit-ted unsigned. The average article length con-tinued to grow as years went on. Several factors probably contributed to the develop-ment. Leslie Stephen, always striving for suc-cinctness, rarely hesitated to cut the length of submissions dramatically. Lee, however, ap-peared to enforce length restrictions with less rigor. Another factor affecting article length was the growing availability of primary sources. The historical profession was at last coming into its own and increasing numbers of indexed and calendared materials were appearing.

Scholars trained in historical research were a rarity when the project began. In England, universities were just beginning the study and teaching of historical research. The *English Historical Review*, begun in 1886, was not yet a force in scholastic circles. The *DNB* served as the first training ground for historical research and in this capacity Lee and Stephen developed the methodological training of those who were to become Great Britain's elite historical scholars. These included C.L. Kingsford, C.H. Firth, A.F. Pollard, J.E. Creighton, Mary Bateson, and T.F. Tout to mention a few. Thomas Frederick Tout admitted:

> Like many Oxford men of my generation I approached historical investigation without the least training or guidance in historical method, and felt very much at a loss how to set to work. The careful and stringent regulations which [Stephen] drew up, and the brusque but kindly way in which he enforced obedience to them, constituted for many of us our first training in anything like original investigation.[29]

Working with hundreds of contributors, many of them unfamiliar with biographical writing or possessing limited experience in historical research, the editorial staff of *DNB* successfully produced volume after volume, each one regarded as better than the one before it.[30] The accomplishment of punctually producing the quarterly volumes seems all the more remarkable when one considers the *Dictionary's* steadily increasing quality.

Stephen's Burden

The task took its toll on Leslie Stephen. The drudgery and strain of the vigilance he deemed necessary to meet deadlines eventually proved too much for him. In addition to contributing many entries himself, he reviewed every submission and edited the contributions sternly, corresponding with the authors, and tactfully dealing with the myriad requests for inclusion of departed loved ones. He also continued with his own writing and studying and with his roles as a husband and the father of four. A selection of his letters appears in Frederic William Maitland's biography of Stephen. In these letters he refers to the *Dictionary* as the "infernal dictionary," "that damned dictionary," and the "accursed drudgery."[31] He refers to himself as a "dictionary-ridden animal," and laments that the damned thing goes on like a diabolical piece of machinery, always gaping for more copy, and I fancy at times that I shall be dragged into it, and crushed out into slips.'"[32]

Maitland elaborates that Stephen's complaining was typical of the way he expressed his frustrations and that he intended people laugh when he used such hyperbole.[33] The frustrations, however, were very real and his health continued to deteriorate under the demanding schedule. At one point he seriously considered delaying a quarterly issue.[34] Realizing that he was placing more and more of the burden on Lee, he insisted that Lee's name begin appearing on the title page. So in March 1890, Lee and Stephen were listed as coeditors, a practice continued for the next four issues. The reduction in Stephen's work load failed to restore his health. In April 1891 he asked his wife to write to George Smith and inform him that his health precluded his continuation as editor of the *Dictionary*. So, beginning with the June 1891 issue, only Lee's name appeared as editor. Lee's enormous capacity for work and his ability to pay attention to detail guaranteed George Smith that the project would continue without interruptions. Stephen's resignation did not prohibit him from continuing to write articles for the *DNB*. Other than Lee himself, Stephen was the *DNB*'s most prolific contributor; his writing comprised approximately 1,000 pages and accounted for one-seventeenth of the entire work.[35] Upon its completion in 1901, the entire work stretched to nearly 30,000 pages commemorating nearly as many lives.[36] In 1901 three supplementary volumes were published, covering an additional 1,000 lives. These supplementary volumes were issued as the final three volumes of the original set. Two hundred of these names were omissions from the original set and the remaining 800 were individuals who had died after their letter of the alphabet had been published. Because George Smith wished the death of Queen Victoria to mark the official end of the work,[37] the *DNB* was extended to include lives of people who had died prior to January 22, 1901. That the death of Victoria should mark the end of this set seems only fitting, for even in its own time the *DNB* was considered a monument to British history.[38]

The size and scope of the *DNB* was such that errors, misprints, and other errata were bound to occur under even the most careful scrutiny. During the quarterly printings of the *DNB*, the corrections, compiled by the Reverend W.C. Boulter, were printed in *Notes and Queries*. In 1904 Lee issued a volume of corrections that was distributed free to subscribers. These corrections were incorporated into the re-issue of 1908–1909.[39] In 1923, A.F. Pollard founded the Institute of Historical Research of the University of London to emulate the training he had had received at the hands of Sidney Lee and to use the Institute's *Bulletin* as a vehicle for reporting addenda and correcting errors in the *DNB*. Today the Institute's publication, re-titled *Historical Research*, no longer serves that function. All corrections are referred to the *DNB* editorial offices at the Oxford University Press.

Critical Reception

From the appearance of its inaugural volume the *DNB* received praise. Its contributors, editors, and publisher were widely recognized, with both Lee and Stephen receiving knighthoods for their involvement in the project. Even continental scholars admitted that the *DNB* surpassed their own national biographies both in terms of scope and scholarship.[40] Most secondary sources refer to the original set as a "monument to Victorian scholarship, enterprise and philanthropy."[41] Reviews of the set as it came out repeatedly drew attention to the exceptional quality of both Stephen's and Lee's writing.[42] It was also noted, as Lee and Stephen had intended, that the shorter articles on those of lesser fame not only embodied the essence of the *DNB*, but would give it lasting value.[43]

There were negative comments. For example, historians of the time objected to the lengthy articles on kings and statesmen that could be better presented in book-length treatments. The emphasis of the editors that the set be geared to the general reader as well as to the scholar raised the eyebrows of more than one historian.[44] There were also comments regarding the length of entries in comparison to an individual's overall historical importance.[45] Current critiques of the *DNB* demonstrate that the set not only maintains its credibility but has taken on a persona of its own. Clearly the steady output of biographical entries has in itself become a significant value of the set and its supplements. Its serialization provides a continuous acknowledgment of British achievement and notoriety since the earliest times, with readers taking pride in the cumulative body of entrants that encompasses eminent statesmen as well as misers.

The reviews of the twentieth-century supplements and, indeed, later retrospective reviews of the original set bring other criticisms into focus. Contemporary awareness of cultural and social issues have raised the consciousness of many reviewers. Comments regarding the exclusion of women, labor leaders, sportsmen, and people of commerce are now noted. Some object that Stephen and Lee's intent to include all segments of the nation fell far short of the mark.[46] Stephen's biographer, Noel Annan, notes that twentieth-century critics call attention to moral judgments that appear throughout the original set and in Stephen's contributions particularly.[47]

Annan replies that Stephen "would have had to step outside of his age to omit moral judgements."[48] Stephen's view on the status of women was reflective of the Victorian era. Even when friends were advocating female emancipation, Stephen resisted with vehemence.[49] Lee, the author of the "Statistical Account" was not unaware of the low number of women appearing in the *DNB*. He noted that in London in 1896 about 600 people would qualify for an entry in the work and that only about 20 of these would be women. He stated:

> In this last calculation I perhaps have made inadequate allowance for the recently developed energy among women which seems likely to generate unlooked-for exploits of more or less distinction. But no statistics are needed to prove that the woman's opportunities of distinction were infinitesimal in the past, and are very small compared with men's something like one to thirty at that present moment. Women will not therefore, I regret to reflect, have much claim on the attention of the national biographer for a very long time to come."[50]

As early as 1890, a review in the *English Historical Review* notes that some women of distinction appear only in their husbands' biographies.[51] And, as late as 1986, a reviewer of the recently published 1971–1980 supplement noted that only 15 percent of the entries were women and that nearly one third of them were writers.[52]

Another omission that has been steadily tracked from the original set through the supplements is the lack of individuals from trade and commerce.[53] The Victorian distaste for revelling in commercial successes seems to have extended well into the twentieth-century supplements. Other omissions that have been noted include the scarcity of trade unionists and a lack of entries recording the violence in Northern Ireland, either in terms of victims or terrorists.[54] Stephen's anticlericalism is well documented. His refusal to list either St. Alban or St. Asaph in the original set was eventually amended by Lee in the supplements.[55] On yet another level, Pollard believed that Lee's interest in literary history accounts for what

could be interpreted as an undue inclusion of very minor literary figures.[56]

The first supplement to deal explicitly with the sexual preference of individuals was the 1961–1970 supplement. Although even here, as one reviewer notes, most contributors were less than direct and perhaps inadvertently revealed a moral judgment themselves. For example, Somerset Maugham's homosexuality is referred to with subtlety when the biographer states that Maugham "stepped off his pedestal with a young American."[57] A reviewer of the 1971–1980 supplement notes that an entrant's "propensity for solitary sex in parks and swimming pools could perhaps be stated more directly."[58] Another reviewer of that decennial supplement notes an absence of attributing drugs or alcohol as a direct influence on the lives or careers of many of the entrants.[59]

Evaluations of the *DNB* concerning its biases or even its editorial practices must be considered in historical perspective. The degree to which these omissions reflect editorial bias or are seen as reflections of current cultural perspective, while debatable, are also what gives the set its historical value. The *DNB* has existed for over 100 years. The mores and even the research strategies used to produce it have changed over that time period and will continue to do so. One of its strengths rests in its lasting value as a source both reflective and indicative of its time.

The original set included many lives from previous centuries and the writers of those biographies had the advantage of secondary sources and historical perspective. As the *DNB* moved into decennial volumes the biographies were overwhelmingly rather recent ones. The change, although subtle, marks a significant difference between the original set and the supplements. Another significant difference rests in the fact that more than half of the original set was written by only 34 regular contributors, while in the supplements the one-time contributor is virtually the norm.[60] During the 16-year production schedule of the original set, the editors were also contributors and their writing style clearly influenced the character of the original set. The supplements have been produced for almost 90 years with contributors and editors changing throughout that time. While the original set serves as an embodiment of Victorian scholarship and carries with it the character and expressions of that era, the supplements are distinguished by the continuity provided by their Oxford base. According to one reviewer "One of the joys of the *DNB*, imparted by its Oxford base, is its tendency to delicate spite, dry periphrasis or oblique understatement."[61]

The *DNB* still serves as model of literary art and historical writing. Its succinct, and sometimes pithy writing is peppered with anecdotal accounts, fact, and individual perspective.[62] Leslie Stephen believed that "No man is a real reader until he is sensible of the pleasure of turning over some miscellaneous collection, and lying like a trout in a stream snapping up, with the added charm of unsuspectedness, any of the queer little morsels of oddity or pathos that may drift past him."[63] The *Dictionary of National Biography* still holds that charm for the the twentieth-century reader. Even though newly available manuscripts may obviate nineteenth-century scholarship, the joy of the writing and the subtle inferences from a time past will be lost to only the most unimaginative of readers. Reviews of the supplements indicate that the twentieth-century endeavors have yielded success in this area as well.[64]

When George Smith died in 1901, he left the *DNB* to his widow. Mrs. Smith served as publisher of the supplement covering deaths from 1901–1911, while Lee continued as editor. In 1917 Smith, Elder was acquired by the Murray publishing house. This was the same firm that had contemplated and then rejected the idea of publishing a national biography in the early 1850s. The *DNB*, not part of sale, was given to Oxford University by the Smith family with the stipulation that it was to continue to be published.[65] Oxford has continued to publish the *DNB* with decennial supplements through 1980, although the supplemental vol-

umes have not appeared with the same punctuality as the original Smith, Stephen, and Lee venture. Oxford has broken the decennial tradition with the publication of the latest supplement. Beginning with the 1981–1985 supplement issued in 1990, the set will be updated through quinquennial supplements.[66]

Extension and Revision

Almost since its completion, speculation both as to the feasibility and to the desirability of revising the whole set has occurred.[67] In a 1949 *Times Literary Supplement* article a reviewer of the 1931–1940 supplement also tackled the subject of a complete revision of the *DNB*.[68] The suggestion prompted a meeting between scholars and publishers who reached the mutual decision that the effort was simply not feasible.[69] The current editor, C.S. Nicholls, states that "books such as ours are very expensive to produce."[70] Efforts are underway to raise funds for a complete revision, but in the meantime the editorial staff has decided to publish a volume of individuals who have been omitted from *DNB* since its beginning.[71] The current editor cautions that it may not be possible to raise all the funds needed for a complete revision. Whether or not funds are found to completely revise the *DNB* thoroughly, it will remain a cherished and significant contribution to British history and scholarship. Its significance as a landmark reference title rests not only in its longevity as a useful reference tool but also upon the unique mix of anecdotal characterization and detailed factual accounting of British lives. The introductions for each supplement provide fascinating overviews of the cumulative body of entries and readers soon lose themselves in the well-written biographies that follow. Only the most insensitive of readers can come away from an hour of browsing in "the most amusing book in the language" without having attained a deeper understanding of British history, life, manners, and achievement.

PUBLICATION HISTORY

Dictionary of National Biography, edited by Leslie Stephen, volumes 1-21; edited by Leslie Stephen and Sidney Lee, volumes 22-26; edited by Sidney Lee, volumes 27-66. London: Smith, Elder and Company, 1885-1901. 66 vols.

Dictionary of National Biography, From the Earliest Times to 1900, edited by by Sir Leslie Stephen and Sir Sidney Lee. [Reissue.] London: Smith, Elder and Company, 1908-1909. 22 vols.

Dictionary of National Biography, Index and Epitome, edited by Sir Sidney Lee. London: Smith, Elder, and Company, 1903-1913. 2 vols.

Dictionary of National Biography, 1901-1911, edited by Sir Sidney Lee. Oxford: Oxford University Press, 1912. 739p.

Dictionary of National Biography, 1912-1921, edited by H.W.C. Davis and J.R.H. Weaver. Oxford: Oxford University Press, 1927. 623p.

Dictionary of National Biography, 1922-1930, edited by J.R.H. Weaver. Oxford: Oxford University Press, 1937. 962p.

Dictionary of National Biography, 1931-1940, edited by L.G. Wickham Legg. Oxford: Oxford University Press, 1949. 968p.

Dictionary of National Biography, 1941-1950, edited by L.G. Wickham Legg and E.T. Williams. Oxford: Oxford University Press, 1959. 1,031p.

Dictionary of National Biography, 1951-1960, edited by E.T. Williams and Helen M. Palmer. Oxford: Oxford University Press, 1971. 1,150p.

Dictionary of National Biography, 1961-1970, edited by E.T. Williams and C.S. Nicholls. Oxford: Oxford University Press, 1981. 1,178p.

Dictionary of National Biography, 1971-1980, edited by Lord Blake and C.S. Nicholls. Oxford: Oxford University Press, 1986. 1,010p.

Dictionary of National Biography, 1981-1985, edited by Lord Blake and C. S. Nicholls. Oxford: Oxford University Press, 1990. 518p.

BIBLIOGRAPHY

The papers, correspondence, ledgers, and day books associated with the *Dictionary of National Biography* were destroyed after the third supplement was completed. Numerous secondary sources exist and several major biographies on key personnel are available. For Leslie Stephen, see Noel Annan's *Leslie Stephen: The Godless Victorian*, a revision of his 1952 biography on Stephen titled *Leslie Stephen: His Thought and Character in Relation to His Time*. Both volumes are valuable. See also Maitland's *Life and Letters of Leslie Stephen*. For George Smith, see Jennifer Glynn's *Prince of Publishers: A Biography of George Smith* and Leonard Huxley's *The House of Smith Elder*. A full-length biography on Sir Sidney Lee has yet to be written. For a summary of the founding of the *DNB*, see both J.L. Kirby and R.H. Fritze cited below. Laurel Brake's article provides the clearest explanation of the publishing history of the *DNB*. Many reviews of the original set and the supplements have appeared throughout the past 100 years; only the more significant ones are listed in the bibliography. For excerpts that capsulize the essence of the *DNB*, see the examples cited in the reviews and especially the article by Pat Rogers. The best method for understanding and enjoying the *DNB* is to read the introductions to the original set and the supplements and to peruse the volumes themselves.

Annan, Noel. *Leslie Stephen: The Godless Victorian*. New York: Random House, 1984.

————. *Leslie Stephen: His Thought and Character in Relation to his Time*. Cambridge, MA: Harvard University Press, 1952.

Bell, Allan. "Leslie Stephen and the DNB." *Times Literary Supplement*, no. 3951 (December 16, 1977): 1478.

————. "A Portable Valhalla." *Times Literary Supplement*, no. 4096 (October 2, 1981): 1115–17.

"Biographies Universelle, Ancienne et Moderne; Nouvelle Biographie Generale; Specimen of a 'Dictionary of National Biography.'" *Quarterly Review* 157 (July, 1884): 187–230.

Brake, Laurel. "Problems in Victorian Biography: The *DNB* and the *DNB* 'Walter Pater'." *Modern Language Review* 70 (October, 1975): 731–42.

Cannadine, David. "British Worthies." *London Review of Books* 3 (December, 1981): 3–4, 6.

Corrections and Additions to the Dictionary of National Biography. Boston: G. K. Hall, 1966.

Davenport-Hines, Richard. "All Sorts and Conditions." *Times Literary Supplement*, no. 4363 (November 14, 1986): 1263–64.

Fenwick, Gillian. *The Contributor's Index to the Dictionary of National Biography, 1885–1901*.

Winchester, Hampshire: St. Paul's Bibliographies, 1989.

Firth, C.H. "Memoir of Sir Sidney Lee." *Dictionary of National Biography Supplement, 1912–1921*. London: Oxford University Press, 1927.

Frank, Robert Worth. "The Most Amusing Book in the Language." *American Scholar* 54 (Winter, 1984/85): 89–97.

Fritze, Ronald H. "The Dictionary of National Biography and Its Early Editors and Publisher." *Reference Services Review* 16 (1988): 21–29.

Glynn, Jennifer. *Prince of Publishers: A Biography of George Smith*. New York: Allison & Busby, 1986.

Hull, Charles H. "Helps of Cataloguers in Finding Full Names." *Library Journal* 14 (1889): 7–20.

Huxley, Leonard. *The House of Smith Elder*. London: Printed for Private Circulation, 1923.

Kirby, J.L. "The Dictionary of National Biography." *The Library Association Record* 60 (June 1958): 181–91.

Lee, Sidney. "The Dictionary of National Biography: A Statistical Account." *Dictionary of National Biography*, v.1, pp. lxi–l xxxxiv. Oxford: Oxford University Press, 1921–1922.

_____. "Memoir of George Smith." *Dictionary of National Biography*, v. 1, pp. xxi–lix. London: Oxford University Press, 1921–1922. First published in September 1901 in the first volume of the original edition of the Supplement.

_____. "National Biography." *Cornhill Magazine* 26 (March, 1896): 258–77.

_____. "Sir Leslie Stephen." *Dictionary of National Biography. Supplement 1901–1911*. London: Oxford University Press, 1920. Reprinted 1927.

Maitland, Frederic William. *The Life and Letters of Leslie Stephen*. London: Duckworth & Co., 1906.

Pollard, A. F. "Sir Sidney Lee and the 'Dictionary of National Biography.'" *Bulletin of the Institute of Historical Research* 4 (1926/27): 1–13.

Rogers, Pat. "Diversions of the *DNB*." *Essays and Studies* 37 (1984): 75–86.

Stephen, Leslie. "Biography." *Living Age* 199 (October/December, 1893): 451–59.

Stephen, Leslie. "National Biography." *National Review* 27 (March/August, 1896): 51–65.

_____. "A New Biographia Britannica." *Athenaeum*, no. 2878 (December 26, 1882): 850.

"Worthies of Empire." *Times Literary Supplement*, no. 2498 (December 16, 1949): 819.

Wrong, George M. "Dictionary of National Biography." *American Historical Review* 7 (April, 1902): 588–90.

NOTES

1 Leslie Stephen, "Biography," *Living Age* 199 (October/December 1893): 451. This is a reprint of an article that originally appeared in the *National Review* in 1893.

2 *The Universal Cyclopedia*.

3 Ibid.

4 "Biographies Universelle, Ancienne et Moderne; Novelle Biographic Generale; specimen of a Dictionary of National Biography," *Quarterly Review* 157 (July 1884): 204.

5 Gillian Fenwick, "Introduction," *The Contributor's Index to the 'Dictionary of National Biography', 1885–1900* (Winchester, Hampshire: St. Paul's Bibliographies, 1989), x.

6 *Encyclopedia Britannica*, 11th Edition.

7 *Quarterly Review*, "Biographies Universelle," 188.

8 Eugene P. Sheehy, *Guide to Reference Books*, 10th ed. (Chicago: American Library Association, 1986), 299.

9 Ronald H. Fritze, "The *Dictionary of National Biography* and Its Early Editors and Publisher," *Reference Services Review* 16 (1988): 22.

10 J.L. Kirby, "The *Dictionary of National Biography*," *The Library Association Record* 60 (June 1958): 181.

11 Ibid., 182.

12 Leslie Stephen, *The Mausoleum Book* (Oxford: Clarendon Press, 1977), 85.

13 Leonard Huxley, *The House of Smith Elder* (London: Printed for Private Circulation, 1923), 181.

14 Ibid., 181–82.

15 Fritze, 23.

16 Huxley, *House of Smith Elder*, 182.

17 Ibid.

18 Noel Annan, *Leslie Stephen: His Thought and Character in Relation to His Time* (Cambridge, MA: Harvard University Press, 1952), 79.

19 Phyllis Gosskurth, *Leslie Stephen* (Essex, England: Longmans, Green & Co. L, 1968), 13.

20 Noel Annan, *Leslie Stephen: The Godless Victorian* (New York: Random House, 1984): 85.

21 Sidney Lee, "National Biography," *Cornhill Magazine* 26 (March 1896): 258–77; Stephen, "Biography," 451–59. Leslie Stephen, "National Biography," *National Review* 27 (March/August 1896): 51–65.

22 Leslie Stephen, "A New Biographia Britannica," *Athenaeum* no. 2878 (26 December 1882): 850.

23 Stephen, "National Biography," 59–60.

24 A. F. Pollard, "Sir Sidney Lee and the 'Dictionary of National Biography,'" *Bulletin of the Institute of Historical Research* 4 (1926/27): 12.

25 Ibid., 2.

26 Stephen, "National Biography," 62.

27 Ibid.

28 Pollard, 7.

29 Annan, *Leslie Stephen: Godless Victorian*, 86.

[30] Pollard, 6.

[31] Frederic William Maitland, *The Life and Letters of of Leslie Stephen* (London: Duckworth & Co., 1906), 378–404.

[32] Ibid., 394.

[33] Ibid., 395.

[34] Ibid., 400.

[35] Fritze, 27.

[36] Robert Worth Frank, "The Most Amusing Book in the Language," *American Scholar* 54 (Winter 1984/85): 89.

[37] George M. Wrong, "The *Dictionary of National Biography*," *American Historical Review* 7 (April 1902): 588.

[38] Ibid.

[39] Laurel Brake, "Problems in Victorian Biography: The DNB and the DNB 'Walter Pater,'" *Modern Language Review* 70 (October 1975): 732.

[40] Annan, *Thought and Character*, 78.

[41] Gillian Fenwick, "Introduction," ix. to *The Contributor's Index to the 'Dictionary of National Biography', 1885–1900* (Winchester, Hampshire: (St. Paul's Bibliographies), ix.

[42] "The *Dictionary of National Biography*," *English Historical Review* 6 (January 1893): 181–82; "The *Dictionary of National Biography*," *English Historical Review* 9 (July 1894): 591–92.

[43] "The *Dictionary of National Biography*," *English Historical Review* 5 (October 1890): 785.

[44] Ibid., 784–785; Wrong, 589.

[45] *English Historical Review*, 1890, 786; Wrong, 589; Annan, *Thought and Character*, 78; Alan Bell, "A Portable Valhalla," *Times Literary Supplement* no. 4096 (2 October 1981): 1116.

[46] Pat Rogers, "Diversions of the *DNB*," *Essays and Studies* 37 (1984): 78; Annan, *Godless Victorian*, 88.

[47] Rogers, 82.

[48] Annan, *Godless Victorian*, 88–89; Rogers, 76.

[49] Annan, *Godless Victorian*, 110.

[50] Lee, "National Biography," 273

[51] *English Historical Review*, 1890, 786.

[52] Richard Davenport-Hines, "All Sorts and Conditions," *Times Literary Supplement* no. 4363 (14 November 1986): 1264.

[53] Ibid., 1264; David Cannadine, "British Worthies," *London Review of Books* 3 (December 1981): 4; Annan, *Godless Victorian*, 88.

[54] Bell, 1115; Davenport-Hines, 1264.

[55] Pollard, 10.

[56] Ibid., 11.

[57] Bell, 1116; Christopher Booker, "Remembering Like Anything," *Spectator* 247 (3 October 1981): 21.

[58] Davenport-Hines, 1263.

[59] Ibid.

[60] Cannadine, 3.

[61] Davenport-Hines, 1263.

[62] Rogers, 82; Brake, 741.

[63] Stephen, "National Biography," 63.

[64] Bell, 1116.

[65] Huxley, 190.

[66] C. S. Nicholls, letter to the author, 25 January 1990.

[67] "Worthies of the Empire," *Times Literary Supplement* no. 2498 (16 December 1949): 819.

[68] Ibid.

[69] Brake, 732.

[70] Nicholls, letter to author, 25 January 1990.

[71] Ibid.

Controlling the Beasties: *Dissertation Abstracts International*

Mary W. George

DEVELOPMENT AND HISTORY

Dissertations are strange beasties, combining the length of a book, the breadth of a grant application, and the depth, supposedly, of a scholarly treatise. An ordinary mortal will encounter just one such creature in a lifetime, taming it only after long and weary labor, despite the wiles of procrastination and the vagaries of a doctoral committee.

As evidence of a person's ability to ask significant new questions about a highly specific area of knowledge, and then to design, conduct, and interpret research appropriate to answer those questions, the dissertation can claim only mixed results. The Germans are very right to qualify the word with the adjective *inaugural*, because the dissertation is at best a good start with no promises. In fact, as a predictor of intellectual energy and potential, it fails miserably; witness the dearth or deficiency of subsequent scholarship by many who "earn" the Ph.D. Then, too, in our culture, those outside academe rank writing a dissertation somewhere near surgery and passing a driving test in terms of pain and challenge, respectively. Yet possessing a doctorate still commands great respect.

Debate will always surround the content and process of graduate education, which is only right. The unexamined pursuit, in academe as anywhere else, too easily becomes routine, drawn out, and ineffectual. Furthermore, the tangible product of the process, the dissertation, is itself a knotty problem: What exactly should it "prove," and to whom? Are traditional expectations regarding its scope, format, readability, time and effort involved— not to mention its value—justified, especially given the low correlation between dissertation quality and any individual's later contributions to the field? These are all ponderable if not solvable questions, ones which Theodore Ziolkowski has placed in historical perspective and named the Ph.D. squid, an image which all who have been in the grip of graduate school will understand too well.[1]

Availability of Dissertations

There is one aspect of the dissertation, however, which Ziolkowski does not address, its availability. To add irony to adversity (viewing the case from a student's perspective), this masterpiece, proof in the medieval sense that a person is worthy to enter a discipline's guild and participate in its rituals, is figuratively a closed book to everyone outside the candidate's immediate circle—closed because it is unpublished and unpublicized.

Here the story begins to twist and tangle. Every degree-granting institution in the world has its own rules about dissertations: how many bound copies the author must provide and whether these may be typed or must be printed; who is responsible for copyrighting the work; where dissertations are kept and under what physical conditions; how—and, for that matter, whether—they will be cataloged, and if so, whether entries for them will appear in any published list or database; who will preserve brittle ones; what legalities must be observed by anyone wishing to read, copy, or quote from them; if they will be sold to, loaned to, or exchanged with other institutions.[2] To add to this crazy quilt, schools which also generate master's, senior, or honors theses usually have a whole different set of rules for those writings,[3] and, of course, each university's idiosyncrasies have shifted over time.[4]

It is not as if people have not tried to solve these problems. There is, for example, an indispensable bibliography of dissertation bibliographies which is arranged by both country and discipline.[5] Several guides to institutions' loan and photocopy policies now exist which indicate exactly what dissertations are available, and how, from the originating school.[6] Special lending agreements within national or regional library consortia make matters somewhat smoother, although no one imagines there will ever be total reciprocity among institutions. A few scholarly journals even review selected dissertations.[7]

On the whole, researchers are faced with a paradox: the possible importance of dissertations to their work is offset by the probable nuisance of identifying and obtaining them. Or, as many have said at a library reference desk, "If it's a dissertation, forget it." That dismissal is typically accompanied by the spoken or unspoken thought, "If it's any good, it should come out, sooner or later, as a real book." This is not the place, however, to digress on the economics or academic politics of that belief, let alone the overhaul necessary to transform a dissertation into a "real" book.[8]

Eugene B. Power

The twists and tangles get still more bizarre owing to a second strange beastie, microfilm, and its impresario, Eugene B. (for Barnum, no less) Power, who first recognized

this format as an ideal way to preserve fragile, fugitive, rare, bulky, and low-demand print sources. Realizing that dissertations qualified on all those counts, Power made filming and selling them the cornerstone of University Microfilms, the business he founded in Ann Arbor, Michigan, in June 1938.[9] In February 1962 he sold the company to the Xerox Corporation, which in turn sold it to Bell & Howell in December 1985.[10] Now called University Microfilms International (UMI), the firm has operations in Ann Arbor devoted to dissertations, serials, and out-of-print materials (Books on Demand).[11]

The idea of miniaturizing documents goes back to the mid-nineteenth century when it was first posited in England by James Glaisher and J.F.W. Herschel who independently suggested the possibility based on technological advances in photography and microscopy.[12] To those who rely on microformat sources to conduct their research, the stuff is both a blessing and a curse. It is a blessing because it allows access to essential works without spending large amounts of money and time to contact and travel to distant repositories. And it is a curse owing to the physical discomfort of reading and transcribing microforms as well as the generally poor quality of paper copies made by reader-printers. It took Eugene Power's insight and entrepreneurial instincts to transform this ugly duckling technology into a corporate swan and in the process to create a marketing tool, *Dissertation Abstracts International (DAI)*, that has become a legend in academe.[13]

As legends go, this one is easy to relate: *DAI* is quite simply the Sears catalog of academe, describing the intellectual goods available for purchase from UMI. Or, put another way, it is a field guide to the strange beasties, standard equipment for anyone who needs to spot, track down, and bag dissertations. All the user who identifies a pertinent product (i.e., a dissertation) needs to do is phone a toll-free number and use a credit card to order the complete version.[14] By 1990 UMI's dissertation database was growing by about 35,000 titles per year. Starting in 1991, another 3,700 Canadian dissertations will be added annually as well.

DAI has come a long way since 1938 when Eugene Power left his job as vice president for sales at Edwards Brothers, the large Ann Arbor printing firm best known to librarians for publishing various Library of Congress author and subject catalogs as well as sets of the *National Union Catalog* between 1942 and 1970. Edwards Brothers was also involved in microform publishing. In the mid-1930s the company launched a major project to film pre-1550 English books. Power had coordinated this program and then acquired it from Edwards Brothers shortly after he set up his own company.[15] In a seven-page pamphlet, *A Plan for Publication of Scholarly Material on Microfilm*, Power explained the purpose of his new company:

> The invention of printing provided the means for the tremendous expansion of scholarly research through the duplication of man's ideas. . . . For centuries printing methods fulfilled the requirements of scholars as a means of reproducing the results of research. With the turn of the century it has been increasingly apparent that the greater specialization of scholarship has resulted in a decrease in the potential market for books and monographs in any one field. This same printing process which at one time provided the release from the restricting influence of book production by scribes is now exerting a similarly restricting influence through a reverse process.
>
> Our printing facilities today are all geared to the production of a large number of copies on an extremely economical basis. However, they are not able to produce a small number of copies economically, and with this decrease in the size of the market, publication of scholarly material becomes an increasingly difficult problem unless accompanied by subsidy. . . .
>
> What scholarly publishing needs is a method of distribution which gives sufficient and adequate publicity to a title or list of titles so that the information regarding what is offered is readily available to prospective users, combined with a means of production which can produce as demand materializes at an economical and uniform rate. . . .

> Briefly, this is a plan to provide a means of production and distribution for the products of scholarly research which, because of their nature, command too small a market to warrant publication through the ordinary and established channels.[16]

Power went on to describe his concept of having dissertation authors submit to UMI "a carefully typed manuscript accompanied by an abstract of 300 or 400 words with the deposit of the usual fee for this service."[17] His proposal continued: "The abstracts thus collected from several sources or authors, will be published in a booklet of abstracts issued at periodic intervals, each abstract occupying one page. At the bottom of each abstract will appear a statement to the effect that a film copy of the complete manuscript can be had at 1¼ cent per page, and a total figure [i.e., price] for the entire book."[18]

Microfilm Abstracts

This, then, was the origin of what is known today as *Dissertation Abstracts International*. The first 11 volumes appeared at very irregular intervals starting in 1938 under the title *Microfilm Abstracts*, with the subtitle originally, *A Collection of Abstracts of Doctoral Dissertations which are Available in Complete Form on Microfilm*. Volume 1, number 1, was only 32 pages long and contained abstracts of 17 dissertations from just five universities (Michigan, Nebraska, Princeton, Stanford, and Toronto). In that first issue's unsigned introduction, Power explained his project by contrasting the characteristics of what he called "ordinary publication"—large print runs, promotion, and distribution to customers—with the "different publishing philosophy" afforded by microfilm which, he said, "offers an effective, satisfactory, and economical method of distributing copies of scholarly manuscripts to a limited market. Because microfilm is a straight-line cost process one copy can be produced as reasonably as a dozen . . . ." Therefore, he continued, "the only investment necessary is the cost of notification and the small cost of making the negative, . . . from which positive copies may be prepared from time to time as individual orders come in."[19]

Power's notion of advertising his wares is also stated in that first introduction: "The abstract is printed in a booklet of abstracts, such as this, and distributed to leading libraries, journals and the current bibliographies, *without cost to those receiving it.* Printed library catalog cards for each abstract accompany the booklet. This completes the process of notification."[20] Since it was free, small, infrequent, and sent out as a promotion, *Microfilm Abstracts* was essentially a publisher's blurb. Happily, libraries did not all treat it like one, so that complete or nearly complete runs exist at most large universities. The part about supplying cards sounds like a gimmick today, but 50 years ago it was probably considered a nice touch by librarians who were used to receiving cards from the Library of Congress for their depository catalogs. Unfortunately, there is no way to know how many libraries actually included these author and subject cards in their catalogs or if the existence of cards increased sales. In 1943 *Microfilm Abstracts* stopped coming with cards and instead gave a Library of Congress card number for each item, with cataloging performed in Ann Arbor—from the dissertation typescript, not just the abstract—and supplied to the Library of Congress.[21]

In the early years, *Microfilm Abstracts* ran a "Cumulative Index of Titles," but because this was arranged by discipline, its only advantage over browsing the individual tables of contents, which were similarly organized, was that it covered several numbers at a time. Every so often the cumulation would stop, then resume again with a new start date.

Beginning with volume 6, number 2, in 1945, the scope and subtitle of *Microfilm Abstracts* changed to include monographs as well as dissertations. Only a handful of monographs were ever listed,[22] however, and UMI eventually started a separate publication, *Monograph Abstracts* (now called *Research Abstracts*) to treat these titles, just as it spun off

Masters Abstracts (now *Masters Abstracts International*) to handle theses. Neither of these segments has ever approached the reputation, success, or indispensability of *DAI*.

Microfilm Abstracts started appearing quarterly in 1950, with an annual cumulated title index, which was still arranged by discipline, not by actual topic. Volume 11 (1951), the last before the title changed to the more familiar *Dissertation Abstracts* (*DA*), included two innovations which have been followed to the present: the four issues were paged continuously, and a cumulated index to dissertation authors was provided in addition to the so-called title index. That particular volume ran to 1,212 pages and carried abstracts for 816 dissertations, under 67 subject headings (with titles most numerous in the field of education) from about 30 institutions.[23] The publication was still distributed free, although the fee for filming and including a dissertation had risen from $15 to $20 in 1949. The cost to purchase a film copy was constant at $.0125 per page, but the price for paper copies had gone up from six cents to a dime per page.

One feature of *Microfilm Abstracts* and its successors *Dissertation Abstracts* and *Dissertation Abstracts International* deserves special notice: arrangement of the abstracts has always been by broad discipline categories. Volume 1, number 1, for instance, included abstracts under the headings Botany, Chemistry, Drama, Economics, Education, History, Mathematics, Philosophy, Political Science, Psychology, and Zoology. Fields and subfields were added as necessary, so that by 1990 there were 10 large groups subdivided into 249 smaller ones. Today there are 10 categories: Communication and the Arts; Education; Language, Literature and Linguistics; Philosophy, Religion and Theology; Social Sciences; Biological Sciences; Earth Sciences; Health and Environmental Sciences; Physical Sciences; and Psychology. When dissertation authors submit their abstracts, they must now indicate which subject category best reflects their area of research, although they may also designate one or two additional categories.[24]

When it debuted, *Microfilm Abstracts* was not reviewed in the usual sense. Instead, there' were announcements of it, probably lifted from press releases, in major trade and professional journals.[25]

Scope Changes

One would think that after the title changed to *Dissertation Abstracts* with volume 12 in 1952, the tool's history would be easier to describe. Far from it. Virtually every year through the 1960s there was some enhancement or oddity introduced. For instance, *DA* appeared six times in both 1952 and 1953— and for the first time had a cover price, $6 per year[26]—then settled into its conventional monthly frequency in January 1954 with volume 14, but without specifying which month anywhere on the publication, a detail which was not added until August 1957. Then, to keep subscribers guessing, volume 18 ran for only six issues, January through June 1958. Starting with volume 19, *DA*'s volumes extend from July to the following June "to facilitate the listing of authors by academic year for the index."[27]

With volume 27, number 1, July 1966, the cover took a turn for the worse: instead of drab gray it was brightly colored, but some benighted staffer decided to omit the volume, number and date from the front cover, an unconscionable decision that was not rectified for a full 20 years! Libraries cannot count the thousands of productive hours lost as check-in clerks had to turn to the title page to discover which issue had arrived. In a more momentous change with volume 27, meiosis occurred and two monthly issues began appearing, section A covering the humanities and social sciences, and section B covering the sciences (including psychology) and engineering. Although this split is logical and benefits special libraries which can choose to subscribe to just one part or the other, it causes a practical problem. Should volumes be shelved by section, then by volume number, or vice versa? Alternatively, volumes can be arranged by

calendar year first, which is how most users expect to see monthly issues run, but then one winds up with numbers 7 through 12 of one volume coming before numbers 1 through 6 of the next—correct but counterintuitive.

Three years later, in July 1969 with the start of volume 30, the title changed again with the addition of "International" to both sections, "to reflect the projected enlargement of University Microfilms' dissertation publication program by the addition of dissertations from European universities."[28] Some Canadian dissertations had, however, been included from the very beginning, although most of them could be obtained only from the National Library in Ottawa. As a result of an agreement between UMI and the National Library of Canada and Micromedia, Ltd., in early 1990, UMI began in 1991 to distribute Canadian dissertations and theses and to include citations and abstracts for them in the various UMI reference tools.[29]

It apparently took seven years for that "projected enlargement" to come about, which it did with another split in the fall of 1976 when section C, *European Abstracts*, first appeared as a slender quarterly designated volume 37. The subtitle of section C switched from *European Abstracts* to the one-word subtitle *Worldwide* in the spring 1989 issue, while remaining a slender quarterly with both title-keyword and author indexes in each issue and a cumulative author index at the end of each volume. The introduction to a recent issue of section C (volume 51, number 4, Winter 1990) makes this puzzling statement: "Sections A and B of *DAI* are published monthly and include dissertations accepted by North American institutions and other institutions throughout the world. Section C covers a portion of European dissertations in all disciplines and is published quarterly."[30] The explanation seems to be that most of the dissertations with abstracts found in section C are not in fact available from UMI. Abstracts for those which are so available appear in section A or B, as appropriate, *and* in section C. In any case, the 400-plus foreign universities whose dissertations have ben included thus far in section C are not ones researchers are generally interested in. Only when *DAI* comprehensively identifies dissertations from Cambridge, Oxford, the Sorbonne, and other renowned European institutions will its international pretensions be meaningful.

DAI's usefulness has also been chronically limited by the omission of several major U.S. universities (notably Harvard, MIT, and the University of Chicago) which maintain close control over reproduction and sale of their dissertations. Yet both Harvard and Chicago are on the list of participating institutions, something which misleads users. It would be good if *DAI*'s front matter would also state not just the year of initial participation, but also the percentage of each university's dissertations which are actually submitted to UMI.

Indexing

Annoying as the publication details are, they are misdemeanors compared with *DAI*'s author, title, and subject indexing "practices"— or rather, experiments—over half a century. Anyone who doubts this should try to memorize Carl Orgren's explanation and chart of the story just up to 1964, which reads like a plot rejected by Kafka.[31] Much has changed, which is a large part of the problem, but not much has improved in the intervening decades. (Note, however, that several venerable discipline indexes such as the *MLA International Bibliography* [New York: Modern Language Association, 1921–] and *Psychological Abstracts* [Washington: American Psychological Association, 1927–] have provided author and controlled-vocabulary subject access to *DAI* for decades, analyzing it like any other scholarly journal. There is, in fact, no reason why one should not cite a *DAI* entry as if it were an ordinary, if exceedingly short, periodical article.)

The case with author indexing, which began in 1951 in the last year of *Microfilm Abstracts*,[32] is not one of method but of madness: the user never knows where to find it. Like the Cheshire Cat, it materializes at will all over the bibliographic forest, sometimes in the final issue of the volume, sometimes as a separate part II of the final issue, sometimes listing authors from sections A and B but not C, and at one point in the middle 1950s not appearing at all for two years!

As noted above with regret, title indexing, which started in the second issue of *Microfilm Abstracts* and continued through volume 29 of *DA* in June 1969, was never more than cumulated tables of contents for one or more volumes, arranged by broad fields—in short, not a true title index at all. The conundrum is that, unlike book titles, dissertation titles are rarely memorable. And even when they are, the fact that they are not "normally" advertised means that few people know enough to refer to them, typically only the writer's advisors, family, and fellow students. The best use one can make of these title indexes is for browsing to see what was being done in an area at a certain time, after which one could refer to the abstracts of interesting items, recognizing that one will miss any dissertation not submitted to UMI. Far better, because complete, tools for browsing are *List of American Doctoral Dissertations Printed in 1912-1938*, *Doctoral Dissertations Accepted by American Universities* (covering 1934-1955), *Index to American Doctoral Dissertations* (covering 1955/56-1962/63), and *American Doctoral Dissertations* (covering 1963/64 to the present). These works are organized by either Library of Congress classification, for printed dissertations, or by field subdivided by university, the arrangement of the last three series, and an extremely useful approach because most graduate students and scholars already know which schools are at the forefront of research in their specialty.[33]

Subject indexing has been equally problematic. There was none at all for more than two decades until volumes 22 through 29 (July 1961-June 1969) appeared with an annual subject index using genuine Library of Congress headings and cross-references. But that era was too good to last. Beginning with volume 30 in July 1969, *DAI* moved one step forward and two steps back. It dropped the farce of a title index, but replaced the Library of Congress subject index with a keyword-in-title (KWIT) computer one. At the same time UMI staff had entered all previous dissertation titles in a database, from which in 1970 the company published an expensive nine-volume *Retrospective Index* covering volumes 1 through 29 and providing a KWIT approach under the all-too-familiar broad discipline categories. The result proved to be a disaster and was roundly attacked by Ralph Scott who said, in one of his kinder comments, that it was "ill conceived and poorly edited . . . [and] promises to be the laughing stock of bibliographers for years to come."[34]

Chastised but not deterred, UMI began its monumental *Comprehensive Dissertation Index* (*CDI*) series in 1973 with the delivery of a 37-volume set covering the astonishing time period 1861-1972 and an astounding 417,000 dissertations by UMI's count. The work was compiled from information already in the UMI database, supplemented by citations to earlier dissertations supplied by U.S. and Canadian doctorate-granting institutions. As with the *Retrospective Index*, the primary organization is by field, with dissertations then listed by each keyword in their titles, in reverse chronological order. An author index occupies the last five volumes. Thus, a dissertation in agriculture with 12 significant title words will appear in the agriculture volume 12 separate times, each time giving author, full title, degree, institution, year, and length. If the dissertation is available from UMI, the order number and citation to *DAI* are provided. There are still major difficulties, the most vexing being the "invisibility" of dissertations with cute or enigmatic titles and the user's need to look up all conceivable keywords in all conceivable disciplines. Nonetheless, much as many librarians regret the demise of professionally assigned uniform subject access to dissertations, reaction to *CDI* was generally favor-

able,[35] although Israel Shenker, reviewing the set in the *New York Times*, had a field day spotting weird or ambiguous dissertation titles and other oddities, including 13 dissertations on cockroaches.[36] Even Ralph Scott, who had rightfully denounced the *Retrospective Index* just three years earlier, gave *CDI* his qualified endorsement.[37]

UMI has continued to publish annual sets of *CDI* (termed supplements), with five- and then ten-year cumulations. These cause some confusion because users are not always careful about which category they open to. For instance, in the 1988 set in volume 4, the keyword sequence for philosophy begins on page 541 and a new keyword sequence for religion starts on page 559. It is all too easy to look up relevant keywords in the wrong discipline.

Nonprint Forms of DAI

Today there are more efficient ways to explore the rich *CDI* lode: by an online search in the BRS DISS or the DIALOG 35 files, by having UMI staff perform a DATRIX offline search, or by using the *Dissertation Abstracts Ondisc* CD-ROM product available in many university libraries. With any of these methods it is possible either to ignore discipline categories altogether or to specify particular ones, using codes. One can also qualify a search by year or institution to further refine the results.[38] One bother accompanies the CD-ROM version: the need to swap as many as four discs in order to search the entire database, but this disadvantage is offset by the fact that there are no connect time or telecommunications costs involved as there are with online access.

Eugene Power's brainchild of 1938 is now middle-aged, revered, and generally flourishing, with offspring well established on their own. Its growth at times took peculiar turns, and its features are far from perfect, but *DAI* will remain a notorious and necessary character in academe as long as dissertations, those strange beasties, exist.

PUBLICATION HISTORY

Microfilm Abstracts. Ann Arbor, MI: University Microfilms, vol. 1, no. 1, 1938; vol. 2, no. 1, 1939; vol. 2, no. 2, 1940; vol. 3, nos. 1–2, 1941; vol. 4, no. 1, 1942; vol. 4, no. 2, 1943; vol. 5, no. 1, 1943; vol. 5, no. 2, 1944; vol. 6, nos. 1–2, 1945; vol. 7, no. 1, 1946; vol. 7, no. 2, 1947; vol. 8, nos. 1–2, 1948; vol. 9, nos. 1–2, 1949; vol. 9, no. 3, 1950; vol. 10, nos. 1–4, 1950; vol. 11, nos. 1–4, 1951. 11 vols.

Dissertation Abstracts. Ann Arbor, MI: University Microfilms, vol. 12 (1952)-vol. 26, no. 12 (June, 1966). 15 vols. Bimonthly, 1952–1953; monthly, January 1954–June 1966.

Dissertation Abstracts: A, Humanities and Social Sciences. Ann Arbor, MI: University Microfilms, vol. 27, no. 1 (July, 1966)-vol. 29, no. 12 (June 1969). 3 vols. Monthly.

Dissertation Abstracts: B, Sciences and Engineering. Ann Arbor, MI: University Microfilms, vol. 27, no. 1 (July, 1966)-vol. 29, no. 12 (June, 1969). 3 vols. Monthly.

Dissertation Abstracts International: A, Humanities and Social Sciences. Ann Arbor, MI: University Microfilms International, vol. 30, no. 1 (July, 1969)- . Monthly. [Also available on microfilm or microfiche; orders can be placed for specific disciplines.]

Dissertation Abstracts International: B, Sciences and Engineering. Ann Arbor, MI: University Microfilms International, vol. 30, no. 1 (July, 1969)- . Monthly. [Also available on microfilm or microfiche; orders can be placed for specific disciplines.]

Dissertation Abstracts International: C, European Abstracts. Ann Arbor, MI: University Microfilms International, vol. 37, no. 1 (Autumn, 1976)-vol. 49, no. 4 (Winter, 1988). 13 vols. Quarterly.

Dissertation Abstracts International: C, Worldwide. Ann Arbor, MI: University Microfilms International, vol. 50, no. 1 (Spring, 1989)- . Quarterly.

Indexes

Dissertation Abstracts International, Retrospective Index, Volumes I-XXIX. Ann Arbor, MI: University Microfilms, 1970. 9 vols.
Comprehensive Dissertation Index, 1861–1972. Ann Arbor, MI: Xerox University Microfilms, 1973.

37 vols. Comprehensive Dissertation Index: Supplement, 1973-. Ann Arbor, MI: University Microfilms International, 1974–. 5 vols./year. Annual. [Also available on microfiche.]
Comprehensive Dissertation Index: Five-Year Cumulation, 1973–1977. Ann Arbor, MI: University Microfilms International, 1979. 19 vols.
Comprehensive Dissertation Index: Ten-Year Cumulation, 1973–1982. Ann Arbor, MI: University Microfilms International, 1984. 38 vols.
Comprehensive Dissertation Index: Five-Year Cumulation, 1983–1987. Ann Arbor, MI: University Microfilms International, 1989. 22 vols. [Also available on microfiche and in separate packages for either the sciences or the social sciences and humanities.]
Library and Information Science: Selected Collection of Doctoral Dissertations and Masters Theses, 1984–1988. Ann Arbor, MI: Dissertation Abstracts International, 1989. 24p. Update frequency varies. [This is one of about six dozen free subject catalogs extracted from the *Comprehensive Dissertation Index* database.]

Machine-Readable Products

DATRIX. Offline flat-fee search service of the entire dissertation and thesis database, available on request from University Microfilms International. 1967– .
Dissertation Abstracts Online. Covers 1861– ; abstracts included, July 1980– . Ann Arbor, MI: University Microfilms International. Updated monthly. [Available as DISS file from BRS Information Technologies and as File 35 from Dialog Information Services.]
Dissertation Abstracts Ondisc. Ann Arbor, MI: University Microfilms International, 1987– . Archival I, 1861-June 1980; Archival II, July 1980-December 1984; Archival III, 1985–1988; Current disc, 1989– . Semiannual updates. [In 1991 two subsets became available as separate subscriptions, each subset corresponding to the discipline groupings in section A (humanities and social sciences) or section B (sciences and engineering) of the print tool. In either case, there is both an archival disc (1861–1985) and a current one (1986–) with semiannual updates.]

BIBLIOGRAPHY

The secondary literature on *Dissertation Abstracts* is not large, surprisingly, given that it is a major reference tool which has been around for half a century. Among the items cited below, Colling's article, almost 20 years old, is the only overview of *DAI* before the present essay, and Meckler's book is the best general history of microforms. Power's autobiography, *Edition of One,* although it is full of interesting anecdotes about his career and company, rambles and lacks precise dates. It has, however, an appendix which reprints his 1938 manifesto on the subject of reproducing dissertations on microfilm. Moore's two-part study is essential for anyone trying to trace dissertation bibliographies over time. Orgren's brief article helps one appreciate the features of *DAI* as it is today by discussing how impossibly confusing it used to be. Shenker's is by far the most informative and delightful review of the *Comprehensive Dissertation Index.*

Asleson, Robert F. "A One-Million-Entry 'Starting Place' for Finding Dissertations." *Wilson Library Bulletin* 46 (September, 1971): 76–77. Reply to Scott, below.

Colling, Patricia M. "Dissertation Abstracts International." In *Encyclopedia of Library and Information Science,* edited by Allen Kent and Harold Lancour, vol. 7, 238–40. New York: Marcel Dekker, 1972.

Davinson, Donald. *Theses and Dissertations As Information Sources.* London: Clive Bingley; Hamden, CT: Linnet Books, 1977.

Dissertation Abstracts Ondisc: Quick Reference Guide. Ann Arbor, MI: University Microfilms International, 1987.

Meckler, Alan Marshall. *Micropublishing: A History of Scholarly Micropublishing in America, 1938–1980.* Contributions in Librarianship and Information Science, no. 40. Westport, CT: Greenwood Press, 1982.

Moore, Julie L. "Bibliographic Control of American Doctoral Dissertations: A History." *Special Libraries* 63 (May/June, 1972): 227–30.

———. "Bibliographic Control of American Doctoral Dissertations: An Analysis." *Special Libraries* 63 (July, 1972): 285–91.

Orgren, Carl F. "Index to Dissertations Abstracts." *College and Research Libraries* 25 (July, 1964): 279–80.

Power, Eugene B., and Robert Anderson. *Edition of One: The Autobiography of Eugene B. Power, Founder of University Microfilms.* Ann Arbor, MI: University Microfilms International, 1990.

———. "Microfilm and the Publication of Doctoral Dissertations." *Journal of Documentary Reproduction* 5 (March, 1942): 37–44.

———. *A Plan for Publication of Scholarly Material on Microfilm.* Ann Arbor, MI: University Microfilms, 1938. Reprinted in *Edition of One: The Autobiography of Eugene B. Power, Founder of University Microfilms,* by Eugene B. Power and Robert Anderson, 379–83. Ann Arbor, MI: University Microfilms International, 1990.

———. "University Microfilms." *Journal of Documentary Reproduction* 2 (March, 1939): 21–28.

Review of *Comprehensive Dissertation Index, 1861–1972. Choice* 11 (July/August, 1974): 734.

Scott, Ralph L. "A $1,000 Misunderstanding: UM's Index to Its Dissertation Abstracts International." *Wilson Library Bulletin* 46 (September, 1971): 73–76. For a reply, see Asleson, above.

———. "Comprehensive Dissertation Index, 1861–1972." *RQ* 14 (Fall, 1974): 61–62.

Sheehy, Eugene P. Review of *Comprehensive Dissertation Index, 1861–1972. College & Research Libraries* 35 (July, 1974): 245–46.

Shenker, Israel. "A Xeroxian Synopsis of Ph.D. Esoterica." *New York Times,* February 11, 1974, p. 37, col. 6; p. 71, col. 4.

Snelson, Pamela. "Online Access to Dissertations." *Database* 5 (June, 1982): 22–33.

User's Guide, Dissertation Abstracts Online: How to Use the Online Dissertation Database Step-by-Step. Ann Arbor, MI: University Microfilms International, 1988.

Wynar, Bohdan S. Review of *Comprehensive Dissertation Index, 1861–1972. American Reference Books Annual* 6 (1975): 309–10.

NOTES

[1] Theodore Ziolkowski, "The Ph.D. Squid," *American Scholar* 59 (Spring 1990): 177–95.

[2] See Table I, "Practices of Publication and Loan of Doctoral Dissertations," appearing annually, with slight title variations, in *Doctoral Dissertations Accepted by American Universities* (New York: H. W. Wilson, 1934–1955); *Index to American Doctoral Dissertations* (Ann Arbor, MI: University Microfilms, 1955/1956–1962/1963); and *American Doctoral Dissertations* (Ann Arbor, MI: University Microfilms International, 1963/1964–1982/1983). This useful information was dropped from more recent volumes of the last named title.

[3] The word *thesis* is often used as a synonym for *dissertation,* but, in the U.S. at least, the former more accurately refers to a report of research conducted at the pre- or sub-doctoral stage, the latter to work at the doctoral level. That distinction will be maintained throughout this essay.

[4] For an excellent overview of the complex situation in the early 1940s, together with an eloquent rationale for filming dissertations, see Eugene B. Power, "Microfilm and the Publication of Doctoral Dissertations," *Journal of Documentary Reproduction* 5 (March 1942): 37–44.

[5] Michael M. Reynolds, *Guide to Theses and Dissertations: An International Bibliography of Bibliographies*, rev. and enl. ed. (Phoenix, AZ: Oryx Press, 1985). A similar tool for just master's theses is Dorothy M. Black, *Guide to Lists of Master's Theses* (Chicago: American Library Association, 1965). The Eugene P. Sheehy, ed., *Guide to Reference Books*, 10th ed., (Chicago: American Library Association, 1986) also identifies numerous dissertation bibliographies via its index. To find dissertation bibliographies in a library catalog, one can use the Library of Congress subject heading "Dissertations, Academic—[country]—Bibliography." *Bibliographic Index* (New York: H. W. Wilson, 1938–) lists dissertation bibliographies on all subjects together under "Dissertations, Academic."

[6] Dietrich Hans Borchardt and John D. Thawley, *Guide to the Availability of Theses*, IFLA Publications no. 17 (Munich: Saur, 1981); G. G. Allen and K. Deubert, *Guide to the Availability of Theses: II, Non-University Institutions*, IFLA Publications no. 29 (Munich: Saur, 1984); Joseph Z. Nitecki, comp., *Directory of Library Reprographic Services*, 8th ed. (Westport, CT: Published for the Reproduction of Library Materials Section, American Library Association, by Meckler, 1982); Leslie R. Morris and Patsy Brautigam, *Interlibrary Loan Policies Directory*, 3rd ed. (New York: Neal-Schuman, 1988).

[7] See, for instance, issues of *Library & Information Science Research* (Norwood, NJ: Ablex, 1979–).

[8] Eugene Power has always stressed that his business exists to *publish* dissertations, a verb which the universities involved treat loosely to mean "make-available-to-save-us-the-trouble." The academic establishment, however, would contend that pseudo-, quasi-, or ersatz publishing would be more accurate, since what Power acknowledges are traditional prejudices against microfilm remain entrenched half a century later, as does the conviction among experts that dissertations are mere novice research reports and only deserve genuine (i.e., book) publication after major reworking and independent peer review. A classic essay on the revisions involved is Frances G. Halpenny, "The Thesis and the Book," *Scholarly Publishing* 3 (January 1972): 111–16.

[9] The company was called simply University Microfilms from its inception to the middle 1960s, after which it was known as Xerox University Microfilms. The name became University Microfilms International in June 1976, although it was still owned by Xerox. (*Dissertation Abstracts* had, however, already added "International" to its title in July 1969.) "UMI," really the corporate logo, appears on letterhead and most publications now, but is not the official name. In legal contexts University Microfilms, Inc., has been used continuously since 1938.

[10] "Microfilm Deal Slated by Xerox," *New York Times*, 21 February 1962, p. 75, col. 2; "Briefs," *New York Times*, 18 December 1985, p. D5, col. 6.

[11] For factual information about UMI, the author wishes to thank Dorie Mickelson, Marna Clowney, and Clare Long of UMI. The opinions and judgments expressed are, however, entirely the author's.

[12] Alan Marshall Meckler, *Micropublishing: A History of Scholarly Micropublishing in America, 1938–1980*, Contributions in Librarianship and Information Science no. 40 (Westport, CT: Greenwood Press, 1982), 6–7.

[13] Eugene Power was born in Traverse City, Michigan, in 1905. He received an A.B. from the University of Michigan in 1927 and an M.B.A. there in 1930. His memoirs, written with Robert Anderson, have appeared as *Edition of One: The Autobiography of Eugene B. Power, Founder of University Microfilms* (Ann Arbor, MI: University Microfilms International, 1990). Anderson, who died in early 1990, was also coauthor with Ray Kroc of *Grinding It Out: The Making of McDonald's* (Chicago: Regnery, 1977), and with Thomas S. Monaghan of *Pizza Tiger* (New York: Random House, 1986), a history of Domino's Pizza. The tone of all three books is unabashedly egocentric. Power and Monaghan are, incidentally, good friends.

[14] From most of the United States the number is 800-521-3042. Customers in Alaska or Michigan are told to make a collect call to 313-761-4700, ext. 781. From Canada the phone is 800-343-5299, ext. 781. There is also a fax number, 313-665-5022.

[15] The gigantic microfilm series continues to this day under the title *Early English Books*, using as its bibliographic basis Alfred William Pollard and G. R. Redgrave, *Short-Title Catalogue of Books Printed in England, Scotland and Ireland, and of English Books Printed Abroad, 1475–1640* (London: Bibliographical Society, 1926; reprinted Oxford: Oxford University Press, 1946).

[16] Eugene B. Power, *A Plan for Publication of Scholarly Material on Microfilm* (Ann Arbor, MI: University Microfilms, 1938); reprinted in Power and Anderson, *Edition of One*, 379–80.

[17] Ibid., 380. The charge was originally $15 and has increased to $25 in 1990, although it is explained today as a fee for having UMI copyright the dissertation, not as a filming fee. Also, the maximum length of an abstract has fluctuated in the past, with 700 words allowed at one time but only 350 in recent years. This reduction coincided approximately with the inclusion of full-text abstracts in the BRS and DIALOG databases and in UMI's own CD-ROM product, effective with titles added in July 1980.

[18] Ibid., 380. Thus, at $.0125 per page, microfilm of a 486-page dissertation came to $6.08. Paper "enlargements" were also offered at six cents per page, or $29.16 for the same item. To compare, as of January 1991, prices for dissertations from UMI, regardless of length, are as follows: when ordered by anyone affiliated with an academic institution, $27.00 for either 35 mm microfilm or 98-frame microfiche;

$32.50 for a paper copy with soft cover; and $39.50 for a paper copy with hard cover. Prices for orders from outside academe are, respectively, $11.00, $21.00, and $25.00 higher. Shipping and handling are extra and vary depending on the delivery method chosen. Orders arrive in three to four weeks.

19 Eugene B. Power, "Introduction," to *Microfilm Abstracts* 1, no. 1 (1938): v–vi.

20 Ibid., vi. Emphasis added.

21 Eugene B. Power, "Introduction," to *Microfilm Abstracts* 8, no. 2 (1948): iv.

22 An example of a monograph abstract appended to the end of occasional issues of *Microfilm Abstracts* is a work in several parts by Joshua Whatmough, entitled "The Dialects of Ancient Gaul." As each section appeared, it was separately abstracted during 1950 and 1951.

23 In early years, both *Microfilm Abstracts* and *Dissertation Abstracts* included "title" and author indexing for two other abstracting publications, one put out at Pennsylvania State University and the other at Colorado State University. Therefore, some of the 816 entries in volume 11 were to dissertations available on film from those institutions only and not from Ann Arbor.

24 *Publishing Your Dissertation: How to Prepare Your Manuscript for Publication* (Ann Arbor, MI: UMI Dissertation Services, n.d.).

25 *Publishers Weekly* 133 (19 February 1938), 938; *ALA Bulletin* 33 (February 1939): 89; *Journal of Documentary Reproduction* 2 (March 1939): 44–45. *Publishers Weekly* said Power's plan "may be revolutionary in the field of scholarly publishing."

26 Compare a subscription at $6.00 per year with the standing order price in late 1990 of sections A and B together at $495, including the author indexes, and of section C, which has four rather than twelve issues, at another $515. Despite these subscription rates, "UMI actually produces *DAI* at a loss, expecting dissertation copy sales to offset the production costs of the reference tools." (Dorie Mickelson, Manager of Database and Bibliographic Operations, UMI Dissertation Information Services Unit, letter to the author, 17 October 1990.) Volume 12 was also the first to list, in issue number 4, which institutions were represented, although the starting year for each university's involvement with UMI was only indicated beginning with volume 26 in July 1965, and then always with caveats to the effect that some participating schools only supply abstracts and do not have their dissertations filmed or distributed by UMI. Lastly, in 1952 *DA* increased in size from its original squat 5.5" x 8.25" dimensions to the 8.5" x 11" format it has today.

27 "Introduction," to *Dissertation Abstracts* 19 (July 1958): iii.

28 "Introduction," to *Dissertation Abstracts International: A, The Humanities and Social Sciences* 30 (July 1969): [iii].

29 "UMI to Distribute Canadian Dissertations," news release (Ann Arbor, MI: University Microfilms International, 1 March 1990).

30 "Introduction," to *Dissertation Abstracts International: C, Worldwide* 51 (Spring 1990): v. There is now a separate abstracting tool for British dissertations, *Index to Theses with Abstracts Accepted for Higher Degrees by the Universities of Great Britain and Ireland and the Council for National Academic Awards*, vol. 35– (London: Aslib, 1986–).

31 Carl F. Orgren, "Index to Dissertation Abstracts," *College & Research Libraries* 25 (July 1964): 279–80.

32 For coverage of earlier years, see *Microfilm Abstracts Author Index, Covering Volumes 1–11, 1938–1951*, compiled by the Georgia Chapter of the Special Libraries Association with the cooperation of University Microfilms (Atlanta: Georgia Chapter Special Libraries Association, 1956).

33 U.S. Library of Congress Catalog Division, *List of American Doctoral Dissertations Printed in 1912–1938* (Washington: Government Printing Office, 1913–39) ; *Doctoral Dissertations Accepted by American Universities*, compiled for the National Research Council and the American Council of Learned Societies by the Association of Research Libraries (New York: H. W. Wilson, 1934–55); *Index to American Doctoral Dissertations* (Ann Arbor, MI: University Microfilms International, 1955/56–1962/63); *American Doctoral Dissertations* (Ann Arbor, MI: University Microfilms International, 1963/64–). For a detailed discussion of the inter-relationships and characteristics of these tools, see the two-part article by Julie L. Moore, "Bibliographic Control of American Doctoral Dissertations," *Special Libraries* 63 (May/June 1972): 227–30 and (July 1972): 285–91.

34 Ralph L. Scott, "A $1,000 Misunderstanding: UM's Index to Its Dissertation Abstracts International," *Wilson Library Bulletin* 46 (September 1971): 73. A rejoinder by Robert Asleson, then president of University Microfilms, follows.

35 See review of *Comprehensive Dissertation Index, 1861–1972, Choice* 11 (July/August 1974): 734; Eugene P. Sheehy, review of *Comprehensive Dissertation Index, 1861–1972, College & Research Libraries* 35 (July 1974): 245–46; Israel Shenker, "A Xeroxian Synopsis of Ph.D. Esoterica," *New York Times*, 11 February 1974, p. 37, col. 6, p. 71, col. 4; Bohdan S. Wynar, review of *Comprehensive Dissertation Index, 1861–1972, American Reference Books Annual* 6 (1975): 309–10.

36 Shenker, p. 37, col. 8.

37 Ralph L. Scott, review of *Comprehensive Dissertation Index, 1861–1972, RQ* 14 (Fall 1974): 62.

38 *User's Guide: Dissertation Abstracts Online* (Ann Arbor, MI: University Microfilms International, 1988); *Dissertation Abstracts Ondisc: Quick Reference Guide* (Ann Arbor, MI:University Microfilms International, 1987).

The Circle of Learning:
Encyclopaedia Britannica

Sandy Whiteley

DEVELOPMENT AND HISTORY

Encyclopaedia Britannica, first published in 1768, is the second oldest continuously published reference work in the English language. As an encyclopedia it had several centuries of precursors. Ephraim Chambers' *Cyclopaedia or Universal Dictionary of Arts and Sciences* (not to be confused with the modern *Chambers's Encyclopaedia*), first published in Great Britain in 1728, was the inspiration for Diderot's famous *Encyclopédie* (1751–1765), which, in turn, directly stimulated the creation of *EB*.

EB's origins lie in Edinburgh, where it was first published in individual parts which subscribers had bound into volumes. Later it was published in half-volumes, then volumes; by the eleventh edition (1910–11) all the volumes in the set except the index were published at once, as we know it today. Early editions were sold on subscription; the publishers used the proceeds from the sale of first parts or volumes to pay for the production of later ones, which sometimes resulted in a drawn-out publication schedule of more than a decade. Although encyclopedias are still called subscription books, they aren't sold that way any more. The term has come to mean books sold in the home and in the contemporary U.S., that is largely encyclopedias.

Encyclopedias can be organized in one of two principal ways: systematically/topically or alphabetically. Within an alphabetically arranged set, an encyclopedia's articles can cover either broad or specific subjects. Each combination of organizational options has its virtues. The alphabetical sequence is easy to use and is neutral (it doesn't favor one philosophical arrangement of knowledge over another), but it scatters various aspects of knowledge. The first 14 editions of *EB* were arranged in one alphabet, but varied from edition to edition to the degree to which broad or specific entries were used. With the fifteenth edition, some elements of a systematic/topical arrangement were introduced.

Andrew Bell and Colin Macfarquhar

The first edition of *EB* was conceived by two Scots, Andrew Bell and Colin Macfarquhar, an engraver and a printer. They were responsible for getting subscribers and hired William Smellie, a printer who had apprenticed for the printer to the University of Edinburgh, as editor. This first edition appeared in 100 parts between 1768 and 1771 with a total of 2,689 pages. There were 160 copperplate engravings scattered through the set.[1] The encyclopedia doesn't appear to have been very well planned. The articles for A-B took up the first volume, those for C-L the next, and the whole second half of the alphabet was squeezed into volume 3. The set contained 75 lengthy articles (on broad topics such as anatomy, chemistry, and law), some of them over 100 pages long, with brief dictionary-type articles, many of which were only one sentence long, interspersed. This edition of *EB*, like several that followed, contained articles digested from other sources plus new material written by the editor. It is not known how much of this set Smellie actually wrote himself, but it appears that his contribution was substantial. There were no biographies but many practical articles gave instructions on surgery, counterfeiting emeralds, and beekeeping as well as other aspects of farming, reflecting Smellie's view that "Utility ought to be the principal intention of every publication."[2] The encyclopedia inevitably reflected the level of knowledge of the day and much superstition and prejudice appeared. California was described as "a large country of the West Indies." But the article "Midwifery" was illustrated with engravings that showed normal and abnormal deliveries in clinical detail, creating a scandal among some subscribers. More than 3,000 sets were sold and the encyclopedia was popular enough to be issued in a pirated edition by London publishers.[3]

Bell and Macfarquhar issued the second edition between 1777 and 1784 in 181 parts which were later bound in ten quarto volumes. It was almost three times larger than the first edition (8,595 pages) and contained maps and 340 copperplates. The new editor, James Tytler, was an unsuccessful surgeon turned writer. Many articles from the first edition were retained and Tytler wrote new ones. This edition included biographies of deceased persons and geographical articles were expanded to include history. Like the first edition, many entries reflected a literal acceptance of the Bible. For instance, in "Chronology," the date of the world's creation was given as 4004 BC, and floor plans of Noah's ark were provided. Longer articles sometimes had indexes printed at the end of them.

Bell and Macfarquhar also published the third edition between 1788 and 1797, hiring a series of editors. It was almost twice as large as the second, with 14,579 pages in 18 vol-

umes and 542 engravings. Many articles continued to be reprinted from the earlier editions. The third was popular all through the British Isles (13,000 sets were printed),[4] and it was the first of many editions to be issued in a pirated edition in the U.S. American publishers rewrote some entries they thought too British (such as the one on the United States). (The U.S. copyright law at that time protected only American authors. *Britannica* continues to be pirated today, this time in Asia.[5]) A two-volume supplement was published in 1801. Its article on chemistry was the first in *EB* to use chemical symbols. This edition was the first to be dedicated to the reigning sovereign, a practice continued in every subsequent edition.

The fourth edition was published in parts between 1801 and 1809. Its 20 volumes contained 16,033 pages. By this time Macfarquhar was dead and Bell was the sole publisher. This edition was edited by Dr. James Millar, classical scholar and physician. Most volumes were little more than reprints of the third edition. Some new articles were added, among them a full description of Jenner's successful use of vaccination against cowpox in 1796. The fourth edition's additions reflect Millar's interests in chemistry and natural history.

After Bell's death, the copyright for *EB* was purchased from his heirs by Edinburgh publisher Archibald Constable. He hired Millar to edit the fifth edition as well. Published in 1815, it was a corrected version of the fourth edition with some new articles. In 20 volumes with more than 16,000 pages, it was the first edition of *Britannica* to be advertised in newspapers, the principal advertising medium of the day.

Refinements in Procedures and Content

By the nineteenth century, several other encyclopedias were being published in Great Britain. To compete, Constable recruited authorities to write about the subjects they knew best for a six-volume supplement to *Britannica*.

For the first time, most articles were signed original contributions rather than, as in the past, digests of previously published material. *Britannica* was the first encyclopedia to print initials at the end of the articles; a key linked these to the names of the authors. Some of the well known contributors were Sir Walter Scott on chivalry, William Hazlitt on fine arts, and Thomas Malthus on population. There also were foreign contributors. Edited by Macvey Napier, librarian and scholar, and published between 1815 and 1824, these volumes served as a supplement to the fourth and fifth editions and to the sixth edition, which was issued concurrently with the supplement. The six volumes were issued in half-volume parts and totaled 5,000 pages containing 125 plates. One-quarter of the 669 articles were biographies, all treating deceased subjects.

The sixth edition, also published in parts between 1820 and 1823 by Constable, was just a corrected version of the fifth with a few new articles. Cross-references were added, leading from the main volumes to the supplement. After the death of Constable, the copyrights were bought by Edinburgh bookshop owner Adam Black, later of the publishing firm of A & C Black. He issued the seventh edition, also edited by Napier, between 1830 and 1842. This set of 22 volumes and 17,101 pages with 506 plates represented a greater increase in size than the numbers might indicate because the pages were now larger. It was a revision of previous editions, incorporating some of the best articles from the supplement. New articles included Thomas de Quincey on Shakespeare, Pope, and Schiller. The seventh edition was heavily advertised and was the first to have a separate index. While the quality of the indexing was not good, this inclusion of an index set a precedent that other encyclopedias were to follow (but that *Britannica* itself abandoned for a time more than a century later).

The eighth edition was edited by Dr. Thomas Stewart Traill, professor at the University of Edinburgh, replacing Napier, who had died.

It was published between 1852 and 1860 in 22 volumes with 17,957 pages. Some classic articles, including pieces by Scott, Ricardo, and Malthus, were reprinted. New articles included biographies by Macaulay of Samuel Johnson, John Bunyan, Oliver Goldsmith, and William Pitt. An American contributor, the president of Harvard, appeared for the first time, writing on George Washington. New topics included photography, Communism, and the telegraph. In addition to separate pages of engraved plates, many illustrations from line blocks were inserted in the text.

The Celebrated Ninth Edition

The aging Black wasn't interested in a new edition, but his sons prevailed upon him and took over the firm. The resulting ninth edition, often called the Scholar's Edition, reflected the changes in intellectual thought occasioned by Darwin's *Origin of the Species*. It is one of the most famous of all encyclopedias and can still be found in many libraries today. For the first time, the set had an English rather than a Scottish editor, Professor Thomas Baynes, a Shakespearean scholar at St. Andrews University. The 25 volumes presented the work of 1,100 contributors and took 14 years to produce, being completed in 1889. The articles are often described as leisurely nineteenth-century essays—long and beautifully written. T.H. Huxley wrote on evolution; Lord Rayleigh, who later won the Nobel Prize, on physics; and Lord Kelvin on chemistry. Algernon Charles Swinburne wrote on John Keats and Dante Gabriel Rossetti contributed biographies of painters. The article on anarchism was written by the revolutionary Prince Kropotkin. James G. Frazer, then an unknown Cambridge don, wrote on anthropology. He later said his research for *Britannica* articles marked the beginning of his systematic study of the subject which led to the publication of *The Golden Bough*. The ninth edition took a progressive stand on religious and scientific questions. W. Robertson Smith wrote many of the ninth edition's articles that presented a historical interpretation of Christianity. As a result, he lost his position as a clergyman and became joint editor of the ninth edition. Some innovations in this edition were the use of colored plates and colored maps. Dates were given for a person's birth and death, an innovation despite the long presence of biographies in *Britannica*, and longer articles were supplied with bibliographies. Because publication of a volume was dependent on revenues from previous volumes, publication was a protracted process, and the earlier volumes were somewhat outdated by the time the later ones appeared. The ninth edition contained 17,000 articles in 20,000 pages in 24 volumes. Some out-of-date articles were retained from the eighth edition but in the main this was a new work. Though scholarly, it did have some articles on practical topics, such as cookery, croquet, and making snowshoes.

Five times as many sets were sold in the U.S., where an authorized edition was distributed by Scribner's and Little, Brown, as in Great Britain. But even after the International Copyright Law was passed in the U.S. in 1891, piracy continued. Despite competition from such U.S. encyclopedias as the *Encyclopedia Americana*, 45,000 authorized sets[6] of the ninth edition were sold in the U.S. as well as an unknown number of pirated sets.

The late nineteenth century saw a boom in subscription book sales in the U.S. There were door-to-door sales of all sorts of books—cookbooks, Bibles, legal books, biographies—especially in the rural U.S. where people had no access to bookstores. While on vacation in England, Horace Everett Hooper, who had worked for subscription distributors, learned of a new printing of the ninth edition of *Encyclopaedia Britannica*. In 1898 he entered into a joint venture with the London *Times* to sell an inexpensive reprint of the ninth edition on credit. He was the first to apply installment buying to books. He also applied the new advertising techniques being used to sell soap and cigarettes to selling *EB*. By this time A & C Black had moved from Edinburgh to Lon-

don, and Hooper bought the rights to reprint the ninth edition from them. The *Times* was in a bad financial state and needed this new source of revenue. They ran advertisements and took orders, for which they received a commission. The reprint was sold at a more than 60 percent price reduction and was enormously successful, so much so that the need for a supplement was seen. A & C Black's ownership of *Britannica* began to be liquidated. By 1901 *EB* was owned by Hooper and another American, Walter Montgomery Jackson. An American editorial office was opened for the first time and Hooper's brother Franklin was made American editor. Journalist Hugh Chisholm was named editor in London, where the main editorial office remained.

The Twentieth Century

The tenth edition (1902–03) reprinted the 25 volumes of the ninth edition (some of which were now 25 years old) and added 11 more. The new volumes contained photographs, a first for *Britannica*. A single index volume covered both the old volumes and the new ones. Hooper designed a frenzied advertising campaign for *Britannica*. There was even a contest with one of the prizes a scholarship to Oxford or Cambridge. Sales agents were sent throughout the Empire and even to Japan. Some Britons scorned the "Yankee invasion" and the use of American advertising tactics. Hooper now took on the additional job of advertising director of the *Times*. Ahead of his time in many ways, Hooper got the *Times* involved in selling discounted books which led to conflict with other publishers and eventually to the sale of the newspaper. *Britannica's* contract with the *Times* was cancelled.

During this time work was proceeding on a totally new eleventh edition. Jackson was now more active in an American firm, the Grolier Society, which was publishing *The Book of Knowledge*, the precursor of today's *New Book of Knowledge*. Conflict arose between Hooper and Jackson because Hooper wanted a completely new eleventh edition and

Jackson wanted to reuse some of the ninth and tenth editions. Their discord led to a series of lawsuits, and work was suspended on the new edition while Jackson and Hooper tried to buy each other out. Finally, Hooper worked out an arrangement with Cambridge University Press that enabled him to publish the eleventh edition. Though Cambridge did not put up any money and was to get a royalty on each set sold, its backing enabled Hooper to borrow money to finish the set. The university had the right to read all articles before publication and to censor ads and as a result the ads were considerably less florid than Hooper liked. For instance, he had to change a hyperbolic ad that read "The Source of all Knowledge" to the tamer "The Key to All Knowledge."[7]

The eleventh edition of *Britannica* has been called the finest ever published. Issued in 1910–1911, it had 1,507 contributors, among them 168 fellows of the Royal Society. Famous contributors included Thomas Huxley, Bertrand Russell, Nicholas Murray Butler, Frederick Jackson Turner, Robert Louis Stevenson, and Alfred North Whitehead. British contributors were still the largest number, but Americans were next, outnumbering Europeans. It was the first edition to acknowledge the importance of the American market by being dedicated to the president of the United States as well as the king. It was also the first edition to be typeset and printed in the United States as well as in Great Britain. It was printed on thin, opaque India paper, the kind used for Bibles. Because the ninth edition had been issued over so many years, it had become a collection of monographs which were not very unified. The eleventh edition was not just a revision of the ninth; editorial planning and control were much improved and more editorial work was done on contributions than in any previous edition. This edition took more of a specific-entry approach than the ninth, splitting up topics from the ninth edition into more short articles. Although the new set was only slightly larger, the eleventh edition contained 40,000 articles versus 17,000 in the ninth edition. It was more of a practical reference work for lay people than just a source for scholars. There was a drift toward popularization, with more biographies of contemporary people. Most critics found it far more readable. The public agreed; more than 75,000 sets were sold.[8]

Sale and Resale of EB

After one last legal battle, Hooper finally bought Jackson out in 1914. Hooper decided to issue a biennial book to update the eleventh edition and published it in 1913 as the *Britannica Year Book*. Nearly a quarter of the pages were devoted to American topics. There were plans for a children's encyclopedia but the outbreak of World War I caused the cancellation of that project as sales of *Britannica* dropped sharply and plans for future editions of the *Year Book* were shelved as well. Hooper returned to the U.S. His next project was a photo-reduced set of the eleventh edition of *Britannica*, the "Handy Volume" edition, to be sold through the Sears & Roebuck catalog for $55. It was very successful, with 200,000 sets sold.[9] With U.S. entry into the war in 1917, President Wilson asked for a curtailment of installment buying and sales of the "Handy Volume" edition dropped dramatically. As he had done previously when faced with a financial crisis, Hooper tried to align *EB* with a major university or scholarly society, but was unsuccessful. Sears, led by philanthropist Julius Rosenwald, came to the rescue and bought the set.

In 1920 Hooper undertook a supplement to treat the war years. Contributors included the president of the new republic of Czechoslovakia, Thomas Masaryk, and General Danilov writing on the Russian Army. Many articles were devoted to blow-by-blow accounts of particular battles, but little attention was paid to the humanities. For instance, 16 pages were devoted to artillery but only four to music. The so-called twelfth edition was made up of the eleventh edition and these three supplementary volumes published in 1921–22. Upon Hooper's death in 1922, his brother-in-law William Cox bought the company. Sears had lost $1,800,000 on *EB* and was happy to sell it to him.[10]

The thirteenth edition (1926) was edited by James Garvin, an Irish journalist with pro-American views. It was really just another three-volume supplement to the eleventh edition. However, it continued the practice of recruiting expert contributors. Leon Trotsky wrote the biography of Vladimir Lenin and H. L. Mencken, Carl Van Doren, Louis Untermeyer, and W.E.B. DuBois wrote on American literature. Andrew Mellon wrote on finance, Amos Alonzo Stagg on football, and Bernard Baruch on war debts. It was the first edition to contain color photographs.

Cox finished a completely new fourteenth edition in 1929 on the eve of the Depression. He approached the University of Chicago to take over the company and publish the new edition in cooperation with Cambridge University, but the plan fell through, so once again Julius Rosenwald of Sears put up over $1 million.[11] Garvin continued as editor in the U.K. and Franklin Hooper remained as the American editor. The 24-volume set had 3,500 contributors, half of them Americans. Advisors for subject areas included Julian Huxley, John Dewey, and Roscoe Pound, and 18 Nobel Prize winners contributed articles, among them Albert Einstein writing on Space-Time. Even celebrities contributed to the set: Gene Tunney on boxing and Irene Castle on dancing, part of an attempt to popularize *Britannica*. This edition furnished instructions on how to swim, play golf, drive a car, and do handicrafts. Famous articles from previous editions—Thomas Babington Macauley on Dr. Johnson, for instance—were reprinted with only slight revision. The set still had a British orientation—for instance, the article on checkers was under Draughts, the one on pensions under Superannuation. Cox ran out of money and had to cancel articles and reuse some from previous editions in shortened form. Sears bought the

set *once more*, this time from Cox. The new edition was enthusiastically received in the U.S. but was criticized in Great Britain for being too American and too popular in tone. In the U.S. most sets were sold through the mail. The Depression cut into sales and they remained low through the 1930s. When Rosenwald died, Sears had a new president who thought the acquisition of *EB* had been a mistake. Cox retired and the new publisher was a Sears executive who dropped mail-order sales and built up the door-to-door sales force, still the main sales method used today.

The Fourteenth Edition and Continuous Revision

With the fourteenth edition, there was a major change in the way *Britannica* was published, with the implementation of a system of continuous revision. This means that some percentage of articles are updated every year on a flexible schedule instead of entirely new editions being published periodically. It is the standard procedure for encyclopedia revision today in the U.S. (though not in Europe). The practice of continuous revision began because Sears did not want to put up large sums for a new edition after the fourteenth; yet the sales staff said that the set must be kept current. After extensive study, they found that with continuous revision they could keep a regular staff instead of hiring a large one for a new edition and firing them when it was done. A number of competitors (*Encyclopedia Americana*, *World Book*) had already started using this system. From this point, the size of the set remained fairly constant until the fifteenth edition. The company offices were centralized in Chicago; Walter Yust became editor; and, over time, the set was restyled, and the index redone.

In 1936 the Library Research Service was established. Its purpose is to provide for purchasers answers to questions that could not be found in *EB*. Purchasers were allowed to ask as many questions as they wanted for ten years after buying the set. Researchers scoured Chicago libraries to respond to these requests. The service became so popular that a limit had to be placed on the number of questions that could be asked. (Today the service answers 135,000 questions a year.) The idea of a yearbook was revived and the *Britannica Book of the Year* was published in 1938 and continues to be issued annually, though publication was suspended during World War II. Through 1968 separate yearbooks were published for the U.S. and the U.K., but since then there has been one international edition.

The University of Chicago Connection

As the nation pulled out of the Depression, sales and profits improved but Sears still felt that *EB* was not an appropriate business for the company and wanted to sell it. It was felt that in order to maintain the set's reputation, it should not be sold to a commercial firm. In 1942, Sears tried to interest the University of Chicago in *EB* again. William Benton, founder of the advertising agency of Benton and Bowles and eventually senator from Connecticut, was vice-president for public relations at the university. After initial discussions with Sears, he recommended to university President Robert Maynard Hutchins that they try to persuade Sears to donate *EB* to the university. Sears agreed to do this, but the university trustees turned the offer down because the university would have had to put up some working capital. Benton was so enthusiastic about the gift that he agreed to put up the money and assume management of the company. Under this plan Benton would own two-thirds of the stock and the university one-third, with an option to buy half of Benton's stock. The university would get a royalty on each set sold and three of the nine directors of the company would be university trustees. The trustees finally agreed to this arrangement.

Benton expanded the company, and bought an educational film company which became Encyclopaedia Britannica Films. During World War II, sales rose rather than fell, as they had in World War I. However, after the war, when consumers were able to buy cars and other consumer items again, sales dropped. A financial crisis developed in 1947 and a new president was brought in, a former executive with *World Book*. That year the first Board of Editors was established, chaired by Hutchins, with the charge to consider questions of general editorial policy. These questions may range from the decision to create a new edition or some other major publication to a debate over the proper treatment of history. The board's members alert editors to changes in the scholarly community that may affect *EB* and help it maintain an international perspective. In 1952, EB published *Great Books of the Western World*, edited by Mortimer Adler, who became chairman of EB's Editorial Board after the retirement of Hutchins. After Walter Yust, who had been editor from 1938 to 1960, retired, Harry Ashmore, a journalist, was editor from 1960 to 1963. Color pictures in the body of text, rather than in separate inserts, were introduced in 1963. In 1961 EB bought *Compton's Encyclopedia*. Today EB also owns dictionary publisher Merriam-Webster, Evelyn Wood Reading Dynamics, Britannica Software, and Britannica Learning Centers.

In 1964 the fourteenth edition was criticized by Harvey Einbinder in his book *The Myth of the Britannica* (New York: Grove Press). He found over 600 articles in the 1963 set that had been taken from the eleventh and ninth editions. Some of these articles were almost 100 years old. Those written by famous contributors were openly retained and still carried their names, occasionally with a note explaining why this classic article was reprinted. But in other cases articles by unknown contributors were reprinted without their initials. Einbinder found obsolete statistics—for instance, almost 20 years after World War II the article on Warsaw said its population was 30 percent Jewish. Articles on classical writers dated back to a time when a classical education was the mark of an educated person and so contained lines in Latin or Greek without translation. He found that inadequate updating had led to inconsistencies among articles. Biographies often didn't reflect the relative importance of people in the contemporary world. For instance, the article on Theodore Roosevelt was more than twice as long as the one on Franklin Delano Roosevelt.

Britannica 3

The editors of *EB* were not unaware of problems and planning was already underway for a totally new edition. After more than 35 years of continuous revision, *EB* was losing its focus. The editors felt that they couldn't continue to just cut and paste; they needed a clear concept of what the encyclopedia should be. As early as 1961 studies had begun on a new plan; Mortimer Adler worked out the scheme between 1965 and 1968. In 1968 work on a revision began in great secrecy; the company managed to keep the new edition under wraps until just before publication in 1974.

The general editor of the fifteenth edition was Warren Preece, former English professor at the University of Chicago, and the executive editor was Philip Goetz, who became editor-in-chief in 1979. This edition had 3,000 pages in 30 volumes, 19,000 photographs, and an editorial price tag of $32,000,000.[12] It had 4,000 contributors, many of them quite distinguished, from 100 countries. While Americans made up the largest number and British next, almost every part of the world except Africa was well represented. Its publication in 1974 was widely hailed as the publishing event of the year with wide media coverage. It was not just a new edition but a new encyclopedia with a totally different orientation.

The editors looked anew at the whole concept of the encyclopedia. A review of the day observed that "They have tried imaginatively to solve the problems that all modern encyclopedias face and to provide with authority and accuracy for all of the varied uses that people make of general reference books, from the fast factual check to the extended search. And they have gone beyond this to attempt to create a tool for systematic self-teaching."[13] The concept was developed by Benton, Hutchins, and Adler, but the rearrangement reflected Adler's interest in self-education, and his love for classification and bringing a unity to knowledge—the encyclopedia as the "circle of learning." It was in a three-part form that tried to combine the best of both a topical and alphabetical arrangement and hence was known as *Britannica 3*. The one-volume Propaedia took a topical approach, the ten-volume Micropaedia strictly an alphabetical one, and the nineteen-volume Macropaedia combined aspects of both. The Propaedia served to impose a topical arrangement on the set by organizing knowledge in outline form under ten broad headings. There is no index to the Propaedia and it is difficult for the unsophisticated reader to use. This volume appears to be the least-used part of the encyclopedia. The Macropaedia had about 4,200 long articles, averaging 5 pages, but with some over 100 pages long. These lengthy articles were intended to overcome the fragmentation of knowledge that often occurs in encyclopedias and were to serve the self-education function. All articles in the Macropaedia were signed and were especially written for the fifteenth edition. For the first time, maps were placed throughout the set with the articles they were intended to illustrate, rather than being isolated in an atlas in the last volume. As an interesting experiment, Russian contributors were asked to write many articles on the Soviet Union. These were not well received; in that pre-*Glasnost* era, they were biased and they have largely been replaced in later revisions. Some reviewers criticized the Macropaedia for retaining an alphabetical arrangement, rather than being arranged topically. Since the *EB* editors had criticized the typical encyclopedia alphabetical arrangement for the way it fragments knowledge, some thought it an indefensible inconsistency to create a hybrid that retained that arrangement in part.

The Micropaedia served the ready reference function and had about 100,000 articles, none of them more than 750 words long. These articles were not signed. A list of 2,600 authorities were given for the Micropaedia, but many articles were written by freelance writers or staff. Some reviewers criticized the Micropaedia because many of the entries were just abstracts of articles in the fourteenth edition, but others, especially librarians, found it to be the most useful part of the set. Most of the illustrations in the set were here. Every subject in the Macropaedia also had a much shorter entry in the Micropaedia with a reference to the Macropaedia section. Most biographies were in the Micropaedia but over 1,000 were found in the Macropaedia. Reviewers complained that it sometimes was not clear why one person merited a long Macropaedia article and another got only brief coverage in the Micropaedia. For example, Aleksander Suvorov, an eighteenth-century Russian military commander, received full coverage in the Macropaedia while nineteenth-century British poet Algernon Charles Swinburne received only brief treatment in the Micropaedia. There were few bibliographies in the Micropaedia. An addendum to the last volume of the Micropaedia contained statistics and directory information that was likely to need frequent updating. Reviewers complained that this information was likely to be overlooked and, in 1985, it was moved to the yearbook, to become the *"Britannica World Data"* section. *Britannica 3* originally had no separate index. Instead, the Micropaedia had an elaborate system of cross-references that was to serve in place of an index. This was the most widely criticized flaw of the fifteenth edition, both by librarians and the public. To capitalize on librarians' need for an index, a publisher advertised an index widely by direct mail and offered substantial discounts for prepaid or-

ders. Many librarians took advantage of this offer, but were taken advantage of by the publisher; he had not produced the advertised index and eventually was convicted in federal court for mail fraud. Later, because of complaints from librarians that in a library setting where several people might be using the set at once it was sometimes impossible to use the Micropaedia as an index, Britannica issued a separate "Library Guide" volume. Because it was not an index but merely listed all the index citations from the Micropaedia, its value was limited.

Revision of Britannica 3

In 1985, a major revision of the fifteenth edition addressed some of the criticisms of *Britannica 3*. A well regarded two-volume index was added. The Micropaedia was expanded to 12 volumes and the Macropaedia was reduced to 17. The 4,200 articles of the Macropaedia were reduced to 681, some of them more than 100 pages long. Many entries resemble short books. Many smaller articles were brought together into a broader entry; e.g., all the states appear under "United States of America." Many articles, including all biographies (except 100 people who profoundly affected world history) were moved to the Micropaedia. The 750-word limit on articles in this part of the set was lifted. Some Micropaedia articles now included bibliographies (usually ones transferred over from the Macropaedia). All the entries were arranged in a word-by-word alphabetization, which is easier to use than the former letter-by-letter arrangement. For topics included in both parts of the set, many Micropaedia articles were rewritten to include more information, so they were no longer just outlines of Macropaedia articles. Highly datable material was moved to the *Britannica Book of the Year/ Britannica World Data Annual* and cross-references were provided to this volume. The Propaedia was also restructured. The new index included the *Britannica World Data Annual* and was judged an excellent finding device. This format and arrangement is currently being used in 1991. In 1991 Editor-in-Chief Philip Goetz stepped down and was succeeded by Robert McHenry, former managing editor.

Today *Britannica* is not only the oldest but is also the largest and most expensive general encyclopedia published in the U.S. A scholarly encyclopedia, it is not for elementary and middle school children, though it is sometimes marketed as being for that age group. Unlike some encyclopedias, there is no vocabulary control and no attempt to include the topics that children are most likely to look up. Many of the science and math articles are too technical for the "curious, intelligent layperson" *Britannica* has always characterized as its audience. Compared with its closest competitors, *Encyclopedia Americana* and *Collier's Encyclopedia*, it contains more esoteric information and does not provide practical, how-to-do-it type information nor much coverage of popular culture. Its real strength is its historical treatment of topics. While most encyclopedias are tailored for a North American audience, *Britannica* also takes a broader world view than competing American sets. For instance, the biographies of the American president and the British prime minister are roughly the same length. The British spelling that is still used is sometimes termed an affectation and is not used consistently. For instance, when a word begins with a different letter in British English ("oestrogen"), the American spelling is used. *EB* is unique in that contributors are allowed to list foreign-language materials in the bibliographies at the end of their articles. For example, the bibliography for the article on the U.S.S.R. lists books in Russian as well as Italian and German. While authors of articles have been instructed not to list obscure materials that would be hard to find, these bibliographies are more scholarly than those in any other encyclopedia.

Who owns *EB* today? Encyclopaedia Britannica, Inc. is a privately held for-profit company. All of the company's stock is held by the William Benton Foundation, an Illinois not-for-profit corporation established in 1948 to support the University of Chicago. In 1957, Encyclopaedia Britannica, Inc. paid the University of Chicago $2 million for its shares of stock in the company. The foundation is controlled by a thirteen-member board of directors, consisting of five members from Encyclopaedia Britannica, Inc., four from the University of Chicago, and four from the public sector. They are responsible for electing the company's board of directors and for working with the University of Chicago to allocate the annual grants made by the foundation. Currently, the foundation gives the university about $2,000,000 a year; it has given the university more than $100 million over its lifetime.[14] This makes EB the university's largest contributor, exceeding even the Rockefellers, whose gifts founded the university. The foundation ownership of the company safeguards it against a takeover by another firm and from stockholders seeking to dictate policies. In order to sell any of its stock, a two-thirds majority vote is necessary. As measured by revenue, Encyclopaedia Britannica, Inc. is the seventh largest publisher in America today.[15] Sales from all divisions now amount to $650 million a year.[16] The company does business in more than 100 countries and has produced encyclopedias in many foreign languages.

EB's Future

Britannica has traditionally been very circumspect about revealing future plans. A company spokesperson stated that there are no plans to change the structure of the set (plans for revisions in Macropaedia articles are already scheduled through 1993) and no electronic version of *EB* is planned. (The company issued a CD-ROM version of *Compton's Encyclopedia* in 1990.) Since the arrangement of a printed work becomes transparent when it is converted to electronic form, perhaps a CD-ROM version of *EB* would end the debate over the set's plan. The 1990 *EB* was the first to be printed on acid-free paper and the company is investigating the digital handling of art in the future. Changes in printing technology under development may also improve the way that the encyclopedia is revised. New technologies may cut production costs so that encyclopedia publishers may be able to do new layouts more frequently. EB, Inc. has always been in the forefront in using new technology; it installed a computer system to do *Britannica 3* and the entire set is in machine-readable form. One can predict that the company will remain in the technological vanguard.

Today's *New Encyclopaedia Britannica* bears little resemblance to the modest "Dictionary of the Arts and Sciences" first published in Edinburgh in 1768. While its editors' willingness to experiment with the arrangement of the set's contents has been cause for controversy, its also shows their commitment to *EB* as more than just a reference tool—as an instrument of self-education as well. After more than 220 years of publishing history, *EB* "continues to provide both outstanding scholarship and balanced coverage of world learning" and retains its undeniable authority.[17] "Throughout the English-speaking world and, for that matter, anywhere in the world, the *Encyclopaedia Britannica* is by far the most famous encyclopedia in the English language."[18]

PUBLICATION HISTORY

Encyclopaedia Britannica: or, a Dictionary of Arts and Sciences . . . By a society of gentlemen in Scotland. Edinburgh, 1768–1771. 3 vols. Reprinted in facsimile. Chicago: Encyclopaedia Britannica, Inc., 1968.

Encyclopaedia Britannica; or, a Dictionary of Arts, Sciences, etc. . . . 2nd ed. Edinburgh, 1777–1784. 10 vols.

Encyclopaedia Britannica; or, a Dictionary of Arts, Sciences, and Miscellaneous Literature . . . 3rd ed. Edinburgh, 1788–1797. 18 vols. Supplement to the third edition. Edinburgh, 1801. 2 vols.

Encyclopaedia Britannica; or, a Dictionary of Arts, Sciences, and Miscellaneous Literature . . . 4th ed. Edinburgh, 1801–1809. 20 vols.

Encyclopaedia Britannica; or a Dictionary of Arts, Sciences, and Miscellaneous Literature.. . . 5th ed. Edinburgh, 1815. 20 vols.

Encyclopaedia Britannica; or, a Dictionary of Arts, Sciences, and Miscellaneous Literature . . . 6th ed. Edinburgh, 1820–1823. 20 vols.

Supplement (to the 4th, 5th, and 6th eds.) Edinburgh, 1815–1824. 6 vols.

The Encyclopaedia Britannica; or, a Dictionary of Arts, Sciences, and General Literature. 7th ed. Edinburgh, 1827–1842. 21 vols.

The Encyclopaedia Britannica; or, Dictionary of Arts, Sciences, and General Literature. 8th ed. Edinburgh, 1853–1861. 21 vols. plus index vol.

The Encyclopaedia Britannica; a Dictionary of Arts, Sciences, and General Literature. 9th ed. Edinburgh, 1875–1889. 24 vols. plus index vol.

The Encyclopaedia Britannica; Dictionary of Arts, Sciences, and General Literature. 10th ed. London, 1902–1903. 34 vols.

The Encyclopaedia Britannica: a Dictionary of Arts, Sciences, Literature and General Information. 11th ed. Cambridge and New York, 1910–1911. 29 vols.

The Encyclopaedia Britannica. 12th ed. London and New York, 1921–22. 32 vols.

The Encyclopaedia Britannica. 13th ed. London and New York, 1926. 32 vols.

The Encyclopaedia Britannica. 14th ed. Annually revised. Chicago , 1929–1973. 24 vols.

The New Encyclopaedia Britannica. 15th ed. Chicago and London, 1974– . 30 vols. through 1984; 32 vols. 1985 to date.

BIBLIOGRAPHY

The best, most easily accessible historical survey appears in *Britannica* itself, in the *Micropaedia.* Kogan's *The Great EB* is the official company history and stresses corporate matters more than the content of the set. Collison has valuable historical information up through the fourteenth edition, as does Walsh. The fifteenth edition was widely reviewed; see the 1974 volume of *Book Review Digest* for citations. Lengthy reviews of recent printings can be found in Kister and Sader. Reviews of many editions of *Britannica* can be found in various issues of *Reference Books Bulletin* in *Booklist*. *Know: A Magazine for Britannica People Everywhere* is the corporate house organ and has many interesting articles but is rarely available in libraries.

American Library Association. Reference Books Bulletin Editorial Board. *Purchasing an Encyclopedia: 12 Points to Consider*. 3rd ed. Edited by Sandy Whiteley. Chicago: Booklist, 1989.

Ashmore, Harry S. *Unseasonable Truths: The Life of Robert Maynard Hutchins*. Boston: Little Brown, 1989.

Collison, Robert. *Encyclopaedias: Their History throughout the Ages*. New York: Hafner, 1964.

Einbinder, Harvey. *The Myth of the Britannica*. New York: Grove Press, 1964.

———. "The New *Britannica*: Pro and Con." *Library Journal* 112 (April 15, 1987): 48–50.

"*Encyclopaedia Britannica*." *The New Encyclopaedia Britannica*. Chicago: Encyclopaedia Britannica, 1990. Vol. 4: 487–88.

Fine, Sheila. "This Day is Published: A Condensed History of *Encyclopaedia Britannica*." *Know: A Magazine for Britannica People Everywhere*. 22 (Spring, 1986): 10–13.

Hyman, Sydney. *The Lives of William Benton*. Chicago: University of Chicago Press, 1969.

Kister, Kenneth. *Kister's Concise Guide to Best Encyclopedias*. Phoenix: Oryx Press, 1988.

Kogan, Herman. *The Great EB: The Story of the Encyclopaedia Britannica*. Chicago: University of Chicago Press, 1958.

Koning, Hans. "Onward and Upward with the Arts: the Eleventh Edition." *New Yorker* 57 (March 2, 1981): 67–83.

Kruse, Paul. *The Story of the Encyclopedia Britannica, 1768–1943*. Ph.D. dissertation, University of Chicago, 1958.

McClintock, Robert. *Enkyklios Paideia: The Fifteenth Edition of the Encyclopaedia Britannica*. National Academy of Education, 1976. Also published in the *Proceedings of the National Academy of Education*, vol. 2.

McCracken, Samuel. "The Scandal of 'Britannica 3'." *Commentary* 61 (February, 1976): 63–67.

"The *New Encyclopaedia Britannica*." *Booklist/Reference Books Bulletin* 171 (June 1, 1975): 1021–28.

Sader, Marion. *General Reference Books for Adults*. New York: R.R. Bowker, 1988. The article on *Britannica* also appears in a slightly different version in *Reference Books for Young Readers*, Marion Sader, ed. New York: R.R. Bowker, 1988.

Walsh, S. Padraig. *Anglo-American General Encyclopedias: A Historical Bibliography, 1703–1967*. New York: R.R. Bowker, 1968.

Wells, James M. *The Circle of Knowledge: Encyclopaedias Past and Present*. Chicago: Newberry Library, 1968.

Wolff, Geoffrey. "Britannica 3, Failures of." *Atlantic* 238 (November, 1976): 107–10.

——— "Britannica 3, History of." *Atlantic* 233 (June, 1974): 37–47.

NOTES

[1] The statistics for this edition and subsequent editions described here are from Robert Collison, *Encyclopedias: Their History Throughout the Ages* (New York: Hafner, 1964), 138–45.

[2] Herman Kogan, *The Great EB* (Chicago: University of Chicago Press, 1958), 10.

[3] Ibid., 13.

[4] Ibid., 24.

[5] For a history of pirated editions in the U.S., see Padraig Walsh, *Anglo-American General Encyclopedias* (New York: Bowker, 1968), 52–54.

[6] Collison, 145.

[7] Kogan, 162–163.

[8] Walsh, 50

[9] Ibid.

[10] Kogan, 212.

[11] Ibid., 222.

[12] Encyclopaedia Britannica, Inc., press release, n.d.

[13] "New Encyclopaedia Britannica," *Reference and Subscription Books Review* (1 January 1975):

[14] "Who Owns EB, Inc?, *News from Encyclopaedia Britannica*, press release, n.d.

[15] "The Biggest Publishers," *Publishers Weekly* (21 December 1990): 12.

[16] "The 400 Largest Private Companies in the U.S.," *Forbes* 146 (10 December 1990): 246.

[17] "Reference Books Bulletin," *Booklist* (15 October 1989): 488.

[18] Walsh, 44.

The Book that Built Gale Research: The *Encyclopedia of Associations*

Carol M. Tobin

DEVELOPMENT AND HISTORY

The *Encyclopedia of Associations* arose out of one man's desire to find the information he needed to do his job. Because of the character of the man and the need of others for the information he sought, that one book became the foundation of Gale Research, a publisher that specializes in reference materials for libraries.

Frederick G. Ruffner

In 1954 Frederick G. Ruffner was a research manager for General Detroit Corporation. He needed to find information about some trade associations and assumed that there would be a listing of such organizations. He came across one, *National Associations of the United States*, that the U.S. Commerce Department had put out in 1949, but it was out of date. He concluded that there was a market for a directory of organizations. "It seemed so basic that I thought if I needed such a book, others must need it too." He decided to publish such a book himself, and with his wife Mary worked on what would become the *Encyclopedia of American Associations*. At first the newlyweds worked in a corner of their bedroom and later expanded to renting desk space in the aptly named Book Building in downtown Detroit. Ruffner eventually quit his job to work on the project full-time.[1]

He sought advice from C. J. Judkins, chief of the Trade Association Division of the U.S. Department of Commerce, the compiler of the Commerce Department directory; Charles M. Mortensen, manager of the Trade Association Department of the U.S. Chamber of Commerce; and Walter E. Forster, chief librarian of the Business and Commerce Division, Detroit Public Library.

Method of Compilation

The method of compilation of the first edition is still used today: identifying associations by scanning various listings and then confirming the information by mail or phone inquiries to the organizations themselves. While compiling the directory, Ruffner moved from a shared office to a private one, and in 1956 he hired his first part-time employee[2] and published the *Encyclopedia of American Associations* (*EAA*). The *EAA* was described in the Preface as "a directory of non-profit organizations of national scope." Readers were given the caveat that "the nature and magnitude of the directory make it impossible for the publisher to guarantee complete accuracy. Listing in this book does not confer status upon any organization, nor should omission imply lack of status." No editor was listed for the first edition. The acknowledgements were signed "Gale Research Company," with the name "Gale" taken from Ruffner's middle name.

From the beginning, Gale has seen libraries as one of its prime markets. The preface to the first edition of *EAA* stated "this book has been designed as a reference tool for librarians, businessmen, educators, government officials and research workers." Ruffner has said "Right from the start we sold by mail, mostly to libraries and government agencies."[3]

The first edition of the *EAA* started a number of practices continued by the later editions and by Gale to this day. The preface asks that "errors of omission or commission" and suggestions be sent to the publisher. The postage paid reply cards for orders and suggestions still found in the 1991 edition appeared in the first edition. There was a reply form to add, change, or delete information about an organization. A footnote added "Upon receipt of this card the publisher will send questionnaire for detailed data on new organizations."

The *EAA* started the Gale practice of using a lengthy title reminiscent of older English works. The full title of the first edition is *Encyclopedia of American Associations: A Guide to the Trade, Business, Professional, Labor, Scientific, Education, Fraternal and Social Organizations of the United States.* The *EAA* announced itself from the start as a first edition and two supplements were promised for December 1956: Supplement I, Functional and Topical Listings, and Supplement II, Additions and Corrections, also to include Labor Unions. Thus *EAA* began another Gale tradition, supplementing works between editions.

A section entitled "How to Use this Directory" has been a standard feature from the start. In the first edition it took two pages; in the 1991 edition it took four. That first edition was divided into six sections: Trade, Business, Agricultural and Governmental Associations; Scientific and Engineering Associations; Education and Social Welfare Associations; Health and Medical Associations; General Associations; and Chambers of Commerce. Section seven was a "Finding Guide Index."

The entries were arranged within each section alphabetically by keyword, except that the Chambers of Commerce were listed alphabetically by state and city. The Finding Guide Index listed each association under its name and by each keyword in the name.

The entries provided information on the name of the organization, its address, the chief paid official or secretary, the staff, the founding date, and a description that included the activities, purpose and membership, and number of local groups or chapters. Old names and predecessor organizations' names were given if a merger had occurred. In the Chambers of Commerce section, population figures for cities and towns from the 1950 Census were listed.

Critical Reception

The work was well received by the library press. The *Booklist and Subscription Books Bulletin* in October 1957 gave the most detailed review. It took the book to task for calling itself an encyclopedia rather than a directory, when even the publisher "always refers to the book as a 'directory', never as an 'encyclopedia.'" The review criticized the lack of running titles in the sections and mentioned some problems with the keyword grouping. Significantly, the review mentioned that there was no truly comparable directory. The reviewer's comparison of *EAA* with the *National Associations of the United States* and its 1956 supplement revealed "a similarity of content but totally different presentations." The review noted that *EAA* had 30 percent more entries under the letter G. Some discrepancies in names of personnel for library organizations between the *EAA* and the *ALA Membership Directory* were mentioned; however, the review noted that a spot check of the New York City addresses with the Manhattan phone directory revealed no errors. The binding, paper, and typeface were judged to be good. The review concluded:

> Until the publication of the *Encyclopedia of American Associations*, there has been no current directory of this type available for use as a reference tool by librarians, businessmen,

educators, government officials, and research workers. While there are some discrepancies and inaccuracies in individual entries, they do not appear to be numerous enough to detract from the value of the volume as a current listing of American associations. It is therefore recommended for purchase by libraries having a definite established demand from their clientele for directory material.[4]

Paul Wasserman's review of *EAA* for *Library Journal* in December 1956 also compared it favorably with *National Associations of the United States,* whose 1956 supplement he judged "very slight and inadequate." He said the *EAA* "should prove a highly useful and frequently thumbed through volume." Wasserman did mention the high price ($15), but said that in spite of it, "this work will be required in virtually every library where business is being served in even a minor way."[5] The *EAA* was also cited in Frances Neel Cheney's "Current Reference Books" column in the *Wilson Library Bulletin* in October 1956.[6]

Perhaps the best indication that Ruffner and Gale had created a classic was the inclusion of *EAA* in a list of 11 titles for 1956 "that gave promise of high reference potential." The list was compiled by the independent Reference Checklist Committee chaired by Louis Shores. In that checklist, the *EAA* is recommended for public, academic, and research libraries; only school libraries were excluded.[7]

No other source of information about associations published prior to the *EAA*, including the Commerce Department's *National Associations of the United States*[8] and the Public Administration Clearing House's *Public Administration Organizations*[9] could boast the breadth of *EAA*, which encompassed fraternal, women's, sports, educational, and religious organizations among others.

The Second Edition and Beyond

With the critical and financial success of the first edition, Gale was able to proceed with

a second edition, although the *EAA* did not become the hoped-for annual until the ninth edition, nearly 20 years later. The second edition was published in 1959. The price had gone up to $20 but for this one got half again as many listings, a subject index, and a number of items added to the description. The work now had 19 sections instead of 6 as well as a section of items "received too late to classify." The descriptions were expanded to include acronyms; affiliated organizations; sections, divisions or special committees; publications, including frequency; and convention or annual meeting. The how-to-use section showed a sample listing to illustrate the different elements of the description, a feature retained to this day. The introduction now specified a Reader Service Bureau maintained by Gale that could supply at no charge additional data that might result as part of the continuing program of editing the *EAA*. The Reader Service Bureau is mentioned through the thirteenth edition in 1979, but the twelfth and thirteenth editions cautioned: "The staff cannot, however, answer inquires concerning the general history of associations and does not compile statistical surveys." The second edition was also financially successful and helped Gale become "a full-fledged publishing company."[10]

The third edition came a little more quickly. It was published in 1961 under the now familiar name of the *Encyclopedia of Associations (EA)*. Once again the price rose, this time to $25. However, for this buyers received 30 percent more listings and a second volume, the Geographic and Executive Index. The introduction mentioned other volumes in preparation, Volume III, "State and Local Associations of the U.S.-East"; Volume IV, "State and Local Associations of the U.S.-West"; and Volume V, "National Organizations of Canada." These volumes never appeared, but they show the idea behind titles that did appear much later, i.e., *Encyclopedia of Associations: Regional, State, and Local Organizations* (1987–) and *Encyclopedia of*

Associations: International Organizations (1983–).

The title change occasioned some more reviews. Eric Moon cited some errors of information but concluded "Despite such errors and omissions, which are probably unavoidable to some degree, this is a valuable reference work which should be in all but the smallest libraries."[11] *EA* appeared on the "Outstanding Reference Books of 1961" list, as "a useful compilation of information hard to find elsewhere."[12]

The fourth edition in 1964 was significant both because Ruffner was listed for the first time as editor along with three others and because of the mention of the idea that the *EA* can be used as a guide to information as well as a directory of organizations. In the fifth and subsequent editions the information functions of organizations have been likened to "switchboards" to connect "persons needing information to highly-qualified sources of information." The fifth edition billed this function as *EA*'s primary value. The acceptance of *EA* by librarians was acknowledged in the introduction to the fourth edition: "Surveys of reference librarians repeatedly show that the *Encyclopedia of Associations* is among the three or four most-used books in any reference department." In December of 1964 a supplementary loose-leaf volume entitled *New Associations* was launched. Originally appearing quarterly, it listed newly formed associations.

In subsequent years the *EA* continued to receive good reviews, along with some suggestions for improvements, most of which were eventually incorporated in *EA*. Running titles were added and the early troubles with keywords were corrected. Librarians were not always happy with some of the "improvements." Eugene Sheehy says that a new edition is always "cause for rejoicing in the reference department," but the enthusiasm for the seventeenth edition was dampened when it was found that volume one came in two physical volumes, which Sheehy felt made *EA* less convenient to use.[13] There was also considerable discussion in the reviews about the usefulness of volume three, *New Associations*, because its price soon approached that of volume one alone.[14]

By 1959 *EA* was listed in A. J. Walford's *Guide to Reference Material*, and appeared in the eighth edition of Constance Winchell's *Guide to Reference Books* in 1967 where it was characterized as the "most comprehensive list for the United States." It was recorded in the fifth edition of the Enoch Pratt Free Library's *Reference Books: A Brief Guide* in 1962 and by 1965 the appearance of the fourth edition was noted without comment in *Choice* as befitted a "new edition of standard reference works . . . recommended for purchase." Bohdan Wynar in the second edition of *American Reference Books Annual* in 1971 described it as the "standard directory well-known to all librarians."[15] A 1982 feature article on *EA* in *Reference Services Review* noted that "because of its uniqueness, diversity, and accuracy the *Encyclopedia of Associations* merits recognition as a 'landmark of reference.'"[16]

Expanding Scope

With few exceptions, expanding scope has characterized *EA* throughout its history. The fifth edition added nonmembership groups if they might seem to be voluntary membership groups; some foreign groups if they were deemed to be of interest to Americans (e.g., the Tennyson Society); and some regional and local groups if their subjects or objectives hold interest outside their immediate vicinity, (e.g., Anti-Coronary Club). The state and local chambers of commerce were dropped because of space considerations and because they are adequately covered by other directories. The sixth edition added international groups having a large American membership, (e.g., the Campaign for Nuclear Disarmament); citizen action groups (e.g., the National Interreligious Service Board for Conscientious Objectors); and governmental advisory bodies (e.g., the

President's Council on Youth Opportunity). The sixteenth edition added "information entries," which describe a group or project for which no address was given. This category included groups that moved around, ad hoc committees, and underground groups like the Students for a Democratic Society. With the addition of volume four, *International Organizations*, in the eighteenth edition in 1983, those groups formerly in volume one moved to volume four except for listings for groups with American sections or bi-national groups. In 1987, *Encyclopedia of Associations: Regional, State, and Local Organizations*, a multi-volume set, started publication. Except for "a hundred or so regional organizations" considered to be of national interest and thus also listed in *EA*, the material in this work was all new.

The 19 sections of the second edition stayed more or less stable with only the subtraction of chambers of commerce in the fifth edition, the dropping and reassigning of horticultural organizations and general organizations in the eighth, and the addition of cultural organizations in the eighth and fan clubs in the twenty-second. The items included in the description continued to grow with zip codes and phone numbers (fifth edition); computerized services and telecommunications service (twentieth edition); budget of the organization and presence of exhibits at conventions (twenty-first edition); and additional information about publications (i.e., circulation figures, prices, former and alternative names, ISSN, online and microfiche availability) (twenty-fourth edition).

The indexing of *EA* has become increasingly sophisticated over the years. Additional keywords were added over time, and, with the twentieth edition, the separate name and keyword indexes had grown to occupy a separate volume. A catchword was added to the top of the index pages in the twenty-third edition to make use more efficient. One of the reasons for the separate index volume with the twentieth edition was the inclusion of all the entries from the international organizations volume and from eight other related Gale directories. This was expanded in the twenty-first edition to include more Gale directories and some non-Gale publications such as the *US Government Manual* and the *Federal Yellow Book* for a total of 15. In the twenty-fourth edition, the editors reverted to the practice of indexing only Gale directories.

As the *EA* grew from several thousand entries to nearly 22,000, its editorial staff also grew. It has had ten editors (sometimes working in pairs or, as on the twenty-fourth edition, in a group of three). The range of editorial titles is perhaps best illustrated by the twenty-first edition (1986). It had one editor, three associate editors, a contributing editor, three senior assistant editors, thirteen assistant editors, two editorial assistants, a contributing editor, two contributing senior assistant editors, two contributing assistant editors, a contributing research editor, an editorial director, an associate editorial director, and, finally, a senior editor of the *Encyclopedia of Associations* Series. In reading the masthead of the various editions, one can follow an editor's movement up through the various editorial ranks thus providing a historical perspective and a consistency of vision for *EA*. The current staff is smaller than that of the twenty-first edition because of rearrangements in the workflow. The *EA* National staff is ten people but only 5.5 FTE; the International is four and the Regional three. There is no longer a research department devoted just to *EA*. Instead Gale's research department works on a variety of directories and other projects as needed.[17]

The work is still done basically the same way as it was for the first edition, although greatly expanded. The staff scans for new associations and sends out questionnaires. Current organizations are sent revision forms with two follow-up mailings. The research department also makes calls both to new groups and to check up on previous listings. Through the years the introductions have cited 90 percent as the number of entries that receive some kind of revision or updating. Each year about 1,000 new organizations are added, while 500 to 600 groups drop out. The current practice is to list as "missing" those groups which cannot be located. Requests for updated information from these organizations have "remained unanswered for at least three editions or have been returned by the Post Office" as undeliverable. In the index these organizations' entries bear the annotation "address unknown since [date]."

Computerized Production

Computerization has helped the staff of *EA*. Ruffner wrote in 1976 that "In the late 60s and early 70s, it took two years to produce a 600-page *Encyclopedia of Associations*. Today, it takes less than half that time to produce a 3000-page, three-book set, a companion international volume, and a printed 'update' service."[18] The ninth edition (1975) is the first to mention computerized photo composition and it was from this date that *EA* became an annual.

As with so many other sources, the existence of a computer tape led to new services. In September 1979 Gale made the thirteenth edition of *EA* available as File 114 on DIALOG. This file now includes *International Organizations* and *Regional, State, and Local Organizations*. In the 19th edition (1984) Gale announced the availability of tapes and also stated that it would do custom computerized selection sorts, e.g., on locations. *Gale Global Access: Associations* a CD-ROM product that used the Knowledge Access International software became available from Gale in January 1989 at a price of $1495 a year. It included all the *EA* volumes, supplements, and updates and also the records from *Association Periodicals*. It was reviewed favorably.[19] A press release from SilverPlatter dated January 3, 1990, announced that SilverPlatter would coproduce Gale's CD-ROM products. *EA* was the first product chosen for production; the SilverPlatter CD continued to use the name *Gale GlobalAccess: Associations*.[20]

EA not only kept pace with modern technology, using computer composition and providing fax numbers in the listings, but it also kept up with the demand for more information. But as quick as Gale and Ruffner were to pick up on a good idea, they were also able to drop ideas that did not work. In 1978 a *Youth Serving Organizations Directory* based on the twelfth edition of *EA* appeared for one edition. Along the way, *EA* had at various times a *Rankings Indexes* volume (twenty-first edition), and a *Research Activities and Funding Programs* (Volume V) published only for the seventeenth edition. A related publication, *Association Periodicals* (1987) was discontinued after only a year. It provided more information about association publications but with the twenty-fourth edition of *EA* increasing the amount of information given about periodicals, it is not needed. The *Updating Service* for volumes I and III begun in 1985 and the *New Associations and Projects* begun in 1964 were combined in the twenty-fifth edition (1990).[21]

In the first edition Ruffner included a quote from Alexis de Tocqueville's *Democracy in America* that appeared in the next twenty-three editions:

> The Americans of all ages, all conditions and all dispositions constantly form associations. They have not only commercial and manufacturing companies in which all take part but associations of a thousand other kinds, religious, moral, serious, futile, restricted, enormous, or diminutive. The Americans make associations to give entertainments, to found establishments for education, to send missionaries to the antipodes. . . . Wherever at the head of some new undertaking you see the government of France or a man of rank in England, in the United States you will be sure to find an association.[22]

This observation on the American propensity for associations helps explain why the *EA* was such a success and found such a welcome niche in reference departments. It also explains why the national organizations' entries take two volumes while the international organizations' entries fill only one volume. And perhaps it explains why this type of reference work found its fullest flowering in United States. The *EA* itself is a fascinating ground for social history. Some of the reviews in nonlibrary journals emphasize the more humorous aspect of this. Richard Kern in *Sales and Marketing Management* picked out the American Association of Dental Victims, the Texas Barbed Wire Collectors Association, and the National Association of Insect Electrocutor Manufacturers as worthy of mention.[23] A *New York Times* article was entitled "Banana Club Meets Electrical Women."[24]

The *EA* is, however, worthy of deeper study. Starting in the twenty-first edition, (1986) the editor(s) wrote mini-essays on the types of new associations listed and how they "mirror the current interest and concerns of the American public." In that edition hunger, national economic issues, children's rights, and Central America were particularly highlighted. In the twenty-fourth edition, Central America was still mentioned and environmental concerns (spurred by the Alaskan oil spill), senior citizens rights, and surrogate parenthood were among the areas that had newly formed groups. Just a comparison of the subjects listed under Social Welfare Organizations in the table of contents in the sixth edition (1970) and the twenty-fourth edition (1989) reveals some of the changes in the United States during that period. Anti-poverty, nutrition, rehabilitation, sex information, crime and delinquency, family life, alcoholism, and narcotics were listed only in the sixth edition and child welfare, community action, criminal justice, disabled, family planning, gay/lesbian, homeless, population, recreation, selfhelp, service clubs, social work, substance abuse, surrogate parenthood, and voluntarism only in the twenty-fourth edition. In some cases only the terminology had changed (e.g., "substance abuse" instead of "narcotics");

but in others (e.g., selfhelp and homeless) the changes demonstrated newly articulated concerns.

The *EA* has been used to trace trends in American life. For example, the author of a 1985 article in the *Annals of the American Society of Political and Social Science* consulted it to study the growth of religious reform movements.[25] Other authors use it to compile mailing lists for surveys, as did the author of "Fee Sharing Between Lawyers and Public Interest Groups." Lawyers seem to find it a particular favorite because it has the facts that can bolster their arguments, e.g., the number of groups concerned with drinking and driving, the founding dates of associations, the number of people who have taken transcendental meditation courses.[26] It seems that the only limits on *EA*'s uses are its users' imaginations.

Gale's Growth

As the *EA* grew and matured so did Gale. However, in a 1984 profile of Ruffner, John Baker was still able to say "Gale is still so much the creation of one man . . . that it's difficult to imagine where it would go without Ruffner at the helm."[27] When Ruffner was asked about how Gale would be without him he said that he hoped it would survive as the Bowker Company did without R. R. Bowker. In 1985 Gale was sold to International Thomson.[28]

Ruffner left Gale and *EA* shortly after the company was sold and he has since started another publishing company, Omnigraphics, with offices in the same building in downtown Detroit as the Gale offices. However even without its creator, *EA* continues to this day, changing to meet new demands while maintaining its established strengths to satisfy the old needs it was created to fulfill.

PUBLICATION HISTORY

Encyclopedia of American Associations. Detroit: Gale Research. 1st ed.,1956; 2nd ed., 1959.

Encyclopedia of Associations. 3rd ed.,1961; 4th ed.,1964; 5th ed.,1968; 6th ed.,1970; 7th ed.,1972; 8th ed.,1973.

Encyclopedia of Associations. Annual. Detroit: Gale Research Company, 1975–. Vol. 1, *National Organizations of the United States.* Vol. 2, *Geographic and Executive Index,* Vol. 3, *New Associations,* Dec. 1964– , 1970 changed to *New Associations and Projects,* 1990 changed to *Supplement,* Vol. 4, *International Organizations,* 18th ed., 1983–. Vol. 5, *Research Activities and Funding Programs,* 17th ed., 1982 only. *Updating Service* for vols. 1 and 3, 1985–

1989. *International Organizations Supplement* 1985– . *Rankings Indexes* 21st ed., 1987 only.

Encyclopedia of Associations: Regional, State, and Local Organizations. Detroit: Gale Research, 1987– . Biennial.

Encyclopedia of Associations: Association Periodicals, edited by Denise Allard and Robert Thomas. Detroit: Gale Research Company, 1987.

Encyclopedia of Associations. DIALOG File 114. Palo Alto, CA: Dialog Information Services, Sept. 1979– .

Gale GlobalAccess: Associations. CD-ROM. Detroit: Gale Research, 1989–1990.

Gale GlobalAccess: Associations. CD-ROM. Wellesley Hills, MA: SilverPlatter Information, 1990– .

BIBLIOGRAPHY

Through its introductions the *Encyclopedia of Associations* provides a good explanation of the publishing history and editorial policy changes. Baker gives important background about Frederick G. Ruffner and Davis's review article is a good summary of *EA* to 1982. Bradley is good on both Ruffner and Gale. There are many reviews of different editions of *EA* and its parts. Only reviews that go beyond description are listed here.

Adams, John. Review of *Encyclopedia of Associations,* 14th ed. *Reference Services Review* 8 (July/September 1980): 78–79.

Angelo, Frank. "A Fact? A List? Answer Man Has It." *Detroit Free Press,* July 17, 1974. Reprinted in *Biography News* 1 (August, 1974): 944.

Baker, John F. " Portrait of a Publisher: Frederick G. Ruffner." *Publishers Weekly* 226 (December 7, 1984): 25–27.

"Bibliophile Prevails with Written Words." *Nation's Business* 68 (May, 1980): 94–95.

Bradley, Philip. "A Founding Father: Frederick Ruffner and the Gale Research Co." *Indexer* 16 (April 1, 1988): 22–31.

Byerly, Greg. Review of database *Encyclopedia of Associations. RQ* 20 (Summer, 1981): 409.

Davis, Mary Ellen Kyger. "Encyclopedia of Associations." *Reference Services Review* 10 (Summer 1982): 11–14.

Moon, Eric. Review of *Encyclopedia of Associations,* 3rd ed. *Library Journal* 87 (January 15, 1962): 209–10.

O'Leary, Mick. "Encyclopedia of Associations Expands Online Research." *Database* 12 (October, 1989): 59–61.

Quint, Barbara. "Connect Time." *Wilson Library Bulletin* 63 (March, 1989): 78–79, 125.

Rettig, James. Review of *Encyclopedia of Associations: Association Periodicals,* 1st ed. *Wilson Library Bulletin* 62 (January, 1988): 99.

Review of *Encyclopedia of American Associations: A Guide to the Trade, Business, Professional, Labor, Scientific, Educational, Fraternal, and Social Organizations of the United States,* 1st ed. *Booklist and Subscription Books Bulletin* 54 (October 1, 1957): 60–64.

Review of *Encyclopedia of Associations,* 7th ed. *Booklist* 69 (April 1, 1973): 724–25.

Ruffner, Fred.,"The Buzz Industry and the Book Industry." *Reference Librarian* no. 15 (Fall, 1986): 131–37.

"Ruffner, Frederick G." *ALA Yearbook* 10 (1985): 13.

"Ruffner, Frederick Gale." *ALA Yearbook* 13 (1988): 76.

Shores, Louis. "Reference Checklist '56." *Library Journal* 82 (January 15, 1957): 145–57.

Sturtevant, Anne F. "Reference Books of 1961." *Library Journal* 87 (April 5, 1962): 1533–41.

Wasserman, Paul. Review of *Encyclopedia of American Associations: A Guide to the Trade, Business, Professional, Labor, Scientific, Educational, Fraternal and Social Organizations of the United States,* 1st ed., *Library Journal* 81 (December 15, 1956): 2961.

NOTES

[1] John F. Baker, " Portrait of a Publisher: Frederick G. Ruffner," *Publishers Weekly* 226 (7 December 1984): 25.

[2] Ibid., 25.

[3] Ibid.

[4] Review of *Encyclopedia of American Associations: A Guide to the Trade, Business, Professional, Labor, Scientific, Educational, Fraternal, and Social Organizations of the United States, Booklist and Subscription Books Bulletin*, 54 (1 October 1957): 60–64.

[5] Paul Wasserman, review of *Encyclopedia of American Associations: A Guide to the Trade, Business, Professional, Labor, Scientific, Educational, Fraternal and Social Organizations of the United States*, in *Library Journal* 81 (15 December 1956): 2961.

[6] Francis Neel Cheney, "Current Reference Books," *Wilson Library Bulletin* 31 (October 1956): 196–98.

[7] Louis Shores, "Reference Checklist '56," *Library Journal* 82 (15 January 1957): 146, 149.

[8] U.S. Department of Commerce, *National Associations of the United States* (Washington: Government Printing Office, 1949).

[9] *Public Administration Organization*, 7th ed., (Chicago: Public Administration Clearing House, 1954).

[10] Mary Ellen Kyger Davis, "*Encyclopedia of Associations*," *Reference Services Review* 10 (Summer 1982): 12.

[11] Eric Moon, review of *Encyclopedia of Associations*, 3rd ed., *Library Journal* 87 (15 January 1962): 209–10.

[12] Anne F. Sturtevant, "Reference Books of 1961," *Library Journal* 82 (15 April 1962): 1533–41.

[13] Eugene Sheehy, "Selected Reference Books of 1981–82," *College and Research Libraries* 44 (January 1983): 54.

[14] Mary Allen, review of *Encyclopedia of Associations*, 11th ed., *Serials Review* 3 (April/June 1977): 22; review of *Encyclopedia of Associations*, 9th ed., *Booklist* 72 (15 October 1975): 326; Edwin G. Tyler, review of *Encyclopedia of Associations*, 7th ed., *RQ* 12 (Spring 1973): 314.

[15] A. J. Walford and L. M. Payne, eds., *Guide to Reference Materials* (London: Library Association, 1959), 51; Constance M. Winchell, *Guide to Reference Books*, 8th ed. (Chicago: American Library Association, 1967), 77, 79; Mary Neill Barton and Marion V. Bell, *Reference Books: A Brief Guide for Students and Other Users of the Library*, 5th ed.

(Baltimore: Enoch Pratt Free Library, 1962), 98; review of *Encyclopedia of Associations*, 4th ed., *Choice* 1 (February 1965): 545; Bohdan S. Wynar, review of *Encyclopedia of Associations*, 6th ed., *American Reference Books Annual* 2 (1971): 55.

[16] Davis, 11; Nancy Jean Melin, "Ending the Old Year with Some New Beginnings," *Reference Services Review* 8 (October/December 1980): 3.

[17] Deborah Burek, coeditor of *Encyclopedia of Associations*, 24th ed., telephone conversation with the author, 30 March 1990.

[18] Fred Ruffner, "The Buzz Industry and the Book Industry," *Reference Librarian*, no. 15 (Fall 1986), 132.

[19] Jim Bloom and Vickey Bloom, "Gale Global Access Associations in Review," *CD-ROM Librarian* 4 (November/December 1989): 57–59.

[20] SilverPlatter Information, Inc., "SilverPlatter Add Gale Databases on CD-ROM," Press release, 3 January 1990; "Gale Joins Forces with SilverPlatter," *The SilverPlatter Exchange* 3 (June 1990): 2.

[21] Burek, telephone conversation with author, 30 March 1990.

[22] The ellipsis points have disappeared over time. The quote does not appear in the twenty-fifth edition. Deborah Burek, telephone conversation with author, 23 April 1990.

[23] Richard Kern, "National Association of . . .," *Sales and Marketing Management* 136 (3 February 1986): 15.

[24] Margaret Wills and Stewart Wills, "Banana Club Meets Electrical Women," *New York Times*, 11 August 1986, A19.

[25] Robert Wuthnow, "The Growth of Religious Reform Movement," *Annals of the American Society of Political and Social Science* 480 (July 1985): 112.

[26] Roy D. Simon, Jr., "Fee Sharing Between Lawyers and Public Interest Groups," *Yale Law Journal* 98 (March 1989): 1071–72; Douglas E. Lahammer, "The Federal Constitutional Right to Trial by Jury for the Offense of Driving While Intoxicated," *Minnesota Law Review* 73 (October 1988): 123; Marina Angel, "White-Collar and Professional Unionization," *Labor Law Journal* 33 (February 1982): 83; "Note: Transcendental Meditation and the Meaning of Religion Under the Establishment Clause," *Minnesota Law Review* 62 (June 1978): 911.

[27] John Baker, "Portrait of a Publisher," 27.

[28] John Mutter, "International Thomson Buys Gale Research for $66 Million," *Publishers Weekly*, 227 (24 May 1985): 19.

Code of Courtesy from the Roaring Twenties: Emily Post's *Etiquette*

Richard W. Grefrath

DEVELOPMENT AND HISTORY

The history of Emily Post's *Etiquette* and the biography of Emily Post are virtually inseparable. Edition after edition, her famous book has embodied the values she lived by. Emily Post was born Emily Price on October 3, 1873, in Baltimore to an aristocratic family which could be traced back to the seventeenth century. Bruce Price, her father, was a famous architect who designed Chateau Frontenac in Quebec and most of the buildings in Tuxedo Park, New York, a high society country club estate.

The Prices moved to New York City when Emily was five. As a child she often accompanied her father during work on his buildings, and she enjoyed scampering around the scaffolding. She grew up in the conventional manner of the wealthy, with summers in Europe or Bar Harbor, Maine, and winters at her family's four-story, red brick house at 12 West 10th Street in Greenwich Village. Her mornings were spent with lessons from her German governess and afternoons featured a walk in the park.

Tall and strikingly beautiful, she created a sensation as a debutante in 1892. Four men were often required to carry her cotillion favors to her carriage after a ball! When some years later she wrote about the etiquette of debutante balls, she did so from personal experience, as was the case with the many other high society topics on which she became an authority.

Marriage and Divorce

Within a year of her debut she married Edwin Main Post, a handsome young banker from one of New York's Vanderbilt families. Soon the Posts had two children, Edwin Main Post, Jr., and Bruce Price Post, named after Mrs. Post's father.

The first setback for the family came when Edwin Post lost most of his money following the panic of 1901. Then, being somewhat of a playboy, his philandering came to the attention of a scandal sheet titled *Town Topics* which published accounts of Post's infidelities. The resulting scandal ended the Posts' marriage in 1906.

Divorced and without means of support, Emily Post and her young sons had to economize. Although hardly destitute, the enterprising Mrs. Post attempted to forge a career for herself. At the time of her divorce, Mrs. Post had published two novels, which had been drawn from long entertaining letters written to her mother while vacationing in Europe. Since novel writing was not considered an acceptable occupation for a woman in her social realm, she reluctantly accepted payment of $3,000 for one of them. For this same reason she hesitated to turn to writing as a career after her divorce.

Nevertheless, she continued to write novels, and she published four additional books by 1920. These successes made her a minor celebrity and additional income from gossipy fictional articles published in magazines had greatly improved her financial situation by 1921 when Richard Duffy, an editor at Funk & Wagnalls, sent a message to Mrs. Post asking for an appointment to speak with her about an "encyclopedia." She sent back word that she already owned five encyclopedias and hardly needed another. But Duffy persisted: "'We do not want you to buy an encyclopedia, we want you to write one.'"[1] Mrs. Post was enthused with the prospect and wondered what type of encyclopedia it might be. However, as she herself relates, "All the lovely balloons of vague fantasy collapsed at the word 'etiquette.' . . . To me at that time the word meant a lot of false and pretentious fuss over trifles."[2] Duffy persuasively argued that all her published writings abounded with people of fashionable manners, with scenes set in the high society of New York, Tuxedo Park, London, Paris, and Rome. But Mrs. Post was adamant. She was not interested in "thousands of silly and perfectly mechanical little rules or in trying to exalt the obvious."[3] Mrs. Post declined Duffy's subsequent appeals for further meetings.

But after a time, Duffy called again, bringing with him a stack of the then popular books on etiquette to demonstrate the need for a new one. "I really thought him a little mad," Mrs. Post recalled; but to get rid of him, she agreed to peruse the volumes.[4]

In her account of these events she was too discreet to name the book she examined first, but whatever it was, Mrs. Post was aghast over the "shocking misinformation" contained in the book she examined and was appalled at its condescending tone. In disgust, she slammed the book shut and at 3:00 a.m. telephoned Mr. Duffy at his home. "I *will* write the book for you," she said, "and at once! It will only be a little primer—just a few of the essential principles of taste. I'll begin it tomorrow morning."[5]

The First Edition of Etiquette

With dogged persistence, she worked on the book day after day for a year and a half. The final manuscript ran 692 pages, hardly "a little primer." Her richest source was her own memory of incidents and personalities. To organize her data she thumb-tacked various headings, "weddings," "correspondence," and so on around her workroom and under these headings fastened notes on each subject. She would disappear for days in her study, working at the typewriter, emerging only for tea by the open fire and some welcome conversation at the Tuxedo Park clubhouse.

The first edition of Emily Post's *Etiquette* was published in July 1922, during the Prohibition Era. Persistent publisher Richard Duffy contributed "Manners and Morals," an introductory essay. Without really naming names, Duffy deplored the "blunt, unpolished hero of melodrama and romantic fiction" and offered readers a jaunty, belletristic discussion of trends in English and American manners from the Ten Commandments, through Confucius, English knighthood, and Samuel Coleridge, among others.[6] He offered the public Mrs. Post as this tradition's new standard bearer and quoted her definition of its premises: "'Best Society is not a fellowship of the wealthy, nor does it seek to exclude those who are not of exalted birth; but it is an association of gentlefolk, of which good form in speech, charm of manner, instinctive consideration for the feelings of others, are credentials by which society the world over recognizes its chosen members.'"[7] In her first chapter, "What is Best Society?" Mrs. Post pursued this theme:

> "Best Society is not at all like a court with an especial queen or king, nor is it confined to any one place or group, but might better be described as an unlimited brotherhood which spreads over the entire surface of the globe, the members of which are invariably people of cultivation and worldly knowledge, who have not only perfect manners but a perfect manner. Manners are made up of trivialities of deportment which can be easily learned if one does not happen to know them; manner is personality—the outward manifestation of one's intimate character and attitude toward life."[8]

Many people today, as many did during the Roaring Twenties, consider Emily Post's etiquette rules to be mere "trivialities." Mrs.

Post herself was ever mindful of the ease with which etiquette can degenerate into mindless following of rules. Her emphasis on the true spirit of etiquette, a system designed to smooth over the awkward moments of life by taking into account the feelings of others and the happiness of all involved, is a major theme in her book and probably accounts in large part for its endurance through so many editions and through so many eras of varying manners and mores. The appeal of an egalitarian brotherhood of the courteous has proved to be timeless, expressed as it is by a true lady of not only wealth and social standing but of humanity and sensitivity as well.

Throughout her subsequent career as the preeminent arbiter of taste and decorum, Mrs. Post was known to belittle the "trivialities" of etiquette, perhaps most notably in her 1929 article in *Collier's*, "Any Fork Will Do." Since publication of the first edition of *Etiquette*, the question she was asked most frequently in letters had been "How can I tell which is the proper fork to use?" when confronted by several at a table setting. "Those who ask me about the most unimaginable trivialities of table manners are most often the very same people who unknowingly break the rules of genuine importance."[9] What, then, is important? The effect of conversation and behavior on others is the primary and abiding concern throughout Mrs. Post's writings. Among other breaches of taste, she deplored "screaming voices and loud, raucous laughter" and the use of poor grammar both of which she considered embarrassing to those one is with.

After laying a philosophical foundation in the first chapter, the practical advice followed. The second chapter started, logically, with "Introductions," such as "Mr. Distinguished, may I present Mr. Young?" Here Mrs. Post introduced the technique of using names indicative of a person's social standing, age, and personality. In subsequent chapters the reader comes to know Mr. and Mrs. Toplofty; Mr. and Mrs. John Appleyard (who until now had not left their home state of Iowa); Mr. and Mrs.

Newlyrich; Mrs. Wellborn; Mr. and Mrs. Oneroom; and Mr. Richard Vulgar, among many others. This was not an innovative literary conceit; similar symbolic names had been used at least as far back as the medieval morality plays such as *Everyman*, and in more recent history Charles Dickens had invented character names such as Mr. and Mrs. Hamilton Veneering to indicate a polished superficiality. Nonetheless, Mrs. Post was a master of the technique, populating her text with an exceptionally large number of such symbolic names, each one skillfully fitted to the situation, disarmingly witty, and drawn from her own experiences in society. In fact, the book's dedication reads: "To you my friends, whose identity in these pages is veiled in fictional disguise."[10] Readers could easily identify themselves in the proceedings, whether Newlyrich or Toplofty, and the comical overtones helped to make this whole world of etiquette rules less stuffy and formidable for the uninitiated wishing to learn the ropes. Reading Mrs. Post's book could be downright entertaining.

"Introductions" progressed to "Greetings," including from Younger to Older, in church, informal greetings, and so on. She gave particular attention to handshakes. A gentleman on the street never shakes hands with a lady without first removing his glove, but the glove stays on if the handshake occurs at the opera. Mrs. Post's witty banter reigned supreme in a heartfelt discussion of the "personality of the handshake." She asked "Who does not like a 'boneless' hand extended as though it were a spray of sea-weed, or a miniature boiled pudding?" Rather, the proper handshake is made briefly, but there should be a "feeling of strength and warmth in the clasp, and—one should at the same time look into the countenance of a person whose hand one takes."[11]

Two subsequent chapters pursued salutations of courtesy (including the proper way for a gentleman to tip his hat, informal bows, the Bow of Ceremony, the Bow of a Woman of Charm) and how to conduct oneself in public (including how a gentleman offers his arm, how to deal with the restaurant check, and behavior in stores and shops). "Do not attract attention to yourself in public," Mrs. Post insisted, "is one of the fundamental rules of good breeding."[12] In discussing conduct in stores, the book emphasized its theme of kindness towards others, saying that "lack of consideration for those who in any capacity serve you, is always an evidence of ill-breeding, as well as of inexcusable selfishness."[13]

The chapter on "Conversation" carried the credo "Think Before you Speak." It spoke much common sense, such as advising to try not to repeat oneself, either by telling a story again and again or by going back over details of a narrative that seemed especially to amuse a listener. This is surely another reason for the continuing popularity of Emily Post. Since the rules prescribed follow common sense, they do not appear arbitrary and artificial. Obviously people of high society spend a great deal of time sitting around talking, so the art of conversation is a serious matter. Bores and "tactless blunderers" were censured. Rather than let an amiable conversation turn into an argument, the tactful person should keep his opinion to himself, suggested Mrs. Post. And readers were advised to switch to another topic of conversation than argue with a speaker whose opinion was opposed to their own.

An entire chapter on "Words, Phrases, and Pronunciation" included "Phrases Avoided in Good Society" and a brief table of phrases one could use: "Let me help you" (not "permit me to assist you") "I will find out" (not "I will ascertain"); and "had something to drink" (not "partook of liquid refreshment").[14] This straightforward approach appealed to the many newly wealthy people who had attained a higher social standing suddenly and who were assured by its unpretentiousness that they did not have to learn a whole new sophisticated language to converse properly in the their new-found society.

A quaint little parable about "the Bank of Life" highlighted the chapter on "One's Place in the Community." Life is a bank in which one deposits funds of "character, intellect, and heart, or other funds of egotism, hardheartedness, and unconcern."[15] One can only withdraw from (the bank of) life what one has deposited. This also applies to the community, where one gets out what one puts in. In this instance Mrs. Post invoked a somewhat moral tone, that etiquette is a system of rules and traditions based not only on good common sense but also on ethics and morality. Formal written invitations and the procedures of visiting one's friends on formal and informal occasions were discussed in subsequent chapters. The book's title page reads, "Illustrated with Private Photographs and facsimiles of social forms," and, true to that promise, there are innumerable examples of engraved cards and invitations for all types of occasions. Examples of acceptances and regrets were also furnished.

An entire chapter was devoted to letter writing, with examples of business and social letters; and several chapters explored the many procedures involved in maintaining a proper household, including teas, afternoon parties and formal dinners. Many household procedures are described thoroughly, including "How a Cook Submits a Menu" and the daily duties of the butler. Also specified in detail are the dress and decorum of other servants, such as the house footman, the kitchen maid, the parlor maid, the housemaid, the lady's maid, the valet, the housekeeper, and the nurse.

The whole matter of servants has received considerable attention throughout the various editions of Emily Post's *Etiquette*. To those readers of the first edition who had lately earned a position in society, its extensive instructions about servants were undoubtedly most welcome. But each new edition of *Etiquette* reduced the emphasis on servants, reflecting the changing times as well as the expansion of the book's audience to social strata below the highest levels. As in all relations with others, courtesy to one's servants was counseled consistently.

Acknowledging that not all readers of *Etiquette* were able to accumulate a large servant staff, Mrs. Post suggested ways to entertain graciously with few or no servants. One of the key ingredients in her formula is use of the buffet, allowing all guests to serve themselves. Mrs. Post was so enamored of this food service technique, she expanded on the topic in her book *How to Give Buffet Suppers* (Waterbury, CT: Chase Brass & Copper Co., 1933), which included eight pages of selected menus and recipes.

The architect's daughter also paid special attention to the way a distinguished house reflects the good taste and charm of its owners. Furniture should be suitable for the architecture of the house. Mrs. Post even proposed a four-question test to determine an art object's suitability for a particular house. She pursued these concerns in her *The Personality of a House: The Blue Book of Home Design and Decoration* (New York: Funk & Wagnalls, 1930).

One of the more controversial topics in *Etiquette* through the years and one which critics like to cite to demonstrate the hopelessly outdated conventions prescribed by Emily Post is the matter of the chaperon. "A young lady who is unprotected by a chaperon," she wrote, "is in the position precisely of an unarmed traveler walking among wolves."[16] The chaperon does a great deal more than simply being present when young people congregate; she coordinates the social life of the young lady, sends out invitations on her behalf, and even stays up until the young lady returns home from a date to let her in the door since no proper young lady lets herself in with her own key! Yet Mrs. Post did insist that the best chaperon is "the young girl's own sense of dignity and pride,"[17] and were it not for the conventions of propriety, this should be more than adequate. Later editions of *Etiquette* progressively toned down the importance of the chaperon.

Arguably the most popular and widely read section in *Etiquette*, from the first edition to the present day, is the chapter on weddings. For many this is one of the very few occasions in life when formal dress is rented, professional caterers hired, and florists engaged, all at once, at a time which seems the most important celebration of a lifetime. Mrs. Post covered all the details so graciously that the whole ordeal seems almost enjoyable rather than intimidating.

The other major rites of passage, christenings and funerals, each warranted their own chapters. According to son Edwin, Mrs. Post was not a religious person, but she interpreted the details of church ceremony with her characteristic simplicity and thoughtfulness.[18]

Chapters entitled "The Country House and Its Hospitality," "The House Party in Camp," and "Clubs and Club Etiquette" provide good advice for these activities. The "Games and Sports" chapter covers mostly how to play bridge courteously, as well as golf. The most important considerations are playing for the sake of playing rather than winning, never losing your temper, being a good loser, and giving your opponent the benefit of the doubt.

The "Fundamentals of Good Behavior" chapter is especially central to the philosophy of *Etiquette*. A lengthy succession of do's and don'ts attempted to advise those who would be true ladies and gentlemen! A gentleman does not borrow money from a woman; no gentleman goes to a lady's house when he is affected by alcohol; a gentleman never takes advantage of another's helplessness or ignorance. These are manifestations of a fundamental code of honor which demands the "inviolability of his word, and the incorruptibility of his principles."[19] She added that "the instincts of a lady are much the same as those of a gentleman."[20]

When *Etiquette: In Society, in Business, in Politics, and at Home* was published in midsummer, 1922, the timing did not appear ideal, coming after the rush of June weddings, one of the major social occasions with which *Etiquette* was designed to help.[21] Nonetheless,

Etiquette was an immediate success, steadily scaling the bestsellers lists.[22]

As Funk & Wagnalls had expected, a large number of *Etiquette*'s purchasers were people who had suddenly made a lot of money on the stock market during the post-war boom. These people were traveling abroad, buying new large houses, hiring servants, joining clubs, and putting on large-scale fashionable weddings. For them, *Etiquette* was a practical guidebook, a manual for the newly rich.[23]

Another aspect of the book's appeal was the glimpse it offered into the world of the aristocracy. For a middle-class housewife who bought *Etiquette* to plan a wedding, it was fascinating to read about "double service dinner service" for 12 persons, where the food starts at opposite ends of the table, progresses clockwise, the butler stationed directly behind the hostess at the end of the table. Other chapters, such as the one on the debutante ball, held similar interest for those who would never attend such affairs.

Many fell under the spell of Emily Post the storyteller. Critic Edmund Wilson said that *Etiquette*'s first edition had "the excitement of a novel" and "snob appeal," both important factors in its success. Wilson reported that F. Scott Fitzgerald was so taken by the atmosphere and drama in Emily Post's book that he was "inspired with the idea of a play in which all the motivations should consist of trying to do the right thing."[24]

Nowhere was Mrs. Post's skill with witty, entertaining prose more apparent than in the five-page tale, "How a Dinner Can be Bungled," in the "Formal Dinners" chapter. Mr. and Mrs. Newwed give a formal dinner and everything goes wrong. The fire in the drawing room fills the house with smoke so everyone starts blinking and sneezing. The clear soup is not clear, is barely tepid, and tastes like dishwater. The fish with Hollandaise sauce arrives in a huge mound too big for its platter with a narrow gutter of water around the edge and a curdled yellow mess dabbed over the center. None of the guests eats any-thing, except for Mrs. Kindheart who sips at the cold soup. After the guests have gone, Mr. Newwed tries to console his weeping wife. "Remembering the trenches" of World War I, he tries to convince her that dinner was not so bad![25]

The authoritative tone of Mrs. Post's writing also accounts for the book's success. She wrote effortlessly and with great wit and charm about a social world she and her family had been solidly a part of for several generations. Not since Mrs. Sherwood, whose *Manners and Social Usages* (New York: Harper & Bros., 1884) was popular when Mrs. Post was a girl, was an etiquette manual published by a woman of such high social position.[26]

Critical and Popular Reception

Contemporary book critics were enthusiastic and laudatory reviews from hundreds of newspapers began pouring in to the publisher.[27] "Up-to-date, sensible, comprehensive," praised *Booklist*.[28] In a lengthy treatise entitled "A School for Better Manners in America," novelist Gertrude Atherton claimed that "as a nation, we are the most ill-mannered in the world," populated by the "awful" characters portrayed in Sinclair Lewis's *Babbitt*, another popular book of the day. But, she implied, Mrs. Post's excellent text would lift the country out of its rudeness. Atherton echoed others in her observation that "Not only is its style delightful, but it reads like a first-class society novel."[29] Will Cuppy of the *New York Tribune* also found it entertaining and said "Mrs. Post is a delightful writer—humorous, wise, witty, worldly, sympathetic, human."[30] *The Literary Digest* perceptively saw behind the innumerable rules in *Etiquette* to its true purpose; "Not to teach us to display our sophistication, but to enable us to live without friction."[31]

Soon after the publication of *Etiquette*, hundreds of readers wrote to Mrs. Post asking for rulings on specific situations not covered in the book. This was an unexpected development since nowhere in *Etiquette* had Mrs. Post invited inquiries. Dutifully she read, considered, and answered all the letters. Those in haste sent telegrams, including one reading "REPLY WIRE COLLECT. WEDDING TOMORROW WHICH SIDE OF BRIDE DOES GROOM LEAVE CHURCH ON?"[32] This flood of letters served a crucial function in the following years, providing material to revise and make additions to revisions of *Etiquette*. This corpus of letters composed the kind of market survey which in more recent years publishers have paid considerable sums for.

As the sales of *Etiquette* continued to increase steadily (within ten years it had sold more than 500,000 copies), Mrs. Post was able to parlay her new found celebrity status into other successful ventures. Soon she began a monthly column on etiquette for *McCall's* magazine; a full-time secretary was hired to assist her with this. The column was a convenient way to share with many the answers to questions she received in her bulging daily mailbag.

Mrs. Post was continually besieged by manufacturers who wished her to endorse their merchandise. She ordinarily declined to endorse a particular brand, as in the case of a ginger ale company which paid $3,000 for a pamphlet written by Mrs. Post saying that "ginger ale is a refreshing drink to serve at parties," without specifically mentioning the brand of the company sponsoring this "endorsement." She wrote pamphlets for linen, silver, and glass manufacturers as well, never endorsing a brand name, but describing the correct use of these items in entertaining. These manufacturers paid up to $5,000 apiece for these advertisements.[33]

By 1929, her fame was sufficiently established for *Collier's* magazine to state, in the caption to her photograph accompanying her article "Any Fork Will Do," that Mrs. Post "is perhaps the highest authority on just what you should do at the right moment."[34]

In the early 1930s Mrs. Post stopped writing her *McCall's* column in favor of doing her own radio program on NBC, a program that aired for eight years until the outbreak of World War II.[35] Shortly after leaving *McCall's*, she contracted with the Bell Syndicate for a syndicated newspaper column on etiquette; called "Social Problems." This column's popularity increased continually and, at the time of her death in 1960, was still being syndicated to more than 200 papers.[36]

Early Revised Editions

None of these many activities deterred Mrs. Post from paying attention to the book that had brought her celebrity. In 1927, 1931, and 1934 revised editions of *Etiquette* were published and, though the revisions were minor, each of these new editions enabled Mrs. Post to incorporate into her famous book some of the situations readers had frequently asked about in letters. The deluge of letters that followed publication of the first edition remained steady; an average of 6,000 arrived each week through the 1930s.[37] The 1927 edition of *Etiquette* carried a new subtitle, "The Blue Book of Social Usage," which was used in all further editions until Mrs. Post's death in 1960.

The 1927 edition added a chapter on "American Neighborhood Customs," including bridal showers, singing groups, and sewing circles, topics which readers had brought to Mrs. Post's attention through letters. In this edition the first edition's "The Chaperon and Other Conventions" was changed to "The Vanishing Chaperon," though much of the content remained, including the infamous sentence about a young girl without a chaperon being like "an unarmed traveler walking among wolves."[38]

Servants still occupied a major section, somewhat expanded by new members such as the business or social secretary; yet there is also a new, modern wife, Mrs. Three-in-One, who manages to be cook, waitress, and hostess when conducting servantless entertaining. The chapter "When Mrs. Three-in-One Gives a

Party" shows the multitude of *Etiquette* readers who were of moderate means and without servants how to throw a party. "Again the Buffet!" counseled Mrs. Post— "One of the nicest and most fashionable entertainments that can be given," whether for lunch, supper or dinner.[39] Following Mrs. Post's instructions, Mrs. Three-in Once could give a dinner yet never leave the table. One trick that helped make this possible was keeping a tea wagon at the hostess's side. For many years the oft-repeated query, "How can I serve a formal dinner for eight without a maid?" met the reply, "You can't." But eventually Mrs. Post determined to find a solution to this dilemma. To test her plan she invited six good friends to dinner with her and her son Bruce. Mrs. Post ladled soup from a tureen and all courses were served from, and plates stacked on a tea wagon at her side. Her success went a step beyond the buffet![40]

Like its predecessors, the 1937 edition was a "complete new edition: rewritten, revised, reset," according to the note on its title page, and completely "modernized," according to the announcement of its publication in the September 18, 1937, *Publishers Weekly.* Funk & Wagnalls launched an energetic promotion campaign with special emphasis on New York and advertisements in *The New York Times Book Review, This Week,* the *New Yorker, Bride's Magazine,* and others. Book sellers received window and counter displays and imprinted circulars. *Publishers Weekly* said that "All of the editions, from 1922 to 1936, retained the rather unbending attitude towards certain forms of behavior which has been relaxed in the present rewriting."[41]

"The Vanishing Chaperon" of the 1927 edition became "The Vanished Chaperon" in 1937. The old idea of "protection," Mrs. Post then explained "is out of tune with the world today." A girl, she believed, should chaperon herself. Still, Mrs. Post gave up the point grudgingly, suggesting that when girls are too free, trouble results. "Continuous pursuit of thrill and consequent craving for greater and greater excitement gradually produces the same result as that which a drug produces in an addict," she warned, and likened the promiscuous girl to cheapened merchandise thrown on the mark-down sale table in a clothing store.[42]

"Modern Man and Girl," a new chapter reflecting the jazz age's effect on mores since 1922. "How Can a Man with Almost No Money Take a Nice Girl Out"? asked one section. Rather than direct a young man to a particular type of date, it suggested that if Sally Hiborn is really worth the trouble she won't care if they dine in a neighborhood cafeteria instead of the Fitz-Cherry Hotel. This is typical Emily Post, the parrying of the question and an answer based on common sense and the feelings of all concerned.

New characters joined *Etiquette*'s cast in 1937. One was Gloria Gorgeous who needed to learn to stop applying makeup in public lest men wonder: If she really is gorgeous, why does her face need such constant attention?[43]

The 1937 edition includes a few letters from readers, including one asking what if she is high society and "he is from over the car tracks." "Go out on those car tracks and take a good look at them," stormed Mrs. Post, and "ask yourself if you are really such a snob that you can't see true values except as some of your friends happen to appraise them for you. And if the car track boundaries still seem that of a foreign country, break your engagement!"[44] What a firebrand! It calls to mind the Emily Post who campaigned for the repeal of Prohibition although she herself was a nondrinker. And how perfectly modern this advice is, yet based on one of Emily Post's basic principles—that the most important value is the happiness of all. A similar letter from a female reader who was from the wrong side of town drew a similar response.

Some of the 1937 edition's additions exhibited a timeless modernity, for example, the new section on smoking. Characteristically, Mrs. Post, a nonsmoker, saw both sides of the argument. She advised smokers to be more discreet and careful about smoking habits (e.g., don't put out cigarettes on lamp bases, etc.) and advised nonsmokers to be tolerant of smokers.

New technology generates new questions of courtesy. Of those who blasted radios at full volume, Mrs. Post said, it "is something that causes too much misery to need comment further than to beg them to remember the rudeness they are perpetrating in putting others to the torture of blaring noise."[45] On the other hand, she considered it acceptable to turn down a dinner invitation to stay home to hear a program on the radio. Mary Littlehouse liked the opera, but, not being able to afford tickets, listened on the radio. So she was not being rude when she declined the dinner invitation from Mrs. Onthehill.

She also addressed other technologies. She cautioned that those who did not own a telephone should not make frequent calls on a neighbor's phone, especially not toll calls. And she added a new chapter on "Manners for Motorists." Though she herself never learned to drive, Mrs. Post loved traveling by car; one of her early publishing successes was her account *By Motor to the Golden Gate* (New York: D. Appleton, 1916). Predictably, she advised motorists to be courteous and to avoid unnecessary horn honking because of impatience. Motorists are to make the hand signal for "stop" the moment they know they are about to apply the brakes, and no drinking and driving.[46]

Other new chapters covered "Etiquette in Washington and State Capitals" and "Restaurant Etiquette." Another new chapter on the "Fraternity House Party and Commencement" analyzed the concept of "popularity." Here Mrs. Post warned college freshmen of both sexes not to make an excessive effort to be popular, but to be themselves. This, she assured them, would cultivate fine and generous friends. Who pays what and appropriate dress and behavior at major college events were also thoroughly described.

The 1937 edition (in numerical sequence the fifth edition of *Etiquette*, although not so

designated) was very well received by the book-buying public as well as the critics. Euphemia Van Rensselaer Wyatt envisioned "an exquisitely ordered universe in which everyone from debutantes to motorists put courtesy first," thanks to following Emily Post's principles which she likened to a "modern code of chivalry" rather than a mere compilation of social do's and don'ts.[47] Though the price of *Etiquette* had remained $4 for 15 years from the first edition to the fifth, Mrs. Wyatt thought the cost high, but nonetheless well worth it. In *Etiquette*, *The New York Times* perceived "a philosophy of behavior which insists that no line of conduct can be correct that is not kindly and wise."[48]

After the outbreak of World War II, sales of *Etiquette* continued to climb. One reason was U.S.O. Clubs throughout the United States and overseas made a special point of obtaining the book and they reported that requests for it ran second only to requests for the Rand McNally atlas. Public libraries discovered that more copies of *Etiquette* were borrowed and not returned (or simply stolen) than any other book except the Bible. The great war correspondent Ernie Pyle boosted sales of *Etiquette* by writing in one of his published dispatches that when he was in Ireland, the candidates for officer training schools had to know their Emily Post. Later he coined the term "Emily Posters." The *Chicago Daily News* picked up the idea and did a story reporting that while Betty Grable was their Number One Pin-up Girl, Emily Post was their Number One Look-Up Girl.[49]

The 1942 revised edition of *Etiquette* came with a special separate 20-page War Time Supplement addressing many of the specific situations occurring in a nation at war. One of her Bell Syndicate columns titled "Our Wounded Come Home: How to Treat Them," was widely reprinted in 1943, appearing in *This Week Magazine* and the *Reader's Digest*. "From now on more and more of our serious wounded will appear in public," Mrs. Post said. "What are we going to do and say when they leave the hospitals and take their places in the world for which they have given so much?" She advised, "Don't stare, don't point, don't make personal remarks." She added that it is rude to ask a man how he lost an eye or leg or what injuries caused the scars on his face and that commiseration from strangers is obnoxious. Wives and mothers, she warned, must school themselves to keep tears under control.[50]

The 1945 edition of *Etiquette* carried the expected addition, "Concerning Military and Postwar Etiquette." It covered many situations involving returning veterans. In it she noted that it is inconsiderate to tell a veteran how difficult the hardships of war-time living were at home and cautioned against imitating the girl at a soda fountain who said, "I guess you're glad to be home to get a real job."[51] There was a new, brief section on Reformed and Orthodox Jewish weddings and "Simplified Wedding Details for a Bride in Everyday Clothes," this being a not uncommon carryover practice from the war years. An expanded section on telephone etiquette suggested that "Hello" remained the correct way to answer the phone at home; furthermore, giving one's name, as in "Mrs. Jones speaking," leaves one without chance of retreat from salesmen and strangers.

The 1955 edition of *Etiquette* appeared with minor revisions. Mrs. Post was then 82 years old and more and more of the activity concerned with the world of "Emily Post's *Etiquette*" was being handled by the Emily Post Institute, founded by son Edwin Post in 1946 and operated under his direction. The institute handled the voluminous mail Mrs. Post received, did research for her books, and prepared a cookbook, published as the *Emily Post Cookbook* in 1951 (New York: Funk & Wagnalls).[52] Some of the 1955 edition's revisions diluted the vigor and originality of Mrs. Post's original text. The famous bungled dinner episode was abridged; the concluding line from every previous edition had been "Whatever you do, don't dine with the Newweds unless you eat your dinner before you go, and

wear black glasses so no sight can offend you." The 1955 edition shortened this to "Whatever you do, don't dine with the Newweds unless you eat your dinner before you go,"[53] without the cleverly extravagant, amusingly snide remark about wearing dark glasses. And the ill-mannered fire, which up through the 1945 edition had smoked everyone out of the drawing room, was eliminated. In a *New Yorker* article entitled "The Waning Oomph of Mrs. Toplofty," Geoffrey Hellman cleverly explored this watering-down. He cited another example along the same lines: the first edition's statement, "To be a slattern in a vulgar household is scarcely an elevated employment, but neither is working in a sweatshop," had by the 1955 edition been changed to "To be a slattern in a vulgar household is scarcely an elevated employment, but neither is belonging to the lower ranks of any other calling."[54] The sharp, poetic "sweatshop" image is gone, perhaps revealing acute politic instincts in not making smart comments which might offend labor or management.

The Tenth Edition—Mrs. Post's Last

The tenth edition of *Etiquette* was the last edition "by Emily Post;" it appeared in the spring of 1960, the year of her death. Mrs. Post died in New York City on September 25, 1960, at the age of 86. A front-page obituary in *The New York Times* pointed out how Mrs. Post had pioneered the simplification of good manners which at the time of the 1922 edition were unnecessarily elaborate. "Every edition of her book emphasized the basic rule of etiquette: make the other person comfortable."[55]

A helpful improvement in format in the 1960 edition was expansion of the table of contents by several pages, allowing listing of all subheadings in each chapter, thus permitting easier browsing. New topics reflecting the times were discussed, including the "blind date" (but only if the third party gets approval from Gloria Gorgeous before giving her phone number to John Handsome). The chapter on "Military and Postwar Etiquette" from the previous edition was boiled down to a small chapter limited to the display, care, etc., of the U.S. flag. Most revisions were minor. Telephoning and smoking, for instance, previously covered in a single chapter, received their own chapters. The classic chapter "Mrs. Three-in-One Gives a Dinner Party," a staple since the 1927 edition, was eliminated. Indeed, little by little many of the famous characters with the symbolic names had departed—too corny, perhaps was the thought; but with them left much of the charm of the first edition.

The tenth edition added a brief four-page concluding chapter titled "For and About Young People." It emphasized "fair play," respect for others' property and rights, and counseled children "to give credit to others and not take too much credit to themselves."[56] In short, the philosophy of courtesy and consideration towards others, the Emily Post philosophy, applies to children as well as adults.

Funk & Wagnalls, publisher of every edition through the tenth (1960), was acquired by Reader's Digest in 1965; Reader's Digest published the eleventh edition that same year. In 1971 Reader's Digest sold Funk & Wagnalls to Standard Reference Library, Inc., then later the same year ownership of Funk & Wagnalls was transferred to the Donnelly Corporation. Donnelly subsequently assigned trade publishing operations to Thomas Y. Crowell Company. Eventually Harper & Row acquired *Etiquette* and published the fourteenth edition, the current edition, in 1984.

Reader's Digest published the eleventh edition in 1965 although it still carried the Funk & Wagnalls imprint. This, the first edition published after Emily Post's death, was revised by Elizabeth L. Post, Emily Post's granddaughter-in-law.

Elizabeth L. Post

Elizabeth Post seemed true to the spirit of the Emily Post philosophy. In her "Preface"

she described her first apprehensive meeting with Mrs. Post. "I found that the supposedly unapproachable authority on all our manners and behavior was the sweetest most natural warm-hearted unaffected person I had ever met." Elizabeth Post understood that perfect manners can only be achieved "by making consideration and unselfishness an integral part of your behavior."[57]

Elizabeth Post made several bold additions. An entirely new chapter advised how to make successful appearances on radio and television. Emily Post, for eight years a successful radio celebrity, could have written a chapter such as this, but never did. The new chapter on public speaking was an excellent primer on the subject, advising how to prepare, what kind of notes to bring, opening words, use of humor and props, what to do with one's hands, and even how to dress, as well as how to introduce a speaker. A new chapter on pets and people described how to keep a dog or cat without allowing the animal to become nuisance to others. Consideration of others' feelings was extended to animals.

Emily Post's "Sports and Games" section had consisted mostly of the card game of bridge and some discussion of golf. The 1965 edition added a major discussion of skiing along with advice on "conduct at a professional match," including football, baseball, basketball, ice shows, and even rodeos! Acknowledging the increasingly important role of etiquette in the business world, Elizabeth Post added a chapter on "Conducting Meetings" that covered both business meetings and meetings held in the home for planning charity fund raisers and the like.

The 1965 Elizabeth Post edition made a decided effort, as have subsequent editions, to be trendy and *au courant*. In a sense, therein lies a problem. In the 1922 first edition, Emily Post truly captured the personality of the post–World War I realm of high society and of its breeding and manners which today, as they did in 1965, seem old-fashioned and artificial. Though the aristocracy she described appeared exclusive, there was a genuine noblesse oblige in her writing. Emily Post's etiquette code was tied to Victorian tradition, which made hers a conservative approach. Through the many editions of *Etiquette*, one sees traditions upheld for the sake of tradition, long after they have ceased to be common practice.

Elizabeth Post has made a conscientious effort to be relevant to the times but has been burdened by the old baggage of much of the Emily Post approach. Among other conventions indicative of this dilemma, the chaperon was still discussed, at unnecessary length, in the 1965 edition. The Emily Post text retained in Elizabeth Post editions has often been revised, smoothing out its delightfully rough edges.

Some of Emily Post's symbolic characters have been retained along with her text, but few if any new ones have been created. Little by little through the years they have faded into the wings. In the 1965 edition, the "Blind Date" section, for instance, retained the section Emily Post wrote about Gloria Gorgeous and John Handsome, but Elizabeth Post added paragraphs describing Cindy, Charlie, and Jane. This supplanting of colorful, witty, symbolic names with dull, generic, android names is characteristic of the increasing lack of excitement in *Etiquette*, a gradual dehumanizing process making it progressively more difficult for the reader to sense the author's personality.

As if inviting comparison, in 1969 Funk & Wagnalls/Reader's Digest published two editions of *Etiquette*, one the twelfth edition by Elizabeth Post and the other a reprint facsimile of the original first edition of *Etiquette* by Emily Post. (The latter sold for $10, $6 more than in 1922.) Reviewing the two in the *Saturday Review*, Jerome Beatty found the 1922 edition "a delight to read" and "more interesting" than the newcomer.[58] Justin Kaplan couldn't resist comparing the two in a fascinating *Harper's* article, "A Rose for Emily." He perceived that the book's concept had shifted over the years "from a guide to forms and etiquette to a general encyclopedia of

modern living which now gives practical and for the most part sensible advice on how to conduct yourself." He observed the effect of retaining in the newer editions the sections Emily Post had written. That nowhere in those sections is "sex" mentioned except in the term "the opposite sex," that one should avoid discussing religion and politics, and that one should never write a letter that would be embarrassing if printed in the newspaper suggest that "things haven't changed all that much in Emily Post's world in nearly fifty years . . . under twelve layers of writing and revision there is still Emily Post's Troy, a rather crusty place."[59]

This captures the perpetual dilemma. The truly captivating passages, those of genuine literary merit, are holdovers written by the cantankerous, lively Emily Post. Conscientiously excising these would make the book less old-fashioned and Victorian, but then much of the appeal would be lost. The brightest literary gem, the bungled dinner episode, which appeared in one form or another in all of Emily Post's editions, was removed by Elizabeth Post in the 1965 edition, never to reappear. One can speculate about the reasons; but whatever they were, *Etiquette* lost a memorable story.

The twelfth edition added a section on the Bar Mitzvah and expanded discussion of teenagers' social interactions. An analytical aspect crept into this edition, at one point causing Elizabeth Post to disagree with Emily Post on introductions. "Best Society has only one phrase in acknowledgement of an introduction: 'How do you do?' It literally accepts no other," according to Emily Post in the first edition.[60] She did allow, however, that "Hello" suffices for greetings on informal occasions. Challenging this supposedly absolute dictum, Elizabeth Post declared, "If you think about it, the phrase 'How do you do?' has little meaning. Therefore, except on very formal occasions when tradition is important and desirable, I prefer the less formal responses: 'Hello,' or 'I'm very glad to meet you.'"[61] Insisting that expressions make literal sense was a new concept; Emily Post's approach had been to affirm the traditional greetings with which people were familiar and comfortable.

The 1975 edition was called *The New Emily Post Etiquette*. In it Elizabeth Post advised, "Don't panic if you find your child has smoked marijuana," though she thought it prudent to persuade him or her not to graduate to harder drugs.[62] Other formerly forbidden topics were now discussed, including sex, but only in the context of "sexual relations during engagement." Typical of the attempt in recent editions to be all things to all people, Elizabeth Post concluded that "each couple must decide this question for themselves." Although relevant factors in that decision are discussed, including the alleged nonapproval of society in general, the reader is left without the opinionated lectures Emily Post delivered when she was at the helm. In other words, "permissiveness" had crept into the rules of etiquette; allowing that may have been a serious tactical error. As Charles Bunge observed, Elizabeth Post "has tried to revise this edition to keep up with today's informal, open way of life, thereby diminishing the distinction between Post and other guides."[63] Other new sections included "You and Your Neighbor," geared to suburbanites. In this section the advice is more a collection of homilies than true insights, with Elizabeth Post advising, "Apply the Golden Rule, treat them as you would like them to treat you."[64]

A sampling of quotes from the 1922 edition were scattered throughout the 1975 edition, perhaps to resurrect some of the character which had been disappearing from recent editions. But this is an awkward device since the quotes are not integrated into the text but just sit here and there as amusing but insular epigraphs.

Elizabeth Post is also author of the current edition, the fourteenth, *Emily Post's Etiquette*, published in 1984 by Harper and Row. A huge new section, "Your Professional Life," incorporates what is often called "business etiquette" and which in previous editions received little attention. This section includes chapters on getting ahead in business, business clubs and associations, leaving your job, and traveling on business. This in-depth treatment of business issues is consistent with the modernization of *Etiquette*, which the fourteenth edition's dust jacket describes as "A Guide to Modern Manners."

Described by one critic as "blunt and homely"[65] compared to the Emily Post's original work, the Elizabeth Post 1984 edition continues the practice of reproducing quotes from the 1922 edition, as if to recapture past glories, but with no greater success than before.

The Elizabeth Post revisions are competent and comprehensive. They can be useful guides in coping with the rapidly changing social situations of recent decades. The one thing they lack is the true genius of Emily Post, whose skills as a literary stylist, combined with a playful sense of humor which matured to jaunty cantankerousness in her later writings, made her editions of *Etiquette* a true delight. Emily Post was a celebrity whose personality caught the American imagination in the Roaring Twenties and maintained that hold until her death.

PUBLICATION HISTORY

Etiquette in Society, in Business, in Politics, and at Home, by Emily Post. New York: Funk & Wagnalls, 1922. 627p.

Etiquette: The Blue Book of Social Usage, by Emily Post. New and enlarged ed. New York: Funk & Wagnalls, 1927. 692p.

Etiquette: The Blue Book of Social Usage, by Emily Post. New and enlarged ed. New York: Funk & Wagnalls, 1931. 740p.

Etiquette: The Blue Book of Social Usage, by Emily Post. Complete new ed., rewritten, revised, and reset. New York: Funk & Wagnalls, 1937. 877p.

Etiquette: War-Time Supplement, by Emily Post. New York: Funk and Wagnalls, 1942. 20p.

Etiquette: The Blue Book of Social Usage, by Emily Post. Complete new ed., rewritten, revised, and reset, including War-Time Supplement. New York: Funk & Wagnalls, 1942. 913p.

Etiquette: The Blue Book of Social Usage, by Emily Post. New York: Funk & Wagnalls, 1945. 654p.

Etiquette: The Blue Book of Social Usage, by Emily Post. 9th ed. New York: Funk & Wagnalls, 1955. 671p.

Etiquette: The Blue Book of Social Usage, by Emily Post. 10th ed. New York: Funk & Wagnalls, 1960. 671p.

Emily Post's Etiquette: The Blue Book of Social Usage, revised by Elizabeth L. Post. 11th rev. ed. New York: Funk & Wagnalls, 1965. 707p.

Emily Post's Etiquette, by Elizabeth L. Post. 12th rev. ed. New York: Funk & Wagnalls, 1969. 721p.

The New Emily Post's Etiquette, by Elizabeth L. Post. New York: Funk & Wagnalls, 1975. 978p.

Emily Post's Etiquette, by Elizabeth L. Post. 14th ed. New York: Harper & Row, 1984. 1,018p.

BIBLIOGRAPHY

Truly Emily Post, the only book-length biography of Post is her son Edwin's entertaining and loving tribute to a memorable personality. Owing to Edwin Post's sometimes overly respectful approach to his subject, other sources, especially the articles in the *Dictionary of American Biography* and *Notable American Women* are valuable for filling in some of the factual details of her life. Among commentators on *Etiquette,* Atherton and Wyatt evoke the book's initial impact. The front-page *New York Times* obituary did justice to one of New York' most celebrated citizens, skillfully summarizing and evaluating her distinguished career. A long standing institution is always ripe for iconoclastic attack, but among modern critics, Kaplan's thoughtful piece is the most balanced.

Ames, William E. "Post, Emily Price." In *Dictionary of American Biography, Supplement 6: 1956–1960,* edited by John A. Garraty, 514–15. New York: Charles Scribner's Sons, 1980.

Aresty, Esther B. *The Best Behavior: The Course of Good Manners from Antiquity to the Present as Seen Through Courtesy and Etiquette Books.* New York: Simon and Schuster, 1970.

Atherton, Gertrude. "A School for Better Manners in America." *The Literary Digest International Book Review* 1 (March, 1923): 10–11+.

Burrell, Martin. "Manners and Etiquette." *In Betwixt Heaven and Charing Cross,* 123–31. Toronto: Macmillan Company of Canada, 1928.

Carson, Gerald. *Polite Americans: A Wide-Angle View of Our More or Less Good Manners over 300 Years.* New York: William Morrow, 1966.

Cate, James L. "Keeping Posted." *University of Chicago Magazine* 64 (May/June, 1972): 24–34.

Dolson, Hildegarde. "Ask Mrs. Post." *Independent Woman* 20 (April, 1941): 103–104+. A condensed version appeared in *Reader's Digest 38* (April, 1941): 7–12.

Downs, Robert B. "Social Arbiter: Emily Post's *Etiquette: The Blue Book of Social Usage,* 1922." In *Famous American Books,* 266–73. New York: McGraw-Hill, 1971.

"Emily Post is Dead Here at 86; Writer Was Arbiter of Etiquette." *New York Times,* September 27, 1960, sec. 1, pp. 1, 37.

Harriman, Margaret Case. "Dear Mrs. Post." In *More Post Biographies,* edited by Joseph E. Drewry, 255–73. Athens, GA: University of Georgia Press, 1947. This was originally published in *The Saturday Evening Post* 209 (May 15, 1937): 18–19+.

Harris, Neil. "Post, Emily Price." In *Notable American Women, The Modern Period: A Biographical Dictionary,* edited by Barbara Sicherman and Carol Hurd Green, 554–56. Cambridge, MA: Belknap Press of Harvard University Press, 1980.

Hellman, Geoffrey T. "Onward and Upward with the Arts: The Waning Oomph of Mrs. Toplofty." *The New Yorker* 31 (June 18, 1955): 80–86.

Kaplan, Justin. "A Rose for Emily." *Harper's* 238 (March, 1969): 106–09.

Mencken, H. L. Review of Etiquette, by Emily Post. In *The American Mercury* 13 (February, 1928): 255.

O'Rourke, P. J. "Come Back, Mrs. Kindheart." *House and Garden* 157 (August, 1985): 18+.

Perkins, Jeanne. "Emily Post: America's Authority on Etiquette." *Life* 20 (May 6, 1946): 59–60+.

Post, Edwin. *Truly Emily Post.* New York: Funk and Wagnalls, 1961.

Post, Emily. "Any Fork Will Do." *Collier's* 83 (April 10, 1929): 21+.

———. "How I Came to Write About Etiquette." *Pictorial Review* 38 (October 1936): 4 +.

"Post, Emily." *Current Biography* (1941): 681–83.

Schlesinger, Arthur M. *Learning How to Behave: A Historical Study of American Etiquette Books.* New York: Macmillan, 1947.

Smith, Helena Huntington. "Profiles: Lady Chesterfield." *The New Yorker* 6 (August 16, 1930): 22–25.

Sypher, Wylie. "Mrs. Post, May I Present Mr. Eliot." *American Scholar* 54 (Spring, 1985): 250–52.

Wilson, Edmund. "Books of Etiquette and Emily Post." *In Classics and Commercials: A Literary Chronicle of the Forties*, 372–82. New York: Farrar, Straus, 1950. This is a revision of "Books

of Etiquette and Emily Post." *The New Yorker* 23 (July 19, 1947): 51–58.

Wyatt, Euphemia Van Rensselaer. "Courtesy First." *The Commonweal* 27 (November 26, 1937): 135–36.

NOTES

[1] Emily Post, "How I Came to Write about Etiquette," *Pictorial Review* 38 (October 1936): 4.

[2] Ibid.

[3] Ibid.

[4] Ibid.

[5] Ibid., 56.

[6] Richard Duffy, "Manners and Morals," introduction to *Etiquette* by Emily Post (New York: Funk & Wagnalls, 1922), ix.

[7] Ibid., xvi.

[8] Emily Post, *Etiquette in Society, in Business, in Politics, and at Home* (New York: Funk & Wagnalls, 1922), 3.

[9] Emily Post, "Any Fork Will Do," *Collier's* 83 (20 April 1929): 21.

[10] Emily Post, *Etiquette in Society*, 1922, iii.

[11] Ibid., 20

[12] Ibid., 28.

[13] Ibid., p. 33.

[14] Ibid., 60–61.

[15] Ibid., 65.

[16] Ibid, 288.

[17] Ibid., 289.

[18] Edwin Post, *Truly Emily Post* (New York: Funk & Wagnalls, 1961), 66.

[19] Emily Post, *Etiquette in Society*, 1922, 506.

[20] Ibid., 509.

[21] Edwin Post, *Truly Emily Post*, 211.

[22] Gerald Carson, *Polite Americans* (New York: William Morrow, 1966), 238.

[23] Edwin Post, *Truly Emily Post*, 213.

[24] Edmund Wilson, "Books of Etiquette and Emily Post," in *Classics and Commercials* (New York: Farrar, Straus, 1950), 374.

[25] Emily Post, *Etiquette in Society* 1922, 179–84.

[26] "Post, Emily," *Current Biography* (1941): 682.

[27] Hildegarde Dolson, "Ask Mrs. Post," *Independent Woman* 20 (April 1941): 104.

[28] Review of *Etiquette in Society, in Business, in Politics, and at Home*, by Emily Post, *Booklist* 19 (April 1923): 206.

[29] Gertrude Atherton, "A School for Better Manners in America," *The Literary Digest-International Book Review* 1 (March 1923): 10.

[30] Review of *Etiquette in Society, in Business, in Politics, and at Home*, by Emily Post, in *New York Tribune*, 2 September 1922, 7.

[31] Review of *Etiquette in Society, in Business, in Politics, and at Home*, by Emily Post, *The Literary Digest* 74 (19 August 1922): 33.

[32] Edwin Post, *Truly Emily Post*, 215.

[33] Margaret Case Harriman, "Dear Mrs. Post," in *More Post Biographies* (Athens, GA: University of Georgia Press, 1947), 263.

[34] Emily Post, "Any Fork Will Do," 21.

[35] Edwin Post, *Truly Emily Post*, 235–37.

[36] "Emily Post is Dead Here at 86,"*New York Times*, 27 September 1960, sec. 1, p. 1.

[37] Hildegarde Dolson, "Ask Mrs. Post," 103.

[38] Emily Post, *Etiquette* (New York: Funk & Wagnalls, 1927), 287.

[39] Emily Post, *Etiquette*: 1927, 646.

[40] Edwin Post, *Truly Emily Post*, 226.

[41] Review of *Etiquette: The Blue Book of Social Usage*, by Emily Post (1937), *Publishers Weekly* 132 (18 September 1937): 1102.

[42] Emily Post, *Etiquette* (New York: Funk & Wagnalls, 1937), 355.

[43] Ibid., 370.

[44] Ibid., 375.

[45] Ibid., 547.

[46] Ibid., 69.

[47] Euphemia van Rensselaer Wyatt, "Courtesy First," *The Commonweal* 27 (26 November 1937): 135.

[48] Review of *Etiquette: The Blue Book of Social Usage*, by Emily Post (1937), *The New York Times Book Review*, 10 October 1937, 23.

[49] Edwin Post, *Truly Emily Post*, 246.

[50] Emily Post, "Our Wounded Come Home: How to Treat Them," *Reader's Digest* 44 (February 1944): 72–73.

[51] Emily Post, *Etiquette: The Blue Book of Social Usage* (New York: Funk & Wagnalls, 1945), 637.

[52] "Obituary Notes: Emily Post,"*Publishers Weekly* 178 (3 October 1960): 41.

[53] Emily Post, *Etiquette: The Blue Book of Social Usage* (New York: Funk & Wagnalls, 1955), 176.

[54] Geoffrey T. Hellman, "The Waning Oomph of Mrs. Toplofty," *The New Yorker* 31 (18 June 1955): 87.

[55] "Emily Post is Dead Here at 86," p. 37.

[56] Emily Post, *Etiquette: The Blue Book of Social Usage* (New York: Funk & Wagnalls, 1960), 641.

[57] Elizabeth L. Post, *Emily Post's Etiquette*, 11th rev. ed. (New York: Funk & Wagnalls, 1965), iii.

[58] Jerome Beatty, Jr., review of *Emily Post's Etiquette*, by Elizabeth L. Post, *Saturday Review* 52 (15 February 1969): 22.

[59] Justin Kaplan, "A Rose for Emily," *Harper's* 238 (March 1969): 106–09.

[60] Emily Post, *Etiquette*, 1922, 8.

[61] Elizabeth L. Post, Emily Post's Etiquette, 12th rev. ed. (New York: Funk & Wagnalls, 1969), 10.

[62] Elizabeth L. Post, *The New Emily Post's Etiquette* (New York: Funk & Wagnalls, 1975), 917.

[63] Charles Bunge, review of *The New Emily Post's Etiquette*, by Elizabeth L. Post, *Wilson Library Bulletin* 49 (June 1975): 757.

[64] Post, *The New Emily Post's Etiquette*, 1975, 937.

[65] P.J. O'Rourke, "Come Back, Mrs. Kindheart," *House and Garden* 157 (August 1985): 19.

"Of Permanent Use and Usefulness": Granger's Index to Poetry

Milton H. Crouch

DEVELOPMENT AND HISTORY

Granger's Index to Poetry has been a standard reference work since its appearance in 1904 and the purpose of the index has remained substantially unchanged: "to assist the reader in identifying and locating poems or selections from poems which have appeared in the most generally accessible anthologies."[1] Every edition has been a long and heavy book. The first edition indexed 369 volumes and contained 30,000 titles; the second edition, 460 volumes and 50,000 titles; the third, 592 volumes and 75,000 titles. The most recent edition, the ninth, indexes 781 volumes containing 150,000 titles.

The index is the outgrowth of work by employees in the poetry department of McClurg's retail book store in Chicago who needed information to help customers locate poetry and short prose works. P.W. Coussents prepared the manuscript that was subsequently edited by Edith Granger, an employee assigned to McClurg's book publishing operation.[2] Little more about this famous index's obscure namesake has been preserved for posterity. By the time McClurg and Company terminated publishing activities in the early 1940s, *Granger's*, along with the Tarzan books and the Hopalong Cassidy books, had become one of the company's most important publications.[3] The Columbia University Press began editing and publishing the index in the early 1940s, and the second supplement, published in 1945, was the first of the series it has published. Columbia University Press shortened the title to *Granger's Index to Poetry and Recitations*.

Indexes

After 1945, some important changes were introduced. Recitations and all prose works were dropped from the listing, and the practice of having separate indexes for title and first lines ceased when the two indexes were combined into a single alphabetical list. A most important new feature was a subject index produced by Elizabeth J. Sherwood, which took the place of what had been termed an "Appendix" in earlier editions. These changes were made with the fourth edition, published in 1953, and arguably the watershed edition of the entire series. Combining the two major indexes (title and first line) eliminated duplication of entries and served to cut "out the paralysis over which index to begin on."[4]

Prior to editor Sherwood's subject index in the fourth edition, users needed to study titles grouped under broad subject categories: "Special Days," "Charades, Dialogues, Drills, etc.," "Noted Personages," "Temperance Selections." Poems concerning temperance were dropped from the third edition and a substantial new subject entry—"Choral Reading," listing 170 selections—was added. The index was expanded for the fifth edition and by the sixth poems were itemized under approximately 5,000 subject headings.

Subject indexing of poetry is difficult and the better the poem, the more difficult the classification under an arbitrary subject heading. William James Smith, editor of the sixth edition, wrote: "We have tried to avoid the more obvious pitfalls of subject arrangement, but we have included a number of somewhat doubtful subject classifications on the theory that the individual can make his own judgment as to the suitability of our suggestions."[5] One reviewer of the sixth edition found the subject index an anomaly and complained that the editors had placed Robert Frost's "The Road Not Taken," under "Roads."[6]

Expansion

Edith Granger intended for the index to prosper. The first short preface promised that future editions would index more anthologies and invited librarians to take an interest in the work. Both of *Granger's* publishers have used questionnaires to glean comments from reference librarians and both have responded to these suggestions.[7] In addition to requesting more complete subject indexing, librarians expressed the need for the index to include more contemporary poets and to expand coverage to include poetry in translation.

The third edition began to address these requests and indexed 35 titles by 14 of the best known contemporary poets. The sixth edition contained recent poetry written on such timely subjects as ecology and women's liberation. It also included a number of volumes devoted to Afro-American poetry. The seventh edition represented a major effort by the editors to include more contemporary poets. The number of anthologies carried over from previous editions was limited in order to include 128 new volumes of poetry.

With the eighth edition, a major effort was made to include more poems by Asian Americans, Chicanos, and Native Americans; an anthology of poems written by American prisoners was also included. The ninth edition, entitled *Columbia Granger's® Index to Poetry*, is perhaps more international than previous editions, indexing more than 50 collections of translated poetry. Its subject index leads users to English translations of hundreds of poems, including translations from Urdu, Hebrew, Gaelic, Yiddish, and Maori.

Major British and American poets have always been well represented. All major or minor poets included in Donald E. Stanford's *British Poets, 1914–1945* (Detroit: Gale Research, 1983) are found in the early editions of *Granger's*. Many winners of the Pulitzer Prize for poetry between 1922 and 1976 have been included in *Granger's* prior to receiving the prize and those few who were not included in an earlier edition are to be found in the very next supplement or new edition. The index enables users to trace the disappearance of minor poets from recently published anthologies and to identify the ever popular minor poets, such as John Greenleaf Whittier, Edwin Arlington Robinson, and James Whitcomb Riley.

Critical Reception

Granger's has received little critical attention, but an enthusiastic reviewer of the first edition helped establish its status as a classic reference work: "This may fairly be said to be an indispensable reference work, and one assured of permanent use and usefulness in large and small libraries."[8] The work reached its sixth edition before being reviewed by the American Library Association's *Reference and Subscription Books Reviews*.[9] Comments gleaned from brief reviews in library publications center on production and format concerns. For example, reviewers complain of narrow inside margins, small print, lack of thumb indexing guides (which disappeared with the publication of the seventh edition), and point out that heavier paper stock should be used for "Keys to Symbols," a frequently consulted section of the index.

The index has not had an exciting publication history. However, as one of the first indexes to composite books, it has been a major influence in the area of reference book publishing. The name *"Granger's"* has become synonymous with poetry indexing and is now a registered trademark. Two early examples of indexes intended to supplement Granger's are Herbert Bruncken's *Subject Index to Poetry; a Guide for Adult Readers* (Chicago: American Library Association, 1940) and John and Sara Brewton's *Index to Children's Poetry* (New York: H.W. Wilson, 1942). Herbert Hoffman compiled his index to Latin American poetry to serve as a non-English language complement to *Granger's*.[10] A new monographic series entitled *Poetry Index Annual*, published since 1982 by Poetry Index Press, Great Neck, New York, provides access to anthologized poetry which is not indexed elsewhere. It is in effect a supplement to *Granger's* since it functions as a kind of updating service between Granger's installments.

The latest edition of *Granger's* has been joined by a volume briefly reviewing each of the anthologies it indexes. William and Linda Katz's *The Columbia Granger's® Guide to Poetry Anthologies* groups the anthologies by type (e.g., Afro-American poetry, ballads and songs, children's poetry, Finnish poetry, holiday poetry, love poetry, Scottish poetry, vampire poetry) and describes the internal organization of each. The Katzes also comment on the overall quality of each anthology's contents and single out examples of quality and representative poems. This book should help

librarians whose budgets cannot support a full collection of the indexed anthologies decide which to buy.

Since 1904, *Granger's* has had ten editors. The illnesses and deaths of these men and women who have worked at the Columbia University Press are reported in various editions of the index. However, no information is given in any of the editions concerning Edith Granger. None of the major library publications have featured her or reported her death. Staff of the Chicago Public Library have been unable to locate information in indexes to local newspapers. We know from the prefaces to the first two editions that she completed university; we also know she initiated an index that has enabled thousands to locate needed poems and to learn from poets what it is like to be alive.

Although the history of its creator is unknown, the future of the index she created is assured. In 1991, the index will be released on CD-ROM. An inherent limitation of *Granger's* has always been the need to search titles or first lines by their first significant words but not by other words. A CD-ROM *Granger's* will allow new avenues of access to poems that will make *Granger's*, always the most useful of poetry indexes, even more useful and versatile. One feature that will enhance its usefulness is the inclusion of the full texts of 8,500 poems on the CD-ROM.[11] Whatever its medium, *Granger's* will continue to grow and evolve.

PUBLICATION HISTORY

An Index to Poetry and Recitations; Being a Practical Reference Manual for the Librarian, Teacher, Bookseller, Elocutionist, etc., edited by Edith Granger. Chicago: A. C. McClurg and Co., 1904. 970p.

Granger's Index to Poetry and Recitations; Being a Practical Reference Manual for the Librarian, Teacher, Bookseller, Elocutionist, etc., edited by Edith Granger. Revised and enlarged edition [2nd ed.]. Chicago: A. C. McClurg and Co., 1918. 1,059p.

A Supplement to Granger's Index (1919–1928). Chicago: A. C. McClurg and Co., 1929. 519p.

Granger's Index to Poetry and Recitations, edited by Helen Humphrey Bessey. 3rd ed., completely revised and enlarged. Chicago: A. C. McClurg and Co., 1940. 1,525p.

Granger's Index to Poetry and Recitations: Supplement, 1938–1944, edited by Elizabeth J. Sherwood and Gertrude Henderson. New York: Columbia University Press, 1945. 415p.

Granger's Index to Poetry, edited by Raymond J. Dixon. 4th ed., completely revised and enlarged, indexing anthologies published through December 31, 1950. New York: Columbia University Press, 1953. 1,832p.

Granger's Index to Poetry: Supplement to the Fourth Edition, edited by Raymond J. Dixon. Indexing anthologies published from January 1, 1951 to December 31, 1955. New York: Columbia University Press, 1957. 458p.

Granger's Index to Poetry, edited by William F. Bernhardt. 5th ed., completely revised and enlarged, indexing anthologies published through June 30, 1960. New York: Columbia University Press, 1962. 2,123p.

Granger's Index to Poetry: Supplement to the Fifth Edition, edited by William F. Bernhardt and Kathryn W. Sewny. Indexing anthologies published from July 1, 1960 to December 31, 1965. New York: Columbia University Press, 1967. 416p.

Granger's Index to Poetry, edited by William James Smith. 6th ed., completely revised and enlarged, indexing anthologies published through December 31, 1970. New York: Columbia University Press, 1973. 2,223p.

Granger's Index to Poetry, 1970–1977, edited by William James Smith. New York: Columbia University Press, 1978. 635p.

Granger's Index to Poetry, edited by William James Smith and William F. Bernhardt. 7th ed., indexing anthologies published from 1970 through 1981. New York: Columbia University Press, 1982. 1,329p.

Granger's®️ Index to Poetry, edited by William F. Bernhardt. 8th Edition, completely revised and enlarged, indexing anthologies published through June 30, 1985. New York: Columbia University Press, 1986. 2,014p.

The Columbia Granger's®️ Index to Poetry, edited by Edith P. Hazen, and Deborah J. Fryer. 9th ed., completely revised indexing anthologies published through June 30, 1989. New York: Columbia University Press, 1990. 2,082p.

BIBLIOGRAPHY

As noted, *Granger's* has received little critical or historical attention. The reviews listed below are the most significant. Baier offers historical information on A.C. McClurg and Co. Only time can tell whether or not a companion such as the Katzes' book becomes a standard for future editions of *Granger's*.

Baier, Andrew. "Book Wholesaler to the Nation." *Illinois Libraries* 47 (September, 1965): 665–69.

Breit, Harvey. "In and Out of Books." *New York Times,* April 26, 1953, sec. 7, p. 8.

Katz, William, and Linda Sternberg Katz. *The Columbia Granger's®️ Guide to Poetry Anthologies.* New York: Columbia University Press, 1991.

Review of *An Index to Poetry and Recitations; Being a Practical Reference Manual for the Librarian, Teacher, Bookseller, Elocutionist, etc.,* edited by Edith Granger (1904 ed.). *Library Journal* 29 (September, 1904): 489.

Review of *Granger's Index to Poetry,* 6th ed. *Booklist* 70 (April, 1974): 830.

Review of *Granger's Index to Poetry,* 6th ed. *Choice* 10 (January, 1974): 1698.

Tangorra, Joanne. "Granger's World of Poetry Comes to CD-ROM." *Publisher's Weekly* (June 7, 1991): 41.

NOTES

[1] William James Smith and William F. Bernhardt, "Preface," in *Granger's Index to Poetry,* 6th ed. (New York: Columbia University Press, 1973): v.

[2] Edith Granger, "Preface," in *An Index to Poetry and Recitations; Being a Practical Reference Manual for the Librarian, Teacher, Bookseller, Elocutionist, etc.,* (Chicago: McClurg and Co., 1904): 5.

[3] Andrew Baier, "Book Wholesaler to the Nation," *Illinois Libraries* 47 (September 1965): 666–67.

[4] Harvey Breit, "In and Out of Books," *New York Times,* 26 April 1953, sec. 7, p. 8.

[5] Smith and Bernhardt, v.

[6] Review of *Granger's Index to Poetry,* 6th ed., *Choice* 10 (January 1974): 1698.

[7] Helen Humphrey Bessey, "Preface," in *Granger's Index to Poetry and Recitations* (Chicago, McClurg and Co., 1940): vii.

[8] Review of *An Index to Poetry and Recitations; Being a Practical Reference Manual for the Librarian, Teacher, Bookseller, Elocutionist, etc.,* ed. by Edith Granger 1904, *Library Journal* 29 (September 1904): 489.

[9] Review of *Granger's Index to Poetry,* 6th ed., *Booklist* 70 (April 1974): 830.

[10] Herbert H. Hoffman, "Preface," in *Hoffman's Index to Poetry: European and Latin American Poetry in Anthologies* (Metuchen: N.J: Scarecrow Press, 1985): iv.

[11] Joanne Tangorra, "Granger's World of Poetry Comes to CD-ROM," *Publisher's Weekly* (7 June 1991): 41.

A Cornerstone of Musical Scholarship: *Grove's Dictionary of Music and Musicians*

William S. Brockman

DEVELOPMENT AND HISTORY

George Grove did not underestimate the size or the character of the audience for the first edition of his *Dictionary*; in the preface, he maintained that "this work is designed to supply a great and long acknowledged want . . . . It is designed for the use of Professional musicians and Amateurs alike."[1] The music industry had ballooned in the latter half of the nineteenth century, musical journals and societies had proliferated, and despite the nineteenth century's interest in encyclopedias and syntheses of knowledge, no one (in Great Britain, at least) had published anything like the *Dictionary*.

It has become commonplace to assert that the quality of British music during the nineteenth century was far inferior to that of the Continent.[2] Yet Great Britain's burgeoning economic power during the Victorian era created a mass market for music.[3] Higher incomes and an increase in leisure time offered people the means to seek and to afford entertainment. Theaters, music halls, and other venues proliferated. The building of railroads made travel rapid and painless, encouraging the development of seaside resorts (with accompanying theaters to provide evening entertainment), and providing work for an increasing number of itinerant musicians. Decennial censuses in Great Britain identified 11,200 music teachers in England and Wales in 1851; the number rose to 38,600 by 1901. An even more telling statistic identifies musicians per population of 10,000: 6.2 in 1851, and 12.1 in 1901.[4] Moreover, music was a status symbol for the middle class:

> In a society which was profoundly conscious of class yet offered chances of social mobility, it was necessary for the ambitious to recognize and exhibit appropriate symbols of aspiration and achievement. Some of the most potent badges were pinned to music, particularly in respectable settings: ownership of a piano; music lessons for daughters; attendance at the oratorio, the quintessentially Victorian socio-musical event; membership of a concert society, preferably exclusive like all good clubs; appearance at the theatre or ball, suitably clad and preferably bejewelled.[5]

George Grove

George Grove himself, even before he began compiling the *Dictionary*, played no small part in the creation of this world. Born August 13, 1820, in the London suburb of Clapham, the son of a fishmonger and venison dealer, Grove attended Clapham Grammar School from 1834 to 1835 and was apprenticed to civil engineer Alexander Gordon in Westminster in January 1836. He was admitted a graduate of the Institution of Civil Engineers on February 26, 1839, and traveled to Jamaica in 1841 and to Bermuda in 1843 to erect lighthouses. His engineering career developed steadily with his involvement in the construction of a railroad station at Chester from 1847 to 1848 and in the Britannia Tubular Bridge across the Menai straights in Wales from 1848 to 1850. Grove had always been an avid aficionado of music. Biographer Percy Young relates that in 1837 he "invested" the first guinea ever given to him in a piano score of the *Messiah*.[6] At about the same time, he began compiling the first of many commonplace books he was to keep throughout his life. These transcriptions of music that interested him served as his conservatory, the closest Grove ever approached to a formal study of music.

Grove's appointment as joint secretary of the Society of Arts in February 1850 could not have brought him to London at a more advantageous time. The Society was planning an exhibition "which could serve as a shop-window for British industry."[7] The Great Exhibition opened on May 1, 1851, in a newly constructed vast building of glass in Hyde Park, soon nicknamed "the Crystal Palace." In May 1852, Grove was appointed secretary to the Crystal Palace Company, which disassembled the entire structure and moved it to the London suburb of Sydenham where it remained until destroyed by fire in 1936.

From its opening on June 10, 1854, at which an orchestra of 1,700 vocalists and instrumentalists performed for the queen and prince consort, the Crystal Palace served as a major force in the popularization of music in London. On July 21, 1855, Grove offered the job of conductor of the Crystal Palace Band to German-born August Manns. Manns's Saturday Crystal Palace concerts along with Grove's program notes became a most significant force in the musical life of London in the ensuing decades: "the combination of Manns and Grove was to prove formidable, and, perhaps, the true generator of modern British music."[8]

Grove's Preparation for Editorship

In retrospect, one could see Grove's career over the next 20 years as a training ground for his work on the *Dictionary*. What Grove lacked in formal training in music and editing, he compensated for with hard work and judicious use of the plentiful acquaintances he had made in school and through his prominent position at the Crystal Palace. He became a central figure in London's musical life through his friendships with Clara Schumann and Johannes Brahms, and in his championing of the music of Franz Schubert and Robert Schumann at Crystal Palace concerts. He made one of the significant musical discoveries of the century when, on a trip with Arthur Sullivan to Vienna in 1867, he located the complete manuscript of Schubert's *Rosamunde* in a cupboard.

Grove was recommended through a mutual friend to edit A.P. Stanley's study of biblical geography, *Sinai and Palestine* (London: J. Murray, 1856). He edited William Smith's *Dictionary of the Bible* (London: J. Murray, 1860–63) after a trip in 1858 to Palestine and Egypt, and, also for Smith, *An Atlas of Ancient Geography, Biblical and Classical* (London: Murray, 1874). Grove's friendship with Alexander Macmillan and, by 1866, his established experience in editing earned him a position as an assistant editor at *Macmillan's Magazine*, one of the leading periodicals of the day. He became editor of *Macmillan's Magazine* in 1868.

The financial stability of the *Macmillan's* editorship allowed Grove to resign the Crystal Palace appointment in 1873 (although he continued for nearly the rest of his life to write its program notes). He was already making plans for the *Dictionary of Music and Musicians*. In January 1874, the Macmillan publishing firm issued a prospectus for a work intended to comprise two volumes: "Within [the last 25 years] music in England has made immense progress and the number of persons who attend concerts and practise music has very largely increased. It is no longer regarded as mere idle amusement, but has taken, or is taking, its right place beside the other arts, as an object of study and investigation."[9]

That music had become "an object of study and investigation" during the previous two or three decades is certainly no exaggeration. The year 1874 marked the formation of the Musical Association (now Royal Musical Association) and of the first publication of its annual *Proceedings*. More significant in demonstrating interest in the study of music was the spectacular proliferation of its treatment in periodical literature, both in magazines devoted to music (such as the *Musical Times and Singing Class Circular*, begun in 1844 and still published as *Musical Times*; its circulation in 1873 was 15,000) and in magazines of general interest, such as *Macmillan's* and *Fortnightly Review*.[10] These periodicals could count on not only a broad, but also a sophisticated, audience: "Readers must have had an awareness of past and present trends in music, besides technical knowledge and a real musical curiosity; otherwise, the printed music examples, considerations of formal symmetry and emotional meaning, and constant references to specific works, operas, opus numbers, and keys would have been meaningless."[11] Yet, while sophisticated, this was largely an audience of amateurs: "The image of the musical scholar in British life was not that of the professional musician, but rather of the gentleman amateur, best represented by the country clergyman quietly pursuing his own antiquarian interests, or by the semi-retired engineer or business man returning to an interest neglected since his youth."[12] Grove himself might have fit such a description. Seen from this perspective, he was the quintessentially appropriate editor of a musical reference work.

The First Edition

A letter dated July 29, 1877, from Grove to George Craik (a partner in the Macmillan firm) set out Grove's timetable for completing editorial work on the *Dictionary* at semiannual intervals from 1877 to December 1880.[13] The first separate unbound parts of the *Dictio-nary* were published throughout 1878. The first volume gathered parts I-IV, and was published in April 1879. Succeeding unbound parts appeared through 1889. These were gathered in volume 2 in 1880, volume 3 in 1883, and volume 4 in 1889. The full set was then reprinted with the index and an appendix in 1890.

What are some of the salient features of this first edition? First, the chronological barrier of the year 1450. It was not until years later that interest in music of the Middle Ages developed; so it was reasonable and not surprising for a latter-day Victorian work to set such a limit, just as it is not surprising to find Grove maintaining in the preface that "all investigations into the music of barbarous nations have been avoided, unless they have some direct bearing on European music."[14] Grove similarly made clear that an English dictionary should pay special attention to English music and musicians. The scope of the *Dictionary* in these and in other areas expanded considerably in succeeding editions.

Articles in the *Dictionary* ranged in length from several sentences to dozens of pages. A majority of the articles were biographies of composers, performers, publishers, and instrument makers. Those of major composers included bibliographies and lists of compositions. Other articles covered societies; instruments; ethnic musics of Europe (such as "Welsh Music"); musical works with distinctive titles (such as "Messiah"); forms of composition ("Sonata"); theory ("Key"); schools, academies, and conservatories; and terms ("Sharp"). Other articles were broad in scope and not easily classified, such as "Schools of Composition," "Musical Periodicals," or "Musical Libraries." Grove himself wrote three major biographical articles, those on Beethoven, Mendelssohn, and Schubert. Illustrations, including diagrams, music, and engraved portraits, were plentiful. The index volume was a significant feature that succeeding editions dropped; with it was a catalog of articles contributed by each writer, a feature also since dropped.

Grove was concerned that the writing style be "anxiously divested of technicality."[15] Certainly, as in the article on "Form," writers of technical articles had to presume a certain shared vocabulary between themselves and readers; but most held to Grove's ideal. In fact, though the style was divested of technicality it was often clothed in pathos, as in Grove's own description of Schubert on his deathbed: "Poor fellow! no wonder he was so depressed! everything was against him, his weakness, his poverty, his dreary house, the long lonely hours, the cheerless future . . ."

Critical reaction to the *Dictionary* was, on the whole, enthusiastic. Long reviews appeared in the leading periodicals.[16] Several harped on the profusion of minor errors which even Grove acknowledged in the preface to the first volume.[17] To remedy these, and to supplement some important material in the first half of the alphabet on which the *Dictionary* had skimped when it was still being planned at two volumes, the fourth volume included an appendix of some 300 pages giving corrections, supplemental material, and additional articles. Grove was faulted for the disproportionate length of some of the biographical articles.[18] The article on Mendelssohn stretched to over 60 pages, longer even than the Beethoven article at 50 pages. A. Maczewski's article on Bach was only 5 pages in length, and his article on Brahms—although Maczewski asserted he was "one of the greatest living German composers"—only 2.

The *Dictionary* made good use both of fledgling contributors and of established scholars. There were 118 in all, including Grove, by far the most prolific. Hubert Parry had studied music at Oxford and piano with Edward Dannreuther; he was to become one of the major figures of late-Victorian and Edwardian musical life, succeeding Grove as director of the Royal College of Music, and becoming professor at Oxford and president of the Musical Association. William Barclay Squire's article on "Music Libraries" presaged his appointment to a post in the Department of Printed Books at the British Museum. J.A. Fuller Maitland became music critic for *The Times*, and edited the appendix to the first edition of the *Dictionary* and the entire second edition. Edward Hopkins ("Organ"); A.J. Hipkins ("Pianoforte," "Harpsichord," "Musical Instruments, Collections of"); and Carl Ferdinand Pohl, librarian of the Gesellschaft der Musikfreunde in Vienna ("Mozart," "Haydn"), all contributed articles in their areas of established expertise. W.H. Husk, librarian of the Sacred Harmonic Society, was second only to Grove himself in number of articles contributed. William S. Rockstro, contributor of major articles on "Mass," "Notation," "Opera," "Orchestra," and "Schools of Composition," was a successful teacher and arranger in London, but did not publish his biographies of Handel, Mendelssohn, and Jenny Lind and his works on music history and theory until after his Grove contributions, when he was well into his fifties. Women, such as Mrs. Walter Carr, Mrs. Julian Marshall, Miss Middleton, and Mrs. Edmond Wodehouse (compiler of the index) contributed significant portions of the *Dictionary*.

Grove's *Dictionary* was the first of the modern generation of musical reference works. Such encyclopedic compilations are conservative in recognizing the maturity of a discipline—a maturity that is able to sum itself up and to present itself with confidence. They are also forward-looking in providing a springboard from which the discipline can leap. As the first parts of the *Dictionary* were appearing, Hugo Riemann in Germany was publishing the first edition of what has become through successive editions an equally venerable work—his *Musik-Lexikon* (Leipzig: Verlag des Bibliographischen Instituts, 1882). Robert Eitner's *Biographisch-bibliographisches Quellen-Lexikon der Musiker und Musikgelehrten* (Leipzig: Breitkopf & Härtel, 1900–1904), whose short biographies and detailed lists of published works and manuscripts established primary bibliographical and source material in Europe from the Middle Ages to the mid-nineteenth century, became an invaluable complement to succeeding editions of the *Dictionary*. In the United States, Theodore Baker published his *Dictionary of Musical Terms* in 1895 and his *Biographical Dictionary of Musicians* in 1900 (both New York: G. Schirmer). The former has been reprinted numerous times, and the latter has been revised and expanded by Nicolas Slonimsky through an eighth edition due in late 1991 or early 1992.

In 1883, Grove left *Macmillan's* to become director of the newly formed Royal College of Music, and remained in the position until 1894. He continued to gather material for a new edition of the *Dictionary* until his death on May 28, 1900.

J.A. Fuller Maitland

J.A. Fuller Maitland assumed the editorship of the second edition. Five volumes were published from 1904 to 1910. Fuller Maitland integrated the articles and corrections from the appendix to the first edition, added Grove's revisions to the three major biographies, and inserted bracketed additions into many of the original articles. Whereas the first edition had often drawn without attribution on biographical material from other works, particularly Fétis' *Biographie universelle*, the second edition credited such borrowings at the ends of articles. In accord with their subjects' importance, the Bach and Brahms articles were enlarged. Fuller Maitland's significant changes included enlarging the scope to include music of the Middle Ages and of selected American musicians and societies, adding cross-references to the body of the text, and eliminating the index. A review of the first volume found it "not merely a revision of the Grove Dictionary but the beginning of a new dictionary."[19]

Recognition of the significance of American music (including both the United States and Canada) came with the publication in 1920 of the *American Supplement*. Its editor was Waldo Selden Pratt, a theologian, organist, and music historian. The novelty of such a focus on a land in which music was seen less as a succession of the compositions of major composers but more as an intrinsic part of society led the editors to provide an unusual structure for the work. A "Historical Introduction with Chronological Register of Names" occupying the first quarter of the volume was organized chronologically into sections giving biographical data on 1,700 composers, performers, publishers, and other individuals of musical importance, and was interspersed with short narratives summarizing not only musical, but also social, political, and economical history. The main body of the *Supplement*, arranged in alphabetical order, gave fuller treatment of some 700 of the names, served as an index to the others, and included specialized articles, such as "Orchestras," which treated their subjects from an American point of view. The *Supplement* also served to update the second edition of *Grove* through its inclusion of some 100 updated articles. Pratt went on to compile what was originally planned as a one-volume abridgement of the second edition and its supplement, but actually became a separate work in its own right, *The New Encyclopedia of Music and Musicians* (New York: Macmillan, 1924).

Henry Cope Colles

Henry Cope Colles succeeded Fuller Maitland as music editor of *The Times* in 1911, and became editor of the third edition of *Grove*, published from 1927 to 1928. Colles continued to employ the *Dictionary*'s original text, but with some 50 years having intervened since the publication of the first parts of the first edition, he found it necessary to revise substantially or to replace many of the articles. Grove's own articles on Beethoven, Mendelssohn, and Schubert remained, albeit with supplementary footnotes.[20] A number of the new contributors, such as Eric Blom, Edward Dent, Alfred Einstein, E.H. Fellowes, Anselm Hughes, and Oscar Sonneck, were to become some of the century's major musicological figures. Illustrations included 96 plates, some in color. The third edition included the *American Supplement*, reprinted without revision from its 1920 version, but with an appendix which updated and added articles.

This third edition was reprinted numerous times, sometimes with minor revisions, well into the 1940s. A fourth edition was published in London in 1940, but revisions consisted primarily in the addition of dates of death and of bibliographical references. With irony, the editor acknowledged the beneficial proximity in England of such scholars as Egon Wellesz, Karl Geiringer, Hans Redlich, and Alfred Loewenberg who had fled the Holocaust.[21] The most significant addition to *Grove* during this time was the *Supplementary Volume* dated 1940, whose title page in the New York imprint identified it as part of the third edition, and in the London imprint as part of the fourth edition. It added many articles and updated biographies and lists of compositions. Articles in the supplement on "Broadcasting" and "Twelve Note Music" show *Grove* catching up with the twentieth century. Its short article on "Jazz" was regressive at best ("unrestrained Corybantic frenzy alternating with passive hopeless melancholy"), but undermined its derision by listing the major composers whom jazz had influenced—Igor Stravinsky, Paul Hindemith, Darius Milhaud, Ernst Krenek, Kurt Weill, and Constant Lambert.

The irregular publication of the *Supplementary Volume* signalled an uncertainty (undoubtedly influenced by the war) as to the direction of *Grove*. A. Hyatt King seized upon this uncertainty in a 1946 article which attacked the fourth edition and the *Supplementary Volume* for inaccuracies, but most importantly for the disproportionate amount of space allotted to Beethoven, Mozart, Haydn, Schubert, Mendelssohn, Schumann, Weber, and Wagner, "a legacy from Grove's own predilection."[22] These sentiments undoubtedly influenced Eric Blom's extensive revision and expansion to nine volumes of *Grove* for its fifth edition in 1954, which Macmillan of

London, due to the severing of its relationship with its American office, published in New York through St. Martin's Press.

Eric Blom

Blom, a critic and editor, had published in 1946 *Everyman's Dictionary of Music* (London: Dent), which, through successive editions into the 1970s, continued to be a most valuable, concise, and popular reference work. His elegant and detailed preface shows the care he took in the selection of articles, the treatment of geographical names, the transliteration of Russian words, the choice of terminology, and the physical appearance of the text. Negotiating between the amateurs and the increasingly influential musicologists, Blom addressed the fifth edition to "a user who possesses a general musical knowledge, or hopes to acquire one."[23] In all, half of the fifth edition was completely new material. The rest (including articles by original contributors Sir Hubert Parry and William S. Rockstro) was thoroughly revised. In striving for balance, one of Blom's most dramatic steps was to replace Grove's venerable articles on Beethoven, Mendelssohn, and Schubert with shorter, updated versions.[24] The "Jazz" article, expanded to 6 pages, was contributed by French jazz critic Hugues Panassié. New was a massive (some 240 pages) article by several contributors on "Folk Music." Cross-references were plentiful. Bibliographies were greatly expanded and typeset in a manner that distinguished them easily from the text; yet, citations were often scanty, and sometimes inaccurate. For the first time *Grove* took a serious interest in non-Western material in the form of surveys (such as "Arabian music") and in more specific articles on theoreticians, composers, and instruments.

The fifth edition became notorious for touting its British origin; Blom's preface maintained that "though Grove gives information on an international scale, it is in the first place an English work."[25] This national bias which developed from Blom's aversion to German-trained American musicologists was to work against his favor, particularly with the publication by 1954 of the first three volumes of the West German *Die Musik in Geschichte und Gegenwart* (edited by Friedrich Blume [Kassel: Bärenreiter-Verlag, 1949–86]; abbreviated as *MGG*), which rapidly became recognized as the major scholarly reference work in music. Any evaluation of *Grove* of necessity compared it to *MGG*, usually to *Grove's* detriment. In an editorial in *The Musical Quarterly*, Paul Henry Lang complained of *Grove's* "somewhat belligerent British bias that is very different from the engaging parochialism of the old edition."[26] A review in *Notes* had similar objections, and concluded that *MGG* "is a far sounder publication on all counts."[27] In a direct tabular comparison of a selection of articles from the two works, A. Hyatt King found *MGG* to be more thorough in its coverage of historical topics, but *Grove* to be better in coverage of the twentieth century.[28]

The prominence of *Grove* and the appearance of other comprehensive works with which it could be compared made tempting the search for errors and omissions in its text. *Musical Times* published several hundred of these, collected from contributors, not long after the publication of the fifth edition.[29] To correct these, and to update and add articles, Blom compiled material for a *Supplementary Volume* which was assembled by Denis Stevens in 1961 two years after Blom's death.

Stanley Sadie

Valid criticism of the fifth edition and the comparatively esoteric nature of *MGG* (not to mention its inaccessibility for those unable to read German) left an open field for a new *Grove*. Macmillan engaged scholar and critic Stanley Sadie, *Musical Times* editor and author of, among other works, *Mozart* (London: Calder and Boyars, 1965), *Handel* (London: J. Calder, 1966), and *Beethoven* (London: Faber and Faber, 1967). Sadie set out in 1969 to

develop an entirely new work. He established a panel of consulting editors, each of whom was responsible for outlining a given topical area and for recruiting contributors. Seven national advisors were each responsible for a given geographical part of the world. In an article published in 1975 that whetted appetites for a work that did not appear until five years later, Sadie announced a rigorous attempt "to set ourselves a series of objectives and standards that will make the dictionary as useful as possible within itself." Furthermore, "it will not share the xenophobia of *Grove* 5."[30]

The *New Grove Dictionary of Music and Musicians*, published in 1980 by Macmillan in London and two subsidiaries, Grove's Dictionaries of Music in New York and Peninsula Publishers in Hong Kong, reflected not only new standards but also the availability of a prodigious amount of additional information made available through the intensive efforts of scholars within the varied branches of musicology that have flourished through the twentieth century. The thousands of biographies in Riemann's and Baker's works, the identification of manuscript and printed original sources in the volumes of the *RISM* (*Répertoire international des sources musicales*, or *International Inventory of Musical Sources*) series, and the establishment of terminology in dictionaries such as the *Harvard Dictionary of Music* (edited by Willi Apel [Cambridge, MA: Harvard University Press, 1944]) indicated a breadth of material that was unavailable in the 1880s. Moreover, the growth of the field of ethnomusicology and the academic legitimatization of popular culture involved disciplines that had henceforth had no place in musical studies.

The New Grove could not reasonably be compared with earlier editions. In size alone, its 22,500 articles in 20 volumes made it more than twice as large as even the fifth edition. The nearly 2,500 contributors included most of the premier scholars throughout the world. Thirty-six percent of these were American, 20 percent were British, and 12 percent were German.[31] More than half the articles (over 11,000) were devoted to composers; those for the Viennese masters are nearly as long as George Grove's original essays. Other persons to whom it devoted individual entries include performers, musicologists, critics, librettists, dancers, patrons, publishers and printers, and instrument makers. Plentiful black and white illustrations were adequate to the task of showing persons, performance on instruments, and manuscripts. Of particular interest to librarians and researchers were extended articles supplemented by extensive lists on the materials and process of research—"Dictionaries and Encyclopedias," "Editions," "Libraries," "Periodicals," and "Sources-Manuscript."[32] As a dictionary, *The New Grove* gave definitions for musical terminology. As a history, it covered genres and forms. As an encyclopedia, it explored broad issues in a range of survey articles.

One of *The New Grove*'s most notable features was the attention it gave to music on an international scale. Hundreds of articles surveyed the musics of countries and regions of the world, defined terms, examined instruments, and offered biographies from non-Western cultures. The articles on individual countries generally drew a distinction between "Art" music and "Folk" music. In the last volume of *The New Grove* was an extensive index of ethnomusicological topics.

Sadie and his staff paid extraordinary attention to the physical format of *The New Grove*. The introduction expanded on Blom's with an even more detailed presentation of alphabetization, usage, and other items of format. Virtually every biography included references, and, in the case of composers, work lists. Although (especially in the case of major figures) these extended to hundreds of listings, the rigorous standards for style and the carefully planned typographical format eased their use.

Critical Reception of The New Grove

Reviewers of *The New Grove* tempered near-unanimous praise with several recurring complaints. The increased space devoted to popular music and jazz was still inadequate.[33] Moreover, reviewers criticized the lack of space devoted to American music; Michael Tilson Thomas, for instance, regretted that "in general, American music takes a back seat."[34] With electrical sound recording available in one form or another since the 1920s, *The New Grove* was faulted for its omission of thorough discographies, particularly in areas such as jazz or non-Western music in which standard musical notation is of limited use.[35] A more cutting criticism was that *Grove* had abandoned its traditional audience of learned amateurs for a more select and literate coterie of musicologists.[36] A review essay by Leon Botstein brings to the fore this change in audience: "The *New Grove* is a monument to the fact that while the study of music has become more professionalized, the audience for music has suffered from waning passion and sophistication."[37]

Some of these criticisms undoubtedly spurred the well-tuned corporate editorial apparatus created for *The New Grove* to continue work on offshoots which in their own specialized areas have dwarfed the parent work. *The New Grove Dictionary of Musical Instruments*, also under Sadie's direction, appeared in 1984. Its articles included some 10,000 non-Western instruments and delved into great detail regarding topics treated more briefly in *The New Grove* ("Violin," for example, extended to over 35 pages with a bibliography of several pages). *The New Grove Dictionary of American Music* (1986) traversed a region that the *American Supplement* had only peered at from afar—"a different cultural model, of a more pluralistic character than that of Europe, and without the same foundation in ecclesiastical, aristocratic, and state patronage."[38] Sadie drew as co-editor for this work noted American musicologist H. Wiley Hitchcock. Criticism of scanty coverage of jazz in the *American* volume presaged *The New Grove Dictionary of Jazz* (1988), edited by Barry Kernfeld.[39] *Jazz* applied the critical vocabulary and rigorous historical standards of *The New Grove* itself to a music that previously had been served primarily by an anecdotal literature, and employed extensive discographies in the same way that *The New Grove* supplemented articles with bibliographies and lists of compositions.

Other Grove projects are presently underway.[40] Most notable is a four-volume *New Grove Dictionary of Opera* edited by Sadie and scheduled for publication in late 1991. Most of its articles on major composers will be newly written, and it will include nearly 2,000 entries on individual operas, as well as new articles on singers, librettists, and librettos. Copublished with W.W. Norton in New York are more modest spinoffs of *The New Grove*. The *Grove Concise Dictionary of Music* (London: Macmillan Press, 1988; in the United States as *The Norton/Grove Concise Encyclopedia of Music* [New York: W.W. Norton, 1988]) is a one-volume abridgement and condensation of its parent volume which, in deference to an audience of students and listeners, includes articles for individual works. Some two dozen volumes in the *Composer Biography Series*, such as *The New Grove Mozart* (London: Macmillan, 1982; New York: W.W. Norton, 1983), extract, revise, update, and index articles from the parent volume. Volumes in the *Handbooks in Music Series* derive in varying degrees from *The New Grove*; these include the *History of Opera*, edited by

Stanley Sadie, (Basingstoke: Macmillan, 1989; New York: Norton, 1990), and *Music Printing and Publishing*, edited by Sadie and D.W. Krummel (Basingstoke: Macmillan; New York: Norton, 1990). In Japan, the Kodansha publishing firm is translating *The New Grove* into Japanese.[41] A new edition of *Grove* itself is presently "an active possibility . . . but no firm plans are made as yet."[42]

Both George Grove and Stanley Sadie saw their work as being all-inclusive. *Grove's Dictionary* covered "all the points . . . on which those interested in the Art, and alive to its many and far-reaching associations, can desire to be informed."[43] *The New Grove* "seeks to discuss everything that can be reckoned to bear on music in history and on present-day musical life."[44] Rather than a progression of more fully developed editions, the Grove dictionaries should be seen as a series of individual works sharing a common heritage. Each was a product, not only of its editors and contributors, but also of its time. The availability of the world's music through broadcasting and recording, the presence of *MGG* and other reference works, the increasing sophistication of musicology, the upheaval of the Second World War, and the Victorian confidence of a musical amateur were only some of the social and intellectual factors that determined the substance of the various Groves. Taken together, the editions and their derived works nevertheless have been a collective cornerstone of musical scholarship— not the whole building, certainly, but an integral part within which the edifice has been summarized and upon which it has been built.

PUBLICATION HISTORY

A Dictionary of Music and Musicians (A.D. 1450–1889) by Eminent Writers, English and Foreign, edited by Sir George Grove with Appendix edited by J.A. Fuller Maitland and Index by Mrs. Edmond Wodehouse. London: Macmillan; New York: Macmillan,

1879–1889, 1890. 4 vols. and index. Reprinted 1890–1898, 1900; Philadelphia: T. Presser, 189–?.

Grove's Dictionary of Music and Musicians, edited by J.A. Fuller Maitland. [2nd ed.] London: Macmillan; New York: Macmillan,

1904–1910. 5 vols. Reprinted 1911; Philadelphia: T. Presser, 1916.

Grove's Dictionary of Music and Musicians: American Supplement, edited by Waldo Selden Pratt; associate editor, Charles N. Boyd. New York: Macmillan, 1920. 412p.

Grove's Dictionary of Music and Musicians, edited by H.C. Colles. 3rd ed. London: Macmillan; New York: Macmillan, 1927–1928. 5 vols. Reprinted 1929, 1932, 1948.

Grove's Dictionary of Music and Musicians: American Supplement, edited by Waldo Selden Pratt; associate editor, Charles N. Boyd. New ed. New York: Macmillan, 1928. 438p. Reprinted 1935.

Grove's Dictionary of Music and Musicians, edited by H.C. Colles. 4th ed. London: Macmillan, 1940. 5 vols.

Grove's Dictionary of Music and Musicians: Supplementary Volume, edited by H.C. Colles. London: Macmillan; New York: Macmillan, 1940. 688p.

Grove's Dictionary of Music and Musicians, edited by Eric Blom. 5th ed. London: Macmillan; New York: St. Martin's Press, 1954. 9 vols. Reprinted 1961.

Grove's Dictionary of Music and Musicians: Supplementary Volume to the Fifth Edition, edited by Eric Blom; associate editor, Denis Stevens. London: Macmillan; New York: St. Martin's Press, 1961. 493p.

The New Grove Dictionary of Music and Musicians, edited by Stanley Sadie. London: Macmillan Publishers; Washington, DC: Grove's Dictionaries of Music; Hong Kong: Peninsula Publishers, 1980. 20 vols.

The New Grove Dictionary of Musical Instruments, edited by Stanley Sadie. London: Macmillan Press; New York: Grove's Dictionaries of Music, 1984. 3 vols.

The New Grove Dictionary of American Music, edited by H. Wiley Hitchcock and Stanley Sadie. London: Macmillan Press; New York: Grove's Dictionaries of Music, 1986. 4 vols.

The New Grove Dictionary of Jazz, edited by Barry Kernfeld. London: Macmillan Press; New York: Grove's Dictionaries of Music, 1988. 2 vols.

The New Grove Dictionary of Opera, edited by Stanley Sadie. Forthcoming.

BIBLIOGRAPHY

The following is a selective list of works that examine individual *Grove* dictionaries or that offer background material on the development of the first edition. Percy Young's biography is invaluable in establishing the facts of George Grove's life and the details of publication of the *Dictionary*. Of special importance are articles by editors Blom, Sadie, and Hitchcock which set out their intentions. Peggy Daub's article in *Reference Services Review* is a history of the publication of the successive editions which benefits from her editorial involvement with the *New Grove* staff. *Encore* is a newsletter distributed to purchasers of *The New Grove*; it features articles on performers and on publishing activities of the Grove organization. Highly useful in evaluating changes between editions and in gauging overall response are reviews.

While these have not been included in the bibliography, an attempt has been made to cite in the endnotes those that are most significant.

Blom, Eric. "Grove V: A Task of Restoration." *Musical Times* 95 (June, 1954): 300–03.

Daub, Peggy. "*Grove's Dictionary of Music and Musicians*: From George Grove to the 'New Grove'." *Reference Services Review* 10 (Fall, 1982): 15–22.

Duckles, Vincent. "Musicology." In *The Romantic Age, 1800–1914*, edited by Nicholas Temperley, 483–502. Athlone History of Music in Great Britain, vol. 5. London: Athlone Press, 1981.

Ehrlich, Cyril. *The Music Profession in Britain since the Eighteenth Century: A Social History*. Oxford: Clarendon Press, 1985.

Encore. The Grove Music Society. v. 1-, March 1986–. New York: Grove's Dictionaries of Music.

Giddens, Gary. "The Grove of Academe." *Village Voice* 32 (January 13, 1987): 75–76.

Graves, Charles L. *The Life and Letters of Sir George Grove, C.B.* London: Macmillan; New York: Macmillan, 1903.

"Grove's Dictionary of Music and Musicians (Fifth Edition)." *Musical Times* 96 (November, 1955): 591–96; (December, 1955): 643–51.

Hitchcock, H. Wiley. "On the Path to the U.S. Grove." *Notes* 41 (March, 1985): 467–70.

Howes, Frank, and Dyneley Hussey. "Grove's Dictionary." *Music and Letters* 9 (April, 1928): 98–110; (July, 1928): 195–210.

King, A. Hyatt. "Grove V and MGG." *Monthly Musical Record* 85 (June 1955): 115–19; (July-August, 1955): 152–57; (September, 1955): 183–85.

King, A. Hyatt. "Grove: Some Suggestions and Reflections." *Monthly Musical Record* 76 (June, 1946): 99–102; (July-August, 1946): 132–34.

Langley, Leanne. "The Musical Press in Nineteenth-Century England." *Notes* 46 (March, 1990): 583–92.

"New $1900 Grove Music Dictionary to be Distributed by St. Martin's." *Publishers Weekly* 218 (November 14, 1980): 40, 42.

O'Meara, Eva Judd. "Marginal Notes to Grove's Dictionary." *Music Library Association Notes* no. 1 (1934):1–7.

Parry, Ann. "The Grove Years 1868–1883: A 'new look' for *Macmillan's Magazine?*" *Victorian Periodicals Review* 19 (Winter, 1986):149–56.

Sadie, Stanley. "Ethnomusicology and the New Grove." *Ethnomusicology* 23 (January, 1979): 95–102.

Sadie, Stanley. "The New Grove." *Notes* 32 (December, 1975): 259–68.

Stevenson, Robert. "The Americas in European Music Encyclopedias." *Inter-American Music Review* 3 (Spring-Summer, 1981): 159–207.

Thompson, Kenneth L. "Grove and Dates." *Musical Times* 104 (July, 1963): 481–84.

Young, Percy M. *George Grove, 1820–1900: A Biography.* Washington, DC: Grove's Dictionaries of Music, 1980.

NOTES

[1] "Preface," in *A Dictionary of Music and Musicians (A.D. 1450–1889) by Eminent Writers, English and Foreign,* ed. by Sir George Grove with Appendix ed. by J.A. Fuller Maitland and Index by Mrs. Edmond Wodehouse (London: Macmillan; New York: Macmillan, 1879–89, 1890), v.

[2] See, for example, H.C. Colles, *The Oxford History of Music, Vol. VII: Symphony and Drama, 1850–1900* (London: Oxford University Press, 1934), p. 445: "While the Continent was reaping its rich harvest of music, and incidentally exporting it across the channel, English music was represented only by some rather thin sowings in a soil, rich enough indeed, but very poorly tilled."

[3] Cyril Ehrlich, *The Music Profession in Britain since the Eighteenth Century: A Social History* (Oxford: Clarendon Press, 1985), 54–59.

[4] Ibid., 236.

[5] Ibid., 68.

[6] Percy M. Young, *George Grove, 1820–1900: A Biography* (Washington, DC: Grove's Dictionaries of Music, 1980), 28.

[7] Ibid., 52.

[8] Ibid., 64.

[9] Charles L. Graves, *The Life and Letters of Sir George Grove, C.B.* (London: Macmillan; New York: Macmillan, 1903), 205–06.

[10] Leanne Langley, "The Musical Press in Nineteenth-Century England," *Notes* 46 (March 1990): 585–86.

[11] Ibid., 587.

[12] Vincent Duckles, "Musicology," in *The Romantic Age, 1800–1914,* ed. by Nicholas Temperley. Athlone History of Music in Britain, vol. 5. (London: Athlone Press, 1981), 483.

[13] Young, 140–41. Also in the letter, Grove emphasizes the time needed for the project—in terms with which any editor can sympathize: "To drive a team of contributors half of whom are amateurs, and half can get 3 times the pay we can give them elsewhere, takes a frightful amount of goading and coaxing and correspondence: and the editing and correcting and checking and completing—as I feel bound to do it—is a matter of great labour and *incessant* thought and occupation."

[14] "Preface," *Dictionary,* vi.

[15] Ibid., v.

[16] These included *Edinburgh Review* 153 (January 1881): 212–40; *Quarterly Review* 148 (July 1879): 39–53; and *Temple Bar* 64 (April 1882): 541–56.

[17] "The body of the dictionary absolutely swarms with mistakes," *Athenaeum* 3221 (20 July 1889): 106.

[18] "What it has wanted has been a stronger guiding hand, a general and comprehensive editing," review in *Edinburgh Review* 153 (January 1881): 239.

[19] George P. Upton, review of the second edition of *Grove, Dial* 38 (May 1905): 311.

[20] Frank Howes and Dyneley Hussey look askance at "the Mendelssohn article, which stands a huge monument to Victorian musical taste, like a sort of Albert Memorial in the very middle of the book," in *Music and Letters* 9 (July 1928): 195.

[21] "Preface," in *Grove's Dictionary of Music and Musicians*, ed. by H.C. Colles, 4th ed. (London: Macmillan, 1940), v.

[22] A. Hyatt King, "'Grove': Some Suggestions and Reflections," *Monthly Musical Record* 76 (July-August 1946): 132.

[23] "Preface," *Grove's Dictionary of Music and Musicians*, ed. by Eric Blom, 5th ed. (London: Macmillan; New York: St. Martin's Press, 1954), v.

[24] The original essays were reprinted in a separate volume: George Grove, *Beethoven, Schubert, Mendelssohn* (London: Macmillan, 1951).

[25] "Preface," *Grove's Dictionary*, 5th Ed., vi.

[26] Paul Henry Lang, *Musical Quarterly* 41 (April 1955): 216.

[27] Richard S. Hill, *Notes* 12 (December 1954): 91.

[28] A. Hyatt King, *Monthly Musical Record* 85 (July-August 1955): 183–84.

[29] "Grove's Dictionary of Music and Musicians (Fifth Edition)," *Musical Times* 96 (November 1955): 591–96; (December 1955): 643–51.

[30] Stanley Sadie, "The New Grove," *Notes* 32 (December 1975): 260–63.

[31] Peggy Daub, "*Grove's Dictionary of Music and Musicians*: From George Grove to the 'New Grove'," *Reference Services Review* 10 (Fall 1982): 20.

[32] See Ann Basart, "An Index to the Manuscripts in the *New Grove* Articles on 'Sources'," *Cum Notis Variorum* nos. 117–34 (November 1987—July-August 1989).

[33] See, for example, reviews by Billy Taylor regarding jazz and by Paul Wittke regarding American musical theater in *Musical Quarterly* 68 (April 1982): 271–73 and 274–82; the entire issue is devoted to individual reviews of *The New Grove*.

[34] Michael Tilson Thomas, *Notes* 38 (September 1981): 55; Robert Stevenson examines in detail *The New Grove*'s coverage of North and South American composers in "The Americas in European Music Encyclopedias," *Inter-American Music Review* 3 (Spring-Summer 1981): 159–207.

[35] Joshua Rifkin, review of *The New Grove, Journal of the American Musicological Society* 35 (Spring 1982): 188.

[36] Charles Rosen, review of *The New Grove, New York Review of Books* 28 (28 May 1981): 26–38.

[37] Leon Botstein, "Orpheus in Academe," *Harper's* 262 (June 1981): 74.

[38] "Preface," *The New Grove Dictionary of American Music*, ed. by H. Wiley Hitchcock and Stanley Sadie (New York: Grove's Dictionaries of Music; London: Macmillan Press, 1986), vii.

[39] Gary Giddens, "The Grove of Academe," *Village Voice* 32 (13 January 1987): 75–76.

[40] Stanley Sadie summarized ongoing publication activities related to the *The New Grove* in a letter to the author, 22 March 1990.

[41] Hiroko Kishimoto, "Grove in Japanese," *Encore* 3 (March 1988): unpaged.

[42] Sadie, letter to author, 22 March 1990.

[43] "Preface," *Dictionary*, v.

[44] "Preface," *The New Grove*, viii.

"Monument": *Guide to Reference Books*

Stuart W. Miller

DEVELOPMENT AND HISTORY

The names Kroeger, Mudge, Winchell, and Sheehy evoke nearly mythic and possibly even reverential thoughts in the minds of almost any librarian trained in the United States since 1902. In that year, the American Library Association (ALA) published what would become the first edition of *the* premier compendium of reference materials for North American libraries, a work that has endured down to the present day in the form of a tenth edition, with a supplement planned for March or April 1992 and an eleventh edition scheduled to appear sometime in 1995.

In the nearly 90 years since the first edition in 1902, only four librarians have acted as chief author/editor of the *Guide to Reference Books*. For almost 75 years of that period, three of those four librarians have all in turn served as head of the Reference Department of the Columbia University Libraries. Such continuity has created an almost worshipful atmosphere that continues to hover around the *Guide* down to the present day and represents both a strength and a weakness for those now charged with the task of keeping the *Guide* in the mainstream of library reference work.

The individual circumstances surrounding the inception and production of most of the ten editions and their interim supplements can probably never be known in their entirety. Other than reviews and news announcements, there appears to be virtually no secondary literature discussing any aspect of the *Guide*.

Both Robert Balay (editor of the forthcoming supplement to the tenth edition) and Eugene Sheehy (compiler of the ninth and tenth editions) report that they received almost no written materials or information when they accepted their responsibilities.[1] Furthermore, while Sheehy has some copies of his correspondence with ALA Publishing, most of the replies to his letters came via telephone.[2] When one talks with Sheehy, Balay, and Robert Michaelson (coordinator of the science section for the next supplement and also a contributor to the tenth edition), one receives the impression of an almost informal undertaking (from a business/operations point of view) with past practices and traditions handed down only orally.[3] This researcher may, therefore, be forgiven for suspecting that even with access to the repositories where remnants of earlier editors' efforts may survive, little would be found, since little appears to have been preserved.

Genesis and Characteristics

One can speculate that Alice Bertha Kroeger, the originator of what would eventually become the *Guide*, simply had an idea for a guide to reference works, convinced ALA to publish it, and she and her successors took it from there. Or, given the eventual size of the work, one cannot help but speculate that it was the *Guide* that really took hold of its compilers.[4]

Of course, some obvious facts can be ascertained about the history of the *Guide*. First, it has always been published by ALA. While this may seem a trivial point, it does in fact verify that the association has always recognized the professional value of the *Guide* and has undoubtedly also recognized its monetary value as well. The *Guide* is one of ALA's best-selling titles of all time. ALA has sales figures readily available only for the last four editions: the total number of copies sold to date for the seventh through tenth editions is 127,572, a very large number indeed when most reference books rarely exceed printing runs of 5,000 copies.[5] Since nearly every public, college, university, and even some school libraries can be expected to buy any new edition sight unseen, ALA Publishing has a virtually captive market to exploit.

Second, it has always been compiled by working reference librarians and has consistently aimed to be a practical guide for everyday use.

Third, the longevity of the work indicates a strong perception on the part of its intended audience that the *Guide* has always served and continues to serve a very useful purpose. While some have taken issue with the *Guide*'s selection criteria and unevenness of coverage, the overwhelming critical response to the *Guide* has been very positive, if not downright adulatory. The perceived usefulness of the work is also reflected in the attempts to keep it up to date.

Keeping Current

There have been many schemes to keep the *Guide* current, an ongoing theme in its history and a recurring request from the reviewing community. After the first edition appeared in 1902, supplemental listings appeared at least annually in issues of either *Library Journal* or the *A.L.A. Booklist* until 1928. The second, third, and fourth editions appeared at irregular intervals in 1908, 1917, and 1923 with two supplements to the second

edition in 1911 and 1914. After the fifth edition of 1929, ALA published three supplements in 1930, 1931, and 1934. After the sixth edition of 1936, four supplements appeared in 1939, 1941, 1944, and 1947. The seventh edition in 1951 was followed by four supplements in 1954, 1956, 1960, and 1963. The eighth edition came out in 1967 with supplements in 1968, 1970, and 1972, and the ninth edition was issued in 1976. A four-year hiatus then occurred until the first supplement to the ninth edition was published in 1980, followed by a second in 1982. In 1986, ALA issued the tenth edition, keeping with the "pattern" established since the seventh edition, of issuing a new edition four years after the last supplement to the previous edition. This pattern is also discernible in the 40-year period 1936–1976: three or four supplements to an edition followed by a new edition. None of it really suggests a carefully planned approach from the publisher's point of view; on the other hand, this could be interpreted as an unsuccessful implementation of the intent to observe a regular schedule.

As any reference librarian will attest, substitutes for a regular pattern of updating for the *Guide* have chiefly consisted of regular feature articles in *Wilson Library Bulletin* and *College & Research Libraries* that have appeared over the years, edited by various people (among them, Charles Bunge, Frances Neel Cheney, and Eugene P. Sheehy), reviewing and/or annotating selected reference works issued in a specific time frame. And the same reference librarians will also attest that this coverage, while helpful, is no substitute for regular supplements or revised editions.

A number of reasons have been suggested as to why the *Guide* has never successfully achieved a regular schedule of supplements and revisions. Certainly, the Great Depression and World War II interrupted many publishing operations for at least 15 years between 1930–1945.[6] It speaks well of ALA that it saw fit to issue several supplements and a new edition during that period. Since 1945, the ever-growing scope of the compilation task occasioned by the enormous increase in the number of reference titles suitable for inclusion in the *Guide*, coupled with the absence of a computerized database for editing purposes, have made the preparation of each new edition an enormous task. (Indeed, the compilers working on the tenth edition received pages of the ninth edition with pasted-on additions cut out from the two supplements.) While reviews of the various editions of the *Guide* have generally complained about the lack of regular updating,[7] not until very recently has ALA made a commitment to create a computerized database to allow for vastly easier updating and revising processes. As a matter of fact, ALA Publishing itself did not begin to move towards computerized processes until the late 1970s.

The Columbia Connection

Another interesting fact about the *Guide* is that, despite the long association with reference librarians at Columbia University and popular impressions to the contrary, no formal agreement has ever existed between ALA and Columbia University concerning compilation of the work. Whatever formal contractual agreements have existed have been between individuals and ALA. However, since most academic libraries recognize that work on a project such as the *Guide* is a legitimate use of staff time (presumably to an extent established by policy or custom), it is clear that at least some of the cost of compiling the *Guide* over the years has been subsidized by Columbia University. (How much can probably never be determined.) This in no way minimizes the extraordinary amounts of personal time devoted to the compilation by the editors and their collaborators.[8] (Constance Winchell in fact took a year's leave of absence to work on the seventh edition.[9])

Following completion of the tenth edition, ALA Publishing and Columbia University discussed the possibility of negotiating an agreement to establish a formal, contractual relationship for the production of a future edition with possible remuneration to the university; no agreement was reached. While Columbia University librarians are still involved with the planned supplement to the tenth edition, future editions of the *Guide* will probably no longer have the strong identification with Columbia University that has been a feature for almost 75 years. Under these new arrangements, the hidden costs of compiling the work will undoubtedly be spread among more institutions.

Given the continuity of author/editorship over the years, the stated purposes of the *Guide* have remained consistent. The *Guide* has always served as a selection tool for reference librarians and has also been meant to serve as a "reference manual for the library assistant, research worker, or other user of library resources who needs a finger post to point out the reference tools available for some particular investigation."[10] As Sheehy notes in the preface to the tenth edition, "the criterion of *usefulness* which governed Miss Kroeger's first edition remains salient."[11]

The *Guide* has always been compiled and edited by working reference librarians who have taken a very practical approach to decisions regarding inclusion or exclusion. Even by the time Sheehy began working on the *Guide*, no editor had articulated a policy on inclusion/exclusion. Sheehy avers that the only real guiding principle was whether or not a title was useful for the compiler's clientele. Robert Michaelson, one of the current section coordinators, agrees that selection criteria have always purposefully been left vague, leaving it to individual reference librarians to identify those works which have shown value in actual reference situations.[12] This goes a long way toward explaining phenomena such as the otherwise perplexing presence of standard topical texts in the *Guide* and, on the other hand, the omission of many titles viewed as vital in some libraries.

At no time in its history has the *Guide* had an editorial advisory board in the sense of a group empowered to determine policy issues and develop guidelines on such matters as inclusion/exclusion criteria. Various *ad hoc* groups have met over the years, apparently either at the suggestion of the editor or of ALA Publishing; some were formed to advise on specific issues. Winchell describes one group in the "Preface" to the seventh edition.[13] None appears to have perpetuated itself.

Critical Reception

Even a cursory glance through the reviews of the various editions and supplements will show that the inevitable result of such an approach has been viewed as a weakness, particularly when editions one through eight were very much a reflection of reference work as performed in one (albeit very large and multi-disciplinary) reference department.[14] Bill Katz remarked in a review of the ninth edition: "The *Guide* is beginning to suffer from lack of criticism. Since 1902 it has been handed down from the American Library Association mountaintop via the Columbia University Reference Department. The superb work of Mudge and Winchell is in danger of being codified."[15] Katz was particularly concerned about the reuse of annotations from prior editions, the lack of timeliness, and the lack of truly critical annotations. While acknowledging the overall worth of the *Guide*, Katz suggested that division of the compilation among more people and more libraries might be a solution—a strategy that in fact began to evolve with the seventh edition and continues today.[16]

On the other hand, the very practical nature of such an approach has been a strength as well, and the *Guide*, more often than not, has received extremely positive reviews. Some border on the embarrassingly effusive. The seventh edition in particular garnered almost fulsome evaluations: "It is a book for Everyman, for general reading, . . . this work is a great one; it deserves the confidence and the affection of librarians, scholars, and general readers;"[17] and ". . . an accomplishment of

the first magnitude . . . Miss Winchell has made the present work so much her own that it is fitting that her flag should fly from the masthead; only a sense of dedication of her profession, certainly not hope of pecuniary reward of which there is not likely to be a surfeit, could have inspired her to undergo the vast amount of labor required, even with the help of numerous collaborators whose assistance she so graciously acknowledges."[18]

Role as a Textbook

In addition to being a tool for practicing reference librarians, the *Guide* was originally designed to be a textbook for the student who wished to pursue a systematic study of reference works. This explains why earlier editions carry sections on the reference department in a library and suggestions on how to read a reference work. In the past several years, the use of the *Guide* as a textbook has, for the most part, been abandoned. However, a reviewer of the seventh edition concluded that its "pleasing format and readable style should recommend it to reference librarians for daily reading."[19] While one may wonder if any reference librarian has ever really read the *Guide* as part of a daily routine, such a statement suggests the authority that the work commands. (Even 15 years ago in library school, it was suggested in an enumerative bibliography class that students forego purchasing the then current eighth edition, but only on the grounds that a new edition was expected shortly and, after all, the students could expect to find a copy in virtually any library in which any would eventually work.[20])

Earlier editions also attempted to define what good reference work really means. The "Introduction: Reference Department" was reprinted essentially unchanged in almost all of the earlier editions. The feature was not dropped until the tenth edition in 1986. Another feature eventually abandoned was the "Suggestive List of 100 Reference Books" that appeared in the first through sixth editions. Meant for the small to medium-sized public library, the concept obviously became unworkable once the number of titles included increased drastically. It also reflected the inevitable fact that a work compiled in a university library will typically reflect the needs of an academic audience, although the compilers have always been fairly successful in incorporating more general-interest titles as well as the more esoteric ones useful in an academic setting. However, the *Guide* is "essentially a working aid for larger libraries and serious research."[21]

Over the years other less comprehensive guides to reference works for other types of libraries and audiences have been issued, including the American Library Association's *Reference Sources for Small and Medium-sized Libraries* (4th ed., Chicago: American Library Association, 1984). The tenth edition of the *Guide* identifies more than 30 guides to reference material in the "Selection of Books" section (pp. 43–47); these guides typically focus on a particular kind of library or subject/geographic area. Many of these works have obviously been patterned after the *Guide*, another indication of its far-reaching influence. Most are of fairly recent origin; some are review media. Their existence indicates a need for more selective guides consistent with the missions and budgets of smaller libraries, ongoing tracking and evaluation of new titles, and more in-depth coverage in certain topical areas. All of these titles offer their own strengths, but none can be said to supersede or replace the *Guide*. Plans for the future of the *Guide* (see below) suggest that the latter two needs are well within the scope of the *Guide*'s purpose and its future capabilities; the first need probably falls outside the *Guide*'s purpose, although perhaps there will someday be a "Concise Guide."

Meanwhile, consistent growth has characterized the *Guide*. The increase in numbers of titles included in the *Guide* is certainly one of the most noticeable differences among the editions. The very modest 104 pages of the first edition has expanded to 1,560 pages in the tenth. The sixth edition in 1936 already listed 4,000 items; the seventh increased the total to about 5,500; the eighth reached 7,500; the ninth expanded to approximately 10,000; and the tenth ended up with about 16,000 titles. It is thought that the tenth edition supplement will contain about 4500 titles. The numbers explain why the acknowledgments, even in the earlier editions, identify persons who provided assistance, the numbers of which have increased significantly over the years. By the seventh edition, Winchell began acknowledging assistance from librarians outside of Columbia; and for the ninth edition, Sheehy had further expanded the coterie of assistant compilers to the point where title-page acknowledgment was made.

The Future

The current work on the supplement to the tenth edition has coordinators for the various sections from Syracuse University and Northwestern University as well as at Columbia. In addition, associate editors in charge of subsections now represent a broad range of libraries noted for various specializations, e.g., the Family History Library of the Church of Jesus Christ of Latter-Day Saints; the Yale Law Library; the Yale Divinity Library; the Applied Life Sciences Library at the University of Illinois at Urbana-Champaign; and the John Crerar Library of the University of Chicago. The ever expanding group of compilers from a variety of library settings should continue to broaden the scope of the *Guide* and perhaps address the criticisms of uneven coverage that inevitably resulted from a work compiled primarily in one institutional setting. And those concerned with tradition *qua* tradition, should recognize that such an approach was really begun long ago by Constance Winchell herself and continued by Eugene Sheehy.

After publication of the tenth edition, ALA Publishing sent out questionnaires to a variety of people asking for input about how the *Guide* should be handled in the future—Sheehy had already announced that the tenth edition was his last—and also talked with Columbia about a formal arrangement, as noted above. Eventually, ALA decided to assign responsibility for the *Guide* to the *Choice* editorial office, certainly a logical enough decision based on *Choice*'s role as a review medium for academic library collection development.[22] Robert Balay, former head of the Reference Department at Yale University and now an editor at *Choice*, took on the position of editor of the *Guide*. Balay currently spends approximately 50 percent of his time each week working on the *Guide*. To assist him he has recruited many of the tenth edition's compilers as section and subsection compilers/editors for a supplement to that edition, scheduled to appear in 1992. An eleventh edition is scheduled for 1995 but, for now, efforts are focused on the supplement.[23]

Another very important project for the future is the creation of a machine-readable database to make the compilation process far easier than before. Even as late as the 1986 tenth edition, Sheehy still used the 4-x-6" card file system that had been utilized by his predecessors.[24] Attempts to combine the computer tape used for production of the ninth edition with its two supplements to create a working tool for compilation of the tenth edition came to naught when the company hired for the task went bankrupt. For the tenth edition's supplement, LC-MARC tapes are being used to supply the bibliographic citations; this should also greatly aid the compilation process. Plans now call for the eventual availability of an online database or a CD-ROM product, updated at regular intervals, with a printed edition produced at regular intervals.

There is every reason to believe that the *Guide* will continue to be a useful work. Two of the most consistent and persistent criticisms of the *Guide*—lack of timeliness due to the irregular updating patterns and unevenness of content due to its singular compilation methods—can be addressed by the creation of an online database and a broadening of the number of compilers. Should the former become a reality and the latter trend continue, the *Guide* should remain a source to be reckoned with in the reference department. A greater number of compilers may also allow for more in-depth assessment of related titles, resulting in a more consistently critical rather than descriptive approach to the *Guide*'s annotations. The existence of a larger pool of compilers also suggests that more formal editorial policies will eventually have to be developed in order to provide for a more rigorously consistent approach regarding compilation criteria. Otherwise, quality may suffer as increasingly larger numbers of compilers incorporate their own decisions and approaches into the *Guide*. On the other hand, the commitment to using practicing reference librarians as compilers is surely the only way to insure the *Guide*'s continuing appeal to the profession as a useful tool for everyday work.

As one reads through the prefaces and introductions to the various editions of the *Guide*, change is a constant theme, whether it is the arrangement of the work itself, significant additions of titles in particular topical areas due to ever-shifting current events, or just concerns about maintaining adequate coverage. It is certain that none of the editors ever thought that any one edition of the *Guide* was a work for all time. The constant renewal through supplements and new editions proves the existence of a world in which demands for information grow and change constantly and the willingness of the *Guide*'s compilers to change with it. The latest steps in the evolution of the *Guide* demonstrate, paradoxically, continuity amidst change and a realization that the *Guide* can continue indefinitely if it continues to meet the needs of its audience. May we all be fortunate enough to see a centennial edition in 2002.

PUBLICATION HISTORY

Guide to the Study and Use of Reference Books: A Manual for Librarians, Teachers and Students, by Alice Bertha Kroeger. A.L.A. Annotated Lists. Boston: American Library Association, Publishing Board, 1902. 104p.

Guide to the Study and Use of Reference Books, by Alice Bertha Kroeger. 2nd. ed., rev. and enl. Boston: American Library Association, Publishing Board, 1908. 147p.

Guide to the Study and Use of Reference Books, by Alice Bertha Kroeger. *Supplement 1909–1910*, by Isadore Gilbert Mudge. Chicago: American Library Association, Publishing Board, 1911. 24p.

Guide to the Study and Use of Reference Books, by Alice Bertha Kroeger. *Supplement 1911–1913*, by Isadore Gilbert Mudge. Chicago: American Library Association, Publishing Board, 1914. 48p.

Guide to the Study and Use of Reference Books, by Alice Bertha Kroeger, Isadore Gilbert Mudge. 3rd. ed., rev. and enl. Chicago: American Library Association, Publishing Board, 1917. 235p.

New Guide to Reference Books, by Isadore Gilbert Mudge. [4th ed.] Chicago: American Library Association, 1923. 278p. "Based on the Third Edition of *Guide to the Study and Use of Reference Books* by Alice Bertha Kroeger as Revised by I. G. Mudge."

Guide to Reference Books, by Isadore Gilbert Mudge. 5th ed. Chicago: American Library Association, 1929. 370p.

Reference Books of 1929, by Isadore Gilbert Mudge, Doris M. Reed, Constance M. Winchell. Chicago: American Library Association, 1930. 47p. "An informal supplement to *Guide to Reference Books*, Fifth Edition."

Reference Books of 1930, by Isadore Gilbert Mudge, Doris M. Reed, Constance M. Winchell. Chicago: American Library Association, 1931. 39p. "An informal supplement to *Guide to Reference Books*, Fifth Edition."

Reference Books of 1931–1933: Third Informal Supplement to Guide to Reference Books, Fifth Edition, by Isadore Gilbert Mudge assisted by Constance M. Winchell. Chicago: American Library Association, 1934. 87p.

Guide to Reference Books, by Isadore Gilbert Mudge. 6th ed. Chicago: American Library Association, 1936. 504p.

Reference Books of 1935–1937: An Informal Supplement to Guide to Reference Books, Sixth Edition, by Isadore Gilbert Mudge. Chicago: American Library Association, 1939. 69p.

Reference Books of 1938–1940, by Constance M. Winchell. Chicago: American Library Association, 1941. 106p. "Second Informal Supplement to *Guide to Reference Books*, Sixth Edition, by Isadore Gilbert Mudge."

Reference Books of 1941–1943, by Constance M. Winchell. Chicago: American Library Association, 1944. 115p. "Third Informal Supplement to *Guide to Reference Books*, Sixth Edition, by Isadore Gilbert Mudge."

Reference Books of 1944–1946, by Constance M. Winchell. Chicago: American Library Association, 1947. 94p. "Fourth Informal Supplement to *Guide to Reference Books*, Sixth Edition, by Isadore Gilbert Mudge."

Guide to Reference Books, by Constance M. Winchell. 7th ed. Chicago: American Library Association, 1951. 645p.

Guide to Reference Books: Supplement, 1950–1952, by Constance M. Winchell and Olive A. Johnson. Chicago: American Library Association, 1954. 117p.

Guide to Reference Books: Second Supplement, 1953–1955, by Constance M. Winchell. Chicago: American Library Association, 1956. 134p.

Guide to Reference Books: Third Supplement, 1956–1958, by Constance M. Winchell assisted by John Neal Waddell and Eleanor Buist. Chicago: American Library Association, 1960. 145p.

Guide to Reference Books: Fourth Supplement, 1959–June 1962, by Constance M. Winchell assisted by John Neal Waddell, Eleanor Buist, Eugene P. Sheehy. Chicago: American Library Association, 1963. 151p.

Guide to Reference Books, by Constance M. Winchell. 8th ed. Chicago: American Library Association, 1967. 741p.

Guide to Reference Books: First Supplement 1965–1966, by Eugene P. Sheehy. Chicago: American Library Association, 1968. 122p.

Guide to Reference Books: Second Supplement 1967–1968, compiled by Eugene P. Sheehy with the assistance of Rita G. Keckeissen. Chicago: American Library Association, 1970. 165p.

Guide to Reference Books: Third Supplement 1969–1970, compiled by Eugene P. Sheehy with the assistance of Rita G. Keckeissen and Eileen McIlvaine. Chicago: American Library Association, 1972. 190p.

Guide to Reference Books, compiled by Eugene P. Sheehy with the assistance of Rita G. Keckeissen and Eileen McIlvaine. 9th ed. Chicago: American Library Association, 1976. 1,015p.

Guide to Reference Books, Ninth Edition: Supplement, edited by Eugene P. Sheehy with the assistance of Rita G. Keckeissen, Eileen McIlvaine, Diane K. Goon; Pure and Applied Sciences compiled by Richard J. Dionne, Elizabeth E. Ferguson, Robert C. Michaelson; Major Data Bases compiled by Martha E. Williams. Chicago: American Library Association, 1980. 305p.

Guide to Reference Books, Ninth Edition: Second Supplement, edited by Eugene P. Sheehy with the assistance of Rita G. Keckeissen, Eileen McIlvaine, Diane K. Goon; Pure and Applied Sciences compiled by Richard J. Dionne, Elizabeth E. Ferguson, Robert C. Michaelson. Chicago: American Library Association, 1982. 243p.

Guide to Reference Books, edited by Eugene P. Sheehy with the assistance of Rita G. Keckeissen, Eileen McIlvaine, Diane K. Goon, Janet Schneider; Science, Technology, and Medicine compiled by Richard J. Dionne, Elizabeth E. Ferguson, Robert C. Michaelson. 10th ed. Chicago: American Library Association, 1986. 1,560p.

BIBLIOGRAPHY

Other than the reviews and a very few news articles, the only secondary literature of any substance on the *Guide* is Plotnik's article on the compilation of the ninth edition. Biographical information on Kroeger and Mudge can be found in Grotzinger's and Waddell and Grotzinger's respective articles in the *Dictionary of American Library Biography*; on Winchell in Richards's article in the *Supplement to the Dictionary of American Library Biography* and in her *New York Times* obituary; and on Sheehy in *The ALA Yearbook 1978*. Significant reviews are listed below; others can be found through standard book review indexes. However, since most of the reviews are basically descriptive and/or laudatory, they are not particularly illuminating. Katz is probably correct in his assessment that rigorous criticism of the *Guide* has been rare.

"Constance Mabel Winchell." *New York Times*, May 25, 1983, p. A24. Obituary.

Grotzinger, Laurel A. "Kroeger, Alice Bertha (1864–1909)." In *Dictionary of American Library Bibliography*, edited by Bohdan S. Wynar, 295–98. Littleton, CO: Libraries Unlimited, 1978.

Jensen, Joan W., et al. Review of *Guide to Reference Books*, 10th ed., by Eugene P. Sheehy. *Choice* 24 (May, 1987): 1361–64.

Katz, Bill. Review of *Guide to Reference Books*, 9th ed., by Eugene P. Sheehy. *Journal of Academic Librarianship* 3 (March, 1977): 37–38.

Plotnik, Art. "From Winchell's 8th to Sheehy's 9th." *American Libraries* 8 (March, 1977): 129–32.

Richards, Pamela Spence. "Winchell, Constance Mabel (1896–1983)." In *Supplement to the Dictionary of American Library Biography*, edited by Wayne E. Wiegand, 163–65. Englewood, CO: Libraries Unlimited, 1990.

"Sheehy, Eugene." *ALA Yearbook* 7 (1978): 66–67.

Tolley, C. W. Review of *Guide to Reference Books*, 7th ed., by Constance M. Winchell. *New Zealand Libraries* 16 (April, 1953): 66–68.

Waddell, John N., and Laurel A. Grotzinger. "Mudge, Isadore Gilbert (1875–1957)." In *Dictionary of American Library Biography*, edited by Bohdan S. Wynar, 377–79. Littleton, CO: Libraries Unlimited, 1978.

"Winchell, Constance M[abel]." *Current Biography* (1967): 465–68.

Wynar, Bohdan S. Review of *Guide to Reference Books*, 9th ed., by Eugene P. Sheehy. *American Reference Books Annual* 8 (1978): p. 3–7.

NOTES

[1] Robert Balay, Editor, *Guide to Reference Books, Tenth Edition: Supplement*, and Eugene Sheehy, (retired) Head, Reference Department, Columbia University Libraries, telephone interviews with the author, April 1990.

[2] Sheehy, interview with the author, April 1990.

[3] Balay and Sheehy interviews with the author, April 1990; and Robert G. Michaelson, Head Librarian, Seeley G. Mudd Library for Science and Engineering, Northwestern University, personal interview with the author, April 1990.

[4] Asked by the author if he would do it again, Mr. Sheehy replied that he suspects he would, even given the "agony" that occasionally went with it.

[5] Figures obtained from a telephone interview (March 1991) with Robert Herschman, Manager, Sales & Operations, ALA Publishing.

[6] The author thanks Eugene Sheehy for suggesting this fact, one that does not come naturally to a member of the post-World War II generation.

[7] Several reviews of the ninth edition make this point. Charles Bunge, writing in his "Current Reference Books" column (*Wilson Library Bulletin* 51 [January 1977]: 442), noted that "because of the necessary time lag in publishing such a large work . . . this fine guide will need to be supplemented in day-to-day reference work by other specialized guides and by the librarian's own strategies for staying current." The review in *Choice* 14 (June 1977): 516 observed that "The work was nearly two years in production, and the lists are already three years out of date." See also Bohdan S. Wynar's review of the ninth edition, *American Reference Books Annual* 8 (1977): 3–7. The tenth edition received somewhat

better marks for currency. See, for example, Joan Jensen and others' review in *Choice* 24 (May 1987): 1361–64, and Bohdan S. Wynar's review in *American Reference Books Annual* 18 (1987): 8–9.

[8] In Eugene Sheehy's conversation with the author, Mr. Sheehy spoke of the "all-consuming" nature of the task of editing the *Guide*, mentioning how he sometimes felt almost guilty if he took an evening stroll after dinner instead of resuming work.

[9] Constance M. Winchell, "Preface," *Guide to Reference Books*, 7th ed. (Chicago: American Library Association, 1951), v–vi.

[10] Isadore Gilbert Mudge, "Preface," *Guide to Reference Books*, 6th ed. (Chicago: American Library Association, 1936), iii.

[11] Eugene Sheehy, "Preface," *Guide to Reference Books*, 10th ed. (Chicago: American Library Association, 1986), ix.

[12] Michaelson and Sheehy, interviews with the author, April 1990.

[13] Winchell, "Preface," v–vi. Sheehy states that he was invited to attend several meetings about the *Guide* organized by ALA Publishing at various ALA conferences that considered a variety of topics. He cannot clearly recall any particular topics discussed but is certain that none of the groups continued on a regular basis.

[14] For examples, see C. W. Tolley, review of *Guide to Reference Books*, 7th ed., by Constance M. Winchell, *New Zealand Libraries* 16 (April 1953): 66–68 and Bohdan S. Wynar, review of *Guide to Reference Books*, 9th ed., by Eugene P. Sheehy, *American Reference Books Annual* 8 (1978): p. 3–7.

[15] Bill Katz, review of *Guide to Reference Books*, 9th ed., by Eugene P. Sheehy, *Journal of Academic Librarianship* 3 (March 1977): 37–38.

[16] Ibid. The preface to the seventh edition indicates that an advisory committee (with members from outside of the Columbia University libraries) reviewed parts of the work. The preface to the eighth edition identifies members of an advisory committee and special mention is made of the work on the science sections by the staff at the University of Wisconsin libraries. The number of other libraries involved has increased in each of the two subsequent editions.

[17] W.B. Ready, review of *Guide to Reference Books*, 7th ed., by Constance M. Winchell, *Library Quarterly* 23 (January 1953): 64.

[18] Harold Russell, review of *Guide to Reference Books, Seventh Edition*, by Constance M. Winchell, in *College and Research Libraries* 13 (July 1952): 274.

[19] Review of *Guide to Reference Books, Seventh Edition*, by Constance M. Winchell, in *Library Journal* 77 (March 1, 1952): 419.

[20] Robert Herschman of ALA Publishing reported total number of copies sold for the last four editions as follows: Seventh edition (1951) 40,149; Eighth edition (1967) 51,597; Ninth edition (1976) 24,030; Tenth edition (1986) 11,796. He believes the drop between the eighth and ninth editions is explained by the abandonment of the *Guide* as a textbook in reference classes. Herschman, interview with the author.

[21] Art Plotnik, "From Winchell's 8th to Sheehy's 9th," *American Libraries* 8 (March 1977): 132.

[22] Robert Balay, "Guide to Reference Books," *Choice* 27 (November 1989): 433.

[23] Balay, interview with the author, April 1990.

[24] Sheehy, interview with the author, April 1990.

"Unbeatable": The *Guinness Book of Records*

Christine C. Whittington

DEVELOPMENT AND HISTORY

The idea for publishing the record book that the *New York Times* once called "a wacky collection of superlatives"[1] originated with an argument among sportsmen hunting ducks and geese in the autumn of 1951 near Wexford, in the southeast tip of the Irish Coast. After his shot at a golden plover missed its mark, Sir Hugh Beaver, managing director of the Anglo-Irish brewery Arthur Guinness, Son and Company, Ltd., debated with his companions whether the golden plover was the fastest game bird in Europe. Sir Hugh consulted various encyclopedias and other reference sources, discovering that none provided information about records and extremes that would prove him correct. He was surprised that such a source did not exist and felt that a book like this would be useful for settling bets and arguments, especially those taking place in pubs or bars where Guinness's famous lager and stout were consumed. Several years later, thinking that it might be a good business undertaking for Guinness to publish a book that would be popular in pubs, Sir Hugh asked Guinness executive Christopher Chataway, holder of the world 5000-meter track record, if he knew of anyone who would be able to compile a book of superlatives. Chataway recommended his friends from Oxford, the twins Norris and Ross McWhirter, "a pair of track fanatics," and owners of a fact-finding enterprise.[2]

The McWhirter Brothers

The McWhirters were born in London, 20 minutes apart, on August 12, 1925. Their father was the editor of three national newspapers—the *Sunday Pictorial*, *Daily Mail*, and *Sunday Dispatch*—and eventually became the managing director of Associated Newspapers.[3] The twins grew up in a home full of reference books "devoted to the establishment of facts."[4] According to J.A. Maxtone Graham's article in *Sports Illustrated*, the young McWhirter twins asked so many questions that their mother complained to their father, who advised her to "tell them to look it up for themselves."[5] They kept a file of newspaper clippings containing unusual information, including lists of the largest buildings, and memorized every important date in British history, the names of every river, mountain range, and nation's capital.[6] They insisted upon checking everything they were told against reference books, causing their teachers to call them the "McWhitakers"[7] in reference to the famous British almanac.

The McWhirters were already supplying information on extraordinary record-setters and unusual topics when Sir Hugh Beaver began to search for someone to write a book of superlatives. After study at Oxford and wartime service with the Royal Navy, the McWhirters returned to London in 1951, where they set up and registered McWhirter Twins, Ltd., a "press and periodicals features service" for supplying facts and figures to newspapers, publishers, and advertisers.[8] The McWhirters were also involved in sportswriting and sportscasting. Norris McWhirter was commenting on an Iffley Road, Oxford, track meet for the BBC and Ross was reporting for the *Star* on May 6, 1954, when their friend Roger Bannister broke the four-minute mile.[9]

On September 12, 1954, the McWhirters attended a lunch with Sir Hugh Beaver and other Guinness executives to discuss Beaver's plan to publish a book of superlatives. The Guinness representatives quizzed the McWhirters about records, including those for the longest river that has ever frozen and the longest time a human squatted on top of a pole.[10] When Norris revealed that he knew that the Turkish language had only one irregular verb, not because he knew Turkish but because he had made an effort to discover which language had the fewest, Sir Hugh Beaver "seemed to decide that he had discovered people with the right kind of quirkish mind for producing the book."[11] It was agreed that the McWhirters would write it and that Guinness Superlatives, Inc., a Guinness subsidiary, would publish it.[12]

From an office at 107 Fleet Street, the McWhirters began the enormous task of compiling a collection of superlatives, "extracting the 'ests' (highest, lowest, smallest, oldest, fastest, heaviest, etc.) from the 'ists' (ichthyologists, paleontologists, dendrochronologists, etc.)"[13] They wrote thousands of letters to governments officials, university professors, various experts, museums, and libraries in 110 countries.[14] The twins compiled entries as they received responses to their queries and arranged for the printing and binding of the book. The first printing of 50,000 copies of the *Guinness Book of Records* was finished on August 27, 1955.[15] The book contained 198 pages, cost $35,000 to publish, and sold for about 75 cents.[16] Its green cover was embossed with the Guinness trademark, a gold Brian Boru harp. It contained a foreword by

Guinness chairman Rupert Guinness, the Earl of Iveagh, introducing the book as a tool for settling arguments. Among the 96 agencies, businesses, and organizations listed in the acknowledgments are the British Speleological Association, the United States Coast Guard, and the Embassy of Japan. The McWhirters were not listed by name but identified only anonymously as "the compilers."

The First Edition

The book contained sections on the human being, the animal kingdom, the natural world, the universe, the scientific world, the human world, the business world, the world's structures, the mechanical world, accidents and disasters, human achievements, and sport. Each chapter was further divided. For example, the chapter on the human being included sections on dimensions, longevity, reproductivity, and physiology. The longest chapter was that on sports, including records for more than 60 activities. Each section included individual records. For example, the section on dogs included entries for age, largest litter, highest price, most popular, and most dogs in a single team. Superlatives included "earliest," "tallest," "shortest," "heaviest," "thinnest," "oldest," "largest," "smallest," "most," "lowest," "highest," "rarest," plus other less common "-ests" such as "busiest" (junction), "remotest" (island), "bloodiest" (assize), and "brightest" (planet). The book included black and white photographs and an index. For many categories, world records were listed first, followed by those for England, Wales, Scotland, and Ireland. For example, the chapter on the world's structures includes entries for the Great Britain's tallest structure (the General Post Office radio masts near Rugby) as well as the world's (the television transmitting tower of station KWTV in Oklahoma City). Many of the world records included in the *Guinness Book of Records* were American, including the largest mail order house (Sears Roebuck), the fastest selling recording ("The Ballad of Davy Crockett"), the largest insurance company (Metropolitan Life), the country with greatest number of telephones (the United States, with 50 million), and the most expensive hotel (Fountainebleu, Miami Beach).

Within four months, the *Guinness Book of Records* was the bestselling book in England, with approximately 187,000 copies sold. The McWhirters each earned about $10,000 in royalties from the sale of the book.[17]

A second, enlarged edition of the *Guinness Book of Records* was published in England in 1956. This edition contained more photographs, new material from the United States and the Soviet Union, which the McWhirters had visited, and new records. The tallest tree in the British Isles, for example, had grown eight feet, six inches since last measured, and 73 new records were added to track and field athletics.[18] Other records changed as a result of technological advances, such as new measurements for the deepest Atlantic sounding, the diameter of the Earth, and the speed of light.[19]

First American Edition

An American edition of 50,000 copies was produced in 1956, entitled *The Guinness Book of Superlatives*. Although the book included the same categories as the British edition, the content was adjusted to appeal to the American audience. The 1956 British edition contained records for fox hunting, snooker, polo, public houses, the largest and fastest British motorcycles, a lengthy section on cricket, and the London Stock Exchange. The American edition of the same year contained much longer sections on baseball, basketball, and American football, and entries for harness racing, rodeo, ranches, and grain elevators, none of which were included in the British edition.

At first, the *Guinness Book of Superlatives* did not sell rapidly and distribution was not well organized. Then, a copy of this American edition on the shelves of the DeWolfe and Fiske bookstore in Boston drew the attention of David Boehm. Boehm had founded Sterling Books in 1949 with six titles, mostly how-to books. Intrigued by the book, Boehm offered to take over the distribution of the 32,000 copies remaining to be sold in the United States. Sterling re-titled the American edition the *Guinness Book of World Records*, packaged it with a new cover, and spent four years selling the excess copies. In 1960, Boehm and Norris McWhirter agreed that Sterling would produce a paperback version of the book in the United States with only world, not national, records, using proofs of the British edition. The success of the paperback version in American bookstores and the requests of bookstore owners convinced Sterling to publish a hardcover edition in 1961. In that year, Sterling sold paperback rights to Bantam Books. Until 1973, the book was not published annually in the United States as it was in Great Britain, but only as supplies were exhausted.[20]

Enduring Popularity

Thirty-five years after it was first published, the *Guinness Book of Records* continues to be immensely popular. In December 1974, it became the fastest selling nonfiction book in history, excluding versions of the Bible. It surpassed Dr. Benjamin Spock's *Baby and Child Care* to reach total sales of 24 million and achieve its own record in the book. Hardcover sales have averaged 100,000 copies per year and paperback sales two to three million per year; an additional 250,000 to 400,000 are sold per year through premium sales.[21] By October 1989, 61 million copies had been sold in 262 editions in 35 languages, including Icelandic, Tamil, Malayalam, and Telugu.[22] Arrangements for compiling the first Russian edition were completed in 1989.[23] Sales of the Finnish and Serbo-Croatian editions have been credited with boosting the sales to the record.[24] In his introduction to the 1990 edition, Benjamin Guinness points out that the book was "No. 1 on the best sellers list . . . every year except 1957 and 1959, when it was not published, and that the global sales to date would equal 171 stacks, each as high as Mount Everest."[25]

There have been many attempts to explain the fascination *Guinness* holds for its readers. McWhirter believes that "People are fascinated by extremes. People crave delineation and points of reference. It's a matter of orientation, but it's also part of the natural competitiveness that most of us have."[26] The United States provides the largest market for *Guinness*. In an interview with Digby Diehl for the *Los Angeles Times*, Ross McWhirter stated that "This curious American dedication to the fact, as well as your competitive spirit, your betting sense, seems to account for our book's popularity," but added that worldwide commitment to literacy has aided expansion of the market for paperback books, including the paperback version of *Guinness*.[27] Promotions and product licensing, including "Oddball Olympics" in various cities, seven Guinness World Records exhibition halls, a comic strip, greeting cards, t-shirts, and television shows have increased the book's exposure.[28] Fundraising events have attracted attention and publicity through attempts to break records listed in *Guinness*.

Guinness has also increased its exposure through the numerous spinoffs that have been published under its name. Many of these expand upon the numerous sports records found in the parent book. These include *The Guinness Book of World Championship Boxing* (London: Guinness Superlatives, 1990); *The Guinness Book of Olympic Records: 1988* (New York: Bantam, 1988); and the annual *Guinness Sports Record Book* (New York: Sterling, 1972–1990; New York: Facts On File, 1991–). Other spinoffs appeal to teenagers, young adults, and trivia fans who also enjoy the parent book. These include titles in the Guinness Oddfax Series such as *The Guinness Book of Almost Everything You Didn't Need to Know About Dogs* (London:

Guinness Superlatives, 1987) and *The Guinness Book of Almost Everything You Didn't Need to Know About the Movies* (London: Guinness Superlatives, 1987).

Critical Reception

Reviewers have mentioned the book's use of "deadpan humor," "arcane erudition," and "air of indisputable authority."[29] In a single sentence, another reviewer noted both the book's "useless information" and its ability to "captivate all ages."[30] Curiosity about the grotesque no doubt plays a role. One reviewer wrote that the book offered a "chance to peep behind the curtain concealing life's freak show" to find gruesome records for obesity, gluttony, deformity, and inhumanity.[31] Most reviewers, even one who surmised that "the *Guinness Book of World Records* includes more useless information than any other book in the world,"[32] cannot resist listing the records they find most fascinating. The *Village Voice* gave *Guinness* a one word review: "Unbeatable."[33]

Types of Records

Teachers have found that the *Guinness Book of World Records* can be used to tempt children and young adults to read.[34] School classes and other children's groups have turned breaking a "Guinness record" into a learning experience. A fifth grade class researched and measured the 201-foot Roe River in Montana and submitted evidence that earned it a place in the 1989 *Guinness* as holding the record for the world's shortest river.[35]

While most records included in earlier editions of the book were for naturally occurring phenomena (the fastest snake); athletic (most lawn bowling titles); or unintentional (the youngest vice president); many of the records in the more recent editions reflect an activity J. Kirshenbaum has dubbed "Guinnessport."[36] The book's popularity has resulted in campaigns all over the world, extreme in themselves, to set new "Guinness records" or "get into Guinness." Norris McWhirter believes that because "Americans have such a high level of achievement. The underachievers are driven into zanier outlets."[37] Perusing newspaper and periodical indexes turns up many accounts of record-breaking activities such as eating a tree,[38] catching in one's mouth a grape dropped from a 60-story building,[39] making the world's longest pasta noodle,[40] or stacking bowling balls.[41] Individuals have attempted not only to break records in order to have them listed in the book, but have attempted to achieve the record for holding the most "Guinness" records. Ashrita Furman of New York City holds the record for the most records in diverse categories,[42] including squats done in one hour, skip running, and pogo stick jumping in the Amazon River. Peter Dowdeswell of London holds many eating records, including those for raw eggs (13 in one second), eels (1,300 in 13.7 seconds), and sushi (1.5 pounds in 1 minute, 13.5 seconds). South Korea is attempting to achieve the most records in the *Guinness Book of Records*, hoping by the mid-1990s to surpass the 30 percent held by Americans. Records already held by South Korea include those for shipbuilding, the largest drydock, and the most sets of twins within a single community.[43]

In response to the popularity of record-setting, each edition of the book includes guidelines for determining whether an activity will be considered a record, rules and procedures, and documentation and verification. The guidelines state that the book is likely to publish "only those records which improve upon previously published records or which are newly significant in having become the subject of widespread and, preferably, worldwide competition."[44] Hence one wonders why pogo stick jumping in the Amazon river, making a jumpsuit out of pennies, or catching grapes in the mouth from great heights qualify. The book no longer publishes any records in the "gratuitously hazardous categories, such as the lowest starting height for a handcuffed, free-fall parachute jump"[45] or new records for other "extremely inadvisable" activities, such as those for sword swallowing[46] or "gluttony."[47]

Guinness Book of World Records has a reputation for excluding morally questionable records. Robert Lacey in the London's *Sunday Times Magazine* noted that the *Guinness Book of Records* included records for the oldest and most prolific mothers, but not the youngest mothers, unwed mothers, or abortions,[48] while Peter Buckman in *Punch* found Ripley's Believe It or Not (described by Norris McWhirter as "cynical, successful, and thoroughly unreliable")[49] a better source of information on sexual feats,[50] and a reviewer for the *Listener* noted that "sex scarcely enters the *Guinness Book of Records*."[51]

Format and Organization

The purpose and format of the *Guinness Book of Records*, if not the records themselves, remain similar to that of the early editions. Like the first edition, the 1990 edition began with an introduction by the Earl of Iveagh, President of Arthur Guinness & Sons. In his foreword to the first American edition, Rupert Guinness, the current Earl of Iveagh, defined the purpose of the book, adapted for the American audience:

> Wherever people congregate to talk, they will argue, and sometimes the joy lies in the arguing and would be lost if there were any definite answer. But more often the argument takes place on a dispute of fact, and it can be very exasperating if there is no immediate means of settling the discussion. Who was the tallest President? Who is the richest man and the most married woman? Where is the highest point in our state? How many died in the world's worst earthquake? Who hit the longest measured home run? Who holds the corn-husking record? And so on. How much heat these innocent questions can raise! The House of Guinness in producing this book hopes that it may assist in resolving many such disputes and may, we hope, turn heat into light.[52]

In their preface, the McWhirters defined the scope of the book as ". . . a collection of facts—finite facts expressed in quantitative terms predominantly those which by measurement are superlative or are records in their respective fields. The world's greatest man is, for this book, the man with the greatest girth rather than the man with the greatest intellect."[53] The book continues to be divided into sections similar to those of the early editions, with sections on the arts and entertainment, newly verified records, and sports games and endurance marathons (e.g., playing Monopoly for 600 hours) the only added categories. The index of the American edition includes entries for the superlatives themselves, e.g., "fastest," "longest," "earliest," followed by the subject. About one quarter of the book's records change each year. Obviously, many records have changed because of technological advances, such as the record for the fastest aircraft. Also many athletic records, such as those for speed skating or bicycle racing, were set in recent years.

Ways to Use Guinness

In the library reference environment, the *Guinness Book of World Records* can supply information not easily available in any other source. Sir Hugh Beaver was correct in his assumption that there was no comprehensive book of superlatives when he conceived his idea for a record book, and no competitor has been published since. It is easy to locate information about museums in directories, for example, but no other single source lists the oldest museum (Ashmolean, Oxford), largest single museum (American Museum of Natural History), or the most popular museum (the Smithsonian's National Air and Space Museum). The charts included in recent editions are especially useful for those who want information in one place; for example, a chart in the 1990 American edition entitled "Worst Accidents and Disasters in the World" ranks by number of deaths disasters resulting from causes as diverse as the Black Death (75 million deaths); panic in an air raid shelter

(4,000 deaths); and the mass suicide at the People's Temple in Jonestown, Guyana (913 deaths). *Guinness* is often used as a first step, providing enough information about a question to enable a librarian or library patron to identify appropriate sources for further information. For example, a person investigating the popularity of motion pictures could use *Guinness* to identify the films with the highest box office gross, highest film rentals, the most expensive film, the highest earnings by actors, and the largest number of Academy Awards before looking for information on the individual films in sources devoted to film.

A New American Publisher, A New American Title

Sterling Books' involvement with the *Guinness Book of World Records* ended with publication of the 1990 edition. Beginning with the 1991 edition, the American edition of *Guinness* has been published by Facts On File. Facts On File is best known as the publisher of the weekly news digest entitled *Facts On File*. Facts On File has brought the American edition closer to the current British edition in size, format, and appearance. The book is larger (9" x 12"), the photographs are larger and in color, and the book contains color charts and other graphics. Like the British edition, the new American edition lists both world and national records for many categories. To reflect this change, the title has officially been changed to *Guinness Book of Records*, the same title used for the British edition. Facts On File plans to maintain strong editorial involvement and communication with Guinness, Ltd., the publisher of the British edition. Two editors are working full time on the American edition—one for Facts On File in New York and the other for Guinness Ltd. in London. The Facts On File editor, Mark Young, is responsible for "Americanizing" *Guinness*. He tracks down records in much the same way the McWhirters did for the first edition. He screens numerous letters (including one containing a cockroach that fell short of the record length) and telephone calls (Facts On File has installed a separate telephone line and answering machine for this purpose); consults other reference sources; and has tapped into networks of experts. Unlike the McWhirters as they compiled the first edition, Young uses computer files to keep track of records and update information. Donald McFarlan is the present editor of the British *Guinness Book of Records*. Norris McWhirter maintains his involvement with the book he created by serving as editorial adviser. Ross McWhirter, who participated actively in conservative politics and litigation, was shot to death at his home on November 27, 1975. Fifteen months later, Irish Republican Army members were convicted for his murder.[54]

Facts On File has enhanced the reference quality of the *Guinness Book of Records* by increasing the number of substantive records and weeding out those of less interest while maintaining many of those that appeal to casual readers, especially children and adolescents. To correspond to this more authoritative approach, copies of the book are not to be offered at discount prices. The Facts On File editions will retain the introductory material regarding rules and verification for record-setting; acceptance of records will be determined by the editors. A mass market paperback edition will continue to be produced by Bantam, using material purchased from Facts on File, but with black and white photographs.[55]

A CD-ROM, the *Guinness Disc of Records*, has been produced by Pergamon Compact Solution of London. It contains animation and music as well as photographs and text. Each word is searchable, so a user can retrieve all the records set by a particular person or find out why the Mississippi Queen is famous.

The *Guinness Book of Records* is not only one of the best selling books in the world, but a reference source that is indeed "unbeatable" for finding superlatives throughout the years. It is up to Facts On File to set the future direction for the American edition. If the company continues to increase the book's visual appeal and to enrich its authority while still retaining enough trivia records to attract casual readers, the recently retitled *Guinness Book of Records* should become an even more effective reference tool.

PUBLICATION HISTORY

Guinness Book of World Records, 1956–1990. Annual. Published irregularly in the United States until 1973 (1st ed., 1956, 2nd ed., 1961, etc.) First edition entitled *The Guinness Book of*

Superlatives. Issued as *Guinness Book of Records,* 1991–. Annual. Also issued in a British edition, *Guinness Book of Records* 1955–. Annual.

BIBLIOGRAPHY

There has been no comprehensive, scholarly investigation into the origin, development, influence, or social impact of the *Guinness Book of World Records*. The most detailed information about its genesis appears in Norris McWhirter's biography of his brother, *Ross: The Story of a Shared Life*. This book also addresses the twins' personal and professional lives apart from their involvement with Guinness. *Guinness: The Stories Behind the Records* devotes more space than the *Guinness Book of Records* can to some of the more interesting record-setters, including a female powerlifting champion and the 1980 eruption of Mt. St. Helens (largest volcanic eruption in U.S. history). It also contains brief chapters entitled "How Guinness Came to America," the latter written by Sterling editor David Boehm. The book also includes a section of some of the stranger letters sent to *Guinness* ("Dear Guinness: I believe I have the longest eyelash in the world . . ."). Reference librarians may find it most useful for its section on "Answers to Some Commonly Asked Questions," ("What are the rules for rest breaks?"). Each edition of the *Guinness* contains the most recent information on categories, rules and procedures, documentation and verification, and revision, and should be consulted by potential record-breakers. Readers seeking brief, entertaining introductions to the origin and development of *Guinness* will enjoy the two articles in *Sports Illustrated*. The biographical sources provide summaries of the McWhirters' lives. Maria Simson's article in *Publishers Weekly* covers the current editorial and publication status of *The Guinness Book of World Records*.

Graham, J.A. Maxtone. "Here is the Odd Paradise of the Record Maniac." *Sports Illustrated* 22 (February 8, 1965): 54–62.

Kirshenbaum, Jerry. "There's Music in the Where?" *Sports Illustrated* 51 (July 30, 1979): 56–70.

Lacey, Robert. "Superlatives, Ltd." *Sunday Times Magazine* (London), January 16, 1972, pp. 22–27.

McWhirter, Norris [Dewar]. "Facts and How to Find Them" [text of an address given to the Society of Indexers]. *Indexer* 12 (April 1981): 125–27.

———. *Ross: The Story of a Shared Life*. London: Churchill Press, Ltd., 1976.

McWhirter, Norris [Dewar] et al. *Guinness: The Stories Behind the Records*. New York: Sterling, 1981.

"McWhirter, Norris [Dewar]," *Current Biography Yearbook* (1979), 247–50.

"McWhirter, Norris [Dewar]," *Contemporary Authors* 13 (1965), s.v.

"McWhirter, Ross," *Dictionary of National Biography*, 1971–80 supplement, s.v.

Simson, Maria. "Guinness Goes to Facts on File After 30 Years at Sterling." *Publishers Weekly* 237 (February 16, 1990): 49–50.

NOTES

1. Robert Lasson, review of *Guinness Book of World Records*, 11th ed., 1973, *New York Times Book Review*, 29 April 1973, p. 22.
2. J.A. Maxtone Graham, "Here is the Odd Paradise of the Record Maniac," *Sports Illustrated* 22 (8 February 1965): 56. The story of the idea for the *Guinness Book of Records* originating with Sir Hugh Beaver's hunting party has appeared, with some variation, in Norris [Dewar] McWhirter, *Ross: The Story of a Shared Life* (London: Churchill Press, 1976), 141–44; Norris [Dewar] McWhirter and others, *Guinness: The Stories Behind the Records* (New York: Sterling, 1981), 113; Jerry Kirshenbaum, "There's Music in the Where?" *Sports Illustrated* 51 (30 July 1979): 66; Robert Lacey, "Superlatives, Ltd.," *Sunday Times Magazine* (London), 16 January 1972, 27; Christopher Booker, "The Speed of a Golden Plover," *Spectator* 250 (19 February 1983): 19.
3. Lacey, 27.
4. Norris [Dewar] McWhirter, "Facts and How to Find Them," [text of the address given to the Society of Indexers, 11 July 1980], *Indexer* 12 (April 1981): 127.
5. Graham, 56.
6. McWhirter and others, 112.
7. Lacey, 27; McWhirter, 21.
8. McWhirter, 101.
9. Kenny Moore, "4 Minutes and 20 Years," *Sports Illustrated* 41 (15 July 1974): 64; McWhirter, 128–44.
10. McWhirter, 143; McWhirter and others, 113.
11. Ibid.
12. Graham, 57; McWhirter, 149.
13. McWhirter and others, 114.
14. Graham, 57.
15. McWhirter and others, 114.
16. Graham, 57; McWhirter and others, 114.
17. Graham, 57–58.
18. *Guinness Book of World Records*, 2nd ed. (London: Guinness Superlatives, Ltd., 1956), 4.
19. Ibid.
20. See David Boehm's chapter entitled "Guinness Comes to America," in Norris McWhirter and others, *Guinness: The Stories Behind the Records*, 114–17. The American Guinness edition was published in October 1956. Sterling editions were published in October 1960, April 1962, September 1963, October 1965, June 1966, March 1968, September 1969, May 1970, April 1971, November 1972, and annually since October 1973. Bantam paperback editions were published in October 1963, April 1964, June 1966, March 1968, May 1970, April 1971, and annually since March 1973.
21. Maria Simson, "Guinness Goes to Facts on File after 30 Years at Sterling," *Publishers Weekly* 237 (16 February 1990): 43.
22. Benjamin Guinness, Earl of Iveagh, "The Story Behind the Guinness Book" in *Guinness Book of World Records* (New York: Bantam Books, 1990), vii.
23. Ibid.
24. Digby Diehl, "McWhirters: Matter-of-Fact Twins," *Los Angeles Times*, 9 December 1974, sec. 4, 1.
25. Guinness, vii.
26. Kirshenbaum, 59.
27. Diehl, sec 4, 1.
28. N. R. Kleinfield, "Guinness Pace: A Record?" *New York Times*, 14 June 1980, 29; Kirshenbaum, 60.
29. Peter Buckman, "The Biggest, the Fastest, the Most Fatuous," *Punch* 271 (17 November 1976): 942–43.

[30] Elizabeth Minot Graves, "Children's Books: A Selected List," *Commonweal* 93 (November 1970): 207.

[31] Laurence Ulster, "The Bore's Bible," *Listener* 118 (17 December 1987): 51.

[32] Guernsey Le Pelley, "Chandelier Munching," *Christian Science Monitor*, 8 November 1988, 13.

[33] *Review of Guinness Book of World Records*, 13th ed. 1975, *Village Voice* 20 (15 September 1975): 52. The *Voice* again called *Guinness* "unbeatable" three months later. *Village Voice* 20 (22 December 1975): 59.

[34] Karin Agosta, "For Reinforcing Basic Skills, There's No Place Like Home," *Instructor* 91 (November 1981): 80; Review of *Review of Guinness Book of World Records*, 9th ed. 1970 *Grade Teacher* 89 (September 1971) 157; review of *Review of Guinness Book of World Records*, 10th ed., 1971, *Library Journal* 96 (15 May 1971): 1834; review of *Review of Guinness Book of World Records*, 12th ed., 1974, *Library Journal* 98 (15 December 1973): 3730.

[35] "5th Graders Zap Town's Claim to World's Shortest River," *Chicago Tribune*, 13 August 1988, sec. 1, p. 4.

[36] Kirshenbaum, 68.

[37] Ibid.

[38] Le Pelley, 13.

[39] "Arlington Man Raisin' Record for Catching Grapes in His Mouth," *Boston Globe*, 4 September 1988, p. 23.

[40] "Pasta Heights," *Chicago Tribune*, 5 October 1989, sec. 7, p. 5.

[41] "For David Kremer, Stacked Bowling Balls Are Right Up His Alley," *People Weekly* 30 (18 July 1988): 91.

[42] "Not Explainable," *New Yorker* 65 (27 February 1989): 25.

[43] "Just for the Record: South Korea's Making Its Move," *Boston Globe*, 7 July 1989, p. 2.

[44] *Guinness Book of World Records* (New York: Bantam, 1990), viii.

[45] Ibid.

[46] Ibid., 30.

[47] Ibid., 463.

[48] Lacey, 27.

[49] McWhirter, "Facts and How to Find Them," 127.

[50] Buckman, 942.

[51] E. S. Turner, "Cod and Blod," *Listener* 84 (26 November 1970): 747. Kirshenbaum, 64, notes that the editors rule out gore, sexual feats, and stunts deemed unseemly.

[52] Rupert Guinness, Earl of Iveagh, foreword to *Guinness Book of World Records* (New York: Superlatives, Inc., 1956), iii.

[53] "Preface" to *Guinness Book of World Records* (New York: Superlatives, Inc., 1956), v.

[54] Kirshenbaum, 67.

[55] Simson, 49–50; Rachel Ginsberg and Gerard Helferich of Facts On File, conversation with the author, 9 May 1990.

A Household Word for Four Generations: Moody's

DEVELOPMENT AND HISTORY

Now comprised of eight separate manuals providing annual in-depth coverage of companies and other entities whose stock and/or bonds are available for public investment, the Moody's manuals started nearly a century ago in 1900 with a single volume entitled *The Manual of Industrial and Miscellaneous Corporation Securities*. After each day's work as a statistician in the banking firm of Spenser Trask, John Moody produced his manual at home with the help of a single assistant editor/compiler and John's wife, Anna, as typist. Financing for the venture was a crazy quilt of advertising revenues, money borrowed from two friends, and promises of deferred billing from the printer. Although eager for a better income and more influence on Wall Street, Moody was not motivated solely by self-interest. His autobiography portrays a family at the mercy of the father's flyers on the stock market, moving annually to a drab, cramped rented house during bad times or to rather grand (albeit temporary) premises when fortune smiled—ample motivation for a life's work of providing timely, uniform, reliable information for investors. A bright, venturesome lad, John had to leave school at the age of 15 to begin contributing to the family's income. Eventually achieving popularity as a writer of financial and autobiographical books as well as prominence in publishing annual financial manuals, he educated himself by dint

of voracious reading on self-selected topics and a loosely structured home-study course in accordance with Chautauqua guidelines. Yarning about his first job, Moody remembered the irony of his boss's comment at discovering that John was lending money on company premises at exorbitant rates: "You belong in Wall Street, you do."[1]

Henry Varnum Poor

There could hardly have been a greater contrast to Moody's background than the situation of Henry Varnum Poor, founder of Moody's chief competitor in financial and investment publishing. A lawyer, Poor was editor of the *American Railroad Journal* when he started the first of a projected three-volume set that became the progenitor of *Poor's Manual*. In an era when big business was king in this country, Henry Poor was the lone advocate of disclosure of company financial and operating information by railroads offering their stock and bonds for public sale. To compile this manual, Poor wrung information from reluctant companies by virtue of his influence as editor of the leading trade journal—goodwill and tact by themselves having failed with a number of firms. By 1860 he had gleaned enough information to publish *A History of the Railroads and Canals of the United States* (New York: J.H. Schultz, 1860), a 200-page book providing operating and financial statistics about more than 120 railroad and canal companies. Although the other two volumes never were written, the first is now regarded as the "grandfather of all investment publications."[2]

In 1868 (the year John Moody was born), Poor and his son Henry William Poor resumed publishing after a hiatus caused by the Civil War, this time calling the work *The Manual of the Railroads of the United States* (New York: H.V. and H.W. Poor, 1868). Lacking either an industry tradition or a legal requirement for uniform reporting of railway statistics, data was not comparable across companies. Before the Interstate Commerce Act of 1887, railway regulation was the province of state governments, and the only common operating principle was "practically unrestricted competition."[3] Undeniably the *Manual of the Railroads of the United States* reflected this flaw. But like Poor's earlier work, in all other respects it was a godsend to the hapless individual investor.

Poor's early manuals were a curious admixture of facts and advertising. For example, the 1891 manual devoted 219 initial and concluding pages as well as all four sides of the front and back covers to advertising; sandwiched in between were directory information and financial statistics. The scope was eclectic, ranging from extensive coverage of larger systems such as the Southern Pacific to basic information about lines covering a single town and environs or even a section of a town. Besides the general index of companies, there were separate listings for advertisers and various railroad company officials, ranging from president to such lower echelon positions as assistant engineer or master mechanic. Standard elements of entries for prominent companies included a physical description of the railroad (weight and gauge of track, miles of track owned, etc.); a one-paragraph company history; a description of equipment owned ("rolling stock"); a summary of activities both in volume (tons of freight and number of passengers) and in dollars; and the latest available statements of income, expense, financial

backing, and debts. Entries for smaller lines included a bare-bones paragraph giving charter date, officers, weight and gauge of rails, carfare, date of annual meeting, and brief description of outstanding debt.

Although *Poor's Manual* continued to be published through 1917, H.V. Poor's association with it declined after his retirement in 1886 and ceased altogether with his death in 1905. Poor's son continued to publish an annual directory of American railroad officials and a handbook of investment securities until 1906 and 1893, respectively. However such efforts presented no real obstacle to Moody's entry into financial publishing. In his autobiography and in *A Fifty Year Review of Moody's Investors Service* (New York: Moody's Investors Service, [1949]), a personal reminiscence about his early entrepreneurial activities, Moody credited a *Wall Street Journal* editor with encouraging him to pursue the venture that ultimately made the manuals a household word. Clearly a large part of his inspiration must also have come from the founding father of financial publishing, Henry V. Poor.

Moody's First Manual

Moody's first *Manual of Industrial and Miscellaneous Corporation Securities* was a modest volume of 1,086 pages listing only 1,800 companies (the majority of them newly incorporated) along with some 200 domestic and foreign bond issues. Described in a newspaper article as "largely a directory,"[4] *Moody's Manual* in most respects represents an evolutionary stage in financial publishing rather than a radical departure from *Poor's*; although Moody's inclusion of industrial companies together with the railroads and utilities covered by Poor was a real breakthrough. Moreover this first effort had the same sort of broad coverage that is the hallmark of today's Moody's manuals—including not only industrial companies but also banks and financial entities, and even U.S. and foreign government securities, in addition to utilities and railroads. The most complete company descriptions included type of business, financial condition of the firm, and a list of management personnel. Less important companies were accorded a cursory description. Coverage spanned "practically all" securities traded on the New York Stock Market; important companies from Boston, Philadelphia, and Chicago markets; and the larger companies from St. Louis, Louisville, and Cincinnati.[5] The collective capitalization (i.e., funds invested in firms listed) amounted to over $9,325,000, quite a sum for that time. Another harbinger of things to come was a section devoted to laws of incorporation in three eastern states and West Virginia, material typically included in either introductions or special features sections of later manuals. Despite subsequent fulminations about advertisements jeopardizing the objectivity of financial reports, in 1900 John Moody placed ads on the cover and on the 16 pages preceding the manual's title page. (In what Moody's Investor's Service calls the "modern manuals" published from 1909 onward, a stronger financial position allowed the company to drop this practice.) As H.V. Poor had before him, Moody found data-gathering difficult. The magnitude of the task can be inferred from a statement in the preface that except for the 5 percent returning mailed questionnaires (some 100 companies), most firms required a "house to house canvass" and some took 12 to 15 visits before they responded.[6]

The soul of honesty, Moody acknowledged that the first manual "of necessity contains both errors and omissions" while asserting that in no other single publication was "more than ten percent of the information embraced in this volume" available.[7] However his early frankness was gradually diluted by the increasingly litigious nature of American society. In 1915 the disclaimer-cum-defense of the publication's value read: "we do not guarantee the correctness of every figure," yet steadfastly maintained that it had "a much smaller percentage of errors than any other

financial publication in existence."[8] In 1927 Moody wrote that, while the magnitude and complexity of the compilation task precluded guarantees of the "absolute accuracy of the statements . . . it is not likely that any serious inaccuracies will be found" and promised in subsequent editions to correct "any errors brought to his attention."[9] In 1960 evidently it was dangerous to concede more than that Moody's sources were reputable but not infallible and that opinions expressed were independent and unbiased. And by the 1970s the standard disclaimer had become a note that Moody's could not assume liability for correctness of reports, ratings, or data in the manuals.

In the virtually total blackout of public information regarding securities, investors apparently greeted both Poor's and Moody's early efforts with nearly unanimous approval. The first editions of both titles were sold out just months after being released. A prepublication announcement for Moody's first manual is purely descriptive,[10] but four years later political science scholars would express approbation of another Moody book, *The Truth About the Trusts* (New York: Moody Publishing, 1904). These scholars' reviews are important because they bolstered the reputation of his yearly manual considerably and because one mentioned the manual as well as the monograph. The first reviewer praised the *Truth About the Trusts* for its "succinct analyses of . . . elements of strength or weakness" of the corporations, corroborated Moody's claim of providing "the most thorough and accurate list of industrial trusts ever published in this country," and proclaimed the data to be "of the greatest interest and importance to every student of the trust problem."[11] A second gentleman (albeit not totally uncritical of *The Truth About the Trusts*) echoed students' gratitude for the monograph and commented on the *Manual of Industrial and Miscellaneous Corporation Securities* saying that it had "within the short space of four years come to fill a useful place in the current literature regarding corporations."[12]

Riding a tide of critical and financial success with his publishing ventures and enjoying huge success with his own extensive investments, Moody suffered the loss of his personal and professional fortunes with the stock market downturn of 1907. After a short while in receivership, the company reorganized; and in 1908 the new Moody Manual Company (forerunner of Standard & Poor's Corporation) published a manual with Louis Holschuh (former treasurer of the old company and future president of Moody's Investors Service) as editor and with Roger W. Babson (John Moody's competitor, founder of a stock and bond statistical service disseminated on index cards) as owner. A third former Moody's employee, George Hoskins, became an editor with the new firm in 1909. From this time until 1924 (when he bought back the copyright) Moody was obliged to suffer his name being on Poor's publication. Roy Porter, who bought the Moody Manual Company in 1914 and changed its name to Poor's Publishing Company in 1919 after buying the Poor's Railroad Manual Company, cheerfully admitted using both names on the manual cover from 1915–1924 because of the "nuisance value,"[13] the chance to annoy John Moody. (The cover title for the 1922 edition, for example, was *Poor's and Moody's Manual Consolidated*.) Another practice that was probably salt in Moody's wounds was incorporation of one-inch ads—not in the front and end matter—but on the very page where a company's securities were described and evaluated, pulling in additional revenue to the tune of $20,000 a year.

Because John Moody began publishing his own manuals again in 1909, confusion about which was the "real" Moody's manual reigned for years. A 1911 *New York Times* article announced the twelfth annual *Moody's Manual* which was, in fact, not John Moody's manual, but the publication of his namesake competitor.[14] In appearance and content, the competing publication resembled early Poor's manuals much more than Moody's manuals.

In 1921, on the occasion of a Moody speech, the same newspaper erroneously identified him as the editor of the *Moody's Manuals*. Moody requested and received a retraction of the statement.[15] The stalemate was not to be resolved until a lawsuit in 1924 resulted in an out-of-court settlement wherein Moody repurchased copyright to the name "Moody's" from Poor's Publishing Company.[16]

Moody's Modern Manuals

The modern manuals began with Moody's 1909 reentry into publishing financial manuals. Allegedly barred from engaging in such activity by the terms of the 1907–1908 bankruptcy and company reorganization,[17] Moody nevertheless came out with a new railroad manual. As he later admitted, it covered "only a portion of the American steam railroad field" and lacked the "ordinary statistical facts found in the old-style railroad manuals"[18] He narrowly escaped being prevented from even this modest venture. In 1937, Roy Porter reminisced about the split vote of Moody Manual Company officials in the early 1900s which narrowly defeated a motion to convert a temporary injunction against John Moody's renewed publishing activity into a *permanent* one.[19]

Moody's passion to excel in this field and his bitterness at having lost his old company are evident in introductory comments berating "the average imitator" who "like any other robber of an idea, never permanently gets the confidence of the public" despite, as Moody saw it, having appropriated his ideas to "foist them on the public as the genuine article."[20] On the same page he referred to "some publication which, because of its name or method of promotion, conveys the false impression that Mr. Moody is identified with it;"[21] and having persuaded himself, he attempted to convince the reader that "No other publication of any financial character has any authority or right to the use of Mr. John Moody's name, either directly or indirectly."[22] Having been sued for libel in a brief youthful fling at newspaper publishing, he scrupulously avoided naming names.

Careful not to use the term "manual" in the work's title, Moody further differentiated *Moody's Analysis of Railroad Investments* from the old manuals by introducing a totally new feature—a stock and bond rating system similar to company credit ratings issued by Dun & Bradstreet. (Like the founder of IBM, throughout his career John Moody was more the master of extending and refining a concept with popular appeal than a brilliant innovator.) Presenting his scale of ratings levels (from Aaa to E) to assess investment risk in terms of safety and resaleability of securities, Moody cautioned, "It must not be forgotten that *arbitrary judgement* is used to a large degree;" and he counseled the reader to use the ratings as indications of the security issue's investment quality but not as "specific opinion" or a "recommendation to buy."[23] Not surprisingly, some of the companies rated—none of which had even been obliged to provide the public with information a decade or two earlier—balked at the assignment of ratings. They were displeased with the whole idea and especially with the practice of rating pessimistically in the absence of complete and current information and giving the benefit of the doubt to the investor. The reluctant companies raised "a storm of opposition, not to mention ridicule,"[24] according to Moody. In contrast, a political scientist summed up what probably was the predominant reaction outside the railroad industry: "The volume is indeed of high merit. . . . It will doubtless be appreciated by both individual investors and . . . others . . . interested in railroad values."[25]

In 1914 Moody expanded the work's scope by adding a second volume to cover public utilities and industrials. Like previous editions, *Part I: Steam Railroads* covered Mexican and Canadian steam railroads as well as U.S. lines; in 1915 Cuban companies were added. Dissatisfied with just analyzing companies' investment offerings, Moody used this two-part 1914 edition to re-stake his claim to providing accurate and complete statistics instead of merely predigested "deductions and conclusions."[26] Both parts included digests of company annual reports adjusted to be more comparable than heretofore—no mean feat, since neither utilities nor railroads (unless engaged in interstate business) were as yet required to report information in a uniform manner. Railroad entries included not only ten years of annual income statements and balance sheet data expressed in the common standard of dollars per mile, but also comments on strong and weak points in company operations. Physical characteristics of each "road" were given together with comments on the significance of various figures. Finally, a complete description of the public stock and bond offerings was shown along with their respective ratings and each rating's rationale. The preface pointed out that an expanded version of the railroad manual's introduction (published in 1912 by Analyses Publishing Company as a book entitled *How to Analyze Railroad Reports*) had been adopted as a text by many universities and colleges. A reviewer of that work commented that the textbook "deserves its well-earned success" and added that Moody's "well known manual . . . has been of service to investors as well as students."[27]

Six years after stock and bond ratings had been introduced, the 1915 edition of the public utilities/industrials manual also assigned ratings to companies other than railroads. In addition to the ratings, the following salient facts regarding utilities were disclosed in the manual: physical condition; earning power (a combination of geographic location, population and its growth, quality of management, availability of "franchise"—meaning monopoly,—and rates charged); strength of financial resources; and general credit-worthiness. Two additional factors especially germane to industrial corporations—the regulatory climate and the degree of their dependence on the country's general prosperity—were included in industrial manual entries. Never content to rest on his laurels for long, Moody upgraded the manuals within the next three years as follows: adding to the railroad manual complete five-year financial figures for smaller companies and issuing a monthly updating publication; augmenting the securities rating system by three more categories at the low end of the scale; and increasing industrial/public utility coverage by more than 1,000 additional companies.

The next quantum leap in scope came with the issuance in 1918 of a separate government securities manual. Covering more than 30,000 bond issues, 25,000 of them issued by the U.S. government and its political subdivisions, the manual carried the subtitle "Founded to endure and Investors make secure." The four respective main sections were the federal government and U.S. dependencies (including Alaska, Hawaii, Puerto Rico, and the Philippine Islands); American states and municipalities; the Dominion of Canada together with its provinces and municipalities; and some 127 pages of data for foreign governments and cities. By now the rating scale had been simplified to five grades ranging from Aaa to Ba plus a sixth category consolidating all lower ratings.

Moody attributed the expanded scope to World War I activity in government securities—not only U.S. liberty bonds but also European bonds payable in dollars, particularly those issued by Great Britain, France, and Belgium—and noted that both then and for years afterwards his was the only manual with extensive international coverage. Many U.S. allies supplied enough information to receive a rating; but to no one's surprise, Germany, Austria, and Russia did not. In 1922, to gain depth of background and experience in the international field, Moody's hired Max Winkler, Ph.D. "a walking statistical table of European affairs."[28] After the war Moody announced his intention of considerably broadening the scope of the government

and municipal volume since he felt "a large amount of American capital must necessarily be provided for government purposes in all parts of the world."[29]

In 1920 when industrials and public utilities were split into two volumes, the Moody's manuals became four in number. The "amplified and enlarged" *Public Utility Investments* included a larger number of companies than ever before, particularly small companies. An 18-page introductory essay about the industry included such details as a prediction that the "jitney bus" (a sort of unlicensed taxi) would be a short-lived phenomenon because its operators were "a comparatively irresponsible class of people."[30] There were 1,426 pages of company coverage plus a section giving ten-year price ranges for public utility stocks and bonds.

Shortly after the war Major Maurice N. Blakemore was hired to get compilation of the manuals back on schedule. Unlike two predecessors, one who ended up in a "lunatic asylum" and a second who quit to take up chicken farming, Blakemore succeeded and served as managing editor from 1922 to 1924.[31] Soon put in charge of sales as well, he proved unsatisfactory at the dual responsibilities. At this juncture (1925) John Sherman Porter, an employee since 1916 and an experienced editorial board member, was promoted to editor-in-chief.

John Sherman Porter's Tenure

It is difficult to determine how much any one individual influenced development of the Moody's manuals, because from the beginning editing has been the joint responsibility of the editor-in-chief, the editorial board, and the administrator titled "sales manager" in Moody's day and "publisher" since 1954. Although he yielded to others the title of "editor" (and from Blakemore's tenure on, permitted their respective names to be emblazoned on the title page), for years Moody retained ultimate control and stated in the front matter that the manuals were prepared under his general supervision. Nevertheless, Porter, who served as editor-in-chief for 38 years, seems to have guided the Moody's manuals more than any other single person except John Moody himself. When Porter started, steam-powered engines held sway on land and sea with scant competition from any other form of transportation; in 1962, when Dun & Bradstreet bought out the original stockholders and Porter resigned, advances in aerospace technology seemed about to promise humankind mastery of the whole universe.

Porter's first major project was adding a separate banking and finance manual in 1928. The introduction gave an overview of such topics as banking in the U.S. and Canada, the Federal Reserve Banking System, and the potential importance of insurance stocks and real estate mortgage bonds to the investor. Coverage included American and foreign companies in the following categories, most previously covered although less extensively in the industrial manual: banks and trusts; mortgage and finance; and insurance (fire, casualty, and miscellaneous). In addition, 11 pages dealt with federal reserve banks and some 57 pages presented information about various entities within the federal farm loan system. Unlike other manuals, this one carried no ratings. Porter instituted use of the subtitle "American and Foreign" on all manuals to emphasize Moody's foreign coverage, a significant change that remained in effect through 1970.

In the speculative boom of the late 1920s the company went public in a modest way, floating an issue of non-voting preferred stock with Moody and company old-timers Holschuh, McCruden, Shea, Leavitt, and Porter as company directors and majority stockholders. For Moody's Investors Service, as for all U.S. businesses, the 1930s were difficult. As Moody remembered it, the firm survived only by cutting some staff and slashing salaries for the rest (including company directors) 20 percent or more.[32] Apparently Poor's Publishing Company fared even worse. According to Moody, "Poor's was forced to give up the ghost in 1940;" and when Moody's took over the Poor's Manual subscription list, total circulation had dropped to fewer than 7,000 copies.[33]

During the pre-war years and World War II, financial publishing did not change a great deal except that, like other sectors of the economy, it occasionally was hampered by rationing of such essential commodities as paper. In 1935, under Porter's leadership, the company discontinued rating stocks (securities reflecting equity or a share of ownership in a company) to concentrate on debt securities (bonds). Critical reception remained favorable. One reviewer praised the Moody's manuals handsomely for documenting not only business and economic conditions in Latin America at the beginning of the Second World War, but also circumstances leading up to the war.[34]

During the 1950s Porter continued to refine the manuals. In 1950 an explanation of bank examination procedures and federal investment regulations became a regular feature of each manual's front matter, a practice continued until 1975 (when, first, investors were assumed to be conversant with basic facts and, second, this short feature had become insufficient for explaining the intricacies of the body of securities regulations by then in force). In 1952, the railroad manual (still covering more than 1,000 railroad companies) expanded to include all commercial forms of transportation and was retitled Moody's Manual of Investments. American and Foreign. Transportation. Railroads-Airlines-Shipping Traction, Bus and Truck Lines. In 1954 and 1955 the subtitle "American and Foreign" was relegated to very small type on the title page and all titles were changed so that the industry classification would be the second word in the title (e.g., instead of Moody's Manual of Investments. American and Foreign. Bank, Insurance, and Finance, the 1955 manual was called Moody's Bank & Finance Manual). The next year an interview of John Moody featured glowing comments about the manuals. Prefacing a sketch of Moody's life as an entrepreneur and publisher, the author stated, "next to the Bible, Wall Streeters put their faith in Moody's Investors Manuals" and opined, "it can safely be said that nearly anything of a financial statistical nature available anywhere on a publicly owned corporation will be found in Moody's manuals."[35] While such comments are not the result of a rigorous analysis or critique, they do reflect popular opinion of the manuals at the time.

Purchase by Dun & Bradstreet

The next two decades were a period of rapid change for Moody's. In 1962, four years after Moody's death, the company was sold to Dun & Bradstreet (another company with a long-standing tradition of excellence in financial publishing) in part so that Porter and others could convert their equity in the company into cash. Moody's then became a wholly owned subsidiary (a virtually independent unit of the parent company).

After Porter came a fairly quick succession of editors-in-chief, all of them former editorial assistants. The first, Frank St. Clair (1963–1969), made no major changes. During the one-year tenure of the second, George H. Parson, the title page format was altered—the typeface less ornate, the page uncluttered, and for the first time the names of the publisher and his assistant positioned on the page above the editor-in-chief. More significant, in 1970 the ratings division of Moody's Investors Service, by then a separate part of the company, instituted fees for the considerable effort and expense of studying and rating companies' securities. This change, now standard practice throughout the financial industry, was first disclosed to manual users in the 1971 *Public Utility Manual*. Although it did not affect Parson's department directly, the increased company resources with which to pay salaries and other mounting expenses doubtless indirectly facilitated maintaining the quality of the manuals. The most notable development dur-

ing this period was the publication of the new *Moody's OTC Industrial Manual*, splitting over-the counter companies (meaning those traded on smaller and regional stock exchanges) off from the industrial manual and also expanding the number of such companies covered.

Parson's successor, Roy A. Krause (1971–1973), oversaw expansion of the industrials to a two-volume set in 1972 and division of the municipals into volume one (Alabama-New Hampshire and U.S.A.-its dependencies) and volume two (New Jersey-Wyoming) in 1973. In October of the last year of his editorship, after nearly four decades of rating only debt issues (bonds), the company resumed rating preferred stocks (on a scale with seven gradations of quality/riskiness). Their rationale for reinstating the ratings was both increased investor interest and "dilution of some of the protection afforded them."[36] While Krause had no influence over this decision, it surely increased the utility and value of the manuals to the investor.

Robert Hanson accepted the post of editor-in-chief in 1973, and has devoted 18 years to the position. With a bachelor's degree in finance from City College of New York, Hanson started out in 1962 in the news reports department at Moody's and came up through the ranks to the editorial board in 1971. As editor he has worked with a distinguished list of publishers (Robert H. Messner 1973–1975, William O. Dwyer 1975–1981, Sheila S. Lambert 1981–1989, and Howard Kiedaisch, associate publisher since 1982, and responsible for the manuals since 1989). In 1989, to make the editor-in-chief job more manageable, Moody's top officials gave half of the editor's mantle to a seasoned editorial board member, Earl Stephens, who took on the *Bank & Finance Manual*, the *OTC Industrial Manual*, the *Public Utility Manual*, and the *Transportation Manual*. Hanson retains responsibility for the *Municipal & Government Manual*, the *Industrial Manual*, the *International Manual*, and the *OTC Unlisted Manual*.

Further Expansion

The current pre-eminence of Moody's among financial publishers is the result of constant re-examination of what the market wants and needs and appropriate product development to meet such needs. Publisher Sheila Lambert played midwife at the introduction of two new manuals. In 1981 the burgeoning number of international and multinational enterprises resulted in a separate *International Manual*. Duplicate entries were phased out gradually (companies paying for high visibility still retaining the privilege of being listed in more than one manual if they so choose). Within a year or two, however, all foreign companies were shifted from the other manuals into the *International Manual*; foreign countries and their political subdivisions were moved from the *Municipal & Government Manual* into the new manual. Then in 1986 Moody's issued a new *OTC Unlisted Manual* giving investors access to information on companies not listed on any exchanges but traded exclusively via "pink sheets" or daily price quotes distributed only to stockbrokers. This manual was declared by *Money*, "your best bet for pinpointing smaller pink-sheet stocks."[37]

Beginning in 1976 half a dozen manuals expanded from one or two volumes to multiple-volume sets: in 1976 the *Bank & Finance Manual* went to two volumes (banks, trust companies, savings and loan associations, and federal credit agencies in the first and insurance, finance, real estate, and investment companies in the second); in 1980 the *Public Utility Manual* split into two volumes; in 1984 the almost new *International Manual* came out as two units (Algeria-Ivory Coast and Jamaica-Zimbabwe); in 1986 the *Bank & Finance Manual* was issued in three volumes, the third adding coverage of unit investment trusts, a relatively new form of investment product; in 1988 the *Municipal & Government Manual*, was published in three parts (Alabama-Kentucky, Louisiana-Pennsylvania, and Rhode Island-Wyoming); and in 1988 the *Bank & Finance Manual*'s Unit Investment Trust volume divided into one part covering sponsors A-M and a second covering N-Z, for a total of four volumes.

Technological Advances

Spurred by competition from Standard and Poor's, the other giant of financial publishing, and from smaller, newer firms, Moody's made two important, albeit somewhat delayed, technological changes. Standard & Poor's Corporation, formed by a 1941 merger of Poor's Publishing and Standard Statistics, introduced the *Compustat* service in 1962. *Compustat*, comprised of 20 years of annual data and theretofore distributed exclusively on tape compatible with mainframe computers, was offered in compact disc for microcomputer users around 1988. Moody's, however, loath to dilute a fine reputation by precipitous entry into nonprint technologies, did not follow suit. Apart from one brief attempt to construct a structured, computer-readable financial database (aborted because there seemed to be no demand for such a product), Moody's kept on doing what they had always done best—producing printed manuals and updating services.

The first technological change involved overhauling the printing process in 1975. For years a cumbersome discontinuous arrangement of companies in the manuals was necessitated by the off-site linotype printing process. The logistics of maintaining a steady stream of work to the printer so that each annual volume could be completed and issued on time meant that similar companies were not integrated into their respective industry sections. For example, in the same edition an initial section of American banks was followed first by foreign banks, then by another section of American banks, and again by a section of foreign banks. This process was terribly expensive and inflexible. Both manual users and Moody's stockholders were better served by the new method of computerized typesetting, which reduced costs at the same time it "smoothed out" the production flow and permitted better organization of the manuals. (Happily the separate index, covering all manuals except the *Municipal & Government* one, is still available to help neophytes chart a course among the eight different manuals.)

In 1986 when Moody's brought the computerized typesetting process inhouse and no longer depended on an outside printer, the second, even more significant technological advance was accomplished. Stored in computerized form, the data was no longer confined to the printed page. Moody's began to augment printed products with electronic distribution of the data through cooperation with vendors such as DIALOG to offer interactive retrieval and manipulation of company financial data supplied by Moody's.

In 1988, the inhouse, computerized typesetting process also contributed to the development of the first of a series of compact disc products searchable offline via CD-ROM reader and microcomputer. This development permitted direct access to the manuals' vast compendia of facts without the significant expense of long distance phone charges incurred in online searching. The first product, *Moody's 5000 Plus*, covering all companies traded on the New York and American Stock Exchanges as well as NASDAQ National Market companies was quickly followed by *Moody's International Plus* covering the leading non-U.S. companies. At this writing a third CD product, *Moody's OTC Plus*, designed to provide information about companies traded over-the-counter, has also been released.

The final significant change in the manuals during the past two decades was financial in origin. In 1975, when pressure on publishing firms to show a profit was mounting, Moody's instituted the option of purchasing more detailed coverage of company information. That is, for $1,000 dollars (in addition to the fee levied by the ratings department), a firm could get increased visibility in the manual in the form of "full measure coverage." This option ensured that company narrative would be expanded, that financial data would be displayed across an entire page, and that in addition to a description of the firm, entries would provide up to seven years of financial and operating information together with ratio analysis putting the figures into perspective. Since its introduction, this service has undergone several modifications. Today, four levels of expanded coverage (or Visibility) are offered. They included Corporate Visibility (CV), CV-Select, CV-Plus, and CV-Ultra. Presentation of company data is expanded with each level of coverage. Corporate Visibility includes up to five years of financial statements with a medium-length description of the company's history, business, and other narrative. Corporate Visibility-Select includes up to a seven-year financial presentation and a more detailed narrative section. Corporate Visibility-Plus expands the narrative considerably, even including such details as the chief executive officer's letter to shareholders and the complete set of notes from financial statements. The highest level of coverage, Corporate Visibility-Ultra, offers the listed company an opportunity to include a full-page advertisement on the second page of its listing. (It should be noted that Moody's exercises considerable editorial judgment as to the contents of the ads.)

Critical Reception

Critical reception for the modern manuals has been almost as sparse as reaction to the very first ones. In the business community, the ratings and the ratings process are of paramount importance—the manuals, merely a transmittal mechanism, usually have not been deemed worthy of comment. Occasionally an article will favor a Standard & Poor's product or feature or state that Moody's "long dominant position in the municipal-rating field is being chipped away by an increasingly aggressive Standard & Poor's corporation,"[38] However, most issuers of securities, with millions of dollars in financing costs riding on ratings outcomes, practice the belt-and-suspenders approach of using both services.

Most large investors do too. A business professor noted that "splits [meaning materially higher or lower ratings for the same security] do occur and both issuers and purchasers normally seek ratings from both agencies,"[39] and concluded, "the value of the second rating, or opinion, arises primarily from the fact that it is independent from the first."[40]

Among librarians, Moody's is always mentioned in the same breath as Standard & Poor's, and most are reluctant to pick a favorite. Some prefer the tidiness of Moody's annual bound volume for its suitability in building a collection of retrospective print holdings and the savings in staff time from having one less loose-leaf service to file. Others place a high priority on the regular updating of the *Standard & Poor's Corporation Records*. If a handbook or bibliography mentions only one of the two, however, it is virtually always the old reliable Moody's manuals.

Only three reviewers have been both knowledgeable enough and brave enough to make a detailed comparison of the *Standard & Poor's Corporation Records* and the Moody's manuals. The first, Judith Truelson, pronounced Moody's "the most comprehensive source of this kind of information [summary and analysis of information in company annual reports], available to private investor and financial analyst alike"[41] The second, Bernard Schlessinger, asserted that whether "Moody's or S&P should be the primary source of business materials, given a limited budget, . . . is a matter of personal preference."[42] In another passage, however, he evaluated the Moody's manuals as "One of the most comprehensive sources for information of this kind, this service is recommended for all business, academic, and public libraries medium-sized and larger."[43] Jean Kellough, the third reviewer, dealt with the compact disc products of the respective publishers, Moody's 500 Plus and DIALOG Ondisc Standard & Poor's Corporation Records. Having noted that S&P covers more companies (9,000 versus Moody's slightly over 5,000), she concluded that "Moody's 5000+ [*sic*], which seems best suited

for a financial analyst or researcher who would use it often, offers sophisticated features that the average undergraduate student would not use."[44]

Reorganized for the Electronic Age

In early 1989, the company was reorganized and renamed to emphasize electronic services—with print products (the manuals and updating services) and two electronic products, Datastream and Interactive Data, forming a group called "Dun & Bradstreet Financial Services of North America" and only the ratings service still going by the name Moody's Investors Service. Early the following year, however, Dun & Bradstreet management decided to divest the two electronic database units, restore the print publishing section to Moody's Investors Service, and revert to emphasizing what Moody's has always done better than anyone else—publish the most complete and most reliable financial information available.

Always striving for improvement, Moody's has a five-year strategic plan for operations. Both current and potential new products are subjected to a rigorous set of criteria and testing for compatibility with company mission, a close fit with what customers want and need, and other key considerations. Broad editorial plans have a dual focus. While manuals and updating services will continue to be available in "hardcopy" form, the same wealth of information will become available in nonprint formats as Moody's expands its activity in the arena of electronic products currently offered. The market will dictate what, if anything, is done to expand existing printed manuals or introduce new ones. A more focused product, addressing a narrower niche of investor interest than the well known encyclopedic manuals, is one option under discussion. Whatever direction is taken, the Moody's manuals will remain a household word in this country and abroad for generations to come.

PUBLICATION HISTORY

The Manual of Industrial and Miscellaneous Corporation Securities. Annual. New York: O. C. Lewis Co., 1900–07.

Moody's Manuals. Annual. New York: Moody Manual Co., 1908–24.

Moody's Analyses of Railroad Investments. Annual. New York: Analyses Publishing Co., 1909–13.

Moody's Analyses of Investments. Part I: Steam Railroads. Part II: Public Utilities and Industrials. Annual. New York: Analyses Publishing Co., 1914–20.

Moody's Analyses of Investments. Part III: Government and Municipal Securities. Annual. New York: Moody's Investors Service, 1918–1920.

Moody's Analyses of Investments. Part I: Railroad Investments. Part II: Industrial Investments. Part III: Public Utility Investments. Part IV: Government and Municipal Securities. Annual. New York: Moody's Investors Service, 1920–1921.

Moody's Manual of Investments and Security Rating Service. Government and Municipal Securities. Annual. New York: Moody's Investors Service, 1921–1927.

Moody's Manual of Investments and Security Rating Service. Public Utility Securities. Annual. New York: Moody's Investors Service, 1921–1927.

Moody's Manual of Investments and Security Rating Service. Railroad Securities. Annual. New York: Moody's Investors Service, 1921–1927.

Moody's Manual of Investments and Security Rating Service. Industrial Securities. Annual. New York: Moody's Investors Service, 1921–1927.

Moody's Manual of Investments. American and Foreign. Government and Municipal Securities. Annual. New York: Moody's Investors Service, 1928–1954.

Moody's Manual of Investments. American and Foreign. Banks-Insurance Companies-Investment Trusts-Real Estate-Finance and Credit Companies. Annual. New York: Moody's Investors Service, 1928–1954.

Moody's Manual of Investments. American and Foreign. Public Utility Securities. Annual. New York: Moody's Investors Service, 1928–1953.

Moody's Manual of Investments. American and Foreign. Railroad Securities. Annual. New York: Moody's Investors Service, 1928–1951.

Moody's Manual of Investments. American and Foreign. Industrial Securities. Annual. New York: Moody's Investors Service, 1928–1953.

Moody's Manual of Investments. American and Foreign, Transportation. Annual. New York: Moody's Investors Service, 1952–1953.

Moody's Industrial Manual. Annual. New York: Moody's Investors Service, 1954– .

Moody's Public Utility Manual. Annual. New York: Moody's Investors Service, 1954– .

Moody's Transportation Manual. Annual. New York: Moody's Investors Service, 1954– .

Moody's Bank & Finance Manual. Annual. New York: Moody's Investors Service, 1955– .

Moody's Municipal & Government Manual. Annual. New York: Moody's Investors Service, 1955– .

Moody's OTC Industrial Manual. Annual. New York: Moody's Investors Service, 1970– .

Moody's International Manual. Annual. New York: Moody's Investors Service, 1981– .

Moody's OTC Unlisted Manual. Annual. New York: Moody's Investors Service, 1986– .

BIBLIOGRAPHY

There must be somewhere (perhaps in the apocrypha) a biblical prohibition against in-depth comparisons of the Moody's manuals and their competitors. The prevailing sentiment seems to be: "Let him who is a certified financial genius cast the first stone." There are scores of articles—both popular and theoretical—on the ratings process and bushel baskets full of news notes on specific ratings being changed as well as discussions of esoteric changes in the rating scales or the types of securities that get rated. But few writers seem to have enjoyed the happy combination of sufficient skill, time, and interest to write a thorough critique of the Moody's manuals and the *Standard & Poor's Corporation Records.*

Slavens gives succinct, serviceable descriptions of the Moody's manuals but barely mentions the *Standard & Poor's Corporation Records.* Ganly gives complete, accurate, and readable descriptions of the *Bank & Finance, Industrial, OTC Industrial,* and *Public Utility* manuals, but he too passes over the *Standard & Poor's Corporation Records.* Walford describes only the *Industrial Manual* and its *News Reports.* Sheehy concentrates on directories and encyclopedias, covering neither Moody's nor S&P's manuals. *Ulrich's* covers both briefly and Woy gives directory-type information on both (although the *Industrial Manual* is the only Moody's manual he lists under the heading "International Business").

Daniells's descriptive annotations compare favorably with Ganly in all respects and surpass him in covering all eight manuals and the *Standard & Poor's Corporation Records*.

The three reviewers who go beyond simple description are Truelson, Schlessinger, and Kellough (covering compact disc versions). All compare and contrast Moody's and S&P's respective manuals more thoroughly and insightfully than any other writers on this topic. Since Moody's and other financial publishers always seem to have something new up their sleeves, it is devoutly hoped that someone will provide timely updates for the library student and the practicing librarian.

"A Century of Standard & Poor's." *The Spectator. Employee Magazine of Standard & Poor's Corporation* 7 (April, 1960): 1–16.

Chandler, Alfred D., Jr. *Henry Varnum Poor Business Editor, Analyst, and Performer.* Cambridge, MA: Harvard University Press, 1956.

Daniells, Lorna M. *Business Information Sources.* Rev. ed. Berkeley: University of California Press, 1985.

Ganly, John V. *Serials for Libraries.* New York: Neal-Schuman, 1985.

Inventing Our Future. Centennial Report. New York: McGraw-Hill, [1988].

Jensen, Dennis J. "The Research Library of Standard & Poor's Corporation." In *Banking and Finance Collections,* edited by Jean Deus. New York: Haworth Press, 1984.

Kellough, Jean. "Moody's 5000+ and DIALOG Ondisc Standard & Poor's Corporations: A Comparison of Two Full-Text Business Databases," *Laserdisk Professional* 2 (November, 1989): 78–89.

Moody, John. *A Fifty Year Review of Moody's Investors Service.* New York: Moody's Investors Service, [1949].

———. *Long Road Home: An Autobiography.* New York: Macmillan, 1933.

National Cyclopedia of American Biography. New York: James T. White, 1918.

Schlessinger, Bernard S. *The Basic Business Library: Core Resources.* 2nd ed. Phoenix: Oryx Press, 1989.

Sheehy, Eugene P. *Guide to Reference Books.* 10th ed. Chicago: American Library Association, 1986.

Slavens, Thomas P. "Major Business Reference Works." *Reference Librarian* no. 15 (Fall, 1986): 185–94.

Standard & Poor's 120 Years of Preserving the "Right to Know." New York: Standard & Poor's Corporation, [1980].

Truelson, Judith A. "Hot on the Corporate Trail." *RQ* 15 (Spring, 1976): 223–28.

Walford, Albert John. *Walford's Guide to Reference Material.* Volume 2: Social & Historical Sciences, Philosophy & Religion. London: Library Association, 1980.

Woy, James. *Encyclopedia of Business Information Sources.* Detroit: Gale Research, 1988.

NOTES

[1] John Moody, *Long Road Home: An Autobiography* (New York: Macmillan Co., 1933), 51.

[2] Richard Rutter, "Statistics House Thrives on Facts," *New York Times,* 24 April 1960, sec. 3, p. 1.

[3] G.B. Baker, "The Crisis at the Stock Exchange," *Contemporary Review* 58 (November 1890): 680.

[4] Robert E. Bedingfield, "Personality: Boswell of U.S. Corporations," *New York Times,* 6 May 1956, 3.

[5] John Moody, *Manual of Industrial and Miscellaneous Corporation Securities* (New York: O. C. Lewis Co., 1900): 47.

[6] Ibid., 50–51.

[7] Ibid., 47.

[8] John Moody, *Moody's Analyses of Investments.* Part II: Public Utilities and Industrials (New York: Analyses Publishing Co., 1915): 4.

[9] John Moody, *Moody's Manual of Investments and Security Rating Service. Industrial Securities* (New York: Moody's Investors Service, 1927): iii.

[10] "A Financial Reference Book," *New York Times,* 17 November 1890, 10.

[11] Alvin S. Johnson, "The Truth About the Trusts," *Political Science Quarterly* 19 (June 1904): 307.

[12] Emory R. Johnson, "The Truth About the Trusts," *American Academy of Political and Social Science* 24 (1904): 387.

[13] Roy Porter, dictated by Mr. Porter in 1937, transcript, Standard and Poor's Corporation Library, New York City, 8.

[14] "4,000 Pages About Railways," *New York Times,* 15 December 1911, 619.

[15] "Not Editor of Moody's Manual," *New York Times,* 23 October 1921, 18.

[16] Porter, dictated by Mr. Porter, 8.

[17] Ibid., 5.

[18] John Moody, *Moody's Analyses of Investments.* Part I: Steam Railroads (New York: Analyses Publishing Co., 1916): 17.

[19] Porter, "Dictated by Mr. Porter," p. 5.

[20] Moody, *Moody's Analyses of Investment.* Part I, p. 17.

[21] Ibid.

[22] Ibid.

[23] John Moody, *Moody's Analyses of Railroad Investments* (New York: Analyses Publishing Co., 1909): 193. Italics in original.

[24] John Moody, *A Fifty Year Review of Moody's Investors Service* (New York: Moody's Investors Service, [1949]): 11.

[25] Emory R. Johnson, "Moody's Analyses of Railroad Investments," *American Academy of Political and Social Science.* Annals 34 (1909): 211.

[26] John Moody, *Analyses of Investments.* Part I: Steam Railroads (1914): 17.

[27] "How to Analyze Railroad Reports," *Political Science Quarterly* 29 (March 1914): 180.

[28] Moody, *Fifty Year Review*, 17.

[29] *Moody's Analyses of Investments.* Part II: Public Utilities and Industrials (New York: Analyses Publishing Co., 1919): 2.

[30] John Moody, *Moody's Analyses of Investments.* Part III: Public Utility Investments (New York: Moody's Investor's Service, 1920): 5.

[31] Moody, *Fifty Year Review*, 18.

[32] Ibid., 32.

[33] Ibid., 22.

[34] J. Fred Rippy, "Moody's Manual of Investments, American and Foreign," *Hispanic American Historical Review* 23 (November 1943): 702.

[35] "Boswell of U.S. Corporations," 3.

[36] *Moody's Industrial Manual* (New York: Moody's Investors Service, 1974): viii.

[37] Andrea Rock, "Got a Stock Hunch?" *Money* 17 (August 1988): 117.

[38] Victor F. Zonana and Daniel Hertzberg, "The Rating Game," *Wall Street Journal*, 2 November 1981, p. 1.

[39] Louis H. Ederington, "Why Split Ratings Occur," *Financial Management* 15 (Spring 1986): 38.

[40] Ibid., 46.

[41] Judith A. Truelson, "Hot on the Corporate Trail," *RQ* 15 (Spring 1976): 224.

[42] Bernard S. Schlessinger, *The Basic Business Library: Core Resources* (Phoenix: Oryx Press, 1989): 239.

[43] Ibid., 39.

[44] Jean Kellough, "Moody's 5000+ and DIALOG Ondisc Standard & Poor's Corporations: A Comparison of Two Full-Text Business Databases," *Laserdisk Professional* 2 (November 1989): 89.

"The Bibliographical Wonder of the World": *The National Union Catalog*

John R.M. Lawrence

DEVELOPMENT AND HISTORY

On Monday, January 12, 1981, Pan American flight 106 to London left Washington, D.C., carrying a shipment of cards for the last volume of the massive, 754-volume *National Union Catalog, Pre-1956 Imprints*.[1] The shipment constituted the final leg of a journey that had commenced more than 80 years before. The final printed product of that monumental effort, whose aim had been the compilation and publication of a record of the holdings of American research libraries, had been hailed as "the bibliographical wonder of the world"[2] and the "greatest single instrument of bibliographic control in existence."[3] The final editing and publishing of this catalog had cost more than 34 million dollars and taken over 14 years to complete, but the total effort involved from the beginning is immeasurable.[4]

Antecedents

As early as 1850 the idea of a union catalog of books in American libraries had been proposed by Charles Coffin Jewett, librarian of the Smithsonian Institution from 1847 to 1854. In his 1850 annual report he proposed the printing of a general catalog that would allow a scholar "the means of knowing the full extent of his resources for investigation." Jewett proposed that the Smithsonian, by using stereotyped plates, would distribute records of its holdings to participating librar-

ies, which in turn would submit plates for titles not held in the Smithsonian. The latter in effect would act as a national bibliographic center. Jewett was well aware that this exchange of records would require that the participating libraries adhere to some sort of uniform cataloging rules, and he included that idea in his ambitious plans.[5]

Unfortunately, a quarter of a century passed before Charles A. Cutter provided the impetus for standardizing cataloging with the publication of his *Rules for a Printed Dictionary Catalogue* (Washington: Government Printing Office, 1875).[6] About the same time, various institutions began to consider the possibility of reducing expenses by the use of centralized production and distribution of printed catalog cards. During the late 1890s, the American Library Association experimented with various card printing schemes for both books and journal articles. The first of these efforts was to provide short title-list cards for books cataloged by the publishing section; another project which began in 1898 provided cards for articles for scholarly journals, such as those indexed by *Poole's Index to Periodical Literature* (Boston: Houghton, 1882) or the *International Catalog of Scientific Literature* (London: Royal Society of London, 1902–21).[7] While these projects met with varying success, all of these efforts contributed to the gradual standardization of printed catalog cards, an innovation that would finally make practical not only the exchange of information about library holdings, but also the easy integration of reports from various libraries into a single information source.[8]

In June 1898, the Library of Congress began to print catalog cards for books received for copyright. After January 1901, the Library began printing cards for all accessions, and plans for distributing the cards to other libraries were announced in July of that year.[9] In his 1901 annual report, Herbert Putnam, the Librarian of Congress, unveiled the ambitious scheme that would in fact create a national union catalog:

> Finally, it is fully recognized by the Library that next in importance to an adequate exhibit of its own resources, comes the ability to supply information as to the resources of other libraries.
>
> As steps in this direction may be mentioned:
>
> First. The acquisition of printed catalogues of libraries, both American and foreign.
>
> Second. An alphabetic author catalogue on cards of books in department and bureau libraries in Washington.
>
> Third. A similar catalogue of books in some of the more important libraries outside Washington.
>
> The Library of Congress expects to place in each great center of research in the United States a copy of every card that it prints for its own catalogues; these will form there a statement of what the National Library contains. It hopes to receive a copy of every card printed by the New York Public Library, the Boston Public Library, the Harvard University Library, the John Crerar Library, and several others. These it will arrange and preserve in a card catalogue of the great collections outside of Washington.[10]

A Union Catalog on Cards

The ideas of depository card collections and distributing catalog cards on demand proved immensely popular, and did much to accelerate the further standardization of catalog cards, although not soon enough for the new union catalog.[11] Cards from Harvard were smaller than the standard and had to be mounted on larger cards, while those from Boston Public required trimming and retyping of headings lost by trimming.[12] Initially, the files from each library were maintained separately, but by 1909 were so extensive that it was deemed necessary to arrange them into a single author alphabet.[13] At that time the new merged file included entries contributed by nine libraries: New York Public, Harvard, Boston Public, John Crerar, Washington Public, the Bureau of Education, the Department of Agriculture, the Geological Survey, and the War Department. Despite the fact that there was a surprisingly small amount of duplication in the file (only 20 percent of the titles were held in the Library of Congress, and only 7 percent by any 2 other libraries), Putnam enthusiastically predicted that when completed the union catalog would contain about 600,000 entries, and in combination with an equal number of entries from the the LC public catalogs, would constitute the "closest approximation now available to a complete record of books in American libraries."[14]

Nonetheless, for the first 25 years of its existence, the union catalog remained a tool used chiefly by the Library of Congress cataloging staff as a source for cataloging copy and supplying card orders. Without a special staff for maintenance, the union catalog was maintained by the library's Card Division as a supplement to the public catalogs. As other libraries, including the University of Illinois, the University of Chicago, and the Newberry Library, joined the list of contributors, the catalog continued to expand. By 1926, the union catalog held some 1,960,000 cards, representing far more titles than the modest predictions made in 1909.

Expansion of the Catalog

However, by this time it was also apparent to scholars that this gigantic figure represented less than a fourth of scholarly titles to be found in American libraries. In addition, the rapid expansion of graduate study following World War I made the inadequacy of this bibliographic record painfully obvious.[15] In

1926, scholarship received assistance from John D. Rockefeller, Jr. The businessman provided a $250,000 gift to be administered over a five-year period, for the specific purpose of extending the "bibliographic apparatus." Project "B," as the effort came to be called in order to distinguish it from other specially funded projects administered by the Library of Congress, was headed by Ernest Cushing Richardson, former director of the Princeton University Library and at that time the consultant in bibliography and research at the Library of Congress. To assist him, Ernest Kletsch, a former member of the Library of Congress staff who had entered private business, was named curator of the union catalog.[16] Their chief objective was expressed as locating "at least one copy of every useful book now in the possession of one or more American libraries."[17] In the five-year history of the project some 8,344,256 copies of 6,775,936 works were located and more than 6.3 million cards were added to the union catalog.[18]

A task of such massive proportions required the adoption of some special rules, and the way certain problems were handled permanently shaped the union catalog. For the first time, a complete set of all Library of Congress printed cards was added to the catalog.[19] A decision was made to weed out duplicate entries, and in cases of conflict the LC cards were considered the master entry. While their presence also helped to standardize filing procedures, various deviations had to be developed for such a massive catalog, for example, the use of chronological order for numerous editions of the same work and the arrangement of some special groups by language before subdividing by date. Cards for Slavic and Semitic titles and other titles represented in non-Roman characters were transferred to other divisions of the Library of Congress, which established union catalogs for materials in those languages.

Another very basic problem that had to be solved was the selection of a method of assigning symbols to libraries reporting to the catalog. The method chosen employed a mnemonic based on three groups of letters representing state, city, and library. This same method, proposed by Frank Peterson, a volunteer worker at the University of Nebraska Library, has since been employed in many important reference works, including the *Union List of Serials* and *Newspapers in Microform*.[20]

Several methods of expanding reports were employed. In addition to adding LC printed cards, project staff typed cards for the handwritten entries in the old official catalogs.[21] At least 118 printed book catalogs, including those of both general and specialized collections from state, academic, and large public libraries, were clipped and mounted on cards, creating more than a million new entries.[22] Libraries were encouraged to make routine contributions of all cards duplicated by mechanical means. Those libraries financially unable to submit large numbers of reports were encouraged to supply copies of shelflists of "treasure room" items. Occasionally libraries loaned shelflists of special collections for project staff to transcribe, and, in a few cases, particularly in Washington and at Harvard, project staff visited libraries and copied or made photostats of catalog entries. In the case of Harvard, more than 700,000 cards were copied over a period of 3 years. One final method of expanding the catalog was the solicitation of gifts of groups of cards discarded by institutions in the process of recataloging their collections. The wide variance in cataloging practices among these institutions, plus the large number of cryptic, one-line entries received in this manner would cause future editors many headaches.[23]

When the Rockefeller grant expired on August 31, 1932, the Union Catalog Division was established as a unit of the Library of Congress. The appropriation of $20,000 was less than half of that available during each of the previous five years, and staff was trimmed from 31 to 11 employees. Most projects for expanding the catalog were frozen as staff time was consumed in the routines of filing cards, revising entries, and providing libraries with information on locations.[24] Nevertheless growth of the file continued. Hard financial times for libraries during the 1930s did not mean fewer reports. While the number of libraries reporting declined, the number of reports remained at a steady level as many contributing libraries were forced to adopt mechanical means of reproducing cards in order to save on expenses.[25]

Regional Union Catalogs

During the late 1930s, various projects of the Works Projects Administration had significant impact upon the union catalog. Perhaps the most far-reaching was the establishment in 1935 of regional union catalogs around the country, including those at Chicago, Philadelphia, Denver, North Carolina, Texas, and Cleveland. From the outset, these projects were viewed as possible important contributors to the national union catalog,[26] and early surveys of the Cleveland and Philadelphia catalogs indicated that as much 24 to 34 percent of the titles represented in the regional catalogs were not included in the union catalog.[27] However despite great enthusiasm over their creation and the perennial recommendations from the Library of Congress staff, another decade would pass before these valuable resources could be added to the union catalog.[28]

Of more immediate impact upon the union catalog were a number of projects sponsored through the Historical Records Survey of the Works Projects Administration. One was the filming on 16mm film of some 19 District of Columbia library catalogs. Being mostly the collections of federal agencies, these institutions had been excluded from the efforts of "Project B" because the emphasis of that project had been upon collections outside of Washington. Eventually some 600,000 author entries were filmed and later transcribed for the union catalog by the New Jersey Historical Records Survey.[29]

Another great enhancement to the bibliographic apparatus was provided in 1937 by the absorption of the American Imprints Inventory by the Historical Records Survey. Under the editorship of Douglas C. McMurtie, this undertaking was intended to provide a nationwide inventory of books and pamphlets published in the United States before 1876 and in some western states before 1890. Field workers across the nation canvassed library collections identifying relevant materials, transcribing the appropriate information, and forwarding entries to a central office in Chicago. Before publication in various state checklists, all entries were checked in the union catalog in Washington. This afforded Library of Congress staff the opportunity to add all locations and entries not previously included in the union catalog.[30]

In 1936 the Division expanded its growing location service in order to assist libraries urgently needing materials not reported in the union catalog. In cooperation with the Association of Research Libraries, weekly checklists of unlocated titles were circulated to 50 research libraries. The participating libraries checked their holdings for the needed titles and returned the lists to the Library of Congress which then notified the requesting library of the available locations. The titles that were not located were cumulated in annual lists of desiderata. In return for acting as a clearinghouse for interlibrary loans, the Union Catalog Division was able to add hundreds of entries and holdings for important scholarly resources.[31]

In its earliest years, most use of the catalog was made by Library of Congress staff or researchers who could physically use the catalog themselves. However "Project B" had served to advertise the value of the catalog and to make many more libraries aware of its potential. From 1927 onward the catalog staff received an ever increasing amount of correspondence; so much in fact that the burden of correspondence began to tax staff resources heavily. By 1940, George Schwegmann, the director of the Union Catalog Division estimated that 25 percent of staff time was spent answering such inquiries.[32] In addition the Library's independent Interlibrary Loan Service made regular use of the union catalog and in 1935 alone made some 5,000 referrals based on information in the catalog.[33]

After 40 years in development, the union catalog had truly become a major national bibliographic resource. In fact it was deemed so important that at the start of World War II the catalog was removed from the capital as a precautionary measure. War and its accompanying research efforts further demonstrated the utility of the catalog. Requests for information on locations doubled during the first year of the war, and there was a conspicuous jump in requests for foreign technical and scientific materials. The fact that only two-thirds of the titles requested were located in the catalog highlighted the need to expand its coverage,[34] and Congress nearly doubled appropriations for the division during the 1942–43 fiscal year.[35]

Plans for a Book Catalog

However, the most significant event affecting the union catalog during the war years was the agreement reached between the Association of Research Libraries and the Library of Congress to publish in book form a depository collection of Library of Congress printed catalog cards. Over the years American libraries had found depository card sets increasingly expensive to maintain. In addition to space problems created by the huge files, it was estimated that each depository library spent over $1,200 each year simply for filing and new catalog furniture. In 1941, an Association of Research Libraries committee chaired by William Warner Bishop proposed the publication of the card set in book form. The book catalog allowed costs to be evenly divided between the subscribing libraries and the Library of Congress.[36] In addition, the book format made it possible to extend the bibliographic resources of the Library of Con-

gress to over 300 libraries, far more than had ever subscribed to the printed cards.[37] The resulting *A Catalog of Books Represented by Library of Congress Printed Cards Issued to July 31, 1942* ran 167 volumes and reproduced approximately 1,900,000 cards. Edwards Brothers, Inc. of Ann Arbor, Michigan, produced the catalog over a span of 4 years by photographing the cards, reducing the size of the image, and printing them 18 to a page.[38]

The immediate impact upon the union catalog of the new printed catalog and its 42-volume supplement which appeared in 1948, was a reverse of the decline in reports from contributing libraries that had been brought on by personnel shortages during the war. At the prompting of the Joint Committee on the National Union Catalog of the Association of Research Libraries and the American Library Association, 36 libraries agreed to check their holding against the printed catalog and report titles not represented in the Library of Congress collections. Another 24 research institutions agreed to search at least part of their collections.[39] In the first year alone, the union catalog received nearly 80,000 reports from these institutions.[40]

Increased appropriations during the period from 1943–47 enabled the Union Catalog Division to finally add holdings from the Cleveland and Philadelphia regional union catalogs. In 1948, in recognition of its growing use and importance, the union catalog was officially designated the National Union Catalog and efforts to expand its coverage increased anew. Complete holdings of Harvard University, the University of California at Berkeley, and the North Carolina union catalog were added. Libraries that had been reporting selectively were encouraged to report all new acquisitions, and the result was the rapid expansion of the catalog.[41]

This period also saw renewed calls for the publication of the entire catalog. As early as 1928, Henry Putnam had discussed the need to publish the file.[42] The feasibility of publishing the catalog was considered again in 1941, but a decision was delayed until the end of the war.[43] However, the obvious incompleteness of the catalog, the tremendous burden of keeping up with the ever-rising number of current cards, plus huge filing backlogs of earlier reports always made the task of editing appear impossible.[44] In 1952, as an experimental step in planning the printing of the catalog, the Union Catalog Division began to set aside current reports for imprints for 1952 and later. The intention of the separate file was to establish a means of estimating the eventual size and cost of publishing the entire catalog.[45] The following year the American Library Association Board on Resources was presented with a proposal for reproducing the entire National Union Catalog, but the estimated cost of some 4 to 5 million dollars to complete the project daunted even the most enthusiastic supporters.[46]

Meanwhile, following the proposals laid out in 1946 by Halsey William Wilson in his pamphlet, *A Proposed Plan for Printing Library of Congress Cards in Cumulative Book Form* (New York: H.W. Wilson), the Library of Congress had discontinued the distribution of depository card sets and had begun in 1947 to publish the *Cumulative Catalog of Library of Congress Printed Cards*. In 1950, a separate subject catalog was initiated and the *Cumulative Catalog* was renamed the *Library of Congress Author Catalog*. Three years later, with the appearance of separate catalogs for maps, motion pictures and filmstrips, and music and phonograph records, the series became the *Library of Congress Catalog—Books: Authors*. Recognition by both the Library and the profession that this catalog failed to represent the annual increase in scholarly titles held in American libraries resulted in the suggestion that the *Library of Congress Catalog* be expanded into a current National Union Catalog.[47]

The proposal was first made formally by C. Sumner Spaulding at the summer 1953 ALA annual meeting, and actively advocated the following year by Frederick H. Wagman.

Wagman saw the publication of a current catalog of American library acquisitions as a possible solution to the problem of publishing the entire catalog. The staff of the National Union Catalog might be relieved of the considerable tasks of arranging, filing, and maintaining current entries as well as responding to reference queries about them. Staff time saved might be spent in editing the retrospective file for eventual publication.[48]

It was recognized at the time that not only would this change greatly enhance the proven utility of the current printed catalog, but would also offer the hope of "lifting a great burden of frustration from the shoulders of the existing union catalog staff and of preparing the way for the ultimate publication of that great bibliographical instrument." By providing a terminus point for the older file, a current catalog would allow for the stabilization of that file in terms of growth. In addition, with the passage of time the current publication would assume retrospective importance.[49]

The ALA Board on Resources established a subcommittee chaired by Wagman to examine the proposal and to make recommendations regarding its implementation. Using responses from surveys of subscribers to the *Catalog* and statistics provided by the Library of Congress, the subcommittee found the proposal economically feasible[50] and selected 1956 imprints as the best starting point for the *National Union Catalog: A Cumulative Author List*. The publication plan was for monthly updates with quarterly and annual cumulations.[51] Following the pattern of its predecessor, the annual cumulations were eventually succeeded by five-year cumulations, although the entries for 1956 and 1957 were eventually published in both the 1953–1957 and the 1958–1962 cumulations.[52]

A major breakthrough in terms of nationwide bibliographic control of library materials, the new printed catalog sparked an exponential growth in the number of reports of library holdings. The total number of titles reported to the catalog in 1956 numbered 103,000; in 1957, 326,00; and by 1962,

823,000.[53] The size of five-year cumulations also reflected this same dramatic growth. The first numbered 28 volumes; while the last, for 1973–1977, totaled 150 volumes.[54]

Plans for a Retrospective Union Catalog

The success of the printed catalog of current titles made the need for publication of the retrospective file more apparent. The existence of the self-contained and relatively compact file of 1952–1955 imprints allowed for the possibility of a small step in that direction. In 1959 the ALA subcommittee on the National Union Catalog decided to sponsor its publication. Johannes L. Dewton was chosen as supervisor and editor of the project, and the 30-volume *National Union Catalog, 1952-1955 Imprints* was distributed to subscribers in 1961.[55]

Further encouraged by the sales of this publication and the execution of the project, the subcommittee decided to undertake publication of the entire pre-1956 file. In 1962, the subcommittee began lengthy discussions of possible formats, including microfilm, microprint and even a "mechanized, central storage bank." Late that same year, the Committee on Resources received a report from Johannes Dewton that estimated the editorial costs of the project to be $2,700,00.[56]

In October 1963, the Subcommittee on the NUC decided to invite bids for the publication of the pre-1956 catalog. The successful bidder would be required to finance the editorial costs and allowed to recoup these from the sale of the catalog. If no satisfactory bid was accepted, the plan was to seek grant support for the editorial costs, or failing that, ask subscribing libraries to support these costs up front.

A preliminary agreement between the Library of Congress and the American Library Association was signed in June 1964. The agreement made publication possible, and, according to the terms, ALA agreed to obtain the funds necessary for the Library to edit the catalog. In March 1965, after considering existing technologies and the likelihood of subscription support for each, the subcommittee decided on a book format for the planned publication. After two mailings of invitations for bids, three bids with sample pages were received by the August 1966 deadline. The subcommittee selected the bid from Mansell Information/Publishing, Ltd., of London on the basis of the lowest sale price to libraries and the most satisfactory format. Contract negotiations between ALA and the company were concluded in January 1967. In February, the Library of Congress established the National Union Catalog Publication Project (NUCPP) to edit the catalog. Under guidance from John Cronin, work began with Johannes Dewton being selected as head of the project and Nathan N. Mendelldoff as assistant head. By March the first 27,000 edited cards to comprise the first volume were on their way to London.[57]

Mansell Publishing, although a British firm formed specifically for the purpose of publishing the National Union Catalog, had important advantages that enabled it to win the bidding process. The first of these was the experience its managing editor, John Commander, gained in publishing the British Museum's *General Catalogue of Printed Books* from 1961 to 1966. The second was the optical innovations of its parent company, Balding and Mansell, a subsidiary of Bemrose Publishing Company.[58] Essentially the firm had developed a system of sense-marking cards that made it possible to direct camera equipment to film only portions of cards instead of entire cards. The process not only made the filming of cards faster, but the efficient use of space in the final product resulted in lowered printing costs.[59]

The original contract called for a schedule of 60 volumes per year. The set was expected to take 10 years to complete and run some 610 volumes. Each of the 14-inch volumes would contain about 700 pages and be priced at $15.

An inflationary factor of 10 percent over the ten year length of the project was included in the contract, but proved grossly insufficient.[60] A supplement was also planned to accommodate those reports received after publication began.[61]

Editorial Processes

Once the contracts were in place, the Library of Congress was able to jump quickly into the editorial process. In eager anticipation of the event, John Cronin had years before spelled out the basic guidelines to be followed.[62] The Library also had the previous experience of compiling three 5-year cumulations of the current *National Union Catalog*, and many of the procedures and arrangements established for the publication of the pre-1956 imprints had precedents in these projects.[63]

The task facing the project staff was sifting through some 20 million cards from various files, and to weed and edit them to an acceptable, consistent standard for publication. The lack of standardization in a file built over a 67-year period that had seen three major revisions in cataloging codes plus innumerable changes in filing rules posed tremendous problems. In addition, the individual entries varied greatly in terms of accuracy and completeness. For example, a large number of entries contributed by Princeton during the 1920s were no more than one line long, while other records included incredible detail. Despite the long-standing rule of Library of Congress cards taking precedence, a substantial amount of weeding needed to be done.[64] In some cases, the duplicate entries numbered into the hundreds.

Preparing the file for publication required a number of processes. The first of these was interfiling seven different supplements with the main file. Pre-editors, or searchers, then reviewed the trays card-by-card, removing duplicate entries and transferring holdings information to the best available record. Cross references were verified, filing adjusted, and all trays were compared to the Library of Congress Official Catalog to be sure that all LC printed cards were included in the National Union Catalog.[65]

The 25 to 30 project editors each reviewed one 1,400-card tray each week,[66] checking for correctness of entry and form, resolving conflicts, adding entries and cross references, arranging the filing order, and identifying entries that needed retyping. The cards were then examined by copy editors who, in preparing the cards for the filming process, reviewed location symbols and eliminated extraneous information. If necessary, the cards were then retyped before review by a senior editor.[67]

The five senior editors who performed the final checking of entries ensured the bibliographic standards of the catalog. Checking some five trays each every week, they reviewed the quality of the editors' work and resolved previously unsolved problems.[68]

After the final review, the cards were stamped sequentially, to insure the arrangement, and microfilmed. The film served as protection against loss of the shipment, and also provided an inhouse copy of the file for use until the printed volumes arrived.[69] The cards were then packed up and sent via air freight to London on Friday, and the whole process began again the following Monday.

Amazingly, the staff never missed a deadline, and the pace of five volumes per month was maintained unfailingly until the end of the 685-volume main sequence in June 1979.[70] In order to meet the publication schedule, some voluminous authors and corporate bodies had to be assigned to senior editors as special projects, weeks ahead of the normal timetable.[71] Some sections required more elaborate treatment. Johannes Dewton continued working on the United States section even after his retirement in 1975.[72] By plan, only volumes 53-56 covering the Bible were published out of sequence after completion of the rest of the main set.[73]

The worst problems were encountered during the first 2 years, when the enormous scale of the difficulties involved, previously only imagined, was finally experienced in practice. It became apparent very early in the project that too much optimism and miscalculation had resulted in insufficient staff to handle the editorial work. Perhaps the direst moment was at the end of the first year when the contract with Mansell was under renegotiation and the Librarian of Congress threatened to terminate the Library's involvement. Mansell agreed to finance a larger editorial staff,[74] and the work continued with as many as 57 employees.[75]

Editorial Flexibility

Another key to the success of the project was the willingness of the editors to adapt their procedures. The project had begun with a few basic guidelines:

1. Library of Congress printed cards took precedence for all items and multiple reports were to be transferred to these master cards.
2. When alternative headings existed, Library of Congress headings were chosen.
3. The American Library Association cataloging code of 1949 was the standard for form and choice of entries.
4. Liberal use would be made of cross references from alternative headings.
5. A unique form for author entries would be employed, and all holdings for an item would be listed in one place.[76]

In practice, strict adherence to even these few guidelines proved difficult. The publication schedule required that weekly shipments be made in alphabetic sequence without delay. The unyielding deadline forced staff to become increasingly flexible and simplify procedures as the project progressed.

The result was a shift in the nature of the printed catalog from one part to the next. Later volumes contained far fewer entries revised to meet the 1949 ALA rules, and even included entries following the 1967 Anglo-American Cataloging Rules. Staff had no time to make the new generation of reports received in the course of the project consistent with the old rules. Fewer added entries and cross-references were made as time went by. Filing rules for voluminous authors were simplified, and even the precedence of Library of Congress cataloging was not always acknowledged, particularly when more complete information was supplied by other libraries.[77]

When Johannes Dewton retired in 1975, leadership of the project was turned over to David A. Smith, who had already served several years as a senior editor.[78] By the time that the main sequence editing was completed in 1979, over three million cards had been received for the supplement. Before the main sequence was finished, the project's assistant head, Maria Laqueur, had designed and begun editing the supplement. Although a new publication schedule allowed slightly more breathing room, the supplement involved the additional tasks of checking in the main sequence and publishing a register of additional locations.[79] When the last editorial work was finally completed in January 1981, some 14 years after the project's start, the staff had reviewed over 23 million cards and prepared over 11 million for publication.[80]

In addition to the Library of Congress, the American Library Association, and Mansell Publishing, some 1,350 libraries in 51 nations had supported the project at a cost of over $35,000 each.[81] After 14 years, the result was a resource of unparalleled magnitude, of value to libraries in acquisitions, bibliography, cataloging, interlibrary loan, reference, and research. The new printed catalog represented not only the largest print record of American library holdings, but also the most extensive record of the history of printing, particularly of the Western world.[82]

New Technology

Yet by the time of completion of the pre-1956 catalog, the *National Union Catalog* was already something of a dinosaur. With the advent of OCLC in the early 1970s and the application of large-scale time-share computing to bibliographic systems, there was talk as early as 1976 of the *National Union Catalog* being displaced.[83] In fact, in 1978, the Library of Congress itself had recognized that its inability to commit the necessary machine and human resources meant that OCLC would preempt the Library's own efforts to develop a national online bibliographic service.[84] Eventually, in terms of both number of records and contributing libraries, OCLC would dwarf the *National Union Catalog*.

The 1980s saw the introduction of automation and a new microfiche format for the current catalog. The new format included a register with cumulative annual name, title, series and subject indexes and resulted in substantial savings in time and cost.[85] However, these innovations plus the expansion of coverage to include Oriental and Near Eastern languages, could not make up for the convenience of the online systems, which have gradually usurped most of the NUC's cataloging, interlibrary loan, and even reference functions.

Unfortunately, the development of competing bibliographic utilities has meant the impossibility of a true national union catalog. With many of the major research institutions that once constituted the bulk of contributors to the union catalog not contributing to OCLC, the latter does not reflect a complete picture of American library holdings, and particularly of many esoteric research materials. The result is that librarians and researchers must search multiple sources and systems to identify many hard-to-locate items. The situation will not be helped by the current plan of the Library of Congress for the *National Union Catalog. Books*. As of the 1990 edition, the catalog will include only those reports from sources other than the three major bibliographic utilities, OCLC, RLIN, and WLN. In addition, staff in the division will be reduced significantly.[86]

These developments will leave unaddressed several important problems. As of 1986, the year before the implementation of regular reports to the catalog in magnetic tape form, the collection of reports of pre-1956 imprints not included in the *National Union Catalog, Pre-1956 Imprints* main sequence or its supplement already stood at over 2 million cards.[87] In addition, although a *Near East National Union List* began to appear in 1988,[88] six union catalogs containing another 2 million records for materials in Chinese, Hebraic, Japanese, Korean, South Asian, and Southeast Asian languages remain unpublished.[89] While these problems may eventually be solved by various retrospective conversion projects, in the meantime a wealth of bibliographic information gathered for such projects will go largely untapped.

Unlike some other important reference works, the *National Union Catalog* was not the product of a single person's ideas or efforts. Being based at a large institution, such as the Library of Congress, allowed the catalog to evolve slowly in terms of both purpose and design. Over the decades, several individuals made important contributions to shaping the reference tool. While Henry Putnam provided the official support necessary to establish the catalog, John D. Rockefeller, Jr., gave the financial support needed to build the file into something significant. Ernest Richardson, Ernest Kletsch, and George Schwegmann, Jr., presided for nearly three decades over the massive work of building the catalog. John Cronin and Frederick Wagman were perhaps the most effective of many advocates of bringing the catalog to print form. Johannes Dewton, David Smith, and John Commander ably oversaw the tremendous task of editing the catalog and producing *National Union Catalog, Pre-1956 Imprints*. However, this pioneering effort in resource sharing was truly the result of thousands of hands. From the legion of filers and editors at the Library of Congress to the army of catalogers from hundreds of libraries throughout North America, all played a significant role in building a tremendous bibliographic resource.

PUBLICATION HISTORY

The National Union Catalog; a cumulative author list representing Library of Congress printed cards and titles reported by other American libraries. Washington: Library of Congress, 1956–1982 (Monthly, with Quarterly and Annual Updates).

The National Union Catalog, Music and Phonorecords (title varies). Washington: Library of Congress, 1956– .

The National Union Catalog, Motion Pictures and Filmstrips (title varies). Washington: Library of Congress, 1956–1982.

The National Union Catalog, a Cumulative Author List, 1953–1957. Ann Arbor: J.W. Edwards, Inc., 1958. 28 vols. (v. 1–20, Authors; v.27, Music and phonograph records; v. 28, Motion pictures and filmstrips).

The National Union Catalog, 1952–1955 Imprints. Ann Arbor: J.W. Edwards, Inc., 1961. 30 vols.

The National Union Catalog, a Cumulative Author List, 1958–1962. New York: Rowman and Littlefield, Inc., 1963. 54 vols. (v. 1–50, Authors; v.51–52, Music and Phonorecords; v. 53–54 Motion Pictures and Film Strips).

National Union Catalog, Register of Additional Locations. Washington: Library of Congress, June 1965– . (Published in book form, 1965–1980; in microfiche format, 1980– . Cumulative microfiche edition covers 1968–).

The National Union Catalog, a Cumulative Author List, 1963–1967. Ann Arbor: J.W. Edwards, Inc., 1968. 72 vols. (v. 1–59, Authors; v. 60–66, Register of Additional Locations; v. 67–70, Music and Phonorecords; v. 71–72, Motion Pictures and Film Strips).

Library of Congress and National Union Catalog Author Lists, 1942–1962: A Master Cumulation. Detroit: Gale Research Company, 1969. 152 vols.

The National Union Catalog, 1956–1967. Totowa, NJ: Rowman and Littlefield, Inc., 1970–1972. 125 vols.

The National Union Catalog, a Cumulative Author List, 1968–1972. Ann Arbor: J.W. Edwards, Inc., 1973. 128 vols. (v. 1–104, Authors; v. 105–119, Register of Additional Locations; v. 120–124, Music; v. 125–128, Films and Other Materials for Projection).

The National Union Catalog, a Cumulative Author List, 1973–1977. Totowa, NJ: Rowman and Littlefield, Inc., 1978. 150 vols. (v. 1–135, Authors; v. 136–143, Music; 144–150 Films and Other Materials for Projection).

The National Union Catalog, Pre-1956 Imprints. London: Mansell, 1968–1981. 754 vols.

National Union Catalog. Books. (Microfiche) *Washington: Library of Congress, 1983– .* (Monthly, with Annual Cumulation. Register Format with Name, Title, Series and Subject indexes).

National Union Catalog. Audiovisual Materials (microfiche). Washington: Library of Congress, 1983– .

National Union Catalog. Cartographic Materials (microfiche). Washington: Library of Congress, 1983– .

BIBLIOGRAPHY

While researchers are lucky in having a number of written accounts by individuals closely involved in the National Union Catalog, there is considerable redundancy in what has been written about it, even in the brief list of sources provided here. The introductory section to the *National Union Catalog, Pre-1956 Imprints*, its printed prospectus, and the volume *In Celebration* (done to commemorate the completion of the project) conveniently assemble a large amount of information on the catalog, but overlap considerably. The last is perhaps the most most comprehensive in coverage and includes articles by William J. Welsh, Gordon R. Williams, David A. Smith, and John Commander. Somewhat altered versions of the articles by Smith and Welsh are also listed. For the most detailed discussion on the early development of the catalog, see the article by Schwegmann. For a discussion of developments during the 1950s, see the articles by Cronin (the first of which also appeared in the prospectus) and the collection of papers by Charles David and others. For lively descriptions of the editorial process, see either of the articles by David Smith. Finally, required reading for using and understanding the scope and limitations of the *National Union Catalog, Pre-1956 Imprints* is Johannes Dewton's introductory essay.

Cronin, John W. "History of the National Union Catalog, Pre-1956 Imprints." In *Book Catalogs,* compiled by Maurice F. Tauber and Hilda Feinberg, 118–32. Metuchen, NJ: Scarecrow Press, 1971.

————. "The National Union and Library of Congress Catalogs: Problems and Prospects." *Library Quarterly* 34 (January, 1964): 77–96.

David, Charles W., et al. "Proposed Expansion of the Library of Congress Catalog—Books: Authors into a Current National Union Catalog, 1956." *College and Research Libraries* 17 (January, 1956): 24–40.

Dewton, Johannes L. "Introduction to the National Union Catalog, Pre-1956 Imprints." In *National Union Catalog, Pre-1956 Imprints,* vol. 1, xi–xix. London: Mansell, 1968.

In Celebration: The National Union Catalog, Pre-1956 Imprints, edited by John Y. Cole. Washington: Library of Congress, 1981.

"National Union Catalog: Celebrates 30 Years." *Library of Congress Information Bulletin 46* (June 1, 1987): 228–33.

Prospectus for the National Union Catalog, Pre-1956 Imprints. London: Mansell, 1967.

Schwegmann, George A., Jr. "The National Union Catalog in the Library of Congress." In *Union Catalogs in the United States,* edited by Robert B. Downs, 229–63. Chicago: American Library Association, 1942.

Smith, David A. "The National Union Catalog Pre-1956 Imprints." *The Book Collector* 31 (Winter, 1982): 445–62.

Welsh, William J. "The Last of the Monumental Book Catalogs." *American Libraries* 12 (September, 1981): 464–68.

Williams, Gordon R. "History of the National Union Catalog, Pre-1956 Imprints." In *National Union Catalog, Pre-1956 Imprints,* vol. 1, vii–x. London: Mansell, 1968.

NOTES

[1] William Welsh, "The Last of the Monumental Book Catalogs," *American Libraries* 12 (September 1981): 468.

[2] Richard Shoemaker, review of *National Union Catalog, Pre-1956 Imprints, Library Resources & Technical Services* 13 (Summer 1969): 431.

[3] *Annual Report of the Librarian of Congress* (1971): 29.

[4] Welsh, "The Last of the Monumental Book Catalogs," 466–67.

[5] John Y. Cole, "Introduction," in *In Celebration: the National Union Catalog Pre-1956 Imprints,* ed. by John Y. Cole. (Washington: Library of Congress, 1981), 3–4.

[6] Gordon R. Williams, "History of the National Union Catalog Pre-1956 Imprints," in *The National Union Catalog, Pre-1956 Imprints,* vol. 1 (London: Mansell, 1968), vii.

[7] F. P. Jordan, "The History of Printed Catalog Cards," *Public Libraries* 9 (July 1904): 318–20.

[8] Williams, vii.

[9] *Annual Report of the Librarian of Congress* (1902): 101.

[10] *Annual Report of the Librarian of Congress* (1901): 241.

[11] *Annual Report of the Librarian of Congress* (1910): 71.

[12] *Annual Report of the Librarian of Congress* (1908): 58.

[13] *Annual Report of the Librarian of Congress* (1928): 238.

[14] *Annual Report of the Librarian of Congress* (1909): 57–59.

[15] George A. Schwegmann, Jr., "The National Union Catalog in the Library of Congress," in *Union Catalogs in the United States,* ed. by Robert B. Downs (Washington: American Library Association, 1942), 231.

[16] Ibid., 232.

[17] *Annual Report of the Librarian of Congress* (1927): 240.

[18] Schwegmann, "The National Union Catalog in the Library of Congress," 232.

[19] *Annual Report of the Librarian of Congress* (1927): 240.

[20] Schwegmann, "The National Union Catalog in the Library of Congress," 233–35.

[21] *Annual Report of the Librarian of Congress* (1927): 240.

[22] *Annual Report of the Librarian of Congress* (1932): 78.

[23] Schwegmann, "The National Union Catalog in the Library of Congress," 235–37.

[24] Ibid., 247.

[25] *Annual Report of the Librarian of Congress* (1935): 48–49.

[26] *Annual Report of the Librarian of Congress* (1936): 52.

[27] Schwegmann, "The National Union Catalog in the Library of Congress," 252.

[28] *Annual Report of the Librarian of Congress* (1944): 82.

[29] Schwegmann, "The National Union Catalog in the Library of Congress," 250–51.

[30] Ibid., 252–53.

[31] Ibid., 257.

[32] Ibid., 256.

[33] *Annual Report of the Librarian of Congress* (1935): 47.

[34] *Annual Report of the Librarian of Congress* (1942): 46–47.

[35] *Annual Report of the Librarian of Congress* (1943): 49.

[36] John W. Cronin, "The National Union and Library of Congress Catalogs, Problems and Prospects," *Library Quarterly* 34 (January 1964): 80.

[37] *Annual Report of the Librarian of Congress* (1943): 48.

[38] Cronin, "The National Union and Library of Congress Catalogs, Problems and Prospects," 80.

[39] *Annual Report of the Librarian of Congress* (1943): 48.

[40] *Annual Report of the Librarian of Congress* (1944): 82.

[41] Williams, viii.

[42] *Annual Report of the Librarian of Congress* (1928): 243.

[43] George A. Schwegmann, Jr. "The National Union Catalog in the Next Decade—Some Unsolved Problems," *Library Resources & Technical Services* 1 (Summer 1957): 159.

[44] Charles W. David, "Proposed Expansion of the Library of Congress Catalog-Books: Authors into a Current National Union Catalog, 1956," *College and Research Libraries* 17 (January 1956): 25.

[45] Cronin, "The National Union and Library of Congress Catalogs, Problems and Prospects," 82.

[46] David, 24.

[47] Cronin, "The National Union and Library of Congress Catalogs, Problems and Prospects," 80–81.

[48] George A. Schwegmann, Jr. and Robert D. Stevens, "The Proposal for a Current Author Catalog of American Library Resources," *College and Research Libraries* 17 (January 1956): 29.

[49] David, 25.

[50] Schwegmann and Stevens, 28–29.

[51] Ibid., 31.

[52] Johannes Dewton, "Introduction to the National Union Catalog Pre-1956 Imprints," in *The National Union Catalog, Pre-1956 Imprints*, vol. 1 (London: Mansell, 1968), xii.

[53] Cronin, "The National Union and Library of Congress Catalogs, Problems and Prospects," 81–82.

[54] "1973–1977 National Union Catalog Goes to Press in Record Time," *Library of Congress Information Bulletin* 38 (March 9, 1979): 81.

[55] Cronin, "The National Union and Library of Congress Catalogs, Problems and Prospects," 82.

[56] Ibid., 84–85.

[57] John W. Cronin, "History of the National Union Catalog, Pre-1956 Imprints," in *Book Catalogs*, compiled by Maurice F. Tauber and Hilda Feinberg (Metuchen, NJ: Scarecrow Press, 1971), 129–32.

[58] John Commander, "Publishing the NUC," in *In Celebration: The National Union Catalog, Pre-1956 Imprints*, ed. by John Y. Cole (Washington: Library of Congress, 1981), 28–30.

[59] William Welsh, "The Library of Congress," in *In Celebration: The National Union Catalog, Pre-1956 Imprints*, ed. by John Y. Cole (Washington: Library of Congress, 1981), 10.

[60] Welsh, "The Last of the Monumental Book Catalogs," 467.

[61] John Commander, "Production and Publication of the National Union Catalog Pre-1956 Imprints," in *The National Union Catalog, Pre-1956 Imprints*, vol. 1 (London: Mansell, 1968), xx.

[62] Cronin, "The National Union and Library of Congress Catalogs, Problems and Prospects," 83.

[63] "The 1968–1972 Quinquennnial Edition of the National Union Catalog," *Library of Congress Information Bulletin* 33 (October 11, 1974): A213–A214.

[64] David A. Smith, "The National Union Catalog Pre-1956 Imprints," *The Book Collector* 31 (Winter 1982): 448–49.

[65] Margaret PorterSmith, "The National Union Catalog Pre-1956 Imprints: A Progress Report," *Library Resources & Technical Services* 20 (Winter 1976): 49–50.

[66] Smith, "The National Union Catalog Pre-1956 Imprints," 453.

[67] PorterSmith, "The National Union Catalog Pre-1956 Imprints: A Progress Report," 50–51.

[68] Smith, "The National Union Catalog Pre-1956 Imprints," 454.

[69] PorterSmith, "The National Union Catalog Pre-1956 Imprints: A Progress Report," 51.

[70] Smith, "The National Union Catalog Pre-1956 Imprints," 450.

[71] PorterSmith, "The National Union Catalog Pre-1956 Imprints: A Progress Report," 50.

[72] David Smith, "Editing the NUC," in *In Celebration: The National Union Catalog, Pre-1956 Imprints*, ed. by John Y. Cole (Washington: Library of Congress, 1981), 27.

[73] PorterSmith, 50.

[74] Smith, "The National Union Catalog Pre-1956 Imprints," 449.

[75] PorterSmith, 49.

[76] Smith, "The National Union Catalog Pre-1956 Imprints," 449.

[77] Ibid., 451–53.

[78] Welsh, "The Last of the Monumental Book Catalogs," 467.

[79] Smith, "The National Union Catalog Pre-1956 Imprints," 458.

[80] Ibid., 449–50.

[81] Welsh, "The Last of the Monumental Book Catalogs," 468.

[82] A. Plotnik, "News That Stays News," *American Libraries* 12 (September 1981): 453.

[83] Joe A. Hewitt, "The Impact of OCLC," *American Libraries* 7 (May 1976): 271.

[84] *Role of the Library of Congress in the Evolving National Network* (Washington: Library of Congress, 1978), 7.

[85] "The National Union Catalog: Celebrates 30 Years," *Library of Congress Information Bulletin* 46 (June 1, 1987): 230–32.

[86] "Library of Congress Announces Changes in National Union Catalog," *Library of Congress News* Press Release, PR 90–77 (June 1, 1990): np.

[87] *Annual Report of the Librarian of Congress* (1986): A-12.

[88] "Library Launches Near East Union List," *Library of Congress Information Bulletin* 47 (June 20, 1988): 243.

[89] *Annual Report of the Librarian of Congress* (1986): A-12.

The Record of Record:
The *New York Times Index*

Jo A. Cates

DEVELOPMENT AND HISTORY

On the ninth floor of the *New York Times* building on grubby West 43rd Street, in a room now shared with the newspaper's Rights and Royalties Department, about 20 editors, abstracters, indexers, and clerks produce one of the most influential and remarkable documents of our time. If the *New York Times* is the newspaper of record, then certainly the *New York Times Index* is the record of record.

Under the leadership of Adolph S. Ochs, the *Times* slogan became "All the News That's Fit to Print." "Ochs created the traditions that made the *Times* great—its full coverage, completeness, and accuracy—and that are sustained by his descendents."[1] Even with a daily circulation of more than one million, the *Times* still sells fewer papers than the *Wall Street Journal* or the *New York Daily News*, but it also has won more Pulitzer Prizes than any other newspaper.

Back in 1951, Meyer Berger, one of those Pulitzer Prize-winning *Times* reporters, wrote:

> Because the *Times* has won universal recognition as a newspaper of record, it is in demand in many forms—full size in bound newsprint, in rag paper for better preservation, on tiny microfilm where a full page is reduced to a little more than one inch. Libraries, parliaments, great business houses all over the world subscribe for it in these forms. The semimonthly *New York Times Index* for quick reference to the newspaper's contents, and an annual index that runs to some 1,500 pages, are also available.[2]

Early Days of Benign Neglect

The *Index*, as highly regarded as it is today, has a peculiar history of almost benign neglect. All indexes since the newspaper's birth in 1851 are now widely available, but that was not always so. For decades, the *Index* was used simply as an in-house resource. From September 18, 1851, to September 1858 the *Index* was compiled in longhand. "In the beginning, it was a brief and sketchy affair, entered painstakingly in longhand into a leather-covered ledger volume, and it was intended for staff use only. An index of this kind, with minor changes in format, was maintained for more than sixty years except for two periods of suspension (September 1858 through 1862 and July 1905 through 1912),[3] "the reasons for which cannot now be determined."[4] Indexes for the period covering September 18, 1858, through December 31, 1862, were finally compiled in the 1960s and published in 1967. "The project to bridge this gap in the series of indexes to the *Times* was conceived and begun by Joseph C. Gephart, editor of the *Index* until his retirement in 1964, who also did most of the original indexing for this volume and others in the series."[5]

In 1863, the indexes were compiled semiannually and, for the first time, set in type. "Though still intended for the staff only, this was a far more sophisticated *Index* than its predecessor. . . . It was arranged by year, and each year was divided into three- or four-month periods."[6] But once again the *Index* was suspended from mid-1905 through 1912. More than 50 years later, indexes for those lost years were compiled and published beginning in 1968. The earlier indexes, especially the handwritten ones, present some expected research glitches. For example, the longhand entries are not divided by year—they are strictly alphabetical. And the number directly to the right of those entries are not dates, but refer the user to an issue number. In addition, complete names are not always listed.

Stability and Growth

It was not until 1913 that a semblance of the *Index* that we know today was published. Indexes were compiled quarterly from 1913 to 1929, then monthly from 1930 to 1947. It was during this latter time period that cumulative annual volumes were introduced. From 1948 to the present, indexes have been published semimonthly. Since 1978, there have been quarterly cumulations. A subscription to the semimonthly issues plus the cumulative annual cost $50 in 1952. By 1990 the price had climbed to $645.

The current *New York Times Index* is a unique subject, geographic, organization, and personal name indexing/abstracting tool to the final late edition of the *New York Times*. Almost every article, with the exception of some letters and advertisements, is indexed. Arranged in dictionary form, it refers the user to the date, page, and column where the article is located in the newspaper. It offers cross-references, and such detailed abstracts of articles that the user may not need to locate the entire article.

In addition to serving as an almanac of sorts, the *Index* has also been used as a scientific tool, often playing a major role in social science research. For example, an article in the *Journal of Consumer Affairs* reported that the *Index* had been used to "test the viability of the resource mobilization perspective on the farm workers' movement" and was analyzed for indications of "macro-level changes in activities of the groups involved."[7]

Harvey L. Holmes, Jr., assistant director and editor, joined the *Index* staff in 1967, and became editor in 1975. He notes that "This is the best selling index on the market, and in many ways the most respected. Before we take our bows we must acknowledge that other papers are doing indexes and putting them out earlier."[8] The index to the *Washington Post*, for example, is issued monthly with an annual accumulation, but is available only from 1972 on. (The *Post* index was published by Bell & Howell from 1972–1981 as part of its Newspaper Index project. Most of Bell & Howell's indexed newspapers are available from the mid-1970s on, but it has also indexed the *New York Tribune*, 1841–1924, available on microfilm.) The *Wall Street Journal* also offers a monthly index with annual cumulations, available from 1955 to the present. No other newspaper index today, however, offers the detailed abstracts and documentation available in the *Times Index*.

The *New York Times Index* has had serious weight problems at times. The 1968 *Index* boasted 1,713 pages, which led John Rothman, one of the great *Index* editors, to write in his foreword that year, "This volume lends substance to our new slogan: 'If it's not in the *Times Index*, maybe it didn't happen.'"[9] "As the *Times* continued to grow in size and the news became even more complex, the number and length of the abstracts increased in proportion, and the *Index* got bigger . . . and bigger," wrote Rothman.

> Some of the annual *Index* volumes of the mid-30s were virtually cubic in shape. The paper shortage of the war years forcibly curtailed this, but with the end of World War II the newspaper returned to its former dimensions, and so did the *Index*. This led to the use of cross-references as a substitute for duplication . . . and also led in 1948 to a change in the physical format of the *Index:* larger pages, and an arrangement of three columns, instead of two, per page.[10]

The 1940s almost saw the death of the *Index*, according to Holmes. "There had been very serious talk about ending the *Index*. John Rothman saved it by emphasizing quality and productivity."

The 1965 *Index* offered the first signed foreword by Rothman along with an important new development. More than 200 maps, graphs, charts, and photographs were included.

In the mid-1970s, after Rothman had left the *Index* to work on the computerized Information Bank, and other editors had come and gone, the newly appointed Holmes decided it was time to exercise some control over the *Index*'s once again expanding girth. In 1971, the page size had increased. In 1973, it had split into two volumes. By 1974, the *New York Times Index* weighed in at nearly 3,000 pages. "We reined that in in 1975 and decided to do a lot more editing," Holmes said. "Now the *Index* is 1,200–1,500 pages, but we index more today than ever before." For example, in the 1988 *Index*, the subject heading "Plagiarism" offers *see also* references to articles indexed under "Gallbladder," "Harvard University," "Medicine and Health," "Music," and the "Presidential Election of 1988." One of the entries under "Music" indicates that "Federal Jury in White Plains, NY, finds that Mick Jagger did not steal song, Just Another Night, from Jamaican reggae singer Patrick Alley (M), Ap 27, III, 22:1." This entry also indicates to the user that this is a story of medium length, and that it appeared in the first column on page 22 of section three on April 27, 1988. According to the *Index*, "Whenever possible, entries are made under 'subject' headings (e.g. Airlines, Mental Health, Steel). . . . Names of persons and organizations are usually covered by cross references to the subjects of their activities."[11] As such, this article also is cross-referenced under Jagger's name.

Reform and Renaissance

In the 1980s there was criticism of the *Index* once again. "We experienced a renaissance in the 1980s with indexing," Holmes said. "Beginning around 1982, users felt the *Index* was too complicated. Like *Ulysses*, it was much admired but never read. And

granted, there was a European bias; some headings were seen as labels. For example, under 'China,' it would say 'China, Communist.' 'Homosexuality' was indexed under crime or medical headings. For the subject heading 'Women,' there would be a *see also* reference to 'Domestic Service.' We were behind the times." (For the record, the *see also* references for 'Women' now include the 'Equal Rights Amendment' and the 'Feminist Movement,' along with 'Housewives' and 'Feminine Hygiene Products.') Dr. Roy Peter Clark, of The Poynter Institute for Media Studies, has delighted in the cross references since examining the 1976 edition of the *Index*. In that year, Dr. Clark wrote an article about religion and education. The cross reference under his name was "See also Jesus Christ." The *Index* does tell the user that "Cross references do not indicate the specific content of the entries to which they refer, and should not be so construed. Thus a cross reference from a person's name to a crime heading cannot and does not indicate whether that person is a defendant, a witness, a prosecutor, or a person merely commenting on the subject but not a party to it."[12]

"In the course of 125 years not all *Index* editors thought alike," Rothman wrote, "and so the *Index* users will find some years in which there was no 'Book Review' listing and no 'Deaths' listing. These aberrations of our forebears have been remedied in the separate cumulations of the *New York Times Book Review Index* and the *New York Times Obituaries Index*, respectively."[13] In the 1858–1968 volume of the *New York Times Obituaries Index*, it was reported that

in some years, accidental deaths and suicides were included under 'Deaths,' in other years they were not; in some years titles were given and in others omitted; in some years last name and initials only were given; in some years entries were limited to the news story of the death itself, in others they included stories on the preceding illness and on the aftermath. Our aim in producing this volume was to provide a convenient recompilation."[14]

It is precisely that, a recompilation; unfortunately the material was not re-edited. Volume 2 of the *New York Times Obituaries Index* covers 1969–1978. This volume includes many individuals whose deaths are covered in the "murders" and "suicides" sections of the *Index*. It also contains a section of addenda and errata for the first volume.

The lengthy, detailed abstracts available in the modern *Index* are a far cry from the early abstracts. According to Rothman:

> In the years before World War I, entries consisted generally of only one or a few words, often in 'telegram' style. Since the newspaper itself was small and there was no need or intent to use the *Index* by itself, without reference to the original newspaper articles, these brief entries served quite adequately to identify the articles. But as the newspaper grew in size and complexity, it became necessary to characterize the source articles more fully, and so, during the 1920s and 30s the abstracts gradually became longer and more informative. This development was spurred further during the Second World War, when more detailed abstracts were needed to distinguish one battlefront report from another.[15]

The *New York Times On Microfilm* is available from the paper's beginnings in 1851. The *Times* purchased the Microfilming Corporation of America in the late 1960s and began to produce the microfilm and microfiche inhouse. The *Index* is now distributed by University Microfilms International, which purchased the *Index* licensing rights in 1983.

Training Indexers

Training for indexers and abstracters emphasizes writing. "We stress old fashioned journalism," Holmes said. "Reading skills are important too. The indexers need to know when to stop reading and start writing. Indexers must produce 70-100 abstracts a day while working on deadline. In addition, they have to be aware that users will be doing online searching as well as reference searching." More than 25 years ago Rothman said:

> Indexing is a giant guessing game. Indexers must assess in advance what information a user is likely to seek, where he is likely to look for it, and how much detail the abstract (or 'entry') should include to possibly spare him a trip to the original item in the newspaper. They must devise ways of guiding the user to additional information that he may not be seeking but that would also be relevant to his quest. They must keep in mind that they are serving not only the users of today but also those of future generations (who, to complicate things still further, are bound to have a different perspective and only too likely to have a different vocabulary.)[16]

Some sections of the *Times* are more difficult and time-consuming to index than others, the front page and international stories among those. As early as 1924, *Index* editor Jennie Welland wrote, "An indexer needs psychological insight as much as an advertiser does. Certainly a good imagination is a vital element in his mental equipment." Welland went on to say that "The staff of the *Index* has turned specialist. Each person is held responsible for all articles on certain assigned subjects. For instance, one person takes care of prohibition in all its complications."[17] In 1931, Charles N. Lurie, then editor of the *Index*, wrote, "In the writing of the entries, certain fields of work are assigned to each indexer; when possible, the subjects include fields in which she is personally interested."[18] At one time, indexers did indeed specialize in subjects, but, according to Holmes, "developed their own fiefdoms. We prefer indexers to be generalists."

Computerized Production

The current computer indexing system, a far cry from the typewriter and carbon slips or even the paper tape system of years past, provides instant editing. The 1968 *Index* foreword indicates that the *Index* had just "completed a two-year program of transition to a computer-assisted production process that enables us to abstract and index more material more accurately, more thoroughly and more efficiently."[19] The first edition of *The New York Times Thesaurus* was published in 1968. A new *Thesaurus* was introduced in 1982.

"We have high academic standards but we are not an academic enterprise," Holmes said. "We are a business and not part of the *New York Times* newsroom in any way." And according to Breckinridge Jones, Jr., deputy editor, "We do have more contact now with the newsroom and the library because of the online system." In 1983, Mead Data Central licensed the *New York Times* online databases. This includes the *Information Bank Abstracts*, which contains the *Times* abstracts as well as abstracts from dozens of other newspapers and magazines. A separate file called Advertising and Marketing Intelligence contains abstracts of articles from trade and professional journals. In addition, the *New York Times* is a full-text file on NEXIS, updated daily, which contains every article published in the paper since June 1980. *Index* entries are sent through a computer program at Mead, and the indexing terms are attached automatically to the corresponding full-text item. In January 1972 the *Index* was first processed through the *New York Times Information Bank* system.

Seymour Topping of the *New York Times* wrote, "Readers have been attracted to electronic media, in some cases to the exclusion of newspapers. In general, however, the two media are supplementary and complementary." He went on to say that "There is a sense that we must be thinking about shaping the newspaper of the future so it can be more meaningful, more serviceable, more indispensable to the community."[20] Regardless, "for many people today's newspaper will not be dead tomorrow but will be then and perhaps forever a vital source of information," Rothman wrote. "It must have been this same conviction that prompted Henry Jarvis Raymond to start an index for the infant *New York Times* back in 1851, and that has prompted his successors to maintain this service, to improve it and expand it, and to offer it to the public."[21] Their efforts have enhanced the value of the *New York Times* as a historical document. Thanks to them, this index, this road map to the *New York Times*, this record of record for nearly 150 years, exists in convenient book format, readily available in many libraries, providing access to the newspaper of record.

PUBLICATION HISTORY

The New York Times Index. New York: Bowker, 1966–1976. 15 Vols. (v. I, Sept. 1851–1862; v. II, 1863–1874; v. III, 1875–1879; v. IV, 1880–1885; v. V, 1886–1889; v. VI, 1890–1893; v. VII, 1894–1898; v. VIII, 1899–June 1905; v. IX, July 1905–Dec. 1906; v. X–XV, 1907–1912.)

The New York Times Index. Semimonthly, with annual cumulations. New York: The Times, 1913– .

BIBLIOGRAPHY

Though much has been written about the *New York Times*, its *Index* has largely been overlooked. John Rothman, editor of the *New York Times Index* through the mid-1970s, provides the richest historical overviews in "Preserving the News That's Fit To Print" and "About the Times *Index*." Harvey L. Holmes, Jr., currently the *Index* editor, and Breckinridge Jones, Jr., deputy editor, contributed a large amount of material for this essay in a personal interview at the *New York Times Index* office on 9 February 1990.

Doebler, Paul. "*New York Times* Opens Its Information Bank to Commercial Clients." *Publishers Weekly* 203 (June 18, 1973): 60–61.

Dolan, Donna R. "Subject Searching of the *New York Times* Information Bank." *Online* 2 (April, 1978): 26–30.

Greengrass, Alan R. "The Information Bank Thesaurus." In *The Information Age in Perspective*, Proceedings of the American Society for Information Science, comp. Everett H. Brenner, 137–140. White Plains, NY: Knowledge Industry Publications, 1978.

Lurie, Charles N. "*The New York Times Index*, 1930." *Wilson Library Bulletin* 5 (April, 1931): 501–03.

Morse, Grant W. *Guide to the Incomparable New York Times Index.* New York: Fleet, 1980.

"*New York Times* Sues Over *Index*." *Publishers Weekly* 211 (20 June 1977): 28.

Paneth, Donald. "*The New York Times*." In *The Encyclopedia of American Journalism*, 345–49. New York: Facts on File, 1983.

Rothman, John. "About The *Times Index*." Paper presented at a workshop on "The Uses, Misuses, and Abuses of *The New York Times Index*" jointly sponsored by Metro and Microfilming Corporation of America, New York, April 28, 1977.

———. "Automated Information Processing at the *New York Times*." In *Information Transfer*, American Society for Information Science Proceedings, 85–87. New York: Greenwood, 1968.

———. "Preserving the News That's Fit to Print." *Saturday Review* 48 (November 13, 1965): 89, 102–03.

Schwarzlose, Richard A. *Newspapers, A Reference Guide.* Westport, CT: Greenwood Press, 1987.

Shepard, Douglas. "A Corrective Supplement to Morse's *Guide to the Incomparable New York Times Index*." *Reference Services Review* 9 (October/December, 1981): 33–35.

Slade, Rod, and Alex M. Kelly. "Sources of Popular Literature Online: *New York Times* Information Bank and the Magazine Index." *Database* 2 (March, 1979): 70–83.

Welland, Jennie. "Published Newspaper Index." *Library Journal* 49 (February 15, 1924): 177–78.

The following are indexes to the *New York Times Index*, not the newspaper. Each is an "independent work not published or approved by the *New York Times*." See "*New York Times* Sues Over *Index*" in *Publishers Weekly*, June 20, 1977.

Personal Name Index to The New York Times Index, 1851–1974, edited by Byron A. Falk and Valerie R. Falk. Verdi, NV: Roxbury Data, 1976–1983. 22 vols.

Personal Name Index to The New York Times Index, 1975–1984, edited by Byron A. Falk and Valerie R. Falk. Verdi, NV: Roxbury Data, 1986–1988. 4 vols.

NOTES

[1] Donald Paneth, *Encyclopedia of American Journalism* (New York: Facts on File, 1983), 345.

[2] Meyer Berger, *The Story of The New York Times, 1851–1951* (New York: Simon & Schuster, 1951), 563.

[3] John Rothman, "Preserving the News That's Fit to Print," *Saturday Review* 48 (13 November 1965): 102.

[4] John Rothman, Foreword to the *New York Times Index, 1899–June 1905*, iii.

[5] Foreword to the *New York Times Index, July 1902–December 1906*, v.

[6] Foreword to the *New York Times Index, 1863–1864*, v.

[7] Darlene Brannigan Smith and Paul N. Bloom, "Using Content Analysis to Understand the Consumer Movement," *Journal of Consumer Affairs* 23 (Winter 1989): 305.

[8] Harvey L. Holmes Jr., assistant director and editor, *New York Times Index*, interview with the author, 9 February 1990. Many of the direct quotes in this essay derive from that interview with Holmes and his colleagues.

[9] John Rothman, "Foreword" in the *New York Times Index, 1968*, unpaged.

[10] John Rothman, "About the *Times Index*," A paper delivered at a workshop on "The Uses, Misuses, and Abuses of the *New York Times Index* jointly sponsored by Metro and Microfilming Corporation of America, 28 April 1977: 2.

[11] "How to Use the *New York Times Index*," in the *New York Times Index*, 1988, unpaged.

[12] Ibid.

[13] John Rothman, "About The *Times Index*," 6.

[14] John Rothman and Byron A. Falk, Jr., "Introduction" in *The New York Times Obituaries Index, 1858–1968*, (Sanford, NC: Microfilming Corporation, 1970), unpaged.

[15] John Rothman, "About the *Times Index*," 2.

[16] John Rothman, "Preserving the News That's Fit to Print," 89, 102.

[17] Jennie Welland, "The Published Newspaper Index," *Library Journal*, 49 (15 February 1924): 177.

[18] Charles N. Lurie, "*The New York Times Index*, 1930," *Wilson Library Bulletin* 5 (April 1931): 502.

[19] John Rothman, "Foreword" to the *New York Times Index*, 1968, unpaged.

[20] "Seymour Topping," in Steven Friedlander, comp., "Stop the Presses," *Avenue* 12 (October 1988): 79.

[21] John Rothman, "Preserving the News That's Fit to Print," 103.

"The Jewel in the Crown": The *Oxford English Dictionary*

James Rettig

DEVELOPMENT AND HISTORY

In 1984, Robert Burchfield, editor of the four supplementary volumes of the *Oxford English Dictionary*, called that dictionary the "'jewel in the crown'" of the Oxford University Press.[1] It has not always been so. The Oxford University Press formally emerged from its antecedents in 1690 to produce Bibles.[2] Its twofold mission was to publish learned books as well as the Book of Common Prayer and the Bible. The latter category proved more lucrative. Bibles, still a perennial item on OUP's list, remained its stock in trade through the nineteenth century. The shift from being known primarily as a publisher of The Word to being *the* publisher about words began in the middle of the nineteenth century and was complete early in the twentieth.

The history of English language dictionaries antedates the history of the Oxford University Press by nearly a century and that of its great dictionary by yet another and more. Robert Cawdrey's *A Table Alphabeticall* (1604), generally acknowledged to be the first English dictionary, was simply a list of difficult words. It explained their meanings and labeled those words having a French or Greek origin, but other apparatus familiar to today's dictionary users—etymology, identification of a word's part of speech, and illustrative quotations—were lacking. These features developed in later dictionaries, but until Nathan Bailey published his *An Universal Etymologi-*cal English Dictionary* in 1721, English-language dictionaries largely followed that early model of listing only hard words. Although Bailey listed only about 40,000 words, he included many common, even some vulgar, words as well as difficult ones.[3]

Johnson's and Richardson's Dictionaries

Later in the eighteenth century, Samuel Johnson broke new ground in two ways. First, in his *Plan for a Dictionary of the English Language* (1747), he examined various principles by which he could exclude categories of words from the dictionary and found all of them lacking. His *Plan* implies a theretofore unknown catholicity in lexicography. However, the incredible demands of the task he imposed upon himself forced him to modify his plan in practice and the dictionary was not as inclusive as expected. Nevertheless, his intent was noble and it anticipated later lexicographical efforts managed by teams. Second, he illustrated the meanings of words and their various senses through quotations. This practice dates back to at least 1598 when John Florio used it in his *A Worlde of Wordes*, an Italian-English dictionary that included quotations from Italian authors. But it was Johnson who made the practice the foundation of serious English lexicography. In his famous preface to his dictionary, he advised his readers that "The solution of all difficulties, and the supply of all defects, must be sought in the examples, subjoined to the various senses of each word, and ranged according to the time of their authors."[4] With the first edition of his *Dictionary* (1755), Johnson set a powerful precedent, drawing many of his quotes from noted writers such as Shakespeare, Dryden, and Bacon whose works he "regard[ed] as the *wells of English undefiled*."[5] Because neither he nor anyone else at the time understood the proper pronunciation of Middle English, he had little appreciation of Chaucer and other early authors; therefore in his dictionary Johnson drew illustrative quotes principally from writers of the Elizabethan age and later. Johnson's dictionary went through four editions in his lifetime, the last appearing in 1773; was reprinted numerous times thereafter; and was used as a foundation for later dictionaries, including Noah Webster's.

The next significant advance in English lexicography was Webster's *An American Dictionary of the English Language* (New York: S. Converse, 1828). Webster did not think quotations were necessary and relied instead solely on precision in definitions to convey words' meanings. Webster advanced English lexicography, theretofore an art practiced to advantage only in Great Britain, by treating terms of American origin or use with the same seriousness as those drawn from the canons of Shakespeare and Spenser.

Charles Richardson also contributed to the principles of English lexicography. In his *A New Dictionary of the English Language* (London: W. Pickering, 1836–37), he collected illustrative quotations back to the fourteenth century; Johnson used quotes only as far back as Sir Philip Sidney (1554–1586). However, because Richardson's purpose in compiling his dictionary and selecting his quotes was to demonstrate that each word "had a single immutable meaning,"[6] his dictionary was flawed in conception and thus in execution. It did, nonetheless, offer something more up-to-date than Johnson's dictionary, by then 80 years old.

The Philological Society

Thoughtful men recognized that although Richardson's recorded a greater percentage of the English vocabulary than any other dictionary, it was incomplete. Hence on June 18, 1857, the Philological Society of London appointed a committee consisting of Herbert Coleridge, F.J. Furnivall, and Richard Chenevix Trench "to collect unregistered words in English."[7] The intent was to compile a supplement to Richardson's dictionary and thereby bring the lexicographic record of English up to date. But then, on November 5 and 19 of that year, Trench, then Dean of Westminster and later Anglican Archbishop of Dublin, presented to the Society a two-part paper entitled "On some Deficiencies in our English Dictionaries." Trench faulted existing dictionaries on seven points:

I. Obsolete words are incompletely registered; some inserted, some not; with no reasonable rule adduced for the omission of these, the insertion of those other.

II. Families or groups of words are often imperfect, some members of a family inserted, while others are omitted.

III. Oftentimes much earlier examples of the employment of words exist than any which our Dictionaries have cited; indicating that they were earlier introduced into the language than these examples would imply; and in case of words now obsolete, much later, frequently marking their currency at a period long after that when we are left to suppose that they passed out of use.

IV. Important meanings and uses of words are passed over; sometimes the later alone given, while the earlier, without which the history of words will be often maimed and incomplete, or even unintelligible, are unnoticed.

V. Comparatively little attention is paid to the distinguishing of synonymous words.

VI. Many passages in our literature are passed by, which might be usefully adduced in illustration of the first introduction, etymology, and meaning of words.

VII. And lastly, our Dictionaries err in redundancy as well as in defect, in the too much as well as the too little; all of them inserting some things, and some of them many things, which have properly no claim to find room in their pages.[8]

Trench's trenchant criticism of the state of English lexicography, supported by copious examples, convinced the Society to abandon its inadequate plan to issue a supplementary dictionary in favor of a plan to create an entirely new dictionary. The faults Trench found in existing dictionaries implied the desiderata for the new dictionary. These formed the foundation for what was to become the *Oxford English Dictionary*.

As the *OED*'s legendary editor, James A.H. Murray noted, "the English Dictionary, like the English Constitution, is the creation of no one man, and of no one age; it is a growth that has slowly developed itself adown the ages."[9] Murray was speaking not of the dictionary he was editing, but of English dictionaries collectively, of which the *OED* is but the exemplar. As those that came before it and the many that have with heavy indebtedness to the *OED* followed, the plan that developed for the *OED* had antecedents in earlier dictionaries.

The nineteenth century was the golden age of philology. In Germany Jacob and Wilhelm Grimm pioneered the study of language on historical principles. They established the practices of basing definitions of words on historical principles, that is, of discerning their meanings through use and of charting changes in meaning through changes in use over the life of a word. At the time Trench had influenced the Philological Society to embark upon a new English dictionary, the Grimms had already been at work on a historical dictionary of German for several years. The first part of their *Deutsches Wörterbuch* (Leipzig: S. Hirzel, 1852-1960) appeared in 1852. The project suffered and yet survived setbacks, including two world wars, and concluded in 1960.

The Grimms' *Deutsches Wörterbuch* was not the only model for the Philological Society to imitate. Hans Aarsleff has shown that Herbert Coleridge, the dictionary's first edi-

tor, credited George Liddell and Robert Scott's *Greek-English Lexicon Based on the German Work of Francis Passow* (Oxford: Oxford University Press, 1843) as an exemplar for its reliance on quotations for clues as to usage, meaning, etc. In a letter to Trench, Coleridge said that "the theory of lexicography we profess is that which Passow was the first to enunciate clearly and put into practice successfully—viz., 'that every word should be made to tell its own story'—the story of its birth and life, and in many cases of its death, and even occasionally of its resuscitation."[10] Passow, a German philologist, first propounded these principles in 1812.[11]

From the examples provided by the *Deutsches Wörterbuch* and Passow as embodied in Liddell and Scott's *Lexicon* and from the inspiration of Trench's critique of English dictionaries, the Society on January 7, 1858, resolved "That instead of the Supplement to the Standard English Dictionaries now in course of preparation by the order of the Society, a New Dictionary of the English Language be prepared under the Authority of the Philological Society."[12] Just two weeks later F.J. Furnivall read to the Society "a circular which the New Dictionary Committee proposed to issue, stating the plan of the Dictionary and asking for help in carrying it out."[13] The help sought was readers to record occurrences of words in the works of noted English writers. When the intention had been to issue a supplementary rather than a completely new dictionary, members of the Society voluntarily read books and prepared reports of "unregistered words." Thus was established the manner in which the editors would obtain the basic building bricks they would fashion into the monumental dictionary.

Coleridge's and Furnivall's Editorships

The next year Herbert Coleridge, grand nephew of the famous poet, accepted the dictionary's editorship. That same year saw publication of the *Proposal for the Publication of a New English Dictionary by the Philological Society* (London: Trübner, 1859). The founding principles enunciated in this document attest to the influence of Trench's ideas. The proposal calls for the inclusion of "every word occurring in the literature of the language it professes to illustrate," the gathering of quotations back to "the end of the reign of Henry III [i.e., 1272]," the uniform adoption of the historical principle in the treatment of individual words, and the inclusion in every etymology of "that language which seems to present the radical element contained in the word in its oldest form."[14] The list of principles put forth in the proposal echo Trench again and again.

This proposal and other appeals by the Society generated interest in the dictionary on both sides of the Atlantic. Lists of authors and works to be read for the dictionary were compiled, volunteers enlisted, and assignments made. Three lists of authors and books were drawn up, one for the period of 1250–1526, one for 1526–1674, and the last for 1674–1858. A proposal by Coleridge that "Americans should make themselves responsible for the whole of eighteenth century literature, which probably would have a less chance of finding as many readers in England" came to naught.[15] Nevertheless, American readers contributed to the dictionary, scouring many books both British and American from various periods and reporting on their reading. In his presidential address to the Philological Society for 1880, Murray singled out Americans for special commendation.[16] In 1860 Coleridge estimated that the first installment of the dictionary would appear in two year's time. The estimate was much too optimistic; indeed, Coleridge died in April 1861 at age 31.

With Coleridge's death, the editorship fell to Furnivall; this proved to be a mixed blessing for the dictionary project. Furnivall, by profession a solicitor and by nature a man of great energy with many interests, devoted his life to literature and education. Furnivall's tenure as editor proved very beneficial to the dictionary project, for this indefatigable founder of organizations did much to create the environment the dictionary needed to meet its ambitious goals of all inclusiveness, of using quotations from as far back as the thirteenth century, rigorous application of historical principles, and of supplying full etymologies. Furnivall created or was instrumental in the foundings of numerous literary societies, most significantly for the dictionary, the Early English Text Society (1864). It had become obvious that to carry out the plan of the dictionary, something would have to be done to improve the availability of texts of literature from the Old English and Middle English periods. As it was, the Philological Society was taking rare books from the sixteenth century and cutting them up for distribution to readers and for the editors' use! Fortunately, early manuscripts were safely out of its reach in various repositories. But they were also outside the grasp of readers and thus these texts' wordhoards could not disgorge their treasures to the readers. Hence the importance of the Early English Text Society. Without its successful efforts to provide printed editions of these early documents, the *OED*'s foundation would have been built on the sand of conjecture rather than the rock of research.

But whilst Furnivall busied himself with important ancillary matters, work on the dictionary itself just inched along, and haphazardly at that. With regard to the dictionary proper, Furnivall developed a system of assigning responsibility for words beginning with various letters to subeditors. Readers sent the subeditors "slips," the 4" x 6" cards on which they noted words, provided the words' illustrative quotes, and noted the quotes' sources and dates. The subeditors were responsible for organizing these materials, a responsibility they carried out with varying degrees of quality. With modification and refinement this system later proved to be an important element in the actual creation of the dictionary.

James A.H. Murray

Happily several events in 1876 converged to revitalize the dictionary project. An Anglo-American publishing partnership of Macmillan and Harper and Brothers approached James A.H. Murray, a master at Mill Hill School south of London and a philological scholar of note, about the possibility of editing a dictionary to rival Webster's. Murray, a largely self-educated man of eclectic interests, received his doctorate from Edinburgh University in recognition of his achievements. He was a man who steadfastly believed that any task worth doing was worth doing well, a trait that assured the dictionary's quality but also its slow progress. At the same time they approached Murray, the publishers inquired about the availability of the Philological Society's materials for the enterprise. Some of these materials were made available to Murray. Basing his work on these, he prepared sample entries and, at the publishers' request, scaled these down, but not enough to satisfy them. Since Murray was not willing to cut them further and since the publisher was not willing to support an enterprise on the scale Murray's standards demanded, the proposal came to naught. However the epiphany of Murray's sample entries renewed the Philological Society's interest in the new dictionary.

Initial arrangements with publishers for a dictionary that was to have been published more than ten years earlier had long since lapsed. However in 1878 the Society began negotiations with the Oxford University Press. These concluded successfully March 1, 1879, when the two parties signed a contract for a dictionary

> to occupy not less than 6,000 nor more than 7,000 pages, . . . and the said Dictionary shall be edited and prepared on the same principles and on the same lines of historical and linguistic evidence as to the forms and meanings of its words, as are shown on the Specimen page . . . , and shall contain on its title page 'Founded mainly on the materials collected by the Philological Society.[17]

The contract not-so-modestly underestimated the dictionary's ultimate length by half.

Earlier in 1878 the Society had persuaded Murray to accept the editorship. And thus was the project rejuvenated and set on its sure-but-lengthy course. Murray began preparing for the task ahead. On the lawn of his home at Mill Hill he erected a small building, made of iron to minimize the threat of fire, and dubbed it the Scriptorium. He also lined the walls of the Scriptorium with pigeon holes, "1,029 in number, for the reception of the alphabetically arranged slips"[18] to accommodate each word's slips, to be arranged in alphabetical order, as the dictionary progressed from A to Z. Over the years Furnivall had received many of the materials from subeditors when they gave up on the project; Murray reported that on Lady Day (March 25) he "received from Mr. Furnivall some ton and three-quarters of materials which had accumulated under his roof as sub-editor after sub-editor fell off in his labors."[19]

The value of the materials Murray received varied considerably. They came from diverse sources. The letter H's slips arrived from Florence; the slips for "Pa" had been stored in a barn in Ireland and its stock continuously depleted as slips were used to light fires; one bag of slips arrived inhabited by mice and another held the corpse of a rat![20] Some were damp and many scrawled illegibly. But nearly two tons of slips, sans mice, were not enough. To adhere to his rigorous standards and produce the dictionary envisioned by the Society, Murray needed more slips, byproducts of a still more ambitious reading project. In 1879 Murray appealed for "*a thousand readers* . . . to complete the work as far as possible within the next three years."[21] Readers were directed to

> Make a quotation for *every* word that strikes you as rare, obsolete, old-fashioned, new, peculiar, or used in a peculiar way. . . .
> Take special note of passages which show or imply that a word is either new and tentative, or needing explanation as obsolete or

archaic, and which thus help fix the date of its introduction or disuse.

Make as *many* quotations *as convenient to you* for ordinary words, when these are used significantly, and help by the context to explain their own meaning, or show their use.[22]

Not enough readers took the last instruction sufficiently to heart. As a result, when Murray and his assistants came to write the articles on common words, they often had to do additional reading to obtain a sufficient number of quotations of enough value from enough periods to demonstrate properly such a word's history. Murray also began a practice, also followed by later editors, of issuing lists of books to be read and of words for which examples, both early and recent, were lacking.

Murray had other editorial issues to settle before the dictionary could progress beyond the sample entries that had rekindled the Society's interest and persuaded the Oxford University Press to publish it. The most significant was devising a manner of showing pronunciation. Murray consulted with various experts on the subject and created a system that received the Society's approval on March 17, 1882.[23] A typographical style also had to be established and followed consistently. The typography had to help identify and maintain distinctions among the parts of each entry—headword, etymology, definitions, quotations, etc. More than a century later Murray was to win the gratitude of computer programmers and systems engineers for the precision with which he designed his dictionary's typography.

In May 1882, nearly a quarter of a century after the idea of the dictionary was first proposed, its first batch of copy went to the printer.[24] *A-Ant*, the first 352-page installment of the *New English Dictionary*, appeared on February 1, 1884, two weeks after Murray proudly laid three advance copies on the table before his colleagues in the Philological Society.[25] (Eventually each fascicle numbered 64 pages.) That spring Murray estimated that the dictionary, provided he received enough assistants, would be completed in less than 12 years.[26] This was but one of many instances in which Murray's optimistic estimates proved to be wishful thinking.

Needed Help

Help was needed and it came from an unexpected source. Henry Bradley, a largely self-educated philologist then supporting his family by freelance literary work and reviewing, wrote a two-part review of the first fascicle for the *Academy* in its February 16 and March 1 issues of 1884. Bradley praised the dictionary for its willingness to accommodate all words, its historical sweep, the clarity of its typography, the value of its illustrative quotations, and its concern for etymology. He also noted that "there are few indeed of the etymologies given in this first part of the Dictionary which we are inclined to dispute."[27] Yet in disputing several, he demonstrated his authority.

The Delegates of the Oxford University Press, its governing board, expressed concern throughout the protracted publication of the dictionary about the slowness of its pace and continually urged its editor to move faster. In order to further the dictionary's progress, Murray resigned his teaching duties to devote full time to his editorial duties and moved to Oxford in 1885. At the urging of the Delegates, the staff was enlarged. In May 1886, due largely to his insightful review of *A-Ant*, Henry Bradley joined Murray's staff. Late in 1887 he was put at the head of a team charged with responsibility for the letter E and worked thereafter independently of Murray.

Both Murray's team and Bradley's team followed Furnivall's model whereby subeditors did preliminary work. Their assistants prepared a draft of each word's article and then the editor reviewed and corrected it. Among assistants a division of labor developed based on each one's expertise. However some questions could not be answered within the Scriptorium. The lack of adequate space and library resources often forced the staff to make time-consuming trips to the Bodleian or college libraries. And to answer some questions, such as the intended meaning of a particular word as used by a contemporary writer, Murray corresponded with the likes of Lord Tennyson, Robert Meredith, Thomas Hardy, Robert Browning, James Russell Lowell, and a wide range of experts, including "the Director of the Royal Botanic Gardens at Kew about the first record of the name of an exotic plant; . . . to a Jesuit father on a point of Roman Catholic Divinity; [and] to the Secretary of the Astronomical Society about the primum-mobile or the solar constant."[28]

The dictionary progressed under Murray and Bradley's guidance. The *Deceit to Deject* fascicle published January 1, 1895, bore the title *The Oxford English Dictionary,* the title that in time came to supplant *New English Dictionary*. To speed its progress even more, William Alexander Craigie of the University of St. Andrews joined Bradley in 1897 and assisted with the letter G and assisted Murray with the letters I and K. In 1901 Craigie assumed independent editorial responsibility for the letter Q.[29] Charles Talbut Onions became the dictionary's fourth editor in 1914, having joined Murray's staff in 1895. "Between 1906 and 1913 [he had] prepared special portions of M, N, R, and S" and in 1914 "began with a separate staff to edit the later portion of that letter (Su-Sz)."[30] Even with four editorial teams working on the dictionary simultaneously, Murray's hope to see its completion by his eightieth birthday was frustrated. He died at age 78 on July 26, 1915, after a brief illness; the dictionary was well into the letter S and Murray had begun planning for the letter U. In recognition of his achievement, Murray had been knighted in 1908; at that time the dictionary had been published through the letter P. Murray's death slowed progress, as did the loss of staff members to military service during the Great War and Bradley's death on May 23, 1923. Fortunately the system of several editors working independently assured continuity and the work moved forward.

Critical Reception

Seventy-one years after Dean Trench had criticized existing dictionaries, the dictionary he had envisioned finally appeared. In April 1928 the first copies were presented to King George and President Coolidge, "the highest representatives of the two great English-speaking nations."[31] It was received with universal acclaim. The *Nation*, anticipating its completion a bit prematurely in 1927, said that "No similar work . . . is comparable in magnitude, accuracy, or completeness."[32] The unsigned review in the *Times Literary Supplement* called it a "monumental and inalienable public possession."[33] The *Saturday Review* hailed it as "a monument which will last when a thousand best-sellers are forgotten" and called it "the topmost peak of a long range of gloss-collectors and lexicographers."[34] Ernest Weekley, writing in the *Quarterly Review* called it a "noble monument of the English language."[35] And Floyd Knight said that "one might look for flaws in the 'New English Dictionary', or lament that it does not include proper names; but its scholarship is so monumental as to make fault-finding seem petty."[36]

Yet it had been 44 years since *A-Ant* appeared. During those four decades mankind had learned how to fly, how to talk across the miles over radio, how to make moving pictures, and how to record sound and play back recordings. Inescapably a product of its times, much of the *OED* was behind the times. Well before the dictionary was complete, some had recognized that it would be incomplete. In 1919, Craigie himself outlined the work that needed to be done to supplement the dictionary's historical coverage. In a paper presented to the Philological Society in 1919 he called for work to commence on historical dictionaries for the Old English; the Middle English (1175–1500); the Tudor and Stuart (1500–1675); the 1675–1800; and the older Scottish periods.[37] More than 70 years later the tasks Craigie outlined are not yet complete. The *OED Supplement*, edited by Craigie and Onions, appeared in 1933. A plan for a new

Dictionary of Old English was announced in the late 1960s but thus far has yielded fascicles for only several letters, but progress continues.[38] The *Middle English Dictionary*, (Ann Arbor: University of Michigan Press, 1952–) begun in 1925 and whose first fascicle did not appear until 1952, has reached "So." Some quotations have been collected for a dictionary of the Tudor and Stuart period for the *Early Modern English Dictionary*, but that project has been suspended, perhaps permanently. No effort has been made towards a dictionary of the 1675–1800 period, one that Craigie thought might not differ enough from the nineteenth century, a period well represented in the *OED*, to require its own dictionary. *A Dictionary of the Older Scottish Tongue*, (Chicago: University of Chicago Press, 1931–) begun under Craigie's editorship, had reached "Re" at the end of the 1980s. Several years after calling for these dictionaries, Craigie concluded American English also needed its own historical dictionary and, even while helping bring the *OED* to its conclusion, departed for the University of Chicago to assume the editorship of *A Dictionary of American English on Historical Principles* (Chicago: University of Chicago Press, 1938–44).

Flaws in the Dictionary

Despite the praise it received in 1928, many of the dictionary's users did "look for flaws in the 'New English Dictionary'" and found them. Even though readers in North America had contributed thousands of slips for the dictionary, the sorts of sources they read differed little in nature from the sources being read in England. As a result, peculiarly American senses of words common to the two national vocabularies and distinctly American words were badly underrepresented in the dictionary, as were distinctly Australian, South African, etc., English words. In this significant way the dictionary fell short of Murray's stated goal of "contain[ing] all English words ordinary and extraordinary."[39] A much more

common form of criticism was antedatings of the earliest recorded use of particular words or notations of later uses of words labeled as rare or obsolete. Murray himself anticipated just this form of criticism, inevitable given the sometimes haphazard way in which early volunteer readers did their work. In 1884 he estimated that "Earlier instances will . . . yet be found of three-fourths of all the words recorded, above all, of the words introduced from Latin since the Renascence."[40] And nearly five decades after the dictionary's completion, one prominent scholar declared that "instead of providing an unquestioned basis for further research, the O.E.D. has to become its object."[41] Rather than contribute to the endless line of articles relating hit-and-miss antedating and postdating of single words that, as Murray himself predicted, had become a staple in the pages of *Notes & Queries* and other learned journals, Jürgen Schäfer did a systematic study of the works of Shakespeare and Nashe to derive an overall estimate of how many of the 260,000 headwords in the *OED* (including the 1933 supplement) are subject to antedating. He concluded that more than 96,000 can be antedated, some by more than a century. One imagines that Murray would have been pleased that his own estimate had been so far above that established scientifically, or at least as scientifically as possible, for Murray considered himself not a literary man but a scientist whose object of study was the English language.

Antedating and postdating of *OED* words can become a game and, like any game, can be corrupted. Marghanita Laski, credited with submitting more than 250,000 slips for the four-volume supplement begun in 1957, has been a very adept player at the game. In 1968, noting that the editors like to have five examples of a word to establish its meaning, Laski

"admit[ted] to certain plantings, though not furtive ones. For instance, when the editor asked me if I could produce evidence to show that *OED* was wrong in supposing that *berate,* v. was obsolete in England, I couldn't immediately lay my hands on an example, so slipped it into my next review and carded it—but several unplanted ones turned up in the next few weeks. And when it occurred to me that *ironmonger* (the shop) now has two meanings, corresponding respectively to Fr. *quincaillerie* and Fr. *droguerie*, it seemed to me unlikely I would find quotations illustrating this. So I wrote an article on changes in shop functions ... offered it to the *Guardian's* women's page, explaining why I'd written it, and then, when it was published, carded it."[42]

The *Supplement* and the second edition of the *OED* quote Laski's 1952 use of "berate" as a verb! Although it is not clear that this is the planting she submitted, it seems likely.

No dating in the *OED* of the earliest occurrence of any word can be taken as a certainty of its earliest appearance in written English; rather that dating denotes the earliest reference available to the editors. The method by which the slips for the original were compiled was imperfect. Most readers, Craigie noted, "as a rule did their duty pretty effectively by taking out at the most two or three thousand quotations from a single work."[43] However some fell below the editors' standards and too few fully heeded Murray's entreaty to give sufficient attention to ordinary words. Several years into the project he told the Philological Society "I have often thought that if I could find time to direct it, or if the Society could find someone else to direct it, the reading of all books over again, with the instructions, 'Take out quotations for all words that do *not* strike you as rare, peculiar, or peculiarly used,' would be of enormous service."[44] Furthermore, the readers often worked from incomplete or less-than-authoritative texts of early works. Only if every text of every literary creation of the previous seven centuries had been available to the editors and only if every word in every one of those documents had been concordanced and linked to its contextual phrase—only if this unimaginably unmanageable task had been performed and only if Murray and others had had time to examine every use of every word

thus recorded, could one say with certainty that the editors had recorded the earliest use of each word in each of its senses.

The First Supplement

Upon completion of the dictionary, work began immediately on its first supplement, a contingency provided for in the 1879 agreement between the Philological Society and the Oxford University Press. Craigie and Onions were engaged to produce the supplement. Already a considerable body of additional slips, many providing antedatings of words, had accumulated. However, a supplement incorporating all of this information as well as new words and new senses of old words "could not be contemplated" at that time "and it was therefore resolved to produce a supplementary volume the scope of which would be in the main restricted to the treatment of those accessions of words and senses which had taken place during the preceding 50 years."[45] Onions and Craigie allowed two categories of exceptions: "items of modern origin and present currency that had been either intentionally or accidentally omitted would be included, and account would be taken of earlier evidence for American uses, which Sir William Craigie was in a position to supply."[46] And so "appendicitis," "burg" meaning a town, "chop-suey," "intelligentsia," "movie," "mushiness," "peachy" meaning agreeable, "radio," "Rayon," "speedway," "tyrannosaurus," and "wave-length" entered the *OED*. Scientific and technical terms, treated inadequately in the original *OED* even as such terms proliferated rapidly, figure prominently in the supplement. The tale of how Murray decided against including "radium" because he doubted the word would take hold is legendary. Given the gift of hindsight, the supplement's editors corrected this notorious omission and others less celebrated.

Upon completion of the supplement, the staff was disbanded and the *OED* became a document frozen in time. However the language continued to grow through the coinage of new words; some words took on new senses; some words fell out of favor and others gained respectability. Yet there was no one to record these changes systematically and to keep the dictionary up to date. Its users, meanwhile, continued to report antedatings and postdatings and journal editors continued to publish these reports. Other dictionaries, of course, carried on, but none of these chart the life of each word through every period as minutely as does the *OED*. The decision to dismantle the lexicographic machine that had been operating continuously for more than fifty years was most unfortunate. The only effort by the Oxford University Press to update the *OED* was oblique in that it was done through the revised third edition of *The Shorter Oxford English Dictionary*. This dictionary, derived from its namesake, was first published in February 1933, and reprinted with corrections the next month, in a second edition in 1936, in a third edition in 1944, and with revised addenda in 1955. Entries in the 40-page 1955 addenda and corrigenda section are stripped down versions of *OED* entries all but bereft of illustrative quotations.

As a product of its times, the *OED* inevitably shared some of the prejudices of the period. Victorian prudishness led to its falling short of Murray's goal to make it all-inclusive. For example, two well known four-letter words, one referring to the act of sexual intercourse, the other to female genitalia, were excluded. It has been taken to task for failing "not only the smut-hound but also the student of literature by omitting any blush-making sub-meanings of familiar words, whatever the eminence of the authors who have used them."[47] Not until 1968 did the Delegates of the Oxford University Press approve their inclusion.[48] Also excluded were many dialect and slang terms, with those included always labeled as such. The *OED* gave preference to the Received Standard dialect of England, thereby implicitly endorsing it as "proper" English. Just what is "proper" English and what is not, indeed whether or not such a thing exists or can exist,

has been and continues to be a matter of considerable debate, brought to white-heat intensity in 1961 with publication of *Webster's Third New International Dictionary* (Springfield, MA: G. & C. Merriam, 1961), a dictionary that departed from the practice of making such distinctions. Suffice it to say that the *OED*'s practices have figured in the debate. Upon its initial completion in 1928, that anonymous reviewer for the *Times Literary Supplement* praised it for capturing the language before it had been degraded when "the newly literate received their charter to treat the language as they pleased in hourly print."[49] This reviewer counted himself as one of "those who respect the purity of the language, who try to honour and understand its traditions and its idioms, who feel doubtful whether even so supple an instrument as English can bear without grave deterioration the incessant strain put upon it by modern democracy, [and who] . . . rejoice[s] that the Dictionary has come into being when it has and as it has."[50] The very historical principles upon which the *OED* is founded and from which its well-deserved reputation rests mock such praise! One could just as well say that it would have been better had the *OED* come to completion in 1612 or 1756 or 1857 so as to have captured the language before its corruption by some other forces. Entry after entry after entry in the *OED* demonstrates unequivocally the inevitability of change in language. And that is why, if one *can* commit a crime against the English language, dispersal of the dictionary staff upon completion of the 1933 supplement was surely such a crime.

Robert Burchfield

The Oxford University Press began to atone for this grave mistake in 1957 when it appointed Robert Burchfield, a New Zealander who had studied Old English and related languages while a Rhodes scholar at Oxford, to edit a new supplement to the *OED* to replace the 1933 supplement. Burchfield has related that, "'The very hard-headed publishers at the time looked at me more or less sternly . . . and they said, "Look, 1275 pages, one volume, seven years: there is the format.""""[51] The lessons of 1879–1928 had been forgotten. When the first volume of the supplement appeared in 1972, eight years after the project had been scheduled for completion, it alone contained 1,331 pages covering "a" through "gyver." Burchfield estimated at the time that the supplement would be complete in two more volumes and within six years. Fourteen years later the fourth and final volume of the supplement appeared. He adhered to the same high standards Murray established and went to the same painstaking steps to establish just what a word meant, consulting Buckminster Fuller about "dymaxion," J.R.R. Tolkein about "hobbit," and Murray Gell-Mann about "quark."

The 1972–86 four-volume supplement lists antedatings of words, new senses, and new words. It is the most catholic part of the OED, for in it Burchfield's "aim, doubtless not fully achieved, was to give parity of treatment to the English of the United States and that of the United Kingdom. The same broad democratic line was taken for other varieties of English, in Canada, Australia, New Zealand, South Africa, and so on."[52] But, great as its contribution is in bringing the OED up to date and in including words from vigorous English-speaking traditions outside the United Kingdom, the OED plus its supplements is still incomplete.

An Incomplete Record of the English Language

From its inception, the OED has been a print-based dictionary. In its original *Proposal*, the Philological Society said the new dictionary "should contain *every word occurring in the literature of the language it professes to illustrate*."[53] The examples readers collected in the 1860s and for many years thereafter necessarily came from printed sources. And although the OED's ten original volumes cited popular usages from newspapers and the like, it looked, much as had Johnson, upon the established canon of great writers as the source of the core vocabulary of English. Jürgen Schäfer determined that Shakespeare, whose every word was put on a slip for the editors' consideration, is much overrepresented in the OED, especially as a source of first use. This tradition continued in the 1972–86 supplement for, as Burchfield said, "Every single word and meaning of great ancient writers like Geoffrey Chaucer were recorded in the OED. And I could see no case that could be made to leave out of the supplement the words of the corresponding 20th-century writers, Stephen Spender, W.H. Auden, T.S. Eliot, Graham Greene, Evelyn Waugh, Iris Murdoch, and so forth."[54] Leaving aside the question of the merits of Burchfield's comparative literary assessments, the point is that the OED is a dictionary of written English emphasizing the written English of its well educated and most literary users. At the same time that his editorial policies upheld this tradition, Burchfield also democratized the OED by including popular and ephemeral sources in greater numbers than before.

It has come under some fire for this. Insofar as spoken English differs from written English, the OED presents an incomplete record. Works such as the *Dictionary of American Regional English* (Cambridge: Harvard University Press, 1985–) and the *English Dialect Dictionary* (London: H. Frowde, 1898–1905), of course, compensate for this. The OED's editors have always had to make choices and impose limits; if they had not, their work would still be in the preparatory stages. But, the criticism that the OED practices "black-and-white lexicography"[55] is valid to the extent that it reminds one that the OED falls short of Murray's goal of all-inclusiveness. That goal will always be a chimera if for no reason other than the print medium of the OED. Even while Burchfield and his team labored away at their supplement, a monumental achievement in itself, some of the *OED*'s most ardent advocates questioned its future viability.

Marghanita Laski, a true friend of the *OED* and indefatigable contributor of quotation slips for the four-volume supplement, shared those concerns about "black-and-white lexicography." In describing her practices while reading for the dictionary, she said "I do not hesitate to send in words I have only heard, whether in speech or on the radio, since the date I give . . . is evidence that the word or phrase was in use at the time."[56] Other limitations in the aging *OED* were also evident by the time its supplement began to appear. Laski presented the case forcefully just one day after publication of the first volume of the supplement. In a letter to the *Times Literary Supplement* she asked whether or not the *OED* was in serious danger of becoming "an object of veneration rather than a tool for modern use."[57]

The Second Edition

Work continued on the supplement, of course, but another decade passed before the Oxford University Press began planning for the long-range viability of the dictionary. Study of the problem began in early 1982. In a press conference held May 15, 1984, at the Royal Society in London, the Press announced its plan to issue a new edition combining the ten-volume 1928 dictionary (re-issued in twelve volumes in 1933 with the supplement as volume 13 and reprinted in 1961 and 1970) and Burchfield's four supplements. To do this, however, required new ways of operating. Even in the 1980s Burchfield and his staff continued to produce the dictionary's supplement much as Murray had in his Scriptorium. Just as with editing the supplement the time had come to include more scientific and technical terms, so with preparation of the second edition the time had come to rely on state-of-the-art technology.

The project required the combined efforts of several organizations. IBM United Kingdom, Ltd., donated equipment and assigned personnel to work with OUP on planning and executing the project; Great Britain's Department of Trade and Industry supported it; and the University of Waterloo in Canada provided programming expertise to supplement that of OUP staff. OUP directed and managed the project. Initial hopes to use optical scanners to convert the dictionary's text into machine-readable form were dashed. The complexities of the typography made that technique impractical. The entire dictionary had to be keystroked onto computer tape! International Computaprint Corporation (ICC) in the United States was awarded the contract for this herculean task. The contract specified a maximum of 7 errors per 10,000 keystrokes; its 120 typists performed the entire job with a remarkably good error rate of between 4 and 4.5 per 10,000.[58] Murray's typographic design, faithfully followed save for minor exceptions for more than a century, proved a great boon to the electronic conversion process. The typographical conventions cued the typists to different parts of each article and thereby cued them to insert various codes to identify the start of each part. Computer programs had to be devised to merge the 1928 text and the text of the supplements. This was a complex task since many entries in the supplements had to be inserted into existing entries in the base set. It was further complicated by the fact that in some cases different parts of an article in the supplements had to be inserted into various locations in the original article. Some human intervention was required, but most of this difficult work was accomplished by machine.

The result, published in 20 volumes in the spring of 1989, was *The Oxford English Dictionary*, second edition. Its introduction forthrightly states that "Whereas the *Supplement* can be regarded for practical purposes as up to date, it is a matter of common knowledge that many elements of the original *OED* require revision. That is the very purpose for which the New OED Project, of which the present work is the first printed product, was initiated. Several of these requirements have been addressed in this edition."[59] One of those requirements was to convert Murray's pronunciation system to a more modern system. The editors prudently chose to employ the International Phonetic Alphabet, developed at the end of the nineteenth century. *OED2* includes "an additional 5,000 words, combinations, and senses . . . located chiefly in the first third of the alphabet, where work done for the *Supplement* is now twenty years or more old."[60]

Desiderata for the Future

OED2 is but a first step toward a New OED, for indeed a new *OED* is needed. Take, for example, a representative definition. Its article on "gasoline," published in 1898, defines it as "a volatile inflammable liquid, one of the first products in the distillation of crude petroleum, employed for purposes of heating and illumination." The first part of the definition remains valid, but the latter part is at best misleading. At that time the dictionary provided one 1895 illustration hinting at this fuel's use in motor vehicles; the other four illustrations relate to illumination and cooking. Both the 1933 and 1972 supplements add illustrations related to automobiles, two also dating from 1895. This is not an isolated case. Many of the definitions need to be brought up to date; additional reported antedatings and postdatings need to be recorded; and the English of Great Britain's former colonies needs to be more fully represented.

These examples are indicative of broader problems, problems most clearly enunciated in 1972 by Marghanita Laski in the same letter to the *Times Literary Supplement* in which she expressed the fear that the *OED* might soon be little more than "a magnificent fossil."[61] Like Trench in his criticism of the dictionaries of the mid-nineteenth century, Laski outlined seven areas requiring attention:

1. *Antedatings*. . . . An enormous number of "first examples" in *OED* can now be antedated, of important as of trivial words and usages, and often by centuries.

2. *Postdatings*. Most "latest examples" in *OED*, even in the later volumes, are nineteenth-century, often early nineteenth-century. From *OED* one can have no indication whether the bulk of words and usages cited continue to be current. . .

3. *Reading*. . . . two people can read the same book and record almost non-identical lists of words to be found in it. . . . In addition, . . . many of *OED*'s original readers were inept. . . .
. . . it is clear that extended reading in the trivia of past centuries could be as valuable to a revision of *OED* as the reading of contemporary trivia has been to the new *Supplement*.
In addition, the past century has seen the publication of much useful material, especially in the field of diaries and letters. . . .

4. *Subjects*. . . . One need only consider the kind of people who read for *OED* to guess, usually rightly, what kinds of subjects will be inadequately covered.

5. *Corrections*. A few examples: Words and usages categorized by *OED* as "obsolete" have often proved to be in later use than recorded; as "rare" have proved to be comparatively common; as "nonce" have proved to be more than that. Whole categories of usage have been capriciously treated or virtually ignored. . . . Words missed by *OED* and obsolete before the new *Supplement*'s period could be recorded.

6. *Spellings*. In several cases words are entered only under spellings now unfamiliar and without cross-reference.

7. *Place of entry*. In several cases, compound words and phrases are entered only under their most unlikely component and without cross-reference.[62]

The first step towards a new *OED*, converting the existing *OED* to machine-readable form, has been completed.

Already the complicated process of converting the *OED* to machine readable form has provided benefits that one could only dream about just a few years ago. In early 1988 the text of the original ten-volume *New English Dictionary* was made available on CD-ROM for searching and manipulation through a microcomputer. The entire text can be searched through a number of approaches, including quotation author, quoted work, quotation text, sense/definition, etymology, headwords and usage, and other sorts of labels. This empowers linguists and others to use this rich resource on the history of the language in new ways. One way is to search a word in the quotations then to check the word's date of first appearance in its own article and compare dates of quotations. In this way reports of antedatings and postdatings can, one assumes, be generated in quantities that the late Jürgen Schäfer could only imagine. Furthermore, they can be generated from within the *OED* itself!

Determining more accurate dates for the first or last recorded appearances of words is but one use of the electronic *OED*. Since the database is in machine-readable form, editors are finally free of Murray's slips-and-cubbyholes process and its later analogs. They can work on the *OED* without regard for its alphabetical sequence and, conceivably, from any location on the globe where there is a phone line. The New OED has the potential of being a truly international record of world English. Editors working via computer and telecommunications lines from offices in each nation in which English is the predominant or a significant language could make contributions. If users have access to the database in its daily updated state, the *OED* will, thanks to the electronic medium, be more up-to-date and be kept more up-to-date than it has been in the print medium.

These are possibilities, not yet fully realized in late 1989. The staff today is largely centralized in Oxford. Editorial work continues to rely on 4" by 6" paper slips and "the drafting of new entries goes on all the time."[63] Keyboarding of completed entries is carried out as a separate operation. Ten of the 14 full-time staff entrusted with keeping the *OED* healthy "are concerned solely with the preparation of entries for new vocabulary items."[64] Three of these ten specialize in scientific and technical terminology. The others tend to "database improvement and plans for revision, as

well as senior editorial work."[65] These fourteen are assisted by a number of freelancers who "carry out support activities such as file searching and library research."[66] As for embracing all varieties of English, the editors are aware of the challenge of doing this from Oxford. In at least a partial response to this challenge, they began in 1989 to organize a North American reading program through the Press's New York office to parallel the program conducted from the Oxford headquarters. Lexicographer Dr. Jeffery Triggs directs the program's American component from an office in New Jersey.[67] This international program, explains a staff member, is principally "a directed reading exercise, i.e., a number of freelancers 'read' sources selected by us, and submit illustrative quotations, at the moment about 12,000 per month" from readers in the United Kingdom, plus those from readers elsewhere.[68] Their efforts are supplemented by voluntary contributors throughout the world, the very means by which the original two tons of quotation slips delivered to Murray in 1879 had been collected.

The agenda before that staff, much of it echoing Laski's seven-point critique of 1972, is best summarized in the concluding pages of the second edition's history of its production:

> There is much in the style of the Dictionary, the punctuation, the capitalization, the definitional terminology, and the spelling (within entries and even of some headwords) that calls for modernization. In the cross-reference system, many improvements are desirable, notably in the citation of variant spellings as headwords and in the more precise specification of parts of speech, homonym numbers, and sense numbers. In the etymologies, the varying systems of transcription should be harmonized, the linguistic nomenclature should be brought up to date, and the results of recent research should be added. The organization of senses within many entries needs to be rethought. Numerous scientific and technical definitions need to be brought into line with present-day knowledge (though the *Supplement* amended the treatment of many of the most important terms). Many of the definitions of general vocabulary need to be

reworked to take account of recent technological and social changes. There are a number of references to countries, currency values, institutions, and persons, which are now anachronistic; and there are still a few definitions which enshrine social attitudes that are now alien. The usage and subject labels should be made fully consistent and modernized.

Many current words are illustrated by a latest quotation from the first half of the nineteenth century, or even earlier, and it is difficult to distinguish them from words or senses that are now, in fact, disused. Recent examples ought to be supplied for every sense that is still current. The citation style of many quotations from the original *OED* could well be brought up to the standard of consistency of the *Supplement* (although improving it would require the rechecking of many thousands of quotations). Earlier examples exist (in various places) for thousands of words and senses, and these should be added. The coverage of English before 1700, and at least as far back as 1500, could be markedly improved. Last, but certainly not least, the coverage of English outside the United Kingdom needs to be greatly expanded, especially the English of North America, which is the greatest source of linguistic change, but not neglecting the English of many other parts of the world where it is a first or important language.[69]

It is an ambitious agenda, reminiscent of the challenge Trench put before the Philological Society in 1857.

A timetable for publication (in whatever form) of the New OED has not been announced although the target is about 15 years hence.[70] A CD-ROM version of the second edition is planned for release in the early 1990s. Whatever the editorial team's hopes for the eventual New OED, those hopes will probably not be realized as punctually as they would like any more than Murray's or Burchfield's hopes were. But there are plans and dreams for a new and better *OED* and related products. And there is a vigorous model for these plans. The *OED* began spawning other dictionaries even before it was complete. Among these are the *Concise Oxford Dictionary of Current English* in 1911, the *Pocket Oxford English Dictionary of Current*

English in 1924, the *Little Oxford Dictionary of Current English* in 1930, the two-volume *Shorter Oxford English Dictionary* in 1933, the *Oxford Dictionary of English Etymology* in 1966, the compact edition of the *Oxford English Dictionary* in 1971, the *Oxford Children's Dictionary* in 1976, the *Oxford American Dictionary* in 1980, the *Oxford Minidictionary* in 1981, and the *Oxford Universal Dictionary* in 1981. The family now consists of more than 25 dictionaries. Future enhancements of the *OED* or spin-offs from it include a "talking dictionary," which would provide the pronunciation or various dialectic or national pronunciations for words; dictionaries of national or regional English; specialized dictionaries tapping all of *OED's* terms from a particular field such as religion or medicine; a database consisting just of the quotations file, much of it not yet published, for use by lexicographers and others; a thesaurus including synonyms and antonyms; a dictionary in which illustrations, some of them in video, supplement verbal definitions of things and processes; and a polyglot dictionary.[71] Already in 1989 *Webster's Ninth New Collegiate Dictionary* (Springfield, MA: Merriam-Webster, 1983) was released on CD-ROM for use with the Apple Macintosh microcomputer. It features digitally recorded pronunciations of entry words.

Thanks to the work of Murray and his assistants; thanks to the work Murray's fellow editors and Robert Burchfield and his assistants continued; thanks to the work of the team of programmers, editors, and typists in the late 1980s, the *OED* promises to remain the glittering jewel in the OUP crown. Although the labor involved in bringing the New OED into being will be nearly as monumental as the labor that has made it a possibility, it will be well worth the effort. The New OED ought to sparkle even more brilliantly and merit more praise than any of the books or databases that have preceded it.

PUBLICATION HISTORY

A New English Dictionary on Historical Principles, Founded Mainly on the Materials Collected by the Philological Society, edited by James A.H. Murray, Henry Bradley, W.A. Craigie, and C.T. Onions. Oxford: Clarendon Press, 1888–1928. 10 vols.

A New English Dictionary on Historical Principles, Founded Mainly on the Materials Collected by the Philological Society, edited by James A.H. Murray, Henry Bradley, W.A. Craigie, and C.T. Onions. *Introduction, Supplement, and Bibliography,* by W.A. Craigie and C.T. Onions. Oxford: Clarendon Press, 1933. 542, 330, 91p.

The Oxford English Dictionary, Being a Corrected Re-issue with an Introduction, Supplement and Bibliography of a New English Dictionary on Historical Principles, edited by James A.H. Murray, Henry Bradley, W.A. Craigie, and C.T. Onions. Oxford: Clarendon Press, 1933. 13 vols. Reprinted 1961, 1970.

A Supplement to the Oxford English Dictionary, edited by Robert Burchfield. Oxford: Clarendon Press, 1972–86. 4 vols.

The Oxford English Dictionary, prepared by J. A. Simpson and E.S.C. Weiner. 2nd ed. Oxford: Clarendon Press, 1989. 20 vols.

BIBLIOGRAPHY

To the extent that the history of the *OED* and the life of James A.H. Murray are one and the same, Elisabeth K.M. Murray's thoroughly researched biography of her grandfather offers a fine history. Aarsleff's article is a careful exposition of the intellectual antecedents of the dictionary. Ronald Fritze's brief history leans heavily on several sources and emphasizes the financial aspects of the enterprise. Shenker's history offers a good picture of the evolution of the *OED2*. Fletcher, Gray, and Murphy describe the dictionary's transition from the relatively static state as a printed book to its fluid state as a machine-readable database. Algeo's review of the second edition is the most thorough, critical, and insightful available. In addition to numerous substantive articles this brief bibliography cannot accommodate, hundreds of brief notes on antedatings and the like as well as reviews of the *OED* in its various media and degrees of completion have appeared over the past century.

Aarsleff, Hans. "The Early History of the *Oxford English Dictionary.*" *Bulletin of the New York Public Library* 66 (September, 1962): 417–39.

Algeo, John. "The Emperor's New Clothes: The Second Edition of the Society's Dictionary." *Transactions of the Philological Society* 88 (1990): 131–50.

Benzie, William. *Dr. F. J. Furnivall, Victorian Scholar Adventurer.* Norman, OK: Pilgrim Books, Inc., 1983.

Burchfield, Robert. "Four-letter Words and the OED." *Times Literary Supplement* no. 3684 (October 13, 1972): 1233.

———. "O.E.D.: A New Supplement." *Essays and Studies* 14 (1961): 35–51.

———. "Some Thoughts on the Revision of the O.E.D." In *An English Miscellany, Presented to W. S. Mackie,* edited by Brian S. Lee, 208–18. London: Oxford University Press, 1977.

Burchfield, Robert, and Hans Aarsleff. *The Oxford English Dictionary and the State of the Language.* Washington: Library of Congress, 1988.

Craigie, W.A. "The Making of a Dictionary." *Saturday Review of Literature* 4 (April 21, 1928): 792.

Fletcher, Ewen. "Computerising the Oxford English Dictionary." *Bookseller* (January 18, 1986): 219–23.

Fritze, Ronald H. "The Oxford English Dictionary: A Brief History." *Reference Services Review* 17 (1989): 61–70.

Gray, J. C. "Creating the Electronic New Oxford English Dictionary." *Computers and the Humanities* 20 (1986): 45–49.

Hanham, Alison. "The Cely Papers and the Oxford English Dictionary." *English Studies,* 42 (June, 1961): 129–52.

Harpley, Mary. "The Oxford English Dictionary on Compact Disc." *British Book News* (February, 1988): 90–91.

Harris, Roy. "The History Men." *Times Literary Supplement* no. 4144 (September 3, 1982): 935–36.

Laski, Marghanita. "Reading for OED." *Times Literary Supplement* no. 3437 (January 11, 1968): 37–39.

Murphy, Cullen. "Caught in the Web of Bytes: The Electronic Oxford English Dictionary." *Atlantic* 263 (February, 1989): 68–70.

Murray, James A.H. *The Evolution of English Lexicography*. Oxford: Clarendon Press, 1900.

Murray, K.M. Elisabeth. *Caught in the Web of Words: James Murray and the Oxford English Dictionary*. New Haven: Yale University Press, 1977.

"The OED and How it Grows." *Bay State Librarian* 67 (February, 1978): 17–18.

Schäfer, Jürgen. *Documentation in the O.E.D.: Shakespeare and Nashe as Test Cases*. Oxford: Clarendon Press, 1980.

Shenker, Israel. "Annals of Lexicography: The Dictionary Factory." *New Yorker* 65 (April 3, 1989): 86–100.

Sider, John W. "Reading for the OED : A Case History." *English Language Notes* 18 (December, 1980): 131–38.

Trench, Richard Chenevix. *On Some Deficiencies in Our English Dictionaries*. London: John W. Parker and Son, 1857.

Wardale, E. E. "The 'New English Dictionary.'" *Nineteenth Century and After* 103 (January, 1928): 97–110.

Weiner, Edmund. "Computerizing the Oxford English Dictionary." *Scholarly Publishing* 16 (1985): 239–253.

―――. "New Uses for the New OED." *Bookseller* (January 25, 1986): 332–36.

NOTES

[1] Rosemary Herbert, "Oxford University Press's 'jewel in the crown,'" *Christian Science Monitor*, 4 May 1987, p. B4.

[2] Various printers served the Oxford University as far back as 1478, a date often cited as the beginning of the Oxford University Press. However, on October 2, 1690, a legally binding agreement transferring rights and property from an entrepreneur to Oxford University marked "the beginning of the true University Press." Harry Carter, *A History of the Oxford University Press*, vol. 1, *To the Year 1780* (Oxford: Clarendon Press, 1975), 109.

[3] Sidney I. Landau, *Dictionaries: The Art and Craft of Lexicography* (New York: Scribner's, 1984), 44–48.

[4] Samuel Johnson, "Preface," in *A Dictionary of the English Language* (London: W. Strahan, 1755).

[5] Ibid. Italics in original.

[6] Landau, 66.

[7] "Notices of Meetings," *Transactions of the Philological Society* (1857): 141.

[8] Richard Chenevix Trench, *On Some Deficiencies in our English Dictionaries* (London: John W. Parker, 1857), 3.

[9] James A.H. Murray, *The Evolution of English Lexicography* (Oxford: The Clarendon Press, 1900), 6–7.

[10] "A Letter to the Very Rev. The Dean of Westminster from Herbert Coleridge" in Trench, (1860), 72. Professor Hans Aarsleff of Princeton University was the first to point out the significance of this passage.

[11] Hans Aarsleff, "The Original Plan for the *OED* and Its Background," in *The Oxford English Dictionary and the State of the Language*, by Robert W. Burchfield and Hans Aarsleff (Washington: Library of Congress, 1988), 42–43.

[12] "Notices of the Meetings of the Philological Society in 1858," *Transactions of the Philological Society* (1858): 198.

[13] Ibid., 199.

[14] *Proposal for the Publication of A New English Dictionary* (London: Trübner, 1859), 2–4.

[15] "A Letter to the Very Rev. The Dean of Westminster from Herbert Coleridge," 72.

[16] James A.H. Murray, "The President's Annual Address for 1880," *Transactions of the Philological Society* (1880–81): 122

[17] "Dictionary-Contract with the Clarendon Press," *Transactions of the Philological Society* (1877–79): li.

[18] James A.H. Murray, "The Work of the Philological Society, from May, 1878, to May, 1879," *Transactions of the Philological Society* (1877–79): 568.

[19] Ibid.

[20] K.M. Elisabeth Murray, *Caught in the Web of Words* (New Haven: Yale University Press, 1977), 176–77.

[21] *An Appeal to the English-speaking and English-reading Public to Read Books and Make Extracts for the Philological Society's "New English Dictionary"* (n.p., 1879), 4. Italics in original.

[22] "Directions to Readers for the Dictionary," in Murray, *Caught in the Web of Words*, 347. Italics in original.

[23] "Historical Introduction," *Oxford English Dictionary* (Oxford: Clarendon Press, 1933), xiv.

[24] James A.H. Murray, "Thirteenth Address of the President of the Philological Society, Delivered at the Anniversary Meeting, Friday, 16th May, 1884," *Transactions of the Philological Society* (1882–84): 508.

[25] Ibid.

[26] Ibid., 531.

[27] Henry Bradley, review of *A New English Dictionary on Historical Principles*, Part 1, A-Ant, *The Academy*, no. 617, new ser. (1 March 1884): 141. The first part of Bradley's review appeared in *The Academy*, no. 615, new ser. (16 February 1884): 105–06.

[28] Quoted from James A.H. Murray's personal papers in Murray, *Caught in the Web of Words*, 201.

[29] "Historical Introduction," xviii.

[30] Ibid.

[31] Ibid., xx.

[32] "The 'N.E.D.'" *Nation* 124 (15 June 1927): 660.

[33] "Our Dictionary," *Times Literary Supplement* no. 1368 (19 April 1928): 277.

[34] "The Greatest of Dictionaries," *Saturday Review* 4 (21 April 1928): 487.

[35] Ernest Weekley, "The Oxford Dictionary," *Quarterly Review* 250 (April 1928): 242.

[36] Floyd Knight, "The Greatest of Dictionaries," *Bookman* 67 (April 1928): 141.

[37] W.A. Cragie, "New Dictionary Schemes Presented to the Philological Society, 4th April, 1919," *Transactions of the Philological Society,* (1925–30): 6–13.

[38] Joan Holland, Drafting Editor, *Dictionary of Old English,* letter to the author, 24 October 1990.

[39] "Directions to Readers for the Dictionary," reprinted in Murray, *Caught in the Web of Words,* 348.

[40] James A.H. Murray, "Thirteenth Address of the President of the Philological Society," 516.

[41] Jürgen Schäfer, *Documentation in the O.E.D.: Shakespeare and Nashe as Test Cases,* (Oxford: Clarendon Press, 1980), 3.

[42] Marghanita Laski, "Reading for OED," *Times Literary Supplement* no. 3437 (11 January 1968): 38.

[43] W.A. Craigie, "The Making of a Dictionary," *Saturday Review of Literature* 4 (21 April 1928): 792.

[44] James A.H. Murray, "Thirteenth Address of the President of the Philological Society," 516. Italics in original.

[45] "Preface to the Supplement," in James A.H. Murray, Henry Bradley, W.A. Craigie, and C.T. Onions, eds., *A New English Dictionary on Historical Principles, Founded Mainly on the Materials Collected by the Philological Society,* W.A. Criagie and C.T. Onions., eds., *Introduction, Supplement, and Bibliography* (Oxford: Clarendon Press, 1933), [v].

[46] Ibid.

[47] Alan Brien, "Down with All Bowdlers!" *New Statesman,* 72 (5 August 1966): 199.

[48] R. W. Burchfield, "Four-letter Words and the OED," *Times Literary Supplement* no. 3684 (13 October 1972): 1233.

[49] "Our Dictionary," 278.

[50] Ibid.

[51] Rosemary Herbert, "The Building of a Dictionary," 232 *Publishers Weekly* (2 October 1987): 38.

[52] Robert W. Burchfield, "The *Oxford English Dictionary* and the State of the Language," in *The Oxford English Dictionary and the State of the Language,* Robert W. Burchfield and Hans Aarsleff (Washington: Library of Congress, 1988), 20.

[53] *Proposal for the Publication of A New English Dictionary by the Philological Society* (London: Trübner, 1859), 2–3. Italics in original.

[54] "'All other dictionaries are temporary works,'" *U.S. News and World Reports* 101 (11 August 1986): 59.

[55] Roy Harris, "The History Men," *Times Literary Supplement* no. 4144 (3 September 1982): 935.

[56] Laski, "Reading for OED," 38.

[57] Marghanita Laski, "Revising OED," *Times Literary Supplement* no. 3684 (13 October 1972): 1226.

[58] J.C. Gray, "Creating the Electronic New Oxford English Dictionary," *Computers and the Humanities* 20 (January/March 1986): 45.

[59] "Introduction," in J. A. Simpson and E.S.C. Weiner, *The Oxford English Dictionary,* 2nd ed. (Oxford: Clarendon Press, 1989), [xi].

[60] Ibid.

[61] Laski, "Revising OED," 1226.

[62] Ibid.

[63] Y.L. Warburton, *OED* Editorial Co-ordinator, letter to the author, 27 July 1989.

[64] Ibid.

[65] Ibid.

[66] Ibid.

[67] Marjorie Keyishian, "Oxford English Dictionary Sets Up Shop in Morristown," *New York Times,* 11 February 1990, New Jersey ed., sec. 12, p. 1, 4–5.

[68] Y.L. Warburton, letter to the author, 27 July 1989.

[69] "The New Oxford English Dictionary Project," in *The Oxford English Dictionary,* 2nd ed., lv–lvi.

[70] Y.L. Warburton, letter to the author, 27 July 1989.

[71] Edmund Weiner, "New Uses for the New OED," *Bookseller* (25 January 1986): 332–36.

"Mom in the Library": The *Readers' Guide to Periodical Literature*

Mary Biggs

DEVELOPMENT AND HISTORY

In 1967, reference expert Bill Katz declared:

> Turning to the *Readers' Guide to Periodical Literature* is like nuzzling in the massive monobosom of American motherhood. Somehow, it is the closest thing to mom in the library—soft, all embracing, ready to educate us for anything. . . . Like pumpkin pie, LSD, and television, the index is merely an amorphous collection of American mores and attitudes. It can be analyzed, pummeled, or praised. No matter how approached, it finally adds up to mother draped in the red, white, and blue, a full shopping bag dangling from her arm, wire curlers adorning her head.[1]

Katz went on to criticize some of "mom's" policies, darkly detecting her "cool, calculated hand" in the index. He over-extended his metaphor, but his essential point was well taken: the *Readers' Guide* had long before become a familiar, dependable, reassuring fixture in libraries of all types and sizes. Not surprisingly, academic librarians complain of the difficulty of "weaning" students from "the green books" (as *Readers' Guide* is often called) and onto the subject-specialized indexes more suitable for most college research. Even when mom can no longer solve all problems, she remains comforting—a beacon to the insecure. And so with the *Readers' Guide*.

Indeed, if the H.W. Wilson Company did not also issue a wide range of indexes to scholarly and professional literature, many students might resist even more strenuously.

That it does, that the old friendly format can be found behind covers of other colors, bearing other names, is an invaluable aid to librarians' instruction efforts, enabling them to counsel the timid that "If you can use the *Readers' Guide*, you can use this. The only difference is that it will lead you to the authoritative articles your professor wants you to use." The air vibrates with relief.

How did the index achieve maternal status? First, of course, it meets an important information need and until recently had no real competition. Second, it is reasonably easy to use and its format has remained the same over its 90-year lifetime. And third, it is extraordinarily good at what it does.

Halsey William Wilson

To appreciate the remarkable accomplishment of *Readers' Guide* requires some knowledge of the publisher that initiated and still produces it: the H.W. Wilson Company. The story has many times been told of Halsey William Wilson and the unique business that he founded and nursed patiently to success against great odds.[2]

Born on May 12, 1868, in Wilmington, Vermont, Wilson was orphaned when still a toddler and spent his childhood in Massachusetts with his grandparents, his adolescence with an aunt and uncle in Iowa and Minnesota. While working his way through the University of Minnesota, he joined with his roommate to establish what became essentially the university bookstore. Wilson acquired his half of the $400 start-up capital by taking loans from other students. They flourished, of course, as the American Dream requires, and Wilson eventually bought out his partner and gained the means to marry a coed with whom he thereafter lived for 59 years, until his death in 1954. Work overtook studies and Wilson never received his baccalaureate, but didn't suffer for lack of it.[3]

Beginnings of Wilson's Publishing Career

His first publishing venture—the *Cumulative Book Index* (*CBI*), which has been continuously published ever since—grew out of his need as a bookseller for a cumulative new-book catalog. *Publishers' Weekly*, the industry's trade journal, had provided semi-annual cumulations, but stopped in 1895, giving Wilson an idea and practical impetus. Three years later, he began issuing *CBI* from his apartment with a staff consisting of himself as production and business manager and his wife as editor.[4] Its first issue consisted of a 16–page pamphlet.[5] *CBI* is important here because it was Wilson's first title and set the pattern for his second, the *Readers' Guide to Periodical Literature* (*RG*).

The presence of "cumulative" in *CBI*'s title suggests that this was a noteworthy feature for the time, and indeed Wilson is sometimes credited incorrectly with having invented the practice of cumulation.[6] In fact, others had gone before him, including Frederick Leypoldt of *Publishers' Weekly* and, more notably, William Howard Brett of the Cleveland Public Library, whose *Cumulative Index to Periodicals* (Cleveland: Cleveland Public Library, 1869–1897; Cleveland: Helman-Taylor Co., 1898–1903) was an important precursor of *Readers' Guide*.[7] But earlier attempts had soon foundered on economic problems. In those pre-computer days, cumulation seemed to demand a complete resetting of type, an

effort much too expensive to be recouped through the prices that could successfully be charged. Drawing on printing experience he had gained while self-financing his education, Wilson decided that the lines of type could be retained after their first use and speedily interfiled with other lines to produce cumulations. This entailed difficulties but proved feasible; a practiced Wilson "combiner" could merge up to 100 galleys of type, or about 6,000 index entries, in an eight-hour shift.[8]

Through his work with *CBI*, Wilson also discovered the optimal index arrangement. The first five issues were divided into two parts: an author-title index followed by a classified index. It was soon clear that subscribers were confused, and the combined author-title-subject "dictionary" format, which would be applied to subsequent Wilson indexes as well, was adopted.[9]

Finally, the development of *CBI* set enduring financial and editorial precedents. By the time she finished assembling its second number, Justina Wilson had decided that full-time housekeeping combined with full-time editing added up to too much work. Marion E. Potter, a 29-year-old graduate student, became Wilson's first employee and stayed with him for 55 years, until her death one year before his.[10] Accounts of the company invariably highlight her contribution, and her long experience and legendary industriousness must, along with Wilson's own direct daily involvement, have formed a backbone that supported the enterprise through its years of development.

Strong supports were needed, for nothing came easy. Bibliographic publishing was and long remained time-consuming, unglamorous, and commercially unpromising. Forty years after the company's founding, Creighton Peet observed in a *New Yorker* "profile:" "[Wilson] has had his field pretty much to himself, and been more or less welcome to it."[11] By that time, of course, the H.W. Wilson Company's profitability was well-established though modest. But each index, beginning with *CBI*, lost money for awhile. In 1898, figuring that this first endeavor would cost him $500 for typesetting and printing, he had set his annual subscription fee at $1 and set out optimistically to enlist a minimum 500 subscribers. But, in a pattern that would repeat, that first year yielded only 300 subscribers and Wilson, undeterred, made up the difference from his bookselling proceeds.[12] He would continue to do this as each new reference serial sought its audience, subsidizing them first through his store and later, after he had given up retail sales and moved to New York, through the profits from more lucrative publications. This practice has continued down to the present in the H.W. Wilson Company, which, 37 years after the founder's death, still functions according to his principles. In 1990, *Readers' Guide Abstracts* on microfiche was six years old, its paper edition two years old, and it was still regarded as an expensive undertaking though it had recovered its costs through sale as a computerized database. George Lewicky, who at the time had headed Wilson's index division for 25 years, explained philosophically that building a sufficient subscriber list would take time, as it had for other indexes, and the company, confident of its product's value, could wait.[13]

It was, then, on this base of knowledge and practice that the three-year-old business built the index that would become its most famous.

Existing Periodical Indexes

Although Wilson did not establish *CBI* with libraries' needs in mind, he soon acquired librarians as subscribers and began attending to their concerns. At meetings, he heard them say that identifying useful periodical articles was so difficult that keeping back runs sometimes seemed pointless. Though indexes existed, they were sadly inadequate. The first to be created had been the famous *Poole's Index to Periodical Literature*, which is still used today. First issued in 1848 as *An Alphabetical*

Index to Subjects Treated in the Reviews and Other Periodicals to Which No Indexes Have Been Published (New York: George P. Putnam), it was revised by its author, William Frederick Poole, in 1853 and then lay dormant, becoming increasingly out of date, until the first meeting of the American Library Association (ALA) in 1876. There Poole proposed, and the Association endorsed, a cooperative project, with indexing to be performed by librarian-volunteers around the country and submitted to Poole as editor-in-chief. The result appeared in 1882, with quinquennial updates through 1907 (Boston: Houghton, 1882–1908).[14] Ambitious, progressive, and important as it undoubtedly was, *Poole's* nonetheless suffered from poor subject indexing; no author indexing; omission of periodical dates; inclusion of some less-useful, and exclusion of some more-useful, periodicals; and, of course, infrequency. Two other efforts— Brett's aforementioned *Cumulative Index to Periodicals* and W.I. Fletcher's *Cooperative Index to Periodicals*, offered as a *Library Journal* supplement from 1883 to 1892— began as monthlies but soon slid back to quarterly, then annual, schedules.[15] An opportunity, and dangers, were apparent to Wilson.

First Issue of Readers' Guide

The February 1901 *CBI* carried, for the first time, a supplement curiously entitled "A Monthly Cumulative Index to Ten Important Periodicals"—curious because it actually indexed only seven: *Atlantic Monthly, Harper's Monthly, North American Review, Century, Forum, Review of Reviews*, and *Scribner's*.[16] Of these, only the first three survive, and only the first two are still indexed by *Readers' Guide*.

Three months later, *CBI* printed the first advertisement for a separately published monthly Wilson periodical index, now named the *Readers' Guide to Periodical Literature* and including, in addition to the seven magazines listed above: *Bookman, Cosmopolitan,*

Critic, International Monthly, McClure's Magazine, Outlook, Popular Science Monthly, and *World's Work*.[17] (Again, the company's math seemed defective, as the ad promised indexing for "fourteen leading periodicals," but clearly listed 15.) Then as now an author-subject index, *RG* was said to be "useful in the library, in the club and in the home." It could be had for $1 per year, or, "for a limited time," free with a subscription to any of the indexed magazines save *Cosmopolitan* and *McClure's*. A sample copy would be sent for the price of a two-cent stamp.

At the end of 1901, a paper-covered volume was published that cumulated the entries in the *CBI* supplement with those from the new *Readers' Guide*. Each subsequent year saw similar cumulations. When the second was issued, in December 1902, the list of indexed periodicals had lengthened to 21.[18] In 1903, *Readers' Guide* absorbed Brett's tottering index, and the first quinquennial cumulation was subtitled: "A Consolidation of the *Cumulative Index to a Selected List of Periodicals* and the *Readers' Guide to Periodical Literature*."[19]

The early multi-year cumulations are notable for sudden steep increases in the number of periodicals indexed, followed by a general leveling off at just over 100 titles. The number would rise slowly after that, reflecting the increase in popular magazines. Those early issues were also unusual—given the index's name and what we have come to expect from it—in handling some books and report literature as well as periodicals. For the first 23 years of *RG*'s existence, it provided statistics in its subtitles. Thus the 1905–9 cumulation proclaimed itself "An Index to Ninety-Nine Periodicals, and Also in the Same Alphabet an Index to 430 Books, Reports, etc., Constituting a Supplement to the Second Edition of the *A. L. A. Index to General Literature*."[20] The 1910–14 edition provided "An Author and Subject Index to 111 Periodicals and Reports and 167 Composite Books," but also explained that because the forthcoming *Standard Catalog* would include analytics for books, they would no longer be indexed in *Readers' Guide*, excepting "government and association reports" (e.g., conference proceedings).[21] Twenty years later, book indexing was enhanced by the new *Essay and General Literature Index*, which thoroughly analyzed collections of essays in book format. In 1915–18, *RG* users were told to expect an "Author and Subject Index to 104 Periodicals and Reports"; in 1919–21 and in 1922–24, "An Author and Subject Index to 108 Periodicals and Reports"; and finally, in 1925–28, the more noncommittal subtitle of "An Author and Subject Index" was adopted.[22]

Change and Continuity

Today, the scope of *Readers' Guide* remains determinedly unchanged. It is, as it was in 1901, "an author subject index to selected general interest periodicals of reference value in libraries."[23] The number of publications indexed has grown to 188. As has ever been true, they are all English-language, almost all published in the United States, and cover all subjects of any conceivable popular interest.

One of the few changes in *Readers' Guide* over the years has been frequency of cumulation. The question of the optimal schedule appears to have perplexed the company. Although annual cumulations were always compiled, the span of final cumulations varied. As indicated in the publication history below, three five-year cumulations covering 1900–14 were followed by one four-year (1915–1918). Then, in her preface to the fifth multi-year cumulation, which included only 1919–21, editor Elizabeth J. Sherwood announced that "the three-year cumulative plan [is] now permanently adopted."[24] She could not have anticipated the coming proliferation of magazines or the resistance librarians would eventually develop to the cost of replacing cumulations with broader cumulations. The "permanent" decision held only through the next cumulation (1922–24). Following that were three more four-year volumes and then, beginning in July 1935, 30 years of biennial compilations. For March 1965–February 1966, only a hardbound annual cumulation was offered, a practice persisting down to the present. It necessitates more laborious searching by the user interested in several years' worth of information (a problem circumvented by the newer online and CD-ROM versions of the index), but has resulted in volumes much more manageable physically.

Small changes notwithstanding, what is perhaps most remarkable about the source is the durability of its original design. Despite its status as very nearly a pioneering effort; despite the great changes that have occurred in the publishing industry, education, and American demographics; and despite the recent emergence of several competitors, *Readers' Guide* has never significantly changed its look, its arrangement, or its purpose. A 1905 library user would be entirely comfortable with a 1990 issue, though subject headings and article titles would be startling. And here, for publisher, user, and, by the way, intellectual historian, is the most challenging and interesting aspect of indexing: selecting and systematizing subject headings.

Indexing Practices

Poole had created what was essentially a keyword subject index, using authors' title terms as descriptors rather than developing a controlled subject-indexing vocabulary. Ironically, the ease of keyword indexing automatically by computer has revived the popularity of this method, but its deficiencies are serious, and Wilson recognized them. His astuteness and that of his early editors is easy to overlook in a period that bristles with indexes of all types, with well developed subject heading lists for all topics, that has seen many analyses of their relative strengths and has at its command a vast array of high technology to facilitate all indexing and printing tasks. But that Wilson, with almost no useful precedents to

learn from and every reason to minimize costs and labor, still recognized the great advantages of controlled-vocabulary indexing and pursued them, seems positively prescient.

The principal advantage, of course, is that all citations to articles on a given subject are brought together under a uniform descriptor, regardless of the terminology selected by the articles' authors. Furthermore, when a title offers few or no clues to content, as is often the case in all periodicals and especially in popular magazines, the indexer's exercise of judgment assures that it will nonetheless be placed under the appropriate heading(s). But all of this requires the strenuous, enormously time-consuming intellectual labor of carefully reading every article to be indexed; deciding upon the most appropriate terms to represent thousands of concepts and the cross-references needed to guide the user to them; and continually scrutinizing and revising headings and, of course, their associated cross-references, to reflect changes in usage.

Following the practice of *CBI* and borrowing its headings when suitable, *Readers' Guide* commenced with the system of subject indexing and elaborate cross-referencing that continues to distinguish all Wilson indexes. In 1990, George Lewicky isolated *RG*'s cross-reference structure, along with the accuracy and currency of its subject headings, as the characteristic that set it apart from and raised it above all competing guides to general-interest magazines.[25]

The *Library of Congress Subject Headings* (*LCSH*) derived in 1898 were used when possible, though being designed for books, *LCSH* terminology often lacked the specificity needed to describe narrowly focused magazine articles. Encyclopedias were also consulted, as were any other indexes the editor could find.[26] Indexing is never straightforward, however, and different editors embraced different ideal theories of subject delineation, which led to some conflict. Years later, Marion Potter, the first *RG* editor, would remember her successor, Anna Lorraine Guthrie, demanding: "Use the encyclopedia subject headings. Every reader can find things in an encyclopedia and does not need to have the proper page pointed out to him."[27] This is debatable, but does agree with the preference implied by Guthrie herself in her preface to the 1905–09 volume.[28]

According to John Lawler, the two women argued at length about headings, with Guthrie initially favoring the simply-formatted headings of the Peabody catalog (e.g., "Child labor"), Potter preferring the Athenaeum catalog's system of subdivision ("Children-Employment"): "The discussion continued until in time the two editors had converted each other. Then it was resumed with Miss Guthrie defending Miss Potter's former position and Miss Potter advocating Miss Guthrie's discarded theories." Potter also sought advice from the University of Minnesota faculty. "What about 'contagious diseases'?" Lawler has her asking the "startled head of the medical school" . . . "should it be 'infectious diseases,' or perhaps 'communicable diseases'?"[29] Experience helped, but the task never became easy. Potter recalled hearing Alice Dougan, who served longer than anyone else as *RG*'s editor, declare after many years: "Subject heading work is a hard job."[30]

In 1954, *RG* editor Sarita Robinson explained the index's current policy on subject heading "selection and use." It had not changed much, with other Wilson indexes and *LCSH* still the main guides. She pointed out, however, that because it dealt with more timely literature, *RG* often had to treat an idea before *LCSH* did, resulting, eventually, in differences between them. Other problems included the difficulty of determining how narrow the indexing should be, how many cross-references were really needed, and which ideas or events were of purely ephemeral interest, which of sufficiently enduring importance to merit their own subject headings.[31]

Tracing the evolution of new terms down through the years of the index is fascinating in itself and illuminates some of Robinson's

points, not to mention Dougan's frustration. For example, the 1900–04 index offered only two subject sections dealing with aviation: "Aerial navigation" and "Air-ships." By 1905–09, there were many relevant headings and many dozens of entries. What would come to be "Pilots" were "Aeronauts," and cross-referencing for the still used "Aerial navigation" instructed the user to "see also": "Aeronautics," "Aeroplanes," "Balloons and Air-ships," and "Flying machines." Throughout subsequent volumes, the numbers of entries continued to multiply, and in 1915–18, the primary terms at last became "Aeronautics" (with a reference from "Aerial navigation") and "Airplanes."

Similarly, one can imagine Wilson indexers scrambling to keep up with automotive developments. In 1900-04, the form of fuel that would emerge as standard was not yet certain; although "Automobiles, Gasoline" took the largest share of citations, with 29; "Automobiles, Electric" had only one less; "Automobiles, Steam" had 10; and "Automobiles, Alcohol" had 5. In 1905–09, there were suddenly dozens of headings relating to automobiles. By 1915–18, "Automobiles" were apparently assumed to be gasoline-fed vehicles, for no qualifier was deemed necessary. Two new headings, however, turned out to reflect only a short-lived fantasy and immediately fell into disuse: "Autoplanes," with a citation to *Scientific American*'s article on "A Limousine for Land and Air Travel," and "Automobiles, Aerial," leading the user to a single article entitled "Aero-Auto-Craft—The Car of the Future."

"Wireless telegraphy" was used through 1919–21, though there was by then some confusion about it, and "Radio" also appeared, with one citation. In 1922–24, the latter heading subsumed the former. "Atomic power" appeared for the first time in 1939–41, with entries for 18 articles, all of them speculative. Headings and citations proliferated after that, but with a dramatic leap in number, and the first use of "Atomic bomb," in the 1943–45 cumulation. "Calculating machines" did not give way to "Computers" until 1965–66, though long before that, many cross-references had to be provided. (Before 1932, "Calculators" were "Mathematical prodigies"!)

Recent economic and political events also raise questions for the indexer, who cannot know at the time they are first reported how future users will search for them. Thus the stock market's "Black Friday" lies buried under "Stock exchange," subheading "Crisis, October, 1929," in the 1929–32 cumulation, confounding some current users seeking contemporary accounts of that day. And "World War I" remained "European War, 1914–1918" until 1977–78. In 1951–53, a cross-reference was provided from "World War, 1914–1918," but several subsequent cumulations omitted it, presumably by accident. When asked how she decided when to revise outdated headings, Marion Potter is said to have replied: "When I shudder at them and can't stand them any longer, I finally change them."[32]

Computerization facilitates subject work, but it remains *RG*'s most problematic task. The company has long been criticized for not following the lead of other services (e.g., *Psychological Abstracts* and ERIC) by publishing its indexes' subject heading lists. Today, online subject files for each index are available to both the Wilson staff and the public—though paper lists continue to be requested. On average, three headings per article are assigned. When asked in 1990 about changes occurring at *RG*, its editor, Jean Marra, mentioned only two: an attempt to establish more uniformity of headings among the various indexes, and increasing care to avoid terminology with a potential to offend certain groups. As an example, she cited "sexist headings." But she added, with typical Wilson caution, "We reflect the literature. We don't feel we're out to change the world." Still, said Marra, "We're trying to become more sensitive."[33]

Establishing the most authentic form of a name is perhaps easier than setting subject headings, but still a challenge. The Wilson Company has always been notable for its carefully developed and maintained personal and corporate names files.[34] Once created separately for each index, these have been collapsed into a single online name authority control file which governs the entire company, guaranteeing consistency among indexes.[35]

Selecting the Sources Indexed

But regardless of its indexing and production quality, a periodical guide is only as useful as its sources are well selected. *Readers' Guide* has been attacked on this score by both interested and disinterested parties, which is perhaps unavoidable for an index that is ubiquitous yet necessarily limited in number of magazines treated.[36] Its defense has always been its unusually responsive means of selection. Early in the history of *Readers' Guide*, all subscribers were polled periodically to determine which titles should be added. As the subscriber list grew unmanageably long, only a representative sample was questioned. In 1951, through a *Wilson Library Bulletin* article, editor Sarita Robinson took her concerns about *RG* coverage directly to librarians. "Are we indexing the right magazines?" she asked, and went on to note irregularities in topical coverage (e.g., no gardening magazine, but nine on education); overlap with the company's subject-specialized indexes; and possible changes in magazine quality over a long run. She concluded by suggesting that a broad-based survey be carried out by ALA as "unbiased and qualified representatives of the profession."[37] One year later, the Committee on Wilson Indexes was established under the auspices of the American Library Association.[38]

In 1984, former member Charles R. Andrews described the committee's functioning in detail.[39] Composed of librarians primarily from the eastern seaboard, to assure their attendance at Bronx meetings (though this is changing and today some come from as far away as California[40]), the committee evaluates Wilson indexes, surveys subscribers, reviews suggestions for change, and communicates its final decisions to the company, which, within its staff and financial limits, complies. In one celebrated instance, Wilson was even persuaded to restore nine previously deleted titles that librarians thought important to library users, though their reference value was questioned by the Wilson Company.[41] Whereas committee members once read all letters and requests from the public, since the 1970s these have poured in so copiously that George Lewicky and Jean Marra screen them and present recommendations for the committee's consideration.[42] Thus the link between the committee and the library profession has become less direct, mediated by the company itself. Though there have been no significant published criticisms of this change, it has the potential to undermine objectivity of assessment. Nonetheless, all letters are available to any committee members who wish to read them, and the company's relationship with its customers remains close and personal, perhaps uniquely so.

In the 90 years since *Readers' Guide* was founded, it has spun off important auxiliary projects. The first was the Periodicals Clearing House, established in 1910 because old articles, whose existence was now signaled by indexing, often could not be found. At its most expansive, the Clearing House had for sale approximately three million single issues, 100,000 bound volumes, and 1,000 complete runs, and searches for still other numbers could be commissioned. Kraus Periodicals purchased the Clearing House in 1955.[43]

Related Wilson Indexes

A more enduring development began unpretentiously as the *Readers' Guide Supplement*—much as *RG* itself had started life as an appendage to *Cumulative Book Index*. Indexing periodicals that were too specialized and academic to be needed by public libraries, the *Supplement* appeared five times each year, then cumulated in a bound volume. The first multi-year cumulation covered 1907–15, the second 1916–19.[44] The third (1920–23) at last gave it an independent identity and announced its new name: *International Index to Periodicals*, with the rather broad explanatory subtitle, "Devoted Chiefly to the Humanities and Science."[45] In 1965, it was re-titled *Social Sciences and Humanities Index* and in 1974 split into two separate indexes.

By this time, the company had long since left Minneapolis, its first home (and "birthplace" of *Readers' Guide*). By the early teens, Wilson had felt the need for proximity to the center of American publishing. He moved the company first to White Plains, New York, in 1913, and four years later to more adequate and convenient quarters in the Bronx, where it still resides. Located just to the east of the bustling Major Deegan Expressway, it is easily identified by the famous sculpture of a huge lighthouse atop an open book that soars upward from its rooftop—which refers, of course, to the famous Wilson lighthouse logo that is imprinted upon each publication.

Other Readers' Guide Products

In 1935, *Abridged Readers' Guide* was started for smaller institutions. Identical in format to its unabridged namesake, it included the indexing for only about one-quarter of the periodicals. It continues to this day, fulfilling the needs of small public and school libraries.

As the years wore on, researchers had felt the lack of Wilson-quality periodical indexing for the nineteenth century. The company resolved, therefore, to create such an index retrospectively, covering 1890–99. When the project was first announced, 20 periodicals were to be included, but by the time it was published in 1944, the number had increased to 51, and *The Nineteenth Century Readers' Guide* spanned two thick volumes.[46]

That no additional *RG* product or format was offered until almost 40 years later is, from one perspective, a testament to the company's caution and stability, and from another, its reluctance to change with the times. Well after other reference works had gone online, Wilson's publications remained stubbornly paper-bound. Finally, in 1983, *Readers' Guide* and several other indexes were computerized and marketed by Wilson acting as its own vendor under the name *Wilsonline*. In 1987, the same indexing span was published on CD-ROM as *Wilsondisc*—with, of course, continuing updates. In both formats, *RG* was well-received by reviewers and users.

But the company's first foray in decades into an indexing format essentially outside its experience came with the introduction of *Readers' Guide Abstracts*—initially on microfiche in 1984, and four years later in a paper version designed primarily for public and school libraries, incorporating only 40 percent of the abstracts available in the microfiche product. In the same year, *Popular Magazine Review* (Topsfield, MA: Data Base Communications Corp., 1984–87) began. It was eventually acquired by Ebsco and underwent a title change to *Magazine Article Summaries* (Palo Alto, CA, 1987–). Offering indexing and comparatively short abstracts for popular magazine articles in both paper and CD-ROM, *Magazine Article Summaries* has perhaps been *Readers' Guide Abstracts'* most comparable competitor, though it has won much less attention and acceptance.

Readers' Guide Abstracts represented an extremely bold step—intellectually, because popular magazine articles had never seemed as suited to abstracting as scholarly papers, and practically, because it was uncommonly labor-intensive. Located in Cambridge, Massachusetts, to take advantage of that area's deep pool of well educated workers, the *Abstracts* in 1990 employed 32 full-time professional abstracters, most of them English or journalism majors hoping to launch writing careers. Explaining why the *Abstracts* were undertaken, Lewicky noted an accelerating trend throughout the information industry toward database enhancements, "value-added" features.[47]

At the age of 90, with 26,119 mail subscriptions to its unabridged paper version and 21,590 to the abridged,[48] the *Readers' Guide to Periodical Literature* is comfortably indispensable, "the closest thing to mom in the library." The index, and more impressively the entire company that produces it, stands as a striking example of success in bibliographic publishing. What, then, were the elements of this success?

The Reasons for RG's Success

Posing the same question in her 1951 article, "Whodunit?," Marion E. Potter settled on a single answer: H.W. Wilson himself.[49] And she was probably correct. The most durable building block of his success was the importance and uniqueness of his products—most notably *CBI* and *Readers' Guide*, which together served as foundation and pilot project for what was to come. But he was not the first to recognize the need, nor were his indexes truly pioneering. He was, however, the first to succeed and endure as an index publisher, and he set high standards of quality that even today *Readers' Guide*'s major competitor, *Magazine Index* (Menlo Park, CA: Information Access Corp, 1977–), does not seem to aspire to and certainly has not reached.[50] Added to this are several impressively far-sighted, hardheaded, business decisions.

First, and least often commented upon, was his willingness to hire women. At a time when they had few opportunities in the private sector, Wilson welcomed them and often placed them in key positions, thus availing himself of the best talents of a largely underrated or ignored, but educated and willing, prospective labor force.

Second, he asserted the futility of competition in costly publishing projects with limited markets, and, equally important, won the agreement of the competitor in question. In 1911, Wilson and R.R. Bowker, producer of *Publishers' Weekly*, agreed to divide up the bibliographic universe. As a result, Bowker would terminate his new monthly periodical index and the cumulated book lists which had begun reappearing in *Publishers' Weekly*, while Wilson would turn over to Bowker some directories and a digest of library literature that he had been publishing.[51] However one may feel about voluntary restraints on competition, the deal apparently benefitted both companies financially.

Third, Wilson knew and stayed close to his customers, a tradition continued by his company after his death. Even before the ALA Committee on Wilson Indexes was formed, he consulted librarians regularly, attended their meetings, and seriously considered their written suggestions. He never grew away from his users, never lost sight of their needs, and so he understood what they would purchase. Coupled with this was his willingness to take losses on new products that held his confidence, allowing them ample time to build adequate subscriber lists. That he already owned and maintained a profitable second business during his early years as publisher helped immeasurably.

Fourth was his development of cumulations, which had been considered economically infeasible.

Fifth, and most famous, was his initiation of "service basis" pricing, an imaginative concept that overcame the other greatest financial obstacle to unsubsidized index publishing. An intellectually demanding and labor-intensive task, index creation is very expensive, yet the potential market is comparatively small and consists mostly of libraries in the not-for-profit sector. Especially in the early days of *Readers' Guide*, neither high-volume sales at low prices nor modest sales at high prices could be counted upon to cover costs, let alone generate a profit. Wilson hit upon the novel idea of pricing the index as a *service* rather than a *product*. He first experimented with and rejected the possibility of issuing indexing on cards, with libraries buying those that covered

the periodicals they owned. Reasoning that even if the entire index were received, libraries would find primarily useful only those parts pertinent to their holdings, he then decided to charge differentially, based on the number of titles owned by the subscribing library. In effect, the smallest libraries with the fewest resources were charged least and the largest libraries were charged most, even though they all received the same product. Service basis pricing withstood indignant challenges from large libraries which, regardless of their indignation, found *Readers' Guide* essential and bought it. Over time, the unorthodox pricing method became accepted and was applied to new Wilson indexes as they developed. It is still used for the specialized sources, though by 1961, the audience for both *Readers' Guide* and *Abridged Readers' Guide* had grown so large that flat pricing became possible.[52] Today, they cost every subscriber $150 and $75 per year, respectively.

So, through its founder's persistence, self-confidence, imagination, good judgment, and conservative financial expectations, the H.W. Wilson Company prospered, and its flagship index became as familiar and indispensable as mom. What *Readers' Guide* has meant to generations of researchers is possible to appreciate only if one can imagine being without it and without all of the indexes whose ways it paved. Obviously, it provides access to mountains of information that would otherwise remain virtually inaccessible. But, beyond this, it must have encouraged the founding of periodicals, serious writing for periodicals, library subscriptions to periodicals, and organized collecting of their entire runs by libraries. Taken for granted like any mom, *Readers' Guide* is rarely appreciated as an instigator of revolution in information access and periodical and reference publishing. It differed from most revolutions in that it exceeded its own early expectations, its effects were overwhelmingly positive, and they endured.

PUBLICATION HISTORY

"A Monthly Cumulative Index to Ten Important Periodicals." Supplement to *Cumulative Book Index*, 1901. Minneapolis: H.W. Wilson Co.

Readers' Guide to Periodical Literature. 1901– . Publisher: H.W. Wilson Co. Place of Publication: Minneapolis, 1901–1913; White Plains, N.Y., 1913–17; Bronx, NY, 1917– Current frequency: Semi-monthly, March, April, September, October, December; Monthly, January, February, May through August, November. Quarterly cumulative issues; annual cumulative bound volumes. Cumulations: 1900–1904; 1905–1909; 1910–1914; 1915–1918; 1919–1921; 1922–1924; 1925–1928; 1929–June 1932; July 1932–June 1935; July 1935–June 1937; July 1937– June 1939; July 1939–June 1941; July 1941–June 1943; July 1943–April 1945; May 1945–April 1947; May 1947–April 1949; May 1949–March 1951; April 1951–March 1953; April 1953–February 1955; March 1955–February 1957; March 1957–February 1959; March 1959–February 1961; March 1961–February 1963; March 1963–February 1965; annual thereafter. Editors: Marion E. Potter, 1901–1902; Anna Lorraine Guthrie, 1903–1914; Marion A. Knight, 1914–1918; Elizabeth J. Sherwood, 1918–1924; Alice M. Dougan, 1924–1945; Sarita M. Robinson, 1945–1963; Zada Limerick, 1963–1979; Jean M. Marra, 1979– .

Abridged Readers' Guide. 1935– Bronx, NY: H.W. Wilson Co. Frequency: Nine per year. Cumulations: Three per year and annual.

Nineteenth Century Readers' Guide 1890–1899, edited by Helen Grant Cushing. Bronx, NY: H.W. Wilson Co, 1944.

Readers' Guide to Periodical Literature on Wilsonline. Online: January 1983– .

Readers' Guide to Periodical Literature on Wilsondisc. CD-ROM: January 1983– .

Readers' Guide Abstracts. Microfiche: 1984– .

Readers' Guide Abstracts, Print Edition. Hard copy: September 1988– . Frequency: Ten per year. Cumulations: Semi-annual.

BIBLIOGRAPHY

The most useful source of information on the development of *Readers' Guide to Periodical Literature,* is *RG* itself, especially the editors' prefaces published in early cumulations and several articles published by long-ago Wilson employees, most in the journal now entitled *Wilson Library Bulletin.* Among these articles are those by Beatrice B. Rakestraw, Sarita Robinson, and Marion E. Potter. Two other sources are also crucial: John Lawler's company history and Arthur Plotnik's encyclopedia article. The latter discusses both Wilson the company and Wilson the man. Plotnik apparently had access to a company archive not available to this author. It is not clear that access to such an archive would be especially revealing since few critical decisions seem to have been made over the years; until recently, when electronic access was provided and *Readers' Guide Abstracts* was introduced, format, scope, and purpose had hardly changed since the index's earliest days.

Andrews, Charles R. "Cooperation at its Best: The Committee on Wilson Indexes at Work." *RQ* 24 (Winter, 1984): 155–61.

Cheney, Frances Neel. "Wilson Publications as Reference Tools." *Wilson Library Bulletin* 22 (June, 1948): 801–05.

Cushing, Helen Grant. "Preface." *Nineteenth Century Readers' Guide 1890–1899.* New York: H.W. Wilson Co., 1944.

Davis, Mary Ellen Kyger, and John F. Riddick, "Readers' Guide to Periodical Literature and Magazine Index: A Comparison." *Reference Services Review* 11 (Winter, 1983): 43–50.

G[uthrie], A[nna] L[orraine]. "Preface." *Readers' Guide to Periodical Literature 1905–1909.* Minneapolis: H.W. Wilson Company, 1910.

"Halsey W. Wilson, Publisher, Dead" [obituary]. *New York Times* (March 2, 1954) p. 25.

Katz, Bill. "Magazines." *Library Journal* 93 (February 1, 1968): 527.

———. "Motherly Index." *Library Journal* 92 (February 1, 1967): 555.

Kesselman, Martin. "Online Update." *Wilson Library Bulletin* (December, 1983): 286–87.

Lawler, John. *The H.W. Wilson Company: Half a Century of Bibliographic Publishing.* Minneapolis: University of Minnesota Press, 1950.

"Nineteenth Century Readers' Guide." *Wilson Bulletin for Libraries* 13 (October, 1938): 143.

Pearson, Lois R. "In the News: Publisher Restores Nine Periodical Titles to Readers' Guide on RASD Committee's Advice." *American Libraries* 9 (February, 1978): 69.

Peet, Creighton. "Profiles: A Mousetrap in the Bronx." *New Yorker* 13 (October 29, 1938): 25–28.

Plotnik, Arthur. "H.W. Wilson." *Encyclopedia of Library and Information Science,* edited by Allen Kent, Harold Lancour, and Jay E. Daily. New York: Marcel Dekker, vol. 10, 1973, pp. 250–78.

Poland, Myra, Henry J. Carr, and O. R. Howard Thomson. "Report on Periodical Indexing." *Library Journal* 39 (December, 1914): 903–04.

Potter, Marion E. "Whodunit?" *Wilson Library Bulletin* 25 (April, 1951): 593–96, 605.

"Preface." *Readers' Guide to Periodical Literature 1900–1904.* Minneapolis: H.W. Wilson Co., 1905, pp. [vii]-ix.

Rakestraw, Beatrice B. "Making a Wilson Index." *Wilson Library Bulletin* 22 (June, 1948): 796–800.

"The Readers' Guide: 1901–1951: The First Fifty Years." *Wilson Library Bulletin* 25 (April, 1951): 591–92, 605.

Rettig, James. Review of *Readers' Guide Abstracts, Print Edition. Wilson Library Bulletin* 63 (January, 1989): 128.

Robinson, Sarita. "Are We Indexing the Right Magazines?" *Wilson Library Bulletin* 25 (April, 1951): 597–98.

———. Subject Headings: Their Selection and Use in 'Readers' Guide,'" *Special Libraries* 45 (May-June, 1954): 203–05.

S[herwood], E[lizabeth] J. "Preface." *Readers' Guide to Periodical Literature 1915–1918.* New York: H.W. Wilson Co., 1919.

Whiteley, Sandy, ed. "Reference Books Bulletin: Featured Reviews: Wilsondisc: Readers' Guide to Periodical Literature (CD-ROM)." *Booklist* 84 (December 1, 1987): 609–12.

Wilson, H.W. "Preface." *Readers' Guide to Periodical Literature 1910–1914.* White Plains, NY: H.W. Wilson Co., 1915.

Wilson, H[alsey] W[illiam]." *Current Biography* (1948): 679–82.

NOTES

[1] Bill Katz, "Motherly Index," *Library Journal,* 92 (1 February 1967): 555.

[2] John Lawler, *The H.W. Wilson Company: Half a Century of Bibliographic Publishing* (Minneapolis: University of Minnesota Press, 1950); Creighton Peet, "Profiles: A Mousetrap in the Bronx," *New Yorker* 13 (29 October 1938): 25–28; Arthur Plotnik, "H.W. Wilson," in *Encyclopedia of Library and Information Science,* vol. 10 (New York: Marcel Dekker, 1973), 250–78; "Wilson, H(alsey) W(illiam)," in *Current Biography* 1948 (Bronx, NY: H.W. Wilson Co., 1949), 679–82.

[3] Lawler, 9–19; "Halsey W. Wilson, Publisher, Dead," *New York Times* (2 March 1954), 25.

[4] Lawler, 25–28; "Wilson, H(alsey) W(illiam)," 680.

[5] The title page of the first *CBI,* dated February 1, 1898, is reproduced in Plotnik, 252.

[6] For example; Peet, 25.

[7] John Lawler, 25; "Preface," in *Readers' Guide to Periodical Literature 1900–1904* (Minneapolis: H.W. Wilson Co., 1905), [vii]; Carl Vitz, "Brett, William Howard," in *Encyclopedia of Library and Information Science,* vol. 3 (New York: Marcel Dekker, 1970), 264.

[8] Plotnik, 254; Beatrice B. Rakestraw, "Making a Wilson Index," *Wilson Library Bulletin,* 22 (June 1948): 796. Rakestraw's article includes a photograph of a combiner intent upon her rows of linotype slugs.

[9] Lawler, 26–27.

[10] Ibid., 28–29; Arthur Plotnik, 255.

[11] Peet, 25.

[12] John Lawler, 27–28, 31–32.

[13] George I. Lewicky, Vice-President and Director of Indexing Services, H.W. Wilson Co., interview with the author, 19 April 1990.

[14] Lawler, 37; Plotnik, 256.

[15] Lawler, 38; Plotnik, 256; "Preface," 1905, [vii].

[16] "The Readers' Guide: 1901–1951: The First Fifty Years," *Wilson Library Bulletin,* 25 (April 1951): 591.

[17] Ibid.

[18] Ibid.

[19] "Preface," 1905, [vii]; [Title page], *Readers' Guide to Periodical Literature 1900–1904* (Minneapolis: H.W. Wilson Company, 1905).

[20] [Title page], *Readers' Guide to Periodical Literature 1905–1909* (Minneapolis: H.W. Wilson Co., 1910).

[21] [Title page], *Readers' Guide to Periodical Literature 1910–1914* (Bronx, NY: H.W. Wilson Co., 1915); H.W. Wilson, "Preface," *Readers' Guide to Periodical Literature 1910–1914* (White Plains, NY: H.W. Wilson Company, 1915), [v].

[22] [Title page], *Readers' Guide to Periodical Literature 1914–1918* (Bronx, NY: H.W. Wilson Co., 1919); [Title page], *Readers' Guide to Periodical Literature 1919–1921* (Bronx, NY: H.W. Wilson Co., 1922); [Title page], *Readers' Guide to Periodical Literature 1922–1924* (Bronx, NY: H.W. Wilson Co., 1925); [Title page], *Readers' Guide to Periodical Literature 1925–1928* (Bronx, NY: H.W. Wilson Co., 1929).

[23] [Cover], *Readers' Guide to Periodical Literature,* 90 (10 March 1990).

[24] E[lizabeth] J. S[herwood], "Preface," *Readers' Guide to Periodical Literature 1915–1918* (Bronx, NY: H.W. Wilson Co., 1919): unpaged.

[25] Lewicky, interview with the author, 19 April 1990.
[26] A[nna] L[orraine] G[uthrie], "Preface," *Readers' Guide to Periodical Literature 1905–1909* (Minneapolis: H.W. Wilson Co., 1910): unpaged.
[27] Marion E. Potter, "Whodunit?," *Wilson Library Bulletin*, 25 (April 1951): 593.
[28] G[uthrie], "Preface," unpaged.
[29] Lawler, 101.
[30] Potter, 595–96.
[31] Sarita Robinson, "Subject Headings: Their Selection and Use in 'Readers' Guide,'" *Special Libraries*, 45 (May-June 1954): 203–05.
[32] Lawler, 106.
[33] Jean M. Marra, Editor, *Readers' Guide to Periodical Literature*, interview with the author, 19 April 1990.
[34] Lawler, 90–93; Rakestraw, 799–800; Mary Ellen Kyger Davis and John F. Riddick, "Readers' Guide to Periodical Literature and Magazine Index: A Comparison," *Reference Services Review*, 11 (Winter 1983): 45.
[35] Davis and Riddick, 46; Marra, interview with author, 19 April 1990.
[36] See, for example: Myra Poland, Henry J. Carr, and O. R. Howard Thomson, "Report on Periodical Indexing," *Library Journal*, 39 (December 1914): 903–04; Katz, "Motherly Index," 555; Lois R. Pearson, "In the News: Publisher Restores Nine Periodical Titles to *Readers' Guide* on RASD Committee's Advice," *American Libraries*, 9 (February 1978):
[37] Sarita Robinson, "Are We Indexing the Right Magazines?," *Wilson Library Bulletin*, 25 (April 1951): 597–98.
[38] Charles R. Andrews, "Cooperation at its Best: The Committee on Wilson Indexes at Work," *RQ*, 24 (Winter 1984): 155.
[39] Ibid., 155–61; Davis and Riddick, 44.
[40] Lewicky, interview with author, 19 April 1990.
[41] Pearson, 69.
[42] Lewicky and Marra, interviews with the author, 19 April 1990.
[43] Lawler, 79–79; Plotnik, 262.
[44] "Preface," in *International Index to Periodicals 1907–1915* (White Plains, NY: H.W. Wilson Co., 1916): unpaged (originally published under the title: *Readers' Guide to Periodical Literature Supplement*); E[lizabeth] J. S[herwood], "Preface," in *International Index to Periodicals 1916–1919* (Bronx, NY: H.W. Wilson Co., 1920): unpaged (originally published under the title: *Readers' Guide to Periodical Literature Supplement*).
[45] E[sther] A[nne] S[mith], "Preface," in *International Index to Periodicals 1920–1923* (Bronx, NY: H.W. Wilson Co., 1924): unpaged.
[46] "Nineteenth Century Readers' Guide," in *Wilson Bulletin for Librarians*, 13 (October 1938): 143; Helen Grant Cushing, "Preface," *Nineteenth Century Readers' Guide 1890–1899* (Bronx, NY: H.W. Wilson Co., 1944): [v]-vii.
[47] Lewicky, interview with author, 19 April 1990.
[48] According to postal statements in 1990 issues.
[49] Potter, 593.
[50] Davis and Riddick, 48–50.
[51] Lawler, 59–60.
[52] Ibid., 115–35; Plotnik, 257, 267–68.

Demystifying Parliamentary Procedure: *Robert's Rules of Order*

Sarah B. Watstein

DEVELOPMENT AND HISTORY

Today, while specific editions and revisions may vary from institution to institution, there is virtually no library in the United States without both a reference copy and multiple circulating copies of *Robert's Rules of Order*. Without question, *Robert's Rules of Order* (hereinafter referred to as *Robert's*), one of the most phenomenally successful reference books of all time, is the standard primary source of information on parliamentary procedure. From its original publication in 1876 to the 1990s, *Robert's* continues to be not only an obvious purchase for academic, public, school, and special libraries, but also the obvious source for answering certain kinds of reference questions on a regular basis.

Over the years, *Robert's* has served an extraordinarily varied audience. It functions as a guide to the parliamentarily perplexed who serve on committees as part of their jobs or as members of organizations or associations and those who attend or chair business meetings of such groups. To the social scientist, *Robert's*, by its own declaration printed on inside jacket cover of the 1970 edition, serves as the book to "help get things done in accord with the American spirit," and thereby functions as a teaching manual of democratic theory. Students of public policy and of legislative behavior also find *Robert's* useful, as does the mathematically oriented political scientist for whom *Robert's* "offers for study a remarkable and fascinating system of queue-ing rules."[1] It is interesting to note that Henry Robert did not aim his book at beginners. Defects in early editions, including coverage of many topics twice, imperfect consistency, incompleteness, inclusion of obscure motions and/or points, awkward syntax, the lack of sample material, and the inclusion of unimportant introductory material no doubt discouraged many a beginner over the years!

Reputation and Influence

Praise and respect for *Robert's* have increased with each new edition or major revision since. In her 1970 profile of General Henry M. Robert, Barbara A. Bannon noted that "'Robert's Rules of Order' has now sold well over 2,600,000 copies in seven earlier editions, and is doing just fine in its new first major revision in fifty-five years, with a first printing of 100,000 copies."[2] In his review of the 1970 edition, Bernard N. Grofman noted that to "virtually all Americans *Robert's Rules* IS parliamentary procedure and using any other manual would be sacrilege. . . . it has been seriously suggested that only the Bible has had a greater influence on the organizational behavior of Americans."[3]

The influence of *Robert's* is evidenced not only by its commercial success but also by its inclusion in nearly any historical sketch of, or core bibliography on, parliamentary procedure. Hundreds of manuals of parliamentary procedure have been published over the years. A historical sketch of parliamentary procedure begins, properly, with the basic principles of parliamentary procedure as defined and practiced as early as the fifth century B.C. in Athens. The English tradition evolved through precedent from as early as the thirteenth century, and was fairly well developed by the eighteenth century. A compilation of these rulings was published by John Hatsell, clerk of the House of Commons, in two volumes (one in 1776 and the second in 1781), and later reissued in four volumes. These volumes were the principal source of Thomas Jefferson's *Manual of Parliamentary Practice*, published in 1801. The three principal writers on the subject of parliamentary procedure in the United States prior to the twentieth century were Jefferson, Cushing, and Robert.

Other Guides to Parliamentary Procedure

Thomas Jefferson's *Manual of Parliamentary Practice* continues to be the principal parliamentary guide of the United States Senate and the House of Representatives, adopted by the Senate in 1801 and by the House in 1837. Luther Stearns Cushing's *A Manual of Parliamentary Practice Rules of Proceedings and Debate in Assemblies* was published in 1845. Generally known as "Cushing's Manual," it was considered more appropriate to the needs of nonlegislative groups than Jefferson's *Manual*. The most widely used book on parliamentary procedure today, however, is that of Henry M. Robert.

Hundreds of rule-and-guidebooks for making meetings work are currently in print, offering quick answers and shortcuts, up-to-date methods, frameworks for deciphering meetings and making choices, tricks and techniques, ploys and stratagems with which individuals can maneuver meetings to their advantage. These rule-and-guidebooks are, in essence, spin-offs of *Robert's* and other "obsolete" nineteenth-century parliamentary procedure guides. These spin-offs exist because the layperson views parliamentary procedure as a jungle and a jumble; and passage through the maze of parliamentary rules and proce-

dures is often confused at best, requiring the use of quick guides which are short and clear, in easy-to-understand language, with frequent checklists and charts. Not all spin-offs are useful to the layperson; many serve to confuse rather than simplify procedures. Sticking to the standard *Robert's* and leaving spin-offs on the shelf often proves to be the most efficient and effective way of learning the fine points of conducting a meeting.

Consideration of competing works must include mention, in addition to spin-offs, of restatements of *Robert's*. These are as numerous as spin-offs, and include Auer's *Essentials of Parliamentary Procedure* (3rd ed., New York: Prentice Hall, 1959) and *Demeter's Manual of Parliamentary Law and Procedure* (Boston: Little, Brown, 1969). Other titles such as Sturgis' *Sturgis Standard Code of Parliamentary Procedure* (3rd ed., New York: McGraw-Hill, 1988) seek to simplify *Robert's Rules*. Still other titles offer down-to-earth, common-sense approaches, pleading for no more formal use of Robert's than necessary, such as Farwell's *The Majority Rules: A Manual of Procedure for Most Groups* (Pueblo, CO: High Publishers, 1980). "Modern" guides include Jones's *Parliamentary Procedure at a Glance* (New York: Dutton, 1971); Keesey's *Barnes & Noble Book of Modern Parliamentary Procedure* (New York: Harper & Row, 1984); Riddick and Butcher's *Riddick's Rules of Procedures* (New York: Scribner, 1988); and Suthers' *The New Primer in Parliamentary Procedure* (Chicago: Dartnell, 1965). Despite the existence of alternatives, in his survey entitled "A Historical Sketch of Parliamentary Procedure," Ray E. Keesey notes that "None of the guides to parliamentary procedure since *Robert's Rules of Order* has had as wide an acceptance as his."[4]

The Value of Procedure

Parliamentary law is a complex subject, the comprehensive knowledge of which requires considerable study as well as practical experience and an understanding of its principles. A thorough understanding of this reference landmark is inseparable from an appreciation of parliamentary law and procedure, for it is through such an appreciation that respect for *Robert's* is both kindled and fueled.

In medieval England, the sovereign summoned his parliament, a general or great council of state. The parliament consisted of an assemblage of persons (members of the nobility, clergy, and commons) who sat for a period of time until it was dissolved. Today the word "parliament" has come to mean an assembly representing a group or the members of an organization and usually convened for the expression of opinion, enactment of policy, and the transaction of other business. "Deliberative assembly," on the other hand, refers to a nonlegislative organization that conducts meetings according to parliamentary law.

The introduction to *Robert's Rules of Order Newly Revised* distinguished parliamentary law from parliamentary procedure. The former is defined as "the name given to the rules and customs for carrying on business in the English Parliament which were developed through a continuing process of decisions and precedents somewhat like the growth of common law."[5] Today parliamentary law is understood as the body of rules and precedents used to govern the proceedings of deliberative assemblies and other organizations.

Although frequently used synonymously with parliamentary law, the term "parliamentary procedure" "refers . . . to parliamentary law as it is followed in any given assembly or organization, together with whatever rules of order the body may have adopted."[6] Mere mention of parliamentary procedure brings to mind the mysterious jargon of the professional parliamentarian: "I rise to a point of order;" "I move to amend the motion;" "I doubt the quorum;" "The Chair requests order." Presiding and leadership practices blur: calling the meeting to order, accepting the minutes, transacting business, adjournment. Duties of members seem equally confusing to the uninitiated: role in debate, role in voting, personal privilege, not to mention honorary, in good standing, ex officio, or absent members! Despite being arcane, it is generally believed that parliamentary procedure as codified by *Robert's* has been important in shaping and refining basic American notions of due process and majority and minority rights as applied to group activities. In his preface to the 1970 edition, Grofman noted that "*Robert's* may be regarded as an implicit theory of democracy. For many Americans, its procedures are synonymous with practical democracy."[7]

Henry Martyn Robert

Outside the ranks of professional parliamentarians, few who can recite which divided motions can't be amended often do not know who Robert was, let alone if there was a Robert at all! Henry Martyn Robert (1837–1923), a scholarly looking nineteenth-century military man, is best known today for taking on the task of codifying and simplifying the rules and procedures of the United States House of Representatives. Born on May 2, 1837, Henry M. Robert came originally from Robertville, South Carolina. When Robert was 13, his father, who had come to the conclusion that slavery was morally wrong, freed his slaves and moved the family to Ohio. At 16, Henry received an appointment to West Point. After graduating from the military academy in 1857, Robert went on to pursue a military career, being commissioned in the Corps of Engineers and serving with distinction in the Union army and becoming Chief of Engineers in the U.S. Army. During the Civil War (1861–65) he constructed defenses for Washington, D.C., Philadelphia, and the port of New Bedford, Massachusetts. In 1863, at the age of 26, while stationed at New Bedford to help in the defense of the local whaling fleet against Confederate raiders, he was asked to preside over his first meeting, a turbulent meeting of his Baptist church. This experience changed his life and affected the lives of his descendents. Henry plunged in, confident that the assembly would behave itself. However it did not, and he resolved to learn something about parliamentary law and procedure. Over the years he became aware of how many different interpretations of parliamentary procedure there were. As a Major serving in the turbulent frontier atmosphere of San Francisco in 1867, he observed that California immigrants from every state in the union had a different idea of what was correct. He began to read all the manuals on parliamentary procedure he could find. Gradually, he became convinced of the need for a new book, based on the rules and practices of Congress, but adapted for the use by societies of ordinary American laypeople.

The First Edition

It was not until 1874 that Robert had the time to write his manual. By this time he had been transferred to Milwaukee. Barbara A. Bannon has provided a detailed history of the publishing of *Robert's Rules of Order*, based in part on her interview with the third Henry M. Robert. She notes that the General initially took the work to a job printer, Burdick and Armitage, at his own expense and had it printed and proofread 16 pages at a time, with the type from those pages then being redistributed and used again for the next sixteen. The manuscript was submitted to D. Appleton & Company of New York and rejected. A second publisher, S.C. Griggs of Chicago, also returned the manuscript with, as Bannon describes, "a letter of polite, vague interest but with the pages uncut."[8] Persistent, the General offered S.C. Griggs the 4,000 copies he had "ready-printed," to be bound by Griggs at his own expense, with the proviso that 1,000 of them could be given away free to educators, legislators, church leaders, and other prominent persons in the United States. The publishing house decided to take the chance.

Originally entitled *Pocket Manual of Rules of Order for Deliberative Assemblies*, the book carried the simpler *Robert's Rules of Order* as the publisher's second, descriptive title on the jacket. The established Cushing manual, published in 1845, was its primary competition. The *Pocket Manual* was immediately suc-

cessful. Within four months of publication in 1876, Griggs had sold out the entire lot; the General had estimated that it would take two years to dispose of 4,000 copies. The book was out of print for one month. It came back into print by the end of July 1876, with some 16 additional pages. In 1893 a third edition, numbering 218 pages, was published. In 1896 Scott, Foresman and Company of Chicago acquired the rights to the book and has been its publisher ever since.

In 1915, *Robert's Rules of Order Revised* was published. This first complete revision was the product of three years of work by the General, then retired from military service. Bannon notes that by that time the book had already sold half a million copies.[9] The book went through numerous editions during the General's lifetime.

Editions under Other Editors

Subsequent editions were handled by the General's second wife and the wife of his son, the second Henry, after the deaths of the two men. Bannon notes that "Conscientiously, each generation of the Robert family since the General has tried to keep up with a voluminous correspondence developing out of the book."[10]

The General died in Hornell, New York, on May 11, 1923. His spirit lives on through the numerous subsequent editions, revisions, and spin-offs of his work. His *Parliamentary Practice*, originally published in 1921 and *Parliamentary Law*, originally published in 1922, were still in print in the 1980s as, respectively, *Parliamentary Practice: An Introduction to Parliamentary Law* and *Parliamentary Law* (both New York: Irvington, 1975).

Among the many editions and printings of *Robert's Rules of Order*, several stand out—the original edition of 1876; the editions issued in Robert's lifetime (2nd in 1876, 3rd in 1893); revisions (1915 which superseded the last of the three earliest editions, and 1970, the first complete revision since 1915); and the current, "Modern Edition," published in 1989.

An understanding of the style, spirit and intent of the original edition is important, because successive editions and revisions have been written to be in complete harmony with the preceding editions so that they can replace those editions "with no disturbance of established practice in organizations that have used the preceding edition."[11] The preface to the 1970 edition of *Robert's Rules of Order Newly Revised* explained:

> "Since this book superseded all previous editions, such replacement is automatic in cases where the organization's bylaws prescribe as its parliamentary authority 'Robert's Rules of Order Revised,' or 'the current edition of Robert's Rules of Order,' or the like, without specifying a particular edition. If the bylaws specify a particular edition, however, such as the '1951 Edition,' or the 'Seventy-Fifth Anniversary Edition,' amendment of the bylaws is necessary."[12]

Darwin Patnode's preface to "Modern Edition" of 1989 indicates that it too continues the very process that led to the succession of previous editions, insofar as reorganization, expansion, and clarification are concerned.

The original edition contained not only an explanation of the methods of organizing and conducting meetings, the duties of officers, and the documents of an organization, but also the rules governing motions, including their forms, objects, characteristics, and other details. A "Table of Rules Relating to Motions" supplemented the text, enabling the presiding officer of a meeting to decide many parliamentary questions by a quick reference without turning a page or using an index. Numerous footnotes concerning legislative procedures were included. A lengthy introduction dealing with legislative procedure began the book. The goal of the text proper—to provide firm and uniform rules of order for deliberative assemblies throughout the land, was met, and, as its popularity attests, met very successfully.

Robert said the object of his book was

> to assist an assembly to accomplish the work for which it was designed, in the best possible manner. To do this it is necessary to restrain

the individual somewhat, as the right of an individual in any community, to do what he pleases, is incompatible with the interests of the whole. Where there is no law, but every man does what is right in his own eyes, there is the least of real liberty. Experience has shown the importance of the definiteness in the law; and in this country, where customs are so slightly established and the published manuals of parliamentary practice so conflicting, no society should attempt to conduct business without having adopted some work upon the subject, as the authority in all cases not covered by their own special rules.[13]

Robert continued to make countless modifications from one printing to the next, inserting new rules, sometimes even reversing earlier rules, from a time shortly after the first printing to the end of his life. In 1915, General Robert wrote, "The constant inquiries from all sections of the country for information . . . that is not contained in Rules of Order seems to demand a revision and an enlargement of the manual. To meet this want, the work has been thoroughly revised and enlarged, and to avoid confusion with the old Rules, is published under the title of 'Robert's Rules of Order Revised.'"[14] Twenty years after the author's death, *Robert's Rules of Order Revised* was reissued, incorporating the changes he made after the 1915 edition was published.

The seventy-fifth anniversary edition of *Robert's Rules of Order Revised*, published in 1951, was prepared, as noted on the verso of its title page, "as an important part of the program of constant attention and frequent revision given this standard work since its original publication." The edition contained two parts: "Rules of Order, A Compendium of Parliamentary Law, Based Upon the Rules of Practice of Congress," and "Organization and Conduct of Business: A Simple Explanation of the Methods of Organizing and Conducting the Business of Societies, Conventions, and Other Deliberative Assemblies." "The Order of Precedence of Motions" is given inside the front cover, and practical points about matters such as by-laws, the nominating committee, the parliamentarian, and special meetings were provided inside the back cover. In their preface, Isabel H. Robert and Sarah Corbin Robert noted that *Robert's Rules of Order* is among the few books privileged to enjoy their greatest influence after 75 years because it is based upon the "same enduring principles on which our nation itself is founded—the right of the majority to decide, the right of the minority to be heard, the right of absentees to be protected,"[15] and because it "has responded to changing needs and conditions."[16]

Significant additions to the 1951 edition included an enlarged index and a new section on Practical Points (annual meeting, by-laws, the nominating committee, the parliamentarian, rotation in office, and special meeting) on the inside back cover. In addition, references to the Congress of the United States were updated to conform to then-current practice, making the book still more useful to organizations that have adopted the rules as their parliamentary authority. Excerpts from the writing of General Robert are contained in the preface; these suggest his basic philosophy and indicate the enduring quality of his work.

The 1970 Edition

Robert's Rules of Order Newly Revised, published in 1970, represented the seventh edition of this standard guide to parliamentary rules, with charts, tables, and lists. This edition was the work of General Robert's daughter-in-law, Sarah Corbin Robert. She was assisted by her son, Henry M. Robert III; William J. Evans, a Baltimore lawyer; and James W. Cleary, president of the California State University, Northridge. The 594-page 1970 edition represented the first complete revision since 1915, and only the second complete revision of the manual since it was first published. The 1970 edition was also the first new edition in nearly 20 years. A replacement for the seventy-fifth anniversary edition, the 1970 edition was published in February on the ninety-fourth anniversary of the first publication of the book. Ten years in preparation, the book was 75 percent rewritten for clarification and easier use, and almost twice the length of the seventy-fifth anniversary edition.

Although the 1970 edition revision superseded the preceding edition of *Robert's Rules of Order Revised*, it was "written to be in complete harmony with" that edition. The verso of the title page also included the following notice: "This book automatically replaces *Robert's Rules of Order Revised* as the parliamentary authority in organizations whose bylaws prescribe 'Robert's Rules of Order Revised,' or 'the current edition of Robert's Rules of Order,' or the like, without specifying a particular edition."

As did earlier editions, the 1970 edition maintained the virtues of its predecessors, continuing to be relevant to those who understood the admonition with which the book opened: "Where there is no law, but every man does what is right in his own eyes, there is the least of liberty."[17] As were its predecessors, the 1970 edition was characterized as necessary to the conduct of American bodies dealing with legislation or regulations of any sort.

Overall, the 1970 edition was more modern, complete, comprehensive, better organized, more clearly presented, more efficient, and far easier to use than previous editions. Notable additions or elaborations in the 1970 edition included a compendium of charts, tables and lists placed conveniently and conspicuously in the center of the book; the inclusion of a section on "Disciplinary Procedures" as a final chapter; an enlarged and improved index; and an introduction offering brief-but-sound accounts of the origins of parliamentary law in Great Britain, of the transfer of British procedures to America, and of the genesis of Robert's work. Additional enhancements included a larger size and a change in type face, both of which contributed to greater clarity and a contemporary feeling as well as enhanced legibility. Most significant, however, are the facts that the 1970 edition was almost completely rewritten in simpler, clearer terms and that the material was reorganized so as to be in accord with the natural flow of business and meetings. Careful review indicates that the entire text of earlier editions was re-examined, reworded, and supplemented where necessary to, as the 1970 "Preface" says, "make the work more useful in its basic function as a reference manual suitable for adoption by organizations as parliamentary authority."[18] The 1970 edition was designed so that one could read it through and acquire a good picture of parliamentary procedure with minimum reference to concepts not previously explained.

Critical Reception of the 1970 Edition

Reviewers praised the edition for taking the mystery out of parliamentary procedure for a significantly larger sector of the population. Many reviewers noted that people could even teach themselves certain parts of it, and that the revision enabled users to feel at home with the subject and not to be afraid of or intimidated by it. Three examples of revision illustrating improvements which led to improved user satisfaction include: (1) charts and tables which are simple to use, and provide quick reference to form, precedence, and applicability of motions (as contrasted to charts which were nearly impossible to use, with stars, asterisks, footnotes and fine print, included in previous editions); (2) the logical arrangement of material in the order one would usually encounter (as contrasted to the paragraph format in earlier editions); and (3) the clear explanation of the basic classification scheme, providing for each motion a section in outline form clearly and succinctly setting forth the motion's basic operational characteristics and its uses (as contrasted to the ambiguous classification and presentation of motions in earlier editions).

Negative criticism of the 1970 edition was scant; nonetheless, certain points deserve mention. The stated intentions of the editors were to combine in the 1970 edition a definitive reference work and teaching edition. Many reviewers felt that although the 1970 edition succeeded as a definitive reference work, it did not succeed as a teaching manual. The continuing presence of some archaic terminology, some unnecessarily complex and confusing rules, and some rules which could best

be disposed of served to minimize this edition's potential as a teaching manual. Reading from cover to cover to learn the basics of parliamentary procedure was not recommended. Furthermore, some reviewers felt that the 1970 edition was not a genuine revision and modernization of American parliamentary practice. These reviewers noted that fealty to the dead General and a desire to maintain terminological accord with the U.S. House of Representatives limited the editors in the scope of their revision and in the extent of their modernization.

The 1989 Edition

Robert's Rules of Order Modern Edition, published in 1989 and edited by Darwin Patnode, a professional parliamentarian, "tries to retain the best of the original style and content of Robert's ideas and supplement them with modern language and rules, seeking a golden mean."[19] The Preface continues to advise that "In most sections, the opening material is that of Robert, and gradually additional material merges with it."[20] Specific points of departure from earlier editions include: (1) the elimination of obsolete footnotes; (2) the incorporation of relevant footnotes into the text; (3) the elimination of "innumerable and maddening" cross-references; (4) the provision of additional definitions to facilitate a clear understanding of terms Robert assumed the reader knew; (5) the insertion of sample bylaws; (6) the addition of longer sample minutes; and (7) the omission of superfluous introductory material. In addition, Patnode claims to have reworked *Robert's* awkward syntax; to have modernized spelling, punctuation, and typography; and to have improved the table of motions. Furthermore, material in the text was "altered slightly to have a more logical sequence."[21] Patnode acknowledges changing the rules in some cases, always, however, being guided by the spirit of the original rules.

Any review of the publishing history of *Robert's* needs to consider the question, which edition is the definitive printing for reference?

In his preface to the 1989 edition, Patnode addresses this quandary: "when an organization's bylaws designate as parliamentary authority *Robert's Rules of Order* without specifying an edition, there can easily be disagreement as to what a particular rule says, not only because several different printings contain somewhat different rules, but also because Robert was not always perfectly clear or consistent within a given printing.[22] Patnode goes on to advise "An organization wishing to follow the spirit of the original rules of Henry M. Robert would do well to adopt as its parliamentary authority the Modern Edition of *Robert's Rules of Order*."[23] Patnode's counsel can be viewed as self-serving, especially since Scott, Foresman issued a ninth edition in 1990. Its title page credits this edition to the same team responsible for the 1970 edition, although the dust jacket notes that "Sarah Corbin Robert was the daughter-in-law of the original author." Just released at this writing, the 1990 edition has yet to be reviewed, let alone tested through application. Meanwhile, others will imitate it, but no other manual is likely to demystify parliamentary procedures as thoroughly or as clearly.

PUBLICATION HISTORY

The list below excludes reissues and reprints and confines itself to new editions. Readers may also wish to refer to the chart of editions and reprints in Margaret A. Banks' article "'Robert's Rules of Order:' Editions, Reprints, and Competitors," cited below in the bibliography.

Pocket Manual of Rules of Order for Deliberative Assemblies Robert's Rules of Order, by Henry Martyn Robert. Chicago: S.C. Griggs & Company, 1876. 176p.

Pocket Manual of Rules of Order for Deliberative Assemblies, by Henry M. Robert. 2nd ed. Chicago: S.C. Griggs, 1876. 192p.

Pocket Manual of Rules of Order for Deliberative Assemblies, by Henry M. Robert. 3rd ed. Chicago: S.C. Griggs, 1893. 218p.

Robert's Rules of Order Revised, by Henry M. Robert. Chicago: Scott, Foresman, 1915. 323p.

Robert's Rules of Order Revised for Deliberative Assemblies, by Henry M. Robert. Chicago: Scott, Foresman, 1943. 326p.

Robert's Rules of Order Revised. Seventy-Fifth Anniversary Edition, by Henry M. Robert. Chicago: Scott, Foresman, 1951. 326p.

Robert's Rules of Order Newly Revised. A New and Enlarged Edition by Sarah Corbin Robert with the Assistance of Henry M. Robert III, James W. Cleary and William Evans. Glenview, IL: Scott, Foresman, 1970. 594p.

The Scott, Foresman Robert's Rules of Order Newly Revised. 8th ed., by Sarah Corbin Robert. Glenview, IL: Scott, Foresman, 1981. 594p.

Robert's Rules of Order Modern Edition, edited by Darwin Patnode. Nashville, TN: Thomas Nelson, 1989. 155p.

The Scott Foresman Robert's Rules of Order Newly Revised. 9th ed., by Sarah Corbin Robert and others. Scott, Foresman, 1990. 706 p.

BIBLIOGRAPHY

The secondary literature on *Robert's Rules of Order* is not as vast as one might expect for a book of its age and influence. This is due, in part, to its longtime bestseller status; its popularity has discouraged ongoing critical examination, despite the appearance of new editions. Furthermore, a limited number of persons have an abiding interest in parliamentary procedure and the literature of that field is itself limited. The best of the secondary literature on *Robert's* is found in two sorts of sources—material which assists readers in distinguishing editions and reprints of *Robert's* from one another, and materials which describe the principal competitors of *Robert's*. Description and analysis in these items is generally thorough and strong, in contrast to reviews of *Robert's* in law, library, or public administration literature. Such reviews tend to be superficial and, at best, only marginally critical. The most significant items available are the works by Banks, O'Connell, and Sikkink. Biographical information on Robert can be found in the introductions to the various editions noted above and in introductions to reprints listed in Banks' "'Robert's Rules of Order:' Editions, Reprints, and Competitors."

Aly, Bower. Review of *Robert's Rules of Order Newly Revised* (1970 ed.). *Quarterly Journal of Speech* 56 (December 1970): 454–55.

Bannon, Barbara A. "Authors & Editors: General Henry M. Robert." *Publishers Weekly* 197 (March 16, 1970): 15–16.

Banks, Margaret A. "'Robert's Rules of Order:' Editions, Reprints, and Competitors." *Law Library Journal* 80 (Spring, 1988): 177–92.

———. "Robert's Rules of Order: A Multiplicity of Editions and Reprints." *Canadian Library Journal* 39 (1982): 367–71.

———. "Robert's Rules of Order: A Survey of Paperback Reprints." *National Parliamentarian* 40 (1979): 22–23.

Cinquemani, Frank L. "Robert's Revised: Parliamentary Practice in Perspective." *RQ* 16 (Fall, 1976): 55–58.

Cleary, James W. "A Commentary on Robert's Rules of Order Newly Revised." *Parliamentary Journal* 9 (April, 1968): 3–9.

Glixon, D.M. Review of *Robert's Rules of Order* (New Revised) (1970 ed.). *Saturday Review* 53 (May 16, 1970): 44.

Grofman, Bernard N. Review of *Robert's Rules of Order* (New Revised) (1970 ed.). *American Political Science Review* 64 (December, 1970): 1288–90.

Holte, Susan, and Bohdan S. Wynar, eds. *Best Reference Books 1970–1980: Titles of Lasting Value Selected From American Reference Books Annual.* Littleton, CO: Libraries Unlimited, 1981.

Keesey, Ray E. "A Historical Stretch of Parliamentary Procedure." In his *Modern Parliamentary Procedure,* Boston: Houghton, Mifflin, 1974, pp. 21–25.

Knowles, Malcolm S. "Move Over Mr. Robert." *Adult Leadership* 1 (June, 1952): 2–4.

O'Brien, Joseph F. "Henry M. Robert as Presiding Officer." *Quarterly Journal of Speech* 42 (April, 1956): 157–62.

O'Connell, Brian, "Robert's Rules of Order Demystified." In *The Board Member's Book: Making a Difference in Voluntary Organizations,* 105–15. New York: Foundation Center, 1985.

Revelle, Keith. "A Collection for La Raza." *Library Journal* 96 (November 15, 1971): 3719–26.

Review of *Robert's Rules of Order. Publishers Weekly* 192 (July 21, 1967): 58.

Review of *Robert's Rules of Order Newly Revised* (1970 ed.). *American Reference Books Annual* (1971): 145.

Review of Robert's *Rules of Order Newly Revised* (1970 ed.). *Booklist* 6 (May 15, 1970): 1141.

Sikkink, Don. "Fundamental Change in Parliamentary Procedure." Paper presented at the Annual Meeting of the Speech Communication Association, 58th, Chicago, December 27–30, 1972. ED 072474.

Wasylenko, Lydia W. Review of *Robert's Rules of Order* (Bantam Books edition, c 1982, 1986). In *American Reference Books Annual* 19 (1988), 278.

Wyllie, Stanley Clark, Jr. Review of *Robert's Rules of Order Newly Revised* (1970 ed.). *Library Journal* 95 (June 1, 1970): 2123.

NOTES

[1] Bernard N. Grofman, review of *Robert's Rules of Order, New Revised,* 1970 ed., *American Political Scince Review* 64 (December 1970): 1289.

[2] Barbara A. Bannon, "Authors & Editors: General Henry M. Robert," *Publishers Weekly* 197 (16 March 1970): 15.

[3] Grofman, 1288–89.

[4] Ray E. Keesey, "A Historical Sketch of Parliamentary Procedure," in *Modern Parliamentary Procedure* by Ray E. Keesey (Boston: Houghton Mifflin, 1974), 25.

[5] Henry M. Robert, *Robert's Rules of Order Newly Revised* (Glenview, IL: Scott Foresman, 1970), xxvii.

[6] Ibid., xxviii.

[7] Grofman, 1289.

[8] Bannon, 16.

[9] Ibid.

[10] Ibid.

[11] Robert, *Robert's Rules of Order Newly Revised,* xxiii.

[12] Ibid.

[13] Henry M. Robert, *Pocket Manual of Rules of Order for Deliberative Assemblies: Robert's Rules of Order* (1876), cited by Isabel H. Robert and Sarah Corbin Robert, *Robert's Rules of Order Revised* (Chicago: Scott Foresman, 1951), 14.

[14] Ibid.

[15] Isabel H. Robert and Sarah Corbin Robert, "Preface," in *Robert's Rules of Order Revised* (Chicago: Scott, Foresman, 1951): 13.

[16] Ibid.

[17] Ibid., 14.

[18] Robert, *Robert's Rules of Order Newly Revised,* xxii.

[19] Darwin Patnode, ed., *Robert's Rules of Order Modern Edition* (Nashville, TN: Thomas Nelson, 1989), 15.

[20] Ibid.

[21] Ibid., 16.

[22] Ibid., 16–17.

[23] Ibid., 17.

"Wings of Flight": Roget's *Thesaurus of English Words and Phrases*

Marta Lange

> The man is not wholly evil—he has a
> *Thesaurus* in his cabin.
> > —Sir James Barrie, describing
> > Captain Hook

DEVELOPMENT AND HISTORY

Peter Mark Roget published his *Thesaurus of English Words and Phrases* in 1852, calling it a "desideratum hitherto unsupplied in any language; namely, a collection of the words it contains and of the idiomatic combinations peculiar to it, arranged, not in alphabetical order as they are in a Dictionary, but according to the *ideas* which they express."[1] It was a tool Roget hoped would not merely assist in communication but would actually give thought "wings for flight."[2]

A medical doctor and Renaissance man whose intellectual interests spanned the sciences, Roget labored almost fours years to produce this work and saw 25 editions or printings published before his death at the age of 91. Tens of millions of copies have been sold since that time, making this work one of the most ubiquitous in the English-speaking world. The word thesaurus, derived from the Greek θησαυρος (*thesauros*) meaning a "treasure," "store," or "collection," is now a common noun in the English language. Few reference titles are as closely identified with a single individual as the *Thesaurus* is with Roget. This landmark work closely reflects both the nature of Roget and the time in which he lived. It is through understanding both that an appreciation of the *Thesaurus* can be gained.

Peter Mark Roget

Roget was born in London in 1779, the only son of Catherine Romilly and the Reverend Jean Roget, a native of Geneva, Switzerland, and pastor of a French Protestant church. Jean died when his son was only four, and Peter was brought up by his mother "who was admirably qualified for the task, not only by her mental accomplishments, but by a systematic habit of mind, which was inherited by her son in a marked degree."[3]

By the time Peter was 14, Catherine was concerned about the direction of his education. His interests and talents lay consistently in the areas of science and mathematics, yet there was no such occupation as scientist in 1793. Catherine therefore chose medicine as the profession Peter would pursue. It was a subject that she found fascinating and a field which proved "profitable to the practitioner, even if not to the patient."[4] She moved the family to Edinburgh whose university had the best medical and scientific programs in the English-speaking world. Peter enrolled at age fourteen and received his M.D. degree at 19.

For the next three years Peter experienced what was perhaps the most adventurous part of his life. He traveled to the Pneumatic Institution in Clifton, where Dr. Thomas Beddoes and Humphrey Davy were experimenting with early forms of anesthesia by treating various ailments through respiration of nitrous oxide, or "laughing gas." Roget's own experience with the gas left him bewildered and frightened. He felt his equilibrium had been destroyed and that, under the influence of the gas, his senses were in a state of confusion. For one so properly trained to be a model professional man, such an experience was plainly destructive. In his years at Edinburgh, "Peter had been convinced that his future lay in regularity and order, not in disequilibrium and confusion."[5]

In the fall of 1800 Peter experimented with creating a "Frigidarium," an idea conceived by Jeremy Bentham for cold storage of foods. He lived in Bentham's house, but desiring more privacy, disenchanted with living in such an unconventional household, and convinced that Bentham was a man who would never finish what he started to do, Roget moved out to his own apartment.[6]

After his return from an 1803 trip to France that almost ended in his imprisonment when war broke out between France and England, Roget moved to Manchester to set up a medical practice where the ratio of physicians to populace was not as high as that in London. He was appointed one of the physicians to the Infirmary and assisted in creating a medical school there. In 1806 he delivered a series of 18 lectures on physiology to medical students. The syllabus of his course showed that his "chief interest in the new science of physiology lay in the *organization* and *order* of the several aspects of that subject and in the *relationship* of the subject to such kindred fields as anatomy."[7] This interest in relationships and classification characterized his work and led eventually to the classification of ideas and words in the *Thesaurus*.

Roget resigned his post at the Infirmary in 1808 and moved to London. He immersed himself in work, and for the next 60 years he practiced as a physician, participated actively in the burgeoning scientific societies, wrote scientific papers, and lectured on physiology and related topics. Roget established a considerable medical practice in London, where he also helped open a neighborhood charity medical clinic, and served as physician to the Spanish embassy. Appointed by King George

IV in 1827 to a commission studying London's water quality, Roget recommended that water be filtered through sand, a method still in use today.[8] The crowning point of his medical career came in 1831 with his election to the Royal College of Physicians.[9]

Roget took a more than usually active part in a number of organizations, including the Royal Institution, Medical and Chirurgical Society, and many others.[10] As a founding member of the Medical and Chirurgical Society, he tended to bookkeeping and oversaw the publishing of several volumes of the Society's transactions. As elected secretary of the Royal Society, he edited the *Proceedings* of the Society and prepared for publication the abstracts of papers communicated to the Society.[11]

Throughout his career Roget contributed papers to the advancement of scientific knowledge. His total bibliography numbers over 100 items, including many treatises written in simple English explaining science at the layperson's level. Fourteen of Roget's articles, ranging in subject matter from "Ant," "Cranioscopy," "Deaf and Dumb" to "Kaleidoscope," were published in the supplement to the fourth, fifth and sixth editions of the *Encyclopaedia Britannica*. These articles were "important in increasing his stature as an authority in physiology and as an all-around savant."[12] He demonstrated his bent for finding relationships and shaping facts into organic laws in a major article on physiology published in the seventh edition of the *Britannica*. He produced several treatises on electricity, galvanism, magnetism, and electromagnetism, evidence of his continuing fascination with science and mathematics.[13]

Roget's *Animal and Vegetable Physiology Considered with Reference to Natural Theology*, a two-volume work appearing in 1834, marked the peak of his professional career. This work was the fifth in the series of the Bridgewater Treatises, commissioned by the Earl of Bridgewater to propound "the power, wisdom, and goodness of God, as manifested in the creation."[14] The treatise offered no original discoveries but brought a sense of unity to physiology and comparative anatomy. In an age of growing scientific discovery and change, however, its view that evolution could not work separately from an all-knowing God was already in question by the time it was published.

Roget served as secretary of the Royal Society for 20 years, a tenure not without its stormy clashes. As early as 1830, Charles Babbage and others charged the Society with dilettantism, private interest, nepotism, and snobbery.[15] For over ten years a series of complicated disputes and arguments advanced until they emerged as a large-scale revolt of young scientists against the old guard. The pressure for reform mounted, and Roget resigned as secretary on November 30, 1847.[16]

A Fascination for Order

Finding himself possessed of more leisure after his retirement, Roget turned his attention to a project which he had begun in 1805, that of classifying and organizing the English language. The *Thesaurus* began as a notebook Roget carried around with him since his earliest days of lecturing. He arranged words within it to help him express himself as effectively as possible. Now in his seventies, he would draw upon a lifetime of experience in lecturing, writing, and editing to make this list into a coherent system others could use.[17] Ironically it is this list, not any of his scientific achievements, that made Roget a household word.

At first glance it is not apparent that Roget had any particular talent equipping him to tackle such an ambitious project. He demonstrated no literary interest, no linguistic training, no fascination with language for language's sake. What he did demonstrate over his entire lifetime, however, was a concern with order; it was "the organization of knowledge (rather than the making of profound discoveries, for which he lacked the

imagination), that was Roget's forte, and which he was able to put to good use in compiling the *Thesaurus*."[18]

Roget's fascination for order was characteristic of the age in which he lived. The successful emergence of modern science depended upon the development of a workable classification of its elements, and systematists worked out schemes for classifying the plant and animal kingdoms and chemical elements. In the same vein, Roget would labor for four years (1848–1852) to organize and classify human ideas into an outline of commonly understood terms.

Although he believed that his work filled a unique niche in the history of word tools, Roget was certainly aware of other related publications. By the time the *Thesaurus* was published, three types of language literature existed: philosophical treatises on the relationship between thought and language, and on the possibilities of creating a universal language; prescriptive grammars, including style manuals and synonym books; and writings in the emerging field of linguistics. Roget probably drew from all three areas when constructing his *Thesaurus*.[19]

While he stressed the utility of the *Thesaurus* for writers, Roget also saw his book as a tool for philosophers:

> Metaphysicians engaged in the more profound investigation of the Philosophy of Language will be materially assisted by having the ground thus prepared for them, in a previous analysis and classification of our ideas; for such classification of ideas is the true basis on which words, which are their symbols, should be classified. It is by such analysis alone that we can arrive at a clear perception of the relation which these symbols bear to their corresponding ideas, or can obtain a correct knowledge of the elements which enter in to the formation of compound ideas, and of the exclusions by which we arrive at the abstractions so perpetually resorted to in the process of reasoning, and in the communications of our thoughts.[20]

He also expressed his philosophy that "the use of language is not confined to its being the medium through which we communicate our ideas to one another; it fulfills a no less important function as an *instrument of thought*; not being merely its vehicle, but giving it wings for flight."[21] Roget also felt it of utmost importance that strict accuracy should regulate use of language. He further worried that

> false logic, disguised under specious phraseology, too often gains the assent of the unthinking multitude, disseminating far and wide the seeds of prejudice and error.... A misapplied or misapprehended term is sufficient to give rise to fierce and interminable disputes; a misnomer has turned the tide of popular opinion; a verbal sophism has decided a party question; an artful watchword, thrown among combustible materials, has kindled the flame of deadly warfare, and changed the destiny of an empire.[22]

Roget shared the dream of a number of earlier writers for a set of symbols upon which to base a universal language. To Roget, none of these earlier schemes seemed practical, yet he considered their ultimate goal highly desirable. Science was developing and expanding during his lifetime, and scientists were seeking a new international language for communication. Rather than basing this language on a set of symbols or characters, Roget believed that such a language should be developed through the organization of ideas based on a consensus of current speaking and writing practice. He felt that his own analysis of the language could assist in determining the principles on which a philosophical language might be constructed, and once constructed, adopted by every civilized nation. Nothing, thought Roget, could do more "to bring about a golden age of union and harmony among the several nations and races of mankind...."[23]

A Multi-Purpose Tool

What Roget conceived as a philosophical arrangement of ideas expressed by language was also meant as a practical tool for the precise use of language. At the time of its publication, practical language works in English fell into three categories: prescriptive grammars, dictionaries, and collections of synonyms. Their collective purpose was to establish an acceptable level of good taste in conversation and in writing. The popularity of these works corresponded with the rise in England of a middle class concerned with bettering its own fortunes, and with binding town and country populations together through education and study of the English language.[24]

The *Thesaurus* is not a prescriptive grammar, but there is some relationship between Roget's goals and those of the various grammars published. Those works sought to develop grammatical standards as well as to purify the English language which some felt had been adulterated by French words and phrases. Roget also sought to create a standard for regulating language, but his concern was more toward regulating the appearance of new words, not grammatical structure.[25]

The *Thesaurus* is not a dictionary, for an ordinary dictionary simply explains the meaning of words or the ideas words are intended to convey. The *Thesaurus* is exactly the opposite: the idea being given, it identifies the word or words by which that idea may be best expressed. Believing that "we cannot but be often conscious that the phraseology we have at our command is inadequate to do them justice,"[26] Roget said his work would offer the writer a helping hand, for

> it is in words that he clothes his thoughts; it is by means of words that he depicts his feelings. It is therefore essential to his success that he be provided with a copious vocabulary, and that he possess an entire command of all the resources and appliances of his language. To the acquisition of this power no procedure appears more directly conducive than the study of a methodized system such as that now offered to his use.[27]

Roget expressly stated that the *Thesaurus* was not a collection of synonyms, and indeed it made no attempt to differentiate among apparently synonymous words.[28] Roget's concern was solely with classifying and arranging words according the their current sense and usage, knowledge of which he presumed the reader to possess. In assuming this knowledge Roget may have been operating with breath-taking optimism, for he was misunderstood even by early reviewers who equated his work with previous synonymies.

The Thesaurus's Antecedents

English synonymies before 1852 tended to be one of two types: word-finding lists and those that tried to explain the distinctions among words.[29] Twenty different titles on English synonymy were published prior to the appearance of the *Thesaurus,* the first in 1766.

In 1805, William Perry's *Synonymous, Etymological, and Pronouncing English Dictionary* greatly extended the traditional definition of synonym (as one of two or more words of identical meaning, or of apparently identical meaning) and broadened it to include a group of words which have resemblances in meaning.[30]

English Synonymes Discriminated, by William Taylor (1813), used etymologies to explain the original meanings of words and thereby establish synonymous relationships. *English Synonymes Explained, in Alphabetical Order; with Copious Illustrations and Explanations Drawn from the Best Writers,* by George Crabb (1816), was the most ambitious precursor to the *Thesaurus.* Crabb's chief contributions were the addition of an etymology, the addition of a statement as to how far words are equivalent in meaning, and the arrangement of words from the most comprehensive to the least comprehensive.[31] Although Crabb's work was far from perfect—his synonymies were often confused and inconsistent and his etymologies often faulty—his work enjoyed great public favor for many decades.[32]

A Selection of English Synonyms, by Miss Elizabeth Jane Whately (1851) proposed that words must often be regarded as signs not of real things but of notions of things, and must have a fixed and generally accepted content.

While Whately was not the first to discriminate meanings of synonyms, she was the first in England to make that the avowed aim of a book of synonyms and to distinguish clearly between the meaning of a word and the thing or idea for which it stood.[33]

One year after Whately's work was published, the first edition of the *Thesaurus of English Words and Phrases, Classified and Arranged so as to Facilitate the Expression of Ideas and Assist in Literary Composition* appeared. Despite the plethora of word books already in existence, it enjoyed immediate acceptance and provoked new interest in opposite and contrasted terms. Roget adapted from previous synonymies the technique of grouping large collections of synonymous words together, but he offered no definitions, no etymologies, no discriminating explanations between words, no citations to reputable authors.

Roget's Classification Scheme

Roget devised his detailed classification of words from Georges Cuvier's zoological classification then used in natural history. He divided his work into six main categories (classes), each of which is divided further into sections (orders), subsections (genera), and heads of signification (species).[34] The sectional divisions he formed corresponded to the natural families in botany and zoology, with the filiation of words being analogous to the filiation of plants and animals within these families.[35] All of these divisions, 1,000 in all, were laid out in outline and tabular form and numbered. Each number designated a particular paragraph of the book, a particular idea under which the reader could find all words expressing that idea. The major portion of the book was arranged in numerical order, presenting an initially confusing format. For the convenience of the reader, Roget provided a tabular synopsis of categories at the beginning of the work. He also appended a short alphabetical index to the text, though it was not his intent that the index ever become the predominant portion of the work.

Roget's chief goal in constructing his classification of ideas was to obtain the greatest amount of practical utility. The diagram below offers a useful picture for understanding his overall scheme.

Just as Cuvier's classification scheme was fixed in form, so was Roget's. The intent behind this fixed design for language may be analogous to the fixed design of nature in the minds of natural theologists. Once the relationships among the various parts of the natural world had been set down in stable classification schemes, human understanding of that world, and God's purpose in it, was considerably increased. A permanent design outlining the organization of the totality of ideas, the components of the internal world, would increase human understanding both of humanity and of God's purpose for humanity.[36]

Roget felt that the terminology composing the framework of his classification was a series of natural signs easily comprehensible from language usage of the time. Although he never explained why he chose the six particular primary classes utilized in the *Thesaurus*, it is possible to trace some portion of his intent to previous writings. Three of the primary classes—matter, intellect, and volition—may be derived from his perception of the laws of physiology described in the introductory chapter of his Bridgewater Treatise. "The second class of laws comprise those which are founded on the relation of means to an end; and which are usually denominated final causes. They involve the operations of mind, in conjunction with those of matter. They presuppose intention or design; a supposition which implies intelligence, thought, motives, volition . . ."[37] All six classes, including abstract relations, space, and affection, are also implied in Tho-

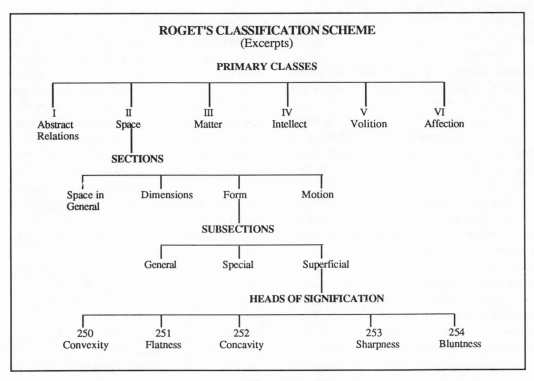

ROGET'S CLASSIFICATION SCHEME
(Excerpts)

PRIMARY CLASSES

| I
Abstract Relations | II
Space | III
Matter | IV
Intellect | V
Volition | VI
Affection |

SECTIONS

Space in General   Dimensions   Form   Motion

SUBSECTIONS

General   Special   Superficial

HEADS OF SIGNIFICATION

| 250
Convexity | 251
Flatness | 252
Concavity | 253
Sharpness | 254
Bluntness |

Figure 1
A Sample from Roget's Classification Scheme.

mas Reid's *An Inquiry into the Human Mind on the Principles of Common Sense* (1764), an essay discussing the principle of natural signs of language.[38]

In selecting words for his text, Roget felt his purpose was to offer as many terms as might be wanted, leaving the proper selection entirely to the discretion and taste of the reader. He therefore included not only single words, but also phrases; vulgar terms, if used in general conversation; words and phrases borrowed from other languages; and neologies coined in the arts and sciences if made familiar through common use. He omitted purely scientific and technical terms along with common proverbs.

Roget addressed and resolved the many problems confronting an organizer of words. Recognizing that many words could fall in more than one category, he used numerous cross-references and also listed some words under more than one head. In order to prevent needless length, he generally omitted conjugate words, or different parts of speech from the same root.

Roget was the first to focus on antonymic as well as synonymic relationships among words. He did not, however, call similar words "synonyms," since he insisted that there are no real synonyms in the sense of two words having identical meanings. Instead he called them "analogous" words. He referred to contrasting words as "correlative." The term "antonym" would not be used until 1867.[39]

Roget arranged the *Thesaurus* in two parallel columns so that correlative ideas could be easily contrasted. (This layout was maintained in the copyright edition until 1962.) The correlative expressions were either intermediate terms whose meaning falls between two opposite ideas (beginning—middle—end), the negative to each of two opposite positions (convexity—flatness—concavity), or the standard with which each extreme is compared (insufficiency—sufficiency—redundance). While these forms of correlative expressions would suggest use of triple rather than double

columns within the text, Roget found this format impractical and remained with two.[40] It is in addressing the correlative nature of words that Roget advanced the linguistic theory that "the study of correlative terms existing in a particular language may often throw valuable light on the manners and customs of the nations using it."[41]

The First Edition

The first edition of the *Thesaurus* was published by Longman, Brown, Green, and Longmans in May 1852, when Roget was 73. "It was a handsome volume, a generous octavo, printed on good quality paper, with the text well spaced-out."[42] Roget's work in a multitude of scientific and literary societies had made him a fairly well known figure, and his *Thesaurus* sold out of the 1,000 copies printed.

Several British journals reviewed the *Thesaurus* within its first year. Most were favorable if not particularly analytical. Many were not quite sure what to make of this new work. "Whatever may be thought, however, of the general aim of Dr. Roget's work, there can be no doubt as to the ability of its execution," said *The Athenaeum*.[43] This unsigned review also suggested that some terms included were already obsolete, and that more care and discrimination could have been taken in the overall selection process. Regarding the book's classification system, the reviewer seemed to feel that if such a scheme proved useful for the writing of a former secretary of the Royal Society, it would certainly be quite useful to others.

The Critic observed that "this is at least a curious book, novel in its design, most laboriously wrought, but, we fear, not likely to be so practically useful as the care, and toil, and thought bestowed upon it might have deserved."[44] *The Eclectic Review* regarded the book very highly, saying that "the utility of such a work is much greater than appears on the surface."[45] It continued,

We can assure our readers that it would be unjust to the author to represent his book as a merely dry catalogue of words. It is full of suggestions. It exhibits the extraordinary richness, fulness, and flexibility of the English language . . . . We recommend it specifically to writers who . . . are so indolent, conceited, so ignorant, or so negligent, as to damage the purity of their mother-tongue by a habit of arbitrarily fabricating new words and a new fangled phraseology . . . . We should rejoice if our warm commendation promoted the circulation of so *thoroughly useful* a book.[46]

The *Westminster Review*, founded by Jeremy Bentham, published its review in April 1853 after the *Thesaurus* had been in print for nearly a year. Stating that no literary man should be without such a help, it added that "the labour must have been immense, but the author's reward is sure. Roget will rank with Samuel Johnson as a literary instrument-maker of the first-class."[47]

Within a few years of its appearance the *Thesaurus* was being defended as a staple without which no serious scholar could live. One of the few reviews critical of its purpose appeared in the *North American Review* in 1854. The writer, identified as E.P. Whipple by Samuel Austin Allibone,[48] ridiculed the *Thesaurus* as a tool engendering mediocrity in writing:

> Seriously, we consider this book as one of the best of a numerous class, whose aim is to secure the results without imposing the tasks of labor, to arrive at ends by a dexterous dodging of means, to accelerate the tongue without accelerating the faculties. It is an outside remedy for an inward defect. In our opinion, the work mistakes the whole process by which living thought makes its way into living words, and it might be thoroughly mastered without conveying any real power or facility of expression.[49]

While Whipple asserted that the *Thesaurus* in the hands of a novice writer may result in anguished prose, it has also been shown to hone the writing of professionals. As one example, Dylan Thomas, a proven master of expression, used the *Thesaurus* as a source of words during his composition of "Poem on his Birthday," in 1951.[50]

Later Editions Edited by Roget and His Descendants

Longman published a second edition of 1,500 copies in March 1853. The third, described as a cheaper edition, enlarged and improved, appeared in February 1855. For this edition Roget revised parts of the text, added thousands of new expressions, and introduced 20 subsidiary heads marked as "(a)" to fill gaps he had found in his scheme. This edition was then stereotyped and used for subsequent printings until the plates were worn out. Roget personally saw 25 new editions and printings through the press, and he collected additions and changes up to his death in September 1869.

His son John Lewis Roget, a lawyer who was active as an art critic and watercolorist, then took over as editor. He compiled his father's multitudinous handwritten notes from the margins and spaces of the *Thesaurus* for his new edition published in 1879. Without changing Roget's system of classification in any way, he nevertheless made his own distinctive contribution to the evolution of the *Thesaurus*. To keep the book within reasonable limits while adding large numbers of words, he confined use of words to a single primary heading and extended the use of cross-references, a practice continued by subsequent editors. John Roget's other major addition to the *Thesaurus* was the significant expansion of the alphabetical index. Roget himself felt that readers would consult the system of classification first and give little importance to the index. John Roget believed, however, that almost everyone who used the book found it more convenient to consult the index first. His new index contained not only all the words in the text but also all the phrases which had previously been excluded.[51] The index took up almost half of the new edition.

John Roget supervised frequent reprints of the *Thesaurus*. New words reflecting topics of the day, such as "veldt," "Afrikander," and "Gatling gun," were added to the text and listed in a supplementary index. Upon John

Roget's death in 1908, his son Samuel Romilly Roget took over as editor. Samuel Roget, an engineer, made no changes in layout but greatly expanded the vocabulary of the book and extended the system of cross-references. He promoted the *Thesaurus* energetically, cementing its place as a landmark work. The crossword puzzle craze of the 1920s gave its sales an enormous boost. Between 1911 and 1929, a least one printing was made per year, with five in 1925 when Samuel Roget brought out his own new enlarged edition. According to a reviewer in *Dial*, "Mr. Samuel Romilly Roget, his father and grandfather, seem in this volume, to have perfected perfection."[52] For the 1936 edition the index was checked line by line. New plates were made and used for frequent reprints even in the war years.[53]

Editions by Others

Samuel Romilly Roget carried on the family's work until 1952 when he sold the family rights to Longmans, Green and Co. With his death in 1953, the family connection with the *Thesaurus* came to an end. Exactly 100 years from the date of the first edition, Longmans commissioned Robert A. Dutch, OBE, to bring the *Thesaurus* up to date. Dutch entirely rewrote the text and recompiled the index while remaining true to the organic structure of the original. In his introduction, Dutch stated:

> it is Roget's great merit that he devised a system of categories, logically ordered, that is both workable and comprehensive. As edition followed edition, more and more words were drawn in without destroying the framework. In the course of a century of testing, modifications have been made only in matters of detail. The present editor's experience confirms that of his predecessors.[54]

While Roget's framework still proved useful for organization, Dutch felt that the system of classification itself was of little interest to most modern readers who wanted a purely practical, not philosophical, communication tool. Dutch, therefore, made many changes to

the format so that the classification system became more transparent for the reader.

In previous editions contrasting heads had been arranged in opposite, parallel columns. Heads that had no opposite were printed the whole width of the page. Dutch kept the parallel columns but printed the heads consecutively. He completely recast the ordering of words in each head so that close synonyms could be grouped more consistently together to lead the mind "by easy transitions from one nuance to another without distraction."[55] He introduced some new heads and renamed or eliminated others, resulting in a reduced total of 990 rather than the original 1,000. Dutch added some 50,000 new words and a large number of cross-references, swelling the total size of the volume to almost double that of the 1936 edition of Samuel Roget.

Dutch's most significant contribution to the evolution of the *Thesaurus* was the use of keywords printed in italics at the beginning of each paragraph. The keyword showed readers where to begin their search within a head. The keyword was used in all cross-references and in the index references, enabling readers to pick out the most suitable of several locations for the meaning they sought.[56] This new edition was judged to present a fuller and more up-to-date vocabulary in a more convenient and readily accessible form.[57]

The *Thesaurus* was revised again in 1982 by Susan M. Lloyd, a modern language teacher and former library worker. She viewed her new edition as an overhaul of an efficient and valuable machine rather than an attempt to completely rebuild it. She refined parts, replaced parts, and took advantage of computer technology to ensure the reliability of the cross-references and index. Her main task was to incorporate the huge number of new expressions that had been generated over a rapidly changing 20 years. She added over 20,000 new terms of the sciences and technology (*data processing, space travel, sources of energy*), commerce and industry (*ergonomics, market research, cost-benefit analysis, hard sell*), and medicine (*transplant, test-tube baby*). She also listed terms describing society and societal changes. She paid special attention to subject areas reflecting her own interests: ecology and conservation (*recycling, greenhouse effect*), sociology and politics (*superpowers, sexism, cover-up, streaking, drug-taking*), and civil rights (*feminism, blackpower, gay lib*).[58]

Lloyd's work proved briefly controversial as journalists charged the *Thesaurus* of being "feminized."[59] In her preface Lloyd states that "in listing nouns denoting people, we have borne in mind the fact that according to recent research the particle 'man,' in such words as 'mankind,' is not always taken, as formerly, to include men *and* women. Care has therefore been taken to include female terms as well, or general terms such as 'chairperson,' where they exist."[60] Other reviews of Lloyd's work questioned her omission of vulgar words and racial epithets, a decision made, according to Lloyd, since those terms are already familiar and since "inclusion gives them an aura of respectability."[61]

While many reviews challenged Lloyd's inclusion or exclusion of words, *The Indexer* challenged what it considered a major flaw in the format: the nonalphabetical arrangement of subheadings. This arrangement could cause the reader to peruse as many as 241 possible points of entry to locate a word/meaning being sought, and was in direct violation of British indexing standards.[62]

Some thirty million copies of the *Thesaurus* had been sold by the time Betty Kirkpatrick began work on the most recent revision of the *Thesaurus* in January 1985.[63] Within her new edition published in 1987, Kirkpatrick added 11,000 entries, placing greater emphasis than in the past on technology, international cuisine, and health. A former editor of the *Chambers 20th Century Dictionary* and a native of Scotland, she included Scottish words that are universally used and recognized. She was also the first reviser to include four-letter words. Few other changes from Lloyd's edition were made. *The Indexer* again lamented the nonalphabetization of subheadings and found this

edition's typeface and page make-up more difficult than in Lloyd's work.[64]

American Editions

The publishing rights to the *Thesaurus* have always remained with Longman, yet even from the beginning other editions sprang forth from publishers in the United States as well as in England. The Reverend Barnas Sears edited the first American *Thesaurus* in 1854, omitting all "vulgar" words and phrases, even phrases as innocent as "to feather one's nest," "to run a muck," or "cool as a cucumber." *Putnam's* severely criticized Sears for meddling with Roget's work on the basis that what he had left out was not vulgar but merely idiomatic and thus useful to writers. When Sears reinserted the "vulgar" words and phrases in his second edition of 1855, he placed them in a separate category as an appendix. *Putnam's* subsequently judged this practice to be "more likely to catch the eye of 'students and younger readers' as they are now placed, than they are as they stand in Roget's original arrangement."[65] Gould and Lincoln, Boston, continued to issue printings of Sears' work until 1867.

In 1886 Thomas Y. Crowell & Company, the major American publisher of the *Thesaurus*, issued, with authorization from Longman, its first American edition, based on John Roget's 1879 work.[66] Crowell released several other printings revised and amended to fit American needs until 1911, when American lexicographer C.O. Sylvester Mawson, revising editor of *Webster's New International Dictionary*, issued a practically new book that deviated considerably from the original Longman edition. Mawson's work, completely revised and reset in 1922, was then called the "International edition" because of the number of non-English words included. The International edition was further enlarged in 1930, 1932, 1936, 1938, and 1939. Crowell then produced *Roget's International Thesaurus: New Edition* in 1946, and, after more than ten years of continuous revision, it published

Roget's International Thesaurus, Third Edition, in 1962.[67] The latest of Crowell's standard American editions is *Roget's International Thesaurus*, fourth edition, revised by Robert L. Chapman and published in 1977.

Some publishers have issued more recent editions under license from Longman. In 1965 St. Martin's Press printed an Americanized edition of the 1962 Longman work. In 1984 Penguin published an abridged paperback version of the 1982 Lloyd edition and in 1988 Penguin released an abridgement of the 1987 Kirkpatrick edition.[68]

While all these editions retained Roget's basic classification system, many others dropped that system yet still used Roget's name. Among these were the *Roget's Pocket Thesaurus* (New York: Pocket Books, 1946); *Roget's Treasury of Words* (New York: Crowell, 1924); *New American Roget's College Thesaurus in Dictionary Form* (New York: New American Library, 1958); and *Roget's II: The New Thesaurus* (Boston: Houghton Mifflin, 1980). *Roget's II* is the electronic version of the *Thesaurus* currently available on CD-ROM as part of *Microsoft Bookshelf*. Longman highly disapproves of the use of "Roget" as a generic term and has recently registered the name as a trademark in several countries including the United Kingdom.[69]

Given the number of publishers and editors who have connections with the *Thesaurus*, along with national and international copyright agreements and arguments, it is not surprising that there is no known bibliography capturing all the editions and printings of the

Thesaurus. According to D. L. Emblen, Roget's biographer, it is doubtful that a clear and complete publication history will ever emerge.[70]

Future of the Thesaurus

The future of the *Thesaurus* may be clearer, however; Longman will regularly revise the *Thesaurus* to ensure that the Longman edition remains up-to-date and authoritative. Longman lexicographers work closely with each editor to determine what should be included and/or removed. In between full revisions, Longman incorporates minor corrections into each new reprint. The next full Longman revision is planned for the mid-1990s.[71]

Computer capabilities make possible an expanded, continually updated database of words. Longman is looking forward to exploiting the capabilities of technology by producing electronic versions of the *Thesaurus*.[72] Through use of the computer, Robert Chapman has envisioned an entirely new tool, a "thessictionary," which would incorporate both thesaurus listings and dictionary definitions.[73] Susan Lloyd has seen opportunities to build a multilingual database in which any language in the world could be analyzed according to Roget's classification. Such a database could be an imperfect forerunner to finally achieving Roget's dream of a universal language, a language which would help bring about the golden age of union and harmony among the several nations and races of the world.[74]

PUBLICATION HISTORY

Thesaurus of English Words and Phrases, Classified and Arranged so as to Facilitate the Expression of Ideas and Assist in Literary Composition, by Peter Mark Roget. London: Longman, Brown, Green, and Longmans, 1852. 418p.

Thesaurus of English Words and Phrases, Classified and Arranged so as to Facilitate the Expression of Ideas and Assist in Literary Composition, by Peter Mark Roget. 2nd ed., revised and enlarged. London: Longman, Brown, Green, and Longmans, 1853. 434p.

Thesaurus of English Words and Phrases, Classified and Arranged so as to Facilitate the Expression of Ideas and Assist in Literary Composition, by Peter Mark Roget. 3rd ed., enlarged and improved. London: Longman, Brown, Green, and Longmans, 1855. 507p.

Thesaurus of English Words and Phrases, Classified and Arranged so as to Facilitate the Expression of Ideas and Assist in Literary Composition, by Peter Mark Roget. New Edition, Enlarged and Improved, partly from the Author's Notes, and with a full Index, by John Lewis Roget. London: Longmans, Green & Co., 1879. 667p.

Thesaurus of English Words and Phrases, Classified and Arranged so as to Facilitate the Expression of Ideas and Assist in Literary Composition, by Peter Mark Roget. Enlarged by John Lewis Roget, newly revised and enlarged by Samuel Romilly Roget. London: Longmans Green & Co., 1925. 691p.

Thesaurus of English Words and Phrases, Classified and Arranged so as to Facilitate the Expression of Ideas and Assist in Literary Composition, by Peter Mark Roget. Enlarged by John Lewis Roget. New ed., revised and enlarged by Samuel Romilly Roget. London: Longmans, Green & Co., 1936. 705p.

Thesaurus of English Words and Phrases, by Peter Mark Roget. New Edition completely Revised and Modernized by Robert A. Dutch. London: Longmans, 1962. 1,309p.

Roget's Thesaurus of English Words and Phrases, by Peter Mark Roget. New edition prepared by Susan M. Lloyd. London: Longman, 1982. 1,247p.

Roget's Thesaurus of English Words and Phrases, by Peter Mark Roget. New edition prepared by Betty Kirkpatrick. London: Longman, 1987. 1,254p.

BIBLIOGRAPHY

Significant secondary literature concerning Peter Mark Roget's *Thesaurus* remains relatively small despite the work's length of tenure and mass distribution. The bulk of the writing consists of short, descriptive reviews of the original and subsequent editions issued by Longman and other publishers. Only reviews of the original edition are included in this bibliography. Noteworthy reviews of subsequent Longman editions have been noted within the text. Two works of some depth stand out: Margaret Anderson's dissertation which delves into the intellectual history and organization of the *Thesaurus,* and D.L. Emblen's biography which places its writing and history within the context of Roget's life and the times in which he lived. Robert Dutch's preface to his 1962 edition gives the best explanation of significant format changes made to the original and retained in subsequent editions. Susan Lloyd's piece, "Dr. Peter Mark Roget and his Thesaurus," within the 1982 edition outlines a concise publishing history of Longman editions, a history brought up to date in McArthur's "The Redoubtable Roget."

Anderson, Margaret Edna. "Roget's Thesaurus: An Explanation of Its Purpose and a Study of Some Applications of Its Principles." Ph.D. dissertation, Case Western Reserve University, 1978.

Chapman, Robert L. "Roget's Thesaurus and Semantic Structure: A Proposal for Work." *Language Sciences* 31 (August, 1974): 27–31.

Douglas, George H. "What's Happened to the Thesaurus?" *RQ* 16 (Winter, 1976): 149–55.

Dutch, Robert A. "Preface to the Revised Edition 1962." In *Roget's Thesaurus of English Words and Phrases,* edited by Robert A. Dutch. London: Longmans, 1962.

Egan, Rose F. "Survey of the History of English Synonymy." In *Webster's Dictionary of Synonyms* Springfield, MA: G. & C. Merriam Co., 1942.

Emblen, D. L. "Dr. Roget: His Book." *The Bookseller* no. 3399 (February 13, 1971): 412–16.

———. "Peter Mark Roget: A Centenary Bibliography." *Bibliographical Society of America Papers* 62 (July, 1968): 436–47.

———. Peter Mark *Roget: The Word and the Man.* New York: Thomas Y. Crowell, 1970.

Lloyd, Susan M. "Dr. Peter Mark Roget and his Thesaurus." In *Roget's Thesaurus of English Words and Phrases,* edited by Susan M. Lloyd. London: Longman, 1982.

McArthur, Tom. "The Redoubtable Roget." *English Today,* no. 12 (October, 1987): 36–39.

———. *Worlds of Reference.* Cambridge: Cambridge University Press, 1986.

Ober, William B. "Peter Mark Roget: Utilitarian and Lexicographer." *New York State Journal of Medicine* 65 (July, 1965): 1804–07.

Proceedings of the Royal Society of London. 18 (June 17, 1969–June 16, 1870): xxviii–xl.

Review of *Thesaurus of English Words and Phrases,* by Peter Mark Roget. *The Athenaeum* no. 1297 (September 4, 1852): 939.

Review of *Thesaurus of English Words and Phrases,* by Peter Mark Roget. *The Critic* 11 (June 15, 1852): 320.

Review of *Thesaurus of English Words and Phrases,* by Peter Mark Roget. *The Eclectic Review* n.s. 4 (July-December, 1852): 623.

Review of *Thesaurus of English Words and Phrases,*
by Peter Mark Roget. *The Westminster Review*
59 (April, 1853): 311

[Whipple, Edwin P.] "The Use and Misuse of Words."
North American Review 79 (July 1854): 137–
157.

NOTES

[1] Peter Mark Roget, "Introduction," in *Thesaurus of English Words and Phrases, New Edition, Enlarged and Improved, partly from the Author's Notes, and with a full Index,* ed. John Lewis Roget (Boston: DeWolfe, Fiske, & Co., 1879), xiii. Italics in original. Roget's introduction to the first edition is reprinted in many subsequent editions and printings.

[2] Ibid, xv.

[3] *Proceedings of the Royal Society of London* 18 (June 17, 1869–June 16, 1870): xxix.

[4] D. L. Emblen, *Peter Mark Roget: The Word and the Man* (New York: Thomas Y. Crowell. 1970), 17.

[5] Ibid., 43.

[6] Ibid., 53–54.

[7] Emblen, *Peter Mark Roget: The Word and the Man,* 96. Italics in original.

[8] *Proceedings of the Royal Society of London,* xxxviii–xxxv.

[9] Susan M. Lloyd, "Dr. Peter Mark Roget and his Thesaurus," in *Roget's Thesaurus of English Words and Phrases,* New edition prepared by Susan M. Lloyd (London & Harlow: Longman, 1982), xiv.

[10] Emblen, *Peter Mark Roget: The Word and the Man,* 138.

[11] *Proceedings of the Royal Society of London,* xxxviii.

[12] Emblen, *Peter Mark Roget: The Word and Man,* 119.

[13] Emblen, "Peter Mark Roget: A Centenary Bibliography," *Bibliographical Society of America Papers* 62 (July 1968): 441–43.

[14] Peter Mark Roget, *Animal and Vegetable Physiology Considered with Reference to Natural Theology* (Philadelphia: Carey, Lea & Blanchard, 1836), 1: xiii. Further mention of this in the text will be to its popular name, Bridgewater Treatise.

[15] Emblen, *Peter Mark Roget: The Word and the Man,* 200.

[16] Ibid., 244–52.

[17] Lloyd, "Dr. Peter Mark Roget and his Thesaurus," xv.

[18] Ibid.

[19] Margaret Edna Anderson, "Roget's Thesaurus: An Explanation of Its Purpose and a Study of Some Applications of Its Principles" Ph.D. dissertation, Case Western Reserve University, 1978, 70–71.

[20] Roget, "Introduction," xxxvii–xxix.

[21] Ibid., xv. Italics in original.

[22] Ibid., xvi.

[23] Ibid., xxix.

[24] Anderson, "Roget's Thesaurus," 89–90.

[25] Ibid., 91.

[26] Roget, "Introduction," xiii–xiv.

[27] Ibid., xv.

[28] Ibid., xxii.

[29] Emblen, *Peter Mark Roget: The Word and the Man,* 264.

[30] Rose F. Egan, "Survey of the History of English Synonymy," in *Webster's Dictionary of Synonyms* (Springfield, MA: G. & C. Merriam Co., 1942), ix.

[31] Ibid., xiii.

[32] Emblen, *Peter Mark Roget: The Word and the Man,* 265.

[33] Egan, "Survey of the History of English Synonymy," in *Webster's Dictionary of Synonyms* (Springfield, MA: G. & C. Merriam Co., 1942), xiv.

[34] Anderson, 114, 117.

[35] Roget, "Introduction," xxviii.

[36] Anderson, 127.

[37] Roget, *Animal and Vegetable Physiology,* 1: 31.

[38] Anderson, 130–31.

[39] Egan, xvii.

[40] Roget, "Introduction," xx.

[41] Ibid., xix.

[42] Lloyd, "Dr. Peter Mark Roget and his Thesaurus," xvi.

[43] Review of *Thesaurus of English Words and Phrases,* by Peter Mark Roget, *The Athenaeum,* no. 1297 (4 September 1852): 939.

[44] Review of *Thesaurus of English Words and Phrases,* by Peter Mark Roget, *The Critic* 11 (15 June 1852): 320.

[45] Review of *Thesaurus of English Words and Phrases,* by Peter Mark Roget, *The Eclectic Review* n.s., 4 (July–December 1852): 623.

[46] Ibid. Italics in the original.

[47] Review of *Thesaurus of English Words and Phrases,* by Peter Mark Roget, *The Westminster Review* 59 (April 1853): 311.

[48] Samuel Austin Allibone, *A Critical Dictionary of English Literature and British and American Authors* (Philadelphia: J.B. Lippincott Company, 1900), 2: 1857.

[49] [E. P. Whipple], "The Use and Misuse of Words," North American Review 79 (July 1854): 138

[50] Mary Dee Harris Fosberg, "Dylan Thomas's Use of Roget's Thesaurus during Composition of *Poem on his Birthday,*" *Bibliographical Society of America Papers* 72 (October 1978): 505.

[51] Roget, John Lewis, "Editor's Preface," in *Thesaurus of English Words and Phrases, New Edition, Enlarged and Improved, partly from the Author's Notes, and with a full Index,* ed. John Lewis Roget (Boston: DeWolfe, Fiske, & Co., 1879), vii–xi.

[52] Review of *Thesaurus of English Words and Phrases,* by Peter Mark Roget, enlarged by John Lewis Roget, newly revised and enlarged by Samuel Romilly Roget, *Dial* 80 (May 1926): 431.

[53] Lloyd, "Dr. Peter Mark Roget and his Thesaurus," xvii.

[54] Robert A. Dutch, "Preface to the Revised Edition 1962," in *The Original Roget's Thesaurus of English Words and Phrases,* New Edition completely Revised and Modernized by Robert A. Dutch (New York: St. Martin's Press, 1965): ix.

55 Ibid., xiii.

56 Lloyd, "Dr. Peter Mark Roget and his Thesaurus," xviii.

57 Bunt, G.H.V., review of *Roget's Thesaurus of English Words and Phrases*, New Edition completely Revised and Modernized by Robert A. Dutch, *English Studies* 44 (1963): 155.

58 Susan M. Lloyd, "Preface to the 1982 Edition," in *Roget's Thesaurus of English Words and Phrases* New edition prepared by Susan M. Lloyd (London & Harlow: Longman, 1982), x–xi.

59 Anthony Quinton, "Articles of Association," *Times Literary Supplement* no. 4131 (4 June 1982): 605; John Weightman, "Canute-like Gestures," *Times Educational Supplement* no. 3438 (21 May 1982): 41; "Zonked by a Ms.: A Woman Updates Roget," *Time* 119 (10 May 1982): 101;

60 Lloyd, "Preface," xi.

61 Weightman, 41; "Zonked by a Ms," 101.

62 Review of *Roget's Thesaurus of English Words and Phrases*, New edition prepared by Susan M. Lloyd *The Indexer* 13 (October 1982): 132.

63 Tom McArthur, "The Redoubtable Roget," *English Today*, no. 12 (October 1987): 39.

64 J.A. Gordon, review of *Roget's Thesaurus of English Words and Phrases*, New edition prepared by Betty Kirkpatrick *The Indexer* 16 (April 1988): 63.

65 Review of *Thesaurus of English Words and Phrases*, by Peter Mark Roget, *Putnam's Monthly Magazine of American Literature, Science & Art* 6 (September 1855): 318.

66 Andrew Delahunty, Longman Dictionaries Publisher, letter to the author, 1 June 1990.

67 "Publisher's Preface," *Roget's International Thesaurus*, 3rd ed. (New York: Thomas Y. Crowell Company, 1962): x–xi.

68 Andrew Delahunty, letter to the author, 1 June 1990.

69 Ibid.

70 Emblen, *Peter Mark Roget: The Word and the Man*, 278.

71 Andrew Delahunty, letter to the author, 1 June 1990.

72 Ibid.

73 Robert L. Chapman, "Roget's *Thesaurus* and Semantic Structure: A Proposal for Work," *Language Sciences* 31 (August 1974): 28.

74 Lloyd, "Dr. Peter Mark Roget and his Thesaurus," xviii.

Eugene Garfield's Contribution to Bibliography: *Science Citation Index*

David A. Tyckoson

DEVELOPMENT AND HISTORY

Of the hundreds of new reference works published each year, very few provide unique access points to information already covered by other sources. Even fewer reference tools are able to influence the evaluation of the information that they contain. And it is extremely rare that a reference work is responsible for creating an entirely new discipline of scientific research. The *Science Citation Index* is one of the rare reference works that has had just such an impact. By allowing researchers to identify materials that are not retrievable through other indexes, by enabling the evaluation of scientific research through the measurement of the citation rates of individual papers and journals, and by providing the primary instrument for the study of citation analysis, the *Science Citation Index* is responsible for each of the above effects. The impact of the *Science Citation Index* has been so widespread that it truly deserves a place as one of the landmarks of references work.

The *Science Citation Index* (along with its more recent cousins the *Social Sciences Citation Index* and the *Arts and Humanities Citation Index*) owes its existence to the genius, entrepreneurial nature, and vision of its creator, Eugene Garfield. In the early 1950s, Garfield was a graduate student in chemistry and participated in a medical indexing project at Johns Hopkins University. By working on this project, he realized that the references at the end of each published scientific article could be interpreted as indexing statements about the contents of that article. However, he did not yet know how to translate these references into a useful information tool. It was only through a chance encounter with a publisher in the field of law that he gained the insight that resulted in the concept of the *SCI*.

An Example from Law

After organizing a conference on the topic of machine methods in scientific documentation in 1953, he was contacted by one of the publishers of *Shepard's Citations* (Colorado Springs: Shepherd's McGraw-Hill, 1873–), who suggested that a scientific index could be established along the same principles as this 80-year-old legal reference tool. Upon examining *Shepard's Citations*, the existence of which Garfield had been entirely unaware, he immediately realized that a similar publication was needed for the sciences. According to Garfield, "It was a eureka experience that was a supreme moment in my career."[1] In very short order, he obtained his library degree from Columbia University, published a paper on "Citation Indexes for Science" in the journal *Science*,[2] organized the Institute for Scientific Information, and began a revolution in scientific information retrieval by publishing the first volume of the *Science Citation Index* in 1961. Over the past 30 years, the Institute has grown into a multimillion dollar enterprise, Garfield has become a millionaire in his own right, and the *Science Citation Index* has become one of the most valuable and respected reference tools in all of the sciences.

The *Science Citation Index* succeeded because it took an entirely different approach to organizing, indexing, and retrieving information than that used in any previous index of scientific information. Several features set it apart from any other scientific indexing or abstracting services. First of all, it is an *interdisciplinary* index of scientific literature. Whereas most other indexes in the sciences attempt to cover a single scientific discipline, such as chemistry, biology, or computer science, the *SCI* includes information from all fields of the sciences. Other than the *General Science Index* (New York: H.W. Wilson, 1978–), which is aimed at an undergraduate rather than a research audience, all other scientific journal indexes are limited to a single scientific discipline. The interdisciplinary aspect of the *SCI* enables researchers to identify material that they could not find by searching only the indexes related to any one specific subject field and also facilitates the exchange of information from one field to another. One of the objectives for creating the *SCI* was to increase scientific communication across existing disciplines, and the nature of its design has enabled it to perform admirably in this area.

Selective Coverage

Secondly, the *Science Citation Index* is a highly *selective* index. Rather than attempt to index all of the literature in any given discipline, the *SCI* covers only a few source journals from each field. With more than 50,000 scientific journals currently being published worldwide, it is impossible for any indexing service to cover all of the sciences comprehensively without being overwhelmed by source material. In order to avoid this problem, the *SCI* only indexes a relatively few key scientific journals. However, the journals that are selected for indexing in the *SCI* are carefully chosen to represent only the most significant and most important titles from each area of the sciences. In order to accurately judge a journal's significance to the field, the editors of the *SCI* choose source journals based upon their impact factor, a statistically derived value related in part to the number of articles that they publish, the number of articles that are cited by other researchers, and the number of times that the journal cites itself.

From the 50,000-plus scientific journals available worldwide, the *SCI* selects only slightly more than 3,000 as source titles. Although representing only between 5 and 10 percent of the world's scientific output, these 3,000 journals contain representatives from all scientific disciplines and originate from more than 40 nations. The only common feature of the journals selected is the fact that they represent the most significant sources for their respective subject areas. Although there has been some debate about the validity of ranking scientific journals, the statistical procedures used to calculate the impact factor of each journal ensures that only the most significant sources are included in this reference tool.

The statistical selection procedure for journal selection has another effect on the *Science Citation Index*. Although most indexing services maintain a stable or slowly growing list of source titles, the list of titles covered by the *SCI* changes every year even though the number of titles indexed remains constant. Individual journal titles move onto or off of the source list as their impact factors change. As a journal becomes a more significant source in its field and rises in importance, it may become one of the source journals for the *SCI*. If a journal loses its status in the field, it may be dropped from coverage. The statistical basis for the selection of source journals for the *SCI* not only allows the index to identify the most important journals, it also serves as an evaluation tool for researchers in deciding which sources are the most important and most relevant to a specific discipline. The mere fact that a journal is indexed by the *SCI* is an indication that it is one of the most valuable titles in its field. The *Science Citation Index* is frequently used not only to identify relevant research, but to rank that research on the basis of the source in which it was published.[3]

Another difference between *SCI* and other scientific indexing services is that once a journal is selected for inclusion in the *SCI*, it is indexed from *cover to cover*. Once selected for indexing, the editors of the *SCI* do not attempt to place any judgments on the value of the information published in a source journal. Whereas other subject indexes tend to only index feature articles, the *SCI* covers everything, including research reports, notes, review articles, letters to the editor, and even book reviews from some of its source journals. Only the news notes and advertising are not indexed by the *SCI*. The theory behind cover-to-cover indexing is relatively simple. Because the *SCI* indexes only the most significant journals in the field, any information contained in those journals has been preselected as belonging to the set of the most important and valuable published scientific information. If information is published in any of the journals selected by the *SCI*, then that information must by definition be of value to the scientific community and should not be lost solely due to a quirk in the indexing process. Because of this policy, information may often be retrieved through the *SCI* that cannot be found by using other reference works that index the same titles on a selective basis.

Subject Access

Subject indexing in the *SCI* is also organized differently than in any other journal index. The *SCI* uses what it calls a "Permuterm Subject Index," which can best be described as a pre-coordinate keyword title index. With the exception of a few stopwords, each of the terms used in the titles of the source articles is placed into a single index file. Those terms are then matched with every other keyword used in each source title. The resulting output is a subject index that allows the researcher to conduct a two-term Boolean search. Within

the limits of keyword indexing, a researcher is able to search the *SCI* under any one term and conceptually combine that term with any others. Although differences in the usage of subject terms must be taken into account, no other scientific subject index allows this type of combination of subject terms.

Citation Access

The final and most noteworthy feature of the *Science Citation Index* is that it indexes not only the articles contained in each of the source journals, but also the bibliographies at the end of each of those articles. Any citation that is contained within one of the source journals is included, regardless of its date of publication, its geographic origin, or the format of the material. Whether a paper cites a recent journal article, a book published during the previous decade, a technical report from World War II, a manuscript from the Middle Ages, or all of the above, each reference is entered independently into the *SCI* database. A computer program is used to reverse the order of the citation information, creating an index in which researchers may identify any new source material that has cited a specific publication from the past. By indexing the references at the end of each article, researchers using the *SCI* are able to identify all new works that have a logical connection with a work from the past. This ability to search citations forwards in time has revolutionized the method in which many scientists find information.

A Multi-Faceted Tool

Through the concept of citation indexing for the sciences, the *SCI* not only created a new reference work for retrieving scientific information, but also provided the primary research tool for the field of citation analysis. Without the existence of the *SCI*, citation analysis would most likely have remained a theoretical rather than practical science. Although it would have been possible to track citations forwards in time without the *SCI*, the time and labor involved in conducting even a single search would have outweighed the usefulness of the results. However, by using the *SCI*, researchers have been able to study citation frequencies of individual researchers, specific journals, scientific disciplines, and even entire nations.[4] None of these studies would have been possible without this tool. In the field of citation analysis, the *Science Citation Index* is not only a compendium of research results, but it is also the laboratory in which that research is conducted.

The *SCI* has also created an entirely new method for evaluating scientific research. Based upon the simple principle that important and useful research results are cited and that unimportant or irrelevant research results are not cited, the quality of research of an individual scientist may be measured by examining the number of times that his or her work is cited. In theory, an individual whose papers have been cited ten times has had a greater impact in the field than an individual whose papers have been cited only once. In addition, since the *SCI* selects only the most important journals for its source information, this evaluation process is refined even further by eliminating citations by those journals that are not considered to be the core materials in their field. The *SCI* thus gives an indication not only of how frequently an individual's work is being used, but also how frequently it is being used by the best researchers in the field.

The use of the *Science Citation Index* to evaluate scientific information has been one of its most controversial applications. Although this method of evaluation was at first advocated by Eugene Garfield as a natural extension of citation analysis, the problems associated with relying strictly upon the number of times an article is cited to determine its scientific value have led him to issue several warnings about the value of this procedure.[5] Nonetheless, citation counts are frequently used as justifications for appointments, promotions,

or research funding.[6] To many librarians, it may seem that one of the most frequent uses of the *SCI* on university campuses is by faculty members searching for citations to their own research so that they can provide that information to promotion and tenure committees. Whether such a use of this reference tool is appropriate or inappropriate, it is a testament to the degree to which the *Science Citation Index* has become an accepted authority within the scientific community.

To fully understand the dramatic impact that the *SCI* has had on scientific information retrieval, it is necessary to have an understanding of the culture of scientific publishing. Scientific tradition dictates that all new research results acknowledge the use of any previously known information, theory, and/or methodology that was used in the derivation of the new material. By including a bibliography of references to previous works, each scientific author is able to give credit to the work of the past researchers who provided background material for the latest results. This tradition is strictly followed in the sciences; it has become extremely rare to see a report of new findings that does not include any references to previous research papers. Citations formally acknowledge that science is a growing body of knowledge and that each piece of new research builds upon past research.

Backward and Forward in Time

In addition to serving as an acknowledgement of earlier work, the scientific citation relationship is one that has been used by researchers for decades as a tool for the identification of other relevant publications on a specific topic. Researchers frequently rely upon the bibliographies at the end of an article to link them with other relevant materials dealing with the same subject matter. The citation relationship provides a unique association between the cited and citing articles that may not be identified by traditional subject or author indexes. When one author makes a reference to another author's work, there is a clear indication that the work of both individuals revolves around some common theme. They may be discussing the same subject material, using the same experimental methods, applying the same theory, disputing the same concepts, or using the same applications of the work of a third party. In any case, the fact that one paper cites another clearly identifies a common thread between the two. When a researcher is able to identify a paper on a topic of interest, the references at the end of that paper will almost always lead to other useful and related sources.

The tracing of bibliographic citations at the end of a research paper has become a standard research method, but it has one major disadvantage—it only works backward in time. An article published in 1990 may cite other sources from a wide range of dates, but it cannot cite materials published in 1991 or 1992 or any other date later than that of its own publication. Researchers who trace citations are able to track down useful sources from the past, but cannot find more recent information. If a search begins with an article that is five years old, there is no possibility of retrieving any newer materials by tracing its references. Although a wide range of sources from the past may be identified, the researcher will never be able to find anything published during the last five years.

The most valuable and most revolutionary aspect of the *Science Citation Index* is its ability to reverse this process. Because *SCI* indexes all of the references at the end of each source article, it allows researchers to trace citations in reverse. By using the "Citation Index" portion of the *SCI* researchers are able to look up an old article and find all of the new articles that have included the original in their bibliographies. Beginning with a single relevant article, a researcher may search backwards in time by studying the bibliography at the end of the source article and may also search forwards in time by searching the citation index to determine if the original article

has been cited recently by any of the papers included in the source journals. Starting with a single relevant research paper, a scientist can use the *SCI* to identify all other important materials dealing with the same concept, regardless of the format in which they are published, their country of origin, or date of publication. No other scientific journal index is able to provide such broad subject, geographic, and temporal coverage.

If the statistical basis for the selection of the source journals is accepted, the *Science Citation Index* becomes more than just a powerful research tool. Based upon the general principle that important scientific research is cited and that unimportant scientific research is ignored, the *SCI* for any given time period becomes a complete record of all scientific research that was considered to be important during that period. Any valuable new information will be indexed if it appears in one of the source journals used by the *SCI*. In addition, any significant research from the past will be included if it was cited by the authors of the articles included in the source journals. If a paper is not included in either one of the source journals or one of its citations, that paper cannot be considered a part of the core of scientific information for that time period. What the *SCI* achieves that no other journal index achieves is the identification, evaluation, and indexing of all relevant information published anywhere in the world from throughout all of history. This may be the greatest achievement of the *Science Citation Index*.

Problematic Issues

Despite its overwhelming success, the *Science Citation Index* is not without its problems. By relying solely upon the bibliographies of thousands of different authors to identify relevant citation information, the *SCI* is completely lacking in consistency in its citation format. Although Eugene Garfield initially proposed a uniform system of citation for scientific journals,[7] that system has never been adopted and the *SCI* cites each source exactly as indicated by each individual author. This results in several variant entries for many papers due to variations in the forms of the names and/or source titles. In addition to spelling differences, the work of many authors is lost because the *SCI* cites only the first author listed for any scientific paper. This policy has become a tremendous problem over the last two decades as the average number of authors for a scientific paper has risen dramatically. Subject indexing is also a problem because the *SCI* relies upon the keywords in the titles of the articles to create its subject index. Differences in terminology and variations in the usage of that terminology may combine to frustrate researchers who are using *SCI* strictly as a subject index. Despite these inconveniences, such inconsistencies have been accepted as a compromise against the tremendous costs in time and labor that would be required to create an authority file for all of the author names, source titles, and subject terms used by the *SCI*.

Other problems with the *SCI* are related to the sheer volume of information contained in the index. In the 1988 annual edition, the *SCI* indexed more than 600,000 source articles and 10,000,000 citations. Due to the tremendous size of the database, the printed edition is published using extremely small and difficult-to-read type. This is particularly true in the "Citation Index" portion of the work, where many users rely on magnification to retrieve the information from the printed page. Once again, this publishing decision is made as a conscious effort on the part of the publishers to reduce the costs associated with printing and distributing such an index. Despite these efforts to save space, a single annual edition now occupies almost four feet of shelf space.

More recently, electronic versions of the database have been introduced through online vendors and on CD-ROM. While these versions may reduce the problems of readability, they magnify the problems associated with the lack of authority control by reducing the capability of the reader to browse the index files and thereby spot variant forms of a person's name. Regardless of its format, the *SCI* requires a significant investment of time by the user to take full advantage of its unique capabilities. However, this investment is well worth the return in the retrieval of additional information sources that do not appear in other reference tools.

As may be expected with a work of this magnitude, one of the most notable features of the *SCI* is its price. The *Science Citation Index* has always been one of the most expensive reference tools on the market. With an annual cost of $8,850 in 1990, a subscription to the *SCI* is one of the largest investments that most institutions will make in any single information source. However, the high cost of the work is offset by the value of the information it contains. In these difficult economic times when libraries are considering the cancellation of expensive scientific journals and indexes, the *SCI* rarely comes up for consideration. This in itself is a testament to the usefulness and value of this unique reference tool.

As it enters its fourth decade of publication, the *Science Citation Index* has become one of the standard reference tools in its field. However, its impact on science has clearly been much greater than if it had been just another index. While most reference works help users to think about the subjects that they cover, the *Science Citation Index* gives its users new ways to think about its subject matter. For this achievement, the *Science Citation Index* has been one of the most significant advancements in the history of bibliography.

PUBLICATION HISTORY

Science Citation Index. Philadelphia: Institute for Scientific Information, 1961– Bimonthly.

The *Science Citation Index* (*SCI*) began publication in 1961 as a quarterly index with annual cumulations. Beginning with the 1979 edition, frequency increased to bimonthly. Quinquennial cumulations are available for the periods of 1965–1969, 1970–1974, 1975–1979, and 1980–1984. Retrospective decennial cumulations covering the years 1955–1964 and 1945–1954 were published in 1984 and 1988 respectively. The publisher intends to continue producing annual editions while at the same time extending retrospective coverage back to the beginning of the twentieth century. Each volume of the *SCI* consists of 4 distinct parts. The "Source Index" contains references to journal articles arranged by personal or corporate author. The "Permuterm Subject Index" provides a keyword subject in-dex to all articles in the "Source Index." All of the keywords used in the subject index are derived directly from the titles of the articles included in the "Source Index." The "Citation Index" consists of an index to all of the bibliographic references contained in these same source materials. These three sections comprise the main body of the *Science Citation Index*. The final portion of the work is the "Journal Citation Reports," which provides statistical information on the citation rates and impact factors of each source journal included by the index. The 1988 complete annual edition consists of 20 bound volumes plus a separate index guide.

BIBLIOGRAPHY

As one of the few reference works that has spawned an entirely new field of study, the *Science Citation Index* has been thoroughly discussed in the professional literature. From works on the theory of the citation relationship to studies of the literature of individual subject fields, the *Science Citation Index* has played a role in hundreds of articles over the past 35 years. Many of these articles have been collected in an eight-volume set by Eugene Garfield, *Essays of an Information Scientist*. This set includes all of Garfield's writings as well as important other materials related to citation analysis and is the first source to consult for material on this work. The editors of the *Science Citation Index* are also highly cognizant of the impact of the *SCI* on the literature and maintain a bibliography of relevant materials in the introductory section of each annual cumulation. This bibliography is useful for anyone interested in finding other published sources about citation anaylsis, the *SCI*, or its related products.

Aaronson, Steve. "The Footnotes of Science." *Mosaic* 6 (March/April, 1975): 22–27.

Adair, W.C. "Citation Indexes for Scientific Literature." *American Documentation* 6 (1955): 31–32.

Brahmi, Frances A. "Reference Use of Science Citation Index." *Medical Reference Services Quarterly* 4 (Spring, 1985): 31–38.

Cawkell, Anthony E. "Science Perceived Through the Science Citation Index." *Endeavour* 1 (1977): 57–62.

———. "Search Strategies Using the Science Citation Index." In *Computer Based Information Retrieval Systems*, edited by Bernard Houghton. London: Clive Bingley Ltd., 1968.

Garfield, Eugene. "Citation Analysis As a Tool for Journal Evaluation." *Science* 178 (November 2, 1972): 471–79.

———. "Citation Indexes for Science." *Science* 122 (July 15, 1955): 108–11.

———. "Citation Indexing for Studying Science." *Nature* 227 (1970): 669–71.

———. *Citation Indexing: Its Theory and Application in Science, Technology, and Humanities.* New York: Wiley, 1979.

———. *Essays of an Information Scientist.* 8 Vols. Philadelphia: ISI Press, 1977–1986.

———. "How to Use the Science Citation Index." *Current Contents* 9 (February 28, 1983): 5–14. Reprinted annually in the *Index Guide to the Science Citation Index.*

———. "Is Citation Analysis a Legitimate Evaluation Tool?" *Scientometrics* 1 (1979): 167–80.

———. "Permuterm Subject Index: An Autobiographical Review." *Journal of the American Society for Information Science* 27 (September, 1976): 288–91.

———. "Science Citation Index: A New Dimension in Indexing." *Science* 144 (May 8, 1964): 649–54.

Herther, Nancy K. "Bringing Citation Indexes to CD-ROM: An Interview with Eugene Garfield." *Laserdisk Professional* 2 (July, 1989): 25–32.

Huang, Theodore S. "Efficacy of Citation Indexing in Reference Retrieval." *Library Resources and Technical Services* 12 (1968): 415–34.

Lazerow, Samuel. "Institute for Scientific Information." In *Encyclopedia of Library and Information Science*, edited by Allen Kent. New York: Marcell Dekker, 1974. Vol. 12: 89–97.

"Librarian Turned Entrepreneur Makes Millions Off Mere Footnotes." *Science* 202 (November 24, 1978): 853–57.

Malin, Morton V. "Science Citation Index: A New Concept in Indexing." *Library Trends* 16 (January, 1968): 374–87.

Margolis, J. "Citation Indexing and Evaluation of Scientific Papers." *Science* 155 (March 10, 1967): 1213–19.

Miller, Elizabeth, and Eugenia Truesdell. "Citation Indexing: History and Applications." *Drexel Library Quarterly* 8 (April, 1972): 159–72.

Narin, Francis, and Mark P. Carpenter. "National Publication and Citation Comparisons." *Journal of the American Society for Information Science* 26 (1975): 80–93.

Poyer, Robert K. "Journal Article Overlap Among *Index Medicus*, *Science Citation Index*, *Biological Abstracts*, and *Chemical Abstracts*." *Bulletin of the Medical Library Association* 72 (1984): 353–57.

Wade, Nicholas. "Citation Analysis: A New Tool for Science Administrators." *Science* 188 (May 2, 1975): 429–32.

Weinstock, Melvin. "Citation Indexes." In *Encyclopedia of Library and Infvolormation Science*, edited by Allen Kent. New York: Marcel Dekker, 1974. Vol. 5: 16–40.

NOTES

[1] "Librarian Turned Entrepreneur Makes Millions Off Mere Footnotes," *Science* 202 (24 November 1978): 853–57.

[2] Eugene Garfield, "Citation Indexes for Science," *Science* 122 (15 July 1955): 108–11.

[3] Eugene Garfield, "Significant Journals of Science," *Nature* 264 (16 December 1976): 609–15.

[4] Henry Small and Eugene Garfield, "The Geography and Mapping of Science: Disciplinary and National Mappings," *Journal of Information Science* 11 (1985): 147–59.

[5] Eugene Garfield, "Is Citation Analysis a Legitimate Evaluation Tool?" *Scientometrics* 1 (1979): 167–80.

[6] Nicholas Wade, "Citation Analysis: A New Tool for Science Administrators," *Science* 188 (2 May 1975): 429–32.

[7] Garfield, "Citation Indexes for Science," 109.

"The Baby Figure of the Giant Mass": Pollard & Redgrave's and Wing's Short-Title Catalogues

Robert W. Melton

And in such indexes (although small pricks
To their subsequent volumes) there is seen
The baby figure of the giant mass
Of things to come at large.
> —Shakespeare, *Troilus and*
> *Cressida* I, iii, 343–46

DEVELOPMENT AND HISTORY

Although the first bibliography examined in this survey was not published until 1926,[1] its roots go back at least to 1884 and thus it might be thought of, along with the *Dictionary of National Biography* and the *Oxford English Dictionary*, as one of the three great reference works of Victorian Britain, together representing our attempts to record the history of our individual achievements, our language, and our printed legacy. Efforts to record the bibliographic output of a particular culture are as old as libraries insofar as individual libraries have attempted to acquire exhaustively all culturally important publications and provide public records of their holdings. However, because of the scarcity of many publications—whether due to short print runs, political or religious suppression, natural or manmade disasters—as well as the financial restrictions on most libraries and the inevitable belief that some types of publications are not worth acquiring, no single repository, even those which benefit from copyright deposit laws, can serve as the basis for such a record.

The Justification for Short-Title Catalogues

If it is necessary to first ask why an enumerative or systematic bibliography of the printed products of a culture is worth compiling in the first place, perhaps the best and simplest answer has been given by Roy B. Stokes, who reminds us that "before books can be studied, they must be known to exist."[2] This principle is important not only for proving the existence of a work which, as in the majority of cases, appeared in only one edition. It is also vitally important for textual scholars and compilers of critical editions, whose goal is the determination or reconstruction of the text of a frequently published work to a state as close to its author's original (or final) intentions as possible. (Such work, of course, involves the study of all extant manuscripts as well as printed editions.)

A bibliography may be devoted to the works of a particular writer, group of writers, or organization; to imprints of a particular press or printer or to those from a particular geographical entity; to works in a particular genre; to works intended or appropriate for a particular reader group; or to works on a particular subject. Although Stokes believes a bibliography must always strive for completeness within its chosen parameters, in the last three cases completeness becomes problematical as issues of definition are involved. Therefore, any of these may be, and often are, further limited by chronology or language in an effort to increase the chances of completeness within the chosen parameters, increase its effectiveness for the desired users, or simply make its compilation realistically manageable. Chronological limits may be arbitrary or may be determined by historical events within either the publishing trade or the greater political or cultural environment. The bibliographies discussed in this survey are based primarily on language and date of publication but otherwise are intended to be comprehensive in coverage.

Efforts to record the printed output of England and its political or linguistic colonies regardless of subject, author, printer, or city of publication began in earnest with the publication in 1884—the same year as the first fascicle of the *Oxford English Dictionary*—of a three-volume *Catalogue of Books in the Library of the British Museum Printed in England, Scotland and Ireland and of English Books Printed Abroad, to the Year 1640* (London: The Museum), principally compiled by George Bullen, the Library's keeper of printed books, and containing some 13,600 entries.[3] A more detailed description of the Library's incunabula—most of which are not British imprints—was planned and begun toward the end of the century by R.G.C. Proctor and A.W. Pollard and, after the former's untimely death in the Alps in 1903, was Pollard's main responsibility in the Library's Department of Printed Books, which he had joined in 1883, for the next ten years. Entitled *A Catalogue of Books Printed in the XVth Century Now in the British Museum* (London: The Museum), the first volume was published in 1908.[4] Four hundred and thirty-one specifically English incunabula located in a variety of British and American collections were cataloged by E. Gordon Duff in *Fifteenth Century Books: A Bibliography of Books and Documents Printed in England and of Books for the English Market Printed Abroad* (London: The Bibliographical Society, 1917), for which Pollard wrote the preface. Pollard, Duff, Proctor, W.W. Greg, and other members of the Bibliographical

Society had also published, between 1895 and 1913, *Hand-lists of English Printers, 1501–1556*.[5]

Origins of the STC

These various efforts led Pollard to write a paper in early 1918 for the Bibliographical Society, of which he had been honorary secretary since a year after its founding in 1892, in which he suggested that it was now possible to attempt to compile a "short-title handlist" of all extant English books from the close of the fifteenth century through the year 1640.[6] The Society's vice-president, G.R. Redgrave, agreed to collaborate with Pollard in such an undertaking and to personally assist in its financing. At its meeting on April 22, 1918, the Society's Council passed a resolution accepting Redgrave's offer and agreed to publish such a catalog as soon as possible after its completion.[7] Pollard presented another paper outlining his proposal in more detail at the January 1919 annual meeting, and by this time he proposed to extend the date of coverage back to the year 1475, thereby adding Duff's coverage and using the same chronological parameters as the 1884 BM catalog, the Cambridge catalog of 1475–1640 books compiled by Charles Sayle, and Edward Arber's transcript of the Stationers' Company registers. (The *terminus ad quem* in all of these catalogs was chosen not so much for the historical fact of the Civil War itself as for the known existence of some 26,000 political and religious tracts printed during the 1640s and 1650s. Collected by the London publisher/bookseller George Thomason, the inclusion of these tracts, as it turned out, would have doubled the size of the project.[8]) The announcement of this enterprise was met with various offers of assistance, perhaps most importantly from the Bodleian Library at Oxford but also from other university libraries and private collectors in Great Britain, from such private research libraries as the Huntington,[9] and from the eminent antiquarian book firm of Bernard Quaritch. From the start, what would ultimately be published as *A Short-Title Cata-logue of Books Printed in England, Scotland, & Ireland and of English Books Printed Abroad, 1475–1640*[10] was, like the *DNB* and the *OED*, very much a group effort.

A. W. Pollard and G. R. Redgrave

The backgrounds and qualifications Pollard and Redgrave brought to the project differed considerably. In addition to his work in the Department of Printed Books, Alfred William Pollard (1859–1944)[11] published an edition of Chaucer in 1898 that was the most scholarly to date. Furthermore, he had been publishing articles on various bibliographical subjects for at least ten years before that and on fifteenth-century history and literature since 1876. But it was his pioneering work on the problems of Shakespeare's texts, particularly his *Shakespeare Folios and Quartos* of 1909 (London: Methuen), which secured his reputation as a literary and textual scholar. In the words of the eminent bibliographer W.W. Greg, this book was "by far the most systematic and critical work that had yet appeared on the subject and one that marked the opening of a new era in Shakespeare studies."[12] His investigations were continued in the 1915 Sandars Lectures in Bibliography at Cambridge, published two years later as *Shakespeare's Fight with the Pirates and the Problem of the Transmission of his Text* (London: A Moring), which fellow Shakespearean J. Dover Wilson called "at once sober and brilliant."[13] It was also Wilson who referred to the Bibliographical Society as Pollard's "brain-child."[14] Pollard also cared for his brain-child, serving as editor of its *Transactions* (later *The Library*) from 1900 until 1934.

Gilbert Richard Redgrave (1844–1941), on the other hand, although likewise a founding member of the Bibliographical Society, was an amateur in things bibliographical. His principal activities and interests were in the fields of engineering, architecture, and art history; he was a minor watercolorist whose works exhibit a pre-Raphaelite influence.[15]

Son of the more famous genre and landscape artist and art historian Richard Redgrave, his first publication was a compilation of his father's writings and addresses, published in 1876 as *Manual of Design* (London: Chapman & Hall). This was followed 15 years later by a monograph on the artists *David Cox and Peter De Wint* (London: Sampson Low; New York: Scribner's, 1891) and the following year by the still useful *A History of Water-Colour Painting in England* (London: Sampson Low; New York: Scribner's, 1892). The first of several editions of *Calcareous Cements: Their Nature and Uses* (London: C. Griffin) was published in 1895, and his coedited booklet *Deterioration of Structures of Timber, Metal, and Concrete Exposed to the Action of Sea-Water* (London: H.M.S.O.) was published for the Institution of Civil Engineers in 1926, the year *STC* was in press. As a young teen, Redgrave assisted in the design and construction of Royal Albert Hall and wrote its opening celebration's program. In 1878, he was architect to the Royal Commissioners of the Paris Exhibition and was awarded Officer of the Legion of Honour. In 1881, he began a career in educational supervision, first as secretary of the Royal Commission on Technical Institutes; from 1884 until 1897 as an inspector of schools, including the National Art Training School, under the Department of Sciences and Art; as chief senior inspector of technical schools under the Board of Education from 1897; and as assistant secretary to the Board from 1900. He presented several papers to the Bibliographical Society, of which he was president in 1908; at least four of these were published. The first, read in 1893, treated a fifteenth-century printer and was published as *Erhard Ratdolt and His Work at Venice* (London: The Bibliographical Society, 1894). Others, presented in 1895, 1896, and 1910, were subsequently published in the Society's *Transactions*. He was also a frequent contributor to the *Times Engineering Supplement*. He died in June 1941 at the age of 97.

Although *STC* is often referred to as "Pollard & Redgrave" and Redgrave's name is given equal prominence on the title page, the work was Pollard's brain-child from the start. According to Wilson, "it was generally recognized at the time, and should be made clear to posterity, that he was in more than formal sense editor-in-chief from the outset, and during the final stages himself shouldered the bulk of the work involved."[16] As the anonymous reviewer for the *Times Literary Supplement* more subtly put it, "it is not the least part of Mr. Pollard's achievement that, performing nobly, he has been the cause of noble performance in others."[17] Redgrave's noble performance was mostly his financial support for the project. In a letter to Pollard dated February 14, 1918, Redgrave offered 600 pounds for the project along with half his time for editorial work or general supervision and the use of his suburban London home as project headquarters. The exact nature or extent of Redgrave's editorial work is difficult to determine. Redgrave's involvement with *STC* is barely mentioned in his *Times* obituary,[18] and his name occurs only once in the preface to the second edition. No entry for Redgrave appeared in *DNB*.

Creating the STC

Once his project received the official blessing of the Society, Pollard set out in the highly methodical way of a trained bibliographer. Having for almost 20 years compiled slips for 1475–1640 English books in the Museum's Department of Printed Books, he proposed a system using cards of different colors for the holdings in the Bodleian, Cambridge, Rylands, and other libraries. (The pre-computer necessity of creating handwritten cards is one very practical reason why bibliographies of this scope have used "short-titles.") Progress was further slowed by other factors, including Pollard's promotion in 1919 to the keepership of printed books at a time of "great administrative difficulty" in the Library[19] and the deterioration of Redgrave's vision. The addition to the effort in 1922 of G.F. Barwick, who had been Pollard's immediate predecessor in

the keepership, was a major factor in its completion by 1924, as no doubt also were Pollard's "forthright style" and "alacrity in tackling new duties."[20] It was another two years in press and final revision.[21]

STC—the acronym received immediate currency—is, like the 1884 BM catalog and as its own not-so-short title makes clear, an attempt to list all works printed from the beginning of printing in England in 1475 through the year 1640 in the English language regardless of the place of printing, as well as all works printed in England, Scotland, Wales, and Ireland in any language, which had been seen by one of the compilers. The final caveat is important: works believed to have been printed, or merely found in previous catalogs, were excluded unless they had actually been examined in one of 148 libraries or collections in the U.K. or the U.S. A system of letter-number abbreviations, or sigla, is used to identify libraries which own each item, but usually no more than three British and two American locations are listed and usually no more than one in the same city, although for particularly rare items either of those rules could be broken. (Reflecting the principally literary interests of the Society's members, the rule was also frequently bent for plays and, as the *Times Literary Supplement* reviewer put it, "other exciting literature,"[22] regardless of rarity.) In this sense, *STC* is neither a true union catalog nor a census of copies; it may best be thought of as a finding-list as well as an enumerative bibliography. It should also be stressed that although sufficient information is (theoretically) presented to differentiate variant editions and issues, *STC* is not a descriptive bibliography such as Duff's catalog of incunabula. In the words of Benjamin Nangle, a compiler of a work of such scope as *STC* "could not aspire to become an expert on the bibliographical niceties of each individual volume."[23] This would be particularly true of a work as dependent as was *STC* on volunteers of varying degrees of bibliographical training. The "mixed character of its sources" in regard to the degree of bibliographic detail given is the basis of Pollard's admirably candid warning in the preface (p. vii) that the book remains "a dangerous work for any one to handle lazily, that is, without verification." After all, the catalog was intended as a "preliminary record of research, in preparation for a full-dress catalogue."

The word "books" has been avoided in the discussion of *STC* for the reason that from the beginning its compilers intended to record all printed items within their scope. As a result, *STC* contains references to extant broadsides, ballads, proclamations, and other works of a similar nature printed on one sheet. Books and sheets of music are included. Although serials as we think of them today, including newspapers, did not develop until after the Restoration in 1660, some publications of a serial nature, such as almanacs, calendars and prognostications, are included and listed together chronologically, as are official publications of the governments and ecclesiastical bodies of England, Scotland, and Ireland. (Unofficial works by a monarch or ecclesiastical official are entered under the individual's name).

The rules governing entry were taken from the 1884 British Museum catalog, which itself was derived from Anthony Panizzi's 91 rules, developed in the late 1830s. Most works are entered by author, including anonymous and pseudonymous works if there is "any general agreement as to the authorship" (p. xi); otherwise, unattributed works are entered by the first proper name in the title if there is one or, if not, by the first substantive—a practice widely criticized and dropped in most short-title catalogs compiled since. The subjectivity inherent in deciding what constitutes a "substantive" and the inconsistency in applying the rules, when multiplied by a dozen or more contributors, resulted in some titles being "hidden" under entries by which few would think to search. For example, "A solemne contestation of diuerse Popes out of their own canon law" (No. 20114) is entered under "Popes," even though it is not really a proper name and isn't the first substantive; "The

returne of the knight of the post from Hell, with the Diuels aunswere" (No. 20905) is entered under "return" even though Hell is a proper name; and "The passion of our lord" (No. 14557) is entered under the phrase "Jesus Christ," even though he wasn't the author and those words are not in the title as presented—and there are no cross-references from either "passion" or "lord." In numerous cases the application of the rules results in anonymous titles being entered under the last word: "A wonderfull and most lamentable declaration of the great hurt done in Erfford," for example, is entered under "Erfurt" (No. 10434). Variant editions or issues of the same work, of which there were many more than the editors had anticipated, are listed chronologically. In all, about 26,500 items are listed—almost double the number in the 1884 BM catalog—including just one not published in Europe: No. 2738, the so-called *Bay Psalm-Book*, printed by Stephen Day in Cambridge, Massachusetts, in 1640.

Impact of the STC

The publication of *STC* had immediate impact, not only among scholars of Renaissance British history and literature but in libraries and, perhaps most of all, in the book trade, where reference to an *STC* number in dealers' catalogs better enabled prospective buyers to know precisely what was being offered for sale. It rapidly gained a reputation as being "among bibliographical works . . . in a class by itself for its combination of authority and range of use"[24] and has been called "without apology . . . the best national imprint bibliography for any extended period of coverage."[25] Many research libraries annotated their copies of *STC* to indicate their own holdings and used the results to attempt to acquire desiderata, and several of those with major holdings, including the Newberry and the Huntington, published separate lists. A union checklist of *STC* titles in some 110 American libraries, compiled by William W.

Bishop, was published in 1944 (revised and updated in 1950) and other union checklists were published for the college libraries at Oxford and Cambridge.[26] Other bibliographers have compiled lists of particular exclusions from *STC*—for example M. A. Shaaber's *Checklist of Works of British Authors Printed Abroad, in Languages Other Than English, To 1641* (New York: Bibliographical Society of America, 1975), which includes items such as European editions of the Latin poems of John Donne. Pollard himself hinted in the preface, and further elaborated in a 1927 paper to the Society, of his plans to rearrange the entries in *STC* chronologically for, as he said, "to get all the books of a nation into as accurate chronological order as possible is one of the biggest things that bibliography can do."[27] But this projected *Annals of English Printing* was crowded out by Pollard's many other endeavors and was made problematical by the fact that so many *STC* entries are either undated or misdated. The frequently expressed need for chronological arrangement of the titles in *STC* was met in 1991 when the final volume of the second edition, including Philip R. Rider's chronological index, was published.

Pollard and Redgrave hoped that within ten years no more than 10 percent more works or 20 percent more variant editions and issues would be discovered. Bishop's checklist turned up roughly 450 additional titles in American libraries (many from the Folger) and this fact, along with the scarcity of copies of *STC* by 1945, led to an attempt to produce an unauthorized American reissue of *STC* incorporating these additions. News of this effort led the Society to issue a swiftly organized reprint of its own (Oxford: Oxford University Press, 1946), although it did not incorporate any additions or corrections, and plans for the American issue were dropped. An anonymous apologist for the Society, writing in the *Times Literary Supplement*, confirmed that revision of *STC* had been going on almost since its appearance, "but it cannot be hurried: and to incorporate any of it in unfinished state was clearly out of the question."[28] The new edition did not begin to appear for 30 more years.

Pollard and Redgrave also stated in their preface that they hoped that "at not too distant a date a supplementary volume may be issued which will make the information collected more easily useful to students of the development of English culture and of the history of printing." In addition to the chronological rearrangement already discussed, what they had in mind was an index to the printers, publishers, and booksellers of all works and variants listed in the catalog. Such an index, compiled by Paul G. Morrison, did not appear until after the deaths of both the chief compilers.[29] It has been superseded by the work of Katharine Pantzer for the second edition of *STC*.

Donald G. Wing

Although Pollard never intended to go past the year 1640, the main negative comments of *STC*'s reviewers can be epitomized by the *TLS* reviewer's remark that "those of us whose effective interest in English books, whether as collector or as student, begins rather later than 1640, are tempted to hope that the enthusiasm of librarians and societies will persevere, to lavish upon later ages a like assiduity of record and discrimination."[30] Such a society and a librarian did indeed heed this call, this time on the North American side of the Atlantic. During the late 1930s, several American scholars had discussed the need to form an organization devoted to the publication of "certain types of labor-saving books . . . which so markedly facilitate the work of research,"[31] and in the summer of 1939 the Index Society was founded in New York City.[32] Despite the impending European war, the Society was particularly impressed by the submission to it of a manuscript by one of its youngest members entitled "A Short-Title Catalogue of Books, 1641–1700," which Donald G. Wing, a member of the Yale University Library staff since 1928, had been compiling since 1933. The Society made publication of at least a part of his catalog by 1941 its first priority. However, partly due to the intrusion of war, partly for normal delays, the first volume of Wing's continuation of *STC* did not appear until 1945.

In later life, Wing would recall that when his Yale class of 1926 were asked about their aspirations, he could only respond that he wanted to read second-hand book catalogs.[33] The fact that *STC* appeared within months of his graduation was, of course, entirely coincidental, but it may have given him the idea for an obvious project for his catalog-reading, library-delving, and bookshop-browsing, which he undoubtedly continued as an affiliate student at Trinity College, Cambridge, in 1926–27 and while working toward a master's degree from Harvard (1928) and a Ph.D. from Yale (1932), both in English literature. Two events in the Yale Library, however—both recounted in the preface to the first volume of his catalog and again in a 1951 talk to the Bibliographical Society of America[34]—were primarily responsible for his undertaking. One was Yale's purchase of the partially cataloged collection of books about the city and colleges of Oxford formed by a former Bodleian librarian, Falconer Madan.[35] The 1641–1700 Oxford imprints, Wing realized, could certainly form the core of an *STC* extension. The second was the Yale Library's own attempt to find roughly 1,600 items then missing which were listed in its first catalog of 1742. Finding these books was now difficult, since items had rarely been listed by author and often were under such partial bibliographic descriptions as "Smith's Sermons in Folio" or such totally nonbibliographic descriptions as "a dirty Old Testament." The need to do further inventory of Yale's pre-1743 holdings and to create bibliographic records for the Oxford books not listed in Madan's catalog allowed Wing to receive permission to create slips for a 1641– 1700 extension of *STC* "on library time"— i.e., while doing his stints at the reference desk—but only if he could think of two other good reasons for the efficacy of such a project.[36]

Unlike *STC*, Wing's extension—hereafter cited eponymously as "Wing"—was from the start essentially a one-person undertaking. He certainly received some help from other libraries and private collectors, but the straightened economic conditions of the 1930s left libraries with staffs too small to participate in such ventures, and some private collectors simply didn't want their ownership of scarce books widely publicized. Wing himself admitted that "only a fool would undertake such a project"[37] and some of the reviewers of the finished catalog agreed, pointing out certain "grave defects" and suggesting that "he would have come nearer to perfection if he had employed collaborators or had included at least one British bibliographer."[38] In his defense, others mentioned that, other than the catalog of the Thomason tracts, check-lists of early Scottish and Dublin imprints, and Evans's rather error-prone *American Bibliography*,[39] there were almost no previous guides to his period, and that its books had been much less studied than had those of the pre-Civil War period.[40] Wing did, in fact, receive a Guggenheim grant to work during the 1936– 37 year in British libraries—40 in London alone—and if this "heaviest year's work which can be imagined"[41] was perhaps not enough to offset the advantages of collaboration, there is a greater, albeit still imperfect, consistency of entry achieved by having a single compiler. In fact, overall the reviews were positive, with one reviewer calling it "a masterpiece of enumerative bibliography . . . destined to be one of the most significant books ever published for the study of English literature"[42] and the Folger librarian, in a review of the first volume, concluding that despite its shortcomings it is "a truly monumental work."[43]

Wing's principles of inclusion, arrangement, and description are much the same as in *STC*, with the exception that due to their proliferation and the challenges they pose to bibliographic description, periodical publications were omitted. As Wing himself accurately predicted, they would "need a separate volume"—a task that furthermore "appeals to me not at all."[44] Although covering only 60 years, as opposed to the 166 of *STC*, Wing lists almost 90,000 works or variants, over three times the number in the earlier catalog; yet he probably missed a greater percentage of extant titles for his period than Pollard and Redgrave had for theirs.[45] (Among American libraries whose significant holdings were not checked were the Universities of California, Michigan, and Minnesota.) The geographical and language parameters are the same. Instead of an entirely numerical sequence, Wing devised a letter-number system for identifying each item (which generally met with positive comments), and a different set of all-letter sigla for locations (which British reviewers typically disliked). More radical departures were his decisions that, in abbreviating, "the opening words of every title have been regarded as sacred" with omissions always indicated by ellipsis and that, in entering anonymous works, the first word not an article is always used (Preface, p. viii). On the other hand, his decision to "assume no responsibility for authority of attribution" led to his listing some works under authors for whom there was less than universal agreement. Wing also declined, understandably, to try to identify the printers of unsigned books or, more regrettably, to differentiate between issues of a work when their title-pages were identical. Nor did he choose to identify the translators of translations into English, thus failing to identify the North and Dryden translations of Plutarch's *Lives*, for example.[46] Perhaps the greatest criticism of Wing was the relative dearth of cross-references. For example, works by Sir John Borough are listed in two places, some under "Borough" and others under "Burroughs." Wing was not unaware that these were indeed the same man, but he felt it to be unnecessary to interfile or even cross-reference alternative spellings of the same person's surname.[47] Deliberately quoting the preface of *STC* in his general introduction to Wing (p. v), Benjamin Nangle, perhaps anticipating such criticisms, emphasized that it is no less a "preliminary

step toward a 'full-dress catalogue'" than was its predecessor and that "'those who use this book as anything more than a finding-list must be on their guard.'"

Wing's Influence

As with *STC*, Wing is not a census of copies—it lists up to five British and five American copies for the more common works—and ultimately the most important effect of Wing on librarians was the immediate skyrocketing in prices of the books which it listed—or failed to list. This inflation was caused not only by the stampede of libraries and private collectors using Wing as a checklist to identify desired works or editions absent from their collections and, with more money now in hand, to seek them out aggressively,[48] but even more from the fact that, working alone, Wing failed to locate as many copies of books as a collaborative team would have done and thus made them appear to be scarcer than they in fact were. Stanley Pargellis of the Newberry estimated that almost half of the 22,000 items in the third volume alone are listed in three libraries only.[49] Despite Wing's explicit warning to users and "to booksellers in particular" (Preface, p. ix), the latter have since its publication delighted in mentioning "only two copies found by Wing," etc., and, as Edwin E. Willoughby of the Folger has pointed out, there are "many guileless and trusting librarians who will actually believe them!"[50] Pargellis has humorously suggested that a study of Wing's impact could be the basis for an article entitled "The Contribution of American Librarians to English Booksellers," and the longtime editor of *AB Bookman's Weekly* commented perhaps ironically in his obituary of Wing that "antiquarian book dealers . . . are everlastingly in his debt."[51] Nevertheless, as a *vade mecum* to both booksellers and collection development librarians, Wing remains unsurpassed.

As with *STC*, publication of Wing led several libraries to publish checklists of their own holdings, among them Christ Church

College at Oxford (1956), compiled by W.G. Hiscock, and the Library Company of Philadelphia (1959), compiled by Edwin Wolf, 2nd;[52] and once again Paul G. Morrison compiled an index of the printers, publishers, and booksellers (Charlottesville: University of Virginia Press, 1955). Neither *STC* nor Wing provides subject access or arrangement, but several projects have been undertaken which use one or both of them as the basis of more specialized checklists; among the more interesting and recent of these is Hilda L. Smith and Susan Cardinale's *Women and the Literature of the Seventeenth Century: An Annotated Bibliography Based on Wing's "Short-title Catalogue"* (New York: Greenwood Press, 1990), which lists both the works in Wing by women and those either for or about women. It also appends a list of the women printers, publishers, and booksellers.

Revision of the Catalogues

Revisions of both *STC* and Wing were begun as soon as, if not before, their first editions appeared, and the reader is referred to the respective prefaces of "New STC" (hereafter referred to as *STC2*) and "New Wing" for a more detailed history of those efforts than can be related here. Pollard's 1927 address to the Bibliographical Society, already cited, noted some omissions already discovered and called for librarians and booksellers alike to notify him of both corrections and additions. In 1934, however, Pollard resigned the secretaryship of the Society and a year later suffered an accident which left him unable to perform much mental work. Meanwhile, a young American student, William A. Jackson, 21 at the time *STC* appeared, had acquired a copy upon its publication and immediately set out to annotate and interleave it with corrections and additions. Long before Pollard's death in 1944 it was apparent that in Jackson the primary instigator of a revised *STC* had been identified. Jackson was well suited for the job, having been a cataloger since his undergraduate days, first at Williams College's

recently founded Chapin Library (1924–30) and from 1930 until 1938 at the Carl H. Pforzheimer Library. At the latter he was co-compiler of the Library's three-volume catalog of books and manuscripts of English literature, 1475–1700 (New York: Morrill Press, 1940). In 1938 he joined the staff of the Harvard College Library, becoming the first Librarian of Houghton Library in 1956.

Unlike Wing, Jackson saw the need for a British collaborator; an obvious choice was F.S. Ferguson, the Quaritch employee (from 1928–1943, general manager) who had arranged for that firm's assistance in the compilation and publication of the 1926 edition and who, according to Pollard's preface (p. vii), was "largely responsible for any bibliographical polish which the catalogue possesses." Soon after the war ended, their efforts came under official sponsorship of the Bibliographical Society, and in 1948, the year Jackson's two-year term as president of the Bibliographical Society of America ended, their project was further cemented when Harvard provided an open-ended grant for Jackson's research. It received the official blessing of Pollard's successor (both as keeper of printed books at the British Library and, eventually, honorary secretary of the Bibliographical Society), F.C. Francis, who gave Jackson Pollard's own annotated copy of *STC*. Jackson's grant allowed for help from a succession of research assistants. Upon his sudden death in October 1964, and Ferguson's in 1967, the work fell to Katharine F. Pantzer, who had taken Jackson's bibliography course at Harvard in 1962 and who had been hired later that year to begin work on the second half of the alphabet.[53] As time drew on, it became clear to Pantzer that much of the work on the early alphabet begun by Jackson, Ferguson, and Jackson's earliest assistants was already in need of further revision, and a decision was made to publish *STC2* in two volumes, with the volume covering I through Z to appear first. It was published in 1976, with a brief preface; A through H, with a more extensive introduction, appeared in 1986. Jackson and, later, Pantzer were immeasurably helped by Lars Hanson and his successor Paul Morgan of the Bodleian Library of Oxford, which served as the British center for the revision.

Pollard's hope that the original *STC* would omit no more than 10 percent of all titles and 20 percent of variant editions and issues turned out to have been overly optimistic. Roughly 10,000 new entries have been added to the more than 26,000 in the 1926 edition. This is partly, but not primarily, due to *STC2*'s inclusion of *all* items bearing printed matter, such as bookplates, blank forms, and engraved items; otherwise the scope remains the same. While the number of newly discovered books was not very large (although no fewer than 46 new editions of Lily's Grammar are listed), the number of ballads, broadsides, and other ephemera not turned up by Pollard and his assistants is significant. (Pollard himself, in his 1927 address, predicted that it would be "later editions and the pamphlets of news which will receive most additions from further research."[54]) Much of the increase is due to the expansion of the number of contributing libraries from 150 to almost 500, but an additional factor is the *STC2* editors' decision to examine and record longer portions of titles, thus catching variants which escaped the admittedly "drastic abridgement" of titles after the opening words employed by Pollard & Redgrave. (Extending the title also helps explain anomalies of entry. "The passion of our lord" being entered under Jesus Christ is perfectly understandable in *STC2*, where a fuller title—"The passion of owr lord iesu christe wythe the contemplatios"—has been transcribed.) The editors also decided to retain listings for some no longer extant works, including several unique titles tragically destroyed by the Nazi air raids on London. Because so many bibliographies, book dealers, and libraries had already adopted *STC* numbers when referring to books within its scope, the same numbering system was used, with decimal numbers added for new titles or variants and cross-references provided from the old number to the new if an item has been

re-attributed or differently entered. A particular strength of the new edition is the greatly expanded number of entries under corporate headings, such as "Bible," "Liturgy," "Indulgences" (an entirely new heading), "England," and "London." Despite the three-fold increase in the number of contributing libraries, symbols are usually provided for no more than five known locations on each side of the Atlantic.

Of equal benefit and importance to the number of new entries is the greater precision of bibliographical description in virtually every citation, not only from closer observation of information in the items themselves but also from taking advantage of the considerable amount of bibliographical research which had appeared between 1926 and 1976 in such areas as type design and size, paper, ornamentation, printing techniques, and the locations and longevity of individual printers. For example, the same "Passion of our lord" was thought, in the 1926 edition, to have been printed by the London printer Richard Pynson in 1508. Further research and the examination of more copies leads *STC2* to identify it as a translation from French, probably printed in Paris by A. Verard. Four additional copies, some fragmentary, are located, the date has been called into question, the collation made more precise, and a note has been added to consult Edward Hodnett's *English Woodcuts 1480–1535* (rpt. Oxford: Oxford University Press, 1973) as a source for its probable Continental printing. It is this level of research which makes *STC2*, in one reviewer's words, a "thoroughly trustworthy bibliography . . . a much greater tool for the investigation of the early booktrade in England . . . [and] a catalyst for new research in a wide range of literary and historical studies."[55] Perhaps the best statement of *STC2*'s merits was made by the anonymous reviewer in a lead article in the Winter 1986 issue of *The Book Collector*, who concluded that

no body of information on the printed produce of any country, or the works in its language produced outside its geographical boundaries, has ever been examined in such detail, recorded with such punctual care, organized in such an exhaustively comprehensive system, or (finally and most important) presented with such patent love and enthusiasm, as that now bestowed on British books and books in English, in that seminal first 165 years of their existence in print."[56]

And in Pantzer, he continued, we have "the most learned and indefatigable and incontestably the best scholar of the field it has ever known."[57]

Both Pantzer's indefatigability and the immense debt of all scholars of early English printing were further demonstrated by the appearance in 1991 of long-awaited printer, publisher, chronological, and other useful indexes as well as further addenda and corrigenda in the third and final volume of *STC2*. Printers and publishers are arranged alphabetically in the first index, and geographically in the second (non-London) and third (London); the latter is supplemented by a map and other useful material on the organization of the London booktrade. Pantzer's material is further supplemented by Philip R. Rider's chronological index of all *STC2* titles. With the completion of *STC2*, it is safe to conclude that Great Britain and Ireland have a more accurate and comprehensive account of their early printed literature than does any other country.

Wing, only 41 when the first volume of his catalog appeared in 1945, had already begun to collect additions and corrections toward a second edition. Most of the work had to be done while carrying out his duties in the Yale Library (where he was ultimately promoted to Associate Librarian for Collections), although in 1967 he received a sabbatical—the first given by Yale to a librarian—to help complete the research. An intermediary step toward the second edition was the publication in 1967 of *A Gallery of Ghosts* (New York: The Index Committee of the Modern Language Association of America), in which Wing listed the titles of about 5,000 works which he had some reason to believe might exist but which had failed to materialize during his research to that time. Hoping that at least 10 percent of these

could be definitively identified either as errors or as legitimate new entries for inclusion in the second edition, Wing was surprised to be able to confirm 700 as extant, legitimate variants and another 675 as ghosts before the first volume of the second edition appeared in 1972. As late as January 1968, he believed that the second edition would consist mostly of quantities of new locations, corrected or fuller imprints for some entries, and "nearly a thousand new entries."[58] Yet by 1972, as James M. Osborn's "General Introduction" to "New Wing" pointed out, a thousand entries had been added in the letter A alone. (The system of re-numbering with each letter of the alphabet and the fact that many numbered entries are either cross-references or have been canceled make it difficult to determine the exact number of imprints finally included. Osburn refers to 120,000 publications, roughly 40 percent more than were in the first edition, but more may have turned up before the final volume appeared in 1988.)

Although Wing graciously thanked several of his chief collaborators in the 1968 BSA address, and although at the end of the "Preface to the Revised Edition" he acknowledged more than 300 persons who sent him additions and corrections, the "New Wing"—particularly the first volume, which appeared less than three weeks before his death—remains very much the work of one man. Many, publicly or privately, have questioned whether, given the criticisms of the first edition and Wing's deteriorating health for several years before his death, it was altogether wise not to have formed an advisory board of expert users of the first edition to assist in both the bibliographical description and the editorial decisions of the second. Instead, Wing's somewhat proprietary attitude[59] toward his catalog resulted in a second edition that differs from the first primarily in the quantity of citations and copies located and not in much editorial re-thinking; thus, although more cross-references are provided, many of the criticisms of the first edition remain valid of the second. In particular, the second edition has been criticized for not including enough of each work's title either to help differentiate it from variants of essentially the same work or to provide readers with a reasonable idea of the work's subject.[60] To be fair, however, to have done so would have essentially abrogated the benefits of a *short*-title catalog. Furthermore, although he attempted to retain the numbering system of the first edition, inserting new entries by use of letters after the number of the preceding entry, about 8 percent of titles were assigned numbers which had belonged to quite different works in the first edition, creating a great outcry since many previous catalogs, bibliographies, scholarly monographs, and the microfilm edition of books in Wing make reference to first edition numbers. At least one bibliographical scholar has called this decision "disastrous,"[61] and another commented that it "shattered a bibliographical reference system."[62] N. Carol Evans, who had access to Wing's manuscript files for her own research, reports that Wing "never had any use for" the numbers, made very little reference to the first edition in his work on the second, and would have preferred to have *completely* renumbered it.[63] Professor Osborn, the chair of MLA's Index Committee, which published the second edition, promised that this practice would be re-examined, and in the second and third volumes, which appeared in 1982 and 1988, the only re-assigned numbers from the first edition are those which were for canceled entries, and a complete list of these number changes was printed in volume two. Work was begun on a third edition of volume one even before volume three was published. Although the editors of volumes two and three, Timothy J. Crist and John J. Morrison, respectively, did admirable work in revising, much of the material from Wing's notes regarding variant editions and states was very rudimentary. The ensuing degree of bibliographical precision, although improved over the first edition, has also received considerable criticism. Volume two was particularly difficult to improve, since it had to be re-edited from galleys left by Wing at his death. (As D.F. McKenzie wrote, many

of the problems inherent in "New Wing" stem from the fact that it was "trapped in an obsolete technology."[64])In order to broaden the base of expertise from which to make editorial decisions, an Advisory Committee for the Wing Revision Project, under the aegis of MLA's Committee on Research Activities, was formed in 1979.

Future Short-Title Catalogues

And what of future editions? The completion of *STC2* in 1991 and "New Wing" in 1988 may well represent the last catalogs of their kind to take the form of the traditional book. Certainly, the planning and appearance of their successor, the *Eighteenth-Century Short-Title Catalogue* (*ESTC*), could not have been realized without the development of computer programs for the creation, manipulation, and retrieval of machine-readable bibliographic records and of the bibliographic utilities which transmit them among virtually all Anglo-American research libraries. A detailed account of the *ESTC* cannot be provided here,[65] and in fact—despite its title—it is not a short-title catalog. (Since electronically stored cataloging makes the issue of physical bulk moot, complete title page transcription is an ideal usually achieved in *ESTC*.) Nevertheless, the advent of *ESTC* has perhaps inevitably become connected to the fate of future *STC* and Wing revisions. Henry L. Snyder, the North American coordinator of *ESTC*, headquartered at the University of California, Riverside, has proposed that the *ESTC* database of almost 200,000 records be used as the basis for an "English Short-Title Catalogue."[66] The entries in volume three of "New Wing" are already in machine-readable form, as are those in the ongoing revision of volume one, and work is underway to convert records in volume two. Some 38,000 records generated by the North American Imprints Project based at the American Antiquarian Society[67] are also being converted from US MARC to UK MARC format in order to make them compatible with the *ESTC* database. The major remaining obstacle to a combined database of all English books of the handprinted era[68] is the conversion of *STC2* records (which would be only about 10 percent of the total). Snyder suggests that the microfilm collection based on *STC* could be used to examine title pages and bring abbreviated *STC2* entries up to the standards of the *ESTC* database. A greater but not insurmountable hurdle would be creation of authoritative headings, of which he estimates there are 10,000 in *STC2* and "New Wing" combined which have not yet been provided by other databases. Incorporation of subject headings to many of the almost 400,000 combined entries is a further possibility in the not-too-distant future.

Perhaps the greatest advantage of a computerized catalog from the compilers' perspective is the fact that future additions and corrections can be made, location symbols added, and re-sequencing accomplished with relative ease and at low cost. From the user's point of view, the ability, already available in *ESTC*, to retrieve in minutes lists of, for example, all titles printed in Philadelphia in 1776, all seventeenth-century titles relating to both women and music, or all eighteenth-century editions of Shakespeare printed in Dublin is a bibliographical capability never dreamed of by Pollard, Wing, Jackson, or even Pantzer when she first hired on in 1962. Their indexes were truly "the baby figure of the giant mass of things to come at large"—but were, and will remain, giants in the field of enumerative bibliography in their own right.

PUBLICATION HISTORY

Pollard, A.W. and G.R. Redgrave, eds. *Short-title Catalogue of Books Printed in England, Scotland, & Ireland and of English Books Printed Abroad*. London: Printed by Arrangement with the Bibliographical Society for Bernard Quaritch, Ltd., 1926. Reprinted. Oxford: Oxford University Press, 1946.
——. 2nd edition, revised and enlarged, begun by William A. Jackson and F.S. Ferguson, completed by Katharine Pantzer, with a chronological index by Philip R. Rider. 3 vols. London: The Bibliographical Society, 1976–91.

Wing, Donald G. *Short-Title Catalogue of Books Printed in England, Scotland, Ireland, Wales, and British America and of English Books Printed in Other Countries, 1641–1700*. 3 vols. New York: Printed for the Index Society by Columbia University Press, 1945–51.
——. 2nd ed., revised and enlarged, begun by Donald G. Wing, continued by Timothy J. Crist, John J. Morrison, and Carolyn W. Nelson. 3 vols. New York: Modern Language Association of America, 1972–88.
——. 3rd ed. of vol. 1. In progress.

BIBLIOGRAPHY

Any study of *STC* and Wing must begin with the prefaces, introductions, and other front matter to each volume of each edition, where much of the history of their conception and evolution is told in more or less detail than in this article. The majority of the items listed below fall into one of three categories. The first consists of reviews of the first or second editions of *STC* and Wing (in some cases of only one volume), which will provide the interested reader with more detailed discussion of both their strengths and faults than can be given here. A variety of reviewers, including scholars, librarians, and booksellers, is represented. Additional reviews may be identified in the standard book review indexes and in *Index to Reviews of Bibliographical Publications: An International Annual*. The researcher should remember that some reviews were published after the appearance of each new volume of these catalogs. The second category consists of biographical information on the compilers, of which Wilson's portrait of Pollard is by far the lengthiest. It, along with the more concise entry by Greg in *DNB*, the obituary in the *Times*, and the tribute by Francis, give some indication of the breadth of Pollard's activities. Cveljo's entry on Wing is probably the best summary of his career; the *New York Times* obituary is short, and Liebert's article is taken from his tribute at a memorial service for Wing at Yale. Redgrave's obituary in the *Times* is the only account of his life the author has identified; there was no memoir of him in the Bibliographical Society's organ, *The Library*, after his death, nor was there a *DNB* entry. Some biographical data on Pantzer can be found in Chernofsky. One item, Munby and Evans, spans two categories and is really two items under one title: Munby's contribution is a memoir of Wing; Evans' a review of the first volume of "New Wing." The third category includes short articles of news about the catalogs which stop short of being reviews. Neither the catalogs which preceded *STC* and Wing nor the separately published indexes, addenda and corrigenda, or supplements to them are cited below, but are cited in either the text or the notes. Most of them are briefly described in Eugene P. Sheehy's *Guide to Reference Books*, 10th ed. (Chicago: American Library Association, 1986) in the section on British and American national and trade bibliography.

[Barker, Nicolas?]. "STC." *The Book Collector* 35 (1986): 417–30.

Chernofsky, Jacob L. "New *STC* Climaxes a Century of Scholarship." *AB Bookman's Weekly* 78 (November 10, 1986): 1872–77.

Clement, Richard W. Review of Vol. I of *STC2*. *The Sixteenth Century Journal* 19 (1988): 520–21.

Cveljo, Katherine. "Wing, Donald Goddard (1904–1972)." *Dictionary of American Library Biography*, 564–66. Littleton, CO: Libraries Unlimited, 1978.

"Donald Wing, 68, Yale Librarian." *New York Times*, October 11, 1972, p. 46, col. 3.

"Dr. A.W. Pollard: An Eminent Bibliographer." *The Times*, March 9, 1944, p. 7, col. 5.

"English Books to 1640." *Times Literary Supplement*, no. 1314 (April 7, 1927): 247.

Francis, F.C. "A.W. Pollard, 1859–1944." *The Library*, 4th ser., 25 (1945): 82–86.

Freeman, Arthur. Review of Vol. I of *STC2*. *The Library*, 6th ser., 9 (1987): 289–92.

Greg, W. W. "Pollard, Alfred William." *Dictionary of National Biography, 1941–1950*. Oxford: Oxford University Press, 1959: 681–82.

Hofmann, Theodore. Review of Vol. III of "New Wing." *The Library*, 6th ser., 11 (1989): 383–88.

Holzknecht, Karl J. Review of Wing. *Papers of the Bibliographical Society of America* 46 (1952): 400–06.

Liebert, Herman W. "In Memoriam Donald G. Wing." *The Yale University Library Gazette* 47 (1972/73): 134–36.

Malkin, Sol M. Untitled obituary of Donald Wing. *AB Bookman's Weekly* 50 (October 16, 1972): 1204.

Mason, Alexandra. Review of vol. II of "New Wing." *Papers of the Bibliographical Society of America* 80 (1986): 255–62.

McKenzie, D.F. "Type-bound Topography." *Times Literary Supplement* no. 4159 (December 17, 1982): 1403.

McKitterick, David. "Changes for the Better?" *The Book Collector* 37 (1988): 461–78.

"Mr. G.R. Redgrave: Engineering, Art, and Education." *The Times*, June 17, 1941, 9.

Munby, A. N. L., and N. Carol Evans. "Wing's STC." *The Book Collector* 23 (1974) 388–93.

Pargellis, Stanley. Review of Wing. *College & Research Libraries* 14 (1953): 98–99.

Pollard, A.W. "Future Work on the Short-Title Catalogue of English Books, 1475–1640." *The Library*, 4th ser., 8 (1927/28): 377–94.

"The Printing of Reference Books." *Times Literary Supplement* no. 23097 (May 4, 1946): 216.

"The 'Short-Title' Catalogue." *Times Literary Supplement* no. 2327 (September 7, 1946): 432.

"The Short-Title Catalogue, 1641–1700." *Times Literary Supplement* no. 2650 (November 14, 1952): 752.

Willoughby, Edwin Eliott. Review of Vol. I of Wing. *Library Quarterly* 16 (1946): 247–50.

Wilson, J. Dover. "Alfred William Pollard, 1859–1944." *Proceedings of the British Academy* 31 (1945): 257–305. Rpt. in *Alfred William Pollard: A Selection of His Essays*, comp. Fred W. Roper. Metuchen, NJ: Scarecrow Press, 1976: 1–57.

Wing, Donald G. "The Making of the Short-Title Catalogue, 1641–1700." *Papers of the Bibliographical Society of America* 45 (1951): 59–69.

Wing, Donald G. "Wing on Wing." *Yale University Library Gazette* 44 (1969/70): 1–7.

NOTES

[1] Pollard and Redgrave's *Short-Title Catalogue* was not published until January 1927, but the imprint date of 1926 will be used.

[2] Roy B. Stokes, "Bibliography," in *Encyclopedia of Library and Information Science* (New York: Marcel Dekker, 1969), vol. 2: 407.

³ Edward Arber's *A Transcript of the Registers of the Company of Stationers of London, 1554–1640* (5 vols., London, etc.: Privately Printed, 1875–94; rpt. 6 vols., New York: P. Smith, 1950) had begun to appear nine years earlier but is, as Sheehy puts it, "difficult to use and sometimes innaccurate." It also lists many titles which were never published, were published differently, or of which no known copies are extant; and some of the manuscript registers, particularly the Decrees and Ordinances, were denied to Arber by the officers of the Company.

⁴ It was primarily this catalog which W.W. Greg credited with transforming bibliography "from a study the main interest of which was artistic to one governed by methods of scientific enquiry." In "Bibliography—A Retrospect," *The Bibliographic Society, 1892–1942: Studies in Retrospect* (London: The Bibliographical Society, 1945): 27. Pollard himself credits his work on this catalog for the "strenuous mental discipline" which was so necessary for his later project. Pollard and Proctor were also chiefly responsible for the descriptions of the printed books in the three-volume *Catalogue of the Manuscripts and Early Printed Books . . . of the Library of J. Pierpont Morgan* (London: Chiswick Press, 1907).

⁵ These appeared in four parts but were also published in one volume under the title *Hand-lists of Books Printed by London Printers, 1501–1556* (London: Bibliographical Society, 1913).

⁶ The paper, which was entitled "Plans for Bibliographical Work on the Sixteenth Century," is summarized in "Journal of the Twenty-Sixth Session: October, 1917, to March, 1918," *Transactions of the Bibliographical Society* 15 (1920): 5–7. Due to the rather serious stammer from which Pollard had suffered since the age of three, the paper, like most he wrote, was read for him by another member of the Society, in this case, G.F. Barwick.

⁷ The resolution was passed at the April 1918 meeting but was published, along with a summary of Pollard's second paper of January 1919, some specimen entries, and a call for volunteers, in the November issue of the Society's *News-Sheet*, p. 3–4, and reprinted in its "Journal of the Twenty-Seventh Session, October, 1918, to March, 1919," *Transactions of the Bibliographical Society* 15 (1920): 142–48.

⁸ The collection was bought from Thomason's heirs in 1761 by King George III, who presented it to the newly formed British Museum. A two-volume catalog of the collection was published by the Museum in 1908 and reprinted in four volumes in 1977 by University Microfilms International to accompany its publication of the collection on 256 reels of microfilm.

⁹ Henry E. Huntington's private collection was bequeathed to the people of California and its building constructed soon after the *STC* project began.

¹⁰ London: Printed by Arrangement with the Bibliographical Society for Bernard Quaritch Ltd., 1926. Eleven of the other contributors are listed on the title page and their contributions explained in the preface.

¹¹ The best biographical sketch of Pollard remains the lengthy obituary by J. Dover Wilson which appeared in *Proceedings of the British Academy* 31 (1945): 257–306. Because of Wilson's own eminence as a Shakespeare editor, it is to be expected that the memoir shed more light on Pollard's importance as a textual critic of Shakespeare and Chaucer than it does on the compilation of *STC*. Wilson's assertion that Pollard's *Shakespeare Folios and Quartos* (1909) was the landmark beginning of modern English textual criticism (p. 288) was seconded by W. W. Greg, who has written that it also "marked the opening of a new era in Shakespearean studies" and that Pollard was the founder of the science of critical bibliography ("The 'Hamlet' Texts and Recent Work in Shakespeare Bibliography," *Modern Language Review* 14 [1919]: 383). Pollard's own autobiographical sketch of his first 50 years and a brief summary of his life "From Fifty to Seventy-Five" by Sir Henry Thomas were printed in *A Select Bibliography of the Writings of Alfred W. Pollard* (Oxford: Privately Printed, 1938), which was presented to him by friends upon his seventy-fifth birthday. See also *Alfred William Pollard: A Selection of His Essays*, compiled by Fred W. Roper, (Metuchen, NJ: Scarecrow Press, 1976), which also reprints Wilson's tribute (pp. 1–57) and includes "Alfred William Pollard: His Influence on Contemporary Bibliography" by Roger Leachman (pp. 58–77).

¹² Greg, "The 'Hamlet' Texts," 383.

¹³ Wilson, "Pollard," 291.

¹⁴ Ibid., 284.

¹⁵ H.L. Mallalieu, *Dictionary of British Watercolour Artists Up to 1920* (Woodbridge, England: Antique Collectors Club, 1976), vol. 1: 216.

¹⁶ Wilson, "Pollard," 299.

¹⁷ "English Books to 1640," *Times Literary Supplement* no. 1314 (7 April 1927): 247.

¹⁸ "Mr. G.R. Redgrave: Engineering, Art, and Education," *The Times*, 17 June 1941, 9e.

¹⁹ "Pollard, Alfred William," in *Dictionary of National Biography, 1941–1950* (Oxford: Oxford University Press, 1959): 682.

²⁰ These two qualities were noted by F.C. Francis in his obituary of Pollard in *The Library*, 4th ser., 25 (1945): 82.

²¹ As with most reference works of such magnitude, editors invariably underestimate the time needed for completion. The 1924 annual report of the Society (in *The Library*, 4th ser., 5 [1925]: 323–25) notes that "Mr. Pollard is finding the final preparation of the copy and correction of the proofs . . . a much heavier task than he anticipated." Since at the time he was editor of *The Library*, those words are undoubtedly his own.

²² "English Books to 1640," 247.

²³ Benjamin Nangle, "General Introduction," *A Short-Title Catalogue of Books Printed in England, Scotland, Ireland, Wales, and British America and of English Books Printed in Other Countries, 1641–1700* (New York: Printed for the Index Society by Columbia University Press, 1945–51), vol. 1: v.

[24] "The 'Short-Title' Catalogue," *Times Literary Supplement* no. 2327 (7 September, 1946): 432.

[25] Arthur Freeman, review of volume 1 of *STC2*, in *The Library*, 6th ser., 9 (September 1987): 289.

[26] William Warner Bishop, *A Checklist of American Copies of "Short-Title Catalogue" Books*, 2nd ed. (Ann Arbor: University of Michigan Press, 1950). Bishop's checklist was a byproduct of a project to microfilm the title page, contents page, and colophon of *STC* books for reference purposes and to help make up for its lack of descriptive detail. Details of the project are in his preface. The 1944 edition stimulated corrections and additions by other American libraries, leading to the 1950 revision. The Oxford and Cambridge checklists were compiled by Strickland and Gibson and Herbert M. Adams, respectively.

[27] A.W. Pollard, "Future Work on the Short-Title Catalogue of English Books, 1475–1640," *The Library*, 4th ser., 8 (1927/28): 385. In addition to the future plans for *STC*, this *post-partum* account gives more detail about its organizational strategy and the cooperative efforts involved in its development than does the preface, including the statement (p. 378) that he owed the idea of a "united catalogue" to Mr. H.R. Tedder, long-time librarian of the Athenaeum Club.

[28] "The Printing of Reference Books," *Times Literary Supplement* no. 2309 (4 May 1946): 216.

[29] Paul G. Morrison, *Index of Printers, Publishers, and Booksellers in A.W. Pollard and G.R. Redgrave, A Short-Title Catalogue . . .* (Charlottesville, VA.: Bibliographical Society of the University of Virginia, 1950).

[30] "English Books to 1640," 247.

[31] Benjamin Nangle, "Preface," *The Index of Middle English Verse*, ed. Carleton Brown and Russell Hope Robbins (New York: Printed for The Index Society by Columbia University Press, 1943), v.

[32] In 1966 the Society became the Index Committee of the Modern Language Association of America. According to Katherine Cveljo's entry on Donald Wing in *Dictionary of American Library Biography* (Littleton, CO: Libraries Unlimited, 1978), his extension of *STC* netted the Society some $30,000, which was used to support publication of other bibliographies, including the second edition.

[33] "Donald Wing, 68, Yale Librarian," *The New York Times*, 11 October 1972, p. 46, col. 3.

[34] Published as "The Making of the *Short-Title Catalogue, 1641–1700*," *Papers of the Bibliographical Society of America* 45 (1951): 59–69.

[35] *Oxford Books: A Bibliography of Printed Works Relating to the University and City of Oxford or Printed or Published There . . . ,* 3 vols. (Oxford: Clarendon Press, 1885–1912). The bibliography listed works only through 1681, but his collection—and thus Yale's—actually contained many titles published after that date.

[36] The reasons he came up with were creating a list of pre-1851 Connecticut imprints and flagging all temporary cards in Yale's card catalog which were ten years old or older—"a sure-fire way to alienate the affections of the maturer cataloguers," he discovered (Wing, "Making of the *STC*," 62).

[37] Ibid., 59.

[38] The anonymous reviewer in the *Times Literary Supplement* no. 2650 (14 November 1952): 752. The *TLS* reviewer of the first volume (in the issue for 7 September 1946, p. 432) had likewise tempered his admiration of Wing's "immense, single-handed" work with his "misgivings as to the limits of human capacity for so herculean a task."

[39] *Catalogue of the Pamphlets, Books, Newspapers, and Manuscripts Relating to the Civil War, the Commonwealth, and Restoration, Collected by George Thomason, 1640–1661 . . . ,* 2 vols. (London: British Museum, 1908; rpt. 4 vols., Ann Arbor: University Microfilms, 1977); Harry G. Aldis, *List of Books Printed in Scotland Before 1700* (Edinburgh: Edinburgh Bibliographical Society, 1904); E. R. McC. Dix, *Catalogue of Early Dublin-Printed Books, 1601–1700* (Dublin: T. G. O'Donoghue, 1898–1905).

[40] Hofmann, review of vol. 3 of New Wing, 384.

[41] A. N. L. Munby, "Wing's *STC*," *The Book Collector* 23 (1974): 390.

[42] Karl J. Holzknecht, review of Wing in *Papers of the Bibliographical Society of America* 46 (1952): 400.

[43] Edwin Eliott Willoughby, review of Wing in *Library Quarterly* 16 (1946): 250. Interestingly, no review of the first edition of Wing ever appeared in the Bibliographical Society's official organ, *The Library*.

[44] Wing, "Making of the *STC*," 63–64. Carolyn Nelson and Matthew Seccombe's *British Newspapers and Periodicals 1641–1700: A Short-Title Catalogue of Serials Printed in England, Scotland, Ireland and British America* (New York: Modern Language Association, 1987) admirably describes each separate extant issue of more than 700 periodicals. See Michael Harris's review in *The Library*, 6th ser., 11 (1989): 378–83.

[45] For example, John Alden, in "Pills and Publishing: Some Notes on the English Book Trade, 1660–1715," *The Library*, 5th ser., 7 (1952): 21–37, which appeared after the final volume of Wing, states (p. 22) that Wing includes only 16 of 64 printed items Alden found on the relation between the book trade and the proprietary medical trade. But six years later, in *Wing Addenda and Corrigenda: Some Notes on Materials in the British Museum* (Charlottesville, VA.: Bibliographical Society of the University of Virginia, 1958), Alden concluded (p. 1), on the basis of a sampling of Wing against the British Museum's holdings, that Wing's "hope for a margin of title omissions within twenty per cent may not have been idle."

[46] Holzknecht, review of Wing, 401.

[47] N. Carol Evans, "Wing's *STC*," *The Book Collector* 23 (1974): 392.

[48] Hofmann notes (p. 384) that in particular the 1970 catalog of the Folger Library still has Wing books listed on accessions slips on virtually every page of its 28 volumes.

[49] Stanley Pargellis, review of the first edition of Wing, *College & Research Libraries* 14 (1953): 98–99.

[50] Willoughby, review of Wing, 250.

[51] Sol Malkin, obituary of Donald Wing, *AB Bookman's Weekly*, 50 (16 October 1972): 1204.

[52] Wing himself provides citations for these and 20 other checklists of pre-1701 books, most of which use his numbering, on p. ix of the preface to the revised edition.

[53] Some biographical information on Pantzer is available in Jacob L. Chernofsky, "New STC Climaxes a Century of Scholarship," *AB Bookman's Weekly*, 78 (10 November 1986): 1872–77. Of particular interest is the fact that, 19 years after entering the doctoral program in Harvard's English Department, Pantzer successfully submitted the first volume of *STC2* as her dissertation.

[54] Pollard, "Future Work on the *STC*," 380.

[55] Richard W. Clement, review of *STC2*, *The Sixteenth Century Journal* 19 (1988): 520–21.

[56] "STC," *The Book Collector* 35 (1986): 421–22. Although unsigned, the reviewer is probably the journal's editor, Nicholas Barker. The review makes the excellent point that *STC* cannot be used as an accurate view of either the English book trade or the reading tastes of the public, particularly the cultural elite, during the period covered since there were several times more books both sold and read in Latin, French, Italian, and Dutch than there were in English.

[57] Ibid, 429.

[58] "Wing on Wing," *The Yale University Library Gazette* 44(1969–70): 2.

[59] In his personal life, too, Wing has been called an "amiable loner" by a Yale colleague, Herbert W. Liebert, in "In Memoriam Donald G. Wing," *Yale University Library Gazette* 47 (1972–73): 134.

[60] David McKitterick, in "Changes for the Better?" *The Book Collector* 37 (1988): 463, provides several examples: "A discovery of the education of the schollars of Cambridge" is not as useful without its subtitle, "By their abominations and wicked practises acted upon, and against, the despised people, in scorn called Quakers."

[61] Ibid., 461.

[62] D. F. McKenzie, "Type-Bound Topography," *Times Literary Supplement* no. 4159 (17 December 1982): 1403.

[63] Munby and Evans, "Wing's *STC*," 392.

[64] McKenzie, "Type-Bound Topography," 1403.

[65] The best source of information on *ESTC* is its own occasional newsletter, *Factotum* (London: Reference Division, British Library, 1978–). Two good descriptions of the database itself are Daniel Uchitelle's "RLIN in the Eighteenth Century: An Introduction to the ESTC Special Database," *Database* 7 (August 1984): 30–33, and David Hunter's "Searching ESTC on RLIN," *Factotum Occasional Paper* 5 (1987). *ESTC* is searchable in the United States through the RLIN database and in Great Britain through BLAISE-LINE.

[66] Slightly different printed versions of the proposal Snyder made orally to the International Committee on the *ESTC* in November 1987 were published in *The Library*, 6th ser., 10 (1988): 191–93 and in *Papers of the Bibliographical Society of America* 82 (1988): 333–36.

[67] The project is essentially converting the pre-1801 American imprints in Evans and all of Marie Tremain's *A Bibliography of Canadian Imprints, 1751–1800* (Toronto: University of Toronto Press, 1952) into MARC format.

[68] The year 1800 is, conveniently, the approximate date for the introduction of printing by machine. The English language may not be the first to have a comprehensive bibliography of its books to 1800: a *Short-Title Catalog of the Netherlands* (*STCN*) should be substantially completed by the end of the century. See J. A. Gruys, et al., "Dutch National Bibliography, 1540–1800: The STCN," *Querendo* 13 (1983): 149-60.

Continuity in a Changing World: *Statesman's Year-Book*

David M. Pilachowski

DEVELOPMENT AND HISTORY

The Statesman's Year-Book enjoys a well earned reputation as a reference book that deserves a place in most libraries. The familiar red 5" x 7½" volumes have appeared like clockwork each year since 1864.[1] Long a staple of reference collections, the *Year-Book* provides unbiased political, social, and economic background on the countries of the world. Besides giving accurate, up-to-date information on individual countries and, more recently, on international organizations, *Statesman's Year- Book,* through its longevity, also provides broad historical coverage of the evolution of the political world. At the same time, the changes within and among countries can also be studied by examination of the *Year-Book*. Indeed, new volumes do not supersede earlier ones since the newer occasionally make reference to earlier editions.[2]

It is difficult to argue with recently retired editor John Paxton's statement that the *Year-Book* "is found in most reference libraries of the world."[3] The *Year-Book* enjoys the longest reign of any annual handbook of countries currently being published. At the same time, praise of the work has been both uniform and vocal. A 1905 review sums it up well: "There are some annuals that have made themselves absolutely indispensable—not a large number, possibly half a dozen—and one of them is *The Statesman's Year-Book.* . . . It has always been good, it grows better each year: when will its improvement cease, because further betterment is impossible?"[4]

Statesman's Year-Book has changed and been improved over time, in part in order to reflect political change and in part due to the introduction of new features. Yet, one remarkable aspect of the publication is the continuity that it has enjoyed. Beyond simple longevity, *Statesman's Year-Book* has been published by one firm and its subsidiary, has had but six editors, included one firm's maps for over 90 years, and has been printed and bound by but two firms since its inception. It is this stability and the quality of these long standing contributions that has helped set *Statesman's Year-Book* apart from other works and has helped ensure its continued success.

Origins of the Year-Book

Macmillan and Company, founded by Alexander and Daniel Macmillan in 1843, has been the original and, with the inclusion of its subsidiary St. Martin's Press, the only publisher of *Statesman's Year-Book*. It seems clear that Macmillan and Company has supported the *Year-Book* from the outset and has recognized the importance of editorial excellence and continuity. Perhaps more amazing than the fact that the *Year-Book* has had the same publisher, is the longevity of its editors. As noted above, the work has had but six editors during its 125-plus years.

The original suggestion that led to the creation of *Statesman's Year-Book* has been attributed to Sir Robert Peel. The preface to the first *Year-Book* reported that "The *Statesman's Year-Book* is intended to supply a want in English literature—a want noticed and commented upon more than fifteen years ago by the late Sir Robert Peel . . . he often felt the want of a hand-book presenting in a compact shape, a picture of the actual condition, political and social, of the various states of the civilized world."[5]

Perhaps further discussion of the Peel connection is tucked away somewhere in the Macmillan archives. While there is no reason to doubt that the original suggestion for *Statesman's Year-Book* came from Peel, this fact is not mentioned in either Morgan's centennial history of Macmillan nor in the published letters or biographies of Daniel or Alexander Macmillan nor of Peel.

With the idea of such a handbook before him, Alexander Macmillan, who directed the firm after his brother's death in 1857, next faced the task of identifying an editor for such an ambitious enterprise. Here, the publisher received advice from historian Thomas Carlyle and politician W.E. Gladstone, who introduced and recommended Frederick Martin to Alexander.[6] Martin was born in Geneva in 1830, educated in Heidelberg, and settled in England.[7] He had been working since October 1856 as Carlyle's secretary and amanuensis.[8] In December 1862, Martin and Alexander Macmillan entered into an agreement for "A Statistical, Genealogical and Historical Account of the States and Sovereigns of the Civilised World."[9]

Editor Martin's Model

Former *Statesman's Year-Book* editor John Paxton has credited Martin with creating much of the format and reputation that the annual has enjoyed over the years. Paxton lauded Martin for "build[ing] the foundations of its reputation for accuracy, impartiality and usefulness. Whatever changes *The Statesman's Year-Book* has undergone at the hands of his successors, the basic features established by Martin have been preserved."[10] The editor's goal was to produce a work that "contains a full account of all the states of Europe, and the principal states of Asia, America, and Australasia, considered under their political, social and commercial aspects."[11]

The format of the first edition consisted of entries on each country divided into the following sections: Reigning Sovereign and Family, if applicable; Constitution and Government; Church and Education; Revenue and Expenditure; Army and Navy; Population; and Trade and Commerce. These categories, conceived in 1864, differ somewhat from today's; but the intent and approach remains the same: to present in narrative and statistical form basic information about the countries of the world. Selected colonies were also included in the original edition of *Statesman's Year-Book*. The colonies of European countries were included in the accounts of their respective imperial powers. India, Canada, and the Australasian colonies of Great Britain were treated separately while its lesser British colonies were ignored.

In that first *Year-Book*, the countries of the world were presented in two unequal sections. Part I, "The States of Europe," listed 16 countries and their dependencies and colonies in 525 pages. One is reminded how different the world was then. Sweden and Norway existed as a personal union under one monarch, with entirely separate governments. Finland and Poland were under the control of Russia, while Turkey was a major power, controlling Egypt, Romania, and Serbia. Germany alone received detailed treatment at the level of individual States of Confederation in an overall entry of nearly a hundred pages. This level of detail may have resulted from editor Martin's background and from the decentralized nature of Germany at that time.

The second part of the 1864 edition of *Statesman's Year-Book*, titled "Principal States Not in Europe," consisted of 156 pages. This section was divided into three subsections: America (Argentine Republic, Brazil, Canada, Chili, Confederate States, Mexico, and United States); Asia (China, India, and Japan); and

Australasia (New South Wales, New Zealand, Queensland, South Australia, Tasmania, and Victoria). While the number of countries included in that first edition was limited, that was by design and would change in subsequent editions. Indeed, one of the few criticisms heard about the early editions of *Statesman's Year-Book* was the omission of many countries.[12]

Besides giving information about countries, editor Martin had other objectives in mind for *Statesman's Year-Book*. In the preface of the 1864 edition he stated:

> It has been considered an object of paramount importance to give only facts, and exclude opinions from the *Statesman's Year-Book*. No form of government is criticised, or compared, from a theoretical point of view, with any other form of political organisation; and no judgment is attempted on any of the thousand features of activity by which the social life of nations manifests itself."[13]

John Paxton identified Martin's legacy as his "dissociation from any party—political and denominational considerations (and) his firm resistance to pressure groups of any description."[14]

A critical factor in gathering and presenting information on the countries included in *Statesman's Year-Book* was the source of the data to be included in the work. Martin placed a premium on the accuracy of his information, stating that:

> The great aim, kept in view throughout, has been to insure an absolute correctness of the multiplicity of facts and figures given in the *Statesman's Year-Book*. For this purpose, none but official documents have been consulted in the first instance, and only where these failed, or were manifestly imperfect, recourse has been had to authoritative books, and influential newspapers, magazines, and other reliable information. In all the latter cases, the source is given, so as to furnish a means for verifying the statement, as well as to present a guide for further investigations.[15]

"Official documents" were put aside by the early 1870s in favor of direct contact with the authors and editors of those documents. Beginning with Martin and continuing to the present, editors have relied upon the people in the "governments departments, embassies, learned societies, (and) statistical offices" for their information.[16] Yet Martin always reserved the right of final decision in using official sources, as he did in rejecting the reported expenses of the Tsarist court "as ridiculously low in view of the boundless pomp and splendour displayed on all occasions."[17]

Beyond the change in sources, the next significant alteration of *Statesman's Year-Book* was the increase in the number of countries covered. Within ten years of its original edition, many new countries had been added. Algeria, Liberia, Natal, and Morocco were added from Africa and coverage of Asia expanded to include Ceylon, Hong Kong, Java, Persia, and Siam. By 1884, several additional counties had been added, and Egypt, Serbia, and Romania were given individual entries separate from Turkey.[18]

Difficulties During Martin's Tenure

Martin's tenure as editor, although lauded, was not without its difficulties, for Martin's dealings with the Macmillan firm were not entirely smooth. He was critical of decisions made by his publisher and "He never ceased to tell the Macmillans how to run their business more profitably, what discounts to give to wholesalers and retailers, or how to make *The Statesman's Year-Book* pay."[19]

Relations between the editor and his publisher were exacerbated in October 1882 during the preparation of the 1883 edition of the *Year-Book*. After rejecting Alexander Macmillan's suggestion that he receive editorial assistance, "Martin lost a large portion of his revised proofs in a railway carriage."[20] Against Martin's wishes, John Scott-Keltie[21] was enlisted to assist the editor with the completion of the 1883 edition. That edition would be the founding editor's last, as he died on January 27, 1883. Scott-Keltie then succeeded to the editorship.[22]

John Scott-Keltie's Editorship

John Scott-Keltie was named the second editor of *Statesman's Year-Book* in 1884, a position that he held until his death in 1927. Scott-Keltie, like the Macmillans a Scot, was born in Dundee in 1840. Scott-Keltie was educated at Perth, with university studies at St. Andrews and Edinburgh. He later completed his studies for the Presbyterian ministry although his developing interest as a journalist while a student persuaded him to follow that career instead.[23]

Scott-Keltie's first position in journalism in 1861 was with W. & R. Chambers, where he worked on *Chambers's Encyclopedia*. In 1871 he joined the editorial staff at Macmillan, with an appointment as sub-editor for *Nature* in 1873.

Statesman's Year-Book underwent several significant changes during Scott-Keltie's editorship. Maps were added as a standard feature of the work beginning in 1892. Four maps appeared in that volume: the density of world population, the British Empire, the partition of Africa, and the frontiers of the Pamirs (north of Afghanistan). Scott-Keltie's interests made the addition of maps to the *Year-Book* very appropriate. His *DNB* entry refers to him as a geographer. Indeed, Scott-Keltie edited the Royal Geographical Society's *Proceedings*, later renamed *Geographical Journal*.[24] He has been called the "architect and builder" of that prestigious journal.[25] When Scott-Keltie was awarded the Victoria Medal of the Royal Geographical Society in 1917, Society President Douglas Freshfield remarked of Scott-Keltie that "He has made himself, and in doing so he has made the Society, a geographical center round which all good travellers revolve. . . . His correspondence has extended over the civilized world, and . . . Dr. Keltie has remained in the eyes of all men the incarnation of British geography."[26] Among Scott-Keltie's admirers was former United States President Theodore Roosevelt. Roosevelt felt indebted to the editor of *Geographical Journal* for having published in that periodical several maps from Brazilian explorations which otherwise would have likely remained unknown.[27]

Maps

The maps commissioned for *Statesman's Year-Book* were noteworthy on two counts. First, they always dealt with a timely topic or place. For example, the Panama Canal schemes were included in the 1902 and 1911 editions, the division of Bengal in 1905, the strategic importance of Singapore in 1938, and the Burma Road in 1939. The number of maps included in the annual volumes ranged from four to ten until 1919, after which it stabilized almost without exception at two.

Secondly, the maps were always beautifully and accurately executed by John George Bartholomew and his successors. John George Bartholomew (1860–1920) was the fourth generation of Bartholomews engaged in mapmaking. Following his education at the University of Edinburgh, he began working with his father in their family firm. He took over the business at the age of 28 and named it "The Edinburgh Geographical Institute."[28] The Bartholomew firm continued to produce the maps incorporated in *Statesman's Year-Book* until the 1984–85 edition at which time maps were discontinued.

Changes in Organization and Contents

Scott-Keltie's interest in geography helps explain another major expansion of the *Year-Book*. Rather than focus on Europe, as Martin had done, Scott-Keltie's tenure as editor saw *Statesman's Year-Book* include every country "that can be regarded as a state, however rudimentary."[29] Beginning in 1890, the arrangement of states changed. The first part of the work was devoted to the British Empire and the second to all other countries. In the words of the centennial essay in the *Year-Book*, "the mid-Victorian distinction between 'civilized' and uncivilized nations was shed."[30]

Rather than being arranged by continent, as had been done previously, the non-British states were for the first time arranged alphabetically.

Another feature of *Statesman's Year-Book* given increased prominence by Scott-Keltie was the information on navies. John Leyland had reported on naval strength through 1899. With the 1900 edition, a name that would become prominent in its own right in reference publishing, Fred T. Jane, appeared for the first time in *Statesman's Year-Book.*

John Frederick Thomas Jane[31] sketched the naval bombardment of Alexandria at the age of seventeen, reportedly placing his brothers and sisters to depict the warships.[32] Jane "wangled a trip on H.M.S. Northampton, which was to take part in British fleet maneuvers" in 1899.[33] According to Janis Bolander, this voyage and others on Royal Navy ships "laid the foundation for a knowledge of the navies of the world that has seldom been equaled."[34] The first edition of Jane's *All the World's Fighting Ships* was published in November 1897 (London: Sampson, Low, Marston, & Company). Scott-Keltie's characterization of Jane as "the well-known naval authority" in his *Statesman's Year-Book* preface in 1900 was certainly justified. Jane presented detailed statistics on the number and types of ships possessed and under construction by the world's naval powers. The detail of information presented by Jane is suggested by one of the charts he prepared for the 1913 edition: "Graphic Diagrams to Illustrate the Varying Ratio between Weight of Heaviest Gun, its Penetrative Power, and the Protection Afforded to Ships during the Last Fifty Years."

Coverage of the United States

The coverage of the United States in *Statesman's Year-Book* was altered considerably under Scott-Keltie. The Macmillan Company opened an office in New York City in 1896. Two years later, Frederick Macmillan suggested to Scott-Keltie that additional space

and attention be devoted to the United States.[35] The first step in expanded coverage was the issuance of an American edition of the *Year-Book*. Instead of the roughly 40-page article on the United States that had customarily appeared, the 1899 American edition included approximately 300 pages on the U.S. in a section that preceded the regular *Year-Book* text.

A second major expansion of the American section occurred in 1906, when each of the then 46 states was given individual treatment. Scott-Keltie explained:

> In compliance with influential suggestions from America, separate notices have been introduced of the States comprised in the American Union, on the same lines, as far as practicable, as the section dealing with the United States as a whole. In view of the fact that these States are, in the main, quite as important as the separate States of the German Confederation, this step will be regarded as justifiable.[36]

The influential suggestions came in the form of "a friendly hint" by the occupant of the White House, Theodore Roosevelt.[37] Beginning in 1906, the United States was given its own numbered section in the *Year-Book,* Part I in the American edition and Part II in the British version.

While Scott-Keltie nominally remained editor of *Statesman's Year-Book* until his death in 1927, Mortimer Epstein became joint editor in 1919. Epstein formally became editor in 1927. This promotion was long overdue, for, "from that time [i.e., 1919] onward [Scott-Keltie] merely lent the lustre of his name to the title-page, whereas all the actual work fell to Epstein."[38]

Mortimer Epstein

Mortimer Epstein was born in Lithuania in 1880 and came to England and settled in Manchester in about 1885. Epstein received his B.A. and M.A. degrees in history and economics at Owen's College in the University of Manchester. He received his Ph.D.

from Heidelberg in 1908.[39] Epstein was by all accounts a hard worker, a necessary trait for anyone in charge of *Statesman's Year-Book* beginning in 1919 and of the *Annual Register* beginning in 1921. Besides being vigorous, Epstein was an organized person. One of his lasting legacies to *Statesman's Year-Book* was his development of a regular team of editorial assistants who remained loyal to the publication for decades.[40]

The major changes in *Statesman's Year-Book* during Epstein's years as editor mirrored the changes in the world. Increased attention was given to transportation, communications, and civilian aviation. These changes also were in keeping with Epstein's description of himself "as a great believer in the participation of university men in business."[41]

In 1938 as the age of empire drew to a close with the approach of the Second World War, Epstein changed the section title for Great Britain and related countries and possessions from "British Empire" to "British Commonwealth of Nations." The arrangement within the section remained very structured, however, with the countries in the empire listed first, followed by the independent countries or dominions.

In the 1946 edition of the *Year-Book*, which would be his last, Epstein included information about the newly formed United Nations, the International Court of Justice, and the International Labour Organization. This information was included in an introductory table at the beginning of the volume. No doubt Epstein did not know how else to handle the international organizations since there was no precedent for such material.

For several reasons, 1946 was a watershed year for *Statesman's Year-Book*. Mortimer Epstein, its third editor, died on June 23, 1946. Furthermore, the official sources and contacts upon which the *Year-Book* relied for accurate data had been disrupted by the Second World War. Finally, the world was a far different place politically after the war concluded, and this necessitated major changes in the *Year-Book*.

Sigrid Henry Steinberg

The fourth editor of *Statesman Year-Book*, Sigrid Henry Steinberg, was a match for the task before him. Steinberg was born on August 3, 1899, in Goslar, Germany. He studied at the University of Munich and the University of Leipzig before receiving his Ph.D. in history from the University of London in 1922.[42] Steinberg, an exile from Nazi Germany, came to England in the mid-1930s.[43] He was a voluminous author whose works included *Five Hundred Years of Printing*, and he also served as assistant editor of *Chambers's Encyclopedia* from 1946–1950.[44]

In some ways Steinberg's most important task was to secure new sources of accurate information for *Statesman's Year-Book* since such sources had been cut off or altered by the war. Steinberg's assistant editor of five years and eventual successor, John Paxton, credits Steinberg with establishing the necessary sources of information:

> [Steinberg] was faced with the task of making entirely new arrangements with the host of new countries, old countries under new regimes, and newly created international agencies. . . . His astonishing gift of acquiring the friendship as well as the professional services of people he never met helped considerably in re-establishing the vast network of correspondents following the war.[45]

The growing importance of international organizations led Steinberg to expand their coverage and in 1949 to devote Part I to them, an arrangement that continues today. Attention was given to the U.N. organs and to the specialized agencies. Member nations are listed, together with the percent of the organization's budget that each has contributed. Six other international organizations were included in 1949, a figure that would grow over time. The British Commonwealth and Empire became Part II, the United States Part III, and Other Countries Part IV.

Once again, the arrangement of countries was revised by Steinberg in the 1962–63 edition. Previously arranged by continent, the nations in the Commonwealth were arranged according to the order in which its members achieved complete sovereignty. While the editor assured readers that this "new arrangement adopts clear historic and constitutional principles,"[46] one wonders how clear and understandable this arrangement was to users. Fortunately, *Statesman's Year-Book* has always included a table of contents and an index that includes countries. The 1960s was a decade in which numerous African countries gained independence. These changes are well documented year-by-year in *Statesman's Year-Book*.

Steinberg was also responsible for a change in the timing of the publication of *Statesman's Year-Book* and the dates appearing on volumes. Beginning in 1960, the volumes include in their title the present and the following year. Thus, 1960 becomes 1960–61, 1961 is labeled 1961–62, and so on. The rationale for this change in dating was explained to the annual's readership in 1964 and that change relates to the timing of publication. *Statesman's Year-Book* was published originally each year in January to coincide with the normal opening of Parliament. That arrangement continued but gave way after decades to a May publication date. Reportedly this shift was made in order to include current budget information from countries whose fiscal year ends at the end of March and in June.[47] Steinberg explained further that July or August publication was still intended to cover 12 months, thereby justifying the hyphenated dates in the title.[48]

John Paxton

With Steinberg's death on January 28, 1969, assistant editor John Paxton was elevated to the position of editor. Paxton was born in 1923. He has published widely, often with A.E. Walsh and C. Cook. Most of his works lie in the fields of political science and history, such as *European Political Facts* (3 vols., New York: Facts On File, 1975–1986), *Commonwealth Political Facts* (New York: Facts On File, 1979), and *Companion to the French Revolution* (New York: Facts On File, 1988).

Beyond updating *Statesman's Year-Book* to reflect the political changes in the world, Paxton made three notable contributions to the publication. The first and most important alteration was the removal of the imperial bias of the work. Beginning with the 1978–79 edition, the *Year-Book's* organization was simplified into two sections. The first continued to cover international organizations. The second listed all of the countries of the world in alphabetical order. This arrangement has greatly facilitated access to the information contained in the work. No longer does one have to know whether a certain country formerly had a dependent relationship with Great Britain or when such a state realized its independence. The year after the change was made, Paxton noted the positive response received from readers to the simplification of the arrangement of countries.[49]

Paxton further facilitated use of the work by introducing two new indexes and a chronology. A commodities index was added in 1976–77. This information had previously been included in the main index but the appearance of the separate index makes product information easier to locate. A personal name index was introduced in 1987–88, a completely new access point. In addition, a chronology was added to the introductory section of *Statesman's Year-Book* in 1984–85. This feature provides a handy way to track political changes that occur during a given year.

The third recent shift in the *Year-Book* was the changing emphasis on maps. Paxton's early years as editor were marked by an increased use of topical maps. These had appeared during John George Bartholomew's time but had given way almost entirely to political maps. Beginning with the 1969–70 edition, interesting and informative topical maps began appearing again in *Statesman's Year-Book*. To mention but a few, the 1969–70 annual included a wonderful map titled "Changes of Sovereignty since 1944." This two-page map contained a wealth of information in easy-to-use format. Another noteworthy map was included in the 1976–77 volume titled "World Natural Disasters (1960–1975)." This map detailed the sites, causes, and death totals of catastrophes. After being placed inside the front and back covers of the annuals during the 1980s, maps were no longer included in the *Year-Book* beginning with the 1984–85 volume.

Paxton also undertook two special projects related to *Statesman's Year-Book*. In 1988, Macmillan commemorated the 125th anniversary of *Statesman's Year-Book* by publishing *Statesman's Year-Book Historical Companion*. This book lists the countries of the world included in *Statesman's Year-Book* in 1988 with a one-to-two-page summary of the political history of the nation. In addition, Paxton wrote an essay for the *Historical Companion* about the first 125 years of the work; his essay is very useful in highlighting key developments in the *Year-Book*. Paxton also edited the *Statesman's Year-Book World Gazetteer*, most recently updated in 1991.[50] This work, in the editor's words, "is available for those who want more details about towns and regions" that are included in the *Year-Book*.[51]

The Future

The future of *Statesman's Year-Book* seems assured. The Macmillan interest in the annual is evidenced by the dedication of the 1987–88 edition to the memory of Harold Macmillan. His was the fifth generation of Macmillans to take an active interest in the *Year-Book* and "gave helpful advice to four of the five editors."[52]

Statesman's Year-Book will undergo two types of changes soon. First, the rapid and dramatic political changes in Eastern Europe and the Soviet Union in the winter of 1990 have resulted in almost unbelievable changes for the staff of the *Year-Book* to incorporate in their publication. Those changes and any others, such as the recent election in Nicaragua, are included in the 1990–91 edition.[53] That such political changes can appear in a bound volume so promptly is testimony to the continuing value of *Statesman's Year-Book* to libraries.

The other change that recently occurred with the *Year-Book* was the retirement of John Paxton after nearly 30 years of involvement with the publication. Paxton stepped down as editor in the summer of 1990; Brian Hunter then assumed the position of editor. Hunter has worked closely with Paxton on the *Year-Book* for years and has worked on the articles on Eastern European nations.

Statesman's Year-Book is truly a work based on continuity that reports on a changing world. While the *Year-Book* personnel and contents will change, the goal of providing a full account of all the the states of the world has been reaffirmed over the years and will remain the guiding principle of this landmark reference work.

PUBLICATION HISTORY

Statesman's Year-Book. London: Macmillan, 1864– . Annual. Through 1959, date on volume was the same as the year of publication. Beginning with 1960 and continuing to the present, dating has been the year of publication and following year (edition published in 1960 titled 1960–61, 1961 titled 1961–62, and so on).

BIBLIOGRAPHY

The most useful sources for understanding the history and development of *Statesman's Year-Book* are the volumes of *Year-Book* itself. In addition, two short articles cover the history of the publication: "First Century of the *Statesman's Year-Book*," written but not signed by Sigrid Steinberg, and John Paxton's "The First One Hundred and Twenty Five

Years of the *Statesman's Year-Book*." The former is particularly useful in describing the first three editors and the latter the trends and changes in the *Year-Book* over time. Charles Morgan's *The House of Macmillan* describes the first 100 years of the publishing house and Alexander and Daniel Macmillan, though little is said about the origins or development of *Statesman's Year-Book*. One of the interesting aspects of the *Year-Book* is the connection to other outstanding reference works. The Bolander and Dempsey articles provide useful information on Fred T. Jane. The contributions of John George Bartholomew and successors to *Statesman's Year-Book* and to publishing in general are described in detail in Allen's article.

Allen, Douglas A. "John George Bartholomew; a Centenary." *Scottish Geographical Magazine* 76 (September, 1960): 85–88.

Bell, Barbara. Review of *Statesman's Year-Book*. *American Reference Books Annual* 14 (1983): 30.

Bolander, Louis H. "Jane's Fighting Ships." *United States Naval Institute Proceedings* 74 (November, 1948): 1384–85.

Brown, R. N. Rudmose. "John Scott Keltie." *Dictionary of National Biography, 1922–1930*. London: Oxford University Press, 1937.

Dempsey, David. "Jane's World." *New York Times Book Review*. Section VII (December 9, 1951): 8.

Espinasse, Francis. *Literary Recollections and Sketches*. London: Hodder and Stoughton, 1893.

"First Century of the *Statesman's Year-Book*." *Statesman's Year-Book, 1963–64*. New York: St. Martin's, 1963, v–xi.

Goodwin, Gordon. "Frederick Martin." *Dictionary of National Biography*. Vol. 12 reissued ed. London: Smith, Elder & Company, 1909.

Graves, Charles L, ed. *Life and Letters of Alexander Macmillan*. London: Macmillan and Company, 1910.

Hughes, Thomas, ed. *Memoir of Daniel Macmillan*. London: Macmillan and Company, 1882.

Macmillan, George A., ed. *The Letters of Alexander Macmillan*. Glasgow: Privately Published, 1908.

Martin, Frederick. "Preface." *Statesman's Year-Book, 1864*. London: Macmillan, 1864.

Mill, Hugh Robert. "Obituary: Sir John Scott Keltie." *Geographical Journal* 69 (March, 1927): 281–84.

Morgan, Charles. *The House of Macmillan (1843–1943)*. London: Macmillan, 1944.

"Obituary: Sir John Scott Keltie." *Geographical Journal* 69 (February, 1927): 189.

Paxton, John, ed. "The First One Hundred and Twenty-Five Years of the *Statesman's Year-Book*." *Statesman's Year-Book* Historical Companion. London: Macmillan, 1988, vii–x.

"Preface." *Statesman's Year-Book, 1964–65*. New York: St. Martin's, 1964.

"Preface." *Statesman's Year-Book, 1979–80*. New York: St. Martin's, 1979.

"Preface." *Statesman's Year-Book, 1987–88*. New York: St. Martin's, 1987.

"Preface." *Statesman's Year-Book, 1989–90*. New York: St. Martin's, 1989.

Review of *Statesman's Year Book*. In *English Historical Review* 20 (July 1905): 617.

Review of *Statesman's Year Book*. In *Nation* 12 (March 16, 1871): 183.

Review of *Statesman's Year Book*. In *Nation* 14 (April 25, 1872): 278.

Review of *Statesman's Year Book*. In *New York Times* 10 (June 3, 1905): 356

Review of *Statesman's Year Book*. In *Scottish Review* 9 (April, 1887): 432.

Review of *Statesman's Year Book*. In *Scottish Review* 19 (April, 1892): 480.

Review of *Statesman's Year Book*. In *Spectator* 117 (August 12, 1916): 192.

Review of *Statesman's Year Book*. In *Times Literary Supplement* no. 1064 (June 8, 1922): 381.

Review of *Statesman's Year Book*. In *Times Literary Supplement* no. 1584 (June 9, 1932): 428.

Review of *Statesman's Year Book*. In *Times Literary Supplement* no. 1898 (June 18, 1938): 421.

Review of *Statesman's Year Book* in *Times Literary Supplement* no. 3581 (October 16, 1970): 1202.

Review of *Statesman's Year Book* in *Times Literary Supplement* no. 3626 (August 27, 1971): 1025.

Statesman's Year-Book World Gazetteer. 4th ed. New York: St. Martin's, 1991.

Scott-Keltie, John. "Preface." *Statesman's Year-Book*, 1906. New York: Macmillan, 1906, v.

Seccombe, Thomas. "Daniel Macmillan." *Dictionary of National Biography*. Vol 12. reissued ed. London: Smith, Elder & Company, 1909.

"Sigrid Henry Steinberg." *Contemporary Authors Permanent Series*, vol. 1. Detroit: Gale, 1975, 599.

Steinberg, Sigrid Henry, ed. "Preface." *Statesman's Year-Book, 1962–63*. New York: St. Martin's, 1962.

Thomas, Wade. Review of *Statesman's Year-Book*. *American Reference Books Annual* 20 (1989): 89.

Wilson, David A. *Carlyle to Threescore-and-Ten (1853–1865)*. London: Kegan Paul, Trench, Trubner & Co., 1929.

Wilson, David A., and David W. MacArthur. *Carlyle in Old Age (1865–1881)*. New York: E. P. Dutton, 1934.

Wynar, Lubomyr. Review of *Statesman's Year-Book*. *American Reference Books Annual* 11 (1980): 44.

NOTES

[1] In the mid-1980s the size increased slightly to 5½" x 8".

[2] Barbara Bell, review of *Statesman's Year-Book, American Reference Books Annual* 14 (1983): 30.

[3] John Paxton, "Preface," *Statesman's Year-Book Historical Companion* (New York: St. Martin's, 1988): xi.

[4] Review of Statesman's Year-Book, *New York Times,* 3 June 1905, sec, 2, p. 356. For other reviews, see: *Scottish Review* 9 (April 1887): 432; *Scottish Review* 19 (April 1892): 480; *English Historical Review* 20 (July 1905): 617; *Times Literary Supplement* no. 1064 (8 June 1922): 381; Spectator 117 (12 August 1916): 192; *Times Literary Supplement* no. 1584 (9 June 1932): 428; *Times Literary Supplement* no. 1898 (18 June 1938): 421; *Times Literary Supplement* no. 3581 (16 October 1970): 1202; *Times Literary Supplement* no. 3626 (27 August 1971): 1025.

[5] Frederick Martin, "Preface," *Statesman's Year-Book, 1864* (London: Macmillan, 1864): v.

[6] John Paxton, "The First One Hundred and Twenty-five Years of the Statesman's Year-Book," *Statesman's Year-Book Historical Companion* (London: Macmillan, 1988), vii.

[7] Gordon Goodwin, "Frederick Martin," *Dictionary of National Biography*, vol. 12, reissued ed. (London: Smith, Elder, 1909), 1160.

[8] David Alec Wilson, *Carlyle to Threescore-and-Ten (1853–1865)* (London: Kegan Paul, Trench, Trubner, 1929), 249. See also Francis Espinasse, *Literary Recollections and Sketches* (London: Hodder and Stoughton, 1893), 260–63.

[9] John Paxton, "The First One Hundred and Twenty-Five Years," vii.

[10] Ibid., viii.

[11] Martin, "Preface," v.

[12] Reviews of *Statesman's Year-Book* in Nation 12 (16 March 1871): 183; and in Nation 14 (25 April 1872): 278.

[13] Martin, "Preface," vii.

[14] Paxton, "The First One Hundred and Twenty-Five Years," viii.

[15] Martin, "Preface," vii.

[16] Ibid.

[17] Ibid.

[18] Sigrid Henry Steinberg, "First Century of the Statesman's Year-Book," *Statesman's Year-Book, 1963–64* (New York: St. Martin's, 1963), x.

[19] Ibid., vi.

[20] Ibid.

[21] Even though John Scott-Keltie's name is almost always listed under "Keltie" in standard reference sources such as the *DNB* and in his obituaries in the *Geographical Journal*, we are told that he always used the hyphen. In that spirit, his name is consistently hyphenated in this essay.

[22] Steinberg, "First Century of the Statesman's Year-Book," vii.

[23] R. N. Rudmose Brown, "John Scott Keltie," *Dictionary of National Biography, 1922–1930* (London: Oxford University Press, 1937), 463–64.

[24] Hugh Robert Mill, "Obituary: Sir John Scott Keltie," *Geographical Journal* 69 (March 1927): 282–83.

[25] "Obituary: Sir John Scott Keltie," *Geographical Journal* 69 (February 1927): 189.

[26] Ibid.

[27] Elting E. Morison, *The Letters of Theodore Roosevelt*, vol. 8 (Cambridge: Harvard University Press, 1954), 904.

[28] Douglas A. Allan, "John George Bartholomew," *Scottish Geographical Magazine* 76 (September 1960): 85.

[29] Paxton, "The First One Hundred and Twenty-Five Years," ix.

[30] Steinberg, "First Century of the Statesman's Year-Book," ix.

[31] Louis H. Bolander, "Janes' Fighting Ships," *United States Naval Institute Proceedings* 74 (November 1948): 1384.

[32] David Dempsey, "Jane's World," *New York Times Book Review*, 9 December 1951, sec. 7, p. 8.

[33] Ibid.

[34] Ibid., and Bolander, "Janes' Fighting Ships," 1384.

[35] Paxton, "The First One Hundred and Twenty-Five Years," ix.

[36] John Scott-Keltie, "Preface," *Statesman's Year-Book, 1906* (New York: Macmillan, 1906), v.

[37] Paxton, "The First One Hundred and Twenty-Five Years," ix.

[38] Steinberg, "First Century of the Statesman's Year-Book," viii.

[39] Ibid.

[40] Ibid.

[41] Ibid.

[42] *Contemporary Authors, Permanent Series*, vol. 1 (Detroit: Gale Research, 1975), 599.

[43] Ibid. See also Paxton, "The First One Hundred and Twenty-Five Years," ix.

[44] *Contemporary Authors*, 599.

[45] Paxton, "The First One Hundred and Twenty-Five Years," ix–x.

[46] S. Henry Steinberg, "Preface," *Statesman's Year-Book, 1962–63* (New York: St. Martin's, 1962).

[47] S. Henry Steinberg, "Preface," *Statesman's Year-Book, 1964–65* (New York: St. Martin's, 1964).

[48] Ibid.

[49] John Paxton, "Preface," *Statesman's Year–Book, 1979–80* (New York: St. Martin's, 1979).

[50] John Paxton, *Statesman's Year-Book World Gazetteer*, 4th ed. (London: Macmillan, 1991).

[51] John Paxton, "Preface," *Statesman's Year-Book, 1989–90* (New York: St. Martin's, 1989).

[52] John Paxton, "Preface," *Statesman's Year-Book, 1987–88* (New York: St. Martin's, 1987).

[53] Garrett Kiely, Marketing Manager for Reference Books at St. Martin's Press, conversations with the author, 6 March 1990.

Permanently Definitive: *Strong's Exhaustive Concordance of the Bible*

Edward D. Starkey

DEVELOPMENT AND HISTORY

James Strong's *The Exhaustive Concordance of the Bible*, first published in 1894, is a reference key to another book, the Bible, in the English-language translation first published in 1611 and known in Great Britain and much of the world as the Authorized Version and in North America as the King James Version. In order to understand the significance of Strong's work, it is necessary to have some feel for the importance of the King James Version.

The King James Version of the Bible

At the beginning of the seventeenth century, English Puritans found every current Bible translation supported at least some theological positions they could not agree with. King James I found the notes in some translations seditious.[1] Accordingly, in 1604 the king set forth a plan whereby 54 scholars from Cambridge and Oxford Universities as well as Westminster Cathedral would engage in a new translation. The translation was completed and printed in 1611. Called in common parlance "the Authorized Version," it was in fact never authorized by royal decree for sole use in churches. For the next few decades it was fiercely criticized from some quarters and saw competition in sales from earlier English translations. Eventually, however, this "authorized" version "acquired a sanctity properly ascribable only to the unmediated voice of God; to multitudes of English-speaking Christians it has seemed little less than blasphemy to tamper with the words of the King James Version."[2] Attempts to document its influence on the development of English literature and the language have been frequent, but in truth its influence is beyond calculation. One need only read the speeches of Abraham Lincoln or Martin Luther King, Jr., to note its influence on American discourse. Indeed the translation acquired a cultural power far beyond anything its originators would recognize.[3]

So widely read a document as the Bible calls for support literature in every language in which it is read. In the Middle Ages, the device known as the concordance came into being. "Concordance" is made up of two Latin words, *cum*, "with," and *cor*, "heart," and carries the sense of agreement or harmony. It originally was used in the plural, *concordantiae*, meaning passages which are in agreement with one another.[4] These passages were understood to form a unified system of truth. For modern usage, the *Oxford English Dictionary* defines a concordance as "an alphabetical arrangement of the principal words contained in a book, with citations of the passages in which they occur." The making of concordances cries out for the use of computer technology, but the lack of it did not daunt nineteenth-century scholars from producing unsurpassable concordances of the English Bible and of the original Hebrew and Greek texts of the Bible.

Early Concordances

The earliest known concordance, to the Latin Vulgate Bible, was compiled by a team of French Dominican scholars under the direction of Hugh of Saint-Cher and was published in 1240. The first concordance to the Hebrew scriptures was compiled by Rabbi Isaac Nathan ben Kalonymus in the mid-fifteenth century and printed in Venice in 1523.[5] It became the source upon which later, fuller Hebrew concordances were based. In 1602 Conrad Kircher published a concordance to the Greek Septuagint, the Greek text of the Hebrew Scriptures published in Alexandria in the third century BC. In 1546 Basel saw the publication of the first Greek concordance to the New Testament. From the sixteenth through the twentieth centuries these concordances of the Scriptures in their original languages were improved upon as more definitive texts of the Bible were themselves published.

The earliest concordances were by no means as useful as we have come to expect from a reference tool. They were neither comprehensive nor exhaustive. Lacking a definitive scholarly text of the Bible, the compilers could refer to a word that was available in one text but not in another. Moreover references could only be made to books of the Bible or to some idiosyncratic referencing system, not to the individual verses. In the thirteenth century Stephen Langton, Archbishop of Canterbury, divided the Bible into the chapters we use today, although other chapter divisions had been proffered and continued in use for some time. Only in 1551 did the present day verse numbering system come into being when Robert Stephanus published his Greek Bible in Geneva. This numbering system came to be accepted in most later Protestant, Catholic, and Jewish translations and imprints and thus could be relied on as a standard reference system.

In 1535 Thomas Gibson, or Gybson, produced the first concordance to the English New Testament *The Concordance of the New Testamant, most necessary to be had in ye handes of all soche as [delyte] in the comunycacion of any place contayned in ye New Testament* (London: Thomas Gybson, 1535). John Marbeck published a concordance to the complete English Bible in 1550 as *A Concordance, that is to saie, a worke wherein by the order of the letters of the A.B.C. ye maie redely finde any word conteigned in the whole Bible, so often as it is there expressed or mencioned* . . . (London: Richardus Grafton, 1550). Both Gybson and Marbeck based their concordances on early English translations of the Bible. One Clement Cotton began work on a concordance to the Authorized Version, and this was taken up and completed by Samuel Newman, who published *A Large and Complete Concordance to the Bible in English, according to the latest translation. First collected by Clement Cotton, and now much enlarged and amended for the good both of schollers and others; far exceeding the most perfect that ever was extant in our language, both in ground-work and building, by Samuel Newman, a poor labourer in the Lord's vinyard* . . . (London: T. Downes and J. Young, 1643) just over 30 years after the initial publication of the Authorized Version.

Cruden's Concordance

Nearly a century later this was supplanted in accuracy and comprehensiveness by Alexander Cruden's *A Complete concordance to the Old and New Testament: or, a dictionary and alphabetical index to the Bible* (London: Warne, 1737). Cruden, whose life, sadly, was punctuated by periods of madness, chose what he considered the most important words in the Bible and recorded many, but not all, instances of their use sequentially through the Old and New Testaments in the Authorized Version. A single line of context is given for each use as well as the name of the book quoted and chapter and verse. Although Cruden remains to this day a popular concordance—it was reprinted through the 1950s—it has major shortcomings: it is not analytical; it does not include all the words in the Bible; it does not include all the references to even the important words; and it lacks most proper names of persons and places.

An analytical concordance leads the researcher back to the Hebrew and Greek original words, and a complete, or exhaustive, concordance contains *all* words and names used in the Bible and records all references to them. While Cruden singled out what he felt were the most important words, neither he nor his subsequent publishers have listed those he excluded.

In essence, in producing the first concordance to the Authorized Version which achieved wide use, Cruden posed the problem. A biblical concordance has many uses: the theologian must find every application of a term to understand its doctrinal impact, the preacher looks for examples in preparing a sermon and has to have all the examples available, and the serious reader searches for full understanding of the whole text. Cruden's concordance could not advance scholarship and could only fill the needs of the preacher and reader in a casual manner. The answer to more serious needs would be met by two concordances published in the late nineteenth century.

Robert Young

In 1879, Robert Young of Edinburgh published his *Analytical concordance to the Bible, containing every word in alphabetical order, arranged under its Hebrew or Greek original, with the literal meaning of each, exhibiting about 311,000 references. With the latest information on Biblical geography and antiquities* (Edinburgh: G. A. Young, and Co., 1879) in which he alphabetically listed all but the most common words of the Authorized Version and under each gave in succession the various Hebrew or Greek words which the English word is used to translate. Then under each Hebrew or Greek word he listed the book, chapter, and verse of the reference as

well as a single line of context. Thus under "morning" Young listed eight Hebrew and four Greek words each with references to their proper uses.

This arrangement has the virtues of leading the researcher back at once to the exact Hebrew or Greek word used in the original text, giving a definition of this original word, and offering references to all the instances of it. Young included all proper names of persons and places and attempted to define and date them. At the end of the concordance he added a Hebrew lexicon to the Old Testament, a Greek lexicon to the New, and a relisting of proper names from the Old Testament with the exact form of the original Hebrew. The lexicons are arranged by the transliterated Roman alphabet. Young's was a strong entry in the field of concordances and remains in print to this day; in 1982 Thomas Nelson Publishers brought it out under the title *Analytical Concordance to the Bible . . . Newly revised and corrected* (Nashville, TN: Thomas Nelson).

Young solved a basic problem of an "analytical" concordance, accounting for the fact that a single English word can be the translation of many Hebrew or Greek words, by lining up each Hebrew and Greek word under the English word which translates it. But this arrangement itself creates another difficulty which biblical scholar Donald Guthrie identifies in his introduction to the 1982 Thomas Nelson edition. The Bible reader who turns to a concordance is often trying to find a full reference by means of a certain keyword he or she has remembered. If many Hebrew and Greek words have been translated by that English keyword, the researcher must look through just so many lists under the keyword. In searching what may indeed be a multitude of lists, the verse becomes elusive. In short, Young's concordance, while being thorough and scholarly, is cumbersome. Moreover, Young did not include every English word used in the Authorized Version; words of great frequency, such as articles and common conjunctions, were excluded but not listed in prefatory matter, a serious drawback.

Strong's Approach

James Strong took a different approach with his *Exhaustive Concordance of the Bible*. He first listed every word used in the Authorized Version except 47 of the most common: a, an, and, are, as, etc.[6] He included proper names. Following each entry he gave a single listing of all uses of the English word, arranged in the order of the books of the Authorized Version, and by chapter and verse within each book. As did Cruden and Young, Strong offered a single line of context, usually not a complete thought. Strong solved Guthrie's problem, mentioned above, by providing this unified list of all references to the English word. Thus the word "morning" in Strong is followed by a list of all its Old Testament uses, beginning in Genesis and ending in Zephaniah, and this is followed by New Testament uses, beginning in the Gospel of Matthew and ending in Revelation.

However, it remains that the English word may in fact be the translation of more than one Greek or Hebrew word. Strong led the reader back to the original word via reference to two lexicons he included at the end of the concordance: Hebrew and Greek. He listed each Hebrew word according to the Hebrew alphabet and gave each a reference number. (By this we know that there are 8,674 Hebrew words in the Old Testament.) A transliteration of the word into the Roman alphabet, a phonetic spelling, and a brief definition follow. Strong did the same for the Greek vocabulary of the New Testament (with 5,624 Greek words). In the main concordance, at the end of each line of context Strong added the reference number of the original Hebrew or Greek word to which the reader can turn for definition. If the reference number is in Roman type, the word is to be found in the Hebrew lexicon; if in italics, in the Greek lexicon. To visit the "morning" example once again, where Young had eight lists for Hebrew words and four for Greek, Strong has a unified list with nine reference numbers for Hebrew words (he has split two Hebrew forms into separate words)

and four reference numbers for Greek words. With entrepreneurial instinct he separately paginated his Hebrew and Greek lexicons for publication independent of the concordance as reference pocketbooks for seminarians and students, and they are thus reprinted to this day. Strong's reference numbers to the Greek and Hebrew words have become standard and have been added to succeeding biblical reference books.

Strong further strengthened his work by adding an appendix in which he listed the 47 common words excluded from the main concordance and including every reference to each by biblical book, chapter, and verse. The difference in treatment between these common words and the words in the main concordance is that Strong did not add a line of context, since doing so would have expanded the work out of reasonable proportion, in some cases almost repeating the entire Bible under a word. The fact remains, however, that this is the first truly *exhaustive* concordance, and the scholar who wishes can trace each single use of "and" and "the" in the Authorized Version.

A second appendix of some 262 pages is a comparative concordance, showing where the changes of the new late nineteenth-century translation known as the Revised Version differ from the Authorized Version. This was of benefit only during the useful life of the Revised Version and was dropped from mid-twentieth century reprints of the concordance when other English translations had gained in popularity.

The Career of James Strong

James Strong's career as a biblical scholar coincided with a quickening of biblical scholarship spurred by advancements in textual studies and archaeology in the century preceding publication of his concordance.[7]

Strong was born in New York City in 1822 and died in Round Lake, New York, in August 1894, four months after his concordance was published. Although raised an Episcopalian, he underwent a conversion to Methodism, and graduated from Wesleyan University in Connecticut in 1844. He studied and taught biblical languages throughout his life, his most important appointment being at Drew Theological Seminary in New Jersey between 1868 and 1893. Conversant in the French and German as well as the English literature of biblical science, he served on the committee which updated the Old Testament translation for the Revised Version (supplanted in the mid-twentieth century by the Revised Standard Version and more recently by the New Revised Standard Version). A member of the American branch of the Palestine Exploration Society, he went on an expedition to Palestine and Egypt in 1874, and he chaired the Archaeological Council of the Oriental Society.

In his quarter century of teaching at Drew, Strong gave evidence of great learning, creative scholarship, and immense drive. Scholars of his kind defined the path for biblical specialists in the twentieth century: accomplishment in all biblical as well as several modern languages, study in Palestine at the sources, concern with biblical texts and their translation to modern languages, and persistent application to tasks. Strong's exactitude as a scholar was coupled with a conservative bent. He maintained that the prophet Isaiah was the sole author of the book that bears his name, that Moses wrote the first five books of the Hebrew Scriptures, and that the creation took place as the book of Genesis records it— all positions attacked by liberal nineteenth-century scholars. Strong remained a critical scholar, however, and stated that his positions were based on his research and not on the blind acceptance of authority.[8]

Although he wrote widely on biblical matters and published some 30 books in his lifetime, Strong's monumental contribution, in nineteenth-century eyes, was the ten-volume *Cyclopaedia of Biblical, Theological, and Ecclesiastical Literature* (New York: Harper and Brother, 1867–1881), begun with

John McClintock in 1867 and completed in 1881. McClintock died after the third volume was published, and Strong took over the editorship. He added two supplementary volumes in 1885–1886. This lengthy work was the first compilation in English of the great amount of information in biblical studies that had been collected in the preceding decades. Lengthy bibliographies follow each alphabetized entry, but the work lacks an index. Although the information in this encyclopedia is now dated and has been much augmented and corrected by the labors of another prolific century, the work was reprinted as recently as 1981.[9]

Although in the nineteenth century Strong's encyclopedia was considered his most important work, his concordance marks his fame in the twentieth. "This is James Strong's monument. It tells of his inventive faculty, his organizing mind, his boundless energy, and his capacity for unremitting toil."[10] Unfortunately, a lecture Strong gave in Round Lake just before his death, "How I Made My Concordance," appears not to have been preserved. However, there are occasional references which indicate that he organized his students, as many as 100 of them, to help him, and that the task took 35 years.[11] Once completed, accurately and exhaustively, the result is definitive, never has to be done again, and will be of use as long as the King James Version is studied.

Strong's Legacy

The reviewing of reference works was not a widespread art form in the 1890s; however, one reviewer in *The Critic*, a New York literary magazine, did make salient comments on the new concordance.[12] Cruden, he noted, "occupied the whole field" until the appearance of Young's concordance in 1880. Cruden's weakness was in being incomplete; Young fully replaced him but included Greek and Hebrew words in their original alphabets in the text itself, thus putting off those who did not know these languages. Strong, the critic noted, "contrived the same end [completeness] in his book by another method, that will not perplex those who have no special knowledge of the sacred tongues, and do not wish to be hindered by the presence of characters in a language they cannot understand." Here he is referring to Strong's reference number system and his Hebrew and Greek lexicons. The appendix of the 47 common words "is an evidence of enormous labor, and will not often be used." The writer offered the useful comparative note that while Cruden quoted the word "King, etc." 665 times, "Strong has 2,813 references to the same group." He finishes by praising the concordance's "exceptional accuracy" but noting that "its great size . . . will probably prevent its coming into universal use."

This anonymous critic need only be faulted for his final words because Strong's concordance has indeed been widely published in the twentieth century. Copyrighted in 1890, it was first released in New York and Cincinnati in April 1894. Hodder & Stoughton brought it out in London the same year. The Methodist Book Concern held the rights to the concordance and reprinted it several times during the first four decades of the twentieth century. In 1938 following a merger of two Methodist Churches, Abingdon-Cokesbury became the imprint, to be followed simply by Abingdon Press. Sales of the concordance increased during the 1950s, 1960s, and 1970s with a surge in Bible reading; a 1977 Abingdon edition is the thirty-sixth reprint with 50,000 copies brought off the press at that time and 35,000 sold annually throughout the 1980s.[13] At the beginning of the 1980s Abingdon reset the type and in 1986 produced a "red letter" edition, wherein quotations of the words spoken by Jesus in the New Testament are printed in red letters. The rights to print this edition were then sold to World Bible Publishers which has subsequently brought it out unchanged under its imprint.

A second event occurred which greatly influenced the distribution of Strong's concordance was the lapsing of the copyright in 1946. The concordance came into the public domain.[14] This was the occasion for a host of reprints, often from photographs of the early text, some of passable, some of lesser quality. Thus the concordance has appeared under the imprints of 16 publishers in the United States, with another version printed in England. So popular did this concordance become by mid-century and so important was it to its publishers to distinguish it from its competitors that its cover title changed on most editions from the original *The Exhaustive Concordance . . .* to *Strong's Exhaustive Concordance. . . .*Many of these imprints were sold with descriptions such as "compact edition," "student version," "popular edition," or "abridged." A comparison of the page numbers indicates that it is usually the comparative concordance to the Revised Version and sometimes the appendix to the 47 common words which are left out rather than a reworking of the main text to lead the user to fewer references.

It is the continuing popularity of the Authorized Version of the Bible among Protestant conservatives that keeps the market alive for reference works based on this version. Reader's Digest reworked the actual text of Strong to produce its *Reader's Digest Family Guide to the Bible: A Concordance and Reference Companion to the King James Version*, edited by John C.L. Gibson and Ian A. Moir (Pleasantville, NY: Reader's Digest, 1984). Here the editors limited entries to 7,000 keywords followed by 100,000 context lines and included essays on various aspects of the Bible as well as reproductions of master paintings.

The most important edition outside the Methodist Book Concern-Abingdon-World Bible track has been *The New Strong's Exhaustive Concordance of the Bible* put out by Thomas Nelson Publishers in 1984. This publisher reset the type by computer and rearranged the design of Strong's lines: scripture references (book, chapter, and verse) are placed in a uniform manner (left justified) after the context line and before the reference number to the Hebrew or Greek lexicon. Strong originally had the scripture reference first followed by the context line and, lastly, the lexicon reference number, with the context line often intruding into the column of lexicon reference numbers. Thomas Nelson also has inserted variant spellings of biblical names from twentieth-century translations so that the reader of the Revised Standard Version or the New International Version can find a biblical name in the concordance according to the spelling from the newer version and then be cross-referred to the entry as it is spelled in the Authorized Version. Strong can in this manner be used as a concordance for newer translations. Definitions have been added for proper names such as "Joseph" for which there is more than one person. A "Key Verse Comparison Chart" is a major addition to the Thomas Nelson edition, which profits the general reader more than the scholar; here 1,800 major verses, chosen from every book in the Bible, are printed in six translations for comparison: the King James Version, the New King James Version, the New American Standard Bible, the New International Version, the Revised Standard Version, and Today's English Version. The editors at Thomas Nelson did not reset the type for the Hebrew and Greek lexicons, but since the originals are clear this has not proven problematic. They do claim that "no section from the original Strong's has been eliminated" (Publisher's Preface), which is not entirely true since the 262-page "Comparative Concordance of the Authorized and Revised Versions" has been dropped as it indeed had been for most reprints after the 1940s when the Revised Version had fallen into disuse and been replaced by the Revised Standard Version.

One of the enduring contributions James Strong made in the design of his concordance is his numbering system for Hebrew and Greek words. The numbering system has proven so popular it has been adopted by editors of other biblical reference books who can assume that a copy of Strong will be handy to most readers. Notable among these are such recent editions of biblical dictionaries as *An Expository Dictionary of Biblical Words.* (William Edwin Vine, Merrill F. Unger, and William White,

Jr., [Nashville, TN: Thomas Nelson, 1985]).[15] Thomas Nelson Publishers included Strong's reference numbers in their edition of the competing, as it were, *Young's Analytical Concordance to the Bible*.

Concordances produced for twentieth-century translations of the Bible would have to live up to Strong's standards unless they were designed for a less scholarly purpose: they would have to be analytical, exhaustive, and easily read. Strong's influence can be clearly seen in the newest concordance available in book format, *The NIV Exhaustive Concordance* (Edward W. Goodrick and John R. Kohlenberger III, eds., Grand Rapids, MI: Zondervan, 1990). In addition to the similarity in title, the design of this concordance is much like that developed by Strong. Each English word of the New International Version is listed in alphabetical order with all occurrences of it listed by biblical book. With each occurrence is chapter, verse, context line, and reference number. For this last, the editors have departed from Strong and created a new reference numbering system since they felt that after a century of use Strong's system was no longer adequate to the task. Advances in the linguistics of the biblical languages, the need to treat Hebrew and Aramaic as separate languages (Strong interfiled vocabularies from Hebrew and "Chaldee" or Aramaic), and the correction of Strong's factual and typographic errors necessitated their decision. However, so prevalent has Strong's numbering system become, Goodrick and Kohlenberger needed to append two indexes to their concordance: an index of Strong's numbers to theirs and an index of their numbers to Strong's. Nor did they depart from Strong in using Roman type for Hebrew/Aramaic (with the Aramaic alphabet following the Hebrew) and italic type for Greek.

In a pre-computer age, Strong's standards for accurate and thorough scholarship, as well as his energy and dedication to task, were among the highest in the field of biblical studies. His contemporaries, somewhat awestruck, criticized him for his appendix which records each application of the 47 common words—"sheer intellectual waste"[16]—but these were men who could not know the value of word-comparison studies for the simple reason that in that age, without computers, such could not yet be done. All concordances are now done with computers, and even these

take years to produce. Strong did the most that could be done before computers were available. His work significantly advanced English-language biblical scholarship of the twentieth century, and it remains permanently definitive for the Authorized Version.

PUBLICATION HISTORY

As noted in the text, the concordance has been frequently reprinted. The original edition, noted first below, was reprinted throughout the twentieth century by official Methodist publishing houses, known variously as the Methodist Book Concern, Abingdon-Cokesbury Press, and Abingdon Press. Re-editing in the 1980s led to the "red letter" edition of 1986, the rights to which Abingdon sold to World Bible Publishers. Many publishers reprinted the earliest version when the work came into the public domain. Chief among these was Thomas Nelson Publishers, which reset the type and added features.

The Exhaustive Concordance of the Bible: Showing Every Word of the Text of the Common English Version of the Canonical Books, and Every Occurrence of Each Word in Regular Order; Together with a Comparative Concordance of the Authorized and Revised Versions, Including the American Variations; Also Brief Dictionaries of the Hebrew and Greek Words of the Original, with References to the English Words: by James Strong. New York: Hunt & Eaton; Cincinnati: Cranston & Curts, 1894. London, Hodder & Stoughton, 1894.

Strong's Exhaustive Concordance of the Bible: Showing every word of the text of the King James Version of the canonical books of the Bible and every occurrence of each word in regular order, together with the words of Jesus identified in bold face red letter and a key-word comparison of selected words and phrases in the King James Version with five leading contemporary translations: also brief dictionaries of the Hebrew and Greek words of the original with references to the English words. Nashville: Abingdon Press, 1986.

The New Strong's Exhaustive Concordance of the Bible with main Concordance, Appendix to the Main Concordance, Key Verse Comparison Chart, Dictionary of the Hebrew Bible, Dictionary of the Greek Testament. Nashville: Thomas Nelson Publishers, 1984.

BIBLIOGRAPHY

The *Dictionary of American Biography* offers a brief but perceptive overview of Strong's life, based on some of the other biographical reminiscences listed. The article in *The Critic* is a contemporary review of the concordance. *The Cambridge History of the Bible*, three volumes in all, treats the transmission of the biblical text down to our times and its translation into modern languages; although it is written in essay format, it is so filled with factual information on the Bible and is indexed so well that many libraries have included copies of it in their reference collections.

Buttz, Henry A. "Prefatory Memoir." In *The Student's Commentary: The Book of Psalms,* by James Strong. New York: Eaton & Mains; Cincinnati: Curts & Jennings, 1896.

Dictionary of American Biography. s.v. "Strong, James."

"Exhaustive Concordance of the Bible." *The Critic* 26 (March 9, 1895): 178–79.

Greenslade, S. L., ed. *The Cambridge History of the Bible: The West from the Reformation to the Present Day.* Cambridge: Cambridge University Press, 1963.

Joy, James Richard, ed. *The Teachers of Drew: 1867–1942.* Madison, NJ: Drew University, 1942.

MacMullen, Wallace. "A Legacy of Inspiration." In *Drew Theological Seminary: 1867–1917,* edited by Ezra Squier Tipple. New York: Methodist Book Concern, 1917.

Vernon, Walter Newton. *The United Methodist Publishing House: A History. Vol. II: From 1870 to 1988.* Nashville: Abingdon Press, 1989.

NOTES

[1] S. L. Greenslade "English Versions of the Bible, 1525–1611" in *The Cambridge History of the Bible: The West from the Reformation to the Present Day* (Cambridge: Cambridge University Press, 1963), 164.

[2] Ibid., 168.

[3] The apotheosis of a Bible text is not limited to the King James Version. Erasmus of Rotterdam printed the first Greek text of the New Testament in 1515, using for his edition what Greek manuscripts he could lay his hands on. For one small section where he could not locate a Greek manuscript, he translated the Latin Vulgate back into Greek, producing a version quite unlike the original. This edition, with Erasmus's later emendations, came to be known as the "Textus Receptus," the Received Text, and was used for many translations into the vernacular throughout Europe including the King James Version. So important was it considered for so long a period that when in the nineteenth century scholars produced more accurate texts derived from very ancient manuscripts, they were accused of meddling with the sacred.

[4] *Encyclopaedia Britannica*, 11th ed., see "Concordance." This essay offers the best brief historical treatment of the development of concordances.

[5] Ibid.

[6] The entire list of forty-seven: a, an, and, are, as, be, but, by, for, from, he, her, him, his, I, in, is , it, me, my, not, O, of, our, out, shall, shalt, she, that, the, thee, their, them, they, thou, thy, to, unto, up, upon, us, was, we, were, with, ye, you.

[7] A good biographical essay is to be found in the *Dictionary of American Biography* (New York: Charles Scribner's Sons, 1936), but additional facts can be gleaned from *The Twentieth Century Biographical Dictionary of Notable Americans* (Boston: The Biographical Society, 1904) and from *Appleton's Cyclopaedia of American Biography,* rev. ed. (New York: D. Appleton, 1900). Interestingly, this last does not even mention the concordance among Strong's publications. Evaluations of Strong's work by his colleagues are found in the reminiscences noted in books listed in the bibliography.

[8] *Dictionary of American Biography*, see, "Strong, James."

[9] *Cyclopedia of Biblical, Theological, and Ecclesiastical Literature*, (Grand Rapids, MI: Baker Book House, 1981).

[10] *The Teachers of Drew*, ed. James Richard Joy (Madison, NJ: Drew University, 1942), 80.

[11] "Publisher's Preface" to the *New Strong's Exhaustive Concordance of the Bible* (Nashville: Thomas Nelson, 1984), v.

[12] *The Critic*, 26 (9 March 1895): 178–79.

[13] Walter Vernon, Jr., *The United Methodist Publishing House: A History*, vol. 2 (Nashville, TN: Abingdon, 1989), 267.

[14] Though the concordance was first published in 1894, Strong had copyrighted it, the two lexicons, and the comparative concordance separately in 1890. The 56 years of copyright protection expired in 1946.

[15] This combines the earlier dictionaries of Vine on the New Testament and Unger and White on the Old.

[16] Quoted by but not agreed to by Wallace MacMullen in Ezra Squier Tipple, ed., *Drew Theological Seminary: 1867–1917* (New York: Methodist Book Concern, 1917), 98.

The World in One's Hands: *Times Atlas of the World*

Mary L. Larsgaard

DEVELOPMENT AND HISTORY

Atlases hold a firm place in today's libraries and homes, and not just by virtue of their heft and size—both of which generally exceed that of most other volumes—but rather by the solid worth of their contents. There are several different major kinds of atlases—general reference, thematic, national. This essay is concerned with an exemplar, the general reference atlas.

"Atlas" is a word usually applied to a collection of maps, all adhering to some governing idea, usually either bound or boxed together. In libraries, the most frequently used type of atlas is the general reference atlas. The general reference atlas of choice must be accurate, have as much topographic detail as possible, treat place names uniformly, have a logical sequence of scale and balanced coverage, have a distinct style, be composed mainly of geographical maps (with a minimum of thematic maps), be comprehensive within the limits of the scales used, and be carefully and systematically arranged and equally carefully edited.[1]

Today's general reference atlas is usually thought to have for its remotest forebear Ptolemy's *Geographia* of the fifteenth century, which with its listing of place names and spellings aroused interest in map making. According to legend, it was accompanied by a group of maps, but no physical copies survive. Even if these maps existed, they were an accompaniment to another book, not an independent publication as a true atlas is. In the sixteenth century, Antonio Lafreri's collections of maps—constructed to match a buyer's needs, tastes, and funds—were also progenitors; but the maps making up these volumes were not done in a uniform style as maps in today's atlases must be. It was Lafreri who used a special title page (in about 1570), showing Atlas with the world on his shoulders, although it would not be until Mercator's 1594 atlas that such a publication would be called an atlas.[2]

It is only with Abraham Ortelius' *Theatrum orbis terrarum* of 1570 that a volume recognizable as a general reference atlas by today's definition of the genre appeared. The *Theatrum*—rolling off the press of Christopher Plantin in Antwerp—was a stupendous success, with its 70 maps on 53 sheets; there were two additional printings in 1570. It included maps of the world arranged in what was called Ptolemaic order, an order supposedly based on Ptolemy's system of descriptive geography. Since tables of contents were not yet standard, this was a handy *aide-mémoire* for educated users.

Such a *succès fou* encouraged more of the same, and the sixteenth and seventeenth centuries became the first important period of commercial map publishing. Before the end of the century, Mercator, whose idea the atlas originally was, had issued his *Atlas sive Cosmographicae meditationes de fabrica mundi et fabricati figure* ("Atlas, or cosmographical meditations upon the creation of the universe, and the universe as created"). With this impetus, the atlas became the dominant cartographic form of the seventeenth century. Anyone who would like to compare these early examples of the atlas with today's version may look at the excellent facsimiles published by Theatrum Orbis Terrarum Publishing Company, Ltd.

The German atlases (e.g., those by Homann) of the seventeenth and eighteenth century had considerable detail, while the English atlases (e.g., those by Speed, Ogilvie, Senex, Jefferys, Kitchens) were more crowded in appearance, but similar to the Dutch atlases: accurate (in as far as knowledge of the time permitted); well presented; and, often, decorated. In the eighteenth and nineteenth centuries, the Dutch hegemony gave way to the German.[3]

The Bartholomew Family

Enter the Bartholomew family. George Bartholomew (1784–1871) began as an apprentice map engraver at the age of 13 for the engraving and publishing firm of W. & D. Lizars; his son John Bartholomew (1805–1861) began an apprenticeship with that firm in 1820, at the age of 15. John did excellent work and was recognized for it. He established the firm of John Bartholomew in 1826, which in 1860 became John Bartholomew and Son, with offices at 4A North Bridge and printing works in nearby Carrubber's Close. John died in 1861. Another John (1831–1893) was first a trainee and later a partner. In 1870 the business moved to 17 Brown Square and in 1879 to 31 Chambers Street. Toward the end of the 1870s a third Bartholomew introduced the use of contour layer coloring to depict relief in commercial maps, a very important innovation.

In the next generation, John George Bartholomew (1860–1920), after education at the University of Edinburgh, joined the family business shortly after 1879. In 1888 John George, at the age of 28, took over the business's management and a year later moved the firm

to Park Road and named it the Edinburgh Geographical Institute. From 1888 until 1892 John George had a partnership with Thomas Nelson; from 1893 to 1919 a cousin, Andrew G. Scott, was his partner. In 1911 the firm was moved to a new building in Duncan Street, and in 1919 became John Bartholomew & Son, Ltd.[4] Before his father's death in 1920, Captain Ian Bartholomew, John George's eldest son, became a partner in the firm.[5]

By the early 1900s, the firm was doing a large number of map-and-atlas jobs for British and American publishers; and Bartholomew atlases—with titles such as *The Handy Atlas* (1871), *The Student's Atlas* (1875), *The Century Atlas and Gazetteer of the World* (1890), *The Handy Reference Atlas of the World* (1912, the ninth edition of *The Handy Atlas*), and *The Citizen's Atlas of the World* (1912)—were omnipresent in the bookshelves of educated persons.[6] It was this solid experience and reputation that persuaded *The Times* to break the precedent of having a German publisher continue to work on the editions of its atlas.

The Times Atlas—The Early Editions

The Times first published a world atlas in 1895—mainly using German cartographers and printers, at the time reputed to be the best in the world—and again in 1900. With its 117 (1895) or 132 (1900) pages of maps (about half of which were of Europe), it remained a standard work until after World War I, when it became clear that substantial political changes necessitated a new atlas. Lord Northcliffe, proprietor of the *Times*, negotiated with John George Bartholomew to produce what would be called *The Times Survey Atlas of the World*. This was published in loose-leaf format with an index-gazetteer in a separate volume between 1920 and 1922. The volume drew upon 15 years of geographical research and was a standard work for a generation. It was soon hailed as the foremost British-produced world atlas. Its layer color system of relief representation was especially welcomed, and the only negative criticisms concerned the omission of railway lines in Asia, transliteration of Russian names, and the lack of dates on maps. Important features were the inclusion of thematic maps and the extremely limited use of textual material with the emphasis overwhelmingly placed on the maps. Its 259-page index had over 130,000 place names and included map grid and latitude and longitude references.[7] This atlas was apparently also published in one volume under the same title by Macmillan in New York.

The Mid-Century Edition

The end of the Second World War again required a new atlas, so the third one was planned. This effort resulted in the massive and supremely important five-volume Mid-Century Edition, very thoroughly revised from the 1920–1922 edition. The five volumes (each with its own index-gazetteer bound in) were: vol. 1, World, Australasia and East Asia (1958); vol. 2, Southwest Asia and Russia (1959); vol. 3, Northern Europe (1955); vol. 4, Southern Europe and Africa (1956); vol. 5, The Americas (1957). The volumes were numbered in accordance with approximate order of longitude from the International Date Line westward.

The atlas makes good use of more than 20 types of projections; for the seven introductory world plates, eight different projections are used, ranging from the Mercator projection (first employed at Duisburg in 1569) on Plate 6, "World Surface Routes," to the Bartholomew "Lotus" projection (in its first appearance) on Plate 2 ("World Oceanography"). Each map shows latitude and longitude as well as key letters and numbers. Scale is given on the back and at the foot of each plate, with a bar scale (showing distance in statute miles and in kilometers) also at the foot; scale ranges from 1:250,000,000 used for four of the five maps of Plate 2 ("World Oceanography") to 1:21,000 for an inset map of Rome on Plate 80 ("Italy, Central"). In the main, scale

for large countries ranges from 1:1,000,000 to 1:5,000,000. Elevation is shown by layer (color) tints and by spot heights, the latter especially for such areas as mountains; color tints and spot depths are used for oceans.

Other symbols are shown at the foot of each plate, and include roads, railways, canals, oil pipe lines, airports, deserts, swamps, glaciers, and ice caps. Boundaries are drawn as they stood at the time of going to press, with disputed international boundary lines indicated; different types of boundaries (e.g., international, states) are clearly differentiated. Where practicable, the population of a town or city is indicated on the maps by virtue of various type sizes; no population figures are given except for the ones in the section on states, territories, and principal islands in the first volume.

Meant to serve as an atlas of international coverage for use in office, home, and library, the Mid-Century Edition accomplishes this purpose through several approaches, but principally through cartographic images. Textual material is extremely limited, pleasing atlas purists. Volume 3, actually the first published, carries an introduction to the entire atlas in its preface (statement of purpose, sequence of volumes, etc.); the preface of volume 1 offers a brief history of atlas making; and the other volumes' prefaces contain suitably brief information to enable the user to deal with the maps in those volumes. Volume 1 also contains an illustrated article, "Progress of World Mapping," by Major-General R. Ll. Brown, formerly director general of the British Ordnance Survey, and an alphabetical list of states, territories, and principal islands of the world. This serves as a finding list for all volumes, with information including political status, location, area, population, and volume and plate number.

The 120 double-page plates—24 plates to a volume—are numbered consecutively throughout the set, including two frontispiece maps (volume 1 with a 1957 geographical disposition of world power blocs, and volume

5 with a map showing the Americas). The contents page of each volume indicates the title and scale for each map plate and for each inset map; this is followed by a list of "Acknowledgments," including names of persons and institutions.

Each plate of this monumental edition measures 24" by 19¼"; on the back of each plate are plate number, title of map, projection, standard parallel, scale, and outline map. The outside of plates depicting the USSR (Plates 38 through 47) also carry a glossary of Russian geographical terms and abbreviations for the principal administrative areas; and the plate for Southern Arabia (Plate 33) carries a glossary of Arabic geographical terms. The outline map on the back of each plate shows the area mapped, or serves as a key to adjoining plates by showing volume and plate numbers, or shows insets, as required.

In the first seven plates thematic world maps deal with physiography, oceanography, climatology, vegetation, mankind, and world surface and air routes. What makes this atlas, and the other editions of the *Times Atlas*, so outstanding in the field is that aesthetically pleasing maps present accurate information in a balanced, impartial fashion.

The inset maps, on a larger scale, providing detail for major regions, cities, and islands, are another important feature—with eleven for the U.S. (ten of cities, and one for the San Francisco Bay area); six for Canadian cities, five for India (four for cities and one for the Damodar Valley); and four for the Soviet Union (two for cities, one each for the Fergana Basin and the industrial Urals). Eleven of the then 15 largest cities of the world are shown in inset maps. In a slight touch of surely forgivable favoritism, London has its own separate plate (Plate 55).

It is with this edition that the atlas solidified its reputation as the next best source to a country-specific gazetteer for place names; it gave as many place-names as possible, preferably for each country in the spelling used by the places' inhabitants. Place names followed the Permanent Committee on Geographical Names (London) and the United States Board on Geographic Names, with the exceptions of China (forms used by Chinese Post Office); Mongolia (simplified); and Syria and Ethiopia (French and Italian transliterations changed to letters with English values). The English form of important places followed the local name in brackets, with both names appearing in the index. William Clowes & Sons, Ltd., Beccles, England, produced the indexes. Directions and a list of abbreviations appeared on the first page of each index, followed by a list of place names arranged alphabetically letter-by-letter. Each entry gave the name of the place's major political or geographical area (e.g., country, state, ocean), latitude, longitude, map plate number, and key letter and number. Throughout, the atlas achieved its aim of a high degree of comprehensiveness and accuracy. In 1965, the supremely useful index (345,000 place names) was published separately as the *Times Index-Gazetteer of the World*.

To look at and to use, the volumes are large (19¼" x 12¾") but relatively lightweight (since they are only ¾" thick), unlike other atlases which require two healthy persons to lift. The volumes published in England have a blue binding with gold lettering on front and spine, while those published by Houghton Mifflin in the U.S. have a red binding with gold lettering. In both cases, as one can observe in almost any library, the atlas has held up well under heavy use.

Reviewers of the Mid-Century Edition were unanimous in considering it to be the most significant world atlas in English at least since the Second World War.[8] It was upon this singularly firm foundation that Bartholomew and the *Times* launched their first "Comprehensive" edition in one volume, with the stated reason that updating a five-volume set would be extremely complex, and thus even more expensive than atlas-making customarily is. No other five-volume edition has appeared.

The Comprehensive Edition

The Comprehensive Edition—largely based, of course, on the plates of the Mid-Century Edition—first appeared in 1967. The plates were updated and a collection of maps on world resources and an illustrated guide to space flight and lunar exploration were added. The index of more than 200,000 place names was bound in, rather than issued as a separate volume. The index maps were a singularly useful feature, one that has continued through subsequent editions. An index map is a two-page spread of the world, with plate areas and numbers overlain so that simply by looking at it one may quickly learn which plate or plates cover one's area of interest. Brief text illustrated with thematic (i.e., subject) maps appeared at the beginnings of the volume. These number 16 pages or plates, e.g., "Resources of the World," "The Earth and Its Atmosphere," "The Universe." The transliteration and spelling recommended by the Permanent Committee on Geographic names and by the U.S. Board on Geographic Names have been used. Wade-Giles transliterations were used for locations in China and Mongolia.

The second edition (1968) of the Comprehensive Edition showed some updating (e.g., population figures), but changes were relatively slight, perhaps based on the feeling that since it wasn't broken, there was no need to fix it. By this time it was common for the *Times Atlas* to be referred to as a "best atlas value," and "by far the best English-language atlas, perhaps even the best atlas in the world."[9] The third edition (1971) was published in the U.S. only, and shows no obvious signs of change.

The fourth edition (1972) featured only slight changes—in the introduction (p. v), it is termed the fourth revision of the 1967 edition. Typical of revision was the plate on the "The Solar System" (p. xxxiv) of the 1967 edition, considerably reworked and moved earlier in the volume (p. xxix in the 1972 volume). As with other Comprehensive editions, the width of the page margins was narrower than those

in the Mid-Century Edition, and the maps were printed on both sides of sheets (rather than having sheets tipped in, as was done for the Mid-Century Edition) without reducing the size of the maps or diminishing the contents.[10]

The 256-page fifth edition (1975) contained the expected: the excellent index-gazetteer, good balance of coverage, attractive maps, and careful attention to design. Except for updating of maps, the only changes were in the introduction and the index. The index of about 210,000 place names was for the first time compiled by computer to facilitate future revisions. The introductory pages on world physiography and oceanography had been completely revised; African frontier changes plus plans for more cities appeared.[11] The reviewer for *Choice* called it, "the essential foundation of any general reference atlas case."[12]

The sixth edition appeared in 1980. At first glance it looks very much the same as its predecessor (e.g., an increase in the length of the gazetteer by only four pages). But the maps were printed in eight colors rather than in six, making for brighter and denser layer colors, and the boundaries were reinforced by a purple rather than a gray tone for improved legibility. The index was preceded by a one-page discussion of the transcription of Chinese place names, since a major innovation in the maps was the replacement of Wade-Giles romanization with Pinyin for mainland China names. An estimated 30,000 changes were made on maps and in the index, including the addition of much new cartographic information (some of it gathered from satellite photographs, such as a huge reservoir in Siberia shown for the first time). The new edition cost an estimated $1.4 million to produce. At the time of publication a reviewer proclaimed that it "remains the authoritative reference" of its kind.[13]

The seventh edition (1985) retained the previous edition's format and structure, with substantial updating of information throughout. Some changes were introduced in the preliminary text pages. The geographical-comparisons data (e.g., text on population of major countries, heights of mountains, area of oceans and seas) expanded to a second page and were accompanied by inset-sized maps; population tables were dropped; the thematic pages at the front were revised; and the population figures in the alphabetical listing of states and territories were updated. A group of world thematic maps (minerals, food, energy, climate) was moved from the introductory section to the atlas proper, and sheets on physiography, oceanography, and air routes present in the 1980 edition were dropped. A new set of double-page physical maps of the continents was added, and inset maps of Jiddah and Riyadh replaced those of Aden and Kuwait on the Arabian Peninsula plate (Plate #33).

The eighth edition (1990) interestingly enough notes its editorial board as the *New York Times* staff. This author looks forward to examining it, and is reasonably confident that the new edition will enable the *Times Atlas* to retain its position as "the best world atlas in print."[14]

Reasons for Its Preeminence

From the moment the Bartholomew firm took it on, the atlas rose to the top of its field and has retained that position. It has set the standard by which all other world atlases are judged; in particular, its use of relief maps as a standard feature has denoted superiority in the world-reference-atlas world for some time. In the English-language publishing world, *Rand McNally's International Atlas* (Chicago: Rand McNally), first published in 1969 and known since 1980 as *The New International Atlas*, comes closest; but the Bartholomew reputation for accuracy and for beautiful maps gives the *Times Atlas* a definite edge. In particular, the unrivaled ability of the maps to show relief sets it apart from other atlases and always has, since showing relief on maps is expensive and is generally done only in the more expensive atlases; yet it is essential if the atlas user is to have a good comprehension of the area being studied.

The Times Atlas has always emphasized physical-political maps and its index, with very brief introductory text and a bit longer section of thematic maps. Balance of coverage is a matter frequently mentioned in reviews of the atlas; this seems to be a matter of the publisher's balancing number of pages of coverage per continent with the continent's share of world land coverage, the density of its population, and the interests of the atlas's audience. Thus Europe—just 3 percent of world land coverage, 10 percent of world population, but an area of substantial interest to British and American users—receives about 30 percent of the plates in the atlas. This percentage is down from 43 percent in the 1920–1922 edition, a comforting sign that its audience is becoming more global in its interests.

A key to the atlas's success has been the close association with it, since the 1920–1922 edition, of the Bartholomew family and firm working with the *Times*. Its critical reception and reputation have been excellent, especially since the Bartholomew name became associated with the atlas. The atlas's influence is substantial in the scholarly world; if one can have only one world atlas, it should be the *Times Atlas*. As for future plans for new editions, nothing had appeared in print on this matter as of mid-1990, a time when certainly all map librarians—along with a good many other persons—were looking forward to seeing the imminent eighth edition of this classic atlas. The computer may play a more important part in forthcoming editions as the use of computer cartography increases. Although rapidly becoming essential for base mapping (i.e., large-scale topographic mapping), computerized cartography has been used in atlases from time to time over the last ten years or so, but generally not to completely successful aesthetic effect. Perhaps once again the firm of Bartholomew can take a lead in innovation.

PUBLICATION HISTORY

Only new editions, not reprints, non-British/U.S. editions, nor atlases derived from *The Times Atlas,* are included in the following list.

"The Times" Atlas. London: The Times, 1895. iv, 117p. of col. maps, 118p.

The Times' Atlas. New ed. London: The Times, 1900. iv, 132 p. of col. maps, 120p.

The Times Survey Atlas of the World, edited by John Bartholomew. [2nd ed.] London: The Times, 1920–1922. 2 v.; vol. 1, 112 col. maps; vol. 2 (index), xii, 259p.

The Times Atlas of the World, edited by John Bartholomew. Mid-Century [3rd] ed. London: The Times; Boston: Houghton Mifflin., 1955–1959. 5 v.: v. 1, World, Australasia and East Asia (1958); v. 2, Southwest Asia and Russia (1959); v. 3, Northern Europe (1955); v. 4, Southern Europe and Africa (1956); v. 5, The Americas (1957).

Index-gazetteer of the World. London: The Times, 1965. xxxi, 964p. Boston: Houghton Mifflin, 1966. xxxi, 964p.

The Times Atlas of the World. [1st comprehensive ed.] London: The Times. 1967. xliii, 123 col. maps, 272p.

The Times Atlas of the World. 2nd ed. rev. London: Times Newspaper. 1968. xliii, 123 col. maps, 272p.

The Times Atlas of the World. 2nd ed. rev. [sic; 3rd ed.; for U.S. only] Boston: Houghton Mifflin, 1971. xliii, 123 col. maps, 272p.

The Times Atlas of the World. 4th ed rev. London: Times Newspapers, 1972. xl, 123 col. maps, 272p.

The Times Atlas of the World. 5th ed. London: Times Books, 1975. xl, 123 col. maps, 223p.

The Times Atlas of the World. Comprehensive ed., 6th ed. London: The Times, 1980. xl, 123 col. maps, 227p.

The Times Atlas of the World. Comprehensive ed., 7th ed. London: The Times, 1985. xl, 123 col. maps, 227p.

The Times Atlas of the World. Comprehensive ed., 8th ed. London: Times Books, 1990. xlvii, 245 col. maps, 225p.

BIBLIOGRAPHY

The secondary literature is composed almost entirely of reviews in serials and other reference works; the most notable exception is Gardiner's history of the Bartholomew firm. While this is surprising—considering the prominence of the atlas—the indexes, most notably *Bibliography of Cartography, Bibliographica Cartographica,* and *Social Sciences and Humanities Index,* are obdurate on this point.

Allan, Douglas A. "John George Bartholomew, A Centenary." *Scottish Geographical Magazine* 76 (1960): 85–88.

Alonso, Patricia Greechie. "The First Atlases." *Canadian Cartographer* 5 (1968): 108–21.

Bagrow, Leo. "The Century of Atlases." In *History of Cartography,* by R.A. Skelton, 179–89. 2nd ed. rev. & enl. Chicago: Precedent, 1985.

Balchin, W.G.V. *Review of The Times Atlas of the World,* 6th ed. In *Geographical Journal* 147 (1981): 120–21.

"Bartholomew (John) and Son, Ltd." *Choice* 13 (May, 1976): 344.

Brown, Lloyd A. *The Story of Maps.* Boston: Little, Brown, 1949.

Brown, R. N. Rudmose. "Bartholomew's New Atlas (The Times Survey Atlas of the World, 1920)." *Scottish Geographical Magazine* 36 (July 15, 1920): 180–81.

"Dr. J. G. Bartholomew, 1860–1920." *Scottish Geographical Magazine* 36 (July 15, 1920): 183–85.

Gardiner, Leslie. *Bartholomew, 150 Years.* Edinburgh: Bartholomew, 1976.

Goméz-Ibáñez, Daniel A. "World Atlases for General Reference." *Choice* 6 (August, 1969): 625–30.

Gray, Richard A. Review of *The Times Atlas of the World: Comprehensive Edition. American Reference Books Annual* (1976): 277.

Katz, William A. "World Atlases." In *Introduction to Reference Work;* vol. 1, *Basic Information Sources.* 4th ed. New York: McGraw–Hill, 1982.

Kister, Kenneth F. *Kister's Atlas Buying Guide.* Phoenix: Oryx Press, 1984.

Piggott, Charles. "Atlas Classic." *Geographical Magazine* 53 (November, 1980): 148–49.

Review of *The Times Atlas of the World,* Mid-Century ed. *Booklist* and *Subscription Books Bulletin* 58 (September 1, 1961): 1–5.

Review of *The Times Atlas of the World,* 6th ed. *Booklist* 78 (May 15, 1982): 1273.

Review of *The Times Atlas of the World.,* 7th ed. *Booklist* 82 (June 15, 1986): 1524–25.

Walsh, S. Padraig. *General World Atlases in Print, 1972–1973: A Comparative Analysis.* New York: Bowker, 1973.

Watson, J. Wreford. "Obituary, John Bartholomew." *Geographical Review* 53 (January, 1963): 145–46.

NOTES

[1] Daniel A. Goméz-Ibáñez, "World Atlases for General Reference," *Choice* 6 (August 1969): 625–27.

[2] Leo Bagrow, "The Century of Atlases," in *History of Cartography*, 2nd ed. rev. & enl., by R.A. Skelton (Chicago: Precedent, 1985), 179.

[3] Patricia Greechie Alonso, "The First Atlases," *Canadian Cartographer* 5 (1968): 108–10, 119; Bagrow, 187–89; Lloyd A. Brown, *The Story of Maps* (Boston: Little, Brown, 1949), 165–73.

[4] Douglas A. Allan, "John George Bartholomew, A Centenary," *Scottish Geographical Magazine* 76 (1960): 85–86.

[5] "Dr. J.G. Bartholomew, 1860–1920," *Scottish Geographical Magazine* 36 (1920): 183–85; Douglas Allan, "John George Bartholomew, A Centenary," 87.

[6] Leslie Gardiner, *Bartholomew, 150 Years* (Edinburgh: Bartholomew, 1976), 6–53.

[7] R.N. Rudmose Brown, "Bartholomew's New Atlas (*The Times Survey Atlas of the World*, 1920)," *Scottish Geographical Magazine* 36 (15 July 1920): 180–81; Allan, 86.

[8] See, for example, review of *The Times Atlas of the World*, Mid-Century ed., *Booklist and Subscription Books Bulletin* 58 (1 September 1961): 1–5.

[9] Goméz-Ibáñez, 628.

[10] S. Padraig Walsh, *General World Atlases in Print, 1972–1973: A Comparative Analysis* (New York: Bowker, 1973), 33–35.

[11] Richard A. Gray, review of *The Times Atlas of the World: Comprehensive Edition, American Reference Books Annual* (1976): 277.

[12] "Bartholomew (John) and Son, Ltd.," *Choice* 13 (May 1976): 344.

[13] Charles Piggott, "Atlas classic," *Geographical Magazine* 53 (November 1980): 148–49.

[14] Review of *The Times Atlas of the World*, 7th ed., *Booklist* 82 (15 June 1986): 1525.

The Legacy of Noah Webster: The Merriam-Webster Family of Dictionaries

Marie C. Ellis

DEVELOPMENT AND HISTORY

When George and Charles Merriam purchased the publishing rights to Noah Webster's *American Dictionary of the English Language* from his heirs in 1843, they could not have foreseen that 150 years later their name and that of Webster would continue to be linked in a successful dictionary publishing enterprise. Over the years, the G. & C. Merriam Company (which officially changed its name to Merriam-Webster Inc. in 1982) has survived the challenges of controversies and intense competition through its successful combination of dedication to editorial excellence and adroit marketing skills. In preserving and enhancing the legacy of Noah Webster, Merriam-Webster has become one of the preeminent publishers of English-language dictionaries and other wordbooks, creating an entire family of dictionaries that bear the Merriam-Webster colophon and trademark.

Although the first Merriam-Webster dictionary was published in 1847, its roots can be traced back to the 1780s when Noah Webster first contemplated the idea of compiling a dictionary reflecting American usage of the English language. Webster publicly revealed his intentions to publish a series of dictionaries with an announcement in the New Haven newspapers on June 4, 1800, indicating that he planned to compile "a small Dictionary for schools, one for the counting-house, and a large one for men of science." Observing that "a work of this kind is absolutely necessary, on account of considerable differences between the American and English language," Webster concluded that those differences "will continue to multiply, and render it necessary that we should have *Dictionaries* of the *American language.*"[1] A man of many talents and wide interests, Webster drew on a broad range of experience for his new endeavor, having served variously as a schoolmaster, journalist, lecturer, editor, lawyer, and legislator, before becoming a lexicographer.

Noah Webster

Born on a farm near Hartford, Connecticut, in 1758, Webster was more inclined to scholarly pursuits than to agrarian life and attended Yale University from 1774 to 1778, "a time when religious fervor was declining and secular interests were paramount."[2] With a college degree, but apparently with no particular professional inclination, Webster undertook both school teaching and law practice during the 1780s. His teaching experience led him to prepare a series of textbooks, an accomplishment for which he became widely known and which served as the springboard for his interest in language. In 1783 the first of these texts appeared. Bound in blue cloth, *A Grammatical Institute of the English Language... Part I* soon came to be known as "the blue-backed speller," and the first edition of 5,000 copies sold out in nine months.[3] In 1788, its title was changed to *The American Spelling Book*, and later it became *The Elementary Spelling Book*.[4] By 1801, one and one-half million copies had been sold, and Merriam-Webster now estimates that total sales of the speller eventually reached 70 million copies.[5] The other parts of Webster's textbook system, a grammar and a reader, were published in 1784 and 1785, respectively, and also enjoyed a great deal of success.[6]

In preparing his speller, reader, and grammar, Webster had accumulated numerous notes relating to etymology, language usage, spelling inconsistencies, and variances in pronunciation. In addition, he had become aware of the many new meanings and terms that had come into the English language since Samuel Johnson compiled his *A Dictionary of the English Language* in 1755, and he became convinced that what the nation needed was an American dictionary of the English language that would reflect the rapid changes that were taking place in the vocabulary of the average citizen.[7] It was this goal that Webster revealed in his press release of 1800. His work was not to be the first American dictionary, however, since, by the time of its publication, six other small dictionaries had already appeared.

Webster's first dictionary, *A Compendious Dictionary of the English Language*, containing approximately 40,000 words, was published in 1806. Basing his compilation on John Entick's *New Spelling Dictionary* (a work originally published in London in 1764 and widely available in the United States in a variety of editions), Webster added about 5,000 words, improved Entick's definitions, revised the orthography to reflect his own ideas regarding uniformity and analogy, and appended tables of currencies and weights and measures, chronologies, population statistics, and a directory of post offices. Since Webster was greatly interested in simplifying American spelling, it is not surprising that he chose to sanction only one version of words in certain categories that had evolved with variant spellings. For example, he listed words like "honor" and "favor" without giving their historical variants ending in "-our," "music" and "public" without the final "k," "defense" and "offense" with an "s" instead of a "c," "theater" and "center" instead of their counterparts ending in "-re," and "check" and "mask" rather than "cheque" and "masque." While these spellings were controversial at the time, they ultimately came to be the preferred spellings in the United States. However, many of Webster's proposed spellings, such as "imagin," "crum," "wimmen," and "soop," never gained acceptance, and they were eventually dropped from later versions of his dictionaries.[8] The 1806 *Compendious Dictionary* was followed in 1807 and 1817 by concise versions for schools. Although his early lexicographical efforts were only moderately successful commercially, the indefatigable Webster was undaunted and turned his attention to compiling the first unabridged American dictionary, the work from which today's *Webster's Third New International* is directly descended. Published in 1828 when Webster was 70 years old, *An American Dictionary of the English Language* was priced at $20 for two large quarto volumes.[9] An announcement in a contemporary newspaper noted that the compilation had been completed "at the expense of twenty years of labor, and thirty thousand dollars in money."[10] However, the price and size of the work prohibited ready sales, and it was 13 years before the printing of 2,500 copies had sold.[11]

Although contemporary critics generally praised Webster's skill at writing definitions, they were less receptive to some of his unorthodox spellings and even more skeptical of his etymologies. However, both proponents and detractors generally acknowledged the magnitude of Webster's accomplishment. Twentieth-century scholars have corroborated the assessments of their nineteenth-century counterparts. James A.H. Murray, editor of the *Oxford English Dictionary*, praised

Webster as "a born definer of words" who "produced a work of great originality and value." George Krapp called it a "significant contribution to the growth of English lexicography" but noted that Webster's 1828 work was "only partially successful." While acknowledging that "Webster's work had serious flaws," Joseph Friend concludes that "he wrote definitions that were more accurate, more comprehensive, and not less carefully divided and ordered than any previously done in English lexicography." Richard Rollins observes that Webster's "finished product was, by all standards, a monumental achievement. With 70,000 words all written out by his own hand, it was indeed a massive work, the last major dictionary ever compiled by a single individual."[12]

Prominent individuals such as John Jay praised Webster's work, and publishers, courts, colleges, schools, and other establishments began using it as their authority.[13] An abridged edition, compiled by Joseph Emerson Worcester, became available in 1829 in a reasonably priced octavo volume. This version sold well and insured the distribution and influence of Webster's dictionary among ordinary individuals in addition to the institutions and monied class who had been able to purchase the two-volume edition. In 1841 a second edition of the unabridged appeared, containing an additional 5,000 words. However, the price of $15 for the two-volume set placed it beyond the reach of many potential purchasers, and a number of unbound copies remained at the time of Webster's death in 1843.[14]

George and Charles Merriam

Fortuitously, it was at this point that George and Charles Merriam made a decision to enter the dictionary publishing business. The Merriam brothers had moved to Springfield, Massachusetts, in 1831 to establish a bookstore and printing office. Advertisements from the period indicate that they sold a variety of merchandise ranging from wallpaper and church music to pencils and toothbrushes.[15] They also began publishing textbooks, Bibles, and legal works. Thus, when the opportunity arose for them to purchase the remaining unbound sheets of the *American Dictionary* of 1841 from the Amherst, Massachusetts, firm of J.S. & C. Adams, the Merriams were ready to expand their publishing venture in that direction. Astute businessmen, the brothers also purchased from Webster's heirs the rights to publish revisions.[16]

Soon after making the investment that would permanently change the nature of their enterprise, the Merriams developed plans to issue a revised and enlarged edition of the dictionary. Recognizing that the task was too large for any one individual, they enlisted Chauncey A. Goodrich, a professor at Yale and Webster's son-in-law, as principal editor and then assembled a distinguished group of scholars and specialists to assist him. Among the other editors were William Tully, who had edited the scientific terms for the 1841 edition; Noah Porter and S.W. Barnum, both professors at Yale University; and William G. Webster, Noah Webster's son. Other Yale scholars were asked to serve as specialists for certain disciplines, such as chemistry, mathematics, astronomy, and law, while James D. Dana, a renowned scientist and editor of the *American Journal of Sciences and Arts*, was responsible for geology.[17] Thus began the Merriam-Webster tradition of using a scholarly corps of editors and specialists to produce lexicographical works.

The new one-volume revised edition of *An American Dictionary of the English Language* was published in 1847 at a price of $6. "Merchandisers with a keen eye for a market and a sound knowledge of how to sell books in quantity," the Merriam brothers predicted correctly that the lower price would stimulate sales so that the total amount of profits would increase even though the profit per copy would decrease.[18] In 1850, in accordance with an act of the state legislature, about 3,000 copies of the dictionary were distributed to the school districts of Massachusetts, and similar programs were adopted by New Jersey and the state of New York.[19]

Praise poured in from all directions. A statement signed by 104 members of Congress read: "It is with pleasure that we greet this new and valuable contribution to American literature. We recommend it to all who desire to possess the most complete, accurate and reliable dictionary of the language."[20] Three presidents—James K. Polk, Zachary Taylor, and Millard Fillmore—also provided glowing endorsements, but perhaps the most unexpected approval came from England when John Ogilvie wrote in his preface to the *The Imperial Dictionary*, published in 1850, that Webster's was "acknowledged both in this country and in America to be . . . superior to . . . every other dictionary hitherto published."[21]

Reviews in the press were equally favorable. A lengthy commentary published in the *New Englander* noted that Professor Goodrich "has given to the work, a completeness, fullness, and accuracy, hitherto unattained in a work of this kind" and concluded that

> we can not but view it as a sort of representative of the English mind in its present advanced state—as a transcript in miniature of the intellectual progress of the age—as a synopsis of arts, science, philosophy, truth in nature and truth in morals; in fine of all knowledge within the range of human investigation, so far as these may be exhibited through the great medium of thought.[22]

Moreover, the London *Literary Gazette* declared the work "a noble monument of erudition and indefatigable research; and the style and accuracy of its typography would do honor to the press of any country in Europe."[23]

The success of the 1847 edition of the *American Dictionary* was due not only to its reasonable price but also to Goodrich's removal of "most of the Websterian crotchets which still remained from the original (1828) work."[24] Mindful of the numerous objections to Webster's orthographic practices, Goodrich eliminated many of Webster's more radical

reform spellings (e.g., "chimistry," "fether," "melasses," "ribin," "zink") and restored those words to their more acceptable forms. In addition, he showed both forms of other controversial spellings (e.g., "center" and "centre," "defense" and "defence"). Pronunciations were also revised to reflect the most recent authorities.[25] The new work included approximately 85,000 entries in the main section and also contained supplementary tables of scripture names, Greek and Latin proper names, and modern geographical names.[26]

War of the Dictionaries

Following the 1847 publication of the *American Dictionary*, competitive skirmishes between the Merriams and the publishers of another lexicographer, Joseph Emerson Worcester, increased and eventually escalated until they came to be called "the War of the Dictionaries." Stemming from events that had transpired prior to Noah Webster's death, the war was fought in several stages and on various fronts and is generally conceded to have lasted from 1834 to 1864. A number of studies of this fascinating bit of Merriam-Webster's history treat this period in far greater detail than space allows in this chapter.[27]

The opening stage for the first battle in this war was set when Joseph Worcester, the lexicographer who had been responsible for the 1829 abridged edition of Webster's *American Dictionary*, published his own dictionary in 1830. Worcester's *Comprehensive Pronouncing and Explanatory Dictionary of the English Language* (Boston: Hilliard, Gray, Little, and Wilkins) was favorably received, particularly by those factions who had opposed Webster's somewhat unorthodox spellings and pronunciation, including "the Anglophile group in Massachusetts and those of conservative tendencies around the country."[28] As sales of Worcester's dictionary climbed, Webster for the first time had a formidable American rival. On November 26, 1834, an article appeared in the *Worcester Palladium* accusing Worcester of taking advantage of his earlier association with Webster and "appropriating to his own benefit the valuable labors, acquisitions, and productions of Mr. Webster."[29] Worcester's dignified response, published in the *Palladium* of December 3, 1834, denied any plagiarism while providing particulars on his agreement with Webster in working on the abridgement and pointing out the variety of differences between his work and Webster's. In a letter in the December 11, 1834, issue of the *Palladium*, Webster responded to both the original editorial and Worcester's reply, acknowledging that he felt some plagiarism had occurred. For more than a year, letters between Worcester and Webster on this issue were published in the *Palladium*, with the cycle ending on March 25, 1835.[30] Of this first phase of the War of the Dictionaries, Friend concludes: "In general, Worcester's defense is a good deal more impressive than Webster's accusations, which tend to grow querulous toward the end of the duel and reveal clearly that the older man felt his livelihood endangered by the popular acceptance of the *Comprehensive*."[31]

The second phase of the war was not quite as civil as the first. Carried out primarily by the publishers of the competing dictionaries, this phase of "Worcester *vs.* Webster came to mean not only linguistic conservatives and moderates *vs.* radicals and liberals, but, with some inevitable extremist distortion and over-simplification, Anglophiles *vs.* Americanizers, Boston-Cambridge-Harvard *vs.* New Haven-Yale, upperclass elegance *vs.* underbred Yankee uncouthness."[32] This second stage of the controversy was sparked by fierce competition for sales following the publication of Worcester's *Universal and Critical Dictionary of the English Language* in 1846 and Goodrich's unabridged edition of Webster's *American Dictionary* in 1847. Accusations and counter-accusations were made through the press, and pamphlets fanning the flames were distributed by both G. & C. Merriam and

the publishers of Worcester's dictionaries. Each side extended the competition to garnering and publishing endorsements and testimonials from prominent individuals, including college presidents, statesmen, authors, and booksellers. Matters were exacerbated by an unfortunate incident in 1853 when Worcester's dictionary was published in London with the added notation on the title page "compiled from the materials of Noah Webster, LL.D., by Joseph E. Worcester."[33] Although the British publisher was obviously at fault, the Merriams were quick to claim this statement as an acknowledgement of Worcester's debt to Webster.

In the course of planning a new printing of the 1847 edition to be published in 1859, the Merriams learned that Worcester was preparing a third edition of his work that would be illustrated. Deciding that the new words and supplements, including a 300-page section of synonyms, they were adding would not be sufficient to compete with an illustrated Worcester, the Merriams hastily made arrangements to insert a special section of illustrations at the front of their edition since there was no time to place the illustrations within the text. Thus, the title page of the 1859 edition includes the claim that it is the first illustrated American dictionary.[34] Upon the publication of Worcester's illustrated *A Dictionary of the English Language* in 1860, the controversy between the two rivals began anew. Again reviewers in newspapers and periodicals made claims for their favorites, and the publishers issued pamphlets supporting their respective publications by reprinting favorable notices and reproducing endorsements from prominent individuals. While the business tactics and advertising strategies used during this period appear to have frequently been unscrupulous, there is no doubt that the fierce competition led to improvements in both works, prompting a reviewer for the *New York World* to conclude: "In some respects, Worcester and Webster supplement each other, and every literary man who can, will choose to have the two."[35]

The Merriams, however, were already making plans for an entirely new edition. Chauncey Goodrich had died in 1860 but not before choosing Noah Porter to be his successor. On Porter's advice, the German philologist C.A.F. Mahn had been selected to replace Webster's outmoded etymologies with ones that reflected current scholarship. In addition, a team of approximately 30 scholars had been chosen to serve as consultants in specific fields, while an additional corps of readers, writers, and editors worked on various other aspects of the compilation.

In September 1864, during the midst of the Civil War, the Royal Quarto Edition of *An American Dictionary of the English Language* rolled off the presses. Known as the Webster-Mahn edition, it marked the beginning of the end of the War of the Dictionaries, "ironically by abandoning everything characteristic of Webster and adopting Worcester's virtues."[36] As Raven I. McDavid has observed, the Webster-Mahn edition was "the foundation of the Merriam tradition; with professional editors and a growing file of citations, it soon achieved preeminence—aided by the death of Worcester and the failure of Worcester's publishers to provide for further revisions."[37] The removal of many of the controversial aspects of Noah Webster's lexicography paved the way for more general acceptance of the *American Dictionary*. Prominent literary figures such as Ralph Waldo Emerson and John Greenleaf Whittier acknowledged its authority and superiority, and business establishments, schools, legislative bodies, courts, and publishers adopted it as their standard. It even came to be the authority for the United States Government Printing Office and the Supreme Court.[38] In addition, the *American Dictionary* enjoyed commercial success in Great Britain, where it was distributed by George Bell & Sons, and it was also sold throughout the British Empire as well as to various Asian countries.[39]

Continuous Revision and Expansion

Following the death of George Merriam in 1880, Orlando M. Baker became the driving force in the company. Baker had joined the firm as a representative of Ivison, Blakeman, Taylor & Co. after they purchased Charles Merriam's shares in 1877.[40] Concerned because the copyright on the 1847 edition was due to expire in 1889, after which any printer would be able to sell "Webster's Dictionary," Baker established a program of continuous revision, with the goal of eventually producing an entirely new edition, while in the interim offering several updated versions with new features. Thus, the 1879 edition introduced a biographical supplement that included listings for 10,000 individuals, while the 1884 version added a gazetteer identifying more than 22,000 place names. Other projects completed during this period included an 1882 edition designed specifically for subscription purchase and several revisions of the *National Pictorial* abridgement, which later was to become *Webster's Collegiate Dictionary*.[41]

Clearly the Merriam-Webster family of dictionaries was expanding rapidly. By 1858 ten versions in addition to the unabridged were available: the Royal Octavo, National Pictorial, University, Counting House, Academic, High School, Common School, Primary, Pocket, and Army and Navy Pocket.[42] Some of these abridgements were leased to other publishers, and the series of Webster school dictionaries was later contracted to the American Book Company, a New York firm which agreed to publish and sell the books while the Merriam Company maintained the editorial content.[43]

In 1890 the culmination of ten years of preparation by a large staff of editors, subject authorities, and editorial assistants appeared under the new title *Webster's International Dictionary*. William A. Neilson, editor-in-chief of the 1934 edition, observed that this title change reflected "both the extension of the vogue and authority of the work through-out the English-speaking world, and . . . the inclusion of foreign scholars among its con-tributors."[44] Produced again under the able editorship of Noah Porter, assisted by Loomis J. Campbell serving as general editor, the work contained more than 175,000 entries, 56,000 more than the 1864 edition. The effort had cost the Merriams approximately $334,000. As Robert Leavitt concluded, "Dic-tionary making had become a task that could be carried out only by a major business and editorial institution."[45] The first *Webster's Collegiate Dictionary* was published in 1898. The largest of the abridged dictionaries based on the unabridged edition, its intent was "to present the most essential parts of Webster's International Dictionary in a compact and convenient form, suited to the general reader and especially to the college student."[46]

Webster's New International Dictionary

In 1900 a revision of *Webster's Interna-tional* with an additional 25,000 entries ap-peared, and in 1909 a completely new edition, *Webster's New International Dictionary*, was published at a cost of approximately half a million dollars. Dr. William T. Harris, former United States commissioner of education, served as editor-in-chief of this edition, while F. Sturges Allen was general editor. Their staff included 50 specialists, 10 revising edi-tors, and a large number of readers, proofread-ers, and other assistants. Noted scholars asso-ciated with this edition included George Lyman Kittredge and John Livingston Lowes of Harvard and A.T. Hadley, president of Yale.[47] Containing more than 400,000 entries, the *New International* initiated the use of the divided page with less frequently used terms, such as obsolete words and spellings, foreign words and phrases, and abbreviations, re-moved from the main alphabetical sequence and placed in a separate section at the bottom of each page. Since the lower section was in finer print, this technique saved space. While

the 1909 edition was not widely reviewed, the critiques that did appear were mixed. The reviewer for the *Educational Review* reacted favorably, while the reviewer in the *Nation* was less enthusiastic, finding the "treatment of synonyms very satisfactory," but noting that "the New International is extremely sus-ceptible to the appeal of slang."[48] Reviewers for *Life* and the New York *Sun* were generally positive and were particularly impressed by the increase in the number of words covered, twice as many as in the 1890 edition.[49]

The Second New International

Many of the specialists who had compiled the 1909 edition were retained to continue adding to the company's growing citation files and to work on revising the other titles in the Merriam-Webster family: the *Collegiate* (of which new editions based on the 1909 un-abridged edition were published in 1910, 1916, and 1931), the Reference History Edition of the unabridged for subscription purchasers, and the various dictionaries for schools that were published by the American Book Com-pany. Preparation for the next major revision of the unabridged got underway in the 1920s, and it developed into "perhaps the most ambi-tious project in co-operative scholarship ever undertaken in America up to that time."[50] William Allen Neilson, a Shakespeare scholar and president of Smith College, was ap-pointed editor-in-chief, while Thomas A. Knott, formerly professor of English at the University of Iowa, served as general editor. Paul W. Carhart continued as pronunciation editor while also serving as managing editor, and Harold H. Bender of Princeton University was appointed to revise the etymologies. In addition to the staff in Springfield, the enter-prise also depended on a corps of consultants composed of 207 scholars, scientists, and other authorities from throughout the country who were responsible for "collecting, choosing, and defining terms in their respective fields."[51] Another group of trained, professional read-ers, as Thomas Knott recounts, "attacked thousands of books, magazines, newspapers, and catalogues in search of new or unrecorded words, new meanings of old words, and evidence about capitalization, accents, hyphens, italics for foreign words, and plurals," a search that resulted in the collection of approximately "1,665,000 citations with 'defining quotations,' and nearly as many more from special fields that called for further research." Knott went on to describe the final stages of preparation as a

> pouring together of all the contributory streams—literary and vernacular, geographical and biographical, scientific and technical, pictorial, etymological, and pronunciational; the exact 'styling' of the manuscript for spelling, compounding, capitalization, etc.; the checking and correcting of hundreds of thousands of cross references; and the final adjustment and condensation of materials to make them fit into the allotted space of 3,350 pages.[52]

Heralded by its publishers as "the most notable publishing event of the century" and even "greater than its famous predecessors," the second edition of *Webster's New International Dictionary* appeared in 1934.[53] Prepared at a cost of $1,300,000, the completely revised work contained more than 550,000 vocabulary entries, "the largest number ever included in a dictionary of any language."[54] The 36,000 names in the gazetteer, 13,000 in the biographical dictionary, and 5,000 listings in the new table of abbreviations brought the total number of entries to more than 600,000. All aspects of the work, including the illustrations, had been examined and updated or replaced as necessary. In the preface, Neilson pointed out the difficulties of finding space "for thousands of new terms and new uses of old terms" stemming from scientific advances, new inventions, and changes in art, as well as the effects of World War I on almost every field of endeavor. In order to make room for these new terms, most words that had become obsolete before 1500 were omitted, thus greatly reducing the size of the section containing obsolete words and cross-references at the bottom of each page. Neilson noted that "tra-

ditional features that have stood the test of time have been retained . . . but more important has been the task of making the dictionary serve as an interpreter of the culture and civilization of today, as Noah Webster made the first edition serve for the America of 1828."[55]

For the most part, reviewers of the second edition of the *New International* agreed that it admirably achieved this goal. The *Saturday Review of Literature* and the *American Mercury* both praised the work.[56] Writing in the *Nation*, H.L. Mencken criticized the inconsistent coverage of derivative terms and the inclusion of English forms without specifying the American preference (e.g., "tire," "tyre"). He also questioned the utility of the illustrative quotations. However, Mencken concluded that "the new Webster comes close enough to completeness to be a very useful work."[57] William Lyon Phelps' commentary in *Scribner's Magazine* extolled the encyclopedic nature of the volume and added "it would be difficult to praise it too highly."[58] The *New Yorker* reviewer was particularly impressed with the way in which the Merriam "corps of citation-hunters" had gathered more than a million examples of word usage by reading "among other things, every word in Shakespeare, the King James Bible, Fannie Farmer's Cook Book, Sears Roebuck's catalogue, the works of Milton, Spenser, and Tennyson, the Encyclopaedia Britannica, four hundred magazines, five hundred manufacturer's catalogues, countless menu cards, and fifty daily newspapers." In addition, the reviewer noted that the editors had solicited the advice of 114 consultants throughout the country in determining pronunciations of questionable words.[59]

Reviews in scholarly journals tended to be more critical, particularly regarding the system of pronunciation, which Kemp Malone in *Modern Language Notes* characterized as a "relic of a pre-scientific age."[60] The review in *American Speech* concurred, observing that the pronunciations were often "provincial and unrepresentative" and that the failure to use the International Phonetic Alphabet "hampers the whole enterprise."[61] However, this was the only serious complaint, and the remainder of the review praised other aspects of the dictionary, such as format, definitions, and etymology. By the time the third edition of *Webster's New International* was published in 1961, the second edition had become as revered as its namesake.

Introduction of Specialized Dictionaries

In the nearly 30 years that elapsed before the publication of a new edition of the unabridged, the Merriam staff was busy with revisions of the other dictionaries in their charge as well as with compiling entirely new works. The fifth and sixth editions of the *Collegiate* appeared in 1936 and 1949, respectively, while the first *Webster's Dictionary of Synonyms* was published in 1942. This new compilation allowed the editors to treat synonyms in greater depth than in the *New International* and to provide more extensive coverage of antonyms and analogous and contrasted words. In addition, the work incorporated many illustrative quotations gleaned from the firm's vast file of citations. In 1942, the company issued *Webster's Biographical Dictionary*, which provided brief biographical information for more than 40,000 significant individuals from throughout history and also indicated pronunciation and syllabic division for the names included.

Perhaps in response to the criticisms of the pronunciation system used in the second edition of the *New International*, the Merriam Company published *A Pronouncing Dictionary of American English* in 1944. Compiled by John Samuel Kenyon and Thomas Albert Knott, the work utilized the International Phonetic Alphabet "to show the pronunciation of cultivated colloquial English in the United States."[62] Since regional differences frequently affect pronunciation, the editors made an ef-

fort to record all acceptable variant pronunciations. As this highly productive decade—which is even more remarkable considering the far-reaching effects of World War II—drew to a close, the firm produced its first *Webster's Geographical Dictionary* in 1949. This gazetteer provided historical and geographical information on more than 40,000 places throughout the world. In addition, entries indicated pronunciation for each place and included population, area, and economic data. A variety of maps and tables supplemented the text. The *Geographical Dictionary*, the *Biographical Dictionary*, and the *Dictionary of Synonyms* soon became staples in even the smallest of reference collections.

Webster's Third

During the 1950s the Merriam staff concentrated on preparing a completely new edition of the unabridged dictionary. Philip Gove, a member of the firm since 1946, became general editor in 1952, and was appointed editor-in-chief early in 1961.[63] *Webster's Third New International Dictionary* was published in September of that year. In his preface to the new edition, Gove calculated that it had been produced at a cost of more than $3,500,000 and had "absorbed 757 editor-years," a figure that did not include the time of the approximately 200 consultants or of typists and other clerical assistants. Describing *Webster's Third* as "a completely new work, redesigned, restyled, and reset," Gove emphasized that "every line of it is new." In order to provide adequate treatment of the more than 450,000 words covered, the editors deleted most words that had become obsolete by 1755. They also revised the pronunciation key and included a greater variety of acceptable pronunciations, reflecting regional differences in "general cultivated conversational usage . . . throughout the English-speaking world."[64]

In preparing *Webster's Third*, the editorial staff continued the kind of citation-gathering that had been used in compiling the previous edition. The resulting file of over 10,000,000 citations provided the basis for writing definitions of new words and identifying new usages of old words, a monumental undertaking since the 1961 edition included approximately 100,000 new words or new meanings. The definitions were supplemented by more than 3,000 black-and-white illustrations and 20 full-color plates.[65] Remarking that the English language "has already become the most important language on earth," Gove asserted that the "new Merriam-Webster unabridged is the record of this language as it is written and spoken."[66]

Instead of the acclaim that might have been expected for this new edition of a venerated work, the appearance of *Webster's Third* sparked an unprecedented critical controversy that had repercussions for more than a decade. Early rumblings of discontent following Merriam's press releases soon reached earthquake proportions. Thus began a new episode in the history of the Merriam company that was to test the firm's staff much as the War of the Dictionaries had tested their nineteenth-century forebears. The news media and popular press launched scathing attacks on the *Third*'s permissiveness, with reviewers' sentiments reflected in such headlines as "Webster's Lays an Egg," "Keep Your Old Webster's," "Sabotage in Springfield," and "It 'Ain't' Good."[67] The *New York Times*, which termed the work a "disastrous" development and faulted the editors for not living up to their public responsibility to provide "a peerless authority on American English," later directed its staff "to follow Webster's Second Edition for spelling and usage" and use *Webster's Third* "only for new, principally scientific words."[68] An editorial in *Life* announcing that the publication would continue to depend on *Webster's Second* for such matters as style and good English, deplored the inclusion in *Webster's Third* of such "non-words" as "irregardless" and "finalize" and accused the dictionary of "joining the say-as-you-go school of permissive English" and all but abandoning "any effort to distinguish between good and bad usage."[69]

In his response to the *New York Times* editorial, Philip Gove commented:

> When a peerless newspaper that in 110 years has proved itself again and again to be the most respected and reputable everyday professional user of words in the United States attacks an established organization that has been from an even longer time a respected and reputable observer and recorder of word usage, the impact is bound to disturb a good many people.

He observed that the compilers of *Webster's Third* relied heavily on the evidence gathered from daily newspapers and general periodicals to determine current patterns of language usage and had in fact quoted the *New York Times* more than 700 times. Gove concluded that "whether you or I or others who fixed our linguistic notions several decades ago like it or not," the language of the 1960s is not the language of the 1920s and 1930s.[70] In a shorter missive to the editor of *Life*, Gove asserted: "The responsibility of a dictionary is to record the language, not set its style. For us to attempt to prescribe the language would be like *Life* reporting the news as its editors would prefer it to happen."[71]

Gove must have soon decided, however, that he could not respond to every negative review of *Webster's Third*, for such reviews continued to appear with depressing regularity. The editor of the *American Bar Association Journal* aligned that publication with the *New York Times* and *Life*, calling the third edition "a serious blow" that "has recently befallen the cause of good English" and concluding that it "will be of no use to us." The reviewer for *Library Journal* termed the dictionary "indispensable for its new (and revised old) material, deplorable for its wholesale *abridgements*—as well as its obfuscation of the boundaries between prestige and non-prestige usages." In one of the most vicious reviews, Wilson Follett, writing for the *Atlantic*, proclaimed that "the anxiously awaited work that was to have crowned cisatlantic linguistic scholarship with a particular glory turns out to be a scandal and a disaster." Follett faulted the editors for whittling away at "traditionary controls," for excessive use of contemporary quotations, and for defining terms with "some of the oddest prose ever concocted by pundits."[72]

In a lengthy review for the *New Yorker*, Dwight Macdonald found little to praise and much to disparage, concluding that the lexicographers who compiled *Webster's Third* "have untuned the string, made a sop of the solid structure of English, and encouraged the language to eat up himself."[73] Macdonald's review expounded on many of the objections and concerns voiced by other critics. Most of these early complaints fell into five major categories: (1) the elimination of certain usage labels, such as "colloquial" and "vulgar," and the drastic reduction of terms labelled "slang," which resulted in words such as "ain't," "finalize," "goof," and "enthuse" being listed with no restrictive labels; (2) the use of illustrative quotations from many contemporary individuals who were not noted for their facility with language, e.g., Ethel Merman, Polly Adler, and Willie Mays; (3) the omission of much of the encyclopedic material, including the biographical dictionary and gazetteer; (4) the use (with the exception of "God") of lower-case letters for words traditionally capitalized, e.g. "hawaiian," "christmas"; and (5) the omission of the pronunciation key at the bottom of each page. In short, as one favorable reviewer put it: "The essential complaint against *Webster's Third* is that it professes to be authoritative, while its critics want it to be authoritarian."[74]

Not all of the reviews in the popular press were negative, however. The *Louisville Times* noted that "no language remains constant from one generation to another" and concluded that *Webster's Third* "is the new authority on our language." Describing the work as "all that the seekers after truth could hope for," the *St. Louis Post-Dispatch* considered it "a staggering accomplishment," while the *Christian Science Monitor* characterized the third edition as "an intensely interesting and distinguished scholarly work, an important milestone in the history of a particularly living, flexible, and beautiful language." Referring to the various negative reviews and editorials as "a flurry of nitwitted commentary," the review in *Editor & Publisher* pointed out that "the Webster editors are conforming with scholarly conclusions that have developed over the last half-century and are now so firmly established as to be beyond question." Moreover, in an article in the *Atlantic*, Bergen Evans called "the storm of abuse" that the popular press had showered on *Webster's Third* a "curious phenomenon." After responding to a number of the specific criticisms regarding the dictionary's "permissiveness," Evans concluded: "anyone who solemnly announces in the year 1962 that he will be guided in matters of English usage by a dictionary published in 1934 is talking ignorant and pretentious nonsense."[75]

In addition, the reception of *Webster's Third* abroad was generally very positive. Observing that "the new *Webster* is first and foremost a dictionary of present-day English," the London *Times Literary Supplement* noted that its American origin should not trouble British users since "the British forms are included as well." Randolph Quirk, writing in the *New Statesman*, termed the new edition "magnificent and meticulously complete," and, while he criticized certain editorial decisions, he concluded that "the publication of the new Webster is a major event in the lexicography of English." Reviewers for other British publications, such as the *Glasgow Herald*, the *Scotsman*, and the *Manchester Guardian Weekly*, wrote in a similarly admiring vein, with no evidence of the vitriolic prose penned by their American counterparts.[76]

Most of the initial reviews of *Webster's Third* in the popular American press were written by journalists or other lay writers. Following a delay of about a year, however, calmer, more rational commentary began to appear in scholarly journals. Written by English teachers and professors, linguists, and lexicographers, these reviews tempered criticism of various aspects of the *Third* with recognition and understanding of the linguistic principles upon which the dictionary was based and with admiration for the work's many positive features. Clarence L. Barnhart, who considered *Webster's Third* "by far the largest and best descriptive dictionary of modern English," provided a detailed synthesis of many of the scholarly reviews in an article published in *American Speech*.[77]

Representative of some of the scholarly commentary is an article in *College English* in which Atcheson L. Hench criticized the work's inadequate labelling and inconsistency in providing historical explanations but concluded that it was "on the whole a magnificent compilation." R.W. Burchfield, editor of the *Supplement to the Oxford English Dictionary*, commended the editors of *Webster's Third* for using contemporary quotations as a basis for much of the dictionary; however, he questioned other editorial decisions, such as the use of lower-case initial letters for proper names and the abandonment of many restrictive labels. In his critique, Harold Allen remarked that *Webster's Third* "already has established its worth among responsible scholars and critics." The noted Hungarian lexicographer, Ladislas Országh, was more wholeheartedly enthusiastic about *Webster's Third* than his American and English colleagues, calling it "not only a monument of learning, the significant and welcoming breaking of fresh ground in English lexicography, but also a matchless precision instrument, a standard work not likely to be surpassed in the remaining years of our century."[78]

The controversy over *Webster's Third* generated a remarkable number of reviews and scholarly articles. It even resulted in works devoted to the controversy itself. In 1962, James Sledd and Wilma Ebbitt compiled a casebook of many of the early newspaper and magazine reviews, while Raven I. McDavid later analyzed the critical commentary that had appeared prior to the official date of publication of *Webster's Third*. Noting the many similarities in content and wording among the various news stories about the

Third published between September 6 and September 28, 1961, McDavid concluded that the articles were based on information contained in Merriam's initial press release, which apparently focused on such aspects of the dictionary as the use of illustrative quotations from contemporary sports and entertainment figures, the inclusion of various terms (such as "beatnik" and "goof") generally considered slang or informal, and the description of "ain't" as "used orally in most parts of the United States by cultivated speakers." The news media seized on these and other statements in the release as novelties or innovations and then reacted to them. Thus, ironically, by identifying and promoting those very features that were most controversial, the press release played a significant role in provoking the early negative publicity.[79]

Other scholars have tried to identify the reasons why many reviewers responded with such intense hostility. Karl W. Dykema attributed the excessive criticism in part to cultural lag, terming some of the reviewers "medieval" in their thinking about language. Walter J. Ong agreed with Dykema but also proposed the theory that people were accustomed to dictionaries based almost entirely on the written language and thus were not prepared for *Webster's Third*, which had achieved a breakthrough by representing oral communication to a much greater degree. A decade later, Rosemary M. Laughlin traced the vehemence of the negative reviews to the "social and psychological milieu" of the early 1960s. More recently, David Gold viewed the debate from the perspective of 25 years later, concluding that most of the justified criticisms centered on the *Third*'s underlabeling, which was seen as permissiveness.[80] Today, most people would agree with the recent assessment in *General Reference Books for Adults* that "*Webster's Third New International Dictionary* is widely recognized as the most authoritative general American dictionary of its kind."[81]

For the Merriam-Webster staff who had labored so long and hard over the third edition of the unabridged, the "lexicographical donnybrook" that greeted its publication must have been disheartening.[82] To make matters worse, in 1962 they were faced with the possibility of a takeover by American Heritage Publishing Company, whose president, James Parton, had been particularly critical of the *Third. Forbes* reported that if Parton gained control of the Merriam firm, he intended to "retire the Third Edition, reissue the Second, and undertake a revision of the badly botched Third." Parton's attempts to purchase controlling shares were unsuccessful, however, and in September 1964 Encyclopaedia Britannica, Inc., acquired the G. & C. Merriam Co.[83]

Other Merriam-Webster Dictionaries

Meanwhile, the task of compiling and revising dictionaries continued unabated. In 1963, the first collegiate dictionary based on *Webster's Third* was published. *Webster's Seventh New Collegiate Dictionary*, containing approximately 130,000 entries, received a much warmer reception than did its parent volume, perhaps because some of the features that had been criticized in the *Third* were not replicated in the collegiate version. For example, the *Seventh New Collegiate* retained its encyclopedic material, such as its gazetteer and biographical section; capitalized proper names; and provided a brief pronunciation key at the bottom of every other page.[84] However, one disgruntled reviewer compared the 1963 *Collegiate* with its 1949 predecessor, particularly in the wording of definitions and in usage labels, and concluded that the *Seventh* "presents a mess the like of which has perhaps been unknown since the Augean stable before Herakles' visit."[85]

Appearing in 1973, the eighth edition of the *Collegiate* was entitled simply *Webster's New Collegiate Dictionary*. With sales of more than a million copies a year, the eighth edition became the best-selling dictionary in the United States. Kenneth Kister attributed this phenomenal success to one reason: "*Webster's*

New Collegiate is an outstanding dictionary." Realistically, however, some credit must be given to the innovative advertisements used to promote the dictionary, described by *Publishers Weekly* as "one of the most imaginative ad campaigns conducted for any hardcover book every published."[86] The *New Collegiate* added approximately 22,000 new words and meanings, including almost all of the previously taboo common terms referring to sexual and other bodily functions and organs. It also revised its treatment of synonyms to a brief statement providing the shared meaning of similar terms.[87]

Having added an eight-page Addenda Section to *Webster's Third* in 1966 and then doubling it to 16 pages in 1971, the Merriam editors produced a separate supplement, *6,000 Words*, in 1976. Reflecting the tremendous growth in the English language over a 15-year period, *6,000 Words* also demonstrated that its publisher could be receptive to criticism, since the editors used capital letters for proper nouns and adjectives. Merriam continued to update the Addenda in *Webster's Third* every five years and published additional cumulative supplementary volumes, *9,000 Words* and *12,000 Words*, in 1983 and 1986, respectively. *Webster's New Dictionary of Synonyms* appeared in 1968, while *Webster's New Geographical Dictionary*, expanded to 47,000 entries, was published in 1972. These revisions were followed by two new titles: *Webster's Secretarial Handbook* in 1974 and *Webster's Collegiate Thesaurus* in 1976.

The 1980s were an especially active decade for the Merriam Company, which officially changed its name to Merriam-Webster Inc. in 1982. In 1983, two of its established publications appeared in new editions: *Webster's Ninth New Collegiate Dictionary* and *Webster's New Biographical Dictionary*. The *Ninth New Collegiate* introduced several new features: usage notes accompany approximately 100 entries "for words posing special problems of confused or disputed usage," and generic terms are followed by the date of the earliest established occurrence of that sense of the word.[88] Surprisingly, shades of the controversy over the 1961 edition of the unabridged surfaced in some of the reviews of the *Ninth Collegiate*. The review in the *Nation* referred to the new *Collegiate* as "a model of scholarship, a delight to read and a genuine description of our language," while *American Speech* termed it "the best *Collegiate* to date." On the other hand, *Fortune* commented that "it is hard to believe that the lexicographers' new permissiveness is good for our language," and a mixed review in *New York* regretfully observed that "the new Collegiate seems to demonstrate a preference for allowing two words to function interchangeably rather than reserving each to mean something slightly different."[89] Nonetheless, *Webster's Ninth New Collegiate Dictionary* is the best-selling dictionary in the United States today, with more than 6.4 million copies sold between its publication in 1983 and the end of 1989.[90]

Other publications revised during the 1980s included the three dictionaries designed to span the years from elementary grades through high school. Variously titled and formatted over the years, the series now includes: *Webster's Elementary Dictionary* (previously *Webster's Beginning Dictionary* and before that *Webster's New Elementary Dictionary*), intended for students in the fourth through sixth grades; *Webster's Intermediate Dictionary*, aimed at students in grades five through eight; and *Webster's School Dictionary* (formerly *Webster's New Students Dictionary*), designed for high school students.

In the second half of the decade Merriam-Webster published a number of new titles. *Webster's Standard American Style Manual* and *Webster's Medical Desk Dictionary* appeared in 1986, followed in 1989 by *Webster's Word Histories* and *Webster's Dictionary of English Usage*. The approximately 2,300 entries in the latter treat many of the disputed usages that made *Webster's Third* so controversial. Entries include illustrative quotations of both historical and contemporary usage and also summarize the opinions of noted authorities on usage. Clearly Merriam-Webster is not prepared to rest on its laurels and confine itself simply to publishing revisions of its standard publications.

Merriam-Webster Today

As the twentieth century draws to a close, Merriam-Webster is in the process of converting all of its publications to machine-readable form. The company plans to begin publishing electronic versions of its dictionaries in conjunction with its corporate affiliate Britannica Software, and it may eventually release some electronic products on its own.[91] Meanwhile, Merriam-Webster has authorized other companies to use its works in electronic formats. For instance, in 1989 *Webster's Ninth New Collegiate Dictionary* became available on CD-ROM for use with the Macintosh personal computer. Frederick C. Mish, Merriam-Webster's current editorial director, points out that this product's graphic capability "makes it different from other electronic dictionaries. It reproduces the dictionary page in its entirety, including pronunciation characters, etymologies, illustrations, and tables."[92] In addition, the CD-ROM includes "digitally recorded pronunciations of each main entry word."[93] Mish observes that the CD-ROM gives only one pronunciation for each entry; therefore, the Merriam-Webster editors were faced with the difficult decision of choosing which pronunciation to include since the first one listed in the dictionary is not necessarily more common or better than the others. The editors also checked all of the recorded pronunciations for accuracy.[94]

Another product utilizing Merriam-Webster publications is the NeXT computer academic workstation introduced by Steven P. Jobs in 1988. At the time of its release, William A. Llewellyn, president of Merriam-Webster, noted that the system provides access to the "entire contents of the *Ninth Collegiate Dictionary*, including the illustrations and the tables, plus the entire contents of the *Collegiate Thesaurus*."[95] In addition, *Compton's MultiMedia Encyclopedia*, produced in 1989, provides access to the definitions of the approximately 60,000 words in *Webster's Intermediate Dictionary* and includes an audio component that gives the pronunciation of approximately 1,500 of the terms.[96]

The Merriam-Webster firm currently publishes more than 30 dictionaries, handbooks, and other reference books. The editorial staff continues to rely heavily on the citation file, which now includes more than 14 million citations. In addition, each editor spends a portion of the day reading a variety of magazines, newspapers, and books and marking new citations to be recorded on 3" x 5" slips, adding between 12,000 to 25,000 slips to the file each month. Editors look not only for "examples of new words and for unusual applications of familiar words" but also for "evidence of the current status of variant spellings, inflected forms, and the stylings of compound words" as well as for "examples that may be quotable as illustrations of typical use" and other useful information. Beginning with the mid-1980s, citations have also been stored in machine-readable form. Since the citation file includes not only the specific citation but also the surrounding text, the machine-readable version can be searched to establish evidence of frequency of certain collocations as well as to determine changes in traditional words and meanings.[97]

In addition to its mammoth citation file, the Merriam-Webster staff maintains a pronunciation file, which currently includes approximately 750,000 slips. Each 3" x 5" slip contains a transcription of the pronunciation of a word and also notes the date, the name of the speaker, and other appropriate identifying information. Pronunciation editors gather the evidence for these slips by listening to radio and television broadcasts, by monitoring shortwave radio broadcasts, and by taking notes during meetings, conferences, and other encounters with live speech.[98]

When asked in early 1990 about rumors that Merriam-Webster was not planning to publish a fourth edition of the unabridged, Frederick Mish responded: "I am confident that there will be a fourth edition in time but not very soon," explaining that the company first had to create a machine-readable version of *Webster's Third* and that preliminary steps had been taken in that regard. Mish added that he did "not expect the fourth edition to be as different from the third as the third was from the second," noting that the Merriam-Webster editors still subscribe to the same definition of the role of the dictionary promulgated by the previous edition.[99]

Even before 1889, the year that the copyright expired on the 1847 edition of Webster's *American Dictionary of the English Language*, the Merriam Company had to contend with the problem of other publishers producing "Webster's" dictionaries and thus taking advantage of the prestige and salability of the Webster name. For more than a century, the firm was involved in various litigations in an attempt to retain the name "Webster" for its exclusive use. Decisions in such suits as those involving the Saalfield Co. in 1917 and the World Publishing Company in 1949 have, while restricting the advertising claims of other publishers, indicated that the name "Webster's" is in the public domain and therefore can be used by any publisher. In its 1949 ruling, the Federal Trade Commission concluded: "The greater weight of the evidence is that to the public the word 'Webster's' simply means a dictionary. It does not mean any particular dictionary, nor the dictionary of a particular publishing company."[100] Therefore, to protect its heritage as literary successors to Noah Webster, the Merriam firm uses several registered trademarks to identify its publications, including the familiar colophon consisting of a wreath encircling Noah Webster's monogram, the words "A Merriam-Webster," and the word "Collegiate."[101]

As the 150th anniversary of the publication of the first Merriam-Webster dictionary approaches, the firm's position as one of the most prestigious publishers of dictionaries in the world remains secure. Thus, it is safe and comforting to assume that Merriam-Webster trademarks, symbolizing a commitment to scholarship and editorial excellence, will grace the title pages of dictionaries and other reference works for many years to come.

PUBLICATION HISTORY

The Unabridged

An American Dictionary of the English Language, by Noah Webster. 2 vols. New York: S. Converse, 1828.

An American Dictionary of the English Language: First Edition in Octavo, Containing the Whole Vocabulary of the Quarto, with Corrections, Improvements, and Several Thousand Additional Words..., by Noah Webster. 2 vols. New Haven: The Author, 1841.

An American Dictionary of the English Language, by Noah Webster; revised and enlarged by Chauncey A. Goodrich. Springfield, MA: George and Charles Merriam, 1847.

An American Dictionary of the English Language, by Noah Webster; thoroughly revised, and greatly enlarged and improved by Chauncey A. Goodrich and Noah Porter. Royal Quarto Edition. 2 vols. Springfield, MA: G. & C. Merriam, 1864.

Webster's International Dictionary of the English Language, revised and enlarged under the supervision of Noah Porter. Springfield, MA: G. & C. Merriam & Co., 1890.

Webster's New International Dictionary of the English Language, W.T. Harris, editor in chief; F. Sturges Allen, general editor. Springfield, MA: G. & C. Merriam Company, 1909.

Webster's New International Dictionary of the English Language, edited by William Allan Neilson, Thomas A. Knott, and Paul W. Carhart. 2nd ed., unabridged. Springfield, MA: G. & C. Merriam Company, 1934.

Webster's Third New International Dictionary of the English Language, edited by Philip Babcock Gove and the Merriam-Webster editorial staff. Springfield, MA: G. & C. Merriam Co., 1961.

Supplements to the above have been published as follows:

6,000 Words: A Supplement to Webster's Third New International Dictionary. Springfield, MA: G. & C. Merriam Co., 1976.

9,000 Words: A Supplement to Webster's Third New International Dictionary. Springfield, MA: Merriam-Webster Inc., 1983.

12,000 Words: A Supplement to Webster's Third New International Dictionary. Springfield, MA: Merriam-Webster Inc., 1986.

The Collegiate

Webster's Collegiate Dictionary. Springfield, MA: G. & C. Merriam, 1898.

Webster's Collegiate Dictionary. [2nd ed.] Springfield, MA: G. & C. Merriam Co., 1910.

Webster's Collegiate Dictionary. 3rd ed. Springfield, MA: G. & C. Merriam Co., 1916.

Webster's Collegiate Dictionary. 4th ed. Springfield, MA: G. & C. Merriam Co., 1931.

Webster's Collegiate Dictionary. 5th ed. Springfield, MA: G. & C. Merriam Co., 1936.

Webster's New Collegiate Dictionary. 6th ed. Springfield, MA: G. & C. Merriam Co., 1949.

Webster's Seventh New Collegiate Dictionary. Springfield, MA: G. & C. Merriam Co., 1963.

Webster's New Collegiate Dictionary. [8th ed.] Springfield, MA: G. & C. Merriam Co., 1973.

Webster's Ninth New Collegiate Dictionary. Springfield, MA: Merriam-Webster Inc., 1983.

Selected Other Dictionaries

Webster's Biographical Dictionary. Springfield, MA: G. & C. Merriam Co., 1943.

Webster's New Biographical Dictionary. Springfield, MA: Merriam-Webster, Inc., 1983.

Webster's Dictionary of Synonyms; A Dictionary of Discriminated Synonyms with Antonyms and Analogous and Contrasted Words. Springfield, MA: G. & C. Merriam Co., 1942.

Webster's New Dictionary of Synonyms; A Dictionary of Discriminated Synonyms with Antonyms and Analogous and Contrasted Words. Springfield, MA: G. & C. Merriam Co., 1968.

Webster's Geographical Dictionary. Springfield, MA: G. & C. Merriam Co., 1949.

Webster's New Geographical Dictionary. Springfield, MA: G. & C. Merriam Co., 1972.

Note: At frequent intervals between major editions, Merriam-Webster dictionaries are issued in revised versions with new copyright dates.

BIBLIOGRAPHY

The amount of secondary material pertaining to Merriam-Webster and its publications is remarkably rich and varied. More than 100 articles and reviews have been written on *Webster's Third New International Dictionary* alone. This bibliography is, of necessity, highly selective. The following articles and books were chosen either for their coverage of various periods in Merriam-Webster's history or for their representative commentaries on Merriam-Webster's major dictionaries. This selection includes a mixture of scholarly and general publications to insure that a certain percentage of the items will be readily available in most public and academic libraries.

Algeo, John. "American Lexicography." In *Wörterbücher: Ein internationales Handbuch zur Lexikographie/Dictionaries: An International Encyclopedia of Lexicography . . .,* vol. 2, edited by Franz Josef Hausmann, 1987–2009. Berlin: Walter de Gruyter, 1990.

Barnhart, Clarence L. "American Lexicography, 1945–1973." *American Speech* 53 (Spring, 1978): 83–140.

Benét, William Rose. "Noah's Ark: The Origin and Making of Webster's International Dictionary." *Saturday Review of Literature* 15 (January 2, 1937): 3–4, 14–16.

Burkett, Eva Mae. *American Dictionaries of the English Language before 1861.* Metuchen, NJ: Scarecrow Press, 1979.

Carter, Robert A. "The War of Words." *Publishers Weekly* (October 2, 1987): 27–28, 33–36.

Chadbourne, Robert. "Keeping Up with the Conversation: Merriam-Webster Is on the Job." *Wilson Library Bulletin* 62 (September, 1987): 41–44.

Dykema, Karl W. "Cultural Lag and Reviewers of Webster III." *AAUP Bulletin* 49 (December, 1963): 364–69.

Friend, Joseph H. *The Development of American Lexicography, 1798–1864.* The Hague: Mouton, 1967.

G. & C. Merriam Co. *100th Anniversary of the Establishment of G. & C. Merriam Company, Springfield, Massachusetts, 1831–1931.* Springfield, MA., 1931.

Gold, David L. "The Debate over *Webster's Third* Twenty-five Years Later: Winnowing the Chaff from the Grain." *Dictionaries* 7 (1985): 225–36.

———. "An End to Dictionary-Bashing or Just a Lull? (On Some Published Reactions to *Webster's Ninth New Collegiate Dictionary*)." *Dictionaries* 10 (1988): 81–91.

Gove, Philip B. "Lexicography and the English Teacher." *College English* 25 (February, 1964): 344–57.

Gove, Philip B., ed. *The Role of the Dictionary.* Indianapolis: Bobbs-Merrill Co., 1967.

Gunderson, Robert D., ed. "New Books in Review: Webster's Third New International Dictionary: A Symposium." *Quarterly Journal of Speech* 48 (December, 1962): 431–40.

Kraus, Janice A. "Caveat Auctor: The War of the Dictionaries." *Journal of the Rutgers University Libraries* 48 (December, 1986): 75–90.

Laughlin, Rosemary M. "The Predecessors of *That* Dictionary." *American Speech* 42 (May, 1967): 105–13.

———. "Prescriptivism, Psychology, and *That* Dictionary." In *Studies in Linguistics in Honor of Raven I. McDavid, Jr.,* edited by Lawrence M. Davis, 377–95. University, AL: University of Alabama Press, 1972.

Leavitt, Robert Keith. *Noah's Ark, New England Yankees and the Endless Quest.* Springfield, MA, 1947.

Marckwardt, Albert H. "Dictionaries and the English Language." *English Journal* 52 (May, 1963): 336–45.

McDavid, Raven I., Jr. "False Scents and Cold Trails: The Pre-Publication Criticism of the Merriam Third." *Journal of English Linguistics* 5 (1971): 101–21.

Moss, Richard J. *Noah Webster.* Boston: Twayne Publishers, 1984.

Pei, Mario. "The Dictionary as a Battlefront: English Teachers' Dilemma." *Saturday Review* 45 (July 21, 1962): 44–46, 55–56.

Read, Allen Walker. "*That* Dictionary or *The* Dictionary?" *Consumer Reports* 28 (October, 1963): 488–92.

Sledd, James, and Wilma R. Ebbitt, eds. *Dictionaries and THAT Dictionary: A Casebook on the Aims of Lexicographers and the Targets of Reviewers.* Chicago: Scott, Foresman and Co., 1962.

Wells, Ronald A. *Dictionaries and the Authoritarian Tradition: A Study in English Usage and Lexicography.* The Hague: Mouton, 1973.

NOTES

1 Quoted in Harry R. Warfel, *Noah Webster: Schoolmaster to America* (New York: Macmillan, 1936), 289. Italics in original.

2 Richard J. Moss, *Noah Webster* (Boston: Twayne, 1984), 2.

3 Richard M. Rollins, *The Long Journey of Noah Webster* (n.p.: University of Pennsylvania Press, 1980), 34–35.

4 Robert Keith Leavitt, *Noah's Ark, New England Yankees and the Endless Quest* (Springfield, MA: G. & C. Merriam Co., 1947), 7.

5 Rollins, 35.

6 Noah Webster, *A Grammatical Institute . . . Part II* (Hartford, CT: Hudson and Goodwin, 1784); Webster, *A Grammatical Institute . . . Part III* (Hartford, CT: Barlow and Babcock, 1785).

7 Leavitt, 14, 16.

8 H.L. Mencken, *The American Language: An Inquiry into the Development of English in the United States*, 4th ed. (New York: Alfred A. Knopf, 1938), 381–87; Chris M. Anson, "*Errours* and *Endeavors*: A Case Study in American Orthography," *International Journal of Lexicography* 3 (Spring 1990): 35–63.

9 Leavitt, 29.

10 Quoted in Leavitt, 29.

11 G. & C. Merriam Co., *100th Anniversary of the Establishment of G. & C. Merriam Company, Springfield, Massachusetts, 1831–1931* ([Springfield, 1931]), [2].

12 James A.H. Murray, *The Evolution of English Lexicography* (Oxford: Clarendon Press, 1900; reprint ed., College Park, MD: McGrath Publishing Co., 1970), 43; George Philip Krapp, *The English Language in America*, vol. 1 (New York: Frederick Ungar, 1925), 362–63; Joseph H. Friend, *The Development of American Lexicography, 1798–1864* (The Hague: Mouton, 1967), 36; Rollins, 123.

13 Leavitt, 34–35.

14 Ibid., 37.

15 G. & C. Merriam Co., *The House That Merriam-Webster Built* ([Windham, CT: Printed at Hawthorn House] 1940), 7.

16 Leavitt, 45.

17 Ibid., 49.

18 Ibid., 48.

19 Eva Mae Burkett, *American Dictionaries of the English Language before 1861* (Metuchen, NJ: Scarecrow Press, 1979), 184; G. & C. Merriam Co., *The House That Merriam-Webster Built*, 9.

20 Quoted in Leavitt, 50.

21 Ibid., 51.

22 *New Englander* 6 (January 1848): 30, 40.

23 Burkett, 185.

24 Leavitt, 50.

25 Burkett, 183.

26 Leavitt, 50; Burkett, 184.

27 See, for example, Burkett, 221–57; Friend, 82–103; Janice A. Kraus, "Caveat Auctor: The War of the Dictionaries," *Journal of the Rutgers University Libraries* 48 (December 1986): 75–90; Sidney I. Landau, "Webster and Worcester: The War of the Dictionaries," *Wilson Library Bulletin* 58 (April 1984): 545–49; Allen Walker Read, "The War of the Dictionaries in the Middle West," in *Papers on Lexicography in Honor of Warren N. Cordell*, ed. by J.E. Congleton, J. Edward Gates, and Donald Hobar (Terre Haute, IN: Dictionary Society of North America, 1979), 3–15.

28 Janice A. Kraus, 82.

29 Quoted in Burkett, 222.

30 Burkett, 223–26.

31 Friend, 83–84.

32 Ibid., 85. Italics in original.

33 Ibid., 86.

34 Leavitt, 58.

35 *New York World*, June 15, 1860, quoted in Burkett, 249.

36 Sidney I. Landau, *Dictionaries: The Art and Craft of Lexicography* (New York: Scribner's, 1984), 64.

37 Raven I. McDavid, "Dictionary Makers and Their Problems," in *Language and Language Teaching: Essays in Honor of W. Wilbur Hatfield*, ed. by Virginia McDavid ([Chicago]: Chicago State College, 1969), 73.

38 Leavitt, 67.

39 Ibid., 69.

40 Ibid., 69, 71.

41 Ibid., 73, 75.

42 Merriam-Webster Inc., "Merriam-Webster Time Line" (three-page typescript), [1].

43 Leavitt, 75.

44 William A. Neilson, "Preface," *Webster's New International Dictionary of the English Language*, 2nd ed. (Springfield, MA: G. & C. Merriam Co., 1934), v.

45 Leavitt, 77.

46 Quoted in "Merriam Celebrates 100 Years of Publishing Merriam-Webster Dictionaries," *Word Study* 22 (February 1947): 3.

47 Leavitt, 82; G. & C. Merriam Co., *The House that Merriam-Webster Built*, 10–11; "Merriam Celebrates 100 Years of Publishing Merriam-Webster Dictionaries," 2.

48 *Educational Review* 38 (November 1909): 425; *Nation* 89 (4 November 1909): 435.

49 Rosemary M. Laughlin, "The Predecessors of *That Dictionary*," *American Speech* 42 (May 1967): 106–07.

50 Leavitt, 83.

51 Neilson, "Preface," vi.

52 Thomas A. Knott, "The New Webster Dictionary," *American Scholar* 4 (May 1935): 372–73.

53 Advertisement in back of *Webster's New International Dictionary*, 2nd ed.

54 "Publisher's Statement," *Webster's New International Dictionary*, 2nd ed., iv; Neilson, "Preface," vi.

55 Neilson, "Preface," v.

56 *Saturday Review of Literature* 11 (12 January 1935): 419; *American Mercury* 36 (December 1935): 507.

57 *Nation* 139 (17 October 1934): 450–51.

[58] William Lyon Phelps, "As I Like It," *Scribner's Magazine* 96 (December 1934): 381.

[59] *New Yorker* 10 (6 October 1934): 18.

[60] Kemp Malone, "Some Linguistic Studies of 1933 and 1934," *Modern Language Notes* 50 (December 1935): 515.

[61] *American Speech* 10 (April 1935): 140.

[62] Quoted in *Word Study* 19 (May 1944): 4.

[63] *Word Study* 36 (February 1961): [8].

[64] Philip B. Gove, "Preface," *Webster's Third New International Dictionary* (Springfield, MA: G. & C. Merriam Co., 1961), 6a-7a.

[65] "Announcing the Publication of Webster's Third New International Dictionary," *Word Study* 37 (October 1961): 1–2.

[66] Gove, "Preface," 7a.

[67] "Webster's Lays an Egg," *Richmond News Leader*, 3 January 1962, reprinted in James Sledd and Wilma Ebbitt, *Dictionaries and THAT Dictionary* (Chicago: Scott, Foresman and Co. 1962), 121–22; "Keep Your Old Webster's," *Washington Post* (17 January 1962), reprinted in Sledd and Ebbitt, 125–26; Wilson Follett, "Sabotage in Springfield," *Atlantic* (January 1962), 73–77, reprinted in Sledd and Ebbitt, 111–19; "It 'Ain't' Good," *Washington Sunday Star* (10 September 1961), reprinted in Sledd, 55–56.

[68] "Webster's New Word Book," *New York Times*, 12 October 1961, reprinted in Sledd and Ebbitt, 78–79; "A Directive Issued to the Staff of the New York Times," *Winners & Sinners* (4 January 1962), reprinted in Sledd and Ebbitt, 122–23.

[69] "A Non-Word Deluge," *Life* (27 October 1961), 4, reprinted in Sledd and Ebbitt, 84.

[70] Philip B. Gove, "A Letter to the Editor of the New York Times," *New York Times* (5 November 1961), reprinted in Sledd and Ebbitt, 88–90.

[71] Philip B. Gove, "A Letter to the Editor of Life Magazine," *Life* (17 November 1961), 13, reprinted in Sledd and Ebbitt, 91–92.

[72] "Logomachy-Debased Verbal Currency," *American Bar Association Journal* (January 1962), 48–49, reprinted in Sledd and Ebbitt, 105–08; B. Hunter Smeaton, "A Review of Webster's Third New International Dictionary," *Library Journal* 87 (15 January 1962): 211, reprinted in Sledd and Ebbitt, 123–25 (italics in original); Wilson Follett, "Sabotage in Springfield," *Atlantic* (January 1962), 73–77, reprinted in Sledd and Ebbitt, 111–19.

[73] Dwight Macdonald, "The String Untuned," *New Yorker* (10 March 1962), 130–34, 137–40, 143–50, 153–60, reprinted in Sledd and Ebbitt, 166–88.

[74] Harold E. Maynard, "The Battle of the Dictionaries," *Public Relations Journal* 19 (August 1963): 11.

[75] Norman E. Isaacs, "And Now, the War on Words," *Louisville Times*, 18 October 1961, reprinted in Sledd and Ebbitt, 79–80; Ethel Strainchamps, "Words, Watchers, and Lexicographers," *St. Louis Post-Dispatch* (29 October 1961), reprinted in Sledd and Ebbitt, 86–88; Millicent Taylor, "The New Dictionary," *Christian Science Monitor* (29 November 1961), 13, reprinted in Sledd and Ebbitt, 99–101; Roy H. Copperud, "English As It's Used Belongs in the Dictionary," *Editor & Publisher* (25 November 1961), 44, reprinted in Sledd and Ebbitt, 96–99; Bergen Evans, "But What's a Dictionary For?" *Atlantic* (May 1962), 57–62, reprinted in Sledd and Ebbitt, 238–48.

[76] "New World of Words," London *Times Literary Supplement* (16 March 1982), 187, reprinted in Sledd and Ebbitt, 197–98; Randolph Quirk, *The New Statesman* (2 March 1962), 304, reprinted in Sledd and Ebbitt, 151–54; Christopher Small, "A Review of Webster's Third New International Dictionary," *Glasgow Herald* (27 February 1962), reprinted in Sledd and Ebbitt, 136–37; Moray McLaren, "Twenty Guineas Worth of Webster," *Scotsman* (10 March 1962), 4, reprinted in Sledd and Ebbitt, 161–62; Alan S.C. Ross, "Words without End," *Manchester Guardian Weekly* (15 March 1962), 10, reprinted in Sledd and Ebbitt, 194–96.

[77] Clarence L. Barnhart, "American Lexicography, 1945–1973," *American Speech* 53 (Spring 1978): 100–13.

[78] Atcheson L. Hench, "Notes on Reading Webster III," *College English* 24 (May 1963): 613–18; R. W. Burchfield, "Webster's Third New International Dictionary," *Review of English Studies*, n.s., 14 (1963): 319–23; Harold B. Allen, "Webster's Third New International Dictionary: A Symposium," *Quarterly Journal of Speech* 48 (December 1962): 431–33; Ladislas Országh, "Webster's Third New International Dictionary of the English Language," *Hungarian Studies in English* 1 (1963): 133–39.

[79] Sledd and Ebbitt, *Dictionaries and THAT Dictionary*; Raven I. McDavid, Jr., "False Scents and Cold Trails: The Pre-Publication Criticism of the Merriam *Third*," *Journal of English Linguistics* 5 (1971): 101–21.

[80] Karl W. Dykema, "Cultural Lag and the Reviewers of *Webster III*," *AAUP Bulletin* 49 (December 1963): 364–69; Walter J. Ong, "Hostility, Literacy and *Webster III*," *College English* 26 (November 1964): 106–11; Rosemary M. Laughlin, "Prescriptivism, Psychology, and *That* Dictionary," in *Studies in Linguistics in Honor of Raven I. McDavid, Jr.*, ed. Lawrence M. Davis (University, AL: University of Alabama Press, 1972), 377–95; David Gold, "The Debate over *Webster's Third* Twenty-five Years Later: Winnowing the Chaff from the Grain," *Dictionaries* 7 (1985): 225–36.

[81] Marion Sader, ed., *General Reference Books for Adults: Authoritative Evaluations of Encyclopedias, Atlases, and Dictionaries* (New York: Bowker, 1988), 395.

[82] James B. McMillan, "Dictionaries and Usage," *Word Study* 39 (February 1964): [1].

[83] "Battle of the Book," *Forbes* 89 (15 April 1962): 47; "Encyclopaedia Britannica Will Buy G. & C. Merriam," *Publishers Weekly*, 21 September 1964, 36–37.

[84] David M. Glixon, "The Best of References," *Saturday Review* 46 (23 March 1963): 36; *Booklist and Subscription Books Bulletin* 59 (15 July 1963): 909–11; Priscilla Tyler, "An English Teacher Looks at Webster's Seventh New Collegiate Dictionary," *Word Study* 38 (April 1963): [1]–8.

[85] John J. Enck, "The Ruptured Duck Flies Again: Webster's Seventh Collegiate," *College English* 27 (January 1966): 302–09.

[86] Kenneth F. Kister, *Dictionary Buying Guide: A Consumer Guide to General English-Language Wordbooks in Print* (New York: Bowker, 1977), 92; *Publishers Weekly* (22 July 1974), 60.

[87] Clarence L. Barnhart, "American Lexicography, 1945–1973," *American Speech* 53 (Spring 1978): 121.

[88] Frederick C. Mish, "Preface," *Webster's Ninth New Collegiate Dictionary* (Springfield, MA: Merriam-Webster, 1983), 6.

[89] Jim Quinn, "Lingo," *Nation* 237 (23–30 July 1983): 90; Thomas L. Clark, "Praise for Webster's Ninth," *American Speech* 59 (Spring 1984): [70]; Andrew Hacker, "A Do–Your-Own-Thing Dictionary," *Fortune* 108 (3 October 1983): 272; Peter Devine, "Webster's Ninth New Collegiate Dictionary," *New York* 16 (21 November 1983): 105.

[90] Daisy Maryles, "A Decade of Megasellers," *Publishers Weekly*, 5 January 1990, 26.

[91] Jane Tencza, secretary to Joseph J. Esposito, President of Merriam-Webster Inc., letter to the author, 2 April 1991.

[92] Dr. Frederick C. Mish, Editorial Director, Merriam-Webster Inc., telephone conversation with the author, 20 March 1990.

[93] Brochure from Highlighted Data, Inc., Washington, DC

[94] Mish, telephone conversation with author, 20 March 1990.

[95] "News Release: *Webster's Ninth New Collegiate Dictionary* and *Webster's Collegiate Thesaurus* Featured on New NeXT Computer System," Merriam-Webster Inc., 1 November 1988.

[96] *Booklist/Reference Books Bulletin* 86 (15 November 1989): 689.

[97] "The English Language in the Dictionary," *Webster's Ninth New Collegiate Dictionary* (Springfield, MA: Merriam-Webster Inc., 1989), 28; also Dr. Frederick C. Mish, telephone conversation with author, 20 March 1990.

[98] "Guide to Pronunciation," *Webster's Ninth New Collegiate Dictionary*, 33; also Dr. Frederick C. Mish, telephone conversation with author, 20 March 1990.

[99] Mish, telephone conversation with author, 20 March 1990.

[100] "Another Decision in Webster's Dictionary Case," *Publishers Weekly* (20 January 1917), 160–65; quoted in "FTC Defines World's Use of 'Webster' Name," *Publishers Weekly* (10 December 1949), 2375–76.

[101] *Word Study* 22 (April 1947): 4; Merriam-Webster Inc., "Is There More Than One Webster?" (1-page typescript, no date).

Afternoon Tea, Parliament, and . . .
Who's Who

Linda K. Simons

DEVELOPMENT AND HISTORY

This is the story of a book which slumbered through its childhood and youth, underwent a midlife transformation at age 47, and emerged to become not only one of the best known reference works in English but also the respected ancestor of a whole family of reference books. Soon to be a century and a half old, it remains the prototype for biographical dictionaries which contain short entries supplied by the subjects themselves. It has spawned dozens of imitators in countries all over the world. This is the story of *Who's Who*.

Antecedents

Information about famous people has existed for a long time. The earliest biographical dictionaries in modern Europe concerned themselves with royal and noble families. One of the oldest was the *Almanach de Gotha*, begun in 1763, which listed the families of the royal houses of Europe and also listed "the principal executive, legislative, and diplomatic officials"[1] of selected countries of the world. This work was published regularly until 1960. In England two publishers in particular are associated with records of landed and titled families. Debrett's published *The New Peerage* starting in 1769. Known by various names in later editions, Debrett's *Peerage* continues to be published. It was supplemented by *The New Baronetage of England* also begun in 1769. This work has also changed names but

continues to exist. John Burke began publishing Burke's *Genealogical and Heraldic History of the Peerage, Baronetage, and Knightage* in 1826. Several years later Burke published his *Genealogical and Heraldic Dictionary of the Landed Gentry of Great Britain and Ireland*. The men (and some women) listed in these works were included because they were born into the aristocracy. There were also books which listed people by virtue of the positions they held. Some examples of these works include the *New Law List*, a directory of the legal professions, started in 1798; the *Medical Directory*, started in 1845; and, later, *Crockford's Clerical Directory*, started in 1858, and listing the name and address of every clergy member in the Church of England.

The first *Who's Who* appeared in 1849, a small book published by Alfred Head Baily. His firm, Baily Brothers, had offices in the Cornhill section of London.[2] As editor for the first edition Baily Brothers chose Col. Henry Robert Addison, an Irishman in his forties. He had been a soldier and a police magistrate as well as a writer of verse, plays, novels, and even an opera.[3] The first edition of *Who's Who* was merely a group of lists: members of the Houses of Parliament, bishops, and so forth. No biographical information was given except for members of Parliament whose age, political affiliation, and constituency were listed.[4] *Who's Who* was evidently a success because it was published annually in an unchanged format through 1896.

The Blacks

By that year the copyright for *Who's Who* had passed from Baily Brothers to the firm of Simkin, Hamilton, Kent, and Company who decided to put it up for sale. One of the publishers interested in buying the copyright was A and C Black. Adam Black had founded the company in Edinburgh in 1807. Under his leadership and then his sons' management, the firm had prospered and had moved to London in 1889. It was known chiefly for being the publisher of Sir Walter Scott's novels, but its list also included serious books of scholarly interest. Blacks had published three editions of the *Encyclopaedia Britannica*, including the great ninth edition. That work, even today considered one of the greatest encyclopedias ever published, consumed much of the firm's energies between 1875 and 1888. By 1896, however, the sales of the *Britannica* had slowed. The first and second generations of the family were dead or retired, and the firm was in the hands of two grandsons of the founder, cousins who were both named Adam. Looking for new works to publish, the cousins had contemplated buying *Men and Women of the Times*. This publication, which attempted to be a sort of national biographical dictionary of the living, had appeared irregularly since 1852. When its current owner, G. Routledge and Sons Ltd., insisted on a price of 1,000 pounds sterling, however, the Blacks decided against purchase. (Blacks did eventually buy *Men and Women of the Times*, in 1900).[5] When Adam Black learned that *Who's Who* was to be auctioned at the London auction house of Hodgsons, he saw an opportunity to acquire a work similar to *Men and Women of the Times*. The day of the sale he met his friend George Whitaker, publisher of *Whitaker's Almanack*, at Hodgsons. The two men discovered that they were both interested in purchasing *Who's Who* and sensibly decided not to bid against each other. They tossed a coin to decide who would bid. Black won the toss and bought the copyright for 30 pounds.[6] Thus chance dictated that A and C Black rather than J. Whitaker and Sons became the publishers of *Who's Who*.

Adam Black immediately started working on changing the scope and format of the book. He hired a new editor, Douglas Sladen, a man whose background looked curiously similar to that of the first editor, Addison. Sladen was 40 years old and a prolific writer of novels, poetry, and travel books.[7] He had taken a first in history at Oxford and had taught at the University of Sydney in Australia.[8] Since some of his books had been published by Blacks, the publishers had some idea of his abilities.[9] Together with the Black cousins, Sladen compiled a list of potential biographees. Names from the original lists were supplemented by people whose biographies might be of interest to the public. The Blacks decided that people would be chosen for their reference merit alone. No one could pay for an entry, and biographees would not be able to purchase the book at a reduced price. This fundamental decision placed *Who's Who* above charges of being a vanity work.

A second fundamental policy was that the biographees themselves would supply the information for the entries. The Black cousins and Sladen created a list of headings (virtually unchanged today) and designed a questionnaire which biographees were asked to complete. The form asked for standard biographical items such as address, birth date, parents' names, spouse's name, schools attended, clubs, occupation, publications, and so on. In 1896 *Who's Who* invited 5,000 people to participate. The firm mailed the questionnaire and invitation in a specially designed blue envelope with a dark blue seal, similar to those used for British Cabinet mailings, to distinguish it from other mail. They hoped that recipients would be curious enough to open the envelope, read the invitation, and accept the Blacks' offer. Since Sladen had obtained permission from the Duke of Rutland and A.J. Balfour to use their biographies as samples, these were included in the mailing as well.[10]

The originality of the Blacks' plan lay first in a wider choice of subjects than those covered by the existing reference books, which were limited to the titled and the wealthy, and secondly in giving a degree of latitude to the biographee so that, while critical comment was excluded, the entries might have some personal and revealing quality—an intention which was greatly assisted by the decision to ask an entrant to declare his recreation.[11]

Of the 5,000 asked to participate in the 1897 edition, all but two, Lord Salisbury and Joseph Chamberlain, eventually agreed to do so. Sladen used a number of tactics to induce people to complete their forms. When W.S. Gilbert refused to fill out his questionnaire, Sladen sent him a completed form which said, "W.S. Gilbert, journalist, writes the libretti for Sir Arthur Sullivan's operas." Gilbert, who always believed that his most important work consisted of his serious plays, immediately filled out his questionnaire in greater detail![12] Sladen also completed a form for one woman, deliberately adding 10 years to her age. When he sent it to her for her approval, she sent back a corrected form, omitting her age altogether but adding other interesting biographical details.[13] In the end, nearly everyone submitted to Sladen's flattery or threats and returned the questionnaire.

Besides overseeing preparation of the lists and entries, Sladen composed the preface to the 1897 edition. In it, he explained the changes in the book and noted what distinguished it from its competitors. He emphasized the great number of writers included in *Who's Who*, noting that journalism and literature had not been adequately covered in the other works. He stated his goal of including all prominent English people, regardless of their family background, and he pointed out that many women were included in the list. (On this last point, Sladen's perception of "many women" was not shared by Julian Huxley. In 1935 he asserted that only 3 percent of that year's entries were claimed by females.[14] A random check of the 1990 edition suggests that percentage has increased to 6 percent, still a relatively small number.) Finally, Sladen noted the many

tables and lists carried over from the old *Who's Who*. These were placed in the front of the volume and the biographies of the persons named in the lists were integrated into the alphabetical order. A and C Black issued the 1897 edition in the late fall of 1896, advertising it in the firm's fall catalog:

> *Who's Who 1897*. Forty-ninth year of issue. Entirely remodelled. Crown 8vo. Price 3s. 6d. net. Contains a complete list of all who have the right to bear any British title; also biographies, mostly autobiographies, of all the prominent persons in the United Kingdom.[15]

Sladen's Departure

Although the book did not make money at first, it eventually became an important item of Black's list. In 1898 the Black cousins and Sladen disagreed over terms of employment and payment and the Blacks decided to take the editorship inside the house.[16] Sladen went on to a distinguished career as a travel writer. Adam Rimmer Black took on the job of editor, one he kept until his death in 1936. As the years passed, he devoted more and more time to *Who's Who* until he was spending virtually all his time on it.[17] He worked anonymously, and at his death the editorial duties were assumed by another anonymous staff member. To this day, the firm guards closely the name of the editor.

Who's Who has been published continuously since 1897, including through the two world wars. During the Second World War the female staff of the publication was evacuated to a village in the Cotswolds where work could proceed without fear of bombing attacks.[18] The wartime paper shortage was another problem. Before 1943 no entries had ever been dropped except when a person died, but the paper shortage impelled the firm to drop several thousand names of marginal interest. Nevertheless, it took the personal intervention of Prime Minister Winston Churchill to assure the full publication and distribution of *Who's Who* despite the paper rationing.[19]

An Enduring Format and Process

The format of the work has remained essentially the same since 1897. The preface is followed by a table of abbreviations; an annual necrology; a genealogical chart of the British Royal Family; and the alphabetically arranged biographies. The many tables carried over from the original work were dropped from the volume in 1903 to provide more space for the biographies. The number of persons included has grown from 5,500 to more than 28,000. Currently the number of biographies is increasing by 150–200 each year[20] and the physical size of the volume has grown to accommodate the additional entries. Throughout its existence, however, *Who's Who* has kept its red binding with gold lettering, and the current issue would be instantly recognizable to Douglas Sladen. The entries would also appear essentially the same to him.

The editorial staff of *Who's Who* monitors newspapers and other sources of information to discover names of potential biographees each year. A Selection Board chooses about half of the new entries for each edition. The other 50 percent are automatically chosen when people are elected or appointed to certain posts (such as member of Parliament) or succeed to certain titles of nobility. Although the majority of biographees are British, a great many foreigners are included. In a 1935 article for *Saturday Review,* Julian Huxley estimated about 12 percent of the entries were non-Britishers, and in a second article written in 1946, he noted the inclusion of Hitler (complete with telephone number!), Mussolini, Stalin, and other heads or former heads of state.[21] An estimated 30 percent of the 1990 *Who's Who* subjects are not British.

A new biographee is invited to complete a questionnaire which is then edited by *Who's Who* so that it conforms to the style of the publication. Each year thereafter a biographee checks and corrects the next edition's proof. The editorial staff also monitors changes through its reading of the press. Since 1943 biographies have occasionally been shortened or otherwise made to conform with the book's overall style. But the entries are essentially autobiographies since each entrant chooses what to say about himself or herself. *Who's Who* does not verify all details, but only those which the editor suspects to be untrue. If a person does not return the questionnaire, the staff will write a biography, but *Who's Who* will not print it without the person's consent. In fact, in the last 20 years the editors have included only four people against their wishes, "all holders of prominent public office."[22]

The questionnaire and resultant biographies emphasize one's career and publications, but the subject which has aroused the most comment is the category "recreation." Devised by Adam Black as a way to personalize the entry, "recreation" has provided amusement to many readers. As early as 1898 the *Times* book reviewer noted that Cecil Rhodes' leisure activities, including riding two hours each morning, collecting old china, and keeping lions and uncaged zebras, scarcely left him time to do any work![23] Julian Huxley delighted in quoting recreations from the 1935 and 1945 editions, including George Bernard Shaw's "Anything except sport" and Ernest Hemingway's "Drinking."[24] He quoted one Lawrence Meynell whose entry "ends on a pathetic note—'walking, canoeing, tree-felling, reading, trying to write a play!'"[25]

Despite all the fuss about recreation, however, the standard biographical details are what constitute the real reference value of *Who's Who*. Generally, an entry follows this form:

> Name; Position; Beginning date of current position; Birthdate; Parents' names; Marriage date and spouse's name; Number of sons and daughters; Education; Information about career, positions previously held, and accomplishments; Publications; Recreation; Address; Telephone; Clubs.

Within this format, there is much leeway. Some people choose to leave out various categories such as recreation or clubs. Some detail their education very carefully while others skim over it with phrases such as "educated privately" or "at home." Some authors meticulously list everything they have written while others list only their most important works. One of the longest entries in the 1990 edition is that of Barbara Cartland, the writer of romance fiction, who seems to have listed everything she has ever published.

When a biographee dies, the publisher transfers the entry with death date added to the next volume of *Who Was Who*. Thus, the record of notable living becomes a record of past notables as well. The first *Who Was Who* was published in June 1920, and additional volumes have been issued at approximately 10-year intervals. Generally, the biographical information is the same as it last appeared in *Who's Who* with the death date added.[26]

Imitators

Who's Who has inspired a great many imitators, including *Who's Who in America* and similar volumes for many other countries. Albert Nelson Marquis published the first *Who's Who in America* in 1899, just two years after Black started its new format, and Marquis admitted his book was a copy of the British title.[27] Besides the national biographies inspired by *Who's Who* there are innumerable specialty biographical dictionaries such as *Who's Who in Finance and Industry* (Chicago: Marquis) and even *Who's Who Among American High School Students* (Lake Forest, IL: Educational Communications, Inc.). The most recent edition of Eugene Sheehy's *Guide to Reference Books* lists 123 titles beginning "Who's Who"; this count does not include foreign titles such as the German *Wer Ist Wer?*[28] Nor does it count local publications nor biographical compendia whose titles begin with other words.

Who's Who remains the reference book of choice if a reader wishes to find basic biographical information about a British subject or a famous non-Britisher. Indeed, it fulfills its task so well that it has eliminated any important competition in its own niche. *Debrett's Handbook* concentrates on the nobility and business people and has many fewer entries. As its patron, Sir Iain Moncreiffe of that Ilk, notes in the preface, *Debrett's* concerns itself

more with social status while *Who's Who* is more concerned with academic status or personal achievement.[29] *Whitaker's Almanack* contains many of the lists that the original *Who's Who* contained, but does not print biographies. The *Dictionary of National Biography* still limits itself to those who have been dead long enough that an objective view of their lives can be attempted. The other biographical dictionaries are more specialized and not as broad-based. Moreover, since the nineteenth century the British, because of their huge empire and, later, Commonwealth, have had a remarkably cosmopolitan attitude toward events and persons. Because *Who's Who* contains biographies of African, Asian, and Indian politicians, writers, and other prominent people, its usefulness is certainly not limited to the British Isles.

Although the term "who's who" was not originated by the publication, it owes its fame to the association with the book. The *Oxford English Dictionary* cites *Who's Who* in one of its definitions for "who" and quotes several uses of the term "who's who" meaning "who each of a number of persons is, or what position each holds." One colorful example is from the 1917 *National Police Gazette*: "We don't believe that Ed W. Dunn's latest effusion would win a place for him in the poet's 'Who's who!' corner."[30] To say that a list is a "who's who" of something implies that it contains people with the best or most of a certain quality. In this respect, "Who's Who" has entered the language of people who have never consulted the original publication.

Who's Who continues to publish annually, adding more names each time. The page size was enlarged in 1985, and the editor does not anticipate enlarging it again soon. Nor are there current plans to issue the book in an electronic form.[31] *Who's Who* will continue to do what it does best, provide basic biographical information about "people who, through their careers, affect the political, economic, scientific and artistic life of the country."[32] Like afternoon tea and Parliament, *Who's Who* represents the best of British tradition and contemporary excellence.

PUBLICATION HISTORY

Who's Who; An Annual Biographical Dictionary. 1849–. Annual. Absorbed Men and Women of the Time with volume 53, 1901. Subtitle varies; volumes for 1849–1898, 1904–1912 issued without subtitle.

BIBLIOGRAPHY

The best source for information about *Who's Who* is the history of Adam & Charles Black Ltd. which provides good background on the company and a fair history of the publication from 1896 to 1957. Julian Huxley's two articles address the issue of who is included and quote many of the more amusing or unusual entries. In an early article, Joseph Jacobs studied *Who's Who* to see what influence place of birth, career choice, and education have had on obtaining an entry in the book. Unfortunately, this study appears not to have been replicated, although a number of similar studies exist for *Who's Who in America.* Douglas Sladen's preface to the 1897 edition is essential to understanding his vision of what the new *Who's Who* should be.

Adam & Charles Black; 1807–1957; Some Chapters in the History of a Publishing House. London: Adam & Charles Black, 1957.

"A Century of 'Who's Who.'" *Times* (London), July 7, 1948, p. 3.

Harris, Leon. "What's What with America's *Who's Who.*" *Smithsonian* 12 (November, 1981): 204–206+.

Huxley, Julian. "The Analysis of Fame; A Revelation of the Human Documents in 'Who's Who.'" *Saturday Review of Literature* 12 (May 11, 1935): 12–13.

———. "Berlin 11 6191 Does Not Answer." *Saturday Review of Literature* 29 (April 13, 1946): 11–14.

Jacobs, Joseph. "The Paths of Glory." *Living Age Littell's* 224 (February 24, 1900): 515–522.

Sladon, Douglas. *My Long Life; Anecdotes and Adventure.* London: Hutchinson & Co., 1939.

———. "Preface" in *Who's Who.* London: A. & C. Black, 1897, iii–vi.

"Who's Not Who in England." *Literary Digest* 104 (February 1, 1930): 44–45.

"'Who's Who' Celebrates 100th Anniversary." *Publisher's Weekly* 154 (December 25, 1948): 2479.

NOTES

[1] Eugene P. Sheehy, ed., *Guide to Reference Books*, 10th ed. (Chicago: American Library Association, 1986), 867.

[2] *Adam & Charles Black; 1807–1957; Some Chapters in the History of a Publishing House* (London: Adam & Charles Black, 1957), 71.

[3] David James O'Donoghue, ed., *The Poets of Ireland; A Biographical and Bibliographical Dictionary of Irish Writers of English Verse* (Dublin: Hodges, Figgis & Co., 1912), 6.

[4] *Adam & Charles Black*, 71.

[5] Ibid., 70–71.

[6] "A Century of 'Who's Who,'" *Times* (London), 7 July 1948, p. 3.

[7] *Who Was Who 1941–1950* (London: Adam & Charles Black, 1952), 1062.

[8] *Adam & Charles Black*, 73.

[9] Ibid., 60.

[10] Douglas Sladen, *My Long Life; Anecdotes and Adventures* (London: Hutchinson & Co., 1939), 190–91.

[11] *Adam & Charles Black*, 72.

[12] Sladen, 191.

[13] Ibid., 191–92.

[14] Julian Huxley, "The Analysis of Fame; A Revelation of the Human Documents in 'Who's Who,'" *Saturday Review of Literature* 12 (11 May 1935): 12.

[15] *Adam & Charles Black*, 73.

[16] Sladen, 193–94.

[17] *Adam & Charles Black*, 99.

[18] Ibid., 103.

[19] Ibid., 108.

[20] A & C Black (Publishers) Ltd., letter to the author, 14 March 1990.

[21] Huxley, "Analysis," 12; Julian Huxley, "Berlin 11 6191 Does Not Answer," *Saturday Review of Literature* 29 (13 April 1946): 11–12.

[22] A & C Black (Publishers) Ltd., letter to the author, 14 March 1990.

[23] "Who's Who, 1899," *Times* (London), 6 December 1898, p. 4.

[24] Huxley, "Analysis," 13.

[25] Huxley, "Berlin," 14.

26 Sheehy, 300.

27 Leon Harris, "What's What with America's *Who's Who*," *Smithsonian* 12 (9 November 1981): 204.

28 Sheehy, 1553.

29 *DeBrett's Handbook 1982* (London: Debrett's Peerage Limited, 1981), 12–13.

30 *Oxford English Dictionary*, 2nd ed. (Oxford: Clarendon Press, 1989), see "who."

31 A & C Black (Publishers) Ltd., letter to the author, 14 March 1990.

32 *Who's Who* (London: Adam & Charles Black, 1990), 7.

All Things for All People: The *World Almanac*

Margaret Morrison

DEVELOPMENT AND HISTORY

"Doth the moon shine the night we play our play?" asks Snout in *A Midsummer Night's Dream* (III, i, 52–53), to which Bottom cries "A calendar, a calendar! look in the almanack; find out moonshine, find out moonshine" (III, i, 54–55). Bottom certainly knew his reference sources; he and his friends needed moonlight for their production of *Pyramus and Thisby*, and an almanac was definitely the place to look. In fact, by the time Bottom called for his almanac in 1590, centuries of common folk and royalty alike had relied on almanacs for their knowledge of the seasons, the phases of the moon, and much more. Today, 400 years later, people still consult almanacs for a great variety of questions, from the colors of their favorite college teams to the height of the world's mountains. Without doubt, the almanac most consulted in the United States is the *World Almanac and Book of Facts*, now well into its second century of publication.

Calendars, the physical recording of periods of time, have existed for at least 5,000 years. They were essential to agriculture and have been found in ancient civilizations throughout the world. So important was the match between calendar time and solar time that in the sixteenth century Pope Gregory himself adjusted the existing calendar to make up for lost days. Calendars and almanacs were once nearly identical, although by Bottom's

time an almanac usually included at least two kinds of calendars: a list of days, weeks, and months with annotations for ecclesiastical festivals, saint's days, and other religious observances; and an astronomical table showing the phases of the moon, position of the planets, eclipse predictions, and weather forecasts.[1]

History of the Almanac

Manuscript almanacs may have existed in Alexandria in the second century A.D. The earliest Christian almanac appeared in 354 on parchment. The thirteenth and fourteenth centuries saw a number of manuscript almanacs, while the ornate Books of Hours, which reflected many features of the almanac, flourished between the thirteenth and seventeenth centuries. Johann Gutenberg composed the astronomical calendar in 1448 in Mainz, and another printer, Johann Mueller, known as Regiomontanus, produced the *Kalendarium novum*, the oldest existing copy of which is dated 1476. Printed in red and black on 12 leaves, or 24 pages, it was illustrated, contained a calendar, table of eclipses, the position of the planets—and a complete and decorated title page. A title page did not appear in another book for 20 years.

The first English almanac, *The Shepheard's Kalendar* by Richard Pynson, appeared in 1495. During the first half of the sixteenth century, the infamous Michel de Nostradamus created almanacs forecasting royal deaths, natural disasters, and political events. During this and the next century, astrology gained in influence, and predictions of all sorts abounded. These worried the royalty and clergy of the time. Henry III of France forbade political prophecies, as did Louis XIII, while the Archbishop of Canterbury and the Bishop of London oversaw the publication of English almanacs.[2] Throughout Europe almanacs grew in popularity, some becoming quite specialized, appealing to particular political parties or religious groups.

Almanacs in North America

In North America in the seventeenth century, almanac printing was a major industry. Almanacs served as almost the only secular source of information in the colonies, and the number of almanacs published in the 1600s and 1700s exceeded the number of all other books combined, including religious literature. Since the first American newspapers and magazines did not appear until the first half of the eighteenth century, the early colonial almanacs found an audience for literary expression as well as for factual data. Early American almanacs were of very high quality, thanks to their capable editors. Before 1687 most almanacs produced in Massachusetts were edited by Harvard graduates who were "tutors," or graduate students. These included Cotton and Nathaniel Mather, the Puritan ministers, and Uriah Oakes, a future president of Harvard, who included extra space below his calendars to provide a summary of the events of each century. These almanacs, known as Cambridge or philomath almanacs, seem to have offered an opportunity for young scholars to display both their mathematical abilities and their poetic talents.

As almanacs became increasingly worldly in the eighteenth century, two new kinds appeared. One, the pocket almanac, specialized in current affairs. The other, the register, was larger than the pocket almanac, contained no literature and included more miscellaneous

government data.[3] This reference volume obviously prefigures almanacs like the *World*. Almanacs of this time often voiced political opposition to British rule and took on a variety of social issues. Benjamin Banneker, America's only black almanac-maker, created almanacs which contained essays on slavery; and Mary K. Goddard, postmistress of Baltimore, printed beautiful almanacs with special features for women.

Prominent families of Americans specialized in printing almanacs. James Franklin, Sr., brother of Benjamin, printed *The Rhode Island Almanac*, "Poor Robin," in 1728. Anne Franklin, his widow, was one of six women, including M.K. Goddard, who printed almanacs before 1800. James Jr., Ben's nephew, wrote the "Poor Job" almanacs in the 1750s.

Benjamin Franklin, however, enjoyed the greatest fame with his *Poor Richard's Almanac*, which survived from 1732 to 1758. Adopting the character of Richard Saunders, Franklin created a uniquely witty and colloquial style for the usual aphorisms that had appeared in almanacs for centuries. Franklin's wit and talent for self-promotion helped *Poor Richard* sell well, approximately 10,000 copies annually, one for every 100 colonists.[4] After 1748 *Poor Richard* became *Poor Richard Improved*, with 36 pages instead of 24 and woodcuts. Although the humor was more sophisticated, it did not seem as much fun, and the almanac ceased publication in 1758.

In the nineteenth century, almanacs broadened their scope, presenting fewer astronomical data, fewer moralizing tracts, and more practical reference information. In 1793 Robert B. Thomas began production of the most popular of all nineteenth-century almanacs, the *Old Farmer's Almanac*, which survives to this day under the same family's leadership. Religious almanacs by denomination were common. The first medical almanac, the *Physician's Almanac* from Boston, appeared in 1817, and in 1844 the first almanac to be produced by a commercial firm, this one advertising patent medicine, came on the scene.

Historian Peter Force printed the *National Calendar* from 1820 to 1836 and included in it brief histories of federal government departments and agencies. Even more contemporary in format, the *American Almanac*, published from 1830 to 1861 and again from 1878 to 1889, contained information on state governments, colleges, railroads, and an annual chronology of events. In addition to these factual compendia, a wide variety of comic almanacs, filled with jokes and pictures, found an eager audience. Among these was *Davy Crockett's Almanack of Wild Sports of the West, and Life in the Backwoods*, which contained tall tales, humorous stories, and vivid drawings of woodsmen and wild animals. Begun in Tennessee in 1835, this almanac survived Crockett's death in 1836 by 20 years.

The newspaper almanacs had their origin in the political almanacs that promoted the people and platforms of political parties. The *Democrat's Almanac* was one such volume; its rival, the *Whig Almanac and Political Register*, was published in New York by Horace Greeley. Started in 1836, the *Whig Almanac* changed its title several times and in 1856 became the *Tribune Almanac*, the oldest of the newspaper almanacs. However the *Herald Almanac* of 1849, also published in New York, was the first to carry a newspaper's name.[5]

The First World Almanac

In 1860 Alexander Cummings, a newspaper publisher from Philadelphia, established the *World* in New York City as a one-cent religious daily. The *World* had immediate and continuing financial problems; and within a year the very capable journalist Manton Marble became its part-owner and editor, redefining it as a calm, conservative newspaper supporting the Democratic Party of New York. By late 1869 Marble had full control of the paper. Its style was sophisticated, its readers upper class, and its circulation weak.

The *World Almanac*, named for its parent, was first published in 1868. While there are very few records of the history of the *Almanac*, it may have been Marble's demands for accuracy in the newspaper that prompted the creation of this handbook used to provide background information, names of prominent people, and statistical data about the U.S. The 1868 *Almanac* cost about 20 cents, was 120 pages long, and carried 12 pages of advertising appearing at the front and back of the volume. After the title page and index, the calendars and astronomical data opened the text. Fourteen pages discussed the ongoing issues of Reconstruction. Election returns for 1866 to 1868 occupied 17 pages. In addition, 4 pages heralded the excellence of the *World*, but other than a listing of state political officials, there is surprisingly little information on New York. The type face was fancy and the print minute.

In 1876 when Republican Rutherford B. Hayes was chosen president by the Electoral College over Democrat Samuel J. Tilden who had won the popular vote, Marble despaired of chances for the Democrats and for a paper that supported them. He offered the paper to his associate editor, William Henry Hurlbert, who found financing from Thomas A. Scott, president of the Pennsylvania Railroad. Hurlbert's style was even more elegant—and stuffier—than Marble's. The *Almanac*, which had been published annually since its inception, died the year of the sale.

Scott had wanted to use the paper as a voice for his own investment plans but grew tired of losing money on it. In 1879 he sold the *World* to Wall Street shark Jay Gould as a minor part of the sale of the Texas & Pacific railroad. Gould claimed that he never wanted the *World,* but the paper did give him a vehicle of his own in the city. Gould's reputation was so bad, however, that even the *World*'s tradition of solid, stodgy journalism could not halt the paper's decline, and it cost Gould $40,000 a year to run.

Joseph Pulitzer contacted Jay Gould about purchasing the *World*. After some negotiations Pulitzer paid $346,000 for the languishing newspaper in 1883. With Pulitzer's acquisition of the *World*, William Henry Hurlbert resigned; his brand of dry, conservative, academic journalism was not compatible with Pulitzer's tight, colloquial, sensational style. With new editorial staff brought in by Pulitzer, the *World* thrived.

The Pulitzer Renewal

As a newspaperman, Pulitzer demanded "Accuracy, accuracy, accuracy. Also terseness . . ."[6] Perhaps to encourage these qualities, he recreated the *World Almanac* in 1886. Pulitzer desired to make the *Almanac* a "compendium of universal knowledge," and although it remained primarily a reference tool for journalists, its scope broadened with each year's publication. More than twice as long as the first issue of the *World Almanac*, with twice the advertising pages and priced at 25 cents, the renewed *World Almanac* wore an illustrated cover and, following some of the advertising, a title page that trumpeted the success of the parent newspaper. For ten years a thermometer on the left side of the title page registered the *World*'s circulation statistics, climbing from zero in 1882 to 605,980 in 1892. The index followed the title page; then came the calendars and astronomical and weather data. As in the earlier issues, election returns concluded the volumes. New features of the Pulitzer-era *Almanac* included more statistical tables on religion, education, labor, and public finance and a six- to eight-page summary of the accomplishments of the *World*, a boastful vehicle that nevertheless pointed out many of the sensational events in New York city and state politics. Also recorded were college cheers ("'Rah, 'rah!, 'rah, 'rah!, 'rah, 'rah!" for Brown, Harvard, Swathmore, Tufts, and Yale); sports data, especially horse racing and sailing; lists of state holidays and marriage laws; a list of members of the British Parliament; and some statistics for foreign countries, including a category titled "Murderous nations" on those countries with the highest homicide rates past and present.

Five years after its revival, the *World Almanac* was strong and healthy. The 1892 edition had 450 pages, about 50 of which were advertisements. The volume's introduction pointed out that it had added 40 pages of local New York City information—names and titles, maps, lists of businesses. Contents included statistical tables of all sorts, a list of living Union and Confederate generals, and sports records, including those for pool and cricket. The discussion of scientific achievements included the discovery that liquid oxygen is blue. As for the results of the recent 1890 census, the preface lamented, "Disappointment will naturally be felt that greater progress has not been made by the Government in the publication of statistics gathered by the census takers."[7] The 1893 edition added several pages of information about and a map of Chicago.

The new title adopted in 1894, the *World Almanac and Encyclopedia*, reflected broader scope. By 1922 the *Almanac* ran about 750 pages with more than 200 pages of advertisements, including a 2-page spread for an etiquette book that described a bride's abject humiliation for some unnamed blunder at her wedding.

Robert Hunt Lyman

With the 1923 edition the title became *The World Almanac and Book of Facts*. While the editor or editors of the earlier volumes toiled anonymously, this new title was in the care of Robert Hunt Lyman, a graduate of Yale and a man of considerable newspaper experience. He had edited the *Yale News* while in college, was a reporter and editor for the *New York Herald*, working for two years as the managing editor of the *Herald*'s London edition. Back in New York he went to work for the *World*, where he became night editor, then assistant managing editor, then acting managing editor, and served on Pulitzer's secretarial staff. Lyman spoke about the *Almanac* to the Special Libraries Association:

After this long experience, when editorial charge of *The Almanac* was given to me in 1922, I had one fixed idea in my mind:—To make *The Almanac* as valuable as possible for the man at the copy desk and for the man preparing an article. The special aim now was to make the accumulation of figures and facts as available as possible.[8]

So closely linked were Lyman and the *Almanac* that Lyman's entry in the *National Cyclopaedia of American Biography* includes a lengthy tribute to the *Almanac*:

Under Lyman's direction it grew steadily and late issues contained more than 1000 pages, some of the pages containing as many as 577 facts. At the time of his death it had an annual circulation of 300,000. It became virtually indispensable for reference in newspaper, magazine, and publishing offices generally and it became perhaps the most widely and frequently consulted book of general reference in existence. Executives in business and finance often use it, and probably no other book extant came into so much use for the settling of bets, particularly on sporting events. Lyman's long and varied newspaper experience, his interest in science and his passion for accuracy made him particularly competent to edit such a work.[9]

Lyman's first volume had more than 850 pages, 200 of which were advertisements, each carrying a structured subject heading at the top of the page—"Advertisements—Muscular Development" or "Advertisements—Cure for Stammering." Three text pages covered the enforcement of the new prohibition laws. Information on foreign policy and international affairs greatly expanded. The 1925 issue marked the first appearance of the regular feature "Biographies of the Presidents and their Wives." These are wonderful, very personal glimpses of national political figures. George Washington "attended horse shows and races, took part in card games, fox-hunting, cock fighting, and was a regular theatregoer." Andrew Jackson, whose marital difficulties are clearly laid out, "was shot at, in the Capitol in Washington, January 29, 1835, by Richard Lawrence, a house painter. The weapon missed fire. Jackson was a Presbyte-

rian, tall and thin." Polk "was a Methodist in his later days, wore his hair long, was democratic and affable."

Lyman struggled to give the book a more predictable structure. He added a table of contents before the index, which still appeared at the front of the volume following advertisements, and he grouped statistical tables by general subject such as agriculture, education, and population. Election results, as always, were last. Lyman explained that this complex organization resulted from the printing schedule for the *Almanac*. Because of the large number of copies to be published and the requirement for current data, the book had to be put together in pieces, or forms, from the inside out. Robert Lyman had to do this by hand. For his 300,000 copies, the first forms had to be printed by October 1 and the last ones by December 20 in order to have the book on the market by the first week of January. To make the *Almanac* as current as possible, the first forms, those at the center of the book, reflected those features (e.g., the text of the Declaration of Independence, the Monroe Doctrine, or the descriptions of foreign countries) that changed very little and so could be ready early. The most recent information, especially election data and sports results, are included in the later forms which appear at the beginning and end of the book.[10]

After Pulitzer's death in 1911, the newspapers, by now the *Morning World*, the *Evening World*, and the *Sunday World*, were held in trust by his three sons. By 1930, the Press Publishing Co., as the new enterprise was known, saw both its circulation and its profits slipping. That year the brothers entered into conference with Roy W. Howard of Scripps-Howard for the possible sale of the papers. In January 1931, a sale contract was signed, but the deal had to go through the court to determine if the sale met the conditions of Pulitzer's will. When the court allowed the sale in February, two days of frenzied activity occurred as the staff of the *World* tried to buy the papers on their own, but the sale of the *World* to

Scripps-Howard became final. If the *Almanac's* staff felt any turmoil, none showed. Lyman continued, apparently unruffled.

New Editors

After Lyman's death in 1937 the editorship of the *Almanac* passed to E. Eastman Irvine. Irvine too was an old newspaper hand, with 35 years experience before becoming the editor, including 14 years with the *New York World-Evening Telegram*. Eastman continued Lyman's general editorial direction. During his tenure, however, the *Almanac* made a major change. On the title page of the 1945 edition, this notice appeared:

> This edition of *The World Almanac*—the sixtieth—appears with all advertising eliminated to maintain the policy of making the publication of greatest interest and value to the greatest number of people. The acute paper shortage has curtailed supplies but the elimination of advertising has permitted *The Almanac* to continue its high volume of coverage of previous years of factual information in all the important fields of American and world activity.

The current *Almanac* editor, Mark S. Hoffman, sees in the decision to cut advertising revenues rather than information a clear outline of the priorities held by the publication.[11]

Irvine, who died on his way to work one day in 1949, was succeeded by Harry Hansen, another journalist of long experience. Hansen had been a war correspondent during the First World War and had come to the *World* in 1926. During Hansen's editorship the *Almanac* continued its traditionally broad coverage. In response to changing tastes and philosophies of journalism, the biographies of the presidents became less personal and more academic—and not as much fun to read. George Washington was described as "resourceful, a stern disciplinarian," and Polk's long hair and affability were not mentioned. Hansen gave up the editorship in 1965 and continued with other publishing ventures until his death in 1977.

Luman H. Long became the *Almanac's* editor in 1966 after working at the *New York Sun* and the *World-Telegram and Sun* for almost 25 years. To Long fell the inclusion of zip codes in 1966, the first colored maps in a center section in 1967, and the addition of colored pages of national flags in 1970. The 1972 edition of the *Almanac* carried Long's obituary. He had had thoracic surgery three days before his death. "Concerned with meeting the deadline of the 1972 edition of the *Almanac*, he had worked intensely up to the day before he entered the hospital."[12] George Delury assumed the editorship in 1973; the first woman editor, Hana Umlauf Lane, began in 1981; and Mark S. Hoffman has served since 1987.

An Abiding Structure

The *Almanac* of today retains Robert Lyman's sense of organization and his vision of making accessible all kinds of data. Tables are still grouped by subject, although the calendars and astronomical data which used to come first now appear 300 pages into the volume. Elections returns have moved to the front part of the *Almanac*. The lists of prominent people have grown to include artists, scholars, and entertainers of all sorts. Feature articles discuss such topics as stress, personal finance, consumer information, and space exploration. Sports items, now among the categories near the back of the book, have become less aristocratic and cover the major team sports, both professional and college (the cheers have disappeared), as well as golf, tennis, and fishing. Clearly, the *Almanac* has grown but it has not abandoned its original intentions.

Publication problems similar to those Lyman faced also remain. Fifty years after his time, in 1985, editor Hana Umlauf Lane talked about the constraints she felt. The final publication date has been moved to November, so her print run of 1.8 million copies had its first deadlines in early August and its last just two days after the elections in November. Although at that time all of the *World Almanac* data resided on a computer, only 20 percent was updated online.[13] With the most recent annual issues of the *Almanac*, the same pattern is repeated. The now more than two million copies are made up of 15 percent relatively stable information, such as the Constitution or the flags, 60 percent updatable information, such as government statistics, biographical data, and geopolitical information, and 25 percent that is completely new each year, like the "Chronology of Events" and specialty articles. Lyman's "Table of Contents" had been renamed "Quick Reference Index" in 1968 and moved to the back of the volume in 1975. The index, vastly expanded from the days when Lyman wrestled to perfect it, still must be produced last and occupies, as ever, the volume's opening pages.

The editors of the *Almanac* who face these deadlines often suffer from the vagaries of world events. Lane lamented that the 1982 Falklands crisis occurred on a final deadline day, and so the story had to wait until the 1983 edition.[14] Mark Hoffman saw the San Francisco earthquake disrupt the 1989 World Series, so that the 1990 *World Almanac* contains incomplete Series information for the first time since coverage of the event began in 1903. Hoffman jokes, "Even though I am a big baseball fan, since working for the *World Almanac*, I find myself torn between rooting for my favorite team and hoping for no rain delays and a sweep. My job has also altered my political feelings come election time, as I am now more concerned (at least for one night) with the election being clearly decided by early Wednesday morning than with who wins."[15]

Along with the timeliness of its information, the *World Almanac* has always valued the accuracy and authority of its data. Since its early issues, the *Almanac* has tried to indicate, at least in some general way, the source of its material. Lyman took pains to explain his use of international reference tools, survey questionnaires, government documents, telephone inquiries, and subject experts to collect his data. He boasted that although typographical errors may occur, he himself let only one get into final print—the date of President Garfield's death being listed as September 10 instead of September 19.[16] The accuracy of the *Almanac*'s data was such that Lyman felt that one of the book's greatest uses was in settling bets. "Daily I get telephone calls. . . . The winner never splits with me. Never! Sometimes the loser will send an indignant protest, hinting that he lost $5.00."[17] No doubt it is due to stories like Lyman's that the verso of the title page of all recent issues of the *Almanac* states "*The World Almanac* does not decide wagers."

Critical Reception

While the *World Almanac* has been around for a good while, reviews have been infrequent until fairly recently. Sol Linowitz, writing for the *Saturday Review* in 1956, humorously discussed the biographical sketches;[18] another very brief note appeared in *Saturday Review* in 1969.[19] The *Almanac* appeared with its three closest cousins, the *Information Please Almanac*, the *New York Times Encyclopedic Almanac*, and the *Reader's Digest Almanac*, in the first volume of Bohdan Wynar's *American Reference Books Annual*,[20] and again in *ARBA* in 1977, where it was noted that the *Almanac* has sold more copies that any other book except the Bible.[21] Wynar again included the *Almanac* in his selection of *Best Reference Books 1981–1985*.[22] *Catholic Library World* called the *Almanac*, "perhaps the best one-volume resource of its kind."[23] The American Library Association's *Reference and Subscription Books Review* called it "one of the best known and most often consulted of ready-reference books."[24] Most of these reviews have cited the variety of information available, the updating of its data, and the usefulness of its index.

Not everything about the *Almanac* has received praise. Wynar, with sympathy, criticized the aesthetics of the publication: "As one can expect, the physical format of *The World Almanac* represents an obvious compromise between the factors of price, size and usability. The volume is especially marred by the 7-point typeface which is slightly difficult to read. The layout is decidedly utilitarian rather than aesthetic."[25] The complaint was echoed by the American Library Association's Reference and Subscription Books Review Board: "Fine print, crowded lines, harsh beige paper do not make *World Almanac* pleasing to sight and touch; but then it is produced as an inexpensive and utilitarian work, not as an aesthetic object."[26]

Julia Miller and Jane Bryan studied in detail four similar almanacs: the *World*; the *Hammond Almanac of a Million Facts, Records, Forecasts* (originally the *New York Times Encyclopedic Almanac*, then the *Official Associated Press Almanac*, then the *CBS News Almanac*), which began in 1970; *Information Please Almanac*, begun in 1947; and the *Reader's Digest Almanac*, started in 1966.[27] The authors asked each almanac 20 questions, like "How many women own major league baseball teams?" "What magazines have the highest circulation?" and "How many Buddhists are there in America?" They also analyzed each volume's coverage of business and economics, and sports, entertainment, and the arts. The *World Almanac* could answer or partly answer 13 of the reference questions, got praise for its entries on business and consumer directories and for its wide coverage of entertainment and sports. *Information Please* fared much the same. *Hammond* responded to 18 of the reference questions but did not rank quite as high on its business and directory information. *Reader's Digest*, the researchers decided, envisioned a different purpose for its much more text-oriented almanac.

Currently, of these 4 titles, only the *World Almanac* and *Information Please* still publish. *Hammond* ceased publication in 1982 and *Reader's Digest* in 1987. In fact, many of the more recent reviews of the *World Almanac* also mention *Information Please*, not as an alternative but as a companion reference tool.

In its long history, the *World Almanac* has had wide influence. Mark Hoffman tells stories he has heard around the *Almanac* offices—that World War II GIs carried the *Almanac* in their footlockers along with pin-ups of Betty Grable; that the oath of office taken by Lyndon Johnson after John Kennedy's assassination was read from the *World Almanac*; that a copy of the *Almanac* was somehow smuggled to the hostages in Tehran, Iran, in 1979—their only news link to the outside world.[28]

The *Almanac* promises to continue its distinguished traditions. The new political organization of Europe, scientific discoveries of space exploration, and new prize winners of all sorts will take their place alongside the dates for Easter for the past and future centuries and the carefully documented phases of the moon. After almost a century and a half, the *World Almanac and Book of Facts* remains a valuable and fascinating reference tool for everyone.

PUBLICATION HISTORY

World Almanac. New York: Press Publishing Co., 1868–1893. Annual. Publication suspended 1876, reinstituted 1886.

World Almanac and Encyclopedia. New York: Press Publishing Co., 1894–1922. Annual.

World Almanac and Book of Facts. Press Publishing Co., 1923; the New York World, 1924–1931; the New York World-Telegram, 1932–1950; the New York World-Telegram and Sun, 1951–1966; Newspaper Enterprise Association 1967–1986; Pharos Books, 1987– . Annual.

BIBLIOGRAPHY

In spite of its age and wide availability, the *World Almanac* has received very little attention in print. The lengthiest treatment comes from Robert Hunt Lyman, the

Almanac's editor for 15 years during the second quarter of this century, who described in detail how information was gathered and the book was produced. No one else has done so in the 65 years since. The *Saturday Review* twice paid it brief tribute as a fact-filled and entertaining volume. The only analytical study ever published was done by Miller and Bryan more than ten years ago. Indeed, more has been written about the distinguished editors of the *Almanac* than about the *Almanac* itself. American almanacs in general offer great opportunity for researchers. Research centers on almanac makers, especially Benjamin Franklin. In contrast to the colonial period, nineteenth-century almanacs, mass produced and usually edited anonymously, have not been studied thoroughly.

"Answers to a Manufacturing Task That Aren't in the World Almanac." *Publishers Weekly* 227 (March 1, 1985): 66–68.

Barret, James Wyman. *Joseph Pulitzer and His World.* New York: Vanguard Press, 1941.

Drake, Milton. *Almanacs of the United States.* New York: Scarecrow Press, 1962.

Linowitz, Sol M. "The Fact Arsenal." *Saturday Review* 39 (March 24, 1956): 42.

Lyman, Robert Hunt. "Saving Time in Research." *Special Libraries* 17 (1926): 352–59.

Miller, Julia E., and Jane G. Bryan. "Wealth of Information: A Review of Four 1979 Almanacs." *Reference Services Review* 17 (1979): 67–78.

Sagendorph, Robb. *America and Her Almanacs.* Dublin, NH: Yankee; Boston: Little, Brown and Co., 1970.

Seitz, Don C. *Joseph Pulitzer, His Life and Letters.* New York: Simon and Schuster, 1924.

Stowell, Marion Barber. *Early American Almanacs: The Colonial Weekday Bible.* New York: Burt Franklin, 1977.

———. "Revolutionary Almanac–Makers." *Bibliographical Society of America Papers* 73 (1979):41–61.

Swanberg, W.A. *Pulitzer.* New York: Charles Scribner's Sons, 1967.

NOTES

[1] Milton Drake, *Almanacs of the United States,* vol. 1 (New York: Scarecrow Press, 1962), p. viii.

[2] Marion Barber Stowell, *Early American Almanacs* (New York: Burt Franklin, 1977), 7.

[3] Ibid., 65.

[4] Ibid., x.

[5] Clarence S. Brigham, "Report of the Librarian," *Proceedings of the American Antiquarian Society,* new ser., 35 (1925): 217.

[6] Don C. Seitz, *Joseph Pulitzer, His Life and Letters* (New York: Simon and Schuster, 1924), 126–27.

[7] *World Almanac,* 1892, 7.

[8] Robert Hunt Lyman, *Special Libraries* 17 (1926): 352–53.

[9] *National Cyclopaedia of American Biography,* see "Lyman, Robert Hunt."

[10] Lyman, "Saving Time in Research," 353.

[11] Mark S. Hoffman, speech given to Rockland County, New York, public librarians, 18 April 1990.

[12] *World Almanac and Book of Facts,* 1972, 3.

[13] "Answers to a Manufacturing Task That Aren't in the World Almanac," *Publishers Weekly* 227 (1 March 1985): 68.

[14] Ibid., 66.

[15] Hoffman, speech, 18 April 1990.

[16] Lyman, 358.

[17] Ibid.

[18] Sol M. Linowitz, "The Fact Arsenal," *Saturday Review* 39 (24 March 1956): 42.

[19] David W. Glixon, "Where to Look It Up," *Saturday Review* 52 (17 May 1969): 31.

[20] *American Reference Books Annual* 1 (1970): 31.

[21] Review of *World Almanac and Book of Facts; American Reference Books Annual* 8 (1977): 62.

[22] Bohdan S. Wynar, ed., *Best Reference Books 1981–1985* (Littleton, CO: Libraries Unlimited, 1986), 5.

[23] Review of *World Almanac and Book of Facts, Catholic Library World* 19 (1978): 358.

[24] Review of *World Almanac and Book of Facts, Reference and Subscription Books Reviews* (1 December 1981): 518.

[25] Review of *World Almanac and Book of Facts, American Reference Books Annual* 1 (1970): 31.

[26] Review of *World Almanac and Book of Facts, Reference and Subscription Books Reviews* (1 December 1981): 518.

[27] Julia E. Miller and Jane G. Bryan, "Wealth of Information: A Review of Four 1979 Almanacs," *Reference Services Review* 17 (1979): 67–78.

[28] Hoffman, speech, 18 April 1990.

"The Best of Its Type":
World Book Encyclopedia

Holly D. Rogerson and E. Paige Weston

DEVELOPMENT AND HISTORY

Early in this century, *World Book* was recognized as the "best of its type."[1] It was also the first of its type: a comprehensive family encyclopedia for North Americans. Over its long history, *World Book* has not strayed from its original intent: to make information accessible to its primary audience of families with children while meeting the needs of users of all ages. Indeed, *World Book*'s early and increasingly sophisticated efforts to keep in touch with its audience are the very story of its success.

On June 24, 1915, James H. Hanson, president of the Hanson-Bellows Company, wrote to Michael Vincent O'Shea, a nationally known educator and expert on child development. Hoping to interest O'Shea in revising *The New Practical Reference Library*, a moderately successful six-volume general encyclopedia first published in 1907, Hanson said, "the needs of the boy and girl in the grades are to be our first consideration. In style we are determined to write down to the mind of the child in all those articles in which children are mainly interested."[2] O'Shea took the bait, and Hanson signed him on as editor-in-chief. Within weeks, however, it was clear O'Shea was shaping not a revision, but a wholly new work—a family encyclopedia eventually named *World Book: Organized Knowledge in Story and Picture.*[3]

The process by which the title of the new work was chosen is perhaps symbolic of the link *World Book* would always have with the education systems in the United States and Canada. The publisher solicited suggestions from over 25,000 leading educators and offered cash prizes not only for a winning title, but also for useful editorial comments. What started out as a publicity device became an early finger on the pulse of the educators. Ninety-six of the nearly 5,000 naming-contest submissions included the word "world" and so *World Book* was born.

From its beginnings, making information accessible to a broad audience has been *World Book*'s goal. Over the years its editors have refined their techniques for assuring attainment of that goal. Today *World Book* is its own best example of a family encyclopedia as defined in its article "Encyclopedia": "Family encyclopedias aim to meet the reference and study needs of students in elementary school, junior high school, high school, and beyond. They are also designed as everyday reference tools for the entire family, for teachers, for librarians, and for other professional and business people."[4] In the 75 years since Hanson first wrote to O'Shea, *World Book* has doubled its size, developed its "style," and broadened its scope; but it has never needed to redefine its audience. In 1947, Dorothy Canfield Fisher wrote,

Don't forget that all of us, in many facets and aspects of our personalities, are "young" in the sense of being uninformed and inexperienced. For instance, I am quite my own age (close to seventy) as to French literature, because that has been a special interest of mine nearly all my life. But in the matter of information about, say, ocean currents, or the ethnology of the people of Nicaragua, I cannot claim a mental age of more than twelve. That is the age for which these cheerful, colorful volumes of bright red and blue were produced. For me too, this outward aspect is encouraging. It suggests to me (as to the eighth-grader) that what I find inside will not, by its cold scholarly rigidity, swamp and drown my not very deep or keen (but all the same living) interest in a subject, aroused perhaps by a casual reference in something I have been reading.[5]

The view from within the *World Book* organization echoes this. Executive Editor A. Richard Harmet attributes *World Book*'s success to its remarkable continuity of purpose, sustained in large measure by the loyalty and longevity of its editorial personnel; by the belief that "World Bookers," from salesperson to CEO, have in the *World Book* product; and by its appropriateness for American homes.[6]

Michael Vincent O'Shea

O'Shea set *World Book* on its path by making a decisive break in content between it and its forebears. However, he recognized those elements in the Hanson-Bellows operation that would further his purpose for his new creation. Notable among these was the Consultation Department of the *New Practical Reference Library*. This department, established by Arno Roach, a forceful Missouri book jobber who handled the *New Practical Reference Library*, the *American Educator*, and *World Book*, answered mail queries from subscribers so that they were not limited to the information contained in the encyclopedia they had purchased. When an inquiry came into the Consultation Department, "Roach would ask himself whether the information requested should actually be included in the encyclopedia itself, and, if so, it was prepared for inclusion in the ensuing edition. This way, he and his staff kept their fingers on the public pulse. "[7] A popular selling point, the consulta-

tion service was an early model for the now finely honed curricular responsiveness of *World Book*.

O'Shea also took note of the successful communication-through-sales strategies used with the *American Educator* and the *New Practical Reference Library*. He felt that the sales force was an important conduit for feedback about readers. O'Shea, "a salesman's editor," believed that the only people qualified to make a judgment and give advice on what should be included in *World Book* "were those who were in daily communication with the public."[8] It is this level of attention to its audience's needs and interests that even today sets *World Book* apart from others of its kind.

Although the current edition of *World Book* looks, naturally enough, vastly different from the first edition, founding editor O'Shea would recognize its commitment to the standards he set. Some of the central features present in the first edition can be seen in today's *World Book*: articles on topics of high interest, written in simple language and with illustrations of key concepts. As an early indication of *World Book*'s close ties with the education system, the first edition of *World Book* contained a variety of special articles on education topics, such as "Modern Education" and "Measurement of Intelligence." Many other articles, on topics such as "Homemaking" and "Cooperation Between Home and School," were aimed at helping families.

Four Major Revisions

Since its inception, *World Book* has undergone four major revisions, each time introducing features that have made it a more responsive reference tool for its family audience. Across intervening editions, however, only *World Book*'s physical growth, from 8 to 22 volumes, can be easily charted. Most of the changes—to the selection of topics, the number and type of illustrations, the vocabulary, the finding aids, and the structure of the articles and of the work overall—were introduced gradually, as editors and staff analysts learned new and better ways to tailor their product to the inclinations, abilities, and needs of American families.

The first major revision to *World Book* resulted in the 13-volume 1929/30 edition. For the first time, the final volume of the set was devoted to a "Reading and Study Guide." This 500-page separate volume, designed primarily for teachers, contained approximately 40 outlines that attempted to integrate the various articles dealing with a given subject area in the encyclopedia. Also included were projects illustrating the application of book knowledge to practical life; reviews of major school subjects with page references to the other volumes of the encyclopedia; and reading lists. Also for the first time—possibly in the history of reference work publishing—the print size, line length, and overall page design of the set were systematically tested through classroom experiments conducted by the School of Education at the University of Chicago, to ensure that *World Book* was easy to read. The next year *World Book* proudly introduced the modified unit-letter arrangement, in which each letter of the alphabet is covered by one volume (with two volumes devoted to a few of the more frequently used letters). *World Book* continues to use a modified unit-letter arrangement today. While the unit-letter arrangement results in volumes of uneven length rather than the uniform volume length favored by some other encyclopedia publishers, editor Harmet believes that this arrangement helps readers in their search for information.[9] In 1933 the set expanded to 19 volumes, and included a bibliography of books for further reading. The much-lauded bibliography, placed in the final volume, was in the form of a classified book list and indicated the level of each book as adult or juvenile.

In 1936 *World Book* secured its ties with the American educational system by establishing its first Editorial Advisory Board, with six distinguished educators as members. Dr. George H. Reavis, assistant superintendent in the Cincinnati school system, served as chairman. Reavis strongly urged that *World Book*

articles, at that time written at the seventh grade level or higher, be written at the level of the grade for which the topic was appropriate (so that, for instance, the article "Dog" would be written in a much simpler style than the article "Donizetti"). Editors agreed, and the Advisory Board began a series of research projects with the goal of grade-appropriate articles in mind. Aside from Reavis, two men played central roles in the original research process. Dr. Hollis L. Caswell, who would later become president of Columbia University's Teachers College, surveyed what was taught at each grade level across the country. William Scott Gray, a reading specialist at the University of Chicago, studied students' reading levels in each grade and established the editorial guidelines to be used in *World Book* to ensure readability. Other researchers examined various subject areas, as well as how students of different ages used encyclopedias.[10] Funds made available by the Field family after the Marshall Field purchase of *World Book* in 1945 strengthened the research activities behind *World Book*. Thus, the *World Book* ethos of writing for "the girl and boy in the grades" was made more practicable with the development of such systematic analysis of the schools and the students.

The results of the studies were incorporated into *World Book's* second major revision, the 1947 "post-war" edition, still nineteen volumes long but enormously different in style and content. For the first time, each article had been written or rewritten at the level of the school grade in which its topic was taught, as specified by Caswell's study. While the celebrated contributors to the edition included such diverse individuals as J. Edgar Hoover writing on the Federal Bureau of Investigation, Emily Post on etiquette, and Monsignor Fulton J. Sheen on a variety of religion-related topics, a painstaking 15-step editorial process retained each author's style but insured the suitability of reading level.[11]

In the 1948 edition, graded bibliographies attached to major articles replaced the longer bibliography at the end of the set. Then, in

1960, came the third major revision, and an expansion to 20 volumes. "Although the only real innovation was the Trans-Vision®, a visual aid showing various layers or levels of a subject [such as the anatomy of a frog] by means of a series of acetate overlays in color, everything in the new set had been freshly approached and executed."[12] By this time, as S. Padraig Walsh has noted, "the work had almost doubled in size (11,600 pages) from the original edition, and the number of illustrations had more than doubled to more than 21,000, with a very substantial increase in the use of color."[13]

In 1971 the set expanded again to 22 volumes, with the final volume consisting of the Research Guide and an Index with 150,000 entries. The Research Guide portion of the volume contained an instructional section entitled "How to Do Research" and more than 200 subject-specific Reading and Study Guides designed to help students and teachers plan independent study units. During the 1970s and 1980s *World Book* introduced a computer-compiled index to supplement its abundant internal cross-references; metric equivalents for all measurements; and many more color illustrations. Also during these years, *World Book* editors worked both to eliminate sexist and racist stereotyping from text and illustrations and to meet, with expanded coverage, the growing public and curricular interest in the history of women, blacks, and Native Americans. But there was not another major overhaul to the set until the 1988 edition for which nearly 1,000 entries were completely revised, and since which approximately one-third of the space in 21 volumes has been devoted to illustrations, in color wherever appropriate.

Critical and Popular Reception

World Book's popularity has never wavered. It is difficult, in fact, to distinguish its critical reception from its popular reception. The many hundreds of book reviews of *World Book* that have been published over the years are more celebratory than critical. Reviewers have tended only hesitatingly to mention minor flaws. The following, from a 1943 review by Lucile Fargo, is typical:

> 'Continuous revision' has an intriguing sound, but is such a complicated process that the encyclopedia maker who does not every once in a while stub his toe is among the thrice blessed. For what he cuts out or inserts or fully rewrites in one spot starts embarrassing repercussions throughout the set. *The World Book*, twenty-fifth anniversary edition, probably does as well in continuous revision as is humanly possible. But anyone who takes the trouble to run down inconsistencies in the resulting patchwork will find them.[14]

The favorable critical reviews were routinely mentioned in sales talks, of course. Long after the first edition, for instance, salesmen quoted a one-liner about it from the October 1918 issue of *Booklist*: "the best of its type." Stringent editing, thoughtful illustrating, and rigorous testing made *World Book* "best of its type"; salesmanship, however, made it best selling. For most of its life, *World Book* has been sold door-to-door to parents. According to William Murray, *World Book* ranked as the bestselling encyclopedia of its kind as early as 1935,[15] and this title has never since been challenged. Interviewed for Murray's 1966 book, *World Book* salesman Bill Hayes said:

> It's been a tremendous growth, though it was a gradual thing. We didn't have an increase every year, just a general trend upward. We didn't have public relations and advertising programs to back us up either. I doubt if there was any one year under Quarrie when the Company spent as much as $25,000 for advertising. It was all accomplished largely by the sweat of the brow of the people who were doing it."[16]

To read the secondary literature is to realize that "World Book" refers to a selling organization, as well as a high caliber publication. When Scott & Fetzer acquired *World Book* from Field Enterprises in 1978, they were buying a sales force as much as a product. Editor A. Richard Harmet now says: "Encyclopedias need to be sold. They're a little like insurance in that way. A person doesn't wake up in the morning and say, 'I feel like buying an encyclopedia today.' The salesperson needs to demonstrate the need, use, and value of an encyclopedia. But since we have a nonprofessional sales force, you have to know they believe in the product."[17]

Maintaining High Standards

How does *World Book* remain the high-quality encyclopedia in which its sellers believe so strongly? Expert contributors, of text and illustration, have never been enough. From the World Book, Inc., internal document "Subject: Editorial Objectives," comes the topic sentence, "*World Book*'s aim is to present information from the vast reservoir of knowledge in the most accessible and usable form." In support of this objective, *World Book*'s researchers and editors put tremendous effort into six complementary strategies:

1. analyzing current school curricula, to ensure that *World Book* covers topics of interest;
2. writing every article "to grade level," so that each article is accessible to readers at the grade level at which the topic is most likely to interest;
3. using all vocabulary advisedly, and defining "difficult" words in context wherever possible;
4. maintaining stringent editorial standards for clarity and organization, while striving to maintain the individual character of contributors' own prose;
5. designing an easy-to-read index volume and an admirable system of cross-references, from one article to others, and from unused headings to valid entries; and
6. systematically testing *World Book* in real classrooms, to learn whether students can, in fact, use it successfully.

The first strategy, school curricula analysis, began with the studies by Caswell in 1936 and to this day are an ongoing process at *World Book*. Caswell himself chaired the Editorial Advisory Board for 19 years and remained on the Board for 30 years. In the 1950s Caswell and Dr. William H. Nault concluded a benchmark study of the curricula in grades kindergarten through 12 in hundreds of U.S. and Canadian schools. This study, the *Caswell-Nault Analysis of Courses of Study*, was followed by a number of similar studies commissioned by *World Book*. Today, the 61-volume *Nault-Caswell-Brain Analysis of Courses of Study* and its 30-volume supplement serve as essential research tools to help *World Book* editors design articles and place them at the appropriate grade level. The studies, collectively referred to as the *Curriculum Analysis* at World Book, show which topics are taught in which grades, and the actual information covered each time the topic is discussed in a cross-section of North American schools. The *Curriculum Analysis* has also served as an important tool for the *World Book* salespeople, enabling them to convey to the customers how closely *World Book* is geared to the school curriculum.

A second study accomplished by a survey of curriculum guides and other instructional materials is the *Typical Course of Study*, which lists by grade and academic discipline topics usually covered in schools. While the *Typical Course of Study* might seem to serve much the same purpose as the *Nault-Caswell-Brain Analysis of Courses of Study*, the two studies' purposes and formats are complementary rather than identical. A careful comparison of subjects in *World Book* reveals how well the encyclopedia covers the topics determined in the *Typical Course of Study*. On the other hand, the *Curriculum Analysis* lets the editors know what questions students are likely to have at each level on a given topic.[18]

Writing each article "to grade level" and using all vocabulary advisedly, including defining difficult words in context, are strategies involving painstaking editorial control. Since 1976, editors have referred to Edward Dale and Joseph O'Rourke's *Living Word Vocabulary* for information on how well known a particular word is—even a particular sense of a particular word. According to Dale and O'Rourke, ". . . a word with a [recognition] score of 50% or less is generally a *hard word* and should be reconsidered before using in written material."[19] Harmet reports that *World Book* uses a score of 67 percent to indicate "an understandable word."[20] Since 1981, when the most recent edition of *The Living Word* was published, Harmet says, "we have updated the database with some 5,000 new and retested words. It remains a key editorial source."[21] However, *World Book*'s editorial policy is not one of using a "controlled vocabulary." Difficult words are used, but all new or difficult vocabulary used in *World Book* articles is defined in context if possible. The World Book, Inc., internal document "Easy Reading is Hard Writing" instructs new editors on word definition.

> We always put a new word (or old word used in a new sense, which makes it also a new word) in italics. Sometimes merely putting a word in italics is enough.
>
> > After roll call, the men wash and shave, and then go to the *mess hall* for breakfast.
>
> Even an unskilled reader would realize that the mess hall is a room in which meals are served. And putting *mess* in italics identifies an uncommon use of the word.[22]

Readability, however, depends on a variety of factors in addition to vocabulary level. Therefore, the length and structures of sentences and paragraphs are carefully monitored by *World Book* editors. The readability of longer, more complex articles is also purposely pyramidal in structure, with the initial paragraphs written much more simply than later ones describing more complex aspects of the topic if it is of interest to various age groups. The obvious effect of such pyramidal structure is that of potential access by a broader audience.

Although *World Book* editors have never made a secret of their role in achieving the remarkable clarity of *World Book* prose, many reviewers over the years have commented on this clarity, as if it were one of life's mysteries. *World Book* has, in fact, always been "heavily edited," says Richard Harmet. "It has never been a collection of scholarly essays like the [Britannica] *Macropaedia*."[23] Articles for the first edition of *World Book* went through seven careful readings before being committed to type.[24] The "Basic steps in the preparation of a *World Book* article," which are listed in the "Encyclopedia" article in the current edition of *World Book*, make clear the editing process is even more involved today. Reflecting on her work for the 1947 edition, Martha Simmonds, then supervising editor for *World Book* style, wrote:

> Of course, styling means rules. They differ. We had to choose what we considered the best authorities in grammar, sentence structure, punctuation, spelling, and pronunciation, because we could not take some rules here and others there. But we made exceptions in special cases, and always on good authority. For instance, our spelling authority prefers *amoeba*, but we decided to use *ameba*, in line with the most up-to-date science textbooks. For the same reason, we wrote *sulfur* instead of *sulphur*, except in the case of a name, such as Sulphur Springs.[25]

But under Simmonds, as today, *World Book* copy editors retained an author's own style, as far as possible. Simmonds quotes with pleasure the following, from the 1947 edition's article "Camel:"

> There is nothing romantic about the camel's personal appearance. It is a shaggy, awkward, stiff-legged, goose-necked, humpbacked beast. It has a split upper lip, popeyes, loosely hung jaws, and a stupid, sad expression on its too-small face. Its temper is sad and sullen, interrupted by fits of anger and rage. The camel's personal habits are so bad that it has few friends, even among other camels.

World Book's editorial policy on access, including indexing and cross-referencing, has resulted in a system allowing easy location of information. Describing a late 1980s' edition of *World Book*, Kenneth Kister noted that its index included an entry for every 70 words of text. "Only the *Academic American Encyclopedia* (1:45), *Collier's Encyclopedia* (1:50), and *Merit Students Encyclopedia* (1:65) have better ratios."[26] In addition to this index are abundant cross-references. Speaking in 1976, Harmet told his audience that *World Book* editors "were aware that Americans generally were not index users, and so we developed a carefully designed system of short articles, cross-references, and other features to guide readers in their search for information."[27] Significantly, even the Preface of the current edition includes a cross-reference to another *World Book* entry.

When the five strategies described so far are not enough to ensure that *World Book* is easy to use, the sixth strategy, testing *World Book* in more than 400 real classrooms across the U.S. and Canada, finds where they have failed. Housed in large metal filing cabinets in the *World Book* editorial offices in Chicago is perhaps the world's most charming database: a database of cards filled out by students. It is a database of the questions *World Book*'s real users pose of it, of the "search strategies" they used, and of the success they met with. Harmet chuckles over questions: How does salt get in the ocean? Do fish close their eyes when they sleep? Editors are on the alert for "tellable facts," he says, to bring out in the articles. "The information may be there, but if a fourth grader's the one who would want to know, and it's not in a place a fourth grader can find it, or in a form a fourth grader can understand, that's not good enough."[28]

However, *World Book* editors see the hands-on testing of materials by their intended audience as much more than a mop-up operation, designed to catch problems that made their way by the first five strategies. Rather, the *Classroom Research Project*, as it is called, constitutes another aspect of audience and curricular responsiveness. The 100,000-plus cards returned to the *World Book* Research Department each year from students in the test classrooms are processed by computers to provide editors with summaries of data on article usage in each grade and subject. Thus, the results of testing affect not only the material tested, but also subsequent editorial decisions on later articles.[29]

Graphics

World Book works hard to match its clear writing with graphics that are equally helpful. The visual appeal of a set of books like *World Book* is significant, as both book reviewers and *World Book* researchers will confirm. As part of the major revision effort for the 1929/30 edition, then owner William F. Quarrie commissioned experiments, at the University of Chicago's School of Education, on the relative readability of various page designs, type styles, and type sizes. At the time, 9-point Baskerville on pages 6.5" x 9.75" was determined to be optimum. Before the 1988 conversion to a new sans-serif font, dubbed "World Book Modern," *World Book* likewise undertook a careful study of modern readers' tastes. *World Book* publishers have also been cautious in introducing new bindings. Overcoming a long reluctance to use the color green, the now-familiar white and green "Aristocrat" binding was made available in 1955, after a specially bound white and green set was presented to, and well-received by, Pope Pius XII.

The other aspect of *World Book*'s visual appeal, of course, is its abundant illustrations. Illustrations have never been superfluous to *World Book*, clear though its prose has been. Reviewing the 25th anniversary edition, Lucile Fargo wrote, "What was of primary importance in 1917 (as now) was that pictures should illustrate the text and not simply decorate it. The skill with which illustrations are now used to illuminate and clarify the text is remarkable. Almost as in a movie, processes are broken down into series of operations pictorially displayed. And of the use of charts and pictographs there is no end."[30]

Important and impressive as they were, the illustrations were accomplished on a shoestring budget. Historically the most thinly staffed department in the company, the Art

Department was allowed to grow briefly while work on the 1947 edition was under way, but then was pruned back again. Not until 1960 and the next major revision, with new Field Enterprises money and new rotary presses that could reproduce illustrations more inexpensively, did the Art Department begin to expand once more. As further technological advances have allowed, illustrations have been added, enlarged, colored, and more fully integrated with the texts they supplement. The relative importance of illustrations, and the relative contribution of illustrators, has also been allowed to grow. Today, article illustrations are reviewed, edited, and verified by experts, as carefully as article texts. The use of color in the 1988 edition, product of a major revision, was greeted with enthusiasm by reviewers.

> The infusion of color in the state and province articles is but a small part of a welcome overhaul of the look of *World Book....* Color photos and drawings appeared through previous *World Book* editions, but not in the numbers used in the 1988 edition. The total number of illustrations, approximately 29,000, remains about the same. However, now 24,000 of them—a remarkable one-year increase of 10,000—are in color.[31]

In the 1990 edition, according to the "Reviewing Aid," illustrations account for approximately one third of the space used. "The use of color extends to all subjects, except for small biographical portraits, historical black-and-white photographs and drawings, and 'one of a kind' illustrations."[32]

Accuracy

Clear prose and visual appeal would mean little without accuracy and *World Book*'s researchers meticulously verify all data included. For this purpose, *World Book*'s own reference library contains 22,000 volumes and 450 periodical titles. Many other libraries in Chicago and throughout the country are used in the research effort, as well as thousands of phone and letter inquiries. The internal document "Research behind *World Book*" (undated, but presumably still current) says, "*World Book*'s researchers, under the direction of Mary Norton, use an average of 20 sources for each article they authenticate."[33] Another internal document, "Subject: Editorial Objectives," urges staff members to maintain accuracy by thinking critically and checking all information against primary sources, when possible. If only secondary sources are available, extensive research in multiple secondary sources is advised.[34]

Though book reviews and sales records suggest *World Book* has sailed from strength to strength, it has, over the years, weathered some storms. For instance, although it is now known for the expert contributors who sign their articles, and for the staff researchers who verify every fact, *World Book* was once open to a charge of plagiarism, and narrowly averted a damaging lawsuit. On November 16, 1930, the *New York Times* published a piece under the headline: "Plagiarism Charged in Encyclopaedia Suit: Britannica Concern Asks Writ and $250,000 Damages from Chicago Publisher."[35] The article elaborated, "The plaintiff . . . charges that the defendant company not only openly plagiarized material contained in the plaintiff's publication but rewrote other material to make it seem original." When it became clear to W.F. Quarrie & Co. that the charge was in earnest, the publishers mobilized a dozen researchers to prove that the *Britannica* and *World Book* articles in question drew their facts, and their phrasing, from a common source. These researchers managed to establish only that about half of the 77 articles in question drew from a common source. Further investigation by *World Book*'s Robert Preble, however, showed that "certain changes had been made in the quotations taken from *Britannica* itself to conform more closely to the claims made in the suit."[36] At this point, though it had become clear that some of the *World Book* articles in question did, in fact, contain instances of "heavy cribbing,"[37] the *Britannica* publisher agreed to drop the suit. After this time, *World Book* contributors were required to fill out three cards with each submission: one certifying they had not committed plagiarism, a second listing their primary sources, and a third giving pertinent biographical data about themselves. This practice continues today.

Foreign Sales and Marketing

World Book has also found marketing abroad to be a challenge. *World Book* is ineluctably an American product. Versions of the encyclopedia have sold internationally (primarily in Great Britain), but overseas sales have always been eclipsed by U.S. and Canadian sales. In 1936 the New Era Publishing Company, of London, did bring out a 10-volume *World Book: British Empire Edition*. Harold Shelton was general editor of this venture; Lord Gorell was advisory editor, "a purely nominal position," according to Walsh. Then, in 1961, Field Enterprises renewed the effort. From 1966 to 1968 they published a 12-volume International Edition, edited by Gilbert C.E. Smith. While not a disaster, the International Edition lacked the strengths of *World Book* at home, and sold accordingly. The International Edition was not so off-puttingly tied to American school curricula, but then neither was it tied to British or Australian curricula. Since 1968 the domestic edition has been sold abroad. *World Book* as sold abroad, however, whether in the International Edition or in the domestic edition, sacrifices some of its famous ease-of-use, since it has been sold abroad in two alphabetic sequences, with the first sequence consisting of the domestic *World Book* and the second sequence consisting of two additional volumes treating topics from the point of view of the readers in that area of the world.

World Book has kept its text up to date with world news and with American attitudes through research and technology. The "Reviewing Aid" for the 1990 edition emphasizes that research "provides the basis for the an-

nual revision of *World Book* and for the long-range planning that makes *World Book* a continuously evolving resource. In this respect, the current edition is one point on a continuum of effort. It reflects the experience gained from the past and points the way for the future as new data and experience provide further guidance."[38] In more concrete terms, however, it is the printing presses, text management software, and telecommunications lines in which *World Book*'s publishers have invested that allow the kind of currency *World Book*'s readers now expect. "From 1947 on," Murray wrote, "the type for every page was kept standing in racks instead of being destroyed, as had previously been done once the printing plates had been made. This enabled the editors to make any changes they desired in a particular page."[39] And as early as 1975, Field Enterprises Educational Corporation announced that *World Book Encyclopedia* would soon begin the move to an electronic editorial/composition system specifically designed for encyclopedia operations.[40] According to Kister, this system was then the most advanced in the encyclopedia industry.[41] Today the text and illustrations of *World Book* articles can be changed, almost at the last minute. The "Reviewing Aid" is worth quoting at length:

> A newly copyrighted and revised edition of *World Book* is available to subscribers late in the calendar year prior to the year of the copyright. For example, shipment of the updated sets for the 1990 edition began on December 20, 1989. An elaborate typesetting and printing schedule was necessary to assure that new sets were available on that date. Because of the large pressrun, it was necessary to begin the printing in early September to assure the availability of books late in December. The binding of completed volumes began in mid-November.
>
> In developing a production schedule, the editors attempted to identify those pages that seemed most likely to require revision and placed them later in the printing schedule. For example, the World Series table in the **Baseball** article was handled in this way. Changes in pages at the end of the printing schedule

could conceivably be made as late as the third week of November.

The editors also reacted to late-breaking events affecting the content of *World Book* that occurred after the deadline for those pages . . . In November, the presses were stopped to revise the **Germany** article to include mention of the opening of the Berlin Wall.[42]

Family purchasers of *World Book*, of course, are unlikely to take advantage of the "continuum of effort" that produces a new edition every year. They are unlikely, that is, to purchase many new editions. Many families and many more libraries, however, decide they can afford an annual supplement to their aging encyclopedia. Supplements have been available to *World Book* purchasers since 1921. From 1922 until 1940 W.F. Quarrie & Co. (later the Quarrie Corp.), published a *Loose-Leaf Annual*. In 1941 this was abandoned for the softcover *World Book Encyclopedia Annual Supplement*. In 1962, in turn, this evolved into the hardbound *World Book Year Book*. Interestingly, *World Book* publishers have long recognized that annual supplements are not used as a reference work the way their base sets are. Murray writes that Roy Fisher, who oversaw the first *World Book Year Book*, knew that the supplement "was almost always opened and read as a magazine. Therefore, he designed the book to be leafed through and to catch the casual browser's attention, exactly as a good magazine does. Visually and textually, the approach was based on good reportorial techniques. 'We knew that once the book went up on the shelf, its active life was generally over,' [Fisher] observed."[43]

Editor Harmet does not fear for the active life of *World Book Encyclopedia*. He is confi-dent there will continue to be a role for printed general reference works. The advent of television did not change *World Book*'s readership, he claims, because people still need to be able to learn the "who, what, where, when, and why" of topics of their own choosing, rather than of topics that come to them on the evening news. In the 1990 edition of *World Book*, Harmet's "Encyclopedia" article contains a section on "How to judge an encyclopedia" which does not take into account any format other than paper. In the event that CD-ROM readers or broadband network connections become commonplace in American homes, however, *World Book* intends to be ready. The new *Information Finder*, "A CD-ROM Reference Based on the *World Book Encyclopedia*," hit the market in December 1989. The CD contains the text of 17,800 articles. It likewise includes tables, cross-references, reading lists, and an index. According to the *Reference Books Bulletin* Editorial Board review, "*Information Finder* is especially impressive in the way it facilely incorporates 139,000 definitions from the *World Book Dictionary*, allowing the user to make quick lookups at any point in a search session."[44] *Information Finder* does not include any of the superb, and hitherto essential, *World Book* illustrations, although some illustrations may be included in an update.

While formats may change, the editorial strategies that have ensured the accessibility of *World Book*'s information to generations of families will assuredly not waver. Editor Harmet intends for *World Book* to remain the "best of its type."

PUBLICATION HISTORY

From the beginning, *World Book* has been published under a system of "continuous revision." The following are editions which resulted from extraordinary revision efforts.

World Book: Organized Knowledge in Story and Picture. Michael Vincent O'Shea, editor in chief. Chicago: Hanson-Roach-Fowler Co., 1917. 8 vols.

World Book Encyclopedia: Modern, Pictorial, Comprehensive. Michael Vincent O'Shea, editor in chief. Chicago: W.F. Quarrie & Co., 1929–1930. 13 vols.

The World Book Encyclopedia. J. Morris Jones, managing editor. Chicago: Quarrie Corporation, 1947. 19 vols.

The World Book Encyclopedia. J. Morris Jones, editor in chief. Chicago: Field Enterprises Educational Corporation, 1960. 20 vols.

The World Book Encyclopedia. Robert O. Zeleny, editor in chief. Chicago: World Book, Inc., 1988. 22 vols.

It should be noted that *World Book* has also been published in several special editions:

The World Book Encyclopedia. (Braille ed.) Louisville, KY: American Printing House for the Blind, 1961.

The World Book Encyclopedia. (Large print ed.) Chicago: Field Enterprises Educational Corporation, 1964.

The World Book Encyclopedia. (Recorded ed.) Louisville, KY: American Printing House for the Blind, 1980.

BIBLIOGRAPHY

Literature about *The World Book Encyclopedia* falls into four categories: book reviews, corporate histories and memoirs, news stories, and inhouse publications. Reviews of *World Book Encyclopedia* are myriad. The few listed below are selected for their depth, and for the edition of *World Book* they treat. Only reviews of milestone editions (anniversary editions or largely revised editions) have been included. Of histories, William Murray's *Adventures in the People Business*, commissioned on the occasion of *World Book*'s 50th anniversary, is the most significant. Murray himself is indebted to "a brief history of the Company's early years" by William V. Miller (1953), but this history was evidently never published, and could not be located in the company archives. Of inestimable value to this chapter were the various inhouse publications (anonymous and undated) furnished by Executive Editor A. Richard Harmet.

Baumbach, Donna, Ann Barron, and Mary Bird. "Electronic Encyclopedia: Searching for the Right One," *CD-ROM End User* 2 (August, 1990): 58–60.

Corrigan, Adeline. "Reference." *Review of World Book. Library Journal* 85 (November 15, 1960): 4235–36.

Dale, Edgar, and Joseph O'Rourke. *The Living Word Vocabulary: A National Vocabulary Inventory.* Chicago: World Book–Childcraft International, 1981. Second edition of *The Living Word Vocabulary: The Words We Know: A National Vocabulary Inventory.* Chicago: Field Enterprises Educational Corporation, 1976.

"Door-to-Door Conglomerate." *Forbes* 122 (August 21, 1978): 112.

"Door-to-Door Selling: Scott & Fetzer Finds It a Lucrative Line of Business." *Barron's* 61 (July 6, 1981): 29, 31.

Fargo, Lucile F. "The World Book Twenty-fifth Anniversary Edition." Review of *World Book. Horn Book* 19 (July, 1943): 246–50.

Fisher, Dorothy Canfield. "Books That Edify." Review of *World Book. Atlantic Monthly* 180 (August, 1947): 122–25.

"General Reference Work to Be Published in Braille." *ALA Bulletin* 53 (June, 1959): 528.

Harmet, A. Richard. "Encyclopedia." *World Book Encyclopedia.* 1989 ed.

———. "Finding Devices and Visual Aids in a Major American Encyclopedia." In "The Making of a General Encyclopedia." *Booklist* 73 (September 15, 1976): 206–07.

Hill, Elsie Isabel. "Salute to the New *Compton's* and *World Book.*" *Horn Book* 23 (September, 1947): 348–53.

Kister, Kenneth F. *Best Encyclopedias: A Guide to General and Specialized Encyclopedias.* Phoenix: Oryx Press, 1986.

———. *Encyclopedia Buying Guide: A Consumer Guide to General Encyclopedias in Print.* 3rd ed. New York: R. R. Bowker Company, 1981.

Murray, William. *Adventures in the People Business: The Story of World Book.* Chicago: Field Enterprises Educational Corporation, 1966.

Nault, William H., Hollis L. Caswell, and George B. Brain. *Analysis of Content of Courses of Study.* Chicago: Field Enterprises Educational Corporation, 1972. *Supplement,* 1978. *Supplement,* 1987.

"Plagiarism Charged in Encyclopaedia Suit: Britannica Concern Asks Writ and $250,000 Damages from Chicago Publisher." *New York Times,* 16 November 1930, sec. 1, p. 3, col. 3.

Rasmussen, Carol. Review of *World Book Encyclopedia.* In *American Reference Books Annual* 15 (1984): 23–26.

Review of *World Book. Booklist* 85 (October 15, 1988): 386.

Review of the *Information Finder. Booklist* 86 (June 1, 1990): 1918–21.
Reviewing Aid for "The World Book Encyclopedia": 22 volumes: 1990 Edition. Chicago: World Book, Inc., 1990.
Rudolph, Barbara. "'It Comes with the Territory.'" *Forbes* 130 (September 13, 1982): 84–85.
Saporito, Bill. "A Door-to-Door Bell Ringer." *Fortune* 110 (December 10, 1984): 83–88.
Scheib, Charlene M. Review of the *Information Finder*. CD-ROM End User 2 (August, 1990): 62–64.
Simmonds, Martha F. "Styling the *New World Book Articles.*" *Spotlight* (June 7, 1947): 2a–2b.

Walsh, S. Padraig. *Anglo-American General Encyclopedias: A Historical Bibliography, 1703–1967.* New York: R. R. Bowker Company, 1968.
"World Book Editors, Artists to Create, Revise Encyclopedia Pages on Terminals." *Publishers Weekly* 208 (September 1, 1975): 46–48.
"World Book Encyclopedia to Publish Special Edition for Partially Blind." *Library Journal* 88 (May 1, 1963): 1850.

NOTES

[1] Review of *World Book, Booklist* 15 (October 1918): 5.
[2] Quoted from William Murray, *Adventures in the People Business: The Story of World Book* (Chicago: Field Enterprises Educational Corporation, 1966), p. 8.
[3] Ibid., 22.
[4] *World Book Encyclopedia* , 1989 ed., see "Encyclopedia."
[5] Dorothy Canfield Fisher, "Books That Edify," review of *World Book, Atlantic Monthly* 180 (August 1947): 122.
[6] A. Richard Harmet, Executive Editor of *World Book,* interview with the author, 24 April 1990.
[7] Murray, 15.
[8] Ibid., 31.
[9] Harmet, interview with the author, 24 April 1990.
[10] Murray, 109.
[11] Ibid., 136.
[12] Ibid., 190.
[13] S. Padraig Walsh, *Anglo-American General Encyclopedias*: *A Historical Bibliography, 1703–1967,* (New York: R. R. Bowker, 1968), 185.
[14] "*The World Book* Twenty-fifth Anniversary Edition," *Horn Book* 19 (July 1943): 249.
[15] Murray, 108.
[16] Ibid., 64.
[17] Harmet, interview with the author, 24 April 1990.
[18] "The Research Behind World Book," photocopied (Chicago: World Book, Inc.), 3.
[19] Edgar Dale and Joseph O'Rourke, "Appendix," *The Living Word Vocabulary: The Words We Know: A National Vocabulary Inventory* (Chicago: Field Enterprises Educational Corporation, 1976).
[20] Harmet, interview with the author, 24 April 1990.
[21] Harmet, letter to the author, 20 June 1990.
[22] "Easy Reading is Hard Writing," photocopied, (Chicago: World Book, Inc.), 45.
[23] Harmet, interview with the author, 24 April 1990.
[24] Murray, 17–18.
[25] "Styling the New World Book Article," *Spotlight* (June 7, 1947): 2a–2b.
[26] Kenneth Kister, *Best Encyclopedias: A Guide to General and Specialized Encyclopedias* (Phoenix: Oryx Press, 1986), 205.
[27] Harmet, "Finding Devices," 207.
[28] Harmet, interview with the author, 24 April 1990.
[29] *Reviewing Aid for The World Book Encyclopedia*: *22 Volumes: 1990 Edition,* (Chicago: World Book, Inc.), 11.
[30] Lucile Fargo, "*The World Book* Twenty-fifth Anniversary Edition," 248–49.
[31] James Rettig, review of *World Book Encyclopedia, Wilson Library Bulletin* 62 (March 1988), 103.
[32] *Reviewing Aid for The World Book Encyclopedia*: *22 Volumes: 1990 Edition,* (Chicago: World Book, Inc.), 13.
[33] "Research Behind World Book," 5.
[34] "Subject: Editorial Objectives," photocopied, (Chicago: World Book, Inc.), 37–38.
[35] *New York Times*, Nov. 16, 1930, sec. I, p. 3, col. 3.
[36] Murray, 87.
[37] Ibid.
[38] "Reviewing Aid for *The World Book Encyclopedia*," 10.
[39] Murray, 138.
[40] *World Book* Editors, Artists to Create, Revise Encyclopedia Pages on Terminals," *Publishers Weekly* 208 (1 September 1975), 46.
[41] Kister, *Best Encyclopedias*, 201.
[42] "Reviewing Aid for *The World Book Encyclopedia*," 16.
[43] Murray, 231.
[44] *Booklist* 86, (1 June 1990), 1918.

Contributor Profiles

Mary Biggs is director of libraries at Mercy College, a multi-campus institution in Westchester County and the Bronx, New York. She is also a lecturer at the Columbia University School of Library Service where she teaches courses in information services. She was formerly on the full-time faculty at Columbia and at the University of Chicago Graduate Library School. She has published widely on reference, bibliographic instruction, education for librarianship, library and information science research, and publishing, with an emphasis on literary publishing.

Pamela S. Bradigan is assistant professor and assistant director at The Ohio State University Health Sciences Library. She received her law degree in 1981 from Capital University and she has written several articles on legal dictionaries, bibliographic instruction, and end-use database searching. Bradigan is currently a consulting editor for the *Bulletin of the Medical Library Association*.

William S. Brockman is English librarian at the University of Illinois at Urbana-Champaign. He is the author of *Music: A Guide to the Reference Literature* (Libraries Unlimited, 1987) and serves as bibliographer of the *James Joyce Quarterly*. He was formerly reference librarian at Drew University.

Charles Bunge is professor in the School of Library and Information Studies at the University of Wisconsin-Madison where his primary teaching area is reference materials and services. He has given talks and workshops in various parts of the country on the selection and use of reference sources. He is the author of numerous articles on this subject in professional journals including "The Publishing of Heavily Illustrated Reference Books," *Reference Services Review* (Spring 1983). He has served as president of the American Library Association's Reference and Adult Services Division and in 1983 received its Isadore Gilbert Mudge Citation for "significant contributions to reference librarianship."

Jo A. Cates served as chief librarian of The Poynter Institute for Media Studies in St. Petersburg, Florida, from 1985 to 1991, and continues to act as an associate of the Institute. She is currently director of the Transportation Library at Northwestern University in Evanston, Illinois. She has served as head of reference at the Lamont Library at Harvard College. Cates is author of *Journalism: A Guide to the Reference Literature* (Libraries Unlimited, 1990) and numerous articles, and reviews books for *Library Journal* and *Choice*.

Kerry L. Cochrane is currently acting head of the Reference Department of the Main Library at the University of Illinois at Chicago. She has been at the University of Illinois since 1984 and has written on hypertext applications in academic libraries.

Milton H. Crouch has held library positions at the University of Florida, The Pennsylvania State University, and, since 1969, the University of Vermont. He served as president of the Vermont Library Association in

1988 and as the VLA's American Library Association councilor from 1983 to 1987.

Richard D. DeBacher is editorial director of Southern Illinois University Press. He began his publishing career at the University of Chicago Press in 1970 where he worked for 11 years. Subsequently, he held various marketing, editorial, and general management positions with the American Library Association and the Oryx Press.

Marie C. Ellis is English and American literature bibliographer at the University of Georgia Libraries where she previously served as head of the Reference Department and as interlibrary loan librarian. She has been a reviewer for *American Reference Books Annual* since 1982 and served on the American Library Association's *Reference Books Bulletin* Editorial Board from 1987 to 1991.

Mary W. George is head of the General and Humanities Reference Division of the Firestone Library at Princeton University. She was coauthor of *Learning the Library* (Bowker, 1982) and wrote the chapter "Instructional Services" in *Academic Libraries: Research Perspectives* (American Library Association, 1990). From 1983 to 1990 she was coeditor of the library instruction journal *Research Strategies*.

Richard W. Grefrath is reference librarian at the University of Nevada, Reno. He is author of "Eating Clams with Your Fingers: A Survey of Contemporary Etiquette Books" in *Collection Building* (Winter 1985).

Marta Lange is head of reference at North Carolina State University Libraries. In 1990-91 she was chair of the Law and Political Science Section of the Association of College and Research Libraries, American Library Association. She has chaired the Standards and Guidelines Committee of ALA's Reference and Adult Services Division. She is the former secretary and a current member of the NCSU Faculty Senate.

Mary L. Larsgaard is assistant head of the Map and Imagery Laboratory Library, University of California, Santa Barbara. She is the author of *Map Librarianship: An Introduction* (2nd ed., Libraries Unlimited, 1987) and serves as editor of the Western Association of Map Libraries *Information Bulletin*. She has served as chair of the Special Libraries Association Geography and Map Division, the American Library Association Map and Geography Round Table, the Western Association of Map Libraries, and the Map Online Users Group.

John R.M. Lawrence is reference/interlibrary loan librarian at the College of William and Mary. He has worked previously as a reference librarian in the University Research Library at UCLA, the Carolina Population Center at the University of North Carolina, and the Documents Department of Perkins Library at Duke University.

William A. McHugh is a reference librarian at Northwestern University and has worked for more than ten years in reference departments in public and academic libraries. He is currently at work on a book on the origin of the *Union List of Serials*.

Robert W. Melton is bibliographer for English and American literature and assistant special collections librarian at the University of Kansas Libraries.

Stuart W. Miller is sales support manager for NOTIS Systems, Inc. He has served as chair of the American Library Association's *Reference Books Bulletin* Editorial Board and is author of the *Concise Dictionary of Acronyms and Initialisms* (Facts On File, 1988).

Margaret Morrison is coordinator of public services at the University of Central Arkansas in Conway, Arkansas. She has participated in the Intern Program at the Library of Congress where she worked for six years as a specialist in automated reference services in the General Reading Rooms. During 1990-91 she served as a Council of Library Resources academic management intern at the University of Chicago Library.

Harold M. Otness is professor of library science and collection development librarian at Southern Oregon State College. He is author of *The Shakespeare Folio Handbook and Census* (Greenwood Press, 1990) and numerous articles in such journals as *Libraries & Culture, Library Journal, Reference Services Review, Asian Culture Quarterly, Public Library Quarterly,* and the Western Association of Map Librarians *Information Bulletin.* Two of his papers have been selected for *Library Lit—The Best of . . .* (Scarecrow Press).

David M. Pilachowski is director of libraries at Denison University in Granville, Ohio. Previously he served as associate university librarian at Colgate University. He has reviewed and written in the fields of political science, Asian area studies, and library automation. He was also a member of the Asian Studies faculty at Colgate and has been an active member of the American Library Association's Machine-Assisted Reference Section.

James Rettig is assistant university librarian for reference and information services at the College of William and Mary. Since 1981 he has been editor/author of the "Current Reference Books" column in the *Wilson Library Bulletin.* He has written numerous articles on reference services and the role of reference sources. He has served in various editorial and advisory positions for *Reference Services Review* and developed that journal's popular "Desert Island" feature. In 1987 the American Library Association's Reference and Adult Services Division awarded him its Isadore Gilbert Mudge Citation for "significant contributions to reference librarianship." He is currently vice president/president-elect of the Reference and Adult Services Division.

Holly D. Rogerson, a librarian and former teacher, is the author of a number of English as a Second Language textbooks in vocabulary and grammar.

Charles Scribner, Jr., was head of Charles Scribner's Sons from 1952 to 1986. His memoir of his career in publishing, *In the Company of Writers: A Life in Publishing* (Scribners, 1990), includes a chapter on Scribner reference books. He served as president of the American Book Publishers Council from 1966 to 1968, as a trustee of Princeton University from 1969 to 1979, and as a trustee of the Princeton University Press from 1949 to 1981.

Johannah Sherrer is head of reference at Perkins Library at Duke University. She has served as editor of *Colorado Libraries* and has published articles on automation and reference services.

Linda K. Simons is coordinator of information services at Roesch Library at the University of Dayton. She has written for *Reference Services Review* and *American Reference Books Annual.* She is currently at work on a book-length guide to reference sources for the performing arts.

Edward D. Starkey is university librarian and associate professor at the University of San Diego. He is author of *Judaism and Christianity: A Guide to the Reference Literature* (Libraries Unlimited, 1991). He is an active leader in the San Diego ecumenical movement. He has served as a librarian at Indiana University, the University of Dayton, and Urbana College; prior to a career in librarianship, he taught high school and college for eight years.

Carol M. Tobin is head of reference at the Thomas Cooper Library at the University of South Carolina. She has served on the Reference and Adult Services Division's Reference Sources Committee. She is author of "Online Computer Bibliographic Searching as an Instructional Tool" in *Reference Services Review* (Winter 1984), and has reviewed books and databases for *RQ, College and Research Libraries, Online,* and *Database.*

David A. Tyckoson is head of the Reference Department of the University Libraries, State University of New York at Albany. He has also served as a reference librarian at Iowa State University and as a science librarian at Miami University in Oxford, Ohio. He has a B.S. in physics and an M.L.S. in library science, both from the University of Illinois at Urbana-Champaign. He has been a reviewer for several sources and has written extensively in the area of reference services. He is also the compiler of annual bibliographies on AIDS published by the Oryx Press.

Sarah B. Watstein is head of the Reference Division at the Library at Hunter College of the City University of New York. She is coeditor of *End-User Searching in Libraries* (American Library Association, 1988) and *On Account of Sex: Annotated Bibliography on the Status of Women in Librarianship, 1982-1987* (American Library Association, 1990), and coauthor of *AIDS & Women, A Sourcebook* (Oryx Press, 1990). She has also written numerous articles on artificial intelligence, burnout, online and instructional services, reference services, and women's studies.

E. Paige Weston is systems librarian and assistant professor at the University of Illinois at Chicago. She has served as an assistant reference librarian at UIC. As a systems librarian, she has wished for systems documentation to be written as comprehensively and comprehensibly as the *World Book Encyclopedia*.

Sandy Whiteley is editor of *Reference Books Bulletin*, the reference reviewing section of *Booklist*. She has worked for the American Library Association's Association of College and Research Libraries and for Northwestern and Yale University libraries. She is the editor of *Purchasing an Encyclopedia* (3rd ed., American Library Association, 1989) and has contributed articles on book publishing, bibliographies, and indexes to the *ALA Yearbook* (American Library Association).

Christine C. Whittington has been arts and architecture librarian and head of the Arts Library at the Pennsylvania State University since 1989. She was a reference librarian at Penn State's General Reference Section from 1983 to 1989. She is author of "General Social Sciences" in *The Social Sciences: A Cross-Disciplinary Guide to Selected Sources* (Libraries Unlimited, 1989) and "John Muir" in *Read More About It: An Encyclopedia of Information Sources on Historical Figures and Events* (Pierian Press, 1989). She was a member of the American Library Association's *Reference Books Bulletin* Editorial Board from 1985 to 1989 and chaired the board from 1987 to 1989.

Elizabeth J. Wood is business librarian and associate professor at Bowling Green State University Library in Ohio. She is author of *Strategic Marketing for Libraries* (Greenwood Press, 1988), has contributed to *Business Serials of the U.S. Government* (2nd ed., American Library Association, 1988), has written articles about business reference works and library marketing, and has given workshops on marketing academic libraries. With Floris Wood she has coauthored *She Said, He Said* (Visible Ink Press, 1991), a compendium of public opinion information.

Index

by Linda Webster